CHRISTIANITY AND INTERNATIONAL LAW

This cross-disciplinary collaboration offers historical and contemporary scholarship exploring the interface of Christianity and international law. This volume aims to understand and move past arguments, narratives and tropes that commonly frame law-religion studies in global governance. Readers are introduced to a range of confessional and critical perspectives explicitly engaging a diverse range of methodological and theoretical orientations to rethink how we experience and find ourselves caught within the phenomena of Christianity and international law.

Pamela Slotte is a professor of religion and law at Åbo Akademi University and vice-director of the Centre of Excellence in Law, Identity and the European Narratives at the University of Helsinki. Recent publications include *Rights at the Margins: Historical, Philosophical and Legal Perspectives* (co-editor, Brill, 2020), *Juridification of Religion?* (co-author, Brill, 2017) and *Revisiting the Origins of Human Rights* (co-editor, Cambridge University Press, 2015).

John D. Haskell is a senior lecturer at the University of Manchester Law School. Previous publications include *Political Economy and Law* (co-editor, Edward Elgar, 2015) and *Political Theology and International Law* (Brill, 2018). His work these days focuses on the sociology of expertise at the intersection of law, money, religion, and technology.

LAW AND CHRISTIANITY

The Law and Christianity series publishes cutting-edge work on Catholic, Protestant, and Orthodox Christian contributions to public, private, penal, and procedural law and legal theory. The series aims to promote deep Christian reflection by leading scholars on the fundamentals of law and politics, to build further ecumenical legal understanding across Christian denominations, and to link and amplify the diverse and sometimes isolated Christian legal voices and visions at work in the academy. Works collected by the series include groundbreaking monographs, historical and thematic anthologies, and translations by leading scholars around the globe.

Books in the series

Christianity and Market Regulation:
Christianity and the Laws of Conscience
Jeffrey B. Hammond and Helen M. Alvare

Infidels and Empires in a New World Order: Early Modern Spanish Contributions to International Legal Thought
David Lantigua

The Possibility of Religious Freedom: Early Natural Law and the Abrahamic Faiths
Karen Taliaferro

Catholic Social Teaching: A Volume of Scholarly Essays edited by Gerard Bradley and E. Christian Brugger

The Immortal Commonwealth: Covenant, Community, and Political Resistance in Early Reformed Thought
David P. Henreckson

Great Christian Jurists in American History edited by
Daniel L. Dreisbach and Mark David Hall

Great Christian Jurists and Legal Collections in the First Millennium
Philip L. Reynolds

English Ecclesiastical Lawyers: A History of Their Life and Work
R. H. Helmholz

Law, Love and Freedom: From the Sacred to the Secular
Joshua Neoh

Great Christian Jurists in French History
Olivier Descamps and Rafael Domingo

Church Law in Modernity: Toward a Theory of Canon Law Between Nature and Culture
Judith Hahn

Common Law and Natural Law in America: From the Puritans to the Legal Realists
Andrew Forsyth

Care for the World: Laudato Si' and Catholic Social Thought in an Era of Climate Crisis edited by
Frank Pasquale

Church, State, and Family: Reconciling Traditional Teachings and Modern Liberties
John Witte, Jr.

Great Christian Jurists in Spanish History
Rafael Domingo and Javier Martínez-Torrón

Under Caesar's Sword: How Christians Respond to Persecution edited by
Daniel Philpott and Timothy Samuel Shah

God and the Illegal Alien
Robert W. Heimburger

Christianity and Family Law
John Witte, Jr. and Gary S. Hauk

Christianity and Natural Law
Norman Doe

Great Christian Jurists in English History edited by Mark Hill, QC and R. H. Helmholz

Agape, Justice, and Law edited by Robert F. Cochran, Jr and Zachary R. Calo

Calvin's Political Theology and the Public Engagement of the Church
Matthew J. Tuininga

God and the Secular Legal System
Rafael Domingo

How Marriage Became One of the Sacraments
Philip L. Reynolds

Christianity and Freedom (Volume I: Historical Perspectives, Volume II: Contemporary Perspectives) edited by Timothy Samuel Shah and Allen D. Hertzke

The Western Case for Monogamy Over Polygamy
John Witte, Jr.

The Distinctiveness of Religion in American Law
Kathleen A. Brady

Pope Benedict XVI's Legal Thought
Marta Cartabia and Andrea Simoncini

Christianity and International Law
Pamela Slotte and John D. Haskell

Christianity and International Law

AN INTRODUCTION

Edited by

PAMELA SLOTTE

Åbo Akademi University

JOHN D. HASKELL

University of Manchester

CAMBRIDGE
UNIVERSITY PRESS

CAMBRIDGE
UNIVERSITY PRESS

University Printing House, Cambridge CB2 8BS, United Kingdom

One Liberty Plaza, 20th Floor, New York, NY 10006, USA

477 Williamstown Road, Port Melbourne, VIC 3207, Australia

314–321, 3rd Floor, Plot 3, Splendor Forum, Jasola District Centre, New Delhi – 110025, India

79 Anson Road, #06–04/06, Singapore 079906

Cambridge University Press is part of the University of Cambridge.

It furthers the University's mission by disseminating knowledge in the pursuit of education, learning, and research at the highest international levels of excellence.

www.cambridge.org
Information on this title: www.cambridge.org/9781108474559
DOI: 10.1017/9781108565646

First published 2021

A catalogue record for this publication is available from the British Library.

Library of Congress Cataloging-in-Publication Data
NAMES: Slotte, Pamela, editor. | Haskell, John (John D.), editor.
TITLE: Christianity and international law : an introduction / edited by Pamela Slotte, Åbo Akademi University; John D. Haskell, University of Manchester.
DESCRIPTION: Cambridge, United Kingdom ; New York, NY : Cambridge University Press, 2021. | Series: Law and christianity | Includes bibliographical references and index.
IDENTIFIERS: LCCN 2020046676 (print) | LCCN 2020046677 (ebook) | ISBN 9781108474559 (hardback) | ISBN 9781108464970 (paperback) | ISBN 9781108565646 (ebook)
SUBJECTS: LCSH: International law – Religious aspects – Christianity. | Religion and law.
CLASSIFICATION: LCC KB265 .C47 2021 (print) | LCC KB265 (ebook) | DDC 262.9–dc23
LC record available at https://lccn.loc.gov/2020046676
LC ebook record available at https://lccn.loc.gov/2020046677

ISBN 978-1-108-47455-9 Hardback
ISBN 978-1-108-46497-0 Paperback

For Piero and J/A/L/E

Contents

Tables

Contributors

SILAS W. ALLARD is a senior fellow at the Center for the Study of Law and Religion and a doctoral student in the Graduate Division of Religion at Emory University. He also serves as managing editor of the *Journal of Law and Religion*, served on the board of El Refugio (a hospitality house for the families of immigrants detained at Stewart Detention Center), and is a former chair of the Georgia Immigration Working Group.

JENNIFER L. BEARD is an associate professor at the University of Melbourne Law School and author of *The Political Economy of Desire: International Development and the Nation State* (Routledge-Cavendish, 2007). Located within the fields of public law, international law and development, and charity law, her work collapses the disciplinary boundaries around fields of law to generate original and productive insights into the different ways in which political power emerges to shape and reshape individual subjectivity and political bodies at both the national and the international levels.

NATHANIEL BERMAN is the Rahel Varnhagen professor in Brown University's Department of Religious Studies. His work focuses on the construction of alterity in discourses ranging from early twentieth-century international law to thirteenth-century kabbalah. Among his publications are *Divine and Demonic in the Poetic Mythology of the Zohar: The "Other Side" of Kabbalah* (Brill, 2018) and *Passion and Ambivalence: Colonialism, Nationalism, and International Law* (Brill, 2011).

ROLAND BOER is a professor in the School of Marxism Studies, Dalian University of Technology, China. He has undertaken research into the relations between biblical narratives and the development of theories of capitalism, as well as the complex interactions between Western Marxism and religion. A recent publication is *Idols of Nations: Biblical Myth at the Origins of Capitalism* (co-author, Fortress Press, 2014).

TIZIANA FAITINI (PhD 2014) teaches Political Philosophy at the University of Trento. She was a post-doctoral fellow at the Leibniz-Institut für

Europäische Geschichte in Mainz and a Marie-Curie COFUND fellow at the Max Weber Kolleg in Erfurt. Among her publications is *Il lavoro come professione: Una storia della professionalità tra etica e politica* (Aracne Editrice, 2016).

DANTE FEDELE studied law (University of Trento) and history of political thought (ENS Lyon). After completing his PhD (ENS Lyon and University of Naples Federico II), he was a research fellow in the legal history department of KU Leuven (2015–19). He is a research fellow of the French CNRS at the Center for Judicial History (University of Lille). He is the author of *Naissance de la diplomatie moderne (XIII e–XVII e siècles): L'ambassadeur au croisement du droit, de l'éthique et de la politique* (Nomos Verlag, 2017).

UDI GREENBERG is an associate professor of history at Dartmouth College. He is the author of the prize-winning *The Weimar Century: German Émigrés and the Ideological Foundations of the Cold War* (Princeton University Press, 2015), as well as multiple articles on modern European thought and politics.

JOHN D. HASKELL is a senior lecturer at the University of Manchester Law School. Previous publications include *Political Economy and Law* (co-editor, Edward Elgar, 2015) and *Political Theology and International Law* (Brill, 2018). His work these days focuses on the sociology of expertise at the intersection of law, money, religion, and technology.

JEDIDIAH J. KRONCKE is an associate professor of law at the University of Hong Kong. Trained as a lawyer and anthropologist, he has undertaken historical work focused on the nature of cross-cultural perceptions of law and their implications for comparative law and contemporary foreign relations. His publications include *The Futility of Law and Development: China and the Dangers of Exporting American Law* (Oxford University Press, 2016).

DAVID M. LANTIGUA is an assistant professor of moral theology and Christian ethics at the University of Notre Dame, where he is a fellow of the Kellogg Institute for International Studies and the Institute for Latino Studies. He is the author of *Infidels and Empires in a New World Order: Early Modern Spanish Contributions to International Legal Thought* (Cambridge University Press, 2020). He has published articles in the *Journal of Law and Religion*, *Modern Theology*, and the *Journal of the Society of Christian Ethics*.

LINDE LINDKVIST is a senior lecturer in human rights studies at the School of Human Rights, University College Stockholm. He specializes in questions of human rights history, the right to religious freedom, and children's rights. He is the author of *Religious Freedom and the Universal Declaration of Human Rights* (Cambridge University Press, 2017).

MARK C. MODAK-TRURAN is a professor of law at Mississippi College School of Law. He received his MA and PhD (religious ethics) from the University of Chicago and his JD from Northwestern University School of Law where he was the editor-in-chief of the *Northwestern Journal of International Law and Business*. Two publications of interest are "A Process Theory of Natural Law and the Rule of Law in China," *Penn State International Law Review* 26 (2008) and "Beyond Theocracy and Secularism (Part I): Toward a New Paradigm for Law and Religion," *Mississippi College Law Review* 27 (2007–8).

CRAIG B. MOUSIN is the university ombudsperson at DePaul University, where he previously served as executive director at the Center for Church/State Studies. He is the founder of the National Immigration Justice Center. His publications include "Can One Still Call It Ignorance or Bias? Nexus Test Modified, but Courts Still Fail to Address International Law under the International Religious Freedom Act," in *Migration and Religious Freedom: Essays on the Interaction between Religious Duty and Immigration Law* (Wolf Legal Publishers, 2018).

ELENA NAMLI is a professor of theological ethics at Uppsala University, Sweden. Her research focuses on social and political ethics, and she has published on philosophical and theological ethics. Her publications include *Human Rights as Ethics, Politics, and Law* (Uppsala University, 2014) and *Future(s) of the Revolution and the Reformation* (editor, Palgrave Macmillan, 2019).

JANNE E. NIJMAN is a professor of history and theory of international law at the University of Amsterdam and chair of the board and academic director of the T.M.C. Asser Institute in The Hague. She is also a professor of international law at the Graduate Institute of International and Development Studies in Geneva. She has published papers on Hugo Grotius and is co-editor of the *Cambridge Companion to Hugo Grotius* (Cambridge University Press, 2021) together with Randall Lesaffer.

REUT YAEL PAZ is a professor at the Centre for Research on Antisemitism at the Technical University, Berlin. She is an Israeli scholar who specializes in public international law, European law, international relations, and international legal history. Paz holds degrees in law and political sciences from the University of Helsinki and a PhD from Bar-Ilan University, Israel, and has held a senior research position in the law faculty at the University of Giessen. Her publications include A *Gateway between a Distant God and a Cruel World: The Contribution of Jewish German-Speaking Scholars to International Law* (Martinus Nijhoff, 2012).

PETER PETKOFF is a senior law lecturer at Brunel Law School and director of the Religion, Law and International Relations Programme at Regent's Park College, Oxford. He is also managing editor of the *Oxford Journal of Law and Religion*. Recent publications include *Changing Nature of Religious Rights under International Law* (co-editor, Oxford University Press, 2015).

ANDREW PRESTON is a professor of American history and a fellow of Clare College at Cambridge University. His books include *Sword of the Spirit, Shield of Faith: Religion in American War and Diplomacy* (Knopf, 2012) and *American Foreign Relations: A Very Short Introduction* (Oxford University Press, 2019); he is also the editor of four other books. He is currently writing a book on the idea of national security in American history as well as co-editing Volume 2 of *The Cambridge History of the Vietnam War* and Volume 3 of *The Cambridge History of America and the World*.

AKBAR RASULOV teaches international law at the University of Glasgow. He is the co-editor of *New Voices and New Perspectives in International Economic Law* (Springer, 2020).

PAMELA SLOTTE is a professor of religion and law at Åbo Akademi University and vice-director of the Centre of Excellence in Law, Identity and the European Narratives at the University of Helsinki. Recent publications include *Rights at the Margins: Historical, Philosophical and Legal Perspectives* (co-editor, Brill, 2020), *Juridification of Religion?* (co-author, Brill, 2017) and *Revisiting the Origins of Human Rights* (co-editor, Cambridge University Press, 2015).

STEFAN STANTCHEV is an associate professor of history at Arizona State University. Author of *Spiritual Rationality: Papal Embargo as Cultural Practice* (Oxford University Press, 2014), Stantchev works on topics that integrate the political, economic, and cultural history of the Mediterranean between c.1100 and c.1600.

Acknowledgments

It has been an immensely rewarding experience to work on this book. The editors first met years ago at the Erik Castrén Institute of International Law and Human Rights (ECI) in Helsinki. The ECI research community, with its discerning take on contemporary and historical international legal matters, has ever since formed a source of inspiration and lasting friendships, for which we are ever grateful. The work on this volume presented us with an opportunity to channel some of what we have learned into a study of the relations of Christianity and international law and to acknowledge our gratitude to the ECI community, past and present.

We are particularly indebted to the series editor of the Cambridge Studies in Law and Christianity, Professor John Witte, Jr. for his unfailing encouragement, feedback, and support throughout the process. At Cambridge University Press, we have also had the good fortune to work first with senior commissioning editor in law John Berger, and later with assistant editor Jackie Grant. Thank you for your collaboration and for making the production process run so smoothly.

We are grateful to the Center for the Study of Law and Religion, Emory Law School for generously financing the project. The grant made it possible for us to bring together the authors contributing to this volume for two inspiring workshops in Helsinki, Finland in autumn 2018 and in Atlanta, United States in spring 2019. We are grateful to Silas Allard, Anita Mann, and Sandra Tilley at the Centre for the Study of Law and Religion at Emory University, and to Bea Bergholm, Heta Björklund, Nora Fabritius, Tuomas Heikkilä, and Noora Hakkarainen at the Centre of Excellence in Law, Identity and the European Narratives at the University of Helsinki for their invaluable administrative support in relation to the two workshops and finalizing the volume.

Finally, we are especially grateful to the contributors to this volume, for their time, energy, and care that went into preparing and writing the chapters – and, more generally, for helping to really shape the focus and scope of the volume. A number of colleagues and friends informed the text, not least those attending Peter Petkoff's afternoon garden salons in Oxford. This publication is very much the child of our camaraderie over these last few years.

1

Christianity and International Law: An Introduction

John D. Haskell and Pamela Slotte

The interplay between Christianity and international law ... The terms "Christianity" and "international law," as well as their relationship to each other, are not easy to understand – at least where there might be consensus.[1] The aim here is to diagnose the elusiveness of these phenomena, to explain why this is important to understand, and to set the stage for further investigations.

So why is it that we cannot come to a consensus about this issue of "Christianity and international law"? If you are inclined, pause a moment with this text and build a list of possible reasons ... Some contrarians might answer that we actually do have a relative consensus, that most reasonable people, at least with the opportunity to learn, find common agreement over most things and whatever differences simply reflect the diversity, the spice, the irreducible uniqueness of individual personalities and cultures. Those who might criticize or denounce this consensus are simply acting in so-called bad faith, whether that is deliberate or misguided or some unintentional tic in their nature. In this scenario, "we" have (faith in, understanding of) Christianity, while "they" would take it away or diminish it; "we" respect (follow, obey, promote) international law, whereas "they" would ignore it or undermine its integrity. In other words, we fall back on an insider/outsider logic, with outsiders subjected to a range of negative "you" statements. When disagreement emerges, we either flatten its differences or kick its partisans out of the fold. The word "relative" (and "reasonable," "common," "whatever differences") does a lot of work to hold together our "consensus" in these situations, separating the chaff from the wheat, what is acceptable nonconformity from what is "going too far." It is doing a lot of work because in fact there is

[1] It is a long-standing trope to observe that law, philosophy, and theology are notoriously slippery vocabularies. See, e.g., Manley Hudson, "The Prospect for International Law in the 20th Century," *Cornell Law Quarterly* 10, no. 4 (1925): 419–59, at 423–4. Perhaps it is exactly this irresolvable elusiveness that makes these concepts attractive to the discipline. See Pierre Schlag, "Law as a Continuation of God by Other Means," *California Law Review* 85, no. 2 (1997): 427–40. Slotte co-wrote this chapter as part of her work as vice-director of the Centre of Excellence in Law, Identity and the European Narratives, Academy of Finland 2018–2025 (grant number: 312430).

a lot of dissent, a lot of quite pronounced conflict over the identity and legacies of Christianity and international law.

Catholics may criticize Protestants for – like that old Groucho Marx joke – not feeling comfortable being part of any club that would accept them, constantly splintering off into new denominational factions, and too often privileging faith over works and refusing to follow traditional rites of salvation. Protestants may say that they adhere to the Scriptures while Catholics worship relics and human sacraments. Catholics and Protestants will usually join together, as Christians, to distinguish themselves from Christian Scientists, Mormons, or Jehovah's Witnesses, the latter groups accused of being non-Christian religions or even cults. Likewise, all these different communities identifying as Christian tend to distinguish themselves from Jews or Muslims, but will usually find closely affinity to Judaism due to its centrality in the Christian narrative, and will even embrace Islam as also belonging to a faith in the one God and for their common stand decrying secular ideologies. Secular orientations are subsumed within the Christian legacy to the extent that they share common political agendas – for instance, restricting Islamic practices in the name of gender equality. Who gets to be called reasonable (e.g., "orthodox" rather than "heretic") and offered a place within the tent is constantly shifting without any straightforward standard.

Something similar is at work when it comes to international law. We will often hear arguments that the discipline is part of a (here it is again) "more or less" (aka "relative") common heritage with a shared language and overlapping commitments (e.g., legal rights based on human dignity). Conflict is chalked up to bad faith actors donning the rhetoric of law to advance political agendas, or (usually long-standing) cultural traditions clouding human judgment to recognize progress (when non-European) or perpetuating prejudice (when European), or legal academics getting caught up in fads that would deny the rule of law any deep values or reliable code of ethical reasoning.

Of course, the prospect of really identifying a set of core characteristics that would meet the claim of a truly "universal" and "legal" order is rather daunting. It would have to include not only Christians but Muslims, Jews, Buddhists, and all the myriad other religions and life-views, all the countries of the world with their unique economic, political, and social compositions and traditions, and all this material requiring a dissection of how they influence one another and act internally, not to mention their influence on the entirety of "international legal thought" itself.[2] When confronted by this seemingly

[2] See Justin Desautels-Stein, "The Rule of Law," in *Tipping Points in International Law: Commitment and Critique*, ed. John D. Haskell and Jean d'Aspremont (*forthcoming*, Cambridge: Cambridge University Press, 2021).

infinite diversity, a typical move among those who claim a universal rule of law is to either claim that these differences all share certain innate human experiences or that what is needed is simply further attention and study of these complexities – in essence, an argument (for, perhaps, a Protestant communitarianism) that sees the path to "salvation" through interpersonal recognition and respect for the uniqueness of each person and community and emphasis on the importance of dialogue.[3] This is a circular proposition since it is dialogue that will lead us to a common platform, but such dialogue would itself require that some such commonality already exists. When we claim that beneath existing (often conflictual) diversity is a common humanity, however, we find ourselves back to the problem that it really looks, in many respects, like there are many, rather than one, legal (or other normative) orders. If we are a brotherhood, it is often that of Cain and Abel.[4]

And that is to say that we can even designate something as firmly "legal," rather than "economic," or "political," or "religious," or some other important domain of social organization. Usually, scholars interested in Christianity and international law actually argue that these phenomena are mutually constitutive, and advocate that readers see them as key DNA building blocks of human (cultural, individual, political) identity.[5] All those things that are felt to be not religion or law are not only influenced by but actually partially constituted by, through, and of religion and law – in other words, they are, to an extent, law and religion. If this is unclear, consider the market. It is commonly held out as a foil to government planning, the realm of private individuals seeking to maximize their interests in a "natural state" of barter and exchange since time immemorial, so much so that when we pass laws related to the market, we speak of "regulating" the market – as opposed to "re-regulating." But just as American Legal Realism teaches us that the market is actually a legal institution formalizing background policy choices that allocate the distribution of resources and power in a society (aka politics),[6] we learn from law and religion studies that the contemporary conceptual and organizational architecture of

3 See Katrina Forrester, *In the Shadow of Justice: Postwar Liberalism and the Remaking of Political Philosophy* (Princeton: Princeton University Press, 2019), 257–68.

4 See Arthur Leff, "Unspeakable Ethics, Unnatural Law," *Duke Law Journal* 28, no. 6 (1979): 1229–49, at 1249.

5 Highlighting the challenges of trying to distinguish these dynamics and their interaction, see Pierre Schlag, "The De-Differentiation Problem," *Continental Philosophy Review* 42, no. 1 (2009): 35–62; Winnifred Fallers Sullivan and Robert Yelle, "Law and Religion: An Overview," in *Encyclopedia of Religion*, 2nd ed. (New York: Macmillan Reference USA, 2005), 5325–32.

6 See, e.g., Morris Cohen, "Property and Sovereignty," *Cornell Law Review* 13, no. 1 (1927): 8–30; Robert Hale, "Coercion and Distribution in a Supposedly Non-coercive State," *Political Science Quarterly* 38, no. 3 (1923): 470–94.

the market is itself a legacy of Christian thought that dates back to the early medieval era.[7] In other words, the international economic order is not clearly separated from Christianity and international law – and not only do these dynamics influence each other but they are built into one another. The difficulty with these claims is not that these institutions are in fact distinct but rather, since they are so wrapped up with one another, that they do not represent analytically distinct terrains in the first place with their own ontological clarity.[8]

International law and Christianity literature tries to get around this conceptual problem by pointing to a set of distinct characteristics, such as authoritative texts, identifiable professional cohorts, recognizable rituals and institutional sites, historical markers, and so forth. But this only reintroduces the very problems it was meant to solve. An authoritative text, for instance, always requires an interpretative source. This source will either be found in some cohort of the laity or professionals, who in turn will themselves be governed by a set of criteria to designate the legitimacy and quality of interpretation, as well as who counts as actually working within or outside the community. We know a good legal argument or a well-reasoned theological position by its conformity with protocols of legal or theological argument, and equally, we can use these protocols to determine when someone is "faking" or "misusing" the language of our faiths. Satan tempted Christ by echoing God's own words; national regimes legitimize bombing children's hospitals in the name of *jus cogens*. In both instances, the claimant is challenged as having twisted the meaning of the faith's principles and words. And where do these criteria come from? From none other than the authoritative texts, or the community traditions, or some external source (such as God, natural law, right reason, common human experience). So, the criteria determine the community and allow us to evaluate the texts, while the community and their texts develop the criteria to interpret their faith in action and to know themselves. There is something uncomfortably circular in this reasoning – at least to the extent that we are seeking to try the things that differ and not simply taking this as a matter of metaphysical truth.

Now, we may indeed wish to hold a certain set of legal or religious tenets to be precious exactly because they are beyond interrogation – they simply define

7 See, e.g., Martti Koskenniemi, "International Law and Religion: No Stable Ground," in *International Law and Religion: Historical and Contemporary Perspectives*, ed. Martti Koskenniemi, Mónica García-Salmones Rovira, and Paolo Amorosa (Oxford: Oxford University Press, 2017), 12–13.

8 See Schlag, "The De-Differentiation Problem."

"who we are" – but it is not very helpful for the purposes of analyzing the role of Christianity and international law in the world to date.

This is all the more difficult because any attempt at reflection will offer its own methodological challenges. Take studies in Christianity and international law that aim to recover some historical past – what sort of problems do we face in such efforts? First, any history resurrects some things and buries others. Those ignored or suppressed storylines alter the way in which we then remember past time and how we understand change. If we believe that people and their ideas are the primary movers of history, we will most likely focus on individual authors and their texts, looking to intellectual historians; if we privilege the ways in which institutions are structured to reproduce their conditions for maintenance and survival, we will pay more attention to organizational formation and the political economy of life and order, drawing more from historical sociology. Likewise, the ways in which we prioritize different social factors, such as economic relationships or gender and racial identity, and to what extent we feel that change occurs top down or bottom up, all these orientations will direct where we look for material and how we interpret our pasts. And our disciplinary training will also lead us to periodize differently.[9] A religious scholar looks to different dates than a political economist, just as a legal military historian privileges a different set of actors, dates, locations, and events than a legal historian tracing the story of the corporation. And, regardless of our specific disciplinary interest, do we focus on practices or beliefs? How faith (or law) functioned on the ground or in the books?[10] Within the congregations or as perceived by those outside the fold? There are no criteria that ultimately allow us certainty to distinguish whether a historical fact within our professional lexicon counts as "public" or "private," an act of agency or structure, of freedom or coercion, of peace or strife.

Second, if it is difficult to discern what to include and how to separate out the internal dynamics of Christianity and international law past, it is equally a challenge to pinpoint what even counts as "internal" to this history. Is it a Western story, and, to the extent that it may be, what even counts as the West when so much of this timeline is wrapped up in colonialism and the swap

9 See generally AHR Forum, "Historiographic 'Turns' in Critical Perspective," *American Historical Review* 117, no. 3 (2012): 698–813; Kathleen Davis, *Periodization and Sovereignty: How Ideas of Feudalism and Secularization Govern the Politics of Time* (Philadelphia: University of Pennsylvania Press, 2017).

10 See, e.g., Bardo Fassbender and Anne Peters, "Introduction: Towards a Global History of International Law," in *The Oxford Handbook of the History of International Law*, ed. Bardo Fassbender and Anne Peters (Oxford: Oxford University Press, 2012), 12–14 (identifying three general types of history writing: on concepts, on persons, or on events).

and steal of knowledge, styles, and technologies (not to mention imaginary provocation) from what we would count as categorically non-Western societies (e.g., the Ottomans, Chinese)? Just as the sheer breadth of legal regimes around the world might discourage any contemporary claims to a single universalizing international law, the same goes for Christianity past and present: its Orthodox trajectories, its evangelical mutations through the African and Asian continents, the varieties of social gospel and pagan-infused Catholicisms living across Central and South America ... And perhaps most intimate to Christianity, the historical treatment of Jewish people is yet to be reckoned with. For all the cacophony of professed support for the state of Israel and the invocations of a Judeo-Christian tradition, can we think of any people more dangerous, from an empirical historical study, to the Jewish people than white European Christian society? When we bear witness to the medieval depiction of Jewish people with horns, the perpetual distrust of their presence in the constitution of nation-states, and all these cultural sentiments culminating in their mass industry extermination and subsequent managed diaspora into what would be perhaps the most volatile location imaginable ... is this not the fruit, the heritage, of our Christianities? We have yet to tell histories that fully reckon with these dark historical legacies, "the deeper realities of Western Christian sensibilities, identities, and habits of mind which continue to channel patterns of colonialist dominance,"[11] and not only to recover these stories but to transform our recital into some fundamental normative reordering of the doctrines and institutional composition of Christendom and global governance.[12]

Third, even if we were to build a comprehensive, integrated interdisciplinary technique that rightly divided our past, these accounts would still be subject to any number of predispositions that scuttle our best efforts for clarity and harmony. For example, suppose we were to focus on a discrete moment in the medieval era. Knowingly or not, this moment would be an opportunity to transpose our contemporary anxieties, assumptions, and hopes into an earlier time, making them seem perennial – what historians label the sins of "presentism" but which seem almost inescapable (for example, with any attempt to trace the history of "freedom" or "individuality").[13] For some, it would turn

11 Willie James Jennings, *The Christian Imagination: Theology and the Origins of Race* (New Haven: Yale University Press, 2011), 8.

12 See Udi Greenberg, "Protestants, Decolonization, and European Integration, 1885–1961," *Journal of Modern History* 89, no. 2 (2017): 314–54; Reut Yael Paz, *A Gateway between a Distant God and a Cruel World: The Contribution of Jewish German-Speaking Scholars to International Law* (Leiden: Martinus Nijhoff, 2012), 1–41.

13 For a discussion of different ways, the "medieval" turn may be characterized; see Umberto Eco, *Faith in Fakes: Travels in Hyperreality* (London: Vintage 1998 [1973]), 59–86.

into a type of progressive narrative, a march through history toward some greater awareness of our common humanity or retreat from one or another irrational barbarism of our collective past.[14] For others, the return to an earlier time would be a search for some lost grail, for inspiration in our origins – or if not our origins, some essence that might, as it did for Aristotle and Thomas Aquinas, serve as a principle of movement to align differing opinions.[15] In relation to law, can we even speak of international law in this medieval moment, or is it something of a much more recent trajectory? Would it begin with the School of Salamanca? Or with the Treaty of Westphalia? If with that moment in Westphalia, are we falling into a story of international law replacing the chaos of confessional religious warfare, or is it a story of the Protestant ethos mobilizing law to recreate our politics, or is it just another instance of Christendom reinventing itself to fit the times?[16] Or perhaps our story of international law can only really begin with the nineteenth century Protestant Crusade and the professionalization of the discipline?[17] Or the interwar period and its elevation of international organizations, with the establishment of international mechanisms of arbitration and accountability, and emphasis on the human personality?[18] Or maybe only after decolonization and the formal inclusion of all countries? Is there even a coherent "international law" that we can speak of, or is it merely a linguistic phenomenon that various experts wield to make sense of something or other – are there in fact many varieties of what is international law? The same might be asked of Christianity. We are back to those earlier questions already raised.

Even if we agree to certain criteria or values and might adequately delineate the contours of Christianity or international law, it is still not very helpful for

14 For an examination into how progress narratives slip into international legal thought, see Nathaniel Berman, "In the Wake of Empire," *American University International Law Review* 14, no. 6 (1999): 1521–54; Thomas Skouteris, *The Notion of Progress in International Law Discourse* (The Hague: T.M.C. Asser Press, 2010).

15 See, e.g., Harold J. Berman, *Law and Revolution*, vol. 1, *The Formation of the Western Legal Tradition* (Cambridge, MA: Harvard University Press, 1983).

16 See David Kennedy, "Images of Religion in International Legal Theory," in *The Influence of Religion on the Development of International Law*, ed. Mark W. Janis (Dordrecht: Martinus Nijhoff Publishers, 1991), 137–45.

17 For a discussion of this effort among a Protestant-oriented cultural elite to shape social institutions, and specifically the emerging field of international law, see John D. Haskell, "Divine Immanence: The Evangelical Foundations of Modern Anglo-American Approaches to International Law," *Chinese Journal of International Law* 11, no. 3 (2012): 429–67; Martti Koskenniemi, *The Gentle Civilizer of Nations: The Rise and Fall of International Law, 1870–1960* (Cambridge: Cambridge University Press, 2001).

18 See Nathaniel Berman, "But the Alternative Is Despair: European Nationalism and the Modernist Renewal of International Law," *Harvard Law Review* 106, no. 8 (1993): 1792–903.

guiding us as to how we are supposed to use this consensus in the everyday affairs of global governance. If you disagree with this claim and think that there are such overarching values, then we have just happened upon one of the more significant debates of the twentieth century (which cuts across Christianity, international law, and the social sciences at large): whether or not we can deduce from broad values how to act, and vice versa, whether it is possible to look at specific contexts and then infer reliable guiding principles. In the 1920s and 1930s, a new set of insights arose from natural and physical sciences, which would have reverberations throughout Anglophone and Western European intellectual and popular societies. It was possible for two systems of rules to hold contradictory foundational principles but where each system and set of principles, within its own respective logic, was absolutely unimpeachable. The takeaway here: you cannot rely on a value or principle to guide your behavior in specific situations (since multiple conflicting values could be equally true), and, by extension, things are actually far more complicated so that we find ourselves lost in a complex hierarchy of competing and interlacing values, engulfed in diverse situational contexts, all of which defies any linear straightforward deductions and inferences. The shorthand for this was "relativity" or "functionalism" or "sociological jurisprudence," but in essence it was just anti-deductive reasoning. If one accepted this premise, then one had to try instead to develop sophisticated methodologies to look at how the world actually operated and be overt about one's preferred aims in relation to the claims of others – in short, everything was, to one extent or another, politics. To see the world as irreducibly political and to find the source of values in the lived outcomes of people's lives tended to incline experts and intellectuals to side with political movements that prioritized immediate "wins" for working people in their "secular" lives. This is the era of voter enfranchisement for non-property owners and women, for social democracy and "safety nets" (e.g., social security, universal health care), the expansion of public spaces (e.g., national parks, libraries), and political-legal checks on financial and industrial elites.[19]

During this period (like in other times), intellectuals and policymakers did not share any consensus when it came to Christianity (or religion), or toward international law. For some, whether or not themselves part of a denominational faith, religion was a universal stimulus at the heart of society (e.g., Émile Durkheim), which could be mobilized in radically different ways. For those on the left, the

[19] See Morton Horwitz, *The Transformation of American Law, 1780–1860* (Cambridge, MA: Harvard University Press, 1979); Edward Purcell Jr., *The Crisis of Democratic Theory: Scientific Naturalism and the Problem of Value* (Lexington: University Press of Kentucky, 1973).

sacred would scrap "civilization" and its establishments to reawaken culture to its primordial energy and lead to a more fulfilling and fundamental new future. For those on the right, it meant tempering the hedonism of desire, acknowledging one's duty to long-standing virtue and exercising a more responsible and measured freedom in democratic politics.[20] Many saw Christianity as an important but outdated influence on international law, while many others thought that international law could only function effectively within a Christian heritage and viewed religious identity as fundamental to cultural and national identities. More often than not, Christianity and the rule of law were bulwarks against the excesses of mass democracy and totalitarian governments.[21] This did not always fit easily with anti-deductive progressive trends in the social sciences, and, especially after World War II, policymakers and scholars, at least within Anglo-American circles, increasingly turned back to the importance of identifying values that would guide knowledge and politics, and that were thought to be reflected in the rule of law.[22] By the 1950s onward, legal scholars began to organize professionally and to collectively publish with a shared idea about their times and what was to be done. According to these legal scholars, Western society was undergoing a cultural crisis because it had lost sight of its core values – most importantly, Christianity and "private" institutions, leading to a relativistic apathy and moral decay that allowed totalitarian agendas to run rampant.[23] Democracy required an ecumenical Christian code of values formalized in legal norms that might help transform the tumultuous international society into a universal social order of collective peace. By the 1970s, at the same time law and religion studies were becoming established as an important professional field of study, for those who felt uncomfortable professing a specific faith, they found agreement with their more metaphysically open colleagues through faith and advocacy of a worldview that focused on individuals as if they operated outside political institutions, with the emphasis on protecting "small" private domains (belief,

20 See Nathaniel Berman, "'The Sacred Conspiracy': Religion, Nationalism, and the Crisis of Internationalism," *Leiden Journal of International Law* 25, no. 1 (2012): 9–54.

21 See Marco Duranti, *The Conservative Human Rights Revolution: European Identity, Transnational Politics, and the Origins of the European Convention* (Oxford: Oxford University Press, 2017); John D. Haskell, "A Case in the Politics of Form: Yearbooks of International Law," *Netherlands Yearbook of International Law* 50 (2019): 21–35 John Nurser, *For All People and All Nations: The Ecumenical Church and Human Rights* (Washington, DC: Georgetown University Press, 2005).

22 See Purcell, *The Crisis of Democratic Theory*.

23 See, e.g., Harold J. Berman, "The Influence of Christianity upon the Development of Law," *Oklahoma Law Review* 12, no. 1 (1959): 86–101 (arguing against "communism, nationalism, and humanism," as well as the "overwhelming centralisation of the social order").

contract, family, church, property) that would nurture ethical interpersonal respect for each other's dignity as a human person.[24]

We often forget this recurring feeling of crisis and renewal, and the recurrence of religion in the international legal imagination. In the early 2000s, for instance, societal crisis and the need for reconnecting with "our Christian heritage" was pegged to the "war on terror." Often, scholars in law and politics pointed to the excesses of Islamic terrorism and Christian fundamentalism as transborder challenges to a cosmopolitan international order. A decade beforehand, the crisis was pegged to the dissolution of the former Soviet Union and the challenges that arose with renewed fervor for nationalist and religious self-determination. Step back into the 1970s and 1980s, and the crisis was experienced as an internal fragmentation of domestic political harmony, distrust in the established rule of law, and encroaching communist/socialist ideologies. And so forth. For each generation, the specific character of crisis and its solution is revised, but always according to a rather constant formal narrative structure with a relatively limited range of political commitments and available legal norms.[25]

It is difficult to say why we forget or what this remembering might mean for us (apart from narratives as such being necessary for sense-making),[26] just as it is difficult to figure out exactly what benefit comes from the perpetual call for more comprehensive and deeper studies (e.g., comparative, historical, interdisciplinary) into the field of law and religion, whether through a domestic or an international focus. In some respects, the increasing volume of literature and professional events around the theme of Christianity and international law paradoxically – and perversely – leads to a certain amount of closure in our capacity for academic understanding, personal imagination, and social world-making, all of which dampens our material and spiritual futures. More can mean less, growth does not necessarily mean progress, movement tells us

[24] For an insightful discussion of how conservative free market ideology and broader family and cultural values came together as a powerful background policy framework in the US context, see Melinda Cooper, *Family Values: Between Neoliberalism and the New Social Conservatism* (New York: Zone Books, 2017). See also Pamela Slotte, "Whose Justice? What Political Theology? On Christian and Theological Approaches to Human Rights in the Twentieth and Twenty-First Centuries," in *International Law and Religion: Historical and Contemporary Perspectives*, ed. Martti Koskenniemi, Mónica García-Salmones Rovira, and Paolo Amorosa (New York: Oxford University Press, 2017), 196–216.

[25] See Martti Koskenniemi, "Enchanted by the Tools? An Enlightenment Perspective," *American University International Law Review*, 35, no. 3 (2020): 397–426, at 400.

[26] See, e.g., Eric Selbin, *Revolution, Rebellion, Resistance: The Power of Story* (London: Zed Books, 2010).

nothing about direction. How so? And in reflecting on this question, we will also begin to frame the aims and stakes of this volume.

Any communication, especially when stretched over time, is subject to feedback loops whereby whatever is said not only "means what it says" but is related to previous reactions. These exchanges come to take on a life of their own. In other words, they become subject to rules and pressures specific to their internal production of exchanges decoupled from anything in the world "out there." We see the world through our pre-scripted lexicons, professional or otherwise. To make things even more complicated, a particular instance might reflect multiple feedback loops that are themselves weighed differently without any uniform standard of evaluation.[27]

To make this concrete in the context of Christianity and international law, we can begin by asking what form, in what location, and between whom is this theme being communicated. Now even this is a trickier question than it looks on the surface because we really have not clarified what counts as "being communicated." Dropping a bomb or signing a treaty or coming to a judicial ruling are all types of communication, but they signify very different things – even when all fall under the rubric of, say, international law. Similarly, we can speak about Christianity or international law as a "thing" somewhere doing something in the world to people, but it is also a rhetorical trope in itself, a communicative device that is meant to explain, persuade, and serve as a reference between people. So it is not only "Christianity," or "Christianity" and "international law," but the full term "Christianity and international law," as something coupled together, a linguistic device or trope that occurs between people in various types of conversation, which is in some way the object of our study.

But still we have not completely honed in on what form of conversation, and, by extension, what players and locations. The conversation that we want to highlight is that of academic discussion, a form of communication that takes place around the university but is most readily related to literature printed as book chapters, journal articles, and monographs. Of course, this scholarship refers to all sorts of non-academic materials (judicial decisions, legal treaties, political events, religious texts, and so forth), just as it draws its methodological and theoretical inspiration from a diverse range of cross-disciplinary and non-academic inputs. But the point is that it ultimately operates according to its own specific internal rules of what counts as good citation method, proper research techniques, stylistic acumen, and well-reasoned argument, as well as all those administrative skills that make one a successful player in the game (e.g., one's access to research material

27 See David Kennedy, "When Renewal Repeats: Thinking Against the Box," *NYU Journal of International Law & Politics* 32, no. 2 (2000): 335–500.

and affiliation with prestigious universities, professional awareness of organizational characteristics, and know-how of the peer review process).[28] For our purposes, we might reduce this to the literature, the content on the printed page, which itself is not so much responding to the "real" world as it is participating in an ongoing literary performance: in our case, Christianity and international law literature, which is a sub-genre of both legal scholarship and international law scholarship, as well as a sub-sub-genre of law and religion scholarship, and also an important literary first-order genre between international law scholars and cadre hailing from other disciplinary fields, such as history, international relations, and religious studies.[29] The majority of volumes in this scholarship are oriented to a particular legal regime (e.g., human rights) and a specific religious affiliation (e.g., Christianity, Islam),[30] or, alternatively, are organized to address "religion" in a "global" political-legal context.[31]

28 Pierre Schlag, "Normativity and the Politics of Form," *University of Pennsylvania Law Review* 139, no. 4 (1991): 801–932.

29 This is not to deny there are "real" things in the world or that scholarship is not part of that story. A university or print medium is an instance of "real" life. But our attempt to understand and engage the world "out there" is always through prearranged filters, and, often, our professional tools and social contexts determine what we can see or what is envisioned to be possible. The "things" themselves are always wrapped up in the ways they come into existence.

30 See, e.g. Michael McConnell, Robert Cochran Jr., and Angela Carmella, eds., *Christian Perspectives on Legal Thought* (New Haven: Yale University Press, 2001); John Witte Jr. and Frank Alexander, *The Teachings of Modern Christianity on Law, Politics, and Human Nature* (New York: Columbia University Press, 2005); Javaid Rehman and Susan Breau, eds., *Religion, Human Rights and International Law: A Critical Examination of Islamic State Practices* (Leiden: Brill, 2007); John Witte Jr. and Frank Alexander, *The Teaching of Modern Roman Catholicism on Law, Politics, and Human Nature* (New York: Columbia University Press, 2007); John Witte Jr. and Frank Alexander, *Christianity and Law: An Introduction* (Cambridge: Cambridge University Press, 2008); John Witte Jr. and Frank Alexander, *Christianity and Human Rights: An Introduction* (Cambridge: Cambridge University Press, 2010); Diaz Shah, ed., *Islam and the Law of Armed Conflict* (Cheltenham: Edward Elgar, 2015); Anver Emon, Mark Ellis, and Benjamin Glahn, *Islamic Law and International Human Rights Law* (Oxford: Oxford University Press, 2012); Marie-Luisa Frick and Andreas Th. Muller, eds., *Islam and International Law: Engaging Self-Centrism from a Plurality of Perspectives* (Leiden: Brill, 2013); Ann Black, Hossein Esmaeili, and Nadirsyah Hosen, *Modern Perspectives on Islamic Law* (Cheltenham: Edward Elgar, 2013); Hossein Esmaeilli, Marboe Irmgard, and Javaid Rehman, *The Rule of Law, Freedom of Expression and Islamic Law* (Oxford: Hart, 2017); Timothy Samuel Shah and Allan D. Hertzke, eds., *Christianity and Freedom*, vol. 1, *Historical Perspectives* (New York: Cambridge University Press, 2016); Allan D. Hertzke and Timothy Samuel Shah, eds., *Christianity and Freedom*, vol. 2, *Contemporary Perspectives* (New York: Cambridge University Press, 2016); Norman Doe, ed., *Christianity and Natural Law: An Introduction* (New York: Cambridge University Press, 2017); Robert F. Chochran, Jr. and Zachary R. Calo, eds., *Agape, Justice, and Law: How Mighty Christian Love Shape Law?* (Cambridge: Cambridge University Press, 2017).

31 See, e.g., Mark W. Janis and Carolyn Evans, eds., *Religion and International Law* (The Hague: Martinus Nijhoff Publishers, 1999); Jack Snyder, ed., *Religion and International Relations Theory* (New York: Columbia University Press, 2011); John Witte Jr. and M. Christian Green,

Even here we have not fully clarified the object of analysis in at least two respects. First, we are not speaking about the literature of all international law academics writing on Christianity and international law but really about just those authors within the Anglophone and English-speaking European context.[32] And second, we have not yet fleshed out the broader institutional environment that frames and assigns value to their writing. This second consideration is especially difficult for those of us engaged in higher education because university and scholarship are very much wrapped up with claims about the virtue of knowledge-production. To be sure, while perhaps none of us are truly objective and the very act of writing is an attempt in some way to change the world (even if a single reader), we still are by and large tied to an ideational idolatry: that ideas matter in and of themselves and exist in a more or less hermeneutically sealed environment that allows individuals to approach, consume, and exchange in relative equality. In this sense, our academic self-conception is not all that different from how we tend to view the artist and their creation. Albeit influenced by any number of external conditions, art is often conceived as ultimately embodying the authentic expression of the sovereign individual, with the truly great artists capable of piercing through the banalities of artistic commerce and social hierarchy to arrive at and convey (or restore) some aesthetic truth to creation (and human experience).

Religion and Human Rights: An Introduction (Oxford: Oxford University Press, 2011); Helle Porsdam, *Civil Religion, Human Rights and International Relations: Connecting People Across Cultures and Traditions* (Cheltenham: Edward Elgar, 2012); James Wellman Jr. and Clark B. Lombardi, eds., *Religion and Human Security: A Global Perspective* (Oxford: Oxford University Press, 2012); Timothy Samuel Shah, Alfred Stepan, and Monica Duffy Toft, eds., *Rethinking Religion and World Affairs* (Oxford: Oxford University Press, 2012); Francesca Trivellato, Leor Halevi, and Catia Antunes, eds., *Religion and Trade: Cross-Cultural Exchanges in World History, 1000–1900* (Oxford: Oxford University Press, 2014); Pamela Slotte and Miia Halme-Tuomisaari, eds., *Revisiting the Origins of Human Rights* (Cambridge: Cambridge University Press, 2015); Kyriaki Topidi and Lauren Fielder, eds., *Religion as Empowerment: Global Legal Perspectives* (Abingdon: Routledge, 2016); Fareda Banda and Lisa Fishbayn Joffe, eds., *Women's Rights and Religious Law: Domestic and International Perspectives* (Abingdon: Routledge, 2016); Anne Stensvold, ed., *Religion, State and the United Nations: Value Politics* (London: Routledge, 2017); Martti Koskenniemi, Mónica García-Salmones Rovira, and Paolo Amorosa, eds., *International Law and Religion: Historical and Contemporary Perspectives* (Oxford: Oxford University Press, 2017); Rex Ahdar, ed., *Research Handbook on Law and Religion* (Cheltenham: Edward Elgar, 2018); W. Cole Durham Jr. and Brett Scharffs, *Law and Religion: National, International and Comparative Perspectives*, 2nd ed. (New York: Wolters Kluwer, 2019).

32 When we speak of this tradition, it is easy to imagine a legion of authors – but in fact, this lineage (like the common law tradition itself) would most likely fit a relatively modest-sized hall.

Not everyone follows this path. Marcel Duchamp provided the example of forgoing the restoration of art's aesthetic purity to instead reveal the economy of consumerism within which any piece of art necessarily originates. Or similarly in literary terms, what Louis Althusser and Pierre Macherey referred to as a symptomatic reading of the text, examining what is not said but essential to the very ability of the form to continue producing itself – and, most troubling, what we know but train ourselves not to know, even as it animates our work.[33] Bad faith as ideology at its peak power. In our case, the political economy that frames our study is perhaps not so easy to agree upon, but if we were to chance a label, it would be closely related to liberal capitalism. We simply cannot write outside our work being published, distributed, read, and valued through this dispensation. Indeed, there seems an intimate connection between our institutions and vocabularies of god, money, and law.

What exactly liberal capitalism means and the more immediate organizational contexts that frame academic publication cut in one way or another through all the texts in this volume, though we will forgo (as do most of our authors) trying here to trace out its characteristics. But calling it out nevertheless helps us orient our study together as we move forward. For what is shared throughout most of the texts is a deep feeling of unease about the state of the world today, a paradoxical feeling of investment in and disillusionment with our scholarly trade, and an ambiguous but powerful draw to the theme of this volume and the mixture of spiritual and material dynamics that it suggests essential to human experience. For such grand topics, though, our ultimate aim is quite simple: to spend time together, trying to capture the experience of what it means in the second decade of the twenty-first century, to be within the field of academia, caught up within the lexicon of Christianity and international law.

The chapters may be usefully read in line with two general orientations: histories (genesis) and themes (liturgy). By "genesis" we are not searching for a solitary "origin" but rather lean in to the attraction and usefulness of looking backward – honing in on diplomacy and missionary practices, property and trade, seafare and warfare, charitable action and colonialism, ideas of peace and the building of international institutions, etcetera – whether to better understand how we arrived in our present moment or to witness the contingency of history. We are caught in a past that also reminds us that the future is uncertain. Or perhaps, in a more Biblical register, we should remember the

[33] See Louis Althusser, Étienne Balibar, Roger Establet, Pierre Macherey, and Jacques Rancière, *Lire e Capital*, Tome 1 & 2 (Paris: Maspero, 1965), 37; Pierre Macherey, *A Theory of Literary Production* (London: Routledge, 1978), 1–104.

truth brought home from the first verse of the book of Genesis: that there is always already a world in chaos and that there is always hope for a new beginning.[34] How many times are those in the Christian scriptures given a second chance, the possibility of new life; how many times is a new dispensation offered to those who will answer and be faithful? Often, this faith means feeling abandoned by God, becoming a stranger to the world: calling out for the night watchman to tell us the hour of our deliverance; or, like Christ, asking his father why he has been forsaken; or, as embodied in St. Paul's promise, understanding that those who follow Christ with a militant fidelity will earn their hope but at the cost of being outcasts to the system; or, as with the messiah, offering salvation to all humanity in the very act of being crucified on an implement of imperial rule.[35] Ours is not this kingdom; we are to stand in solidarity with the meek and downtrodden. How often do we forget this as international lawyers? As Christians? As citizens of powerful nation-states?

In contrast to the stranger, the orientation of the volume toward "liturgy" designates the formal public gathering of the faithful to worship, to practice together. With this, we mean to indicate (in a nonexclusive fashion) themes that constantly resurface within international legal thought (e.g., belonging, care, community, freedom, enchantment, humanity, mobility, sovereignty, territory), bringing us into communion, whether to debate strong differences or struggle toward a common goal. And liturgy with a slight twist. In many volumes that canvass the theme of religion and law, chapters will be organized according to confessional denominations (e.g., Catholic, Protestant), or schools of thought (e.g., naturalist, positivist), or some more compartmentalized variation on these general themes (e.g., multiple natural law traditions based on a legal regime, such as the family). This may create the impression that each sect or school is hermeneutically sealed and allows readers to dip in and extract a set of discrete axioms that may then be applied or discarded. While a number of authors in this volume address specific sectarian camps in Christianity and international law alike, our collective effort steers clear of any explicit attempt to lay out canonical and distinct resources. To the contrary, our sense is that each of these labels makes sense only in relation to broader conversations of what they are not or what they deny. In other words, they are

34 For a call to see the promised land not as a distant promise but as a present reality in our hands, see David F. Noble, *Beyond the Promised Land: The Movement and the Myth* (Toronto: Between the Lines, 2005)

35 See Stanislas Breton, *A Radical Philosophy of St. Paul*, trans. Joseph N. Ballan (Columbia University Press, 2011); Alain Badiou, *St. Paul: The Foundation of Universalism* (Stanford: Stanford University Press, 2003).

part of a mutually constitutive conceptual (almost linguistic) system that does not allow for any autonomous set of beliefs or practices, or permit us to simply consume and exchange knowledge, but rather requires a spiritual journey of labor to prepare ourselves, or, perhaps better put, to earn our truth.[36] To see hope as a reward and not an inheritance. As such, the liturgy we imagine is not tied to any specific community beyond the broad congregation that makes up (especially legal) academics struggling to come to terms with the same phenomena that brought you, dear reader, to open these pages as well.

36 See Michel Foucault, *The Hermeneutics of the Subject: Lectures at the College de France, 1981–82*, ed. Frédéric Gros, trans. Graham Burchell (New York: Picador, 2001), 13–39.

2

The Byzantine Commonwealth and the Emerging Features of a Law of Nations in the First Millennium

Peter Petkoff

The Eastern Roman Empire represents a prototype of a Christian state both in terms of its political philosophy of Church–state relations and in terms of a political philosophy regarding legal recognition of other states – both Christian and non-Christian. The process through which Byzantium recognized emerging states in Europe and beyond became an important element of international legal order as this dominant Christian empire addressed the most critical question of political legitimacy: how can a political order established by Christ recognize other political communities that challenge its territory? As a political community established by Christ and driven by the rule of law, the Empire navigated its international relations following a very specific theological program that reflected its attitude toward its neighbors. This program held that any political project should be an imitation of the Byzantine Christ-given political community and through such process it would come closer in affinity to the Empire and become integrated into its Christian commonwealth.[1] New political and commercial treaties with

[1] Some of the general studies of Byzantine political theories include: Dimiter Angelov, *Imperial Ideology and Political Thought in Byzantium (1204–1330)* (Cambridge: Cambridge University Press, 2007); Ernest Barker, *Social and Political Thought in Byzantium, from Justinian I to the Last Palaeologus* (Oxford: Clarendon Press, 1957); H.-G. Beck, *Nomos, Kanon und Staatsraison in Byzanz* (Wien: Osterreichische Akademie der Wissenschaften, 1981); Evangelos Chrysos, "Perceptions of the International Community of States during the Middle Ages," in *Ethnogenese und Überlieferung*, ed. Karl Brunner (Wien: Oldenbourg, 1994), 293–307; Franz Dölger, *Byzanz und die europäische Staatenwelt: Ausgewählte Vorträge und Aufsätze* (Darmstadt: Wissenschaftliche Buchgesellschaft, 1964); Francis Dvornik, *Early Christian and Byzantine Political Philosophy: Origins and Background*, 2 vols. (Washington, DC: Dumbarton Oaks Center for Byzantine Studies, trustees for Harvard University; distributed by J. J. Augustin, Locust Valley, 1966); Dimitri Obolensky, *The Byzantine Commonwealth: Eastern Europe, 500–1453* (London: Phoenix Press, 2000); Georg Ostrogorsky, *History of the Byzantine State*, rev. ed. (New Brunswick, NJ: Rutgers University Press, 1969); Steven Runciman, *The Byzantine Theocracy* (Cambridge: Cambridge University Press, 1977); Jonathan Shepard, "The Byzantine

foreign powers were to be "granted" rather than negotiated and, through this act of giving, Byzantium would expand the horizons of the political and religious imaginations of the emerging powerful states. These states were, in turn, to develop aspirational political and material cultures to be like the Byzantines, while Byzantium preserved a political imagination that it was at the center of a political, religious and cultural architecture. The vision here was a family of nations that draws together loyal partners and reluctant adversaries within a political project that was (at least in theory) revelational and that could bind nations through inventive rules of international recognition and soft power.

This was a complex process of translating across Byzantine legal culture, political and religious ideas, and political and religious ritual through bilateral treaties. And whether the Byzantine outsiders were seeing themselves as conquerors who claimed imperial territory or members of the Byzantine Christian commonwealth, their rules-based relationships with Byzantium shaped the blueprint of what would become the emerging grammar of the law of nations from the twelfth century onward.

In this respect, any history of the law of nations will remain fragmented if it does not incorporate the history of the making of Medieval Europe through the treaties between Byzantium and its neighbors. This investigation incorporates discourses of canonists up to the fifteenth century, attempting to capture their concerns and intuitions (e.g., Francisco de Vitoria, Francisco Suarez and Hugo Grotius). And, in doing so, it takes account of the ways in which different traditions began to think legally and how this shaped particular legal cultures and how these legal cultures have or have not had an impact on the emerging early modern grammar of the law of nations.

2.1 KING OF KINGS RULES OVER KINGS: CHRIST HAS SET THIS EMPIRE

It is critical to understand that the political synthesis of the Byzantine *οικουμένη* and its implications for anything that could resemble a law of nations in the first millennium was that the world order was not man-made.[2] This fact had a number of implications for the ways in which the normative boundaries within and beyond Christendom were perceived and ultimately

Commonwealth 1000–1550," in *The Cambridge History of Christianity*, vol. 5, *Eastern Christianity*, ed. Michael Angold (Cambridge: Cambridge University Press, 2006), 1–52.

[2] The text in heading 2.1 refers to the four betas, the initials displayed on flags and coins from the Paleologan period which represent the motto of the Paleologoi imperial family – *Βασιλεὺς βασιλέων βασιλεύων βασιλεύουσιν*.

expanded. "The empire in which they lived was planned by God. Its government by a God-protected emperor was preordained and there was no sense in speculating on alternative forms of society."[3]

The notion that the polity was set by Christ in some way meant that in Byzantium there was no real sense that humans engaged in political engineering; rather, it was felt that humans, and the symphony of Emperor and Patriarch in particular, held the polity in trust and exercised an extension of divine economy in the *οικουμένη*. Constantine Porphyrogenitus declared that "the imperial power should be exercised with due rhythm and order," and that "the empire represented the harmony and motion of the universe as it comes from its Creator."[4] On this understanding, anything from law-making to acts of judgment or the baptizing of the emerging frontier nations was the extension of the divine economy, an initiation of the Other in the divine economy rather than a conquest of new lands. This perspective offers what we might call today "soft power." This was a commonwealth in the vision of Augustine, with shared objects of love rather than any territorial-based order.

I am well aware that a text that would suggest the existence of a law of nations in the first millennium would at the very least raise the eyebrows of international legal historians who commonly mark the emergence of the law of nations with the Peace of Westphalia and attribute parental rights to Grotius, de Vitoria or Gentili.[5] In contrast, this study proposes a much earlier beginning, and explores the ways in which Byzantines shaped a particular understanding of a global normative order, which was formed by their very distinctive understanding of a Christian empire. The key political and political-ecclesiastical debates that forged the Medieval West were initially set in motion by the conversations between the emerging new states and Byzantium, and the legal terms of their recognition as new political communities. Our perception of international law's history remains fragmented if we do not

3 Donald M. Nicol, "Byzantine Political Thought," in *The Cambridge History of Medieval Political Thought c.350–c.1450*, ed. J. H. Burns (Cambridge: Cambridge University Press, 1988), 56.

4 Constantine VII Porphyrogenitus, *De ceremoniis aulae Byzantinae libri duo*, vol. 2 (1830), proem.

5 The present proposal in some way goes even further than James Muldoon's summary on the influence of the medieval canonists on the works of Vitoria, Suarez and Grotius. James Muldoon, "A Canonistic Contribution to the Formation of International Law," *Jurist* 28, no. 3 (1968): 265–79; James Muldoon, "The Contribution of the Medieval Canon Lawyers to the Formation of International Law," *Traditio* 28 (1972): 483–97; James Muldoon, "Medieval Canon Law and the Formation of International Law," *Zeitschrift der Savigny-Stiftung für Rechtsgeschichte: Kanonistische Abteilung* 81, no. 1 (1995): 64–82.

appreciate the political and ecclesiastical dynamics of Byzantine rule and its effort to carry forward the legacy of Justinianic legal culture.

Ius gentium was used continuously throughout the Roman as well as the Byzantine period, and meant many things; but the term never referred to a law of nations demarcated by the liminality of their sovereignty. It did, however, at least in the Byzantine context, become a vehicle for contemplating in legal terms the possibility of other political communities coexisting on Roman soil. This evolving application of *ius gentium* also meant that Byzantium began to gradually recognize what we would describe today as limited or extended forms of sovereignty, and facilitated the transition from understanding *ius gentium* as *ius inter gentes*.

Byzantines, except in a few very specific cases, did not see the world outside of their own sphere as a world which can possibly exercise sovereignty.

> The treatise thus clearly shows how Byzantine political theory was translated into practice, especially in matters of foreign policy and diplomacy. . . .
>
> The Byzantine superiority complex made it embarrassing for them to treat foreigners on equal terms. The military, political or commercial treaties which they made with foreign powers were not contracts between equal partners. They were considered to be privileges and favours graciously conferred by their emperors in the form of chrysobulls or charters sealed with the imperial golden bull. Not until the thirteenth century were they forced to admit that such advertisements of their universal autocracy were no longer realistic or acceptable.[6]

Sovereignty (as much as one could claim that there was such a concept in Byzantium) was something that the Roman Emperor could exercise. This was a power given to the emperors by Christ; in fact, the entire Empire was a political order established by Christ. As a consequence, Byzantines saw the emerging new states on Roman territories as *gentes*, groups without political culture and traditions that would eventually fall in love with the Byzantine legal and political culture, (ideally) become Orthodox Christians and thereby become part of a family of princes initiated to the Empire established by Christ. The only political regimes that are referenced in Byzantine treaties as being capable of exercising sovereignty are the Persians,[7] the Arabs and (reluctantly) the Franks (and subsequent "anomalous" emperors of the Western Roman Empire). This peaceful coexistence, built on family ties

6 Nicol, "Byzantine Political Thought," 57.

7 Evangelos K. Chrysos, "The Title Βασιλευς in Early Byzantine International Relations," *Dumbarton Oaks Papers* 32 (1978): 29–75; Evangelos Chrysos, "Some Aspects of Roman-Persian Legal Relations," *Kleronomia* 8, issue A (1976): 1–56.

and ecclesiastical infrastructure, produced what is referred to in the literature as the Byzantine commonwealth:[8] a group of medieval kingdoms that emerged on the territory of Byzantium during the Great Migration of the Nations, settled their status through international treaties, acted as *federati* and often as powers challenging Constantinople and gradually "fell in love with Byzantium."

What this meant in practice was appropriating Byzantine legal and political culture – and, most importantly, its complex ecclesiastical infrastructure which linked together the Pentarchy (the Five Senses of the Universe) and the most senior Patriarchates, which together constituted the universal authority of the Church in the First Millennium.

While ecclesiastical law was dependent on its promulgation through imperial law, it developed its own system of what we could describe as universal consensus, exemplified by the system of Pentarchy, those five ancient centers of Christendom (Rome, Constantinople, Alexandria, Antioch and Jerusalem) whose consensus shaped doctrine and other normative precepts of the Universal Church. This early form of a universal normative system was based on a consensus between the parties, which was itself determined by principles of equality between the members of the Pentarchy.

> Wherefore, if we may compare great things with small, the most God-fearing of the emperors and the more eminent of the holy fathers have laid it down as necessary that the heads of the hierarchy should be attended with such circumstance, and that rich and poor alike should be placed on the same footing: to the end that the faithful, when they see this great and reverend solemnity observed for emperors and patriarchs, and for them only, may offer thanksgiving accordingly, as a sacrifice acceptable to the Lord, Who from the middle of the circle of the world's beauty glorifies the defenders thereof; and on bended knees they may pray to the Lord that all the earth on which the sun shines shall rejoice in the light of imperial victories, and all the goings of this world shall be made to shine by the prayers of the patriarchs.[9]

In this passage from the twelfth-century canonist Theodore Balsamon's *Meditata*, the Pentarchy is presented not so much as a historical reality but rather as a permanent feature of the life of the Church that integrates the mystical as well as the physical aspect of the ecclesial gathering as the center of

8 Obolensky, *Byzantine Commonwealth*; Georg Ostrogorsky, "The Byzantine Empire in the World of the Seventh Century," *Dumbarton Oaks Papers* 13 (1959): 1–21; Ostrogorsky, *History of the Byzantine State*; Dölger, *Byzanz und die Europäische Staatenwelt*.

9 *Τοῦ ἁγιωτὰτου πατριάρηου Ἀντιοηέας Θεοδώρου μελέτη ἤγουν ἀποκρισις, χάριν τῶν πατριαρχικῶν προνομίων*, PG cxxxviii, cols 1017 and 1020.

both life and governance in the Christian community. Being together in Christ is no different from being together as an ecclesiastical government.

Pentarchy itself emerged as an early fifth-century concept according to which, within the theoretically universal Christian world, ecclesiastical power was divided among the Patriarchs of Rome, Constantinople, Alexandria, Antioch and Jerusalem.[10] The Pentarchy had three manifestations: institutional, canonical and theological. They received visible force when representatives of the ancient centers of Christianity met to define correct belief and practice, as well as methods of imposing it by disciplinary canons. The first gathering at Nicaea, summoned by the emperor Constantine I in 325, set a pattern that grew into an exclusive system manifested at the fourth ecumenical council at Chalcedon in 451. By the seventh century, the Pentarchy of five great sees claimed to share extraordinary powers as equals, though Rome always commanded most honor as the see of St. Peter.

Precisely at the time when the pentarchic theory received this legal and canonical recognition, however, it lost much of its real substance due to both political and ecclesiastical fragmentation. Nevertheless, the Pentarchy, as an ideal model, continued to be mentioned in canonical texts and to be used in Byzantine polemics against the papacy. And with the interdependence between conciliar decrees and imperial legislation, it maintained a Byzantine sphere of influence through ecclesiastical law and institutions over territories that were no longer under Byzantine political control. It also developed a new principle of ecclesiastical consensus that became a model for producing universally binding rules in the Church (and the Empire) in the First Millennium. The significance of this rule-based ecclesiastical decision-making for the development of the law of nations is that, for the first time in the context of a Christian Empire, a collective ecclesiastical body (rather than the Emperor himself) was agreeing and producing universal rules applicable for the entire Christendom. What was particularly significant about these rules was that they created the possibility for collective bodies to adopt rules through debate and consensus that were universally binding and essentially

10 See John Meyendorff, *The Primacy of Peter* (London: Faith Press, 1963); "Patriarche," in *Dictionaire de droit canonique and Dictionnaire de theologie catholique*. See also J. M. Hussey, *The Orthodox Church in the Byzantine Empire* (Oxford: Clarendon Press, 1990), 297–312. Meyendorff traces the concept of pentarchy as early as Emperor Justinian I (527–65) who gave the system legal sanction in his *Novellae* (6, 109, 123) where he dispatches his most famous text establishing the relationship between Church and state, between *imperium* and *sacerdotum*. John Meyendorff, "Pentarchy," in *Dictionary of the Middle Ages*, ed. Joseph R. Strayer (New York: Charles Scribner's Sons, 1982).

independent from changing political realities.[11] It also reflects the complex interdependence between political and ecclesiastical networks within the Christian *οικουμένη*, which gradually and toward the sunset of the Byzantine Empire were transformed into an ecclesiastical network that propelled the continuity of the Byzantine state. Pentarchy represented a particular universal outlook and an interdependence between the demarcation of the Empire and that of the Church. The Empire legitimized the positions of the Universal Church and the boundaries of the Universal Church legitimized the boundaries of the Empire.

This concept of universality appears rather fluid. It placed a strong emphasis on coexistence, living together, shaping a universal normative framework and at the same time leaving space for local normative distinctiveness, thus enabling the local perspectives truly to shape any perspectives on universality. One reason why the Pentarchy is an important source for understanding early forms of universal normativity has to do with its resilience and transformation during regime change. While Byzantium was losing its territory, the normative framework of the Byzantine *Οικουμένη* or the Byzantine commonwealth persevered not only through the "Third Rome" claims of other Balkan states (and ultimately Russia) but also through the traffic of normative forms – legal, liturgical and visual. Even today, the normative rules of belonging to the Byzantine commonwealth determine the shape of the federation of autocephalous Eastern Orthodox Churches. And while their relationships increasingly resemble the politically charged contentious normative cultures of the modern nation member-states that they inhabit, the normative framework that shaped the ecclesiastical framework of the First Millennium remains exactly the same.

In this respect, the Byzantine commonwealth was certainly a departure from the system of *ius commune* that emerged in Western Europe after the twelfth century. Unlike the emerging parallel jurisdictions of civil and canon law, which cross-fertilized and shaped the legal culture of the Latin West, the Byzantine commonwealth represented the unity of the *οικουμένη* through the body of Roman law appropriated by the Eastern Roman Empire, which developed into a comprehensive system of civil and ecclesiastical law (Nomocanons) where the general imperial normative framework appropriated the distinctive normative cultures of the Churches of the Pentarchy. And when the political framework of Byzantium was shrinking and ultimately disappeared, the normative framework of the Churches of the Pentarchy

[11] The decrees of the Seven Ecumenical Councils apply to the Byzantine commonwealth with or without the existence of the Byzantine state.

and the gradually more independent Churches incorporated into the Byzantine commonwealth preserved the early normative framework of a Universal Christian *οικουμένη*.

With full awareness that it will be a huge exaggeration to speak of a law of nations or of international law in the First Millennium, we may nevertheless capture and identify certain fragments of legal and political thought and theology that relate in a particular way with themes such as a global normative order and normative relationships among different legal orders. Part of this is driven by the dichotomy of Roman law and *ius gentium*, which is to be expected. But while the appropriation and perseverance of the notion of *ius gentium* continued to appear with varying significance in Byzantium, another and more significant process of consolidation of political philosophy continued to evolve. On the one hand, it applied *ius gentium* to provincial customs, to normative practices and to outsiders' normative orders. On the other, the *ius gentium* began to acknowledge the different ways in which these increasingly secessionist outsiders' normative orders related to the Empire's own normative self-perception and how it shaped the fluid legal framework of the Byzantine commonwealth. While the Byzantines used *ius gentium* to imagine the *gentes* through *ius gentium* in its classical sense (as normative customs and traditions existing within the Empire), the realities on the ground and the changing use and references to *ius gentium* were reflecting normative agreements with increasingly independent political communities aspiring to be like (or to become) the Byzantines.[12]

Byzantine relationships with other nations were governed by two key medieval perceptions of the international community of states, the "hierarchy of states" and the "family of princes and nations." These perceptions shaped the Byzantine normative perception of "the Other."[13] All states of the *οίκουμένη* were conceived of as members of a society of nations that acquired higher or lower positions on a pyramid according to the grade of their relations to the Byzantine Emperor.[14] The Byzantines perceived their "Empire and the European world of states" as a "family of princes and nations."[15] The powerful institution of the family as the most important social formation in ancient and

[12] This is apparent in the First Bulgarian Empire's political self-perception in the ninth century when Tzar Symeon of Bulgaria (893–927), educated in Constantinople and who models his court on the Imperial Court of Constantinople, signs his correspondence as an Emperor of Bulgars and Romans and dies of a heart attack while besieging Constantinople.

[13] Evangelos, Chrysos, "Die Nordgrenze des Byzantinischen Reiches im 6. bis 8. Jahrhundert," in *Die Völker Südosteuropas im 6. bis 8. Jahrhundert*, ed. Bernhard Hänsel (Munich: Südosteuropa Gesellschaft, 1987), 27–40.

[14] Obolensky, *Byzantine Commonwealth*; Ostrogorsky, *History of the Byzantine State*.

[15] Dölger, *Byzanz und die Europäische Staatenwelt*.

medieval societies was successfully applied to the construction of close and peaceful ties among the rulers whenever it was feasible.[16] At the head of the family, with an ecumenical mission to unite all people within and outside Byzantium's borders, sat the Emperor.[17] Through these patterns of international relations between Rome and its neighbors emerged a new appropriation of Roman *ius gentium* that gradually acquired some of the features of the law of nations before the emergence of modern nations.

2.2 *IUS GENTIUM* AND THE ACCESSION TO THE CHRISTIAN *Οικουμένη*

The negotiation of Byzantium with "the Other" on its peripheries came to shape the way in which all parties understood themselves as well as concepts of legal status and political legitimacy, and it is this consolidation of empire that set the stage for the early medieval world of the eleventh century onward.

With the change of the idea of Roman citizenship in Byzantium, the references to *ius gentium* began to change as well. This situation is reflected in the legal terminology of the time. The term *civis* – together with *πολίτη* – indicates the freeman (as opposed to the slave) rather than the previous meaning of the Roman (as opposed to the non-Roman, the foreigner). Consequently, the term *civitas (πολιτεία)* became identical with *Romana libertas (ρωμαϊκή ελευθερία)* and referred to a free person or to a slave after he was granted freedom.[18] For the same reason, in the legal sources of the fifth and sixth centuries the word *peregrinus* loses its technical meaning and no longer refers to the non-Roman, the foreigner who in earlier times was the

16 Evangelos Chrysos, "The Roman Political Identity in Late Antiquity and Early Byzantium," in *Byzantium: Identity, Image, Influence: XIX International Congress of Byzantine Studies, University of Copenhagen, 18–24 August, 1996*, ed. Karsten Fledelius and Peter Schreiner (Copenhagen: Danish National Committee for Byzantine Studies, 1996), 7–16.

17 Chrysos, "Roman Political Identity"; Evangelos Chrysos, "Legal Concepts and Patterns for the Barbarians' Settlement on Roman Soil," *Das Reich und die Barbaren*, ed. Evangelos Chrysos and Andreas Schwarcz (Vienna: Böhlau, 1989), 13–24; Evangelos Chrysos, "Conclusion: De foederatis iterum," in *Kingdoms of the Empire: The Integration of Barbarians in Late Antiquity*, ed. Walter Pohl (Leiden: Brill, 1997), 185–206; Evangelos Chrysos, "The Empire, the gentes and the regna," in *Regna and Gentes: The Relationship between Late Antique and Early Medieval Peoples and Kingdoms in the Transformation of the Roman World*, ed. Hans-Werner Goetz, Jörg Jarnut, and Walter Pohl (Leiden: Brill, 2003), 13–19; Evangelos Chrysos, "Byzantines and Foreigners," in *Fifty Years of Prosopography: The Later Roman Empire, Byzantium and Beyond*, ed. Averil Cameron (Oxford: Oxford University Press, 2003), 119–36.

18 Cf. Fausto Goria, "'Romani', cittadinanza ed estensione della legislazione imperiale nelle costituzioni di Giustiniano," in *La nozione di "Romano" fra cittadinanza ed universalità: Atti del II seminario di studi storici da Roma alla terza Roma* (Naples: E.S.I., 1984), 277–342.

subject of the *ius gentium*, but rather to the stranger, the *alienus* – essentially, a barbarian.[19] In this process of distinguishing between Roman and barbarian, between foreigner and neighbor, the subject of the *ius gentium* – the *εθνικών δικαίων* – acquired a new traction and became *ius inter gentes*, heralding the concept of "the law of nations" with its medieval connotations. In this process, the application of *ius gentium* gradually began to form and to push the elements of interstate relations, which in turn shaped the relationships between the New Rome and its neighbors and produced elements picked up by the medieval canonists.[20] The new political developments triggered by the "migration of nations" and by the Arab conquest demanded new forms of negotiation and agreement, of accommodation and integration with neighbors and, ultimately, development of legal tools that tacitly recognized that other states could exercise sovereignty, ceding Roman soil without damaging the unique status of the Christ-made Roman Empire. Hence, a new approach to the *ius gentium* was needed, and it was deployed through a large nexus of legal bilateral arrangements which the Byzantines applied in order to get the best possible results and political advantage out of situations of critical military confrontation.[21]

Roman jurist Gaius defines *ius gentium* as a synthesis between the philosophical approach to law and justice as common to all mankind[22] and the exclusion of the *peregrini* from the application of the Roman Law in the second century AD.[23] Ulpianus refines this definition with an emphasis

[19] Alienus (*ξένῖος*) at any given place: e.g. a Corinthian in Antioch or, more often, a citizen of Rome or any other place on his journey to the sacred places, a pilgrim. See Chrysos, "Roman Political Identity," 10. "This term is generic, lacks any technical precision and in most of the cases where it is used for foreigners has lost its pejorative meaning, retaining only a rather neutral register." Friedhelm Winkelmann, "Die Bewertung der Barbaren in den Werken der oströmischen Kirchenhistoriker," in *Das Reich und die Barbaren*, ed. Evangelos K. Chrysos and Andreas Schwarcz (Vienna: Böhlau, 1989), 221–35. It even enters the vocabulary of the foreigners themselves, who often call themselves barbarians. C. G. Pitsakis, "A propos de la citoyenneté romaine dans l' Empire d' Orient: Un survol à travers les textes grecs," *Méditerranées* 12 (1997): 73–100; Diether Roderich Reinsch, "Ausländer und Byzantiner im Werk der Anna Komnene," *Rechtshistorisches Journal* 8 (1989): 257–74; Liliana Simeonova, "Constantinopolitan Attitudes toward Aliens and Minorities, 860s–1020s," *Études balkaniques* 11, no. 3 (2001): 91–112.

[20] Chrysos, "Perceptions of the International Community"; Max Kaser, *Ius gentium* (Cologne: Böhlau, 1993), 23ff.; cf. Francesco Sitzia, "Romanità dell'impero: ius civile e ius gentium," in *La nozione di romano tra cittadinanza e universalità* (Naples: E.S.I., 1984), 263–75.

[21] Roger C. Blockley, *East Roman Foreign Policy: Formation and Conduct from Diocletian to Anastasius* (Leeds: Francis Cairns, 1992); Raimund Schulz, *Die Entwicklung des römischen Völkerrechts im vierten und fünften Jahrhundert n. Chr* (Stuttgart: Franz Steiner Verlag, 1993); Chrysos, "Conclusion," 185–206.

[22] Aristotle, *Rhet.* I 13, 2 [δίκοαον κοινόν], Cicero, *Be bar. resp.* 14.32; cf. *De off* III 17.69 *[commune ius gentium]*.

[23] Gaius, *Inst.* I, 1.

on "all men's law" in general, and Hermogenianus, a jurist at the time of Constantine the Great, extends it to include several institutions, common to all legal systems, such as "wars, divisions of nations, foundations of kingdoms . . . commerce," and so on.[24] Justinian's jurists included the following definition in the *Institutes* (I 2, 2):

> The law of nations is common to all mankind, for nations have established certain laws, as occasion and the necessities of human life required. Wars arose, and in their train followed captivity and then slavery which is contrary to the law of nature; for by that law all men are originally born free. Further, from this law of nations almost all contracts were at first introduced, as, for instance, buying and selling, letting and hiring, partnership, deposits, loan returnable in kind, and many others.[25]

The trend to move from the original, philosophical concept of *jus gentium* and its connection with *jus naturalis* to a more concrete positive legal concept of the law of nations within the mainstream developments of Roman and Byzantine law and policies is captured by the *Etymologiae* of Isidore of Seville, as well as the inclusion of Isidore in Gratian's *Decretum* into the mainstream canon and civil law of the Middle Ages.[26] Isidore's text also reaffirms what has already been recognized and incorporated in the Justinianic corpus – that the relationships between Byzantium and its increasingly formidable neighbors has prompted new perspectives that have reshaped their emerging perceptions of authority, sovereignty and rule of law.

The starting point for the Byzantine appropriation of *ius gentium* is the acknowledgment that it occurred when the Byzantine Empire reached the point at which it considered all the nations of the world as potential subjects of the Christian emperor.[27] Rulers belonging to the Orthodox Commonwealth were perceived as either vassals within the "hierarchy of states," subordinate to the emperor who presided over this hierarchy, or a family of princes and nations that carried legal status. Whatever the specific characterization of their position, the Commonwealth subjects were understood to exist within the framework introduced by the Byzantines and accepted by all other nations of the *οικουμένη*, who through written treaties and oaths agreed to be placed in

[24] Dig. i, 1, 5.

[25] Thomas Collett Sandars, *The Institutes of Justinian with English Introduction, Translation, and Notes*, 15th imp. (London: Longmans, Green, and Co., 1922), 8.

[26] Etym. V 6.

[27] Alexander Schenk von Stauffenberg, "Die Germanen im Römischen Reich," *Die Welt als Geschichte: Zeitschrift für universalgeschichtliche Forschung* 1 (1935): 72–100.

different positions within the institution, according to their credentials in historical ties with Byzantium, their religious affiliation and so forth.[28]

In these negotiations with what were perceived as barbarian settlements, the imperial government was deliberately trying to select the proper places according to its own purposes and goals.[29] The main gain for the empire was the manpower that the barbarians put at the emperor's disposal, as *foederati*. It is important to acknowledge that *foedus* was used for any kind of international treaty, not only for the treaties which produced federates, and was used interchangeably with treaties' terms such as *societas, pax, atnicitia, συμμαχία, ειρήνη* and *φιλία*. *Amicitia* was not a particular form of treaty but a state of friendly affairs, based on common interests and cooperation.[30] As long as the territorial status was not changed, the peoples who had forced the Empire to accept their settlement on Roman soil were legally regarded as *hospites* and could live within the: Empire without enjoying sovereignty over the land of their settlement.

In this process, the legal vocabulary began to shift by placing a new emphasis on territory and frontier in order to emphasize the liminality of the *οικουμένη*. With the diminishing of the Empire's capacity for confrontations with outsiders, stronger legal terms designating "frontier" and "territory" acquired a new prominence and were applied to serve defense purposes.

> The Byzantines liked to hear expressions such as *κύριος της οικουμένης*, but in the same time they knew very well that they could not possibly identify the *orbis terrarum* with the *orbis Romanus*, the empire with *οικουμένη*. The empire had concrete borders established through legal agreements with the neighbors surrounding it. A study of the meaning of words like *solum, terra, finis, confinis, limes* and the Greek equivalents *γή, χώρα, δριον, μεϋόριος, σύνορον* shows that the empire became increasingly sensitive about the borders of its territory.[31]

In this process, *ius gentium* (in a Byzantine context) operated as a rule of recognition that enabled the Byzantine Empire to maintain its status as the

28 No original texts of any of those treaties have been preserved and the available secondary sources do not give any great details about the content of treaties. For further reading regarding the Byzantine treaties with their *foederati*, see Dölger, *Byzanz und die europäische Staatenwelt*, 35, 167; Otto Treitinger, *Die oströmische Kaiser- und Reichsidee: nach ihrer Gestaltung im höfischen Zeremoniell* (Darmstadt: H. Gentner, 1956), 195; Chrysos, "Legal Concepts and Patterns," 14.

29 Chrysos, "Legal Concepts and Patterns," 16.

30 Chrysos, "Legal Concepts and Patterns."

31 Chrysos, "Die Nordgrenze des Byzantinischen Reiches," 27–40; Jean-Pierre Arrignon and Jean-François Duneau, "La frontière chez deux auteurs byzantins: Procope de Césarée et Constantine VII Porphyrogénète," in *Géographica Byzantina*, ed. Hélène Ahrweiler (Paris: Sorbonne, 1981), 17–30.

only legitimate God-made polity, and, at the same time, deal with realities of depleted territories and political adversaries who were there to stay. By recognizing them as *foederati* through *ius gentium*, Byzantium effectively had the ability to make them *regna* inferior to Rome. They were granted the right to exist on Roman territory and were effectively subordinated, at least symbolically, to the Roman Emperor (who was usually referred to in the language of treaties as a Father of any party to a bilateral treaty). The development of the term *subiectus* in this sense created very fluid legal tools with which to integrate political outsiders into the imperial structure and make them more or less Roman. This evolving of *civis* in the direction of *subiectus* was critical for the development of the early forms of the law of nations because it became a vehicle for integrating barbarian *gentes* and individual rulers to different degrees within the Byzantine commonwealth whereby treaty-based agreements formalized the extent to which they became Roman.

This shift is reflected in the different reactions to barbarians' integration as Roman subjects. On the one hand, barbarians' substantial participation in state affairs was disliked because the essence of the Roman Empire was understood to be *έννομος πολιτεία*, a society governed by law, and these populations were explicitly characterized as being not "born and brought up under Roman law."[32] This definition also reflected the normative liminality of the Empire, the real borders of the Roman Empire, the *solum Romanum*, as "*termini juris dictionis Romanae*." Beyond these borders were the *externae nationes*, the *solum barbaric.*[33] This definition derives from Ulpianus and is included in Justinian's Digest: "*in orbe Romano qui sunt … cives Romani effecti sunt.*"[34]

On the other hand, the Christian Empire has the capacity to integrate its neighbors through a variety of rules of recognition into its Christian commonwealth and make them in some sense Christian and Roman. Quite early in the history of the new era, the terms "Christian" and "Roman" (Byzantine) were synonymous in Byzantium; the expression *Χριστιανών idvos* precisely defined the Byzantine. Similarly, the greatest Byzantine canonist, Balsamon, in the twelfth century commented that those who live an Orthodox life are Romans even if they dwell beyond the Empire's borders, thereby recognizing the fusion

32 De regno, 22A; Alan Cameron, Jacqueline Long, and Sherry Lee, *Barbarians and Politics at the Court of Arcadius* (Oakland: University of California Press, 1993), 113.

33 Amm. Marc. XVIII. 4. 5; Johannes Straub, "*Germania provincia*: Reichsidee und Vertragspolitik im Urteil des Symmachus und der Historia Augusta," in *Colloque Genevois sur Symmaque à l'occasion du mille six cinquième anniversaire du conflit de l'autel de la Victoire*, ed. François Paschoud (Paris: Belles lettres, 1986), 221.

34 This legal definition was included in Leo VI's *Basilica* (XLVI. 1. 1. 14).

of political and ecclesial identities and the raison d'être of debates about ecclesiastical jurisdiction that could easily become debates about the sphere of influence of the New Rome.[35] Thus, the Byzantine *Romanitas* was also a matter of religious affiliation. This self-identification did not change even after the fall of Constantinople in AD 1453.[36]

The principle of the cohesion of the Empire's population under the written law served additionally as an institutional mechanism for the integration of foreigners who lived within Byzantium. They were either subjects to Roman law *dediticii* or *foederati*,[37] and gained autonomy as a conditional privilege in the peace treaties regulating their settlement on Roman soil in the period of the migrations. By the end of the twelfth century the Venetians, followed by others, were allowed to organize their own jurisdiction.

With the decline of the *civitas Romana* for determining the political status of the individual (the quality of being a citizen), the *civilitas* became the central ingredient of projecting Byzantine soft power in relation to its neighbors.[38] *Civilitas* expressed a truly Roman quality of life. The values and ideals of *civilitas* remained an ambition to every emerging new state in Europe, cultivated in particular by the educated and better-off citizens. The Roman upper class set standards and goals for an ordered society according to the rule of written law and with the leisure to enjoy all forms of cultural life, which their neighbors sought to replicate. This was the *civilitas* of the Roman Empire, the cultural qualification of the Roman as opposite to the foreigner, the barbarian. At the same time, *civitas* had a transformative potential. It was not simply in opposition to a culture that was never to be Roman-like but rather indicated the capacity of outsiders to be absorbed by *civitas*.[39] This quality was open to all those who rose to its standards, both old inhabitants and newcomers (i.e. foreigners who made a successful career, usually in the army or at the imperial court), and allowed non-Romans to achieve the highest

35 IV 454 Ralles-Potles.

36 Patriarch of Constantinople Gennadius II, *Oeuvres complètes de Georges Scholarios*, ed. Louis Petit, Xénophon A. Siderides, and Martin Jugie (Paris: Maison de la bonne Presse, 1936), 252.10; Steven Runciman, *The Great Church in Captivity: A Study of the Patriarchate of Constantinople from the Eve of the Turkish Conquest to the Greek War of Independence* (New York: Cambridge University Press, 1968), 121, 379; Athanasios D. Angelou, "'Who Am I?' Scholarios' Answers and the Hellenic Identity," in *Philhellen: Studies in Honour of Robert Browning*, ed. Costas N. Constantinides et al. (Venice: Istituto Ellenico di Studi Bizantini e Postbizantini di Venezia, 1996), 1–19; Jonathan Harris, "Being a Byzantine after Byzantium: Hellenic Identity in Renaissance Italy," *Kambos: Cambridge Papers in Modern Greek* 8 (2000): 25–44.

37 Chrysos, "Byzantines and Foreigners"; Chrysos, "The Empire, the gentes and the regna."

38 Chrysos, "Byzantines and Foreigners"; Chrysos, "The Empire, the gentes and the regna."

39 Chrysos, "The Empire, the gentes and the regna."

possible rank, the emperorship, while hundreds of others finished their careers as patricians, caesars, *sebastocratores* or *basileopatores*.[40] As such, Romanness was a cultural-political rather than ethnic qualification, offering economic, demographic and political advantages to the waves of migrating peoples.[41]

The way one can imagine the Byzantine *οικουμένη* is through the emergence of a not particularly systemic but pretty clear political philosophy – that this is a political order established by Christ. Anything that happens within this political order internally and externally reflects this simple assertion. Justinian's Novel 42 is a reflection of this political theory and helps outline the complex symphony of powers in Byzantium, which in many ways underpinned the complex mission of the Orthodox Church in the post-Byzantine world. "We came to enact the present law on a matter not strange to the emperor. . . . [T]he emperor has united with the bishops in their decision and order, so that the concurrence of the divine and the human may, by just decision, create harmony."[42] The Emperor and the clergy (*βασιλεία* and *ίερωσύνη*) are responsible for distinct areas of public life, the divine and the secular (*τα θειότερα* and *τα ανθρώπινα*).[43] The expected *μία συμφωνία* = *una consonantia* is the end result of the committed cooperation of the two highest but distinct institutions.[44]

With regard to ecclesiastical affairs, law was merely a validation of synodical decisions. The Emperor's law ratified the bishops' decision: "We make the sentence of deposition passed upon him by the Holy Synod . . . our own, and enact the present law against him."[45] Synodical decision was of course valid (*κυρία*) by itself, but through the Emperor's law it would become even more valid (*κυριωτέραν*).[46] In this context, Church law legitimized the Christian

40 Chrysos, "Byzantines and Foreigners," 133.

41 Chrysos, "Byzantines and Foreigners," 134.

42 *Iustiniani Novellae*, recognovit Rudolfus Schoell. Opus Schoellii morte interceptum absolvit Guilelmus Kroll (Corpus Iuris Civilis, vol. III). https://droitromain.univ-grenoble-alpes.fr/Corpus/Novellae.htm.

43 Justinian defines his intervention as a *βασιλική έπικύρωσις* Schoell-Kroll, *Novellae*, p. 265,6–7. *(μία) αγαθή συμφωνία – (una) bona consonantia* reveals the functional connection of Novel 42 with Novel 6. Hagit Amirav and Evangelos Chrysos, "The Christian Commonwealth in Anti-Heretical Texts: The Case of the Emperor Justinian's Writings," in *New Themes, New Styles in the Eastern Mediterranean: Christian, Jewish, and Islamic Encounters, 5th–8th Centuries*, ed. Hagit Amirav and Francesco Celia (Leuven: Peeters, 2017), 19–38.

44 Schoell-Kroll, *Novellae*, pp. 263,25–264,4. ACO III p. 181,34. Amirav and Chrysos, "Christian Commonwealth in Anti-Heretical Texts."

45 The phraseology is significant: Τήν καθαιρέσεως ψήφον παρά της αγίας συνόδου . . . κυρίαν ή ημετέρα τίθεται βασιλεία = ratum nostrum ponit imperium (in terms of ratifacere).

46 Schoell-Kroll, *Novellae*, p. 267,20–2. Amirav and Chrysos, "Christian Commonwealth in Anti-Heretical Texts."

Empire, and other political communities within the commonwealth were also able to gain political legitimacy in the Empire through reception of Church law.

In terms of a balance between *imperium* and *sacerdotium*, Justinian's reference to the authority of the clergy[47] states that the *imperium* (*βασιλεία*) follows the *sacerdotium*. Whatever the bishops decided on automatically obtained the imperial validation,[48] thus equating synodical decisions with political legislation. Justinian ruled that "our laws want the sacred canons to have no less force than our laws."[49] In Novel 131,1, the Emperor established the absolute equality of the canons with the laws:

> We therefore ordain that the canons of the holy church which were enacted or confirmed by the four holy councils, that is to say, of the 318 at Nicaea, of the 150 holy fathers at Constantinople, and of the first held at Ephesus, ... and of that held at Chalcedon ..., shall have the force of law. We accept the dogmas of the aforesaid four holy councils as divine scriptures, and uphold their canons as laws.[50]

The only canons included are those that were decided by the four ecumenical councils, indicating a vision of parallel political and ecclesiastical normative *οικουμένη*.[51] The Justinain corpus also established that the theological decisions (*όροι*) of the four councils are given status equal to the Holy Bible and have great importance for the universal authority of the synodical Fathers in later generations. Here the Christian commonwealth and the Emperor's role in restoring order under divine Providence are central issues. The centrality of the Christian community's welfare was synonymous with the community of his Empire.[52]

This process of validation of the Church canons with the same rank and value as the imperial laws had significant implications for both Byzantine law

47 Schoell-Kroll, *Novellae*, p. 263,22.

48 Schoell-Kroll, *Novellae*, p. 267,30–2.

49 Cod. Justinianus I, 3, 44,1

50 Schoell-Kroll, *Novellae*, 654,24–655,8. Beck, "Nomos, Kanon und Staatsraison in Byzanz"; Amirav and Chrysos, "Christian Commonwealth in Anti-Heretical Texts."

51 Eduard Schwartz, "Die Kanonessammlungen der alten Reichskirche," *Zeitschrift der Savigny-Stiftung für Rechtsgeschichte, Kanonistische Abteilung* 25, no. 1 (1936): 1–114; Amirav and Chrysos, "Christian Commonwealth in Anti-Heretical Texts."

52 Amirav and Chrysos, "Christian Commonwealth in Anti-Heretical Texts." The text of Novel 42 is very indicative about the global religious and political authority of the Emperor. The opening text outlines the power of Justinian as a global leader and his commitment to exercise his power to restore order: In nomine Iesu Christi dei nostri Imp. Caesar Flavius Iustinianus Alemanicus Gotthicus Francicus Germanicus Anticus Alanicus Vandalicus Africanus pius felix gloriosus victoriosus triumphalis semper Augustus Menae patriarchae. Schoell-Kroll, *Novellae*, 263, 29–31.

and Byzantine external relations. The interdependence between civil and canon law related the jurisdiction and legal affairs of the Pentarchy to the legal affairs of the state, and this process continued even after many of the territories of the Pentarchy remained outside of Byzantine political control. After the fall of Constantinople, this interdependence acquired a new traction and continued to hold together the Orthodox commonwealth through complex ecclesiastical "foreign policy" mimicking the Byzantine "soft power."

The subsequent relationships between Church and state in Byzantium and with the world outside of the Byzantine *οικουμένη* were a process of expanding the sphere of influence of the *oukoumene* through soft power rather than conquest. After all, if a divine polity, then the reasoning held that any people were always capable of receiving Christ or returning to Christ and the Orthodox faith.

This "soft power" approach forged the political and religious identities of new states and redefined the normative self-perception of existing states. This integration was carried out through a complex interaction of international treaties, Christianization and the export of high culture (including legal cultures, both canon and civil).[53] By the fourteenth century this cultural cross-fertilization within the Byzantine commonwealth had produced a comprehensive and complex cultural, political and civilizational network.

2.3 BYZANTIUM AND THE ARABS: NEGOTIATION OF A STATUS QUO FROM BYZANTINE PERSPECTIVES

The Byzantine commonwealth would seemingly not work as an approach to non-Christian powers. And yet it seems that the fluid notion of empire developed some rather innovative forms for negotiating political coexistence and international trade with powerful Muslim neighbors. A fascinating feature of the treaty-based relations between Byzantium and the Muslim world were the Muslim compounds that gradually acquired the status of Muslim religious establishments in Constantinople.[54] These compounds emerged as early as the ninth century and gradually evolved from compounds for high-ranking

[53] The complex and sophisticated program of international treaties was a key form of "soft power," forging the political and religious identities of emerging new states and redefining the normative self-perception of existing states. Chrysos, "The Title Βασιλευς in Early Byzantine International Relations"; Chrysos, "Some Aspects of Roman-Persian Legal Relations." See also Clarence Gallagher, *Church Law and Church Order in Rome and Byzantium: A Comparative Study* (Aldershot: Ashgate Variorum, 2002).

[54] Glaire Anderson, "Islamic Spaces and Diplomacy in Constantinople (Tenth to Thirteenth Centuries C.E.)," *Medieval Encounters* 15, no. 1 (2009): 86–113.

Muslim prisoners of war to centers where Muslim traders as noble prisoners of war gravitated and which guaranteed the sanctity of the treaties[55] (their status reflecting the status of major Christian sites, such as the Church of the Holy Sepulchre in Jerusalem, under Muslim control). These treaties tell us that in the eyes of the Byzantines, their powerful Muslim neighbors had to be imagined as state actors, without the wider scheme of the Byzantine *οικουμένη*, in a way different from other emerging Christian state actors.[56] The Byzantines were prepared to see Muslim prisoners of war as subjects under imperial protection, able to exercise their freedom of worship in Constantinople. In return, the Byzantines expected a reciprocal level of protection of Christians under Muslim rule.

What is remarkable about these mosques (which were technically compounds with more general functions including public prayer) was that they represented a complex understanding of diplomatic relations with the Muslim world and an evolution of elaborate political ideas.[57] There is evidence from several sources that the Muslim prisoners participated in calls for prayer, which among other things reaffirmed their allegiance to the caliphs in Bagdad. This meant that, at least at a ritualistic level, the Byzantines recognized the political legitimacy of their powerful Muslim neighbors. In that sense, the rules of war and the tolerant treatment of Muslim prisoners of war in Byzantium contributed significantly to the recognition of Muslim statehood by the Byzantines.[58] "[T]here are two lordships, that of the Saracens and that of the Romans, which stand above all lordship on earth, and shine out like the two mighty beacons in the firmament."[59] In his correspondence with the Caliph, Patriarch Nicholas Mystikos (852–925) links justice with treaty obligations.[60] Mystikos explores what can be identified as the themes of justice for all nations, treatment of noncombatant civilians, war crimes committed by Muslim converts who do not respect Christian or Muslim perceptions of justice, *pacta sunt servanda*, and breach of international treaties. What is significant is that the field of Byzantine diplomacy had taken up a position already adopted by Photius and with Constantine Cyril the Philosopher during his mission to the Arabs. On the one hand, this position acknowledged the Arabs, "the Other," as a different political factor from the variety of political

55 Anderson, "Islamic Spaces and Diplomacy in Constantinople."
56 Anderson, "Islamic Spaces and Diplomacy in Constantinople."
57 Anderson, "Islamic Spaces and Diplomacy in Constantinople."
58 Anderson, "Islamic Spaces and Diplomacy in Constantinople."
59 Nicholas Mystikos, *Letters*, ed. and trans. Romilly James Heald Jenkins and Leendert Gerrit Westerink (Washington, DC: Dumbarton Oaks Center for Byzantine Studies, 1973), 3.
60 Mystikos, *Letters*, 7–17.

formations within the Byzantine commonwealth that aspired to become like the Byzantines. The Arabs, on the other hand, just like the Persians, were a formidable foe that had to be construed differently. They were not simply another group of lawless barbarians to be assimilated through Christianization. Byzantines clearly saw Muslim rulers as legitimate sovereign rulers.

The language thus changes and the reminder that every power comes from God acknowledges the possibility that parallel sovereignties exist as part of a divine plan. This position recognized theologically political realities and at the same time became a powerful tool for negotiating rules-based international relations. If there are two or more legitimate regional powers, their peaceful coexistence and wartime relations have to be rule based. In fact, at least in theory, relationships between the Arabs and the Byzantines on a treaty level appear to have been based on the presumption of equality. This equality was expressed as rule-based and justice-based governance. If both parties represented political communities established by God, they must be compliant with the idea of Divine Justice and mirror this in their governance. This was quite a remarkable conclusion in light of the often fairly crude Christian-Muslim polemics that pervaded other contexts, and a very different take from the soft power approach in relation to emerging European states.[61] What we see here is the maintenance of a God-given framework where the Christian states recognize – on similar terms – non-Christian states. The difference of language is remarkable because it suggests that the Arabs (just like the Persian Empire) were also rules-based societies, that they represented developed legal cultures and that they did not need to receive their legal culture from Byzantium (in the ways that emerging European pagan states did), even if it were the Byzantines who had to remind their powerful Muslim adversaries that this was the case (which in fact was more wishful thinking than reality by the ninth century).

The political determination of the Muslim state was ultimately something that was God given, and while the theological anti-Muslim polemics remained, the state could go so far as to provide religious compounds for its religious adversaries and allow freedom of worship under the protection of the Christian

[61] Юрий Валерьевич Максимов [Yuri Valerievich Maksimov], *Византийские сочинения об Исламе: Антимусульманская апологетическая литература* [Byzantine Writings on Islam: An Anti-Muslim Apologetic Literature] *VII–XV вв*, vol. 1 (Изд-во СПбГУ [St. Petersburg University], 2006); Johannes Koder and Ioannis Stouraitis, *Byzantine War Ideology between Roman Imperial Concept and Christian Religion: Akten des Internationalen Symposiums (Vienna, 19–21 May 2011)* (Vienna: Verlag der Österreichischen Akademie der Wissenschaften, 2012); Metropolitan Museum of Art, *Byzantium and Islam: Age of Transition, 7th–9th Century*, ed. Brandie Ratliff and Helen C. Evans (New York: Metropolitan Museum of Art, 2012); Speros Vryonis, *Byzantium: Its Internal History and Relations with the Muslim World: Collected Studies* (London: Variorum Reprints, 1971).

Emperor. This was a price worth paying to protect the interests of the Byzantine *οικουμένη* in Muslim domains, where the ancient patriarchates of Jerusalem, Antioch and Alexandria remained bastions of the Byzantine commonwealth.

> All earthly authority and rule depend from the rule and authority that are above; and there is no authority among men, nor any potentate who succeeds to his power on earth by his native ability, unless the Author and Ruler and only Potentate in the Highest shall approve his succession. Therefore it is right, if possible, that all of us who have obtained power among men, even though there should be nothing else to promote our mutual contact and converse through words, yet for this very reason-that we have obtained the gift of our authorities from a common Head-is it right that we should not omit day by day to make contact with one another, both by letters and by the emissaries who serve us in our affairs.[62]

The Byzantine Empire struggled to remain the center of the Christian *οικουμένη* and beyond Christendom, in which the Empire was perceived as a symbolic yardstick of legitimacy (Muslim rulers continued to refer to the Emperor as their Father in treaties up until the Fall of Constantinople). At the same time, on a practical level, the Christian Empire was steadily weakened and politically shrinking, and thus all-too-happy to enlist Christian schismatics and non-Christian political powers in order to preserve its international status.

The key element of these treaties seems to acknowledge, at least at a rhetorical level, that both powers are law abiding. This was a departure from the concept that Rome is the only civilization that knows and lives by the rule of law and that the relationship between Roman law and *ius gentium* is a process of translating across Roman legal culture. In many ways, the treaties with Persia had already created the possibility of ceding Roman territory to another power and regarding foreign powers other than Rome as societies based on the rule of law, and therefore exercising sovereignty. In the case of the Arab world, this acknowledgment seemed to represent a paradigm shift. It referred to the fact not so much that Islamic rulers had an extensive legal infrastructure comparable to Roman law but rather that Muslim rulers were (often) recognized by their "God-given authority."[63]

> But before I describe them, I will say this: there are many fields in which one who is set up to rule will properly try to excel, unless he chooses to convict himself of his unworthiness for his office, and, instead of setting his subjects an example of a life directed toward virtue, and of arousing in them a pleasant

[62] Mystikos, *Letters*, 3.
[63] Mystikos, *Letters*, 7–17.

> admiration and love of his personal rule, excites and provokes them rather to hatred and insolence. The summit (as it were) of the ruler's virtue, and the crown of his achievements is Justice.[64]

In the correspondence of patriarch Mystikos, we encounter an emerging political theory that relies on a particular understanding of the origins of political power in Byzantium. Since this political order is set by Christ and cannot be improved through social engineering, it is conceivable that any power on Earth is God-given (which resonates with the conversation between Christ and Pilate in John 19:11). This approach reveals a very subtle strategy of using *ius gentium* as a bridge for translating across Roman legal culture in an Arab context, which facilitates the deployment of Roman legal tools to craft the terms of the agreement.[65]

> You should first have accused them of their fault, convicted them of wrong-doing, exhorted them to amend and to abandon their evil course: and this not once only, but twice or more. Then, if they proved stubborn and, instead of turning to the good, persisted in the worse course, you might, without any fear of vengeance from God or man, have undertaken to punish and repress the folly of those who had conspired in the fault. But nothing of this was done: On the contrary, as I say, you have killed as if they were your enemies men who are innocent, who have committed no fault, who have broken no article of the original agreements.[66]

In several volumes on Byzantium and the Arabs from the fourth to the sixth century, Irfan Shahîd established a theoretical construction of the Saracens who lived within the Roman-Persian border as being *foederati* of the late Roman Empire. Thus, he sees the Arab "*phylarchs*," who were officially bestowed with official titles, as leaders of federates "who remained non-citizens and to whom *civitas* was not extended."[67] At the same time, it is quite clear that the imperial administration did not see them as political aliens.[68] They were "Roman Saracens," not "Persian Saracens."[69]

64 Mystikos, *Letters*, 5.
65 Mystikos, *Letters*, 15–16.
66 Mystikos, *Letters*, 7.
67 Irfan Shahîd, *Byzantium and the Arabs in the Fifth Century* (Washington, DC: Dumbarton Oaks Research Library and Collection, 1989); Irfan Shahîd, *Byzantium and the Arabs in the Sixth Century* (Washington, DC: Dumbarton Oaks Research Library and Collection, 1995).
68 Chrysos, "Legal Concepts and Patterns"; Chrysos, "Roman Political Identity"; Chrysos, "Conclusion"; Chrysos, "The Empire, the gentes and the regna."
69 John Malalas, *The Chronicle of John Malalas: A Translation*, trans. Elizabeth Jeffreys, Michael Jeffreys, Roger Scott and Brian Croke (Melbourne: Australian Association for Byzantine Studies, 1986), 271.

2.4 THE EMPIRE, THE CHURCH AND THE WORLD

The Byzantine commonwealth does not usually form part of the legal sources that shaped the early canon of the law of nations. This might be considered a blind-spot in the history of international law. While the fall of Constantinople represented the fall of the political Byzantine *οικουμένη*, Russia and other regional players, aspiring to be successors of Byzantium, developed the doctrine of the "Third Rome" – in short, pledging the continuity of the Byzantine commonwealth, a tactic that resonates even today in the project Ruskij Mir.[70] And, perhaps even more importantly, the Byzantine commonwealth was shaped by soft power that was oriented to the ways in which local customs and traditions fit within a wider framework of imperial law. As mentioned earlier, this soft power approach attempted to broker ecclesiastica and civil law.

Understanding the grammar of the "soft power" of the Byzantine Orthodox commonwealth tells us a great deal about the complex relations between states[71] and the constitutive interplay between religion and state within Byzantium. It is through this exercise of soft power that other rulers found their models for imitation and wanted to associate themselves with this glittering symbol of imperial and court life and of the Orthodox faith. The decline of the Empire placed an increased emphasis on the role of the patriarch, both within Constantinople (in relation to the imperial office) and outside it (through Mount Athos as a microcosm of the Orthodox commonwealth). It also highlighted the need for the Church to engage diplomatically with a complex variety of external actors.[72] After the fall of Constantinople, it was the ecumenical patriarch and the monks on Mount Athos who still represented that shared consciousness.[73] The Ecumenical Patriarchate, Mount Athos and Moscow's claim as "The Third Rome" continue to serve that representative function today. Orthodox networks and cooperation within the European Union (EU) are only a bleak resemblance of the Byzantine commonwealth that survived the Ottomans (but not the Balkan Wars).[74]

70 Peter Petkoff, "New Worlds and New Churches: The Orthodox Church(es) and the European Union," *God and the EU: Faith in the European Project*, ed. Jonathan Chaplin and Gary Wilton (Abingdon: Routledge, 2016), 70–88.

71 Joseph S. Nye, *Soft Power: The Means to Success in World Politics* (New York: Public Affairs, 2004).

72 Petkoff, "New Worlds and New Churches"; Averil Cameron, "Mount Athos and the Byzantine World," in *Mount Athos: Microcosm of the Christian East*, ed. Graham Speake and Metropolitan Kallistos Ware (Oxford: Peter Lang Verlag, 2012), 11–28.

73 Cameron, Long, and Lee, *Barbarians and Politics at the Court of Arcadius*, 19.

74 Obolensky, *Byzantine Commonwealth*. The last figure to give expression to the idea of the Orthodox commonwealth, Joachim III, Patriarch of Constantinople, died at the outset of the Balkan Wars. The end of the nineteenth century and the emergence of nation-states and de

It would nevertheless be naïve to underestimate the residual energy of the Orthodox commonwealth, which is gradually being reconstituted in different contexts and has all the facilities to thrive within the context of contemporary foreign policy. Religious engagement in Russia's foreign policy – in the context of the EU and in the context of the North Atlantic Treaty Organization (NATO) expansion and the creation of new independent Orthodox churches – shows that the ancient networks and allegiances of the Orthodox commonwealth are alive and well. Even the mission of the patriarch of Jerusalem today is articulated as a departure from national (Greek, Arabic, Israeli) ecclesial identities and uses, as a point of reference, an ecclesial identity based on the more inclusive transnational universal *Romanitas* of the Byzantine commonwealth.[75]

We cannot understand the global outlook of the Byzantines without understanding the idea of the Christian commonwealth, or *οικουμένη*, and its totalizing ideology. It is an all-inclusive project that imagines the possibility of including *all* mankind under its umbrella. This project is both religious and political. Heretics and non-Christian political projects always have the potential to change and become a proper part of the Christian commonwealth. This is a critical junction at which to understand the interdependence between Byzantium's attitude to heresies and toward the religious and/or political "Other." It is also a key toward understanding the normative boundaries and bonds within the emerging plural community of states that began to emerge after the Great Migration of the Nations.

RECOMMENDED READING

Angelov, Dimiter. *Imperial Ideology and Political Thought in Byzantium (1204–1330)*. Cambridge: Cambridge University Press, 2007.

Barker, Ernest. *Social and Political Thought in Byzantium, from Justinian I to the Last Palaeologus: Passages from Byzantine Writers and Documents*. Oxford: Clarendon Press, 1957.

facto national churches marked the end of the Byzantine commonwealth. Obolensky, *Byzantine Commonwealth*.

75 Interview with Anna Kouroulis, 16 October 2015, http://orthochristian.com/86858.html. The last pronouncement on the matter of the Christ-given Empire and symphony of powers was made by Patriarch Antony IV in 1393 to the Grand Duke of Moscow, Basil I: "The holy Emperor has a great place in the church. He is not to be compared with other rulers and local princes. For from the beginning the emperors established and confirmed the true faith in all the *oecumene*. . . . Therefore, my son, it is not proper for you to say that we have a church but no emperor. It is not possible for Christians to have a church and not to have an emperor. For the church and the empire have a great unity and communion. The one cannot be separated from the other." In Barker, *Social and Political Thought in Byzantium*, 194–6.

Dvornik, Francis. *Early Christian and Byzantine Political Philosophy: Origins and Background*. 2 vols. Washington, DC: Dumbarton Oaks Center for Byzantine Studies, trustees for Harvard University, 1966.

Obolensky, Dimitri. *The Byzantine Commonwealth: Eastern Europe, 500–1453*. London: Phoenix Press, 2000.

Runciman, Steven. *The Byzantine Theocracy*. Cambridge: Cambridge University Press, 1977.

3

Christianity and the Birth of Ambassadorial Deontology: Some Historical Notes

Tiziana Faitini and Dante Fedele*

3.1 INTRODUCTION

Embassy lies at the heart of Christianity. Recall the archangel Gabriel, sent as God's messenger to Mary in the village of Nazareth. This event alone, described in Luke's Gospel (1:26–37) and represented in lively pictures and sculptures innumerable times, is enough to remind us of the long historical connection between Christianity and diplomacy. And so it is no surprise that, as a specific literature on the ambassador began to develop in early modern Europe, the analogy between diplomats and angels was very frequently used. The roots of this analogy can be traced back to the writings of the Jewish thinker Philo of Alexandria († c. AD 50), and to the biblical *Letter to the Hebrews* (1:14), traditionally credited to Paul. It was from the late Middle Ages onward, however, that the analogy really gained currency, in parallel with the development of diplomatic theory and practice. In 1214, Pope Innocent III called the legates who had been sent to Southern France to pacify the region troubled by the Albigensian heresy, "angels of peace and faith." In about 1230, the French theologian and bishop of Paris William of Auvergne used the example of the ambassadors dispatched by Italian communes to illustrate, in his *De universo creaturarum*, the role played by angels in carrying out God's orders. Some years later, in his *Liber de doctrina tacendi et dicendi*, the Italian judge Albertano da Brescia instructed ambassadors on how to address their recipient drawing on the text of "Hail Mary" and the episode of the Annunciation. During the period between the late fifteenth and the mid-seventeenth century, the analogy became commonplace in the literature on

* Although this chapter is a common work, Sections 3.1 and 3.4 were jointly written, Section 3.2 is by Tiziana Faitini and Section 3.3 by Dante Fedele. This chapter is part of a project of Tiziana Faitini, which has received funding from the European Union's Horizon 2020 research and innovation programme under Marie Skłodowska-Curie grant agreement No. 665958.

the ambassador that was spreading across Europe; its purpose was usually to confer dignity to the ambassadorial office through its direct comparison with an ideal figure of the Christian tradition.[1]

Angels, though, were not the only characters in Christian history invoked to this end. In his *De legationibus libri quinque* (1548), the German Catholic jurist and theologian Konrad Braun (who would later represent the archbishop of Mainz at the Council of Trent) went even further, mentioning the prophets, the apostles, and even Jesus Christ (defined as the Father's ambassador). This approach was especially popular among subsequent Catholic authors, like the Polish Krzysztof Warszewicki, the Spanish Juan Antonio de Vera y Zuñiga and Christoval de Benavente y Benavides, the Italians Gasparo Bragaccia and Anastasio Germonio, and the Flemish Frederik van Marselaer.[2]

This endeavor to dignify the ambassador's office by comparing it to the offices performed by the angels, the prophets, the apostles, and Christ is but one aspect of the multifaceted relationship between Christianity and diplomacy through history. Other (more practical) aspects include the "right of chapel" – that is the right to practice the ambassador's own religion, or rather that of his principal, within the host state, and to guarantee his fellow nationals access to the embassy chapel, if not always to his coreligionists among local citizens – or the right of asylum in the premises of the mission, in juridical discussions of which constant reference was made to the right of asylum in ecclesiastical buildings. The "right of chapel" in particular proved to be an effective tool in the accommodation of religious dissent in early modern Europe, and both of these rights lie at the origins of the idea of the extraterritoriality of diplomatic premises.[3]

1 See Dante Fedele, *Naissance de la diplomatie moderne (XIIIe–XVIIe siècles): L'ambassadeur au croisement du droit, de l'éthique et de la politique* (Baden-Baden: Nomos Verlag; Zürich: Dike Verlag, 2017), 546–53; and Daniel Ménager, *L'ange et l'ambassadeur: Diplomatie et théologie à la Renaissance* (Paris: Garnier, 2013).

2 See Conradus Brunus, "De legationibus libri quinque," in Conradus Brunus, *Opera tria [...]. De legationibus libri quinque [...] De caeremoniis libri sex [...] De imaginibus liber unus [...]* (Moguntiae apud S. Victorem: Ex officina Francisci Behem, 1548), dedicatory letter [unpaged], ch. I.5, 11–12, who referred – among other passages – to John 8:29, 12:44–5, 12:49, 14:31, and 20:21; Rom. 10:15; and Gal. 1:12. Further references, made by later authors, included 2 Cor. 5:20 (where Paul says "pro Christo ergo legationem fungimur"): on this passage, see Anthony Bash, *Ambassadors for Christ: An Exploration of Ambassadorial Language in the New Testament* (Tübingen: J. C. B. Mohr, 1997), 87–116; and Lactantius, *Divinarum institutionum* IV.25 (where Christ is defined as God's "legatus et nuntius"). See Fedele, *Naissance*, 225–6.

3 See Benjamin J. Kaplan, "Diplomacy and Domestic Devotion: Embassy Chapels and the Toleration of Religious Dissent in Early Modern Europe," *Journal of Early Modern History* 6, no. 4 (2002): 341–61; Dante Fedele, "Religious Freedom and Diplomacy," in *The Wiley-Blackwell Encyclopedia of Diplomacy*, ed. Gordon Martel, 4 vols. (Hoboken, NJ: Wiley-Blackwell, 2018), vol. 4, 1597–1610; and Dante Fedele, "'Templorum praerogativae cum Legatorum domibus communicabantur:' Il tempio nel dibattito sull'inviolabilità della sede

This chapter approaches the connection between Christianity and diplomacy from another viewpoint, exploring the historical formation of ambassadorial deontology in the late Middle Ages. The word "deontology" was coined by Jeremy Bentham at the beginning of the nineteenth century, and its "retroactive" application is, of course, anachronistic. Nonetheless, deontology is useful in that it theorizes duties – and moral duties in particular. And, from the Middle Ages onwards, a theory on the duties of the ambassadors, deeply rooted in the Christian tradition of thought on the duties and offices of ecclesiastical ministers, undoubtedly begins to take shape. After a brief survey of this tradition of thought and some notes on the polysemic concept of *officium* (which can be translated as "duty," "service," or "office"), the chapter will focus on two jurists, Lucas de Penna († c. 1390) and Bernard de Rosier (1400–75), who played important roles in modeling the public figure of the ambassador and his professional, moral, and juridical duties. Lucas and Bernard were the first authors to deal explicitly with the ambassador's qualities and behavior, raising questions that were discussed extensively in early modern literature on the ambassador. Their texts, informed by their active participation in political life, built on the legacy of the abovementioned Christian tradition in defining the office of the ambassador, and drew upon the Bible, theological works, and canon law. Analysis of these texts thus provides an important fresh perspective on the contribution made by Christianity to the early shaping of a figure who was to become a leading actor on the stage of international law.

This analysis of the office of the ambassador will also reveal much about the broader issue of the intertwining of theological and juridical theory and practice: two dimensions whose constant, but very nuanced, historical interplay cannot be explained as a purely linear process of either secularization or spiritualization.[4] The example of the historical semantic stratification of *officium* is, in this regard, extremely significant. What follows will demonstrate that *officium* was originally a moral and juridical Roman concept, before becoming an institutional and moral linchpin of the medieval Christian church. During the late Middle Ages and the early modern period, the concept of *officium* elaborated within the ecclesiastical and religious hierarchies of the medieval church was used to moralize society as a whole, and also became a crucial element of the emerging statal bureaucracy. Both the concept

diplomatica nella prima età moderna," in *La territorializzazione del sacro: Valenza teologico-politica del tempio*, ed. Tiziana Faitini (Brescia: Morcelliana, 2016), 195–222.

4 Henning Ottmann, "Politische Theologie als Begriffsgeschichte: Oder: Wie man die politischen Begriffe der Neuzeit politisch-theologisch erklären kann," in *Der Begriff der Politik: Bedingungen und Gründe politischen Handelns*, ed. Volker Gerhardt (Stuttgart: Metzler, 1990), 169–88; Michele Nicoletti and Luigi Sartori, *Teologia politica* (Bologna: EDB, 1991).

itself and the practice of officeholding to which it had given birth were fundamental to the early development of the administrative apparatus of the modern state and to modern political rationality[5] – not to mention the shaping of the deontological rules for rulers, public officials, and professionals.[6] An intriguing commingling of elements from both the classical and the Christian traditions seems thus to lie at the very foundations of the modern state. Our investigation of the ambassador and his duties will, we hope, include insights into these complex historical processes and their implications.

3.2 *OFFICIUM*: REFLECTING ON DUTIES AND ROLES IN THE LATIN AND CHRISTIAN TRADITION

The concept of *officium* was first introduced in Latin by Cicero in the first century BC. The Roman statesman and writer devoted his treatise *De officiis*[7] to the exploration of this concept, and the *decorum* and *convenientia* of human actions intrinsic to it: that personal actions must be seemly and convenient to the situation and the *persona* (a term which meant both an individual person and a role) who is carrying them out. A clear connection between duty, status, and role can already be discerned here in relation to both individual and public roles. The *officium*, connected to the duty to probity in the management of others' affairs, whether as a public official or in one's private transactions, also entered the Roman law. By the end of the third century, however, the term mainly referred to the duty and tasks connected with a public office or the fulfillment of a function of public interest (which were also called *munus publicum* or, in some cases, *ministerium*).[8] Some specific juridical texts – the books *de officio* – on the duties and functions of imperial officials began to

[5] The impact of the classical and ecclesiastical tradition of the *officia* on the building of the modern state, from the Middle Ages onwards, has been explored from several points of view. In addition to the classic Ernst H. Kantorowicz, *The King's Two Bodies: A Study in Medieval Political Theology* (Princeton: Princeton University Press, 2016 [1957]), see Udo Wolter, "The *Officium* in Medieval Ecclesiastical Law as a Prototype of Modern Administration," in *Legislation and Justice*, ed. Antonio Padoa-Schioppa (Oxford: Oxford University Press, 1997), 17–36, with further references.

[6] See Tiziana Faitini, "Shaping the Profession: Some Thoughts on Office, Duty, and the Moral Problematisation of Professional Activities in the Counter-Reformation," *Journal of Early Modern Christianity* 7, no. 1 (2020): 177–200; see also Michael Stolleis, "Grundzüge der Beamtenethik (1550–1650)," in Michael Stolleis, *Staat und Staatsräson in der frühen Neuzeit: Studien zur Geschichte des öffentlichen Rechts* (Frankfurt am Main: Suhrkamp, 1990), 197–231.

[7] Cicero, *De officiis*, trans. Walter Miller (Cambridge, MA: Harvard University Press, 1913).

[8] See Francesco Grelle, "Le categorie dell'amministrazione tardoantica: *officia, munera, honores*," in *Società romana e impero tardoantico*, vol. 1, *Istituzioni ceti economie*, ed. Andrea Giardina (Roma: Laterza, 1986), 37–56.

circulate, and parts of these texts eventually found their way into the first book of the *Digest*.[9] The books *de officio* collected instructions of various kinds, centered on the person of the magistrate or whichever body held authority over the juridical institution in question. They were probably compiled in order to provide various jurisdictions with regulations of immediate interest, and commonly included brief references to the official's moral integrity. In the Roman context, *officium* thus referred to a concrete duty rooted in an actor's social position, and translated explicitly into a worldly function.

It is upon this legacy that the Christian tradition built its own analysis *de officiis*. In this tradition, worldly functions and ministries were regarded as duties which expressed a transcendent moral imperative; the combination of moral and institutional aspects in the concept of *officium* thus became even more overt. The first of these works was a treatise written at the end of the fourth century by Ambrose, archbishop of Milan and Doctor of the Church, whose *De officiis* is explicitly modeled on that of Cicero.[10] Ambrose deals with the same issues as Cicero, but, addressing the honest Christian, rearticulates them in the light of the Gospels; the fundamental values, examples used, authorities cited, and responses given all differ from those of his model.

Ambrose's main theme is clear: the *officium* is that which is owed to the community, according to one's own position and role within it. The body, a crucial metaphor for the conceptualization of *officium*, is used to refer to mankind and the community of the Church. This trope had been used before by some ancient authors and was introduced into the Christian vocabulary with Paul's use of the image of the Church as Jesus's mystical body (1 Cor. 12:6–30).[11] Ambrose remarks that no one member of the body can "claim the function (*officia*) of any other" without "going against nature"; at the same time, all members "are necessary to the body." Similarly, within the social or ecclesiastic body, each member, in its own particular way, has to assist the others in a reciprocal service ("*mutuo ministerio*"): "if one fails in its duty (*officio suo*), the rest are impeded."[12] The image of the body implies hierarchical

9 See Aldo Dell'Oro, *I libri de officio nella giurisprudenza romana* (Milano: Giuffrè, 1960).

10 On Cicero's impact on Christian thought, see Norman E. Nelson, "Cicero's De Officiis in Christian Thought 300–1300," in *Essays and Studies in English and Comparative Literature* (Ann Arbor: University of Michigan Press, 1933), 59–160.

11 For an overview on the organicistic metaphor, see Anton-Hermann Chroust, "The Corporate Idea and the Body Politic in the Middle Ages," *Review of Politics* 9, no. 4 (1947): 423–52; and the classic Henri de Lubac, *Corpus Mysticum: The Eucharist and the Church in the Middle Ages*, trans. Gemma Simmonds, Richard Price, and Christopher Stephens (London: SCM-Notre Dame University Press, 2006).

12 Ambrosius Mediolanensis, *De officiis*, trans. Ivor J. Davidson (Oxford: Oxford University Press, 2002), III.3.17–19, 363–5.

differentiation between its parts but also respect and interdependence. Since each member has a particular duty and function, which cannot be fulfilled by any other, any impairment affects the body as a whole. In these lines, Ambrose anticipates further political elaborations on this metaphor – one of the most influential of which was John of Salisbury's *Policraticus* (twelfth century).[13] Throughout the Middle Ages, these elaborations provided rulers (and all the various members of society) with instructions on the duties and conduct appropriate to them, and must in fact be understood as central to the history of the deontology of public officials.

At the beginning of the seventh century, another archbishop, the Spanish Isidore of Seville, composed a book entitled *De officiis ecclesiasticis*. Isidore directly addressed the clergy and their function as ministers of the ecclesiastic body and his approach was very specifically ecclesiastic and liturgical. He depicts the sacred order of the clergy according to a precise, hierarchical order of perfection; each ecclesiastic ministry ("*ministerium ecclesiae*")[14] is minutely described, from the priest to the lecturer to the married person, from the bishop to the penitent to the catechumen (who was not yet a member of the Christian community). For each of these figures, their biblical origins, particular liturgical tasks, and required moral qualities are outlined. Each *officium* is defined by its combination of these elements, and is an administrative role precisely positioned in the ecclesiastic community, which implies a vocation and requires the person in question to behave in a certain way and to possess certain qualities.

Following in Isidore's footsteps, the writings on ecclesiologic – and particularly liturgical – *officia* were widely developed in the late Middle Ages.[15] The most important treatise – because of both its comprehensiveness and its popularity – is probably the *Rationale divinorum officiorum*, written by William Durand at the end of the thirteenth century. Its definition of *officium* encapsulates all of the earlier tradition and epitomizes what the *officium* had become by that time:

> The *officium*, according to Isidore, is an action proper or appropriate to each person (*proprius vel congruus actus uniuscuiusque persone*) according to the traditions and laws of their polity or profession (*secundum mores et leges*

[13] On John of Salisbury's important text, centered on the notion of *officium*, see Frédérique Lachaud, *L'éthique du pouvoir au Moyen-Âge: L'office dans la culture politique (Angleterre, vers 1150-vers 1330)* (Paris: Garnier, 2010).

[14] See Isidorus Hispalensis, *De officiis ecclesiasticis*, ed. Christopher M. Lawson (Turnhout: Brepols, 1989), II.5, 56.

[15] See Cyrille Vogel, *Medieval Liturgy: An Introduction to the Sources* (Washington, DC: The Pastoral Press, 1986), 13–16.

> *civitatis vel institute professionis*). The *officia* of monks, priests, hermits, etc. are all different. … Everybody should carry out their own *officium*, or, according to Isidore, "each person should do those things that are detrimental (*officere*) to nobody but are of benefit to all."[16]

Although these lines are from a liturgical treatise, *officium* is clearly not meant only as a liturgical service: one's *officium* belongs to a (public or individual) person and is a set of actions determined by membership of an institutionalized community, whether a city or one of the various religious professions that made up the ecclesiastic community. An *officium*, moreover, has to be oriented to the common good. As this definition reveals, although the concept of *officium* originated and was extensively elaborated in the textual tradition touched upon, its scope was much wider. Indeed, canon law and theology were to make the concept central to the division of tasks and states of life within the Christian community and the body politic as a whole – and to the evaluation of the performance of those tasks and the fulfillment of those states, carried out by the sacrament of confession (which the Fourth Lateran Council in 1215 decreed that all Christians had to annually make).

A relevant example of this approach can be found in Thomas Aquinas's masterwork, the *Summa theologiae*. The concluding section of its second part includes an analysis of the conditions and states of life (both lay and secular) and of their corresponding *officia*. In Aquinas, *officium* has to do with the need for differentiated actions within the community and, in some regards, is very close to the concept of the ministry (*ministerium*), valid in both ecclesiological and liturgical terms. It expresses a person's duty to embody, for the common good, the role of which they are the repository and which responds to the needs of others and society as a whole. For this reason, "offices (*officia*) differ properly in respect of acts that are referred to others; thus a teacher is said to have an office, and so is a judge, and so forth."[17] And if the *officia* of judges and teachers are different, their virtues and sins must also differ. The penitential literature that flourished in the same period, thanks to the activity of the Mendicant orders and the concrete development of the practice of the confession, made this fact plainly evident: the analysis (and evaluation) of duties gradually extended to the whole society, in accordance with a broader

[16] Guillelmus Durantus, *Rationale divinorum officiorum*, ed. Anselme Davril and Timothy M. Thibodeau, 3 vols. (Turnhout: Brepols, 1995–2000), V.II.1, vol. 2, 14 (our translation).

[17] Thomas Aquinas, *Summa theologiae*, trans. Fathers of the English Dominican Province, modified trans. (New York: Benzinger Bros, 1947), Iia-Iiae, q. 183 art. 3 ad 2, https://dhspriory.org/thomas/summa. See Marie-Dominique Chenu, "*Officium*: Théologiens et canonistes," in *Études d'histoire du droit canonique dédiées à Gabriel Le Bras*, 2 vols. (Paris: Sirey, 1965), vol. 2, 835–9.

spectrum of different social and professional categories that took the lay (in addition to the ecclesiastical and the religious) states into account.

In the process of this long development, the moral and social order found an element of structure in the concept of *officium*, which served as a basis for a division of tasks arranged for the good of the entire body politic. In other words, the *officia* concerned the actions which a specific state or profession (lay or religious) required to be effective. The concept and its corresponding practices draw together the moral and the institutional. Within this semantic and actual context, the medieval jurists' conceptualization of the public official – and the ambassador in particular – can be more easily understood.

3.3 EARLY MODELS OF THE AMBASSADOR AND HIS *OFFICIUM*: LUCAS DE PENNA AND BERNARD DE ROSIER

These elaborations on the concept of *officium* (with their juridical, institutional, and moral implications) and the careful problematization of the function of each member of the body politic were to be vital to the conceptualization of the ambassador's function in late medieval legal scholarship. At that time, diplomacy was far from being the organized and theoretically grounded practice we know today. During the twelfth century, the Central and Northern Italian communes had developed a web of diplomatic relations – of which the Lombard League which defeated Emperor Frederick Barbarossa in 1176 is probably the most famous. However, diplomacy was not seen as a career, and did not involve living abroad on a permanent basis. Ambassadors were citizens temporarily entrusted with a commission to carry out a particular mission, which normally consisted of negotiating a treaty or giving a speech. The rules governing these missions were only partly stipulated in local legislation, which showed little interest in this office. It was left to the legal scholars – who were not only university professors but people actively involved in public life, and often sent on diplomatic missions themselves – to lay out the foundations of diplomatic theory. They did this within the context of their expositions on the Roman law texts that Emperor Justinian had collected in the sixth century and that – having been rediscovered in the eleventh century – were studied in Bologna and other medieval universities. These texts did not, however, dedicate any sections specifically to the ambassador. Even the sections *de legato* (i.e., on legates) in the *Digest* and the *Code* concerned internal agents charged with connecting the cities and provinces of the Empire to its center, rather than interstate ambassadors. This meant that jurists, as well as drawing on the few passages related to diplomatic agents, extended – through frequent recourse to analogical reasoning – a number of rules established in other legal areas to the ambassador. From the late twelfth century on, they referred to the embassy as an *officium* and *munus publicum*, emphasizing the office's public character and elaborating on its material and institutional aspects: the ambassador's appointment, the nature and content of the documents with which he had to be provided, his duty to respect his mandate scrupulously, his right to a salary or reimbursement for the expenses and damages incurred during his mission, his immunities and privileges, and the problem of any potential conflicts of personal interest with his diplomatic mission.[18]

The personal qualities, specific duties, and actual behavior of the ambassador himself were also fundamental issues, but the Roman law texts made no mention of these aspects and neither, initially, did legal scholars. In fact, Lucas de Penna's commentary on the *Tres libri Codicis*,[19] written in the second half of the fourteenth century, was the first text to explore these deontological questions, and can be considered the first explicit treatment of ambassadorial deontology.

3.3.1 *Lucas de Penna's Commentary on the* Tres libri

Born in Penne, in Abruzzo, at the beginning of the fourteenth century, Lucas studied law in Naples and held public office in Naples and Central Italy before moving to Avignon as papal secretary, whence he returned in 1377 with the papal Curia. He does not seem to have ever taught at university, but his commentary has all the appearance of a scholarly work and reveals the great breadth of his culture, both legal and extralegal. Of particular interest, however, are some unusual characteristics of the section *de legato* (*Cod.* 10.65) – found nowhere else in the late-medieval legal literature. Before turning to the actual comment on Justinian's text, Lucas analyses the ambassador's qualities and behavior, first setting out a list of twenty qualities (*qualitates*) that an ambassador should possess, then another list of twenty precautions (*cautelae*) that he should observe. This discussion, which has no direct connection to the Roman law texts collected in this section of the *Code*, draws heavily upon classical literature (Cicero in particular) and on the Bible and the precepts for

[18] See Donald E. Queller, *The Office of Ambassador in the Middle Ages* (Princeton: Princeton University Press, 1967); and Fedele, *Naissance*, 13–280.

[19] That is, the last three books of Justinian's *Codex*, which, in the Middle Ages, circulated separately from the other nine books and were included in the last volume of the *Corpus iuris civilis*, called *Volumen*. Here we rely on Dante Fedele, "The Status of Ambassadors in Lucas de Penna's Commentary on the *Tres Libri*," *Tijdschrift voor Rechtsgeschiedenis* 84, no. 1–2 (2016): 165–92.

the clergy laid down in the theological and canonical literature. This highly innovative approach enabled Lucas to adopt principles developed for other offices, which had already been elaborated within the Church, to create a basis upon which to discuss the necessary qualities, training, and ethics for an ambassador in the carrying out of his *officium*.

Lucas appropriates the definition of the embassy as an *officium* already formulated by previous jurists and tries to clarify its specific features. He considers this *officium* to entail the "establishing of friendship, alliance and peace" between the sender and the recipient of a mission. Here we find our first example of Lucas's use of Christian and biblical sources: the definition is based on the words of the constitution *Ego Ludovicus* (collected in Gratian's *Decretum* of c.1140), in which Emperor Louis the Pious invited Pope Pascal I to send him *legati*. Lucas also recalls the first book of *Maccabees*, which mentions the ambassadors that Jonathan sent to Bacchides "to make peace."[20]

Lucas also quotes the Bible and the *Decretum* when pointing out that, for any ambassador to be listened to with favor by his recipient, it was necessary for the latter to hold him in esteem. In support of his view, Lucas borrows the words of the *Song of Songs* (2:10), "my beloved speaketh to me," and cites a canon in the *Decretum* which, arguing that nobody should be forced into monastic life, stated that "what [someone] does not love he easily despises."[21] He then goes on to mention two other canons taken from Gregory the Great concerning bishops and magistrates: they both point out that the intercessor who displeases the person to whom he is sent provokes the latter's anger rather than helping to settle the dispute.[22] The latter references in particular help to reinforce the idea that, when choosing an ambassador, it was necessary to take the intended recipient's opinion of him into account, lest the mission be compromised. These canons were frequently alluded to in the literature of the subsequent century.[23]

Lucas believed that nobility was another ambassadorial prerequisite, particularly that nobility won through wisdom; he refers again to the Bible, and to the book of *Wisdom*, arguing that, among all noble things, this quality is the noblest.[24] At the beginning of his comment on this section, Lucas observed that ambassadors should be chosen among jurists and men of great eloquence,

[20] Lucas de Penna, *Commentaria in tres posteriores libros Codicis Iustiniani* (Lugduni: Apud Ioannam Iacobi Iuntae F., 1582), ad *Cod.* 10.65, 313a, nos. 9–10; c. 30 § 1, d. 63; and 1 *Maccabees* 9.70 (the Bible is always quoted in the Douay Rheims Version, based on the Latin Vulgate).

[21] Lucas de Penna, *Commentaria*, ad *Cod.* 10.65, 312a, no. 3; and c. 4, C. 20, q. 3.

[22] See dictum ante c. 1, d. 49 (from Gregory the Great's *Regula pastoralis*) and c. 5, C. 3, q. 7 (from his *Moralia in Iob*).

[23] See Fedele, *Naissance*, 635 n. 19.

[24] Lucas de Penna, *Commentaria*, ad *Cod.* 10.65, 314b, no. 20.

remarking that the best way to acquire eloquence is to "imbibe" the Holy Scripture.[25] Cicero's *De oratore* is quoted extensively in Lucas's discussion of the ambassador's training, but the Old Testament, the philosopher Boethius, and the *Decretum* are also cited, to support the claim that true eloquence is grounded in wisdom, which mainly consists in the knowledge of philosophy and divine law.[26] Lucas also suggests – in passing – that an ambassador should be able to speak the language of his recipient in order to avoid the use of interpreters. Although brief, this reference is nevertheless noteworthy because the issue – despite its great practical relevance – was otherwise to be ignored in the literature on the ambassador until well into the sixteenth century. Even more intriguingly, Lucas bases his argument on a rule of the Fourth Lateran Council (1215) regarding bishops. As the Roman Church expanded into the Orient after the Crusades, organizational problems had been raised by the coexistence within the same diocese of communities with different languages, customs, and rites; the Council had therefore granted bishops permission to nominate auxiliaries, or even a vicar, who could cater to this diversity by celebrating the divine offices and administering the sacraments. Drawing on this conciliar rule, Lucas exhorts the ambassador to learn different foreign languages in order to be able to dispense with interpreters and carry out his mission "by himself."[27]

The discussion of the virtues necessary to an ambassador is conducted with constant reference to the Bible, and particularly to *Proverbs*: "as the cold of snow in the time of harvest, so is a faithful messenger to him that sent him, for he refresheth his soul," while "to trust to an unfaithful man in the time of trouble, is like a rotten tooth, and wary foot."[28] Stressing the need for the ambassador to be diligent in carrying out his mission, Lucas again cites *Proverbs*: "as vinegar to the teeth, and smoke to the eyes, so is the sluggard to them that sent him."[29] He also mentions three canons from the *Decretum* in which bishops are exhorted to be zealous and solicitous in fulfilling the task with which they have been entrusted.[30] Lucas then extrapolates to the ambassador the qualities – listed in

25 Lucas de Penna, *Commentaria*, ad *Cod.* 10.65, 311b, no. 1, with reference to c. 7, d. 37.

26 Lucas de Penna, *Commentaria*, ad *Cod.* 10.65, 312a–312b, nos. 5–7.

27 Lucas de Penna, *Commentaria*, ad *Cod.* 10.65, 316a, no. 24, and c. 14, X 1.31 (which reproduces canon 9 of the Fourth Lateran Council). On this canon, see Orazio Condorelli, *"Unum corpus, diversa capita": Modelli di organizzazione e cura pastorale per una varietas ecclesiarum (secoli XI-XIV)* (Rome: Il Cigno Galileo Galilei, 2002), 22–45.

28 Lucas de Penna, *Commentaria*, ad *Cod.* 10.65, 312a no. 4; the quotations are taken from Prov. 25:13 and 25:19.

29 Lucas de Penna, *Commentaria*, ad *Cod.* 10.65, 315a no. 21, with quotation of Prov. 10:26.

30 Lucas de Penna, *Commentaria*, ad *Cod.* 10.65, 315a no. 21, with reference to c. 1 and 2, d. 84, and c. 6, d. 83.

the second book of *Maccabees* – of the former high priest Onias, a "good and virtuous man, modest in his look, gentle in his manners, and graceful in his speech, and who from a child was exercised in virtues."[31] The most interesting passage, however, is one in which Lucas closely examines the issue of the ambassador's attire, gestures, and gait. He first states that an ambassador must be decorous in his dress and demeanor, in order to properly manifest the gravity of his office ("*ut ... probet debitum suae legationis officium*"). Here, again, Lucas refers to Gratian's *Decretum*, which reported a canon from the so-called Fourth Council of Carthage according to which a cleric had to demonstrate his profession through his dress and demeanor ("*clericus professionem suam et habitu et incessu probet*"). The extension of this principle from the *clerici professio* to the *legationis officium* is explicit here. After reporting this canon, Lucas (as Gratian had also done) then quotes a passage from Augustine in which the latter says that a man's outward bearing manifests his inner qualities.[32] Next, Lucas adapts some excerpts from *De institutione novitiorum*, written by Hugh of Saint Victor in the first half of the twelfth century, to the figure of the ambassador. Conceived for the education of the novices in the community of Saint Victor, this text is primarily concerned with the notion of *disciplina* (how to walk, gesture, speak, eat, drink, and dress) and the idea of harmony between the internal and the external.[33] Lucas focuses in particular on a passage in which Hugh examines some inappropriate behaviors, associating each with a specific defect of the soul, and urging the ambassador to control his outward conduct. He also cites other passages on the need to moderate one's facial expressions and gestures in order not to subvert the *officia* of the members of one's body.[34] Such behavioral precepts and deontological rules were to become very common in the literature on ambassadors and courtiers of the early modern period, a body of work which – drawing on a wide variety of sources – molded European civility. We must not forget, however, that the origins of these precepts and rules can be traced back to medieval monastic and clerical texts, to which *De institutione novitiorum* was seminal.[35]

[31] Lucas de Penna, *Commentaria*, ad *Cod.* 10.65, 316a no. 26, with quotation of 2 Macc. 15:12.

[32] Lucas de Penna, *Commentaria*, ad *Cod.* 10.65, 315a no. 22, with reference to c. 8, d. 41 and Gratian's *dictum*.

[33] See Hugh of Saint Victor, "De institutione novitiorum," in *L'œuvre de Hugues de Saint-Victor*, ed. Hugh B. Feiss and Patrice Sicard (Turnhout: Brepols, 1997). See Jean-Claude Schmitt, *La raison des gestes dans l'Occident médiéval* (Paris: Gallimard, 1990), 173–207.

[34] Lucas de Penna, *Commentaria*, ad *Cod.* 10.65, 315a no. 22, who draws on Hugh of Saint Victor, "De institutione novitiorum," 58, 70, 72, and 74.

[35] Dilwyn Knox, "Disciplina: The Monastic and Clerical Origins of European Civility," in *Renaissance Society and Culture*, ed. Ronald G. Musto and John Monfasani (New York: Italica, 1991), 107–36.

Another virtue highly valued by Lucas was "discretion" (or "discernment") – the patristic and monastic roots of which have been extensively studied by François Dingjan.[36] Lucas focuses in particular on the correct use of words, describing what appears to be a speaking technique for diplomats. He states that "an ambassador must be discreet in everything and learned, following the example of priests" and that he must be able to adapt to different situations and interlocutors and to recognize that the differences between people mean – as Augustin averred and the *Decretum* reported – that each person needs a different remedy.[37] Numerous references to the Bible, canon law, and classic literature are then made to support the argument that ambassadors need to adapt their style to every audience or occasion. This also necessarily implies the ability to be silent, since (in Gregory the Great's words) "he who knows how to remain silent when appropriate, knows how to talk opportunely," while (in those of the *Ecclesiastes*) "a fool multiplies words."[38]

Lucas's text is not simply an amalgam of references that would have been familiar to his contemporaries (although Lucas appears to be the first jurist to use them so extensively); rather, they are part of a discursive strategy that presented principles and precepts taken from authoritative sources and intended as a contribution to the definition of the ambassadorial office, teasing out its moral and intellectual qualities, and establishing precise rules of conduct. Remembering that Lucas's discussion of these issues is the first of its kind in the late Middle Ages, let us now turn our attention to a short treatise in the following century by the Languedoc canonist Bernard de Rosier, who was the next author to address the topic.

3.3.2 *Bernard de Rosier's* Ambaxiatorum brevilogus

Unlike Lucas de Penna's, Rosier's career embraced both university teaching and public (especially ecclesiastical) office. Born in 1400, in July 1427 he joined Cardinal Pierre de Foix as the secretary of the mission to Aragon which led to the abdication of the antipope Clement VIII and the end of the Western Schism. Rosier wrote an account of this mission, and subsequently a treatise on the office of papal legate; and in 1435–6, during another

36 François Dingjan O.S.B., *Discretio: Les origines patristiques et monastiques de la doctrine sur la prudence chez Thomas d'Aquin* (Assen: Van Gorcum & Comp. N.V. – Dr. H. J. Prakke & H. M. G. Prakke, 1967).

37 Lucas de Penna, *Commentaria*, ad *Cod.* 10.65, 313a–313b no. 11, with reference to d. 38 *per totum* (regarding the example of priests), and to c. 1, § 4, C. 14, q. 6 (for Augustine's letter 153).

38 Lucas de Penna, *Commentaria*, ad *Cod.* 65, 317b no. 27 (with a quotation from Gregory the Great's *Moralia in Job*) and 318b no. 30 (with a quotation from Eccles. 5:2 and 10:14).

mission in Castile, he composed the *Ambaxiatorum brevilogus.*[39] This text remained in manuscript form for centuries, until finally being edited in 1906 by Vladimir E. Hrabar, a Russian historian of international law.[40] Although largely unknown and thus not particularly influential, this text is still well worth studying as it is "the first textbook of diplomatic practice written in Western Europe."[41] Unlike Lucas's commentary, the *Brevilogus* is not a work of scholarship. It includes very few references to other texts and no doctrinal discussion; instead, the text directly addresses ambassadors, to whom the author offers practical advice and precepts of conduct. Although implicit, the theological and canonical background to these precepts is indisputable.

After listing the virtues that a diplomat must possess, Rosier considers the rank and authority of ambassadors and their principals and the reasons behind the sending of embassies, going on to detail the phases of a mission, from preparation to homecoming. He emphasizes the public nature of the ambassador's office, using the expressions *officium publicum* and *public*[*a*] *person*[*a*],[42] and repeatedly points out that ambassadors, although they are sent to individual rulers to deal with specific matters, actually realize the "common good" on behalf not just of a single country but of the "universal commonwealth" or the "whole world."[43] The ancient and Christian concept of *officium*, with its implications for the entire body politic, is implicitly leant upon in these lines. In Rosier's view, it is precisely because ambassadors work for "public utility" that they enjoy inviolability and the other privileges established by "public authority" and warranted by "both laws" (that is, civil and canon law). Those who hinder them are said to hinder the "public good."[44]

39 After teaching canon law at the University of Toulouse, Rosier was appointed to the bishopric and in 1452 became archbishop of Toulouse, an office he held until his death, in 1475. See Dante Fedele, "Rosier, Bernard de (1400–1475)," in *The Wiley-Blackwell Encyclopedia of Diplomacy*, ed. Gordon Martel, 4 vols. (Hoboken, NJ: Wiley-Blackwell, 2018), vol. 4, 1654–8.

40 Bernardus de Rosergio, "Ambaxiatorum Brevilogus," in *De legatis et legationibus tractatus varii*, ed. Vladimir E. Hrabar (Dorpat: C. Mattiesen, 1906), 3–28.

41 Garrett Mattingly, *Renaissance Diplomacy* (Boston: Houghton Mifflin Company, 1955), 28 (see chs. 3 and 4 for a summary of the *Brevilogus*).

42 Bernardus de Rosergio, "Ambaxiatorum Brevilogus," ch. 6, p. 7, and ch. 24, p. 24, and Prohemium,p. 3.

43 Bernardus de Rosergio, "Ambaxiatorum Brevilogus," ch. 6, p. 8 ("Constat et enim ambaxiatores comunibus utilitatibus insistere, per eos rei publice universe comoda plurima provenire, licet ad singulos et pro particularibus negocijs particulariter transmittantur") and ch. 30, p. 28 ("Ambaxiatorum officium quantum rei publice et toti orbi sit utile, evidencia facti manifeste demonstrat").

44 Bernardus de Rosergio, "Ambaxiatorum Brevilogus," ch. 26 and ch. 27, p. 26. See Riccardo Fubini, "L'ambasciatore nel XV secolo: due trattati e una biografia (Bernard de Rosier, Ermolao Barbaro, Vespasiano da Bisticci)," *Mélanges de l'École française de Rome: Moyen-Âge* 108, no. 2 (1996): 649–51.

Among the ambassador's intellectual virtues, Rosier – perhaps even more than Lucas de Penna – attaches crucial importance to "discretion," which is the focus of much of this work, well worth reading for the insight it provides into the wider framework that underpins his deontological approach.[45] Rosier explains, for example, that, after his first formal address to his recipient, an ambassador must listen carefully to the latter's reply, and then behave "prudently" during the subsequent discussion. He should wait to be questioned rather than talking first. If he realizes that a question is intended to make him reveal an aspect of the matter which it would be imprudent to divulge or is intended to deceive, he should at the same time not give full explanations, nor completely fail to answer the question (or delay his answer to another day). Throughout his mission, an ambassador must adapt his attitude to the present circumstances and people, and do what is expedient "according to the right judgement of reason," knowing that "in the things of this world ... discretion is extremely necessary to advance from opposite positions" toward an agreement. Rosier states that awareness of how to proceed in this way is greatly enhanced by direct knowledge of many various peoples and of men's conditions and affairs, acquired through personal experience in various places and at the courts of great men. Through such experience – we read in one of the rare quotes included in the *Brevilogus* – ambassadors will become "wise as serpents and simple as doves."[46] Interestingly, this excerpt from Matthew's Gospel is used in several passages of Gratian's *Decretum* in reference to priests, monks, and, more generally, all men, making the point that, possessing the candor of the dove, they will not intrigue against others, and, possessing the guile of the snake, they will know how to escape the traps of their enemies.[47]

Of interest, too, is the fact that, according to Rosier, discretion can sometimes entail recourse to dissimulation. Although he does not actually use this term, he warns "discreet ambassadors" to ensure that – whatever they might be obliged to listen to – they always answer cautiously and gently, never lose their temper, and never raise their voices or behave insolently. If a negotiation concludes favorably, they should be open in their happiness and great delight. If, on the other hand, a negotiation does not lead to the desired result, they should not therefore refuse any

45 As well as the passages cited in the next notes, see Bernardus de Rosergio, "Ambaxiatorum Brevilogus," ch. 2, p. 5; ch. 13, p. 13; ch. 15, p. 15; ch. 16, p. 16.

46 Bernardus de Rosergio, "Ambaxiatorum Brevilogus," ch. 14, pp. 14–15, with implicit quotation of Matt. 10.16. Rosier insists on the importance of experience also ibid., ch. 2, p. 5; ch. 10, p. 11; ch. 18, pp. 18–19; and ch. 30, p. 28.

47 See c. 2, d. 36 (for priests); c. 13, C. 6, q. 1 (for all men); and c. 5, C. 16, q. 1 (for monks).

agreement, unless they have clear instructions in this regard; and, even in these circumstances, they should act with consideration and modesty, and never reveal their passions to their counterpart.[48] However, the quote from Matthew's Gospel and the many references to the "public utility" of embassies reveal that dissimulation was subject to strict limitations. The indications on this question attest to Rosier's responsiveness to actual practice and his original contribution to political and moral thought. Although theological reflection on the lawfulness of the use of lies, simulation, and dissimulation was already ample in his time,[49] in the political literature the issue would be seriously examined only in the next two centuries, when the snake and the dove – although they did not disappear completely – were largely replaced by the lion (representing strength) and the fox (representing cunning).[50]

Unlike later authors who admitted recourse to deception in pursuit of political goals, Rosier placed his treatment of discretion within a strongly defined moral and ontological hierarchy, based on the twin concepts of (*debitus*) *ordo* and (*debitus*) *modus*.[51] The elaboration of the ethical guidelines he proposes for the ambassadors is thus clearly based on a much wider, theologically inspired framework. "Due order" is, in fact, the stable foundation of not only diplomatic action but all things; since Thomas Aquinas, it had corresponded to the hierarchy of beings and the correct relation between them, the negation of which was not just the absence of order but evil and sin. As Rosier puts it, following the "due order" means putting the fear of God first, preferring heavenly goods to those of the world and the perpetual over the transient; only by respecting this hierarchy is it possible to act properly. Complementary to the "due order" is the *debitus modus*, which refers to the dynamism of action in this world. *Modus* is the manner in which any act should be carried out, and what makes that act what it truly is. Consequently, pursuing high things with cowardice, grave things lightly, sweet things brutally, things of little account pompously, great things carelessly, joyful things with sadness,

[48] See Bernardus de Rosergio, "Ambaxiatorum Brevilogus," ch. 15, pp. 15–16; ch. 19, p. 19; and ch. 20, p. 20.

[49] See Lucien Godefroy, "Mensonge," in *Dictionnaire de théologie catholique: contenant l'exposé des doctrines de la théologie catholique, leurs preuves et leur histoire*, ed. Alfred Vacant et al. (Paris: Letouzey et Anxé, 1903–72), t. X, col. 555–69.

[50] See Michael Stolleis, "Löwe und Fuchs: Eine politische Maxime im Frühabsolutismus," in Michael Stolleis, *Staat und Staatsräson in der frühen Neuzeit: Studien zur Geschichte des öffentlichen Rechts* (Frankfurt am Main: Suhrkamp, 1990), 21–36.

[51] See Bernardus de Rosergio, "Ambaxiatorum Brevilogus," ch. 7, pp. 8–9. We wish to thank Andrea Robiglio (KU Leuven) for his help in the interpretation of this passage.

sad things with hilarity, secret things openly, and evident things secretly … all this is to overlook the *debitus modus*. Since the latter is always related to circumstances, Rosier explains, it cannot be adequately described in writing, only learnt through discretion ("*circumpsecta hominis discrecio prudens*"), which enables men to act appropriately, in all places, at all times, with everyone. Echoes of Cicero and the scholastics reverberate in this moral exhortation aimed at inspiring the ambassador and guiding him through his daily practice of diplomacy.

3.4 CONCLUSION

This overview indicates that Christian thought on the duties (and the corresponding ecclesiastical practice) intermingled with classical ideas on the (public or individual) roles to shape the actual figures of public officials in late medieval European society. As many scholars have shown, the exercise of judicial and executive functions – crucial to the formation of the modern state and its bureaucracy – was profoundly influenced by this combination. Lucas de Penna's and Bernard de Rosier's speculations indicate that this was also true of diplomatic functions. The relation between the first modeling of the status of ambassadors and the Latin notion of *officium* is evident, as is the use of Christian sources. The Bible, canon law, and the theological literature provided rules and principles upon which to model that status, in the absence of specific references in Roman law and before humanism led to the rediscovery of the classical authors. From the mid-sixteenth century on, ancient history also provided abundant material, which, alongside and sometimes in lieu of Christian doctrine, greatly contributed to shaping the status of ambassadors in the early modern period. Throughout this period, the literature on the ambassador increasingly debated the moral aspects of the office and gave detailed practical guidelines. Before then, however, the Christian literature had proved a vital source for the elaboration of ambassadorial deontology, providing the necessary material and conceptual tools for the first investigations of this subject.

RECOMMENDED READING

Bash, Anthony. *Ambassadors for Christ: An Exploration of Ambassadorial Language in the New Testament*. Tübingen: J.C.B. Mohr, 1997.

Faitini, Tiziana. "Shaping the Profession: Some Thoughts on Office, Duty, and the Moral Problematisation of Professional Activities in the Counter-Reformation." *Journal of Early Modern Christianity* 7, no. 1 (2020): 177–200.

Fedele, Dante. *Naissance de la diplomatie moderne (XIII e–XVII e siècles): L'ambassadeur au croisement du droit, de l'éthique et de la politique*. Baden-Baden: Nomos Verlag; Zürich: Dike Verlag, 2017.
Kantorowicz, Ernst H. *The King's Two Bodies: A Study in Medieval Political Theology*. Princeton: Princeton University Press, 1997.
Ménager, Daniel. *L'ange et l'ambassadeur: Diplomatie et théologie à la Renaissance*. Paris: Garnier, 2013.

4

Formation and Refiguration of the Canon Law on Trade with Infidels (c.1200–c.1600)

Stefan Stantchev*

Ideas and practices often perceived as modern carry a complex premodern history that cannot be excised from their present. This is certainly the case of trade embargoes as economic means for the attainment of political goals.[1] For a variety of reasons, however, tracing change over long periods of time remains an exercise in chronological and spatial jurisdiction. Further complicating our understanding of the convoluted relationship between past and present has been the increasingly pronounced tendency to write in the vein either of a "history of ideology" or, conversely, of a "history of action." In fact, "theory" and "practice" existed in a dialectical relationship, a cyclical tug of war that produced not so much winners and losers as complex realities that require a thick reading of legal, political, cultural, and social change.[2] This chapter, by contrast, seeks to explain the transfiguration of the legal tradition from the perspective of international law history by focusing on two interrelated transitions. The first one is the remapping of human space from the spiritual terms of the canon law into the geopolitical ones of modernity. Second is the shift from the verticality of human relations envisioned in the classical canon law to the assumption of equality underpinning its sixteenth-century refiguration. In addition, the papal decrees on trade with infidels became grounded in natural law. Thus, the seemingly

* The author would like to thank Berkeley Law for its generous support of this project through a Robbins Collection Fellowship.

[1] On export control systems in general, see David A. Baldwin, *Economic Statecraft* (Princeton: Princeton University Press, 1985); on the origins of modern trade embargoes, see Stefan Stantchev, "The Medieval Origins of Embargo as a Policy Tool," *History of Political Thought* 33, no. 3 (2012): 373–99.

[2] Stefan K. Stantchev, *Spiritual Rationality: Papal Embargo as Cultural Practice* (Oxford: Oxford University Press, 2014).

traditional canonistic discussion anticipated the hallmarks of the law of nations as it came to be seen around 1600.[3] The evolution of ideas may be complex, but the results of this inquiry are rather straightforward. While the chapter will proceed in chronological order, we shall preview its main arguments thematically.

Thirteenth- and fourteenth-century jurisprudence resulted in creating the *ius commune* – Europe's common legal past – but it did so by following the distinct tracks of the law of the church (canon law) and the Roman law (civil law) whose worldviews and presuppositions were fundamentally different.[4] Oblivious to political and geographical maps, the world of the canon law was one of faith and the historical narrative propelling it. The communities envisioned by the pastoral logic of the canon law were defined in terms of their relations to the papal flock. To simplify, this was the world of *mappamundi*, with Jerusalem as its navel, a mapping of revealed truth and diabolical forces. Therefore, the political map – modernity's paradigmatic entry point into the world of international relations – is a self-defeating device for understanding medieval thought. Faithful existed outside Christian realms and infidels lived within. Souls, not political formations, mattered. The challenge to this pastoral mapping of space originated at first organically, from the dualistic nature of the classical, thirteenth/early-fourteenth-century jurisprudence itself. While the canonists upheld the pastoral underpinnings of the canon law, the civilians brought into the conversation the geopolitical features of the Roman law through the concepts of the Roman people and its enemies. Under the intellectual and political pressures of the fifteenth and sixteenth centuries, the canonists themselves made the leap from, figuratively speaking, the medieval world of *mappamundi* to the geopolitical one of modernity.

3 On the latter, see in brief J. M. Kelly, *A Short History of Western Legal Theory* (Oxford: Clarendon Press, 1992), 199–202, 241–3. On the grounding of the law of nations in natural law, see Patrick Capps, "Natural Law and the Law of Nations," in *Research Handbook on the Theory and History of International Law*, ed. Alexander Orakhelashvili (Cheltenham: Edward Elgar, 2011), 61–92.

4 Manlio Bellomo, *The Common Legal Past of Europe, 1000–1800*, trans. Lydia G. Cochrane (Washington, DC: Catholic University of America Press, 1995) and James A. Brundage, *The Medieval Origins of the Legal Profession: Canonists, Civilians, and Courts* (Chicago: University of Chicago University Press, 2008). On the canon law in general, see Richard H. Helmholz, *The Spirit of Classical Canon Law*, 3rd ed. (Athens, GA: University of Georgia Press, 2010) and Wilfried Hartmann and Kenneth Pennington, eds., *Medieval Canon Law in the Classical Period, 1140–1234: From Gratian to the Decretals of Pope Gregory IX* (Washington, DC: Catholic University of America Press, 2008). On its relationship with international law, see James Muldoon, "The Contribution of the Medieval Canon Lawyers to the Formation of International Law," *Traditio* 28 (1972): 483–97; James Muldoon, *Popes, Lawyers, and Infidels: The Church and the Non-Christian World, 1250–1550* (Philadelphia: University of Pennsylvania Press, 1979); James Muldoon, "Medieval Canon Law and the Formation of International Law," *Zeitschrift der Savigny-Stiftung fur Rechtsgeschichte: Kanonistische Abteilung* 81, no. 1 (1995): 64–82.

Second, a pastoral mapping of the world is self-evidently vertical. For the canon law, the purpose of life was the attainment of salvation and the church was the indispensable guide in the process. While the jurists upheld in theory the principle that "all human beings are equal," in practice such statements were challenged in different ways, for example, by the institution of slavery.[5] Similarly, the genderlessness and theoretical equality of souls did not lead high medieval authorities to consider women as equal to men.[6] Nor did their acknowledgment that Jews and Saracens partake in Christ's nature – both in souls and in bodies[7] – necessarily lead them to postulate equality between the community of faithful and any others. The ideal was that of an ever-expanding flock and therefore the relations envisioned between self and others were those between sheep and wolves or between faithful and potential converts. Consequently, the canon law on trade with infidels could not feed directly into a system predicated upon the equality of its constituent parts. Change within discussions on the law on trade with infidels occurred in the sixteenth century when the relationship between the two legal traditions was turned on its head. Instead of Roman law filling the gaps of the canon law, the canon law tradition infused early modern legal discourse with the idea that trading with the enemy is not only harmful but also immoral.

While the classical synthesis as a whole remained incongruent with modern understandings of international relations until it was refigured in the sixteenth century, it did nevertheless generate two potential building blocks of such systems: the concept of truce and the definition of contraband. Neither subject's history is known to historians of later times. To reference the title on truce and peace in the 1234 *Liber extra* (Decretals of Gregory IX) as an example of an exception whereby the canon law dealt with international law is to pay lip service to the study of the medieval past.[8] *De treuga et pace* had, in fact, no relationship to anything that could be termed international law for it concerned the peace and truce of God, a paradigmatically "domestic" matter. By contrast, it was within commentaries on the law concerning trade with infidels that the jurists explained and refined the concept of truce and its relationship to peace and war. Similarly, to claim that Hugo Grotius (d. 1645)

5 Kelly, *Short History*, 146, 148–53.

6 See Nancy Caciola, *Discerning Spirits: Divine and Demonic Possession in the Middle Ages* (Ithaca: Cornell University Press, 2003).

7 For example, Norman P. Zacour, *Jews and Saracens in the Consilia of Oldradus de Ponte* (Toronto: Pontifical Institution of Medieval Studies, 1990), 62, 86.

8 Alain Wiffels, "Early-Modern Scholarship on International Law," in *Research Handbook on the Theory and History of International Law*, ed. Alexander Orakhelashvili (Cheltenham: Edward Elgar, 2011), 30 and n. 16.

"introduced the concept of contraband to modern international law"[9] is to operate strictly within a history of economic warfare, rather than a broader one of economic statecraft,[10] to ignore a rich body of earlier work, and to misconstrue Grotius's novelty.

4.1 TRADE WITH INFIDELS: THE CLASSICAL SYNTHESIS

Popes and jurists displayed an interest in trade with infidels at the intersection of three developments that were transformational for Western Europe. From the mid-eleventh century the papacy became the center of a church reform movement – often called the Gregorian reform after its most famous exponent Pope Gregory VII (1073–85) – that produced a hierarchical, relatively centralized, and comparatively homogeneous Roman church.[11] Second, from the late eleventh century, Catholic-led armies fought supposedly infidel ones on a pan-Mediterranean scale under papal promises for the remission of penance and/or sins in what would later become known as the crusades.[12] Finally, starting in the twelfth and culminating in the thirteenth century, an explosive growth of Mediterranean trade led to qualitative changes in Europe's economy and society in a process known as the Commercial Revolution.[13]

Against these broad contexts, in 1179, the Third Lateran Council reaffirmed ancient laws banning business with heretics in *Sicut Ait* while its *Ita Quorumdam* innovated by permanently prohibiting the delivery of war material to "Saracens."[14] In 1187, however, Saladin conquered Jerusalem.[15] In *Quod olim*, Clement III (1187–91) banned all trade between Christians and Saracens in time of war and

9 Phillip Drew, *The Law of Maritime Blockade: Past, Present, and Future* (Oxford: Oxford University Press, 2017), 26.

10 See on this subject Baldwin, *Economic Statecraft*.

11 For a detailed account, see Colin Morris, *The Papal Monarchy: The Western Church from 1050 to 1250* (Oxford: Clarendon Press, 1989); for papal power, Kenneth Pennington, *Pope and Bishops: The Papal Monarchy in the Twelfth and Thirteenth Centuries* (Philadelphia: University of Pennsylvania Press, 1984) and Alberto Melloni, *Innocenzo IV: La concezione e l'esperienza della cristianità come regimen unius personae* (Genoa: Marietti, 1990).

12 For a short yet comprehensive overview of the crusades, see Jonathan Riley-Smith, *The Crusades: A History*, 2nd ed. (New Haven: Yale University Press, 2005). For the composition of crusader armies, see Steve Tibble, *The Crusader Armies* (New Haven: Yale University Press, 2018). For the literature on crusader treatises incorporating the law on trade, see Stantchev, *Spiritual Rationality*, ch. 1 and the literature cited therein.

13 Robert S. Lopez, *The Commercial Revolution of the Middle Ages, 950–1350* (Englewood Cliffs, NJ: Prentice Hall, 1971) has lost none of its relevance. For the eastern Mediterranean in the period of interest, see chiefly Eliyahu Ashtor, *Levant Trade in the Later Middle Ages* (Princeton: Princeton University Press, 1983).

14 X 5.7.8 and X. 5.6.6. See Stantchev, *Spiritual Rationality*, 99–101, 44–9, respectively.

15 Malcolm Barber, *Crusader States* (New Haven: Yale University Press, 2012), 289–323.

punished contrabandists through an *ipso iure*, or automatic excommunication, whereby "a person sentenced himself by committing the act."[16] The total embargo, in turn, generated a difficult question. Can Christians export anything to Muslims in order to ransom other Christians? In *Significavit nobis* (1193–94), Pope Celestine III provided an answer to the bishop of Ancona.[17] While Celestine and then Innocent IV (1243–54), the one pope among the foremost canonists, phrased the permission broadly, the majority opinion qualified the canon and excluded war material.[18] In 1198, Pope Innocent III (1198–1216) – faced with the failure of the Third Crusade (1188–92), the economic needs of the maritime cities, and his desire to ensure the support of at least one maritime republic for the planned Fourth Crusade – allowed Venice to restart trade with Egypt under the provisions of Lateran III's *Ita quorumdam*.[19] This dispensation from the provisions of *Quod olim* underpinned all subsequent practice. Finally, Lateran IV's *Ad liberandam* (1215) clarified the requirements for absolution of contrabandists and, to a much lesser extent, the definition of contraband.[20]

Papal letters then applied the "mind" of the law to analogous situations. By the mid-thirteenth century, stipulations identical to those of *Ita quorumdam* governed licit Catholic trade with pagans in the Baltic and Orthodox Christians in the Balkans. Within Christendom, trade restrictions targeted heretics, disobedient Catholic communities, and individual Jews.[21] Thus by the mid-thirteenth century a de facto system of export controls serving as one part of a broader boundary between those within and outside the flock was erected. The jurists, however, neither engaged in cultural analysis nor systematically discussed the various canons curtailing Christians' commerce with infidels. Rather, they stuck to commenting on the canons contained in the *Liber extra* one by one or subject by subject (Saracens, Jews, heretics). Their attention was chiefly attracted by the dispositions concerning Saracens.

The backbone of the resulting "classical" synthesis is as follows. Avarice motivates some to deliver war material to Saracens and others to serve on the warships of Saracens. "Saracens" are descendants of Hagar who prefer to call themselves after Sarah, Abraham's free wife, and "who worship and revere

[16] X 5.6.12. Stantchev, *Spiritual Rationality*, 50–2. Quotation from Helmholz, *Spirit*, 383.

[17] X 5.6.11, Stantchev, *Spiritual Rationality*, 52–5.

[18] Stantchev, *Spiritual Rationality*, 52–5.

[19] Stantchev, *Spiritual Rationality*, 55–8.

[20] Stantchev, *Spiritual Rationality*, 58–61.

[21] Stantchev, *Spiritual Rationality*, 91–9. On interdict, see, in general, Peter D. Clarke, *The Interdict in the Thirteenth Century: A Question of Collective Guilt* (Oxford: Oxford University Press, 2007) and, for a case-study, Richard J. Trexler, *The Spiritual Power: Republican Florence under Interdict* (Leiden: E. J. Brill, 1974).

countless gods and goddesses, and indeed demons, and accept neither the New, nor the Old Testament."[22] "Arms" means goods such as swords, coats of mail, sticks, and stones. The export of such goods is prohibited at all times. In times of war, no trade with Saracens is allowed. Intention, otherwise such an important litmus test for guilt, was found irrelevant in the case of contraband; what matters is that the offender has provided Saracens with things that can be used to wage war on Christians. Facilitating such crimes, furthermore, is no less an offense. What justifies papal intervention in such temporal matters? When a crime concerns Christendom or the honor of the faith, the pope exercises jurisdiction over the laity. The church can impose the punishment of slavery and a free-born Christian can be reduced to slavery on account of a crime. Contrabandists are excommunicated ipso facto, must be deprived of all their goods, and become the slaves of their captors. Contraband, moreover, is a capital punishment in the civil law. The pope alone can absolve contrabandists (from 1308). This, in brief, was the canonistic consensus on the subject of trade with infidels.[23]

The law on trade may have dealt with Christians and their relations with others, but its subjects were individual people, not states or even faiths. There is little doubt that Saladin's Egypt and, later, the Mamluk Empire were the main targets of papal export controls. Other polities, like the Emirate of Granada, were also targeted by individual papal decrees. The situation, in short, was akin to that of the crusades. While Jerusalem was always at the heart of the movement, papally authorized warfare carrying remission of penance and/or sins occurred against all sorts of papal enemies, including Catholic princes. Although popes acting as leaders of Christendom, the territorial expression of a faith-based community, did not refrain from pointing out actual polities, their decrees' incorporation into the canon law typically entailed a transformation. Whereas the canon law was in principle "the vehicle by means of which abstract moral principles would be transformed into the basic rules according to which an entire society would operate," the process was in fact a dialectical one as mundane political measures were sometimes absorbed into the law through their transformation into abstract moral principles: trade with Saracens endangers the soul.[24] The seemingly

22 Henry of Susa [Hostiensis], *Summa* (Aalen: Scientia Verlag, 1962 [1537]), 236v. On Hostiensis, see chapter "Henricus de Segusio" in Kenneth Pennington, *Popes, Canonists, and Texts (1150–1550)* (Aldershot: Routledge, 1993), 16. On "Saracens," see John V. Tolan, *Saracens: Islam in the Medieval European Imagination* (New York: Columbia University Press, 2002).

23 Stantchev, *Spiritual Rationality*, ch. 2.

24 For the quotation, see James Muldoon, *Empire and Order: The Concept of Empire, 800–1800* (New York: Palgrave Macmillan, 1999), 64; Stantchev, *Spiritual Rationality*, ch. 2.

straightforward term Saracens, moreover, proved elastic. Although thirteenth-century jurists may seem to equate Saracens with Muslims, using the term as synonymous to infidels at large was always a possibility. Thus the point of arrival of the medieval tradition, the fifteenth-century work of Nicolò dei Tudeschi, known as Panormitanus (d. 1445), used Saracens and infidels interchangeably.[25] The same is true of some editions of the work of Antoninus of Florence (d. 1459), which early modern authors commonly used as their link to the medieval tradition.[26] In turn, the author of the most insightful work on the subject, Martín de Azpilcueta (d. 1586), took this interchangeability to mean that the definition of Saracens had overexpanded, signifying all infidels.[27] Conceptualizing a world in terms of souls was not conducive to generating any actual or "embryonic" system of international law and relations. The former worked through an understanding that fused the micro level of the soul with the macro one of universal entities (the Roman Empire, the Roman Church) that hypothetically could encompass the entire world. By contrast, any system of international law has to be predicated on the middle level of the state (or the tribe), on the continuous existence of multiple independent entities in need of balancing their relations.

The second major incongruity between the law on trade with infidels and subsequent systems of international law concerns the premise of equality. Whatever the factual imbalances, a modern system of international relations presupposes the notional equality of its constituent parts. By contrast, there could be no equal footing between Christians and others in the thirteenth-century commentaries. Indeed, one finds a direct parallel between the best-known medieval and modern embargoes elsewhere: in the lack of consideration for the target's rights to subsistence. The use of blanket embargoes in the late twentieth century caused a great deal of humanitarian concern and thus advocacy for the employment of targeted sanctions instead.[28] The latter, of course,

25 Niccolò dei Tudeschi (Panormitanus), *Lectura super Tertio Quarto et Quinto Decretalium* (Lyon, 1521–2), V, 36r, 37r/v. On Panormitanus, see Orazio Condorelli, ed., *Niccoló Tedeschi (Abbas Panormitanus) e i suoi Commentaria in Decretales* (Rome: Il Cigno Galileo Galilei, 2000).

26 See Stantchev, *Spiritual Rationality*, 165–9. Antoninus does single out political formations when discussing the total embargo.

27 Martin de Azpilcueta [Doctor Navarrus], *Relectio in cap. Ita Quorumdam* (Rome, 1580; Coimbra, 1550), 7r [#2].

28 See Thomas G. Weiss, "Sanctions as a Foreign Policy Tool: Weighing Humanitarian Impulses," *Journal of Peace Research* 36, no. 5 (1999): 499–509; and, more broadly, David Cortright and George A. Lopez, *The Sanctions Decade: Assessing UN Strategies in the 1990s* (Boulder: Lynne Rienner, 2000) and David Cortwright and George A. Lopez, eds., *Smart Sanctions: Targeting Economic Statecraft* (Lanham: Rowman & Littlefield, 2002).

can only work if a line is drawn between a target's government and its population. Thirteenth-century jurists, however, displayed no interest in distinguishing between Saracens or discussing the humanitarian effects of embargoes on Saracens. Any resumption of trade was predicated instead upon the necessity of the Christian population.[29] There was one target of embargoes, however, toward which the medieval tradition displayed a very clear attitude. Trade with heretics was halted by virtue of specific decrees, but, as excommunicates, the heretics were subject to restricted relations with the Christian community anyway. In the high Middle Ages, excommunication was no small matter: it could extirpate flies, sink ships, render a vineyard fruitless, and, of course, kill robbers of ecclesiastical property. Folk understandings of its effects match the gravity of the matter in the eyes of the canonists: an excommunicate was temporarily delivered to the devil. For all the dramatism of wording and accompanying ritual, the overall goal was the shepherding of souls, not their loss along the way. Only a sheep's cancerous nature justified its permanent expulsion from the flock lest it all became diseased.[30] Therefore, condemned heretics were explicitly denied, as the late medieval Holy Thursday bulls would have it, not only "arms, horses, iron, lead, timber for construction, salt, oil, wine, clothes, victuals" but also "anything else that relates to the uses of man."[31] Ad hoc prohibitions were similar in tenor: condemned heretics were to be provided with no grain, wine, oil, bread, cloth, meat, arms, animals, or any victuals necessary for the nourishment and defense of men.[32]

While the main thrust of the classical synthesis on trade with infidels differed in important ways from the premises of later international law, it did nonetheless provide two genuine building blocks for a system of international relations. The first was the concept of truce. The prompt for its discussion was the wording of *Significavit nobis*, which was read as drawing a clear distinction between truce and peace: one who vows not to travel

[29] See, for licenses, Stantchev, *Spiritual Rationality*, 55–8, 61–6, 145–61, 174–5. On the development and deployment of the concept of necessity, see Frank Roumy, "L'origine et la diffusion de l'adage canonique Necessitas non habet legem (VIIIe-XIIIe s.)," in *Medieval Church Law and the Origins of the Western Legal Tradition: A Tribute to Kenneth Pennington*, ed. Wolfgang P. Müller and Mary E. Sommar (Washington, DC: Catholic University of America Press, 2006), 301–19.

[30] Elisabeth Vodola, *Excommunication in the Middle Ages* (Berkeley: University of California Press, 1986) and Helmholz, *Spirit*, 366–93.

[31] "... arma equos ferrum plumbum lignamina sal oleum vinum vestes victualia et alia quemcumque ad usum hominum pertinentia ...." Reg. Vat. 519, 156r.

[32] Cardinal Albornoz with regard to Francesco Ordelaffi, Lord of Forlì, and Guglielmo and Giovanni Manfredi, Lords of Faenza, A. S. Venezia, Commemoriali, Copie, Reg. 5, 54v–57r, esp. 56v (1 Feb 1355), Riccardo Predelli, ed. *I Libri Commemoriali Della Republica Di Venezia: Regesti* (Venice, 1878), II, #72, 228.

unless there is peace and then does so under the conditions of truce is excommunicated and commits perjury.[33] Unlike war, truce provides for the security of things and people. Unlike peace, truce does not imply the end to discord itself. Whoever makes truce does not make peace and only temporarily desists from war.[34] The problem, warns Raymond of Penafort (d. 1275), is that peace and truce are often used interchangeably.[35] Pulling truce into the opposite extreme of its semantic field, three of the most influential authors, Henry of Susa, known as Hostiensis (d. 1271), and then the two leading fifteenth-century authorities, Panormitanus (d. 1445) and Antoninus of Florence (d. 1459), wrote that what applies in times of war also applies in times of truce or that truce interrupts war but does not remove (the condition of) war.[36] Gottofredo da Trani (d. 1245) was rather exceptional in directly addressing the question as it relates to the law on trade: it is well known that some merchandize cannot be exported to Saracens at any time, but the export of other goods is not prohibited in time of truce.[37] Thus, the classical synthesis on trade law made inroads into defining the murky zone that lay between war and peace.

The second building block that the thirteenth-century synthesis on trade offered to later jurists was a list of items the export of which was prohibited. The word itself is quintessentially medieval: to do something contra the lord's or commune's *banna* meant to violate orders and prohibitions of said lord or city government. Thus, in the Venetian statute of the *Ufficiali al Cattaver* (best translated as Office of Contraband), the expression designated a broad array of possible violations, including those who, against the orders of the church and "*contra* our *banna*," carry *de prohibitis* to Mamluk Egypt.[38] Just as popes did not speak of crusades or embargoes, so thirteenth-century jurists did not necessarily use any noun to designate contraband, but the expressions *res prohibitas* and thus simply *prohibita* eventually became commonplace.

33 Johannes Andreae, *In quintum Decretalium librum Novella Commentaria* (Turin, 1963), Book V, 42A. On the author and his work, see Stephan Kuttner, "Johannes Andreae and His 'Novella' on the Decretals of Gregory IX," *The Jurist* 24 (1964): 393–408.

34 *Decretales . . . cum glossis restitutae*, 5.6.11, col. 1662, Hostiensis, *Lectura*, V, 32.

35 Raymond of Peñafort [Raimundus de Pennaforte], *Summa de iure canonico*, ed. Xaverio Ochoa and Aloisio Diez (Rome: Commentarium pro religiosis, 1975), 212.

36 Hostiensis, *Lectura*, V, 32; Panormitanus, *Lectura*, V, 37r, observation #3 after the narration of the canon; Antoninus of Florence, *Summa Theologica* (Graz: Akademische Druck & Verlagsanstalt, 1959), III, 1339.

37 ". . . sed alie merces non sunt prohibite tempore treuge." Gottofredo da Trani, *Summa super titulis Decretalium* (Aalen: Scientia Verlag: 1968 [1519]), 414.

38 A. S. Venezia, Ufficiali al Cattaver, Capitolari, Busta 1, 46Bis r (1364).

The most distinctive feature of the jurists' discussion of contraband items was its bookishness. Compelled by their scholastic approach to search the far corners of the *Corpus Iuris Civilis* but not the holds of round-ships, the jurists simply appended the items mentioned by the laws to those they found in the canons. Nevertheless, by the mid-thirteenth century, a minimum common definition of contraband items had spread throughout the Catholic shores of the Mediterranean and the list kept expanding in different types of commentary until it was restricted in the sixteenth century. The main points in this development are best presented in tabulated form (see Table 4.1).

All in all, the classical synthesis on the subject of trade with infidels exemplifies a major fault line within the *ius commune*. On the one hand, popes and jurists were responding to actual events and trends of political, economic, and social life. On the other hand, the principles of the canon law, not to mention the very genre within which the jurists wrote, prevented the formulation of an explicit political theory of economic sanctions, let alone anything that can be termed international relations. The jurists' fusion of civil and canon law was sometimes mechanical even at the micro level (are, after all, contrabandists to be enslaved or beheaded?). For all its inapplicability to policy-making, the classical synthesis turned the law on trade with infidels into a feature of the late medieval intellectual, political, and economic landscape and provided genuine building blocks for a system of international relations through its definition and refinement of the concept of truce and through its resurrection and repackaging of Roman law's definition of contraband.

4.2 THE RIGHTS OF INFIDELS: TOWARD AN EQUAL FOOTING OR A DEAD END?

The law on trade with infidels outside Christendom that thirteenth-century jurists synthesized originated in Mediterranean realities and in Christians' relations with Saracens. Meanwhile, the extension of Western knowledge of Eurasia expanded the canonists' geographical and ethnographic horizons, spotlighting the potential for new converts. The canonist who brought these previously unaccounted for peoples into the well-ordered pastoral space of the law was uniquely qualified for the job: Sinibaldo Fieschi, a most preeminent jurist, better known as Pope Innocent IV. Although neither Innocent nor any of the other commentators brought the discussion of trade and the discussion of the rights of infidels together, a brief look at the latter subject is necessary to fully understand the perception of the world underpinning the classical law on trade with infidels and its subsequent reorientation. Due to its scope and depth, the work of James Muldoon shall suffice to present Innocent's thought

TABLE 4.1 *Contraband categories*

Category	Sub-categories	13th-century–early 14th-century synthesis	16th-century synthesis (*Martín de Azpilcueta*)[1]
		Ius commune	Gist of de Azpilcueta's views, with stress on the definition of contraband. First published 1550; 1580 ed. features some additions from the time of Gregory XIII (1572–85).
Total embargo in time of war		X 5.6.12 Extrav. Comm. 5.2.1	No trade in time of war. Things not expressly prohibited can be carried during peacetime so long as this is not done for the purpose of helping Saracens fight Christians.
ARMS	Any type of	Cod. 4.41.2 Goal: prevent Barbarians from becoming more powerful X 5.6.6 Goal: stop Christians helping Saracens wage war on Christians Extrav. Comm. 5.2.1	The category *arma* comprises offensive and defensive tools destined for battle by the intent of either their producers or their exporters. Different statutes speak differently: some of offensive weapons, others of both offensive and defensive ones. Some consider items manufactured for battlefield use and others such assumed to be useful in battle. The goal, anyway, is to prevent the export of the means by which the enemies can attack the city or the kingdom. In the case of instruments produced primarily for the battlefield, the burden of proof (that they are not in fact weapons) lay on the exporter. In the case of those not so produced, such as stones, the presumption is that they are not weapons until proven otherwise. The export of the latter does not lead to excommunication if performed bona fide.
	Cuirasses, shields, helmets	Cod. 4.41.2 Dig. 50.16.41	Included

(continued)

TABLE 4.1 (*continued*)

Category	Sub-categories	13th-century–early 14th-century synthesis	16th-century synthesis (*Martín de Azpilcueta*)
	Bows, arrows, short or other swords	Cod. 4.41.2	Included
	Galleys, round-ships	X 5.6.17	Included
	Sticks and stones	Dig. 50.16.41	Only if exported *mala mente*.
RAW MATERIAL	Iron Stones for sharpening	Cod. 4.41.2 X 5.6.6 Extrav. Comm. 5.2.1, Dig. 39.4.11	The export of iron to Saracens is banned, both raw and worked. Raw iron is iron from which nothing has yet been produced. Only the export of iron is banned; those who export other metals are not excommunicated by the canons. This is why Gregory XIII explicitly added tin, steel, and all other types of metal [to the provisions of the Holy Thursday bull; this is an addition in the 1580 edition]. Those who export iron products not suitable for war are not excommunicated unless they do so *mala mente* [in big enough quantity so as to constitute raw material once the products are melted].
	All other types of metal		See above
	Timber for construction of galleys and war machines	X 5.6.6 X 5.6.17	*lignamina galearum:* the word is *ligna* (wood), the material from which galleys are built, not *ligamina* (ligaments), which keep galleys together [*ligamina* is the word that the early modern Holy Thursday bulls used]. *Galea* in Latin means helmet; *galea* here means a type of ship propelled by oars. The expression *lignamina galearum* in X 5.6.6 is commonly

(continued)

			understood to mean "timber suitable for the construction of galleys." It does not extend to cover other types of timber. However, in light of the Holy Thursday bull, which speaks more broadly of *lignamina*, omitting the word *galearum*, excommunicated are all who export any timber suitable for the fabrication of offensive or defensive arms for either sea or land use.
PRECIOUS METALS	Gold	Cod. 4.63.2: not used in the 13th-century synthesis	Rejected as a general rule by de Azpilcueta in 1550, but covered by the expression *ominaque metallorum genera* introduced in the Holy Thursday bull by Gregory XIII and thus in the 1580 ed. of Azpilcueta's work.
VICTUALS	In general	Extrav. Comm. 5.2.1 Extrav. Jo. XXII. 8.un. (In ad hoc papal letters since at least 1223)[2]	Prohibited if done with the goal of helping Saracens against Christians. Not prohibited if done for other purposes.
	Wine, oil, liquids	Cod. 4.41.1.	See above
	Grain, salt	Dig. 39.4.11 Hence dry foods in general, Placentinus, *Summa Codicis* (Turin, 1962), 175	See above

(continued)

TABLE 4.1 (*continued*)

Category	Sub-categories	13th-century–early 14th-century synthesis	16th-century synthesis (*Martín de Azpilcueta*)
ANIMALS	Horses	Extrav. Comm. 5.2.1 Extrav. Jo. XXII. 8.un. (In ad hoc papal letters since at least 1223)[3]	The export of horses is prohibited by the Holy Thursday bull. The presumption is that any export of horses is done *mala mente*, i.e. for the purpose of waging war on Christians.
OTHER		Individual proclamations can feature items not accepted by the majority opinion. E.g., Lerida 1229: Animals that can be eaten, ridden, or used to cultivate the land.	Things not expressly mentioned but necessary for the waging of war on Christians per the Holy Thursday bull, namely, things that are: (1) necessary for the waging of war on Christians and (2) exported with this intention.

1 Martin de Azpilcueta, *Relectio cap.*11r–14v [arms], 14v–15v [iron, other metals], 15v–19r [timber], 23r–31r [victuals, horses].

2 Acta Honorii III et Gregorii IX, #112 (13 May 1223).

3 Acta Honorii III et Gregorii IX, #112 (13 May 1223).

on the subject.[39] Until the Gregorian reform movement, the canonists displayed little interest in infidels and even less in non-Christians outside Christendom. Attempts to (re)define the place of Jews in Christian society from the late twelfth century, however, triggered a discussion on that subject. In turn, considerations of relations with infidels without "began by extending previous discussions of non-Christians living within Europe."[40] Against the background of warfare in the Holy Land, expansion in the Baltic, and the Mongol threat, Innocent IV innovated and "developed a legal basis for a theory of papal relations with non-Christian societies."[41]

Innocent IV began with the premise that infidels possess the right to rule, *dominium* (which perhaps corresponds best to the modern "self-determination"), and therefore their infidelity alone does not justify Christian conquest. This premise withstood a challenge from another top legal authority, Hostiensis, who borrowed from earlier work to make the essentially Donatist point that the advent of Christ illegitimized all infidel rule. When the Council of Constance (1414–18) condemned John Wycliff's more obviously Donatist ideas, the minority opinion grounded in Hostiensis's authority became altogether unsustainable. Yet, the distinction between the two views is easily overdrawn.

Although Innocent IV bequeathed to posterity the winning notion that infidels have the right to *dominium*, his own analysis of Christians' relations with others outside Christendom undermines it. While infidel rulers exercise legitimate power, the pope is ultimately responsible for the souls of all humans. Therefore, infidel rulers must allow Christian missionaries in their land and must also punish violations of natural law. When a ruler hinders Christian missions or fails to compel his subjects to adhere to natural law, the pope can authorize a Christian invasion even though he cannot compel any infidels to forcefully accept baptism. Neither Innocent nor the later canonists dwelled on the seemingly critical definition of exactly what violations of natural law would justify papal intervention into the affairs of infidels, only suggesting "sexual abuses and idolatry" as potential triggers of papal action.[42] It is at this point where the majority opinion leads de facto to what the minority position had clearly stated: that infidels have, in fact, no right to self-determination. After all, the non-Christians envisioned by Innocent and his successors comprised pagans in the Baltic, shamanist Mongols, and Muslims in the Mediterranean, all of

39 Muldoon, *Popes, Lawyers, and Infidels*.

40 Muldoon, *Popes, Lawyers, and Infidels*, 3.

41 Muldoon, *Popes, Lawyers, and Infidels*, 5.

42 Muldoon, *Popes, Lawyers, and Infidels*, 48.

whom the jurists considered pagans and idolaters. The issue of "sexual abuses" could just as easily be translated into a requirement for many "infidel" societies, in which polygamy was a key component of the social order, to either alter their social structure overnight or face Christian intervention. Indeed, the Catholic missionaries' expectation that any new converts to Christianity would strictly adhere to the norms of the Western Canon Law from the very moment of conversion was a key reason for their failures in Asia.[43] In short, no society known to Innocent IV could at one and the same time enjoy the right of self-determination proclaimed by him and yet avoid charges of violating natural law and thus, hypothetically, a Christian invasion.

Thus, despite the majority opinion's nominal insistence on the rights of infidels, its desired objective was to bolster a continuous expansion of the papal flock coupled with universal conformity to "natural law" as understood by Catholic jurists. This could not result in a theory of international relations, for, as Muldoon aptly points out, "[m]odern international law concerns the relations between states, not between an ecclesiastical institution and individuals that are its potential members."[44] The canon law could oppose the wholesale Christian conquest of others, but its pastoral logic and spiritual conceptualization of space precluded jurists working within its limits from formulating a theory of international space and relations. It took a tilt within the *ius commune*, that fusion of canon and civil law that, in Manlio Bellomo's words, built Europe's common legal past, to alter the status quo.

4.3 THE ROMAN PEOPLE AND ITS ENEMIES: CUTTING PASTORAL SPACE TO SIZE

In the early fourteenth century, a bull by Benedict XI on trade with Saracens employed an unusual language that had not been used in previous documents on the subject: "It is destructive of the Ecclesiastical republic and nearly treason to supply enemies of the cross with weapons which they lack, so as to render them more powerful."[45] What whoever composed the letter did was to substitute "Ecclesiastical republic" for "Roman power" and "enemies of the cross" for "barbarians" in a text of the Codex long incorporated into the law on trade with infidels. The Roman Church acts for the Roman Empire and the

[43] James Muldoon, "From Frontiers to Borders: The Medieval Papacy and the Conversion of Those along the Frontiers of Christendom," *Quaestiones Medii Aevi Novae* 16 (2011): 101–21.
[44] Muldoon, *Popes, Lawyers, and Infidels*, 154.
[45] Stantchev, *Spiritual Rationality*, 124.

Roman people are those who obey the pope. Following in the vein of well-established discourse,[46] the most influential contemporary jurist working in the civil law tradition agreed, with a twist.

On the whole, high medieval jurists debating the extent of imperial power had little interest in Christendom's relations with the outside world.[47] In his commentaries, however, Bartolo da Sassoferrato (d. 1357) developed the building blocks of a mapping of the world that gives the church an honorific precedence over the empire while replacing the canon law's spiritual charting of space with Roman law's geopolitical one.[48] On the face of it, Bartolo's global vision was consonant with Innocent IV's. Bartolo's world history was based on Jerome's periodization into four imperial periods: the Roman Empire following those of the Babylonians, the Persians, and the Greeks. With the advent of Christ – and now Bartolo borrows a modified version – it became Christ's empire and Christ's vicar possesses both the spiritual and the temporal swords, a position that earlier authorities like the preeminent twelfth-century jurist Huguccio had restricted to Rome itself.[49] Before Christ, the emperor was rightly called lord of the world, but after the advent, the empire belongs to Christ who, through his vicar the pope, transfers its administration to a secular prince who has no jurisdiction over ecclesiastical lands.[50] The parallel with Innocent IV is obvious. Nominally, Christ is lord of the world (Bartolo) just as the pope is the shepherd of all humans (Innocent). De facto, the empire's reach is constrained (Bartolo) and, similarly, the pope's actual flock is made of baptized Christians (Innocent). The difference lay in that Innocent IV's recognition of a limited pastoral role did not lead him to abandon the canon law's pastoral mapping of the world or the hope of a continuously expanding flock. Innocent IV's insistence that infidel rulers must protect Christian missions in their lands coupled with his prohibition of rival proselytizing at home precludes charting international relations based on

46 See Muldoon, *Empire and Order*, 94–7.

47 See Kenneth Pennington, *The Prince and the Law, 1200–1600: Sovereignty and Rights in the Western Legal Tradition* (Berkeley: University of California Press, 1993), 8–37.

48 Bartolo da Sassoferrato, [*Collected Works*] (Venice: Apud Iuntas, 1570; Robbins Collection, University of California-Berkeley): Vol. 1, *In Primam Codicis Partem*, 26v (Cod. 1.11.6), Vol. 9 *In Secundam FF. Noui Partem*, 227v–228r (Dig. 49.15.24), Vol. 12, *Consilia, Qvaestiones, et Tractatvs*, 97r/v.

49 Ernst H. Kantorowicz, *The King's Two Bodies: A Study in Medieval Political Theology* (Princeton: Princeton University Press, 2016 [1957]), 292–3 for Jerome and Tolomeo of Lucca's popularization of the Christian empire thesis; Muldoon, *Empire and Order*, 76 for Huguccio.

50 Bartolo da Sassoferrato, [*Collected Works*]: Vol. 12, *Consilia, Qvaestiones, et Tractatvs*, 97r/v (*Totius Orbis*).

equality. By contrast, Bartolo paves the way for such a system through his definitions of two concepts: Roman people and the enemies of the Roman people.

The concept of Roman people was the only tool available to the jurists that denoted a political community irrespective of ethnicity, language (and one might add, social status); the *populus Romanus* was the bouquet of *gentes* that recognizes the emperor.[51] This made it possible to make a major leap toward a concept of international space by including infidels within and excluding current and potential faithful without Christendom. Who, then, comprises the Roman people?[52] The Roman people is made not only of those who are part of the empire but also by those who obey the Roman Empire, follow its laws even if they do not obey the emperor (like the cities of Lombardy), claim independence on account of a (revocable) imperial privilege (like Venice), or claim independence on account of an irrevocable pact (like the provinces donated by Constantine to the church). The population of such provinces remains part of the Roman people, continues Bartolo, even if the administration is exercised by someone other than the emperor. Although the pope exercises jurisdiction over all ecclesiastics, they similarly remain part of the Roman people. The same applies to kings, like those of France and England, who deny being subjects of the King of the Romans. In sum, concludes Bartolo, practically all people who obey the church belong to the Roman people.[53] Crucially, the phrase "those who obey the church" does not denote the flock, following the presuppositions of the canon law, but, rather, following the logic of the civil law, stands for Christendom, the territorial expression of the faith-based community.[54]

Having thus squared spiritual and political space from the perspective of the Roman law, Bartolo could carve a place for peoples truly outside the envisioned "us." What Bartolo saw beyond Christendom's boundaries were not potential converts and pockets of faithful among infidels but simply foreigners, *extranei*. In his taxonomy of foreigners, Bartolo took a veritable conceptual leap toward a concept of equal relations by taking into account the others' own

51 Jan Baszkiewicz, "Quelques remarques sur la conception de dominum mundi dans l'oeuvre de Bartolus," in *Bartolo da Sassoferrato: Studi e documenti per il VI centenario*, Vol. 2, ed. Università degli studi di Perugia (Milan: Giuffrè, 1962), 15.

52 See also Cecil N. Sidney Woolf, *Bartolus of Sassoferrato: His Position in the History of Medieval Political Thought* (Cambridge: Cambridge University Press, 1913), 25–8, whose account renders Bartolo's main points chiefly through Latin citations in the main text.

53 Bartolo da Sassoferrato, [*Collected Works*]: Vol. 9, *in Secundam FF. Noui Partem*, 228r (Dig. 49.15.24).

54 As Woolf puts it, *populus romanus* is "conterminous with Western Christendom." Woolf, *Bartolus of Sassoferrato*, 28.

point of view. The Greeks believe that the Emperor of Constantinople is lord of the world, the Tartars claim that the Great Khan is the universal lord, and the Saracens believe that their ruler is lord of the world. Furthermore, continues Bartolo, some are "our allies," like the Greeks against the Turks. Notably, unlike the canonists working on the law on trade with infidels, Bartolo was able to point out a community with whom Christendom is at peace – the Mongols. "Our merchants," continues Bartolo, also visit places with which "we have neither peace, nor war, nor any dealings, like those of India." Those with whom the Christians are in state of war, concludes Bartolo, are the Saracens and "nowadays the Turks."[55] Elsewhere, Bartolo explains the latter point. Christians are not supposed to engage in violence against Jews and pagans. Yet, the church calls for war on Saracens because they hold "our land," specifically Jerusalem and the land that God promised to Abraham and his seed. Similarly, the church incites war against Turks because they are, literally, on the way to the Holy Land, thus obstructing its recovery.[56]

Bartolo, in other words, was working not from a canonistic point of view but rather from that of the Roman law, mapping humans in pragmatic, political terms. While J. M. Kelly's wording – Bartolo lay "the ground for a system based on a plurality of mutually independent territorial sovereignties"[57] – might be a bit too strong, Bartolo certainly raised the possibility of peaceful relations between parties that, if not explicitly put on the same footing (Christ remains nominally lord of the world), are at least not explicitly placed in a hierarchical order with Christendom (or, as in the Byzantine model, the empire) on its top. In hindsight, it may seem that Bartolo cut down the global scope of Innocent IV's aspirations to the size of the former empire's geopolitical reach. Yet, Bartolo did not systematically engage the canonists' ideas on the subject; he simply commented on decrees and their wording.

Indeed, for all the possibilities raised by the likes of Innocent IV and Bartolo, legal writing in the form of commentary to laws and canons was not conducive to the formulation of broader theories. While Bartolo may have turned earlier legal methodology on its head by making the law fit the facts of life, rather than upholding the glossators' idealistic and literal approach,[58] what was required was a type of legal writing predicated on problem solving, not explication. Sure enough, the gulf that separated commentaries from

55 Bartolo da Sassoferrato, [*Collected Works*]: Vol. 9, *In Secundam ff. Noui Partem*, 228r (Dig. 49.15.24).
56 Bartolo da Sassoferrato, [*Collected Works*]: Vol. 1, *In Primam Codicis Partem*, 26v (Cod. 1.11.6).
57 Kelly, *Short History*, 157.
58 Quentin Skinner, *The Foundations of Modern Political Thought*, vol. I (Cambridge: Cambridge University Press, 1978), 9.

policy-making was a hindrance to medieval people no less than it has been to their modern students. In result, a new type of legal writing, the *consilium*, emerged to bridge theory and practice. Among the most commonly cited by later jurists working on Christendom's relations with others were *consilia* written by Oldradus da Ponte, a "legal authority of some distinction" at the papal court in Avignon.[59] While the questions asked of Oldradus were a tad too specific to result in a theory of Christian-infidel relations, later jurists made ample use of ideas and wording provided by Oldradus's *consilia* on Jews and Saracens. *Consilium* 51 concluded that a Jew converting to Islam is not to be punished. What it gave later jurists was an argument that Saracens are less evil than Jews. This was used to make the point that if trade with Jews, seen as worse than pagans, is allowed, then so must be trade with Saracens (seen as pagans) not in war with Christians.[60] In Consilium 72, Oldradus made another point that not only enjoyed a long shelf life but also became a building block of the reconfigured law on trade of the sixteenth century. Christian war against Saracens in Spain is licit – and not only when the latter attack Christians – because "it is quite likely that whenever they have the chance they will attack and oppress Christians and the Church, for this seems to be in their nature."[61] Oldradus's understanding of Saracens' hostility to Christians as innate may seem to indicate a never-ending clash of faiths, but it was in fact used differently. On a basic level, Oldradus's statement explained the applicability of export controls to the Muslims of Spain. More broadly, his statement was coupled with a historical excursus of the early Arab conquests in the Mediterranean not to draw an apocalyptic picture of Christian-Muslim relations in general but, on the contrary, to circumscribe this perpetual hostility to the former lands of the Roman Empire. The notion that Saracens in the Mediterranean are usurpers was then used to raise the prospect of peaceful relations with them elsewhere. Finally, *Consilium* 264 provided more intuitive support for equal relations between Christians and others: peacefully living Jews and Saracens ought not to be expelled by Christian princes. What later jurists lifted from this advice was a specific idea, that Christians, Jews, and Saracens share the same nature, in effect a reminder that all are equal in Christ. Thus, like Bartolo's commentaries, so Oldradus's *consilia* provided the nuts and bolts that later jurists would use to construct a streamlined, explicit theory of trade with infidels. Not surprisingly, it likely took a question from a maritime power to make this happen.

59 Zacour, *Jews and Saracens*, 9.
60 Zacour, *Jews and Saracens*, 42–3, 51.
61 Zacour, *Jews and Saracens*, 48.

4.4 BRIDGING LAW AND POLICY-MAKING: CAN THE FAITHFUL TRADE WITH *BARBARAS NATIONES*?

Thus begins a *consilium* that the famed fifteenth-century jurist Alexander Tartagnus (1423/4–77) wrote on bequest of Vitale Lando, a fellow jurist acting on behalf of the commune of Venice.[62] Alongside archrival Genoa, Venice was the major commercial and maritime power of the later Middle Ages. The Venetians were no strangers to the use of *consilia* in relation to their commercial operations in the East. The complicated, ad hoc papal licensing system of the mid-fourteenth century had compelled them to do so. This case, however, was different. Rather than seeking advice on a technicality – does a license expire upon a pope's death? – the Venetians' inquiry anticipated those made by Portuguese kings in the sixteenth century. While Alexander took the Venetians on a remarkably sharp tour of the law on the subject, what they must have wanted to know was what Alexander's response eventually got to: can war material be exported to infidels not at war with Christians?

While the immediate context of Venice's request for a clarification is not provided by Alexander's *consilium*, Vitale Lando's years of service in prestigious offices mostly overlap with Venice's war with the Ottoman Empire of 1462/3–79. In addition, Alexander served as the canon law chair at the University of Padua between 1467 and 1470.[63] In the late 1460s and then again in the early 1470s, a main trust of the Venetian strategy consisted of assisting Sultan Mehmed II's (1451–81) nemesis, Uzun Hasan, ruler of the Aqquyunlu.[64] To the nomads of Anatolia, Uzun Hasan represented an appealing, traditional alternative to the now sedentary and increasingly controlling Ottoman dynasty. This made Uzun Hasan both a foreign and a domestic threat and thus by far the most formidable one Mehmed II faced. Uzun Hasan, however, had one distinct disadvantage. He lacked artillery, use of which the

62 Alexander Tartagnus, *Consilia seu responsa*, vol. 7 (Venice, 1590), #130, 97v–98r. For the relevant chronology, see Annalisa Belloni, *Professori giuristi a Padova nel secolo XV: profili bio-biografici e cattedre* (Frankfurt: Klostermann, 1986), 110–12 and Giuseppe Gullino, "Vitale Lando," *Dizionario Biografico degli Italiani* 63 (2004). For his life and works, see Aurelius Sabattani, *De vita et operibus Alexandri Tartagni de Imola* (Milan: Giuffré, 1972), specifically 14–16 [birth date], 98–106 [*consilia*], 108–10 [influence].

63 Gullino, "Vitale Lando."

64 On Venice's conflict with Mehmed II, see Stefan Stantchev, "Devedo: The Venetian Response to Sultan Mehmed II in the Venetian-Ottoman Conflict of 1462–79," *Mediterranean Studies* 19, no. 1 (2010): 43–66; Stefan Stantchev, "Inevitable Conflict or Opportunity to Explore? The Mechanics of Venice's Embargo against Mehmed II and the Problem of Western-Ottoman Trade after 1453," *Mediaevalia* 32, no. 1 (2011): 155–96. On the Aqquyunlu, see John E. Woods, *The Aqquyunlu: Clan, Confederation, Empire*, rev. and exp. ed. (Salt Lake City: University of Utah Press 1999 [1976]).

Ottomans had mastered. The Venetians, having had their own land campaign against the Ottomans suffer a miserable fate in 1463–4, put all their hopes in their naval power and a trade embargo, on the one hand, and in the ability of Uzun Hasan to turn the table on Mehmed II, on the other. Venice was ready to provide naval support to the Aqquyunlu leader in 1463 and a decade later its vessels left Venice loaded with cannons and handguns for Uzun Hasan's troops.[65] Yet, contrary to prevalent historiographical myths, the Venetian government neither traded with Muslims when it fought them nor made a living from wholesale violations of the canon law on trade with others.[66] It is thus likely that Alexander entertained the above question on account of Venice's dealings with Uzun Hasan.

Can, then, "the faithful trade with *barbaras nationes* with whom there is no state of war?" It may seem not, begins Alexander, using the laws, canons, glosses, and Hostiensis's *Summa* to list comprehensively yet succinctly and with remarkable precision all the limitations that since the thirteenth century had amounted to the permanent system of export controls described earlier in this chapter (Table 4.1). Then, briefly, Alexander breaks with the tradition of canonistic commentaries by introducing the concept of enemies of the Roman people in order to distinguish between two classes of barbarians: those who are enemies and those who are not. Alexander resumes the traditional and obvious line with respect to the former. Explicitly prohibited things – *prohibita, res prohibitas* – cannot be exported at any time and nothing at all can be exported at time of war when the majority opinion makes *prohibita* off limits even if exported for the purpose of ransoming Christians. Everything belonging to the categories of war material (on account of the canon law) and victuals (on account of the Roman law) is off limits at any time. In case of uncertainty, notably, the merchants are to get the benefit of the doubt.

Having provided an unusually clear definition of contraband, Alexander turned to defining the enemy and thus to exploring some novel ground in the jurisprudence on the subject. The understanding of Saracens that Alexander deployed was the most canonical. Whereas Oldradus had stated that Saracens

65 A. S. Venezia, Sen. Del. Sec. Reg. 21, 209v (2 Dec 1463). Senate, chronicles, and the Venetian envoy all provide substantially different accounts of what exactly was to be delivered; see Enrico Cornet, *Le guerre dei Veneti nell'Asia 1470–1474: Documenti cavati dall'Archivio ai frari in Venezia* (Vienna: Tendler, 1856), #52, 65–6; Domenico Malipiero, "Annali Veneti dall'anno 1457 al 1500," in *Archivio Storico Italiano* 7 (Firenze: Gio. Pietro Viesseux, 1843), 82; Laurence Lockhart, Raimondo Morozzo Della Rocca, and Maria Fransesca Tiepolo, eds., *I viaggi in Persia degli ambasciatori veneti Barbaro e Contarini* (Rome: Istituto Poligrafico dello Stato, Libreria dello Stato, 1973), 103.

66 Stantchev, *Spiritual Rationality*, chs. "Devedo," "Inevitable Conflict or Opportunity to Explore?"

are not idolaters,[67] Alexander went with Hostiensis's definition in precisely this sense. Yet, the Saracens, continues Alexander now following Oldradus, are less evil than Jews. Then he makes his point. Generally trade with Jews is allowed even though there are multiple restrictions on relations with them (cohabitation, bathing, calling Jewish doctors);[68] it stands to reason that trade with Saracens would be similarly allowed. Moreover, Jews and Saracens share the Christians' nature and, if they live inoffensively, are to be tolerated and not expelled. Having established the humanity of Saracens, Alexander continues to explain why waging war on them is licit, building his answer on Bartolo (because they occupy the Holy Land promised to "us") and Oldradus (because they occupy formerly Christian Spain). When it comes to the Turks, Alexander adds an element not found in Bartolo, namely, "because they persecute Christians."[69]

Having fused the thirteenth-century synthesis on trade with infidels with the fourteenth-century understanding of the concepts of the Roman people and its enemies, Alexander finally distinguishes between Saracens and barbarians, thus breaking novel ground in discussions on trade. Whether he was the first to do so is hard to know. What matters is that he was the one cited by influential later authors. Using Bartolo as his stepping stone, Alexander distinguishes between those with whom Christians have war (Saracens, Turks), those with whom there is peace (the Mongols), and those with whom Christians have no relations whatsoever (India). *Non prohibita* can clearly be exported to such others if they can also be exported to Saracens, absent war. But can *res prohibita* be exported to infidels who are not Saracens or Turks? They can because the law speaks only of Saracens and enemies of the Roman people.

Although the *ius commune* had merged the law of the church and the law of the empire, the commentaries of the canonists and the civilians followed distinct tracks, according to the very different assumptions of each corpus. Alexander's actual or apparent originality lay in fusing the distinct lines of spiritual and political considerations into a single, coherent statement on the content of the law that made it directly applicable to policy-making.[70] While it is not clear who picked up the cannons that the Venetian vessels left for Uzun

67 Zacour, *Jews and Saracens*, 67, 88.

68 For a modern edition and discussion of an authoritative statement on that subject, see Diego Quaglioni, "Inter Iudeos et Christianos commertia sunt permissa: 'Questione ebraica' e usura in Baldo degli Ubaldi (c. 1327–1400)," in *Aspetti e problemi della presenza ebraica nell'Italia centro-settentrionale (secoli XIV e XV)*, ed. Sofia Boesch Gajano (Rome: Ripoli, 1983), 275–305.

69 Alexander Tartagnus, *Consilia*, 7, #130, 97v–98r.

70 Alexander Tartagnus, *Consilia*, 7, #130, 98r.

Hasan on an Anatolian beach – Mehmed II's artillery put the Aqquyunlu army to flight – Alexander's *consilium* reconfigured existing legal thought. Alexander's *consilia* were widely diffused,[71] and, in the mid-sixteenth century, well-read authors of treatises that were novel in their subject-matter would use his work as the backbone of a new synthesis on the law on trade with infidels.

4.5 THE CLASSICAL SYNTHESIS REFIGURED

That Alexander provided a streamlined legal opinion to Venice in the fifteenth century does not mean that a new understanding on the law of trade with infidels took Europe by storm. The canon law's perspective was brought to the laity annually by way of the Holy Thursday bull. By listing all occasions in which Christians are excommunicated by virtue of committing the deed itself, the bull reminded all Catholics of the gist of the law on trade with infidels while upholding a spiritual mapping of space when pointing out the targets of export controls: "Saracens, Turks, and other enemies of the Christian name." Jurists who commented on the bull followed its presuppositions. In 1537 Pierre Rebuffi (1487–1557), a renowned law professor, published a commentary on Pope Paul III's 1536 Holy Thursday bull, clarifying the text word by word.[72] Unlike high medieval jurists, Rebuffi paid particular attention to contraband. Like his predecessors, Rebuffi was interested in the content of ancient texts, not contemporary warehouses. Humanistic boasting reinforced the "ivory tower" nature of his commentary: citing Isidore of Seville as the authority on metals, referring to Alexander the Great's Bucephalus when discussing horses as a contraband item, and pointing out that *Calybes*, according to Strabo and Pliny, were people who lived in the Black Sea area when discussing steel (*calybe*).[73] Yet by 1537, commentaries expanding the law on trade with infidels were anachronistic. The papacy itself had practically aligned its position with that of Alexander Tartagnus.

By the time of Rebuffi's commentary, Portuguese kings were exercising almost unlimited authority over the subject, including the export of weapons to peaceful infidels, allied infidels, and infidels fighting other infidels. They were doing this

[71] Giovanna Murano, "Una raccolta di minute autografe di consilia di Alessandro Tartagni (1423/24–1477)," *Bulletin of Medieval Canon Law* 31, no. 1 (2014): 237–48, at 238.

[72] Pierre Rebuffi, *Bulla Coenae Domini Pape Pauli III* (Paris, 1537), 27v. On the author, see Howell A. Lloyd, "Constitutional Thought in Sixteenth-Century France: The Case of Pierre Rebuffi," *French History* 8, no. 3 (1994): 259–75.

[73] Rebuffi, *Bulla Coenae*, 26r–27r.

under ad hoc papal authorizations.[74] While people of low social status and no stake in the existing social order may have engaged in wholesale transgressions of the law, Catholic governments and rich mercantile elites bent and stretched the law but avoided breaking it. On a spiritual plain, some aristocrats and patricians certainly feared the sentence of excommunication. On the temporal plain, breaking the norms of trade with infidels made high-standing individuals with a lot to lose as well as entire communities vulnerable to a variety of attacks.[75] The classical synthesis on trade with infidels was not forgotten or ignored. By seamlessly merging canons and laws in a straightforward policy advice, Alexander showed how a complex law that originated in the context of crusades to the Holy Land could be repackaged, restricted, and adapted to the "age of explorations". This rearrangement of the classical synthesis appears most notably in three distinct treatises that were innovative in their subject matter and first published in the 1550s.

Benvenuto Stracca's 1553 *De Mercatura* is perhaps the best known. As Charles Donahue has argued, while "generally thought to be the first comprehensive treatise on mercantile law," this it was not; instead, the work was widely consulted probably because it provided "a guide to the [legal] sources from the point of view of merchants' cases and mercantile courts."[76] Indeed, Stracca's exposition of the law on trade with infidels well illustrates Donahue's point about *De Mercatura* as a treatise. Stracca's work may not be original, but it is a structured, comprehensive presentation of the law. Notably, Stracca begins and concludes the sections of interest here by citing Alexander's *consilium* to Venice, the elegance of which he praises. Christian merchants can export all sorts of merchandize to those who are neither Saracens nor enemies of the Roman people.[77] Stracca's separate section on contraband follows the same pattern. Rather than innovating by producing a list of contraband items, Stracca faithfully renders the content of laws and preceding commentaries (Table 4.1), keeping personal interventions to

74 Stantchev, *Spiritual Rationality*, 207–8 and, especially, Giuseppe Marcocci, "Trading with the Muslim World: Religious Limits and Proscriptions in the Portuguese Empire (c. 1480–1570)," in *Religion and Trade: Cross-Cultural Exchanges in World History, 1000–1900*, ed. Cátia Antunes, Leor Halevi, and Francesca Trivellato (New York: Oxford University Press, 2014), 91–107.

75 See Stantchev, *Spiritual Rationality*, 77–87, 133–61, 176–201, 207–11.

76 Charles Donahue, "Medieval and Early Modern Lex Mercatoria: An Attempt at Probatio Diabolica," *Chicago Journal of International Law* 5, no. 1 (2004): 21–37, at 27; Charles Donahue, "Benvenuto Stracca's *De Mercatura*: Was There a *Lex mercatoria* in Sixteenth-Century Italy?" in *From lex mercatoria to Commercial Law*, ed. Vito Piergiovanni (Berlin: Duncker & Humblot, 2005), 79 [on popularity] and 106 [quotation].

77 Benvenuto Stracca, *De Mercatura seu Mercatore Tractatus* (Venice, 1553), 39v–41v [#40–8].

a minimum.[78] Stracca probably helped popularize Alexander's integration of the classical synthesis with Bartolo's concept of the Roman people and its enemies. The picture that emerges from Stracca's work is that of a world far bigger than the Mediterranean, mapped in political terms.

While Stracca put together the laws of concern to merchants, Marquardus dei Susannis wrote *De Judaeis et aliis infidelibus* between 1555 and 1557 as a handbook for judges dealing with Jewry law; the book was "extremely popular and well received."[79] Marquardus argues that Christians are allowed to trade with Jews and Saracens in "licit things" and that the same applies to "barbarous nations and infidels."[80] In times of war and, taking the conservative line, times of truce, or when war is feared, all trade is banned.[81] As Stracca, Marquardus explicitly follows Alexander when he distinguishes between Saracens and barbarians and states that trade restrictions apply only to Saracens and enemies of the Roman people. In turn, Marquardus follows Bartolo's definition of Roman people and understanding of international space. Finally, for a list of contraband items, Marquardus refers the reader to Stracca.[82] A dual difficulty in charting known space, however, remained. How are Saracens to be mapped? Are all Muslims the enemies of Christians?

The answer was provided by the Iberian jurist Martín de Azpilcueta (1492–1586), known as Doctor Navarrus, in the guise of a veritable treatise on *Ita quorumdam*, the foundational document of papal export controls.[83] De Azpilcueta's innovative treatise well reflects the changing intellectual landscape of the sixteenth century. De Azpilcueta's meticulous treatment of the law left no word undiscussed. Of interest here, however, are the implications of his treatise (Table 4.1 summarizes his definition of contraband).

De Azpilcueta's first step was to build a new foundation for the canon law on trade with infidels. Lateran III did not declare new prohibitions; it simply

78 Stracca, *De Mercatura*, 67v–68v [#12–16].

79 Kenneth R. Stow, *Catholic Thought and Papal Jewry Policy, 1555–1593* (New York: Jewish Theological Seminary of America, 1977), 65. Stow's analysis of Marquardus's work is brilliant but limited to the book's chief subject.

80 Marquardus de Susannis, *Tractatus de Judaeis et aliis infidelibus* (Venice, 1568; orig. pub. 1558), 20v.

81 Marquardus de Susannis, *Tractatus*, 20v–21r.

82 Marquardus de Susannis, *Tractatus*, 21v.

83 Martin de Azpilcueta, *Ita Quorumdam*. On the overall context of the work, see Marcocci, "Trading with the Muslim World." For the work itself, Marcocci, "Trading with the Muslim World," 102–3 and Stantchev, *Spiritual Rationality*, 203–6. On the author, Vincenzo Lavenia, "Martín de Azpilcueta (1492–1586): Un Profilo," *Archivio italiano per la storia della pietà* 16 (2003): 15–148.

added new penalties to those who commit acts prohibited by *ius antiquum naturale vel positivum divinum et Caesareum*, for example, the fourth commandment, as the requirement to honor one's parents, extends to one's *patria*.[84] This newly erected, baroque façade of the law's relevance in terms of natural law, rather than papal and conciliar decisions, anticipates the trend found in the works of Alberico Gentili and Hugo Grotius.[85] At the same time, it contrasts with the fact that the bulk of the work was devoted to restricting the law's applicability.

Although de Azpilcueta did not map international space verbally, let alone graphically, his work contains all theoretical considerations needed to merge the pragmatic portolans of merchants with the more abstract concepts of space reflected in canons and laws. While Bartolo and Oldradus had tersely pointed out why the church wages war on Saracens in the Holy Land, Saracens in Spain, and Turks, de Azpilcueta provides a detailed explanation grounded in a historical excursus that leads to a conceptual breakthrough. "Saracens" was originally an ethnic category (*nomen gentis*) signifying the Arabs. Muhammad persuaded the Arabs to consider themselves the only legitimate successors of divine law, separating them from the Roman Empire and the Roman church; the Muslims defeated the Romans and the Persians, conquering Syria, the Holy Land, and "all of [the Roman province of] Africa"; they would have conquered France were it not for Charles Martel. In short, once *nomen gentis*, the Saracens, became *nomen sectae Mahometiae*, they followed Muhammad and occupied or attacked things of the church.[86] De Azpilcueta then took a step forward: the religious category Saracens is made of multiple ethnic ones: Arabs, Turks, Moors, and Persians, among others.[87] Thus, de Azpilcueta disposed of the medieval understanding of the word Saracens as a mixture of an ethnic and a religious component and, in a radical break with the past, dismissed the long-enshrined classification of Muslims as pagans: *Ita quorumdam*'s restrictions do not generally extend to pagans because pagans do not belong to the "sect of Muhammad."[88]

Having distinguished between what would today be called religious and ethnic identity and working against the background of natural law, de Azpilcueta drew a line between religious difference and political hostility. Instead of painting an apocalyptic picture of the relations between "Christianism" and "Sarracenism," de Azpilcueta circumscribed the hostility between the two sides to the

84 Martín de Azpilcueta, *Ita Quorumdam*, 4r.
85 See for the latter Capps, "Natural Law," esp. 63.
86 Martín de Azpilcueta, *Ita Quorumdam*, 7r/v.
87 Martín de Azpilcueta, *Ita Quorumdam*, 8r (#9).
88 Martín de Azpilcueta, *Ita Quorumdam*, 9v (#21).

Mediterranean, where the matter remained both geopolitical (Saracens qua usurpers) and religious (Saracens fight out of hatred for Christianity). The result was far-reaching: there were Muslims, outside formerly Roman lands, who were at peace with Christians.[89] That there could be Saracens at peace with Christians was a radical enough concept, but de Azpilcueta did not stop there: not all Saracens fight Christians on account of *odio religionis*; Saracens can even wage a just war on Christians.[90] Dr. Navarrus's theoretical reconciliation between "Christianism" and "Sarracenism" was tempered when applied to the specific areas of interest to the kings of Portugal: the export of war material to Muslims in India was subject to numerous "ifs" and a lower threshold applied to judging Muslim kings' intentions with respect to Christians as hostile than in the case of the "kings of pagans" in Brazil.[91] These qualifications notwithstanding, de Azpilcueta awarded Muslims a legitimate place on the political map of the world. An "international" relations system is thus lurking between the lines of his work. Even the presence of the Ottoman fleet in Toulon – Dr. Navarrus wrote at the time of an unprecedented Ottoman-French alliance that upset religious norms on both sides – does not violate the law, unless the Ottomans are provided with weapons, triremes, or other war material that would be used against Christians in the future.[92]

In short, unlike Stracca and Marquardus, de Azpilcueta did not simply popularize the main points raised by Alexander nearly a century earlier; he also brought the refiguration of the classical synthesis to its logical conclusion. Although Dr. Navarrus continued to treat the Roman Empire and the Roman Church as synonymous concepts, by introducing natural law to the law on trade with infidels and by disjoining religion and politics in his reconceptualization of Saracens, a subject he claimed caused him tremendous difficulty,[93] the Iberian jurist broke with the tradition he had inherited. To say that de Azpilcueta paved the way for a system of international relations grounded in the principles of self-determination and equality is probably to exaggerate his thought's significance. Rather, the point is that Dr. Navarrus's writings reflect a new understanding of the world and an approach that, unlike Innocent IV's, does not in the last analysis preclude the possibilities that it nominally upholds.

The work of de Azpilcueta illustrates how the broader changes of the sixteenth century impacted the canon law on trade with infidels. Whereas the classical

89 Martín de Azpilcueta, *Ita Quorumdam*, 9r (#16).

90 Martín de Azpilcueta, *Ita Quorumdam*, 8v–9r. See also 8r (#11).

91 Martín de Azpilcueta, *Ita Quorumdam*, 9v (India, #23), 10v (Brazil, #29).

92 Martín de Azpilcueta, *Ita Quorumdam*, 10r (#25).

93 Martín de Azpilcueta, *Ita Quorumdam*, 6v (#2).

canonistic synthesis envisioned a world according to what it ought to be, its sixteenth-century refiguration walked a careful line between Machiavellian realism and an upholding of universal moral standards through the concept of natural law.

4.6 EPILOGUE: CONTRABAND IN THE LONG PERIOD

Having previewed this chapter's arguments in its introduction, we shall conclude not with a summary of its findings but rather with a challenge to the paradigm of approaching the subject within the ambit of modern history, as exemplified by Philip Drew's recent work on maritime blockades.[94] Early modernity did not invent economic sanctions, maritime blockades, or the concept of contraband. Nor did it ditch the medieval canon law on the subject of trade with others. Instead, it paved the way for the deployment of its content in the service of sovereign states in Europe.

The canon law on trade with infidels seems to have been well-known to Grotius for him to cite a rather obscure canon that, among other things, concerns trade with Alexandria.[95] Grotius followed with the widely cited *Significavit nobis*, the canon on which basis the canonists had discussed the concept of truce, and with John XXII's embargo against Granada.[96] The reason that Grotius cited these canons was not to define contraband per se but rather to provide examples of declarations of war in relation to that subject. This probably explains his choice of three canons that feature somewhat geopolitical terms (Alexandria and Egypt, the Emirate of Granada). Grotius, however, did not offer new content on the subject; in fact, he barely offered any. His interests were not in export controls but rather in the interdiction of neutral commerce during wartime. His modernity lay in his approach: after briefly citing the three fragments of the canon law, Grotius refers his readers to an exhaustive list of the actual practice of governments.[97] While Grotius "envisioned an open and egalitarian order[,] not a hierarchical one," and thus had little use for the Roman pontiff,[98] his contemporaries could well use the principles and/or

94 Drew, *Law of Maritime Blockade*.

95 X 1.36.11; see Aloysius Tautu, ed., *Acta Honorii III (1216–1227) et Gregorii IX (1227–1241)* (Vatican City, 1950), #39 (18 Aug 1218) and Stantchev, *Spiritual Rationality*, 66.

96 X 1.36.11, X 5.6.11, Extrav. Jo. XXII. 8un. Hugo Grotius, *De Jure Belli ac Pacis libri tres* (Lausanne, 1752 [1625]), III, 558.

97 Grotius, *De Jure Belli*, III, 558–60.

98 James Muldoon, "Colonial Charters: Possessory or Regulatory?" *Law and History Review* 36, no. 2 (2018), 355–81, at 380–1.

the content of the *ius commune* in the pursuit of their own goals. In turn, the work of Emanuel Gonzalez Tellez, arguably "one of the last massive canonistic commentaries to enjoy European wide distribution," offered another innovative comment on the canon law on trade with infidels, this time citing Grotius, too.[99]

Early modern legal realities, as Richard Helmholz has shown, remained indebted to the *ius commune* even in the case of England.[100] Furthermore, as Muldoon has recently argued, papal practice had a direct bearing upon English expansion into North America:

> The charters that the English kings issued regarding the exploration and colonization of North America reflected . . . papal principles, to the point of quoting *Inter caetera* verbatim. These papal bulls, drawing on three centuries of canon law theory and papal practice to regulate European overseas expansion, were shaping the early stages of what eventually would be international law.[101]

With respect to contraband, in 1584, Queen Elizabeth banned the delivery of war material and victuals to the Spanish Netherlands and in 1589 admonished the Hanse towns not to provide Spain with war material, shipping supplies, or victuals.[102] The word "contraband," as argued by Drew, may well have been, in some rather narrow sense, introduced to international law in 1625, but what it covered included nothing that had not already been discussed at length on account of papal embargoes. What the treaty called contraband was, moreover, hardly different from the *prohibita* of contemporary papal Holy Thursday bulls.

Drew's own careful study of early modern and modern realities helps expose the fallacy of using Grotius as the alpha temporal point of historical inquiry into international law. Indeed, later medieval jurists would have been right at home with the types of stipulation found in the 1909 London Declaration Concerning the Laws of Naval War, the content of which Drew meticulously reports. These are grouped in two articles. Article 22 deals with

99 Kenneth Pennington, "Sovereignty and Rights in Medieval and Early Modern Jurisprudence: Law and Norms without a State," in *Roman Law as Formative of Modern Legal Systems*, ed. Jaroslaw Reszczyńsk, Piotr Ścislicki, and Janusz Sondel (Kraków: Jagiellonian University Press, 2003), 30 [citation], 33–4 [Tellez on trade].

100 See, in general, Richard H. Helmholz, "University Education and English Ecclesiastical Lawyers 1400–1650," *Ecclesiastical Law Journal* 13, no. 2 (2011): 132–45.

101 Muldoon, "Colonial Charters," 12.

102 R. G. Marsden, "Naval or Victualling Stores: The Right of Pre-Emption," *Journal of the Society of Comparative Legislation* 4, no. 1 (1902): 45–50, at 45–6; Drew, *Law of Maritime Blockade*, 27.

TABLE 4.2 *Definitions of contraband*

HOLY THURSDAY BULL, 1610–1722[1]	TREATY OF SOUTHAMPTON, 1625[2]
Horses, **weapons, iron, iron wire, tin, steel, all other types of metal** and war **machines**, timber for construction, **hemp, ropes made of hemp or of other material**, and that material itself, and other things with which they fight Christians	Ammunition, ships, **weapons**, sails, **ropes, gold, silver, copper, iron, lead, and the like**

[1] See Stantchev, *Spiritual Rationality*, 208.
[2] Drew, Law of Maritime Blockade, 26–7.

absolute contraband or what de Azpilcueta had called things meant for war. The list starts with "arms of all kinds" and continues with ammunitions, animals that can be used in war, warships, and ends with a sole example of a conceptual rather than merely technological departure from canonistic commentary: machinery for the production of war material. In turn, Article 24 deals with what de Azpilcueta had termed items that are prohibited only if exported for the purpose of causing harm, namely "articles, susceptible of use in war as well as for purposes of peace." This group includes "foodstuffs" (the *victualia* of the *ius commune*) and continues with other items that would have surprised no late medieval jurist, like "forage and grain, suitable for feeding animals," "clothing," or "gold and silver."[103] Drew is certainly right that "the categories of contraband as described by Grotius some 400 years ago . . . have endured the test of time."[104] The point, however, is that Grotius was nothing more than a milestone in a long period in the history of "customary international law" on the subjects of export controls and contraband. This longue durée began in the late twelfth century against the contexts of church reform, commercial revolution, crusade, and revival of the Roman law. Its chief feature was the formation and then transfiguration

[103] Drew, *Law of Maritime Blockade*, 28 and nn. 19–20. "Although the London Declaration never entered into force, many of its provisions relating to contraband are recognized as being reflective of customary international law." Drew, *Law of Maritime Blockade*, 28.

[104] Drew, *Law of Maritime Blockade*, 29. Similarly, Drew's note on the early history of maritime blockade with brief references to changes in European commerce and economy is built exclusively from works about blockades, some rather antiquated, with no consideration of the studies that define our knowledge of the developments mentioned. Drew, *Law of Maritime Blockade*, 37–8.

of Western legal mappings of humans and their physical space from the spiritual categories of the canon law into the geopolitical ones of Roman law and modernity. In turn, this transfiguration was symptomatic of the vigorous yet ultimately unsuccessful attempt of high medieval popes and lawyers to build a Christendom founded on the principles of the canon law.

RECOMMENDED READING

Clarke, Peter D. *The Interdict in the Thirteenth Century: A Question of Collective Guilt*. Oxford: Oxford University Press, 2007.

Helmholz, Richard H. The *Spirit of Classical Canon Law*. 3rd ed. Athens, GA: University of Georgia Press, 2010.

Muldoon, James. *Popes, Lawyers, and Infidels: The Church and the Non-Christian World, 1250–1550*. Philadelphia: University of Pennsylvania Press, 1979.

Stantchev, Stefan. *Spiritual Rationality: Papal Embargo as Cultural Practice*. Oxford: Oxford University Press, 2014.

Trivellato, Francesca, Leor Halevi, and Cátia Antunes, eds. *Religion and Trade: Cross-Cultural Exchanges in World History, 1000–1900*. New York: Oxford University Press, 2014.

5

God, Sovereignty, and the Morality of Intervention outside Europe

David M. Lantigua

5.1 THE NORM OF INTERVENTION AND GLOBAL HISTORY

The 1648 Peace of Westphalia typifies the "modern" starting point of state sovereignty and humanitarian intervention within conventional historical treatments of International Relations (IR) theory. The treaties ending the Thirty Years' War signaled the dawn of an international society after medieval Latin Christendom with new diplomatic arrangements that assigned legitimate autonomy to specific European states independent of Roman imperial and papal authorities. The ideological archetypes of Westphalia for IR theory during the twentieth century were contemporaries, Thomas Hobbes (1588–1679) the realist and Hugo Grotius (1583–1645) the rationalist. Each of them powerfully envisioned a modern form of international relations: Hobbes accented sovereign political independence and international anarchy between states whereas Grotius affirmed a worldwide association of states absent a global authority yet still regulated by norms of universal law to justify war and intervention. Hobbesian sovereignty and Grotian internationalism illustrate the dynamic tension and terms of modern international relations.[1]

The turn to the global history of international law has challenged the conceptual parameters of the IR Westphalian narrative focused on intra-European relations between sovereign states.[2] In particular, attention to the constitutive role of imperial expansion and colonial settlement outside Europe offers a richer scope for analyzing the development of "modern" international relations and

[1] Mark W. Janis, "Sovereignty and International Law: Hobbes and Grotius," in *Essays in Honour of Wang Tieya*, ed. Ronald St. John Macdonald (Dordrecht: Martinus Nijhoff, 1994), 391–400.

[2] Representative examples include Paul Keal, *European Conquest and the Rights of Indigenous Peoples: The Moral Backwardness of International Society* (Cambridge: Cambridge University Press, 2003); and Antony Anghie, *Imperialism, Sovereignty, and the Making of International Law* (Cambridge: Cambridge University Press, 2007).

their legal-political concepts such as the state of nature, the right of occupation, and the law of nations.[3] Anticipating the critical turn to international legal history during the last few decades, Carl Schmitt made the compelling claim in his 1950 work *Der Nomos der Erde* (*The* Nomos *of the Earth*) that "the structure of European international law was determined by a particular course of events: conquest of a new world."[4] From the historical standpoint of European colonialism in the Iberian-Atlantic world rather than Westphalian Europe, sovereignty and especially intervention – the two pillars of modern international relations – appear very different. European conceptions of sovereignty, as well as property, often justified aggressive colonial interaction with indigenous peoples of the Americas who exhibited allegedly deficient modes of political life and occupation of the land. Whether terminating in war or in economic exploitation of indigenous peoples, intervention received overarching sanction from God and nature, thus entrenching its authoritative force.

The aim of this chapter is not to derail the search for a norm of intervention, subjecting it to either hypercritical legal history or unrelenting genealogical suspicion.[5] On the contrary, as Terry Nardin has argued, intervention remains an important facet of international relations that demands deeper ethical consideration. For his part, Nardin's appeal to common morality as a rational standard for criticizing the practices of particular historical communities or international customs provides a normative ground for further analysis.[6] According to a common morality based on respect for human dignity, humanitarian intervention expresses a fundamental duty to protect the innocent from violence under "truly grave" situations that justify an exception to the norm of nonintervention. Humanitarian intervention is therefore an expansive concept that may entail coercive military force such as war, but only as an extreme measure that does not exclude other diplomatic avenues.[7]

The broadly Kantian tradition of common morality outlined by Nardin has critical purchase for thinking through cases of intervention without

3 Andrew Fitzmaurice, *Sovereignty, Property and Empire, 1500–2000* (Cambridge: Cambridge University Press, 2014); Anthony Pagden, *The Burdens of Empire: 1539 to the Present* (New York: Cambridge University Press, 2015); Jennifer Pitts, *Boundaries of the International: Law and Empire* (Cambridge, MA: Harvard University Press, 2018).

4 Carl Schmitt, *The* Nomos *of the Earth in the International Law of the* Jus Publicum Europaeum (Candor, NY: Telos Publishing, 2003), 101.

5 For a recent notable exception combining the history of sovereignty and the norm of humanitarian intervention within Europe and beyond, see Luke Glanville, *Sovereignty and the Responsibility to Protect: A New History* (Chicago: University of Chicago Press, 2014).

6 Terry Nardin, "The Moral Basis of Humanitarian Intervention," *Ethics and International Affairs* 16, no. 2 (2002): 57–70, at 64–5.

7 Nardin, "Moral Basis of Humanitarian Intervention," 67–8.

succumbing to either a cultural parochialism or a moralizing imperialism concerning normative judgments. It is noteworthy that Nardin identifies Christian natural law and philosophical Stoicism as historic predecessors to the tradition of common morality. He locates this Christian natural law approach to intervention in the biblical mandate to defend one's neighbor from oppression and injustice. Moreover, rather than denuding the morality of intervention of its historical background, Nardin rightly underscores how it took political form in Western Christian interactions with non-European peoples evident in the writings of Pope Innocent IV, Francisco de Vitoria, and Grotius, each of whom argued for intervention in foreign lands on the grounds of punishing wrongdoing or protecting the innocent.

Notwithstanding the insights of Nardin's normative project, it contains certain weaknesses and limitations. Nardin's portrayal of the Christian natural law tradition as a predecessor to common morality, for example, is too homogenous and does not parse important canonistic, scholastic, and humanistic differences among past thinkers in the Christian West concerning foreign intervention. Medieval and early modern Christian thinkers generally made a categorical distinction that permitted intervention as either a *punitive action* or a *defensive action*. This difference, overlooked by Nardin, had considerable political consequences for European interactions with foreign peoples in expansionary contexts even during the modern period.

Nardin's presentation of the natural law tradition also ignores the normative role its prominent thinkers assigned to the law of nations (*ius gentium*), especially in contexts of colonial expansion. As a result, Nardin's common morality approach to humanitarian intervention overestimates the singular force of natural law as the only expression of human reason in traditional jurisprudence. Whereas the natural law was interpreted as promulgating universal norms of reason, the *universal law of nations* could account for unity and diversity in political arrangements, positive law, and understandings of property.[8] It is revealing that Nardin's historic precedent to "enforcing respect for human rights" was a natural law tradition justifying the

[8] Nardin does seem to appreciate this point about the law of nations offering a framework for tolerating various social practices among different cultures, but he does not develop its importance for a historical analysis of the moral norm of intervention. See Terry Nardin, "Legal Positivism as a Theory of International Society," in *International Society: Diverse Ethical Perspectives*, ed. David R. Mapel and Terry Nardin (Princeton: Princeton University Press, 1998), 31–2. For a constructive Thomistic account of legal authority as a natural relation attentive to cultural pluralism, see Jean Porter, *Ministers of the Law: A Natural Law Theory of Legal Authority* (Grand Rapids, MI: Eerdmans, 2010). And for a theological view that preserves the law of nations as a basis of international authority, see Oliver O'Donovan, *The Ways of Judgment* (Grand Rapids, MI: Eerdmans, 2005), ch. 12.

enforcement of "standards of civilized conduct" among foreign rulers who violated rational universal standards.[9]

This chapter begins to vindicate a moral norm of humanitarian intervention from within a "critical discourse" of the law of nations attentive to both its dominative and its emancipatory uses in colonial contexts outside Europe.[10] The Spanish debates concerning the conquests, as considered in this chapter, exposed arguments for nonintervention and intervention that had an influence, often unacknowledged, on later modern thinkers of international relations. Ideas of sovereignty and intervention were deployed to advance not only aggressive colonial expansion but also the rights of non-Europeans. Crucially, the Iberian-Atlantic context brought into focus a scholastic theological account of the law of nations "common to all peoples": it could affirm native inhabitants in colonial settings as first occupants according to a symmetrical political standing, simultaneously scrutinizing European injustices and defending indigenous claims of justice. Although sharing some important features with this scholastic view, the "modern" law of nations increasingly became associated with the "civilized nations" of Europe and the world, which supplied a benchmark for measuring the fittingness of foreign peoples in the emergent international society. From this longer global history, a different view of intervention surfaces that can recognize its political purposes in European colonial contexts as well as some of its contemporary iterations under a global economic order.

5.2 WAR, OCCUPATION, AND THE CHRISTIAN LAW OF NATIONS

The ideas of intervention and sovereignty in the Christian legal past prompt a discussion of just war and political occupation, two practices belonging to the law of nations (*ius gentium*). Gratian's *Decretum* (1140), the definitive collection of discordant canons of the Latin Church, followed Isidore of Seville's Roman legal categorization of war and occupation of land held by enemies or no one as part of the law of nations, not natural law.[11] The law of nations conferred the public character of these practices, since each presumed a

[9] Nardin, "Moral Basis of Humanitarian Intervention," 57.

[10] I use this expression of "critical discourse" to address the early modern colonial context from Enrique Dussel, "Las Casas, Vitoria, and Suárez, 1514–1617," in *Human Rights from a Third World Perspective: Critique, History, and International Law*, ed. José-Manuel Barreto (Newcastle upon Tyne: Cambridge Scholars Publishing, 2013), 172–207.

[11] Gratian, *The Treatise on Laws*, trans. Augustine Thompson (Washington, DC: Catholic University of America Press, 1993), Dist. 1, c. 9. Gratian cited Isidore of Seville's *Etymologies*, V.vi. Notably, Gratian also included immunity of ambassadors and slavery in the law of nations.

sovereign ruler over a people having the authority to declare war and claim occupation of territorial space. For medieval civilian and canon lawyers, occupation of land under the law of nations did not entail its private ownership but rather political jurisdiction over the people inhabiting a specific region. And war, which belonged to the law of nations according to the canon lawyers, permitted only those just wars outlined by the three traditional causes: repelling an enemy, recovering stolen property, and avenging prior injuries.[12] Gratian encapsulated the requirement of legitimate political authority and due cause in his definition of a just war as one "waged from an authoritative edict or by which injuries are avenged."[13] In the medieval context of the Crusades, proper authority and just cause acquired a religious character whereby the papacy could declare war to recover the seizure of the Holy Land from Muslim occupants, beginning with Pope Urban II in 1095.

Natural law, by contrast, accounted for the common possession of all things and the identical liberty of everyone, thus indicating that private property and slavery were not natural institutions but instead rationally devised under the law of nations through custom and utility. Christians of late antiquity, shaped by ancient Stoicism, viewed the institutions of private property and slavery generally as sinful aberrations from the original state of freedom and harmony prior to the Fall. Although medieval canonists and theologians maintained the view that slavery was contrary to natural law, the retrieval of the Greek philosopher Aristotle and the Roman Marcus Tullius Cicero during the twelfth and thirteenth centuries contributed to a more palatable interpretation of private property's conformity to natural reason. Without private property (or the division of things), claimed Thomas Aquinas following Aristotle, human communities would be prone to laziness, confusion, and increased conflict.[14] Notwithstanding its rational utility, private property for medieval Christian theologians and jurists remained under the category of *ius gentium*.

Like property, the conformity between war and natural reason also solidified during the Middle Ages. Cicero, whose appropriation during the Middle Ages among both jurists and theologians was unmatched, expanded medieval Christian discourse about intervention and war. Cicero articulated a common opinion of just war thinkers that revenge and defense were the only two valid causes of just war. According to Cicero's *De inventione*, the origins of these

12 Frederick H. Russell, *The Just War in the Middle Ages* (Cambridge: Cambridge University Press, 1975), 64, 97.

13 C. 23, q. 2, c. 2, in *The Ethics of War: Classic and Contemporary Readings*, ed. Gregory Reichberg, Henrik Syse, and Endre Begby (Malden, MA: Blackwell, 2006), 113.

14 Thomas Aquinas, *Summa theologiae*, translated by Fathers of the English Dominican Province (New York: Benzinger Bros, 1947) II-II q. 66, a. 2.

causes resided in the natural law. More specifically, vengeance belonged to the natural law (*ius*), and it took two forms as either a punitive act or a defensive act.[15] The Roman legal tradition preserved by Gratian also considered vengeance or the repayment of violence with force as part of *ius naturale*. Even though war was an extension of natural vengeance for medieval Christian thinkers, it belonged categorically to *ius gentium* and it concerned the rectification of injuries carried out by public authorities.[16] Natural law admitted vengeance in an act of self-defense yet it had to be restricted through the proportionate use of force.[17] The punitive dimension of vengeance obtained only at the level of public authority, not individuals. Concomitantly, as Saint Augustine observed, another state's neglect to punish the wrongdoings of its own citizens could constitute a lawful cause of war.[18]

In the era of the Crusades, the cause of punishing egregious wrongs would expand considerably to justify wars of intervention among non-Christian peoples beyond Latin Christendom. Sinibaldo Fieschi (later Pope Innocent IV), much like Aquinas, acknowledged the legitimacy of occupation of non-Christian lands and properties based on natural reason and positive law. The canon lawyer pope rejected a quasi-Donatist doctrine of jurisdiction and property founded on grace and true piety as defended later by the canonist Cardinal Hostiensis. Nevertheless, Pope Innocent IV also supplied the ideological armature for foreign intervention according to an international right of punishment when he raised the question, "Is it ever licit to invade lands which are held or owned by infidels?"[19] Under Innocent IV's judgment, publicly accepted violations of the natural law merited punishment and dispossession whenever rulers failed to hold their citizens accountable. Given the context of the Crusades, Innocent IV claimed that only the pope could authorize punitive intervention through war. Idolatry and the prohibition of Christian preaching were the two chief sins against natural law that, according to Innocent, could merit punishment from foreign intervention. When Latin Christendom turned to the Atlantic world during the early modern age, these moral and religious causes of war placed a powerful legal veneer over European colonial expansion.

15 Cicero, *De inventione*, trans. C. D. Yonge (Whitefish, MT: Kessinger Publishing, 2004) Book II, 22.

16 Russell, *Just War in the Middle Ages*, 96.

17 Aquinas, *Summa theologiae*, II-II, 64.7.

18 Augustine, *Questions on the Heptateuch*, and Gratian, C. 23, q. 2, c. 2, in *The Ethics of War*, 82, 113.

19 Pope Innocent IV, *Quod super his, de voto*, X 3.34.8, § 1. For an English translation of most of the medieval decretal, see *The Ethics of War*, 152–5.

5.3 SOVEREIGNTY AND INTERVENTION IN THE IBERIAN-ATLANTIC WORLD

Early modern Iberian-Atlantic powers later deployed the Innocentian doctrine of punishment stripped of its papal authorization in imperial efforts to spread Christianity and civilize foreign peoples. The papacy's concession to the practice of royal patronage by protective Catholic monarchs not only expanded imperial control over the Church, it also facilitated the eventual secularization of crusading interventions once waged exclusively under papal directive. A crucial turning point in the secular transference of war's authorization occurred when King Duarte of Portugal persuaded Pope Eugenius IV in 1436 to endorse his brother Prince Henry's colonization of the Canary Islands to convert the pagans there. Duarte's description of the native Guanches was a telling prognostication of subsequent European views toward non-Europeans in the Atlantic world and beyond: "The nearly wild men who inhabit the forests are not united by a common religion, nor are they bound by the chains of law, they are lacking normal social intercourse, living in the country like animals."[20] In other words, since the natives allegedly were without law and social-political order, they required Portuguese political subjugation to become civilized in the image of Christian Europeans. Eugenius IV acquiesced to this new rationale for war against non-European infidels who did not pose a threat to Latin Christendom. That same year of 1436, Pope Eugenius authorized Prince Henry, a member of the Order of Christ, to lead an African crusade against not only Moors (Muslims) but also "other infidels."[21]

Through the Iberian political appropriation of papal worldwide dominion, the medieval Crusades remained the legal backbone of Spanish conquest and colonization of the New World.[22] When Spanish conquistadors emerged as armed prophets spreading the faith with weapons in the name of the Catholic Crown, they could marshal traditional Christian justifications for war and intervention among foreign peoples. Consider the case of the most well-known conquistador of the Nahua peoples of Mexico, Hernán Cortés, who in 1522 summoned his company of soldiers to war based on several rationales: to subjugate a barbarian people for the dissemination of faith; to protect their own lives; and to support native allies.[23] He stated succinctly, "as Christians we

[20] "Letter of King Duarte to Eugenius IV," in *The Expansion of Europe: The First Phase*, ed. James Muldoon (Philadelphia: University of Pennsylvania Press, 1977), 54.

[21] Peter Russell, *Prince Henry "the Navigator": A Life* (New Haven: Yale University Press, 2000), 161.

[22] Russell, *Just War in the Middle Ages*, 303.

[23] Hernán Cortés, "The Third Letter," in *Letters from Mexico*, ed. and trans. Anthony Pagden (New Haven: Yale University Press, 1986), 166.

were obliged to wage war against the enemies of our Faith; and thereby we would win glory in the next world."[24] This religious motivation of Cortés was explicit and resounding throughout his letters as when he wrote, "I have put an end to many idolatries and offenses against our Creator, bringing many of the natives to the knowledge of God and planting in these lands Our Holy Catholic Faith."[25] Appended to the religious purpose was the task of claiming political sovereignty over the native peoples, now deemed subjects of the Spanish King and Holy Roman Emperor Charles. Like Duarte in the Canaries, Spaniards frequently regarded Amerindians as incapable of governing themselves, which meant that they lacked genuine political occupation of their lands left open for European possession.

Cortés and the many other European colonizers had clear economic motivation for intervention, though it was never considered an official cause of war. Christopher Columbus, for example, indicated a devotion to discovering more gold on other islands in the early colonization of the Caribbean.[26] Out of the snares of these interlocking economic, political, and religious interests, there emerged the rapacious system of forced labor known as the *encomienda*, which imposed tributary service upon the natives in return for their learning European civility and the Catholic faith. Extracting natural resources from the earth, especially gold and silver, constituted the brutal form of labor characteristic of Latin America starting with the *encomiendas* and continuing up to the present day.[27] Cortés gave ominous expression to the unquenchable thirst for wealth bent on dominating Mexico's first occupants. In a letter to King Charles, he stated: "By making slaves of this barbarous people, who are almost savages, Your Majesty will be served and the Spaniards will benefit greatly, as they will work in the gold mines, and perhaps by living among us some of them may even be saved."[28]

Trained rudimentarily in law, Cortés managed to articulate official causes of war that became contentious and sometimes fashionable in the ensuing Spanish debates about the conquests. Yet Spanish theologians formed in scholasticism and the *ius commune* tradition of Roman law and canon law now entered the fray. Chief among them was the Dominican theologian at the

24 Cortés, "The Second Letter," in *Letters from Mexico*, 63.

25 Cortés, "The Fifth Letter," in *Letters from Mexico*, 442.

26 Andrés Reséndez, *The Other Slavery: The Uncovered Story of Indian Enslavement in America* (New York: Houghton Mifflin Harcourt, 2016), ch. 1.

27 Marie Arana, *Silver, Sword, and Stone: Three Crucibles in the Latin American Story* (New York: Simon and Schuster, 2019).

28 Cortés, "The Fifth Letter," 446.

University of Salamanca, Francisco de Vitoria. His 1539 lectures on the Amerindians and just war dismissed Cortés's causes based on religious difference and the desire for glory, along with any theocratic belief in the Christian emperor as ruler over the whole world (first unjust title).[29] Additionally, Vitoria rejected Christopher Columbus's so-called title of discovery or occupancy (third unjust title) and the Innocentian right of punishing foreigners who commit sins against natural law (fifth unjust title) on the authority of worldwide papal dominion (second unjust title).

Vitoria did evaluate possible arguments for waging war to protect ambassadors, preachers, and travelers from harm and to defend indigenous allies from other natives. With respect to the latter, Vitoria cited, as a matter of debate, the example of Cortés establishing an alliance or treaty with the native Tlaxcalans against the Aztec Empire. Cortés reported that these alliances with "Indian friends" (*indios amigos*) were beneficial to native tributary subjects of the Aztec tyrants, who often seized their children and offered them as sacrifices to the imperial gods.[30] Vitoria did not specifically refer to Cortés's letters though he did identify the indigenous as neighbors worthy of defense by Christian rulers from tyrannical laws mandating sacrifice of the innocent or even cannibalizing condemned criminals.[31] The possibility of intervention in these cases was not to punish infractions of the natural law per se, as formulated by Pope Innocent's teaching, but to protect global neighbors from suffering further injuries.[32]

Whereas Vitoria worked out a possible argument for defensive intervention to stop widespread injuries, the standard justification of Spanish colonial sympathizers relied on Innocent's claim of punitive intervention and a medieval conception of worldwide papal power now under secular political entitlement. Beginning with Juan López de Palacios Rubios, the lawyer who penned the infamous Requirement in 1513 forcing the natives to "choose" submission under Spanish sovereignty or risk war and enslavement, the Innocentian doctrine of punishing foreign violations of the universal natural law supplied the conventional argument for conquest.[33] The papal donation of Alexander

29 Francisco de Vitoria, "On the American Indians," 252–8, and "On the Law of War," 302–3, in *Political Writings*, ed. Anthony Pagden and Jeremy Lawrance (Cambridge: Cambridge University Press, 1991).

30 Cortés, "The Second Letter," 50–1.

31 Vitoria, "On the American Indians," 288, and "On Self-Restraint," in *Political Writings*, 214.

32 Vitoria, "On Self-Restraint," 225.

33 James Muldoon, *Popes, Lawyers, and Infidels: The Church and the Non-Christian World, 1250–1550* (Philadelphia: University of Pennsylvania Press, 1979), 140–3.

VI had conceded to Spain, according to aggressive sympathizers, full jurisdictional and executive power over most of the native peoples of the Americas.

Vitoria was cognizant of the underlying conception of ecclesiastical power informing the primary causes of war among Spanish theocratic lawyers and conquistadors. In the first of two lectures on the Church delivered at the University of Salamanca in 1532 and 1533, the Spanish theologian confronted the medieval hierocratic doctrine and posited that the Pope was not lord of the world (*Papa non est orbis dominus*). Vitoria appealed to an all-important canon legal principle based on the Apostle Paul (1 Corinthians 5:12–13), who taught that the Church did not possess power and jurisdiction over the unbaptized, or those outside the faith community. Therefore, Vitoria concluded, "the pope has no dominion in the lands of the infidel, since he has power only within the Church."[34] Vitoria's lecture coincided directly with the use of the Requirement in Francisco Pizarro's seizure, judgment, and eventual execution of the Inca Atahualpa on grounds of high treason, not to mention the utter looting and dispossession of Peruvian treasures. All of these matters, as Vitoria related in a personal letter to his provincial in 1534, made the blood freeze in his veins.[35] Vitoria's sixth unjust title mentioned in his Indies lecture rejected wholesale the Requirement policy used by both Cortés and Pizarro to legalize their conquests based on a "voluntary" choice of the natives to submit to Spanish imperial sovereignty. There was never any true and legitimate consent of the native peoples as a whole, Vitoria claimed; instead, there was miscommunication, fear, and unlawful violence and theft.[36]

Punitive intervention, or the international right of punishment, was at the center of the controversial high-profile imperial debate in Valladolid, Spain, between the Dominican bishop-canon lawyer Bartolomé de las Casas and the imperial chronicler Juan Ginés de Sepúlveda. From 1550 to 1551, Holy Roman Emperor Charles officially suspended the Spanish conquests across the Atlantic to resolve the question of lawful intervention in the service of propagating the Gospel to native peoples. A council of over a dozen theologians and lawyers attended the Valladolid junta. Although the members never reached an official conclusion, the debate exposed an important clash in the Latin Christian West between two divergent expressions of evangelization – the peaceful apostolic method of rational persuasion and the crusader method of political subjugation. It also brought into sharp relief distinct rationales for war from either the Spanish or the indigenous sides of the Indies affair. For our

34 Vitoria, "On the Power of the Church," in *Political Writings*, 84.
35 Vitoria, "Letter to Miguel de Arcos, O.P.," in *Political Writings*, Appendix A, 331–3.
36 Vitoria, "On the American Indians," 275–6.

purposes, the debate displayed opposing arguments in support of either *native sovereignty* (Las Casas) or *European intervention* (Sepúlveda).

A translator of Aristotle and chronicler of Emperor Charles, Sepúlveda couched his imperial-humanist rationale for political subjugation of uncivilized peoples in the spirit of Duarte and the Portuguese conquest of the Canaries. The Amerindians, Sepúlveda railed, were naturally inferior, like children to adults, which was demonstrated by their absence of written language and money and their public approval of unnatural acts such as human sacrifice. Once overly partial to the Aristotelian natural slavery argument, Sepúlveda was more adept at the Valladolid debate in his usage of the Innocentian doctrine of war to punish natural law violations. Sepúlveda stated in his objections to Las Casas during the debate that "by this cause alone of not guarding natural law or being idolaters," as taught by the canonists, the native peoples "can be conquered and punished" by superior European powers.[37]

Sepúlveda's usage of Innocentian doctrine expanded foreign punitive intervention to an unprecedented range through a total denial of the native right of sovereignty in the Indies. He did so by transferring the locus of punitive judgment from the Roman papacy to European empire. Although the papacy could endorse the civilizing mission of European imperial powers, it was not necessary, as evident in the case of the ancient Romans who punished and corrected many barbarous peoples. The power to punish violations of the natural law by means of war and conquest was the distinct task of the law of nations, which Sepúlveda interpreted in imperial-humanist terms as the law of wiser, civilized peoples.[38]

Bartolomé de las Casas spoke on behalf of the indigenous side against Sepúlveda, the conquistadors, and the dominant voices of the royal court. The Dominican friar deployed the language of just war to support the native sovereign right of self-defense against European aggressors. In his five-day apologia of the Indians at the Valladolid junta, Las Casas extrapolated a right of resistance according to natural law and the law of nations. He stated emphatically:

> [E]very nation, no matter how barbaric, has the right to defend itself against a more civilized one that wants to conquer it and take away its freedom. And, moreover, it can lawfully punish with death the more civilized as a savage and

37 Juan Ginés de Sepúlveda, "Aquí se contiene una disputa," in *Tratados de Fray Bartolomé de las Casas*, vol. 1 (Mexico: Fondo de Cultura Económica, 1965), obj. 7, p. 311.

38 For more on Sepúlveda's views and the Valladolid debate in the context of international legal history, see David Lantigua, *Infidels and Empires in a New World Order: Early Modern Spanish Contributions to International Legal Thought* (Cambridge: Cambridge University Press, 2020), ch. 4.

> cruel aggressor against the law of nature. And this war is certainly more just than the one that, under pretext of wisdom, is waged against them.[39]

Las Casas repudiated Spanish justifications of punitive war in the Indies under a religious humanitarian cover to convert and civilize the native peoples.

Aware of the Innocentian cause of war stemming from the medieval crusader context, Las Casas responded directly to Sepúlveda's application of the right of conquest over the Indies. The Dominican friar-bishop devoted more than twenty chapters of his apologia to refuting Sepúlveda's principal argument for war based on punishing violations of the natural law. Like Vitoria, Las Casas relied chiefly on the medieval canon legal principle (1 Corinthians 5:12–13) restricting ecclesiastical and Christian political jurisdiction over outsiders, or the unbaptized, to prohibit punitive intervention in the lands of infidels outside Europe. The application of Innocent's doctrine "to all parts of the world" where native inhabitants had never heard of Christianity, according to Las Casas, was nothing less than absurd.[40]

The preaching of the Gospel had to be peaceful and persuasive, fully respecting the listener's rationality as a creature made in the divine image and possessing the freedom to consent without the fear wrought by armed companies and threats of conquest. Even if Christians proclaimed the true God to Indians convincingly and with good examples, Las Casas averred that infidels were bound by conscience "to defend the worship of their gods and their religion by going forth with their armies against all who attempt to take those things from them or injure them or prevent their sacrifices." Indeed, the Indians could "fight, kill, capture, and exercise all the rights consequent on a just war according to the law of nations."[41] Las Casas's arguments at the Valladolid debate, like the rest of his writings, tirelessly defended the political agency of New World native occupants, all of whom were free and independent as commonwealths. Both the eternal law of divine providence and the natural law of human reason attested to the self-determination of every commonwealth or kingdom, which had rule and jurisdiction over its own territory. Pagan jurisdiction and protection of borders, Las Casas asserted, was "no less natural than the jurisdiction of Christian rulers." Taking the European Christian powers as illustrative of his point, the king of France lacked the authority to pronounce judgment or impose laws on the Spanish Crown, and vice versa.[42]

39 Bartolomé de las Casas, *In Defense of the Indians*, trans. Stafford Poole (Dekalb: Northern Illinois University Press, 1992), 47–8.

40 Las Casas, *In Defense of the Indians*, 120.

41 Las Casas, *In Defense of the Indians*, 244.

42 Las Casas, *In Defense of the Indians*, 83.

Vitoria similarly concluded that since Christian rulers in Europe could not wage wars against each other to punish crimes against natural law, then neither could they do so against unbelievers.[43]

5.4 SPANISH THEOLOGIANS AND THE SCHOLASTIC LAW OF NATIONS

As Spanish Dominicans shaped by the *ius commune* tradition, Las Casas and Vitoria outlined important scholastic principles of political sovereignty in an international context. And they did so by creatively appropriating the law of nations as a symmetrical critical discourse in contrast to Sepúlveda's dominative deployment of it. The scholastic law of nations, founded on the universal authority of the natural law yet belonging to the category of positive law, gave political status to free and independent sovereign peoples apart from any formal recognition by another political power, even if the latter claimed the superior wisdom to judge. Their scholastic theological views also contrasted markedly from later social contract thinkers who abandoned the distinct category of the law of nations and cast sovereignty as indivisible under a form of political monism. According to the Spanish theologians, sovereignty was neither the mortal god of Hobbes's Leviathan nor the collective being of Jean Jacques Rousseau's general will; rather, it resided chiefly in the power of the people (*populus*), or commonwealth, as self-sufficient and independent. The power of the people originated from both God and nature and it was a power anterior to, and generative of, political authority. Two important rights accrued from this scholastic-juristic conception of the people: consent and self-defense. At the level of *ius gentium*, or the positive law of nations, these rights supported provision for the people through political rule and protection by means of war when necessary.

Although the people's consent transmits authority (*auctoritas*) to a form of political rule by way of pact or custom, the people retain power (*potestas*) over their goods and lands in some effective sense. Relatedly, the people or commonwealth cannot lose their right of defending themselves. The evident conclusion here is that the political authority in question does not possess all the power inhering in the commonwealth. Possessing the power to form representative jurisdiction over occupied land was therefore what demonstrated the political agency of a people even when it did not exhibit the geopolitical sovereignty characteristic of, say, a modern nation-state. In the transatlantic context of the Spanish empire, these scholastic principles affirmed native political agency, or the rights of infidels over their properties

[43] Vitoria, "On Self-Restraint," 224–5.

(*dominium rerum*) and jurisdictional rule (*dominium iurisdictionis*). Vitoria turned to the consent of the people as a principle for precluding unjust Spanish claims of ruling over the natives or the unlawful extraction of their natural resources.

Vitoria's sixth unjust title, as noted, rejected the so-called "voluntary election" of the Requirement policy enforced upon native peoples by Cortés and Pizarro. These conquistadors vitiated "any freedom of election" among the natives because of their use of fear and terror through threats of war. Even if the Aztec and Inca rulers in question had voluntarily transferred political authority, it would remain unlawful and empty without the effective consent of the people.[44] According to the letter written to his Dominican provincial in Spain, Vitoria was certain that voluntary transference of political power never happened in the Peruvian case of Atahualpa when Pizarro and his company looted the Inca empire. If the Spaniards ever acquired lawful rule following native consent in the Indies, there were still constraints on the extraction of natural resources. For example, if it were in the interest of the commonwealth to prohibit the export of gold, then a foreign prince could not do so without committing an egregious wrong against the native inhabitants. Just as the King of Castile would cause harm to Spaniards by exporting their country's gold to Italy, the same held for the Indies.[45] Foreign dispossession of wealth and gold violated indigenous peoples' power and agency.

Las Casas went further than Vitoria by promoting the indigenous right of consent and self-defense in the face of Spanish colonial aggression. As Las Casas stipulated clearly at the Valladolid junta, "whatever right a king has, he has by the consent of his people." Consequently, neither a pope nor a Christian emperor could claim power to depose foreign infidel rulers, because "the right of choosing a king, which belongs to the people by natural law, cannot be taken away from them."[46] In a final treatise *On the Treasures of Peru* (*De thesauris*), Las Casas defended, incredibly, the restoration of Inca sovereignty and precious metals like gold and silver back to native descendants on the basis that the Peruvians never freely consented to foreign Spanish rule. The Dominican friar's argument relied on a traditional Roman and canon legal maxim of consent applied to the Indies case. This principle of *quod omnes tangit* ("What touches all must be approved by all") took a radical form in Las Casas, who repurposed it in order to require every single individual's

44 Vitoria, "On the American Indians," 275–6.
45 Vitoria, "On Self-Restraint," 227–8.
46 Las Casas, *In Defense of the Indians*, 338.

consent within an indigenous commonwealth open to transferring its sovereignty to a foreign ruler.[47]

The Dominican friar condemned all the Spanish conquests and wars in the Indies as unjust, thereby concluding that the conquistadors were nothing but tyrants and thieves. The right of self-defense, or resistance, was entirely on the side of the indigenous occupants of the New World. Steeped in scholastic political thought and canon law, Las Casas resorted to the Christian tradition of tyrannicide. This teaching enabled him to identify the cause of indigenous justice evident in the Inca resistance to Spaniards, which he based on a just claim of war beginning with the Taíno inhabitants of Hispaniola. Las Casas referred to the important case of Enriquillo, who, originally free as a Taíno chief, was forced to work under the Spanish tributary colonial system. After a Spanish overseer raped his wife with impunity, Enriquillo violently revolted and went into rural hiding. Las Casas asserted boldly that Enriquillo's royal status gave him the power to "execute punishment and vengeance on every Spaniard found there." That was "because the kings and native rulers" of Hispaniola had "never recognized the Crown of Spain as their sovereign."[48] Although Vitoria never made an explicit declaration in favor of native resistance against Spain, his position on the deposing of tyrants overlapped with that of Las Casas: were a tyrant or unlawful ruler to emerge, the people can resist "because even if the commonwealth has given away its authority it keeps its natural right to defend itself."[49]

Vitoria also explored the possibility of just defense in cases of Spanish intervention to stop the injuries caused by the practices of human sacrifice and cannibalism within native civilizations against both the innocent and captives. The fundamental biblical precept of loving one's neighbor had a concrete expression in the Book of Proverbs applicable to the Indies: rescue those dragged away to their deaths.[50] For Vitoria, God's command that everyone have solicitude for their neighbor meant that the natives of the New World were neighbors and Christian European princes could lawfully defend them from tyranny.[51] Remarkably, Vitoria viewed this form of defensive intervention through war as justifiable apart from either papal approval or the request of

47 For an English translation of the relevant excerpt from *On the Treasures of Peru*, see Document 23 in *Bartolomé de las Casas and the Defense of Amerindian Rights: A Brief History with Documents*, ed. Lawrence Clayton and David Lantigua (Tuscaloosa: University of Alabama Press, 2020), 113–15.

48 Bartolomé de las Casas, *Historia de las Indias*, vol. 3 (Mexico: Fondo de Cultura Económica, 1986), cap. 125.

49 Vitoria, "On Law," in *Political Writings*, 200.

50 Vitoria, "On Self-Restraint," 225, citing Prov. 24:11.

51 Vitoria, "On the American Indians," 288.

native peoples. Vitoria has therefore sometimes occupied a privileged place in the early development of the doctrine of humanitarian intervention.[52] Yet sympathizers of aggressive colonialism like Sepúlveda found his teaching quite handy, if only rhetorically. Sepúlveda claimed toward the end of his life that liberating the innocent from injurious acts – one among several causes of war he mentioned at the Valladolid debate – could provide the *sole* basis for a superior right of conquest over the New World barbarians.[53] In reality, such a contrived right could not have applied generally to the indigenous peoples of the Americas, most of whom did not sanction either human sacrifice or cannibalism.

Often overlooked, Las Casas also supported defensive intervention to protect the innocent from harm in cases of state-sanctioned human sacrifice. His position contrasted with Vitoria's, however, in maintaining the political role of the papacy for international affairs. As the steward of Christ, the Prince of Peace, the Pope could take steps to prevent the slaughtering of innocent persons elsewhere who would never have the chance of receiving the Good News of salvation. The Pope could authorize foreign intervention of a Christian ruler to free innocent persons from death, just as Scripture teaches: "Deliver the oppressed from their oppressors."[54] Such intervention under papal solicitude did not constitute a public declaration of war but instead a private act of defending one's neighbor. This case of defensive intervention to stop the death of innocents, even with use of moderate and proportionate force, belonged to the natural law and divine law, not the law of nations. Las Casas made the relevant point that intervention to prevent the practices of human sacrifice or cannibalism in the New World was not on the grounds of punishment but strictly defense.[55] Las Casas and Vitoria therefore shared a common viewpoint on the lawfulness of defensive intervention, though they differed on the possible means of employing it.

5.5 THE GREAT SOCIETY OF STATES, THE MODERN LAW OF NATIONS, AND WORLD COMMERCE

The Protestant European seaborne empires of the seventeenth and eighteenth centuries reframed the legal-political conversation about sovereignty and

[52] Stephen C. Neff, *Justice Among Nations: A History of International Law* (Cambridge, MA: Harvard University Press, 2014), 124.

[53] Juan Ginés de Sepúlveda, "Del reino y los deberes del rey," in *Tratados políticos de Juan Ginés de Sepúlveda* (Madrid: Instituto de Estudios Políticos, 1963), 36.

[54] Las Casas, *In Defense of the Indians*, 186–7, citing Sir. 4:9.

[55] See Document 25 in *Bartolomé de las Casas and the Defense of Amerindian Rights*, 118–20.

intervention, thus setting the tone for modern international relations. Where the use of the law of nations persisted among prominent and influential jurists like Grotius and Emer de Vattel, it was associated even more closely with the natural law to identify its universally binding and immutable obligations. For them, sovereignty and intervention, or occupation and war, adhered to a rational necessity demarcating certain human groups as savages or enemies who did not conform to the universal precepts and natural duties of the law of nations. Sovereignty and intervention would take on a new meaning in a colonial context defined by a world of rapid commercial expansion under armed merchant companies.

Neither the universal Roman papacy, nor the Holy Roman Emperor, nor the attendant view of a unified transatlantic Christendom sustained the "modern" discourse of the law of nations. Legal humanism predicated on Roman law and history (biblical and classical), along with neo-Stoic natural philosophy, gained ascendency among Protestant jurists and philosophers who supplanted the traditional Catholic sources of canon law and scholastic theology. The Dutch lawyer Grotius, in the defense of his stand-alone work *Mare liberum* (*The Free Sea*) against a Scottish detractor, attested to the providential significance of Justinian's *Institutes*, which contained universal natural laws and precepts of the law of nations.[56] The Prolegomena to Grotius's most well-known work, *On the Rights of War and Peace* (*De jure belli ac pacis*), articulated the dominant paradigm of the modern law of nations as universally binding between states, serving the advantage of neither this nor that particular state but instead the "great society of states."[57] The right of war and its conduct contained in the law of nations occupied most of Grotius's mature work. Specifically, his arguments for a right of war waged by sovereign princes against foreign tyrants violating the principles of humanity has earned him the title of true pioneer of humanitarian intervention, the "father of solidarist international society theory."[58]

Such acclaim and authority, however, should not disregard various features of Grotius's arguments that point to the encumbered ambivalent legacy of the Iberian-Atlantic past for these emergent Protestant seaborne empires. Grotius, as Richard Tuck has often noted, sided with Innocent IV (and Sepúlveda)

56 Hugo Grotius, "Defense of Chapter V of the *Mare Liberum*," in *The Free Sea*, ed. David Armitage (Indianapolis: Liberty Fund, 2004), 105.

57 Hugo Grotius, *Prolegomena to the Law of War and Peace*, trans. Francis Kelsey (New York: Liberal Arts Press, 1957), § 17, p. 13.

58 Nicholas Wheeler, *Saving Strangers: Humanitarian Intervention in International Society* (Oxford: Oxford University Press, 2000), 45.

against Vitoria (and Las Casas).[59] The Dutch jurist thereby endorsed a right of punitive intervention against violators of the natural law. Remarkably, Grotius cited Vitoria's lecture on the Indies and the canon legal principle of nonintervention or immunity from punishment (1 Corinthians 5:12), but it was restricted to papal justification of foreign intervention and not Christian sovereigns as such.[60] Unlike the Spanish, however, the Dutch political context of Grotius's treatment of the right of war did not concern the spread of an empire of evangelization through conquest in the Americas but rather the enforcement of lucrative trade in the East Indies under an empire of commerce. What Vitoria had considered as a right of traveling enforceable by war under certain conditions evolved into an unimpeachable liberty of trading for Grotius and many of his contemporaries.

Like Hobbes, Grotius followed the Erastian doctrine of subordinating ecclesiastical authority to civil power. Whereas Hobbes's Erastianism terminated in the absolute will of the civil sovereign, Grotius's version subscribed to universal natural law theory.[61] Grotius's international right of punitive intervention was a secular translation of ecclesiastical jurisdiction similar to Sepúlveda. Ironically, even though Grotius followed Vitoria in restricting papal claims of worldwide dominion, he repurposed the universal power of bishops over ecclesiastical affairs, extending it to sovereign kings now entrusted with "care of human society in general" through a right to punish offenses against God and nature.[62] This further explains why Grotius's only legal source for establishing an international right to intervene and punish those who depart from the natural law came from Pope Innocent IV.[63] Yet due to neo-Stoic humanist proclivities, Grotius abandoned idolatry and human sacrifice as causes for punitive war. Similar to another neo-Stoic legal humanist, Alberico Gentili, Grotius considered atheism a lawful cause for punishment.[64]

59 Richard Tuck, *The Rights of War and Peace: Political Thought and the International Order from Grotius to Kant* (New York: Oxford University Press, 1999), 103.

60 Hugo Grotius, *The Rights of War and Peace*, ed. Richard Tuck (Indianapolis: Liberty Fund, 2005), Book II, ch. 22, pp. 1108–9.

61 Marco Barducci, *Hugo Grotius and the Century of Revolution, 1613–1718: Transnational Reception in English Political Thought* (Cambridge: Cambridge University Press, 2017), 110. For more on the influential views of early modern Swiss theologian Thomas Lüber (Erastus), see Eric Nelson, *The Hebrew Republic: Jewish Sources and the Transformation of European Political Thought* (Cambridge, MA: Harvard University Press, 2010), ch. 3.

62 Grotius, *Rights of War and Peace*, Book II, ch. 20, p. 1028.

63 Grotius, *Rights of War and Peace*, Book II, ch. 20, p. 1024.

64 Grotius, *Rights of War and Peace*, Book II, ch. 20, pp. 1033, 1036. For example, see Alberico Gentili, *De iure belli libri tres*, vol. 2, trans. John C. Rolfe (Oxford: Clarendon Press, 1933), Book I, ch. 25, p. 125. "Some kind of religion is natural, and therefore if there should be any

Grotius also presented the defensive criterion of intervention clearly outlined by Vitoria. Sovereign rulers possessed a universal right of human society to intervene and prevent a foreign tyrant from oppressing his subjects. Notably, the classical tyrants mentioned by Grotius, whether real or imagined, had committed acts classifiable under cannibalism.[65] Tyrants and barbarians were synonymous on this view. Following Aristotle, Grotius claimed further that war against barbarians who acted "like beasts" was something "natural."[66] Grotius ambivalently retained both the punitive and the defensive causes of intervention so clearly juxtaposed in the Iberian-Atlantic controversy of Valladolid between the sovereign independence of native peoples and European intervention through war.

The eighteenth-century Enlightenment discussion of international relations revolved around a modern "science" of the law of nations. Swiss jurist Vattel opened his classic treatment of the topic by identifying the scope of the new science, "which teaches the rights subsisting between nations or states, and the obligations correspondent to those rights."[67] The universal rights and obligations pertaining to liberty, war, commerce, and occupation belonged to what Vattel, indebted to Grotius, called a "natural or necessary law of nations" not based on positive law as it had been for scholastic theologians. It referred instead to the law of nature applied to states and nations. Beyond Grotius's humanist-inflected treatment of the law of nations, or that of his critic Samuel Pufendorf from the previous century, Vattel represented an important shift toward a broader public legal discourse drawing on modern historical events and figures as its chief source material.[68] *The Law of Nations* (*Droit des gens*) would eventually garner tremendous support from American founders to advance their revolutionary cause against the British.

Despite the seeming universal and scientific parameters of Vattel's public discourse of the law of nations, his account remained captive to the ambivalent contours of Europe's colonial past and present interaction with non-Europeans. The law of nations served both dominative and critical purposes in Vattel's work. On the one hand, it provided a forceful critique of the Spanish Catholic model of European expansion and its denial of native

who are atheists, destitute of any religious belief, either good or bad, it would seem just to war upon them as we would upon brutes."

65 Grotius, *Rights of War and Peace*, Book II, ch. 25, pp. 1159–61.

66 Grotius, *Rights of War and Peace*, Book II, ch. 20, pp. 1024.

67 Emer de Vattel, *The Law of Nations, Or, Principles of the Law of Nature, Applied to the Conduct and Affairs of Nations and Sovereigns*, ed. Béla Kapossy and Richard Whatmore (Indianapolis: Liberty Fund, 2008), 67.

68 Pitts, *Boundaries of the International*, 69–70.

sovereignty. On the other, it was exceedingly partial to the highly interventionist practice of settler colonialism against natives in early British North America.[69] Vattel's apparent double standard toward non-European peoples of the Americas stemmed from a criterion of civilization and development linked to an early modern European agricultural argument for land ownership.[70] The nub of Vattel's tension between sovereignty and intervention received expression at the preliminary outset of *The Law of Nations*. There he asserted that nations "are all free and independent, but bound to observe laws of that society which nature has established between them; and so far bound that, when any one of them violates those laws, the others have the right to repress her."[71]

Importantly, Vattel did not seek to endorse widespread foreign intervention because the right of sovereign self-preservation had to respect the liberty of nations. His definitive colonial example favoring restricted intervention against a purported right to punish foreign nations turned on the Spanish case. Vattel opposed arguments presented by "ambitious" and "greedy" Europeans that usurped the independent "American nations" in order to civilize and convert them.[72] "The Spaniards violated all rules," he wrote later in *The Law of Nations*, "when they set themselves up as judges of the Inca Atahualpa."[73] Like the Spanish theologians from two and a half centuries before, Vattel claimed that native Peruvians never committed any injustices against the Spaniards to justify war.

The Valladolid debate, Innocent IV, and Vitoria were all in the colonial background of Vattel's view on international relations, yet the Swiss jurist failed to appreciate the preceding Spanish discussions. Instead, he joined German academic jurists Pufendorf and Christian Wolff, each of whom associated the doctrine of an international right of punishment exclusively with Grotius. In the spirit of the Spanish theological rejection of Innocent's doctrine, Wolff presented his critique of Grotius succinctly: "[A] punitive war is not allowed against a nation for the reason that it is very wicked, or violates dreadfully the law of nature, or offends against God." Among those wrongs that

69 Vattel, *Law of Nations*, Book I, ch. 7, p. 130: "[T]hough the conquest of the civilized empires of Peru and Mexico was a notorious usurpation, the establishment of many colonies on the continent of North America might, on their confining themselves within just bounds, be extremely lawful."

70 For more on the early modern/modern sources and context of the agricultural-improvement argument addressing the natives of North America, see James Tully, *An Approach to Political Philosophy: Locke in Contexts* (Cambridge: Cambridge University Press, 1993), ch. 5.

71 Vattel, *Law of Nations*, 77.

72 Vattel, *Law of Nations*, Book II, ch. 1, p. 265.

73 Vattel, *Law of Nations*, Book II, ch. 4, p. 290.

did *not* constitute lawful intervention through punitive war, Wolff included idolatry but also deism and atheism, thereby moving beyond the humanist jurists.[74] Vattel, virtually repeating Wolff's position, referred to Grotius's error as "an odd kind of right to punish faults which involve an enormous violation of the laws of nature, though they do not affect either his rights or his safety."[75] Vitoria's claim that foreign intervention must involve an injury committed according to the law of nations informed Vattel's norm even as it went unacknowledged. The defense of oppressed subjects under a sovereign tyrant, Vattel wagered, was demonstrated lawfully in the case of the Dutch United Provinces intervening for the English against King James II because the people rightly implored assistance.[76]

Vattel retained the legal-humanist ire against barbarians when he advanced an unreserved right of punishment, even extermination, against any savage nation bent on plundering and harming the members of the great society of nations. Since "the universal society of the human race" was established by nature, everyone had to uphold certain duties to preserve it and mutually assist one another toward perfection.[77] When robbers and pirates threatened nature's dictates, a confederacy of nations may be necessary to eliminate these common enemies of humanity.[78] Savages who live by theft and plunder thus violate one of the primary dictates of nature – cultivation of the earth.

Imbibing early modern English colonial arguments, Vattel identified the seizure and occupation of land directly with the natural law in order to sanction world commerce. Vattel delineated the universal duty of humankind in the following way: "The whole earth is destined to feed its inhabitants; but this it would be incapable of doing, if it were uncultivated. Every nation is then obliged by the law of nature to cultivate the land that has fallen to its share." Not only pirates threatened this natural order of world commerce but also "the savages of North America." Although the Aztec and Inca nations were "civilized empires" in Vattel's judgment, the scattered native peoples of North America who "ranged rather than inhabited" the vast land were paradigmatic savages. This was no mere rhetorical designation but a clear indication of an inferior and idle mode of life among Native Americans who allegedly did not labor in the land through its cultivation and improvement. By identifying the

74 Christian Wolff, *The Law of Nations Treated According to the Scientific Method*, ed. Thomas Ahnert (Indianapolis: Liberty Fund, 2017 [1749]), ch. 6, pp. 472–3.

75 Vattel, *Law of Nations*, Book II, ch. 1, p. 265; Cf. Wolff, *Law of Nations*, ch. 2, pp. 128–9.

76 Vattel, *Law of Nations*, Book II, ch. 4, p. 290.

77 Vattel, *Law of Nations*, 72–3.

78 Vattel, *Law of Nations*, Book I, ch. 7, p. 129; Book II, ch. 7, p. 301; Book III, ch. 3, p. 487.

occupation of land with natural law, Vattel, like many of his modern interlocutors, departed from the long-standing tradition of viewing occupation as part of the law of nations.[79]

Vattel's colonial repository included English agricultural arguments defending widespread colonial settlement of North America's "vacant" lands based on a European conception of private property, as seen in chapter 5 of John Locke's *Second Treatise of Government*. From this European civilizational standpoint, Vattel referred to the savages of North America as people who made "no actual and constant use" of the land but only hunted, fished, and gathered its wild fruits.[80] The definitive modern historical example from Vattel's colonial source material were the New England Puritans, who lawfully purchased land from the natives but also had just claims to appropriate uncultivated land as needed. Puritan leaders such as Governor John Winthrop and Deacon Robert Cushman of the Massachusetts Bay Colony relied on an agricultural argument to designate native underutilization and waste of the vacant land (*vacuum domicilium*) ripe for English taking.

Yet, whereas the Spanish made themselves judges in the punishment of the Inca Atahualpa, "the Puritans appointed themselves judges of how much land Indians required."[81] The scope of English judgment in this case shifted from the sin of idolatry to the savagery of idleness and wastefulness. Unfortunately, Vattel's esteem for Puritan "moderation" failed to register the radical Puritan separatist and founder of Rhode Island Roger Williams and his valiant defense of Algonquian occupancy, property, and sovereignty in the American Northeast. Williams, a strong proponent of native self-determination, believed that Europeans could occupy lands in America only by means of just purchases, diplomatic treaties, and the generosity of native peoples.

The "extremely lawful" colonization in North America outlined by Vattel revealed the ascendant role of commerce as not only *reason of state* but also *reason of a society of states* during the seventeenth and eighteenth centuries among humanist jurists and Enlightenment thinkers. By focusing on Grotius as the chief interlocutor, Enlightenment thinkers of international relations like Wolff and Vattel largely failed to recognize the ambivalent Spanish colonial legacy. Even as they rejected the doctrine of punitive war against peoples in foreign lands who committed no injury against Europeans in line with the Spanish Dominican theologians, they also maintained the early

79 Vattel, *Law of Nations*, Book I, ch. 7, pp. 129–30.

80 Vattel, *Law of Nations*, Book I, ch. 18, p. 216.

81 James A. Warren, *God, War, and Providence: The Epic Struggle of Roger Williams and the Narragansett Indians against the Puritans of New England* (New York: Simon & Schuster, 2018), 36.

modern Iberian designation of "barbarian" non-European peoples lacking rational conformity to universal natural law and the civilized law of nations.

Vattel, in particular, demonstrates how modern international relations appropriated a new agricultural criterion of occupation according to the universal dictates of nature that made European intervention in extra-European lands far more conducive to colonial expansion beyond the practices of conquest and war.[82] Intervention for the modern public law of nations was no longer strictly a matter of defensive and punitive wars, or travel and trade between independent sovereigns. It could sanction colonial settlement of "vacant" lands for the economic purpose of improving the earth and making its bounty available to sustain humankind in a world of commerce. Industrious peoples from afar possessed a superior claim to the soil that could deny indigenous peoples the freedom to use the land according to their distinct traditions, customs, and ecological habits.

The specter of neocolonialism today that disproportionately affects traditional ways of life among inhabitants of the Global South shares certain features of the dominative use of the modern public law of nations whose colonial roots began in the Iberian-Atlantic world. Under a modern geopolitical system of sovereign nation-states in the age of transnationals, there is increasing aggressive economic intervention by national governments and foreign corporations against indigenous and traditional peoples who do not properly exploit the land. From the Philippines to the Amazon region, resource wars over extractive mining and widespread deforestation are raising the norms of nonintervention and intervention anew. Needed here is not common morality but a recovery of notions of peoplehood that can account for the collective and individual rights of cultures embodying modes of life and property outside the dominant global economic order. In the contemporary context, intervention by states or other major social actors may entail protection of peoples whose representation goes unnoticed before modern geopolitical notions of national sovereignty.

The legacy of the Spanish theologians, though not always explicit, has continued in the recent social teachings of Pope Francis. The Latin American Pope has embraced the cause of indigenous peoples against a technocratic form of economic imperialism supported by transnational corporations and governments. In the Pope's exhortation entitled *Querida Amazonia* (2020), he echoes the Dominican advocacy for indigenous justice in the New World against

82 For the contrasting views of Wolff and Vattel on this point about occupation of land, see Georg Cavallar, *Imperfect Cosmopolis: Studies in the History of International Legal Theory and Cosmopolitan Ideas* (Cardiff: University of Wales Press, 2011), 30–5.

enduring commercial powers that claim that the Amazon region is "an enormous empty space to be filled, a source of raw resources to be developed, a wild expanse to be domesticated." Like a contemporary Las Casas, Pope Francis draws public attention to protecting God's earth and its most vulnerable inhabitants: "The businesses, national or international, which harm the Amazon and fail to respect the right of original peoples to the land and its boundaries, and to self-determination and prior consent, should be called what they are: *injustice and crime*."[83] Of course, the original occupants of the Americas know through their historical experiences of widespread suffering that these injustices and crimes marked the conflictual encounter between them and Europeans in the Anglo-Iberian Atlantic world from the beginning. Contemporary discussions concerning the legal concepts of sovereignty and intervention in international relations would do well to remember the ongoing relevance of the moral and political lessons of global history.

RECOMMENDED READING

Anghie, Antony. *Imperialism, Sovereignty, and the Making of International Law*. Cambridge: Cambridge University Press, 2007.

Fitzmaurice, Andrew. *Sovereignty, Property and Empire, 1500–2000*. Cambridge: Cambridge University Press, 2014.

Keal, Paul. *European Conquest and the Rights of Indigenous Peoples*. Cambridge: Cambridge University Press, 2003.

Lantigua, David M. *Infidels and Empires in a New World Order: Early Modern Spanish Contributions to International Legal Thought*. Cambridge: Cambridge University Press, 2020.

Muldoon, James. *Popes, Lawyers, and Infidels: The Church and the Non-Christian World, 1250–1550*. Philadelphia: University of Pennsylvania Press, 1979.

Pagden, Anthony. *The Burdens of Empire: 1539 to the Present*. New York: Cambridge University Press, 2015.

Tuck, Richard. *The Rights of War and Peace: Political Thought and the International Order from Grotius to Kant*. New York: Oxford University Press, 1999.

83 Pope Francis, *Querida Amazonia*, February 12, 2020, § 14, https://press.vatican.va/content/salastampa/en/bollettino/pubblico/2020/02/12/200212c.html.

6

The Significance of Christian Charity to International Law

Jennifer L. Beard*

6.1 INTRODUCTION

Charity has a rich association with European international law.[1] As a Christian virtue, charity drove the imperial exploits of Christian missions during the Age of Discovery in the sixteenth and seventeenth centuries. This is when the early Christian writers of a modern, European international law such as Francisco de Vitoria (1486–1546), Francisco Suárez (1548–1617), Richard Zouche (1590–1661), Hugo Grotius (1583–1645) and Cornelis van Bynkershoek (1673–1743) emerged, and the Peace of Westphalia is said to have established a law of nations amongst "a European society of sovereign states."[2] Christian charity, it was believed, offered non-Christian peoples in the "New World" eternal salvation,[3] and it became a prime justification for the universalization of

* I wish to acknowledge the enthusiasm and support of the editors John Haskell and Pamela Slotte, the warmth of participants at the 2018 Helsinki workshop, the editing assistance of Ellen Roberts and the generosity of Martti Koskenniemi and Shaun McVeigh.

[1] European international law, often referred to simply and imperiously as international law, or public international law, represents the principal but contested system of contemporary legal relations between modern nation-states. See Dipesh Chakrabarty, *Provincializing Europe: Postcolonial Thought and Historical Difference* (Princeton: Princeton University Press, 2007); Richard Joyce, *Competing Sovereignties* (New York: Routledge, 2012); Paul Berman, *Global Legal Pluralism: A Jurisprudence of Law Beyond Borders* (Cambridge: Cambridge University Press, 2012); Sundhya Pahuja, "Laws of Encounter: A Jurisdictional Account of International Law," *London Review of International Law* 1, no. 1 (2013): 63–98; and Martti Koskenniemi, "Histories of International Law: Dealing with Eurocentrism," *Rechtsgeschichte* 19 (2011): 152–76.

[2] See Jennifer Beard, "The International Law in Force: Anachronistic Ethics and Divine Violence," in *Events: The Force of International Law*, ed. Fleur Johns, Richard Joyce and Sundhya Pahuja (New York: Routledge, 2011), 18.

[3] See Chapter 10 in this volume; Jedidiah J. Kroncke, *The Futility of Law and Development: China and the Dangers of Exporting American Law* (New York: Oxford University Press, 2016); Julia McClure, "The Charitable Bonds of the Spanish Empire: The Casa de Contratación as an Institution of Charity," *New Global Studies* 12, no. 2 (2018): 157–74; and Jennifer Beard, *The*

a European international law – all of which Antony Anghie points out resulted from the process by which European doctrines and beliefs "were transferred to, or imposed upon, the non-European world, principally through the mechanism of colonialism."[4] Today, eschatological notions of charity continue to underpin notions of contemporary international law that place "the quality of life of all people into a developmental framework."[5] Development, in this sense, is a form of charity in so far as it deploys social resources to improve the living conditions of people, particularly the poorest people in a material sense, through the relief of poverty, the advancement of education and expertise, and economic, social and cultural progress. Development may also be understood as a form of charity in so far as it calls a particularly "Christian subjectivity into being with a promise."[6]

The virtue of charity is also associated with the just war tradition and the notion that "judgement and punishment must always be executed *ex caritate*."[7] The just war doctrine, which relies on theoretical notions of the deserving and the undeserving, was developed first in the works of Augustine and Thomas Aquinas, and then by international lawyers such as de Vitoria and Grotius.[8] These discriminatory distinctions are also deeply embedded in the histories of poverty, distributive justice and the welfare state.[9] The words of a homily on charity, written in 1563, provide us with a good sense of these two contrary "offices" of charity:[10]

Political Economy of Desire: International Development and the Nation State (Abingdon: Routledge-Cavendish, 2007).

4 Antony Anghie, "Europe and International Law's Colonial Present," *Baltic Yearbook of International Law Online* 6, no. 1 (2006): 79–84, at 79.

5 Beard, *Political Economy*, 4.

6 Beard, *Political Economy*, 7.

7 Ben Smith, *Traditional Imagery of Charity in Piers Plowman* (The Hague: Mouton & Co., 1966), 36.

8 I would like to thank Martti Koskenniemi for bringing the texts of Augustine and Aquinas to my attention. See also Antony Anghie, "Francisco de Vitoria and the Colonial Origins of International Law," *Social & Legal Studies* 5, no. 3 (1996): 321–36; Anne Orford, *Reading Humanitarian Intervention: Human Rights and the Use of Force in International Law* (Cambridge: Cambridge University Press, 2003); Antony Anghie, "International Law in a Time of Change: Should International Law Lead or Follow?," *American University International Law Review* 26, no. 5 (2011): 1315–76.

9 See, e.g., Maureen Flynn, *Sacred Charity: Confraternities and Social Welfare in Spain, 1400–1700* (London: Macmillan, 1989); and Linda Martz, *Poverty and Welfare in Habsburg Spain* (Cambridge: Cambridge University Press, 1983).

10 *Certain Sermons or Homilies Appointed to be Read in Churches* (London, 1623/1563) quoted in Alexandra Walsham, *Charitable Hatred: Tolerance and Intolerance in England, 1500–1700* (Manchester: Manchester University Press, 2006), v.

> The one office of charitie is, to cherish good and harmlesse men, not to oppresse them with false accusations, but to encourage them with rewards to doe well, and to continue in well doing, defending them with the sword from their adversaries ... The other office of charitie, is to rebuke, correct, and punish vice, without regard of persons, and is to be used against them onley that be evill men, and malefactours or evill doers ... [I] is as well the office of charitie to rebuke, punish and correct them that bee evill, as it is to cherish and reward them that bee good and harmlesse ....[11]

In this chapter I explore these eschatological and discriminating effects of Christian charity, but I focus on the ways in which charity enabled an ethics of the self to be combined with the social and material constitution of spaces, jurisdictions and the early modern administrative state in England.

The aim of this chapter is to roughly sketch the early significance of charity as a manifestation of late medieval and early modern lawfulness, which helps to explain how states became the sites of public authority that we understand them to be today. With this aim in mind, I invite readers to think about charity as a body of law and a source of authority. My argument is that the concept of charity underpinning Christian social relations in medieval and early modern England enabled divine authority to become public (or to assume public office) by assuming a legal mandate to govern or administer parts or aspects of social life that are recognized as such. Charity therefore provides us with an interesting lens through which to study early Western forms of public authority and their relationship to jurisdiction, territory and practices of inclusion and exclusion.[12] My focus is on early modern England because I have a more general interest in the history of the common law meaning of charity and its public aspects.[13] More broadly, this chapter offers food for thought to all readers interested in histories of sovereignty, authority and jurisdiction, and, by association, European-oriented international law.[14]

In Section 6.2, I explain the biblical origins of the English concept of charity. In Section 6.3, I make a few thematic attempts to trace the relationship between charity and the emerging state of England in the late medieval and

11 Walsham, *Charitable Hatred.*

12 Shaunnagh Dorsett and Shaun McVeigh describe this process as authority "shaped and expressed through jurisdictional technique." Shaunnagh Dorsett and Shaun McVeigh, "Jurisprudences of Jurisdiction: Matters of Public Authority," *Griffith Law Review* 23, no. 4 (2014): 569–88, at 570.

13 For a traditional history of the common law of charity, see Gareth H. Jones, *History of the Law of Charity, 1532–1827* (Cambridge: Cambridge University Press, 1969).

14 See Lauren Benton and Richard J. Ross, eds., *Legal Pluralism and Empires, 1500–1850* (New York: New York University Press, 2013); and Dorsett and McVeigh, "Jurisprudences of Jurisdiction."

early modern periods, prior to the construction of the British Empire. In Section 6.4, I trace the disintegration of charity in England as it ceases to authorize and order law as such, and instead becomes a mere subject of law.[15]

6.2 *AGAPE*: A SOURCE OF AUTHORITY, A MANIFESTATION OF LAWFULNESS AND THE ORIGINS OF CHARITY

6.2.1 Agape: *The Law of Love*

The scriptures of a New Christian Testament were written in Greek between roughly 50 and 100 CE. The earliest complete Christian Bible, the *Codex Sinaiticus*, was produced in the fourth century, written entirely in Greek.[16] In the New Testament, the ambiguous concept of "love" (in Greek: ἀγάπη (*agape*); and in verb form *agapao*) was redeployed in new and important ways[17] to describe the relationship between God and humanity, including God as the source of love, God's love of humankind and the love that a Christian has of God and their neighbor.[18] In the writings of Matthew, this love fulfills the Law and the bond between God and humanity.[19] In short, Love and (a binding) Law are One.

6.2.2 Agape *in Latin and English*

In around 405 CE, the Bible was translated into Latin from original Hebrew, Greek, Aramaic and earlier Latin texts, initially by Jerome. Versions of this "Vulgate" Bible remained the most commonly used edition of the Bible in Western Europe for around a thousand years, principally because Christians were generally prohibited by the Western schism of the Catholic Church from reading the Bible in any other language.[20] As Hannibal Hamlin points out:

15 Shaunnagh Dorsett and Shaun McVeigh, "An Essay on Jurisdiction, Jurisprudence, and Authority: The High Court of Australia in Yorta Yorta (2001)," *Northern Ireland Legal Quarterly* 56, no. 1 (2005): 1–20, at 1.

16 See Allan K. Jenkins and Patrick Preston, *Biblical Scholarship and the Church: A Sixteenth-Century Crisis of Authority* (Burlington: Ashgate, 2007), ix–x.

17 See Catherine Osborne, *Eros Unveiled: Plato and the God of Love* (Oxford: Clarendon Press, 1994). Cf. Anders Nygren, *Agape and Eros* (Philadelphia: Westminster Press, 1953).

18 See Osborne, *Eros Unveiled*; and Helen Wilcox, "Sacred and Secular Love: 'I will Lament, And Love,'" in *The Oxford Handbook of Early Modern English Literature and Religion*, ed. Andrew Hiscock and Helen Wilcox (Oxford: Oxford University Press, 2017), 617.

19 See 1 John 4:7; Matt. 22, 34, 36; and Paul in Rom. 13:8–10; and Wilcox, "Sacred and Secular Love," 617.

20 As Helmut Koenigsberger states, throughout the Middle Ages, in addition to the "deep schism" that had developed between the Greek and the Roman Churches, "there existed Christian churches in Africa and Asia which were never in communion with Rome at all."

"Only as Latin died out as a vernacular and became the specialized language of the Church did the Vulgate (literally 'common' or 'of the common people') become ... the preserve of the priestly class."[21]

As well as being the basis upon which Roman Catholic canon law and doctrine were built during the medieval period, the Latin Vulgate strongly influenced the development of vernacular languages across Western Europe, including English from the sixth century. The English concept of charity is rooted in the Latin word *caritas*. *Caritas* was one of several Latin nouns used in the Vulgate to express the original, Greek concept of *agape*. However, *caritas* has no verb form, such that the verb form of *agape* (*agapáō*) tended to be translated into the English verb "to love."[22] Hence the noun "charity" and the verb "to love" became familiar but distinct terms in the English language.

The concept of *agape* would have therefore arrived in England in its Latin form at different points prior to Augustine's mission in 597,[23] but it was integrated into English as "charity" via Old French. The earliest records of various forms of the word "charity" appear in Old English religious homilies of the late twelfth century.[24] The word is used extensively in the first complete translation of the Bible into English, begun during the 1380s by John Wycliffe. Since the word had been integrated into the English language by this time, the translation by Wycliffe of *caritas* into *charite* was not controversial. However, because Wycliffe was considered a heretic, his Bible was outlawed, and the Latin Vulgate remained the official and only lawful Bible throughout the Middle Ages in England.[25]

By the time the complete Bible was being translated into the English vernacular, England had become a predominantly Christian domain and charity was the principal allegory used to instruct Christians on how a Christian society might be constituted on earth. As Richard Helmholtz observes, prior to the twelfth century, "[a]llegory and meditation ... provided

Helmut Koenigsberger, "The Unity of the Church and the Reformation," *Journal of Interdisciplinary History* 1, no. 3 (1971): 407–17, at 413.

21 Catholics were not universally opposed to translating the Bible, and vernacular Bibles existed in many European languages prior to the Reformation. The first printed German-language Bible appeared in 1466. Martin Luther first published his German New Testament in 1522. See Hannibal Hamlin, "The Bible," in *The Oxford Handbook of Early Modern English Literature and Religion*, ed. Andrew Hiscock and Helen Wilcox (Oxford: Oxford University Press, 2017), 548.

22 The Latin term *dilectio* is also used in some contexts.

23 See Richard H. Helmholz, *The Canon Law and Ecclesiastical Jurisdiction from 597 to the 1640s* (Oxford: Oxford University Press, 2004), 1.

24 See Ayoush S. Lazikani, *Cultivating the Heart: Feeling and Emotion in Twelfth- and Thirteenth-Century Religious Texts* (Cardiff: University of Wales Press, 2015), ch. 1.

25 Hamlin, "Bible," 546.

the key to opening up the meaning of difficult texts"[26] and the truth about how individual Christians were expected to embody Christ-like conduct and obtain salvation.[27] These interpretations of charity underpinned canonical collections, penitential books, synodal legislation and the secular law of Christian rulers. The English translations of scripture[28] would have encouraged people, particularly the clergy, to read and write, as well as speak in English, about important matters of religion, authority and conduct.[29] The words and concepts used in the Bible, and what meanings they obtained, were extremely important because the Christian religion together with the personal secular laws, customs and obligations imposed by feudalism and manorialism and an emerging common law remained the primary sources of authority in England throughout the late medieval and early modern periods.[30] And they provided the idiom for making claims regarding public authority, generally in the form of office. The notion of charity both underpinned, and was influenced by, these Christian social relations in a manner that enabled forms of public authority to arise through "jurisdictional technique."[31] In consequence, English "charity" took on greater significance in, and for, the emerging state of England than the Greek concept of "love" or *agape* that underpins it.[32]

We can see how the concept of charity is deployed in the late Middle Ages in the *Vision of Piers Plowman* (written c.1370–90).[33] *Piers* "is an explicitly Christian poem, composed by a cleric and couched in allegorical language

26 Helmholz, *Canon Law*, 1.

27 Hamlin, "Bible," 546.

28 Ferdinand Holthausen, ed., *Vices and Virtues: Being a Soul's Confession of Its Sins with Reason's Description of the Virtues: A Middle-English Dialogue of about 1200 A.D.*, repr. (London: Oxford University Press, 1967 [1888]) and Robert William Burchfield, "The Ormulum," in *Dictionary of the Middle Ages*, ed. Joseph R. Strayer, vol. 9 (New York: Charles Scribner's Sons, 1987).

29 Hamlin, "Bible."

30 See Jocelyn Wogan-Browne et al., eds., *The Idea of the Vernacular: An Anthology of Middle English Literary Theory, 1280–1520* (Pennsylvania: Pennsylvania State University Press, 1999), 93. For further scholarship on the links among property, sovereignty and empire in European international law, see Martti Koskenniemi, "Sovereignty, Property and Empire: Early Modern English Contexts," *Theoretical Inquiries in Law* 18, no. 2 (2017): 355–89, at 355; Rachel Walsh and Lorna Fox O'Mahony, "Land Law, Property Ideologies and the British-Irish Relationship," *Common Law World Review* 47, no. 1 (2018): 7–34; and Jacques Derrida and Gianni Vattimo, *Religion* (Stanford: Stanford University Press, 1998).

31 Dorsett and McVeigh, "Jurisprudences of Jurisdiction," 570.

32 See 1 John 4:8, 16; and I Cor. 13:4. Catherine Osborne explains: "It is unusual in Greek to reify, or perhaps even personify, the concepts expressed by abstract nouns where the normal expression would be a verb. Thus love, war, peace, death, and so on become forces, or gods, to be reckoned with". Osborne, *Eros Unveiled*, 27.

33 William Langland, *The Vision of William Concerning Piers the Plowman* [1377], ed. Walter W. Skeat (Oxford: Clarendon Press, 1874).

heavily indebted to Scripture both in allusion and in verbal parallel."[34] Above all, *Piers* is a poem of the failure of Christian law and the lawlessness of medieval Christian society. Nonetheless, the poem shows us something of the form, organization and administration of English society in an era before the term "political" had entered the English language.[35]

The poem was written in the same period as the complete Bible was being translated from Latin into English. In *Piers*, both love and charity are used in the imagery reflecting biblical allusions to the concept of *agape*, indicating a distinction in meaning between them. Throughout the poem, both terms are used not merely to express manifestations of the spirit of *agape* but to show that pure *agape* "desires nothing but self-expression" – that the power of God is a natural law regulating conduct and interpersonal relationships in public as well as private spheres.[36]

The word love (*loue*) is generally used as a verb in the modern sense but in reference to a more superior divine Love: God's love of humankind. According to William Langland, "Loue" is a mediator, "as the mayor is, between king and commons; Just so does Love lead and direct the law; He sets the fine on man for his misdeeds." As Ben Smith writes, Langland's personification of "loue" as "mediator, law-shaper, and judge" of the people indicates that divine love "brings accord and reconciliation." As mentioned, this "imperative to love God and one's neighbour are the reshaping under the new dispensation of the old Mosaic law" such that "judgement and punishment must always be executed *ex caritate*."[37] In a later verse, the poet Langland writes that "love begins in power, and in the heart is the source and deep fount of love."[38] Hence, according to Langland, God is power, "the source of all things, who gives mankind the natural ability to experience *caritas*."[39]

Whereas Love represents a form of divine grace and the source of law, the figure of Charity represents Christ on earth. Charity is thus used allegorically to signify the Law of Love fulfilled. Christ and Christ-like conduct, most significantly loving kindness, mercy, voluntary poverty, altruistic almsgiving and meekness, are

34 Smith, *Traditional Imagery*, 13.

35 According to the *Oxford English Dictionary*, the word "political" is first recorded in *Dyaloge Dyuers Maters* by Sir Thomas More (1478–1535): "He called hys chirch owt of the gentyllys whych els as for morall vertews & polytycall.were not far vnder many of vs," in Thomas More, *A dyaloge wherin be treated dyuers maters*, 1st ed. (London: John Rastell, 1529), i. xxix. f. xliii; *Oxford English Dictionary* (Oxford: Oxford University Press, 1989), continually updated at www.oed.com/.

36 Smith, *Traditional Imagery*, 50.

37 Smith, *Traditional Imagery*, 36.

38 Smith, *Traditional Imagery*, 36.

39 Smith, *Traditional Imagery*, 37.

a means of gaining full remission of sins for the charitable person as well as bringing peace and lawfulness into the community.[40] In this way, charity could be used to signify both individual manifestations of love and the community of people in "a state of Christian harmony (amity and peace)."[41] Charity is thus understood as more than a mere virtue. Charity is the law fulfilled, how power is to be exercised and how wealth is to be distributed. For the individual Christian, however, charity was first and foremost the path to salvation.

It is important to remember that charity during this period was understood not in the narrow sense of poverty relief or as a set of beneficent acts but as the attempt to embody Christ on earth through divine love. Aquinas in the *Summa Theologiæ*, for example, categorized charity as the friendship of man for God, which acts as a special virtue emanating from the soul that "sets the form on all" virtues.[42] Charity was, therefore, closely associated with the "good works" popularized in the seven corporal acts of mercy concerning the material needs of others, which were also commonly understood as acts of penance: to feed the hungry, give drink to the thirsty, clothe the naked, shelter travelers, visit the sick, minister to prisoners and bury the dead.[43] These acts of mercy were a means of obtaining or embodying the love of God (charity), but they did not mark out the metes and bounds of charity.

Arguably, this combination of "doing good" and "communing or embodying good" into legal order within the meaning of charity enabled the permanent need for inner conversion to be linked to obtaining the social changes necessary for salvation. The Law, we must remember, was fulfilled in Christian society by *agape*. In the poem *Piers*, however, charity itself is determined by the station in life of each individual Christian. Although everyone is expected to be meek and to seek poverty over profit, knights are advised to protect the truth, men of Law who plead at the bar are required to refrain from taking bribes and to use their eloquence on behalf of the poor, laborers are expected to engage in agricultural work regardless of need, and so on. In this sense, charity was an authorized form of living, articulated through the idiom of office.[44] Interpretations or allegories of charity were attached to

40 Smith, *Traditional Imagery*, 50.

41 R. A. Houston, "What Did the Royal Almoner Do in Britain and Ireland, c. 1450–1700?," *English Historical Review* 125, no. 513 (2010): 279–313, at 289.

42 Thomas Aquinas, *The Summa Theologiæ of St. Thomas Aquinas*, 2nd rev. ed., trans. Fathers of the English Dominican Province (London: Burns, Oates & Washbourne, 1920), Question 23.

43 David Lepine, "Cathedrals and Charity: Almsgiving at English Secular Cathedrals in the Later Middle Ages," *English Historical Review* 126, no. 522 (2011): 1066–96, at 1081.

44 For analyses of the concepts of office and jurisdiction and their relationship to law, see Dorsett and McVeigh, "Essay on Jurisdiction"; and Shaun McVeigh, "Office and the Conduct of the Minor Jurisprudent," *UC Irvine Law Review* 5, no. 1 (2015): 499–511, at 499.

a person's station and instructed Christians on that which one ought to or had to do in the way of love. As Bernd Moeller writes: "Material welfare and eternal salvation were not differentiated and thus the borders between the secular and spiritual areas of life disappeared."[45]

6.3 CHARITABLE EFFECTS

6.3.1 *The Public Offices of Charity*

The charitable disposition, which was central to the nature and quality of social relations in the medieval and early modern periods, extended to the creation of legal jurisdictions and public office, which were fundamentally ways of conceiving the "relationship between religion and law."[46] In order to be truly divine, the jurisdiction of kings and other lords, as well as clerics, had to be charitable. Accordingly, although English monarchs and their lords understood and exercised power based on their own feudal obligations, as Christians they were also called upon to transform themselves through Christ-like conduct into an embodied relationship with God.

The office of almoner presents us with the prime example of charity authorizing a public office. Originally referring to anyone who fulfilled expectations of charity and piety by distributing alms, almonership became a public function serving both the church and secular lords, which "were equally committed to a combination of practical provisioning and socio-cultural displays of power."[47] As Robert Houston notes, most secular and ecclesiastical households in Britain and Ireland employed an almoner, who "performed a broadly traditional charitable function, understood not only as beneficence, but also creating and re-creating a Christian community."[48] These grants of charitable jurisdiction were not so much a secularization of office as a "concerned effort to better integrate clergy into society" and the "civil ordering of moral life on religious grounds."[49] As Houston writes: "In

45 Moeller characterizes this as a "sacred society." Bernd Moeller, *Imperial Cities and the Reformation: Three Essays*, ed. H. C. Erik Midelfort and Mark U. Edwards, Jr. (Philadelphia: Fortress Press, 1972), 46ff.

46 Houston, "What Did the Royal Almoner Do," 289.

47 Felicity Heal, "Reciprocity and Exchange in the Late Medieval Household," in *Bodies and Disciplines: Intersections of Literature and History in Fifteenth Century England*, ed. Barbara Hanawalt and David Wallace (Minneapolis: University of Minnesota Press, 1996), 180, cited in Houston, "What Did the Royal Almoner Do."

48 Houston, "What Did the Royal Almoner Do," 281.

49 Houston, "What Did the Royal Almoner Do," 289 citing Eamon Duffy, "The Godly and the Multitude in Stuart England," *Seventeenth Century* 1, no. 1 (1986): 31–55, at 48–9. See also

this the Tudor and Stuart almoner's mission (in the full religious meaning of the word) was to offer a compassionate resolution to disputes that embodied justice, charity and dignity in a social sense and 'penitence, forgiveness and grace' in a religious one."[50]

6.3.2 *Charitable Justice*

The desire to do well and lead a charitable life strongly influenced the penitential techniques of the Catholic Church, which in turn played a role in emphasizing the public administration of charity. The process of "administering" charity required "an array of interpretive strategies to negotiate a growing recognition of the dangers inherent to charity, how it might be misapplied or exploited or misinterpreted."[51] In this way, charity – the Christian expression of lawfulness – became a public, administrative disciplinary technique – a complicated and constant program of interpretation and judgment that required not only a distribution of resources but also correction or punishment as holders of all charitable offices – public and private – were expected to "read strangers like a book."[52] These charitable notions of punishment and justice competed with older conceptions of charity as a divine, legal act of kindness or mercy in an embodied relationship with God. It is possible to see reflected in this tension divisions in contemporary law between justice and mercy, law and equity, Law and Crown as a rule-bound system of criminal justice based on reason (judgment) takes precedence over more discretionary concepts such as mercy, forgiveness or restitution.

An example of the shift can be seen in the poem *Piers*, in which the author instructs his reader to have pity on the poor and be merciful[53] but also uses the figure of Reason to convince the king that if he were king with a realm to protect:

> It's no use asking me to have mercy till lords and ladies learn to love the truth . . . I should leave no wrong unpunished, on peril of my soul. Nor, God willing, would anyone win my favour with gifts, or gain mercy through Fee; only their meekness would influence me. For a man named *Mullum Malum*

Steven Ozment, *The Reformation in the Cities: The Appeal of Protestantism to Sixteenth-Century Germany and Switzerland* (New Haven: Yale University Press, 1975), 34.

50 Houston, "What Did the Royal Almoner Do," 289 citing Duffy, "Godly and the Multitude," 48–9.

51 Evan Gurney, "Thomas More and the Problem of Charity," *Renaissance Studies* 26, no. 2 (2012): 197–217.

52 Gurney, "Thomas More."

53 Verses VI 140 207 of the poem; see William Langland, *Piers the Ploughman* (London: Penguin Books, 1959), 36.

> met with one called *Impunitum*, and bade *Nullum Bonum* be *irremuneratum*. Let your confessor, my lord, interpret this riddle for you, without glossing over it. And if you carry it out, I swear the Law shall turn labourer and drive a muck-cart, and Love shall rule over your land as you have always wished.[54]

Here, Langland is drawing on Pope Innocent III's *De Contemptu Mundi*. "He alone is a just judge ... who leaves no evil unpunished and no good unrewarded."[55] For the poet Langland, the concept of love is used to represent a lawfulness that can only be achieved, according to Reason, by the king's just punishment of crime. Here law, not love, does the dirty work, but it leaves the realm charitable as the king has always desired. Conscience warns the king that "unless you win the support of the common people, you will find it very hard to bring this about and govern your subjects strictly according to justice." In response, Reason demands that the king give him the power to command obedience but insists that Conscience remain as their adviser.[56]

These instructions to the king about the fulfillment of office, and the substitution of law for love, shift the meaning of charity with respect to public judgments of criminal behavior and the exercise of public justice in interesting ways. The poem indicates how the deployment of royal justice is used to preserve and augment dominion whilst running counter to the forgiving dictates of Christianity, as well as earlier forms of Anglo-Saxon law and custom. The poem demonstrates how interpretations of charity authorized and ordered law as such and did not simply determine authority within a legal regime.[57]

Whilst reason and conscience are being deployed in the public office of king, those not holding public, law-making authority are left with a different set of virtues with which to administer private charity ranging from parents not spoiling their children by sparing the rod, to the clergy clothing and feeding the poor,[58] to merchants funding public works and charitable causes with their profits.[59]

6.3.3 *Charitable Exclusion*

By the late Middle Ages, charitable notions of public justice had also become a set of discriminatory spatial practices with which to create bodies of deserving people by excluding the underserving "sinners," including vagrants, sex-workers, wasters and the like, all of whom were considered to be both lacking in charity and

54 Langland, *Piers the Ploughman*, 59.
55 Langland, *Piers the Ploughman*, 271.
56 Langland, *Piers the Ploughman*, 60.
57 Dorsett and McVeigh, "Essay on Jurisdiction," 499.
58 Langland, *Piers the Ploughman*, 58.
59 Langland, *Piers the Ploughman*, 92.

undeserving of charity.[60] These sophisticated distinctions between recipients of alms, which had been fed into civic virtue by theologians and canonists, mark the impossibility of truly Christ-like charity on earth.[61] As the philosopher Gregg Lambert notes: "The hatred that is bestowed upon the criminal marks the recognition, on the part of community, of a form of love that remains 'outside' incorporation," producing "a commonplace morality" "that evacuates the concept of love in this religion and turns it once again into a justification for every social division, for war, and, ultimately, genocide."[62]

David Lepine points us to the three defining principles applied to the poor: "proximity, the known in preference to the stranger; need, the sick, disabled, old, those unable to work; and merit, the just rather than the wicked."[63] Barbara Harvey writes that larger Benedictine monasteries were already performing a form of discriminating almsgiving at this time. This tension between voluntary, merciful giving and discriminating giving is also evident in *Piers*.[64] Miri Rubin argues that a combination of rising population, greater hardship and scarcity of resources compelled greater discrimination.[65] These events meant that the "profundity of Christianity in its original sense," which was "to divinize a man who was both a criminal and a God, is lost."[66] As Evan Gurney argues, "No longer could individuals in England give alms with a glad and indifferent heart."[67] By 1531, it would be prohibited for anyone to "gyve any herborowe monye or lodgyng to any beggers beyng stronge & Able" at risk of being fined a discretionary sum, a figure that was raised in 1536 to ten times the amount of the alms given.[68]

6.3.4 *Charity, Territory and Public Administration*

During the thirteenth century, charitable justice also began to converge with territorial forms of jurisdiction as small, local churches owned by major

60 See Annabel S. Brett, *Changes of State: Nature and the Limits of the City in Early Modern Natural Law* (Princeton: Princeton University Press, 2011).

61 See Annabel Brett's discussion of the writings of the Salamancan, Domingo de Soto (1495–1560), for an excellent analysis of similar developments in Southern Europe: Brett, *Changes of State*, ch. 1.

62 Gregg Lambert, *Return Statements: The Return of Religion in Contemporary Philosophy* (Edinburgh: Edinburgh University Press, 2016), 42–4.

63 Lepine, "Cathedrals and Charity," 1088.

64 Langland, *The Vision of William*, Passus VI, 214–41.

65 Miri Rubin, *Charity and Community in Medieval Cambridge* (Cambridge: Cambridge University Press, 1987), 291; Lepine, "Cathedrals and Charity," 1087–8.

66 Lambert, *Return Statements*, 42–3.

67 Gurney, "Thomas More."

68 22 Henry VIII, c. 12, Stats. Realm, vol. III, p. 328, 330.

landowners were taken over by the Church and placed "into a strict ecclesiastical hierarchy."[69] As the Church asserted its control over pastoral care in this way, the parish became defined in terms of geographical boundaries within that hierarchy under the spiritual charge of a bishop or minister beholden to Rome, allowing for a more overarching, centralized set of public powers structured and administered through the Church hierarchy.[70]

These ecclesiastical processes – which created exclusionary techniques, territorial units and authorized means of distributing justice and resources – enabled early modern Parliaments in the fourteenth and fifteenth centuries to pass laws creating administrative districts responsible for relieving their own "impotent poor" who, because of age or infirmity, were incapable of work.[71] As mentioned, territory was already tethered to "the intellectual and ethical needs of actual officeholders," particularly clerics already in the service of lords and church.[72] During this process, those lacking in charity were thus able to be incorporated into existing legal discourses of criminality, mentioned above, initially directed at runaway serfs. The Statute of Cambridge 1388[73] placed restrictions on the movements of laborers and beggars who refused to work for statutory wages or begged.[74] The Vagabonds and Beggars Act of 1494 decreed that idle persons should be placed in the stocks and then returned to their last place of residence or place of birth. The Vagabonds Act of 1530, entitled "how aged, poor and impotent Persons, compelled to live by Alms, shall be ordered; and how Vagabonds and Beggars shall be punished,"[75] subjected vagabonds to

69 Helmholz, *Canon Law*, 1.

70 See "parish, n." *Oxford English Dictionary* (Oxford: Oxford University Press, 1989), continually updated at www.oed.com/. Barbara Harvey, *Living and Dying in England 1100–1540: The Monastic Experience* (Oxford: Clarendon Press, 1993), 19–21 cited in Lepine, "Cathedrals and Charity," 1087. For an overarching study of the linkages between territory or space and the application of power, see Michel Foucault's lectures at the Collège de France, particularly in Michel Foucault, *Security, Territory, Population: Lectures at the Collège de France, 1977–1978*, ed. Michel Senellart, François Ewald and Alessandro Fontana, trans. Graham Burchell (Basingstoke: Palgrave Macmillan, 2009); Michel Foucault, *The Government of Self and Others: Lectures at the Collège de France, 1982–1983*, ed. Frédéric Gros, François Ewald and Alessandro Fontana (New York: Picador/Palgrave Macmillan, 2011); Michel Foucault, *"Society must be Defended": Lectures at the Collège de France, 1975–76*, ed. Mauro Bertani and Alessandro Fontana, trans. David Macey (New York: Picador, 2003).

71 See Charles J. Ribton-Turner, *A History of Vagrants and Vagrancy and Beggars and Begging* (Montclair, NJ: Patterson Smith, 1972).

72 David Kearns and Ryan Walter, "Office, Political Theory, and the Political Theorist," *The Historical Journal* (2019): 1–21, at 3.

73 Statute of Cambridge 1388, 12 Rich. 2, c. 7.

74 The Statute of Labourers 1349 (UK).

75 Vagabonds Act of 1530, 22 Henry VIII, c. 12.

whippings, rather than the stocks. This act also licensed those who were unable to work due to sickness, age or disability to beg by giving jurisdiction to local Justices of the Peace to grant licenses.[76] Not only could alms only be given to licensed beggars but donors were encouraged to restrict donations to members of their own parish or to direct alms to the parish chest. In this way, ecclesiastical parishes were integrated into an emerging parliamentary form of feudal governance. It is noteworthy that the concepts of politics and the political also enter the English vernacular in the early fifteenth century, as the meaning of charity disintegrates.

6.4 ENGLISH CHARITY

Over a century after the completion of the Wycliffite Bible, when William Tyndale began translating the New Testament into English from the original Hebrew and Greek in 1526, he faced a dilemma. Tyndale was influenced by the humanist endeavors of his time, which included a return to the original text of classical works.[77] Accordingly, Tyndale chose to translate the concept of "*ἀγάπη*" (*agape*) not as "charity" from the Latin but as "love." By privileging "love" in his translation, Tyndale claims, "the matter it selfe in the circumstaunces do declare what loue, what hope, and what fayth is spoken of."[78] The ambiguity of love, Tyndale believed, could be clarified by the individual Christian through a careful reading of the word in context.[79] Tyndale's rejection of the word charity is understood as a rejection of the Catholic doctrine on which extant practices of charity had been founded, including the church's system of alms giving and superstitious intercessory prayer, which depended on the church acting as intermediary between God and subject. Much has been written about the Protestant nature of this position; but Tyndale's translation also posed a threat to the authority of the legislative reforms of King and Parliament concerning the deserving and the undeserving poor. These concerns were overcome by further legislative interventions into the meaning of charity (and poverty) in the Elizabethan era.

[76] Sidney Webb and Beatrice Potter Webb, *English Local Government: English Poor Law History: Part 1, The Old Poor Law* (New York: Longmans, Green & Co., 1927), 45.

[77] See Maria Dowling, *Humanism in the Age of Henry VIII* (London: Croom Helm, 1986); and for a discussion of the deference to authority and patronage within humanism, see Anthony Grafton and Lisa Jardine, *From Humanism to the Humanities: Education and the Liberal Arts in Fifteenth- and Sixteenth-Century Europe* (London: Duckworth, 1986), xiii–xiv.

[78] Gurney, "Thomas More," 211 citing David Daniell, ed., *Tyndale's New Testament* (New Haven: Yale University Press, 1989).

[79] Gurney, "Thomas More," 211.

At the time, Thomas More, in his *Dialogues Against Heresies* (1529) and *Confutation of Tyndale's Answere* (1532 and 1533), railed against the use of the word "love" in place of "charity."[80] A staunch Catholic, as well as Chancellor to Henry VIII and Lord High Chancellor of England from 1529 to 1532, More believed that Tyndale "was attempting 'of purpose' to strip the concept of charity bare of its associations with salvific merit, and to redefine the virtue in a way that undercut church authority."[81] Although a well-known humanist himself, More sites the difficulties of translation as reason for restraint and a conservative approach to translation, "especially when salvation is at stake." Of course, the authority to interpret and forgive was also at stake – an authority intimately connected to the law and the lawmaker. More "favours comen custome" and censures Tyndale's failure to accord with the accepted common usage of an English audience familiar with the term "charity."[82] As Gurney argues, "More clearly advocated a notion of charity that obtained its sanction and power from the communal order rather than the other way around."[83] This argument is ironically prescient given that only months later Henry VIII, if not the English people, would claim jurisdiction over the Christian canon in England and More would ultimately be sentenced to death for his refusal to recognize the King's supremacy (and the legitimacy of his divorce).[84]

King Henry VIII, together with the English Parliament, announced the sovereignty of the English Empire from the Catholic Church in the Act in Restraint of Appeals 1533,[85] by declaring that "this realm of England is an empire, and so hath been accepted in the world, governed by one Supreme Head and King."[86] This is an important event in the history of European

80 St. Thomas More, *The Yale Edition of the Complete Works of St Thomas More*, vol. 6, *Parts I & II, A Dialogue Concerning Heresies*, ed. Thomas M. C. Lawler, Germain Marc'hadour and Richard C. Marius (New Haven: Yale University Press, 1981). According to Hamlin, "English Catholics remained opposed to the English Bible until the Rheims-Douai translation of 1582/1609–10; for them, the Bible was a book in Latin." Hamlin, "Bible," 546. See also Matthew DeCoursey, ed., *The Thomas More/William Tyndale Polemic: A Selection* (Sheffield: Early Modern Literary Studies, 2010); and Stephen Greenblatt, *Renaissance Self-Fashioning: From More to Shakespeare* (Chicago: University of Chicago Press, 1980), 95.

81 Gurney, "Thomas More," 201.

82 Gurney, "Thomas More," 201.

83 Gurney, "Thomas More," 201.

84 Gurney, "Thomas More," 201.

85 Act in Restraint of Appeals 1533, 24 Hen. VIII c. 12.

86 Act of Appeals of 1533, 24 Hen. VIII c. 12, in Alan Smith, *The Emergence of a Nation State: The Commonwealth of England, 1529–1660* (London: Longman, 1984), 388. See also Marcel Gauchet, *The Disenchantment of the World: A Political History of Religion*, trans. Oscar Burge (Princeton: Princeton University Press, 1997), 158; and Walter Ullmann, "This Realm of England Is an Empire," *Journal of Ecclesiastical History* 30, no. 2 (1979): 175–203, at 183–4.

international law,[87] along with the Act of Supremacy 1534.[88] The break represents an intersovereign relationship if not an international law. The former Act declares that the king may henceforth "render and yield justice and final determination to all manner of folk resiants or subjects within this realm, in all causes, matters, debates, and contentions happening to occur, in surge or begin within the limits thereof . . . [w]ithout restraint or provocation to any foreign princes or potentates of the world."[89]

As Claire McEachern argues, Henry VIII's announcement was based "as much in a competitive, mimetic resemblance to foreign authority as in a rejection of it."[90] These parliamentary acts may be understood as founding moments of English nationalism[91] – if not Empire[92] – because they detached the realm of England from the universal ideal of the Roman Catholic Church and attached it to the "ideality" of (Tudor-Stuart) Crown dominion and nationhood, which the concept of charity had helped to build.[93] The Church of England would remain the only recognized ecclesiastical body within the English dominion until the Elizabethan Act of Toleration in 1689. As Helmut Koenigsberger notes: "By the fourteenth and fifteenth centuries, the functional conditions for the survival of a unified Church had all but disappeared."[94] Whereas, in "the eleventh and twelfth centuries it had been considered perfectly natural for Italians, Anselm and Lanfranc, to become archbishops of Canterbury, or an Anglo-Norman cleric to hold the see of Palermo," even by the thirteenth century, the "churches in the different kingdoms reserved ecclesiastical positions more and more for natives of the country, as was happening in the case of secular offices."[95]

87 These Acts preceded the Peace of Westphalia of 1648 by more than a century. See Beard, "The International Law," 18.

88 In 1534, the Acts of Supremacy, 26 Hen. VIII c. 1, renounced the authority of Rome and established the "King or Sovereign Lord" of England as "the only Supreme Head on earth of the Church of England."

89 Claire McEachern, *The Poetics of English Nationhood, 1590–1612* (Cambridge: Cambridge University Press, 1996), 1 citing Acts of Appeals of 1533, 24 Henry VIII c. 12.

90 McEachern, *Poetics*, 2. For a discussion of founding moments, see also Fleur Johns, Richard Joyce and Sundhya Pahuja, eds., *Events: The Force of International Law* (Oxford: Routledge, 2011).

91 Over the next century, nation would shift in meaning from "race or kind . . . to denote that principle of political self-determination belonging to people linked (if in nothing else) by our common government." McEachern, *Poetics*, 1.

92 This would come with the crowning of King James I and the union of Scotland and England and the colonization of Ireland.

93 McEachern, *Poetics*.

94 Koenigsberger, "Unity," 413.

95 Koenigsberger, "Unity," 413.

Authority in Europe was thus shifting in a jurisdictional sense, but charity – Christian lawfulness – remained a significant source of that authority. Henry VIII's appreciation of this can be seen in the fact that his break from Rome was combined with a series of acts aimed at ensuring that his own authority over scripture is substituted for that of Rome. In 1534, King Henry VIII introduced the Act of Submission of the Clergy setting out the method of dealing with canon law given the restraint of appeals to Rome as conceded by the clergy in 1532. Attached to the act was the *Provinciale*, a collection of canon law collected by William Lyndwood in 1432 "as the consolidation of English Canon Law as then practised."[96] This now had the authority of the state by an act of Parliament.[97]

To further his sovereign authority, Henry VIII commissioned the printing of the Great Bible in 1539, in defiance of both Rome and the Vulgate and, more significantly, to control independent, Protestant interpretations of Christian doctrine, particularly Tyndale's. By producing and authorizing the Great Bible, Henry VIII maintained the "idea of a single, undivided Church coterminous with [English] civil society" rather than the Roman Church.[98] In 1541, Henry VIII enacted law requiring these bibles be "fyxed and set vp openlye in euery of the sayd paryshe churches."[99] Although the concept of *agape* was translated as "love" in this Great Bible, this failed to shift the common usage of the word "charity" in early modern literature and English law, which had become vital in disciplining the English population. More had been right to argue that the concept was now controlled by common custom (and English law).

6.4.1 *The Reformation of Charity*

By the reign of Elizabeth I, the reformation in England had changed the relationship between law and the Christian religion, and the principles concerning the constitution of England were thus also changing. During this period, the role of the church in the governance of the population began to be both challenged and defended, and the idiom for making claims of public

96 Willian Lyndwood, *Lyndwood's Provincial*, ed. John Bullard and Bell Chalmer (London: Faith Press Ltd, 1929), xxxvii.

97 Lyndwood, *Lyndwood's Provincial*, xxxi.

98 Deryck W. Lovegrove, *Established Church, Sectarian People: Itinerancy and the Transformation of English Dissent, 1780–1830* (Cambridge: Cambridge University Press, 1988), 1.

99 Alfred Pollard, *Records of the English Bible: The Documents Relating to the Translation and Publication of the Bible in English, 1525–1611* (London: Henry Frowde, 1911), 262.

office shifted. In 1574, Lord Henry Howard argued of bishops in *A Defense of the ecclesiastical regimente in Englande*: "As for dealing in civil causes, so far as they are annexed and coherent to a spiritual function, maintaining peace and keeping quiet in the country, I think it be very profitable and requisite for every state."[100] As Houston explains, "Tudor bishops in general were 'both spiritually strong and bureaucratically fit': their aptitude as administrators did not compromise their piety or their role as promotors of co-operation and reconciliation."[101] Although these religious offices continue to remain closely aligned with the emerging English state, the increased power of the monarchy meant that these administrative and judicial offices became less associated with the concept of charity and the religious associations that that concept maintained, and increasingly associated with the concept of politics and all the secular associations that that concept brought with it.

It was in the context of these developments that the Elizabethan Parliament continued to enact statutes regulating the poor and punishing those who were perceived as idle, as well as introducing early forms of income tax.[102] These Elizabethan acts strike a different balance in terms of authorizing and enforcing public power. An Act for the Punishment of Vagabonds, and for the Relief of the Poor and Impotent in 1572 brought voluntary giving to an end by introducing compulsory assessment and collection of rates to support the deserving poor.[103] In this way, charitable obligations were not only owed to the state as well as to God but also enforced in this world by a secular ruler defending an English public. The Act for the Relief of the Poor 1597 established unpaid, quasi-public "overseers of the poor." And the Poor Relief Act of 1601, which "placed the administration of poor relief in the hands of municipal authorities," was introduced as "[l]ocal ecologies of relief were ultimately, sometimes painfully, subsumed within a national administrative system."[104]

Hence, responsibility for Christian lawfulness was increasingly being assumed and administered by secular rather than ecclesiastical authority. This meant that charity was no longer authorizing and ordering law as such

100 Cited in John Bossy, *Peace in the Post-Reformation* (Cambridge: Cambridge University Press, 1998), 73–96.

101 Andrew Chibi, *Henry VIII's Bishops: Diplomats, Administrators, Scholars and Shepherds* (Cambridge: James Clarke and Co., 2003), 294, cited in Houston, "What Did the Royal Almoner Do." See also McEachern, *Poetics*, 4; Stephen White, "The Book of Common Prayer and the Standardization of the English Language," *The Anglican* 32, no. 20 (2003): 4–11.

102 Steve Hindle, *On the Parish? The Micro-Politics of Poor Relief in Rural England c. 1550–1750* (New York: Clarendon Press, 2004), 3.

103 An act for the punishment of vagabonds, and for the relief of the poor and impotent 1572, 14 Elizabeth I, c. 5.

104 Hindle, *On the Parish*, 7–8.

but simply determining authority within a legal regime in some aspects of public administration.[105] In this sense, the enforcement of public charitable functions moved from the divine to the secular – from God and Pope to king. The notion of charity as a community of people in "a state of Christian harmony (amity and peace)"[106] began to fade from the picture as the meaning of charity shifted from being the ideation of a communal manifestation of the Good Law to a concept implicitly or explicitly describing private welfare distribution. Now monarchy, which was able to animate "the abstractions of the state," acted as the "crucible of an ideology of social unity."[107] During this period, charity thereby became a set of private transactions to be encouraged (or, in the case of superstitious uses, outlawed). Already, the term charity had been taken from the "law and practice as administered by the English ecclesiastical courts" and put to use by the English Courts of Equity to describe "charitable uses" (trusts that served as gifts of land or money bequeathed not to a named beneficiary but for a charitable cause).[108] In 1601, the Elizabethan Parliament began to supervise these causes by statute.

6.4.2 *The English Law of Charity*

Although the poorest Christians were originally considered the most charitable (or Christ-like), prior to the Reformation charitable giving had become an important means for those with power or means to achieve salvation. As a civic and personal virtue attached to personal salvation, charitable giving produced significant public benefits, and not always for the poor, sick or suffering. As Joseph Willard notes, gifts for the construction of bridges, piers and roads were common. These were public duties (or gains, depending on your perspective) adopted from the Roman law and integrated into canon law and charitable practice.[109] Endowed almshouses and hospitals provided lodging for travelers as well as relief and care of the sick. Manorial and guild practices were also evident. The profits of parish stock (usually sheep or cattle), for example, were directed to the relief of the poor, and parish and craft guilds acted as mutual aid societies.[110]

105 Dorsett and McVeigh, "Essay on Jurisdiction," 499.
106 Houston, "What Did the Royal Almoner Do," 289.
107 McEachern, *Poetics*, 7.
108 See Richard H. Helmholz, "The Law of Charity and the English Ecclesiastical Courts," in *The Foundations of Medieval English Ecclesiastical History*, ed. Philippa Hoskin, Christopher Brooke, and Barrie Dobson (Woodbridge: Boydell Press, 2005), 111.
109 Joseph Willard, "Illustrations of the Origin of 'cy près,'" *Harvard Law Review* 8, no. 2 (1894): 69–92, at 71–2.
110 A. L. Beier, *The Problem of the Poor in Tudor and Early Stuart England* (London: Methuen, 1983), 2.

Public gains also arose from the post-mortem dispersal of estates. Testamentary gifts were commonly given for "works of mercy and piety among the infirm and needy poor" to "please Almighty God" and obtain salvation.[111] The poor interceding was also popular because they were considered closer to Christ.[112] Accordingly, wealthier Christians endowed an office or founded a service to pray for the soul of the deceased on the anniversary of his or her death, or at some other appointed time, usually combined with giving alms to those who participated in the prayers. Others founded a chantry for a priest or priests to celebrate masses for the soul of the deceased, which would also include almsgiving.[113] All of these private, pre-Reformation activities were supported by developments in the sacrament of penance and the doctrine of purgatory. Manifesting charity through a "Christian benignity of disposition expressing itself in Christ-like conduct"[114] thereby shifted into "giving charity" by means of secular transactions between individuals, though mediated by the church. These voluntary acts of charity, which complemented the system of charity being administered by Parliamentary power and the criminal justice system, thus became a kind of lawful tender given in exchange for salvation or indulgence, and the almoners and other officers who supervised these transactions functioned as "chamberlains or accountants" as much as settlers of disputes and distributors of alms.[115]

The ability to distribute wealth as a private enactment of charity was particularly attractive to the merchant class gaining strength (and resources) in the late medieval period. Once again, the thirteenth-century poem *Piers* offers us important insights as to the origin of, and motivation for, these transactions. A group of merchants is told by Truth, an allegorical figure representing the Church, that they will be granted freedom from punishment if they "buy up boldly all the best goods and sell them again, and use the profits to repair the hospitals, and to help folk in trouble, to get the bad roads mended quickly and rebuild the broken bridges, to enable poor girls to marry or to enter nunneries, to feed the poor and the men in prisons, to send boys to school or apprentice them to a trade, and to assist religious orders and give them better endowments."[116] However, when a priest asks to read the pardon given to Piers, attested by Truth, the document says no more than: "And they that have done good

111 Beier, *Problem*, 2.
112 Beier, *Problem*, 1085.
113 Lepine, "Cathedrals and Charity," 1083.
114 See etymological developments of the concept in the *Oxford English Dictionary* (Oxford: Oxford University Press, 1989), continually updated at www.oed.com/.
115 See Houston, "What Did the Royal Almoner Do."
116 Langland, *Piers the Ploughman*, 92.

shall go into life everlasting: And they that have done evil into everlasting fire."[117] The chapter ends with the author warning rich men – who trust in their wealth and who have triennials said for them after their death – to not think that a papal bull or indulgence will allow them to break the Ten Commandments. In fact, the practice of redistributing wealth to support explicit public causes would not only continue unabated in English society as a public good, it ultimately became encouraged and privileged by statute as the very (legal) definition of charity.

6.4.3 *The 1601 Statute of Charitable Uses*

Elizabeth's 1601 Statute of Charitable Uses was "An Acte to redresse the Misemployment of Landes Goodes and Stockes of Money heretofore given to Charitable Uses." This act added to the "broader reorganization of the system of public and private responsibilities for the poor and dependent."[118] What is significant about this statute is that the list of charitable uses that the statute seeks to encourage contains essentially the same causes that Truth tells the merchants to pursue with their profits in the poem *Piers*. These uses of profit become the source of what the common law today considers to be a "charitable purpose" either by explicit mention or because a purpose falls within its "spirit and intendment," and thus within the equity of the statute. Charity in this legal sense is concerned only with the identification, privileging and regulation of voluntary private capital transfers for public benefit. Charity was thus becoming a potential privilege of (private) law – a law "to capture, give recognition to, incentivise, and regulate a distinct sector of organised society that receives and raises private and public funds to pursue a defined set of 'charitable purposes' for the public benefit,"[119] rather than the manifestation of love and law fulfilled.

117 Langland, *Piers the Ploughman*, 97.

118 1601 Statute of Charitable Uses, 43 Eliz I, c. 4. Known as the Statute of Elizabeth, it was repealed by section 13(1) of the Mortmain and Charitable Uses Act 1888, c. 42, which maintained the list of purposes recited in the preamble to the Statute of Elizabeth. According to William Quigley: "This, and other Elizabethan poor laws, enacted three principles which shaped much subsequent social legislation: the principle of local responsibility; the principle of settlement and removal; and the principle of primary family responsibility". William Quigley, "Five Hundred Years of English Poor Laws, 1349–1834: Regulating the Working and Nonworking Poor," *Akron Law Review* 30, no. 1 (1996): 73–129, at 91. See also Paul Slack, *The English Poor Law, 1531–1782* (London: Palgrave Macmillan, 1990); and David Englander, *Poverty and Poor Law Reform in 19th Century Britain, 1834–1914: From Chadwick to Booth* (London: Routledge, 1998), 1.

119 Jennifer Beard, "Charities, Election Campaigning and the Australian Constitution," *Melbourne University Law Review* 43, no. 2 (2019): 462–514, at 465.

What is notably absent from the list of purposes in the 1601 Statute is any reference to uses indicative of Catholic beliefs, such as gifts for masses or prayers for the dead, which, as mentioned, had been a common purpose of bequests prior to the Reformation but had subsequently been made illegal.[120] Without the inclusion of "superstitious" uses aimed specifically at buying the donor's salvation, the concept of charity at law was essentially becoming a coalescence of ideas of public utility with respect to a physical, commonwealth body.[121] As the word became associated with the administration of publicly regulated, private welfare distribution, traces of "the good" began to be transformed into ideas about the commonwealth and discourses about public or general interests, or, in more modern parlance, public benefit. Confined to their own systems of precedent, these legal meanings thus helped to develop new doctrines based on a "public" spirit grounded in public bodies (politic), which ultimately led judges to conceive of charity as a class of purposes that not only offered a "public benefit" but required it.[122] This was perhaps inevitable since secular courts were left to define a concept that had once relied on spiritual doctrine to give it meaning.[123] Charity could, or would, no longer be referred to as *agape* (love) and courts would eventually begin referring to the distinction between a "charitable use within the common or narrow sense of those words"[124] and the legal meaning of charity.[125] By adopting this very particular aspect of charitable giving as the meaning of charity at law, the concept was further removed from its biblical connotations of Christ-like conduct and pious uses. This also furthered the division between

[120] Such bequests were void following the 1547 Statute of 1 Edw. VI. c. 14, which avoided certain assurances of lands made for "superstitious uses," including "legacies to priests to pray for the soul of the donor." See *West* v. *Shuttleworth* 2 M. & K. 684, per Lord Cottenham; Michael Blakeney, "Sequestered Piety and Charity: A Comparative Analysis," *Journal of Legal History* 2, no. 3 (1981): 207–26; John Brunyate, "The Legal Definition of Charit," *Law Quarterly Review* 61 (1945): 268–85, at 279; and Norman Bentwich, "The Wilderness of Legal Charity," *Law Quarterly Revue* 49 (1933): 520–7, at 523.

[121] Matthew Mills, "The Development of the Public Benefit Requirement for Charitable Trusts in the Nineteenth Century," *Journal of Legal History* 37, no. 3 (2016): 269–302, at 298.

[122] Mills argues that the first express use of the public benefit requirement to conclusively determine charitable validity occurs in 1862. The case of *Morice* v. *Bishop of Durham* [1805] EWHC Ch J80 is also important as it led to the explicit discussion of a public benefit requirement in *Cocks* v. *Manners* (1871) L.R. 12 Eq. 574. See Mills, "Development," 279.

[123] Meanwhile, the Church of England, which was regulated separately by statute, remained an appropriate object of religious charity. It would not be until the enactment of the Toleration Act 1688 that Protestant dissenters would be permitted to make valid gifts to nonconformist ministers. The "emancipation of Roman Catholics, Jews and Unitarians had to wait until the nineteenth century." Blakeney, "Sequestered Piety."

[124] *Trustees of the British Museum* v. *White* (1826) 2 Sim & St 594, 596.

[125] *Jones* v. *Williams* (1767) Amb 651, 652.

the public functions of charity and private charity, and provided an indication of how the Crown emerged in England as the guardian of public interests with deep ties to territory and dominion over land and people.[126]

6.4.4 *Love and Law Divided*

In 1604, Queen Elizabeth's successor, King James, commissioned six groups of "learned men" to produce a new English translation of the Bible. The task took seven years. The final product became the authorized Bible of the Church of England. Since Tyndale's translation in 1526, the word "love" had been adopted instead of the word "charity" in the 1534 Coverdale Bible, the 1537 Matthew Bible, the 1539 Great Bible, the 1560 Geneva Bible and the 1568 Bishops' Bible, although not always consistently. On the matter of which English word to use to describe the Greek concept of *agape*, the translators of the original King James Bible of 1611 and the revised version in 1769 chose "charity" – the Vulgate translation of "*caritas*." Certainly, it was not the case that the King James translators did not know that "love" might have fit. Rather, they purposely, and unanimously, chose the word "charity" presumably because of the significance it has assumed in the English language and culture. It was, as Queen Elizabeth described it, "the knot of all Christian society."[127] Through "the processes of inclusion and exclusion through which local communities were constructed, sustained, and ultimately absorbed into a national political culture,"[128] English *agape* (charity) did much of the work required to secure a public sense of England by adhering public office, territory and people into an English nation and an English church under an English sovereign.[129]

6.5 CONCLUSION

One approach to the question of what the Christian concept of charity can tell us about international law would be to follow the charitable and imperial

[126] Adam Davis, "The Social and Religious Meanings of Charity in Mediaeval Europe," *History Compass* 12, no. 12 (2014): 935–50, at 936.

[127] Walter Frere and William Kennedy, eds., *Visitation Articles and Injunctions of the Period of the Reformation*, vol. 3 (London: Longmans, Green & Co., 1910), 23. Cited in Walsham, *Charitable Hatred*, 251.

[128] Hindle, *On the Parish?*, 7.

[129] See Timothy Hampton, "What Is a Colony before Colonialism? Humanist and Antihumanist Concepts of Governmentality from Foucault to Montaigne," in *Early Modern Humanism and Postmodern Antihumanism in Dialogue*, ed. Jan Miernowski (Switzerland: Palgrave Macmillan, 2016), 93–115.

exploits of Christian missions into the modern-day relationship between international law, development and humanitarianism. But the history of charity has even more to tell the international lawyer than present ideas about human development, welfare distribution, international justice or humanitarianism. In England, charity authorized the exercise of public power in the late medieval period, and, during England's early modern period, charity provided the ideational intimacy necessary to bring together concepts of divine authority, secular rule, sovereignty and territory through practices of jurisdictional technique, governance and exclusion.[130]

RECOMMENDED READING

Brett, Annabel S. *Changes of State: Nature and the Limits of the City in Early Modern Natural Law*. Princeton: Princeton University Press, 2011.

Dorsett, Shaunnagh, and Shaun McVeigh. "Jurisprudences of Jurisdiction: Matters of Public Authority." *Griffith Law Review* 23, no. 4 (2014): 569–88.

Houston, R. A. "What Did the Royal Almoner Do in Britain and Ireland, c. 1450–1700?" *English Historical Review* 125, no. 513 (2010): 279–313.

McClure, Julia. "The Charitable Bonds of the Spanish Empire: The Casa de Contratación as an Institution of Charity." *New Global Studies* 12, no. 2 (2018): 157–74.

Walsham, Alexandra. *Charitable Hatred: Tolerance and Intolerance in England, 1500–1700*. Manchester: Manchester University Press, 2006.

130 The idea of nation is also introduced during this period. See McEachern, *Poetics*.

7

Hugo Grotius: On Freedom of the Seas and Human Nature

Roland Boer

This contribution examines an important triangulation in the thought of Hugo Grotius, or Hugo de Groot (1583–1645): his biblically based effort to redefine private property; a Remonstrant (or Arminian) theological framework for his definition of the free-willing and rational individual who could choose good or evil, as well as punish evil in others; and his work for the Dutch East India Company (the *Verenigde Oostindische Compagnie*, VOC), which in many ways framed all that he wrote. Through these three items, Grotius developed an initial framework for international law, especially the ideology of "freedom of the seas," or what is now called "freedom of navigation." The question that arises through this analysis is whether the universal category of "freedom of the seas" as well as his idea of human nature are vitiated by the specific context in which they arose and the interests they served, or whether one can indeed develop universals, recognized by others, from specific contexts.

"Freedom of navigation" has once again become an issue as I write. As China has been asserting its historical claims to the South China Sea (or "South Sea" as they call it), the United States and Australia, among other states, have been asserting "freedom of navigation" in order to challenge China at a low level. In order to understand these relatively recent developments – upon which I do not seek to pass judgment – we need to go back some four hundred years to understand the specific origins of what is now called "freedom of navigation." This exercise takes us to the important and intriguing Hugo de Groot, more commonly known in the Latinized form as Hugo Grotius. Why Grotius? He was the first to develop the idea of "freedom of the seas," although it was based on biblical and theological argumentation. In brief, he sought to retell the myth of Genesis 2–3 so as to identify a natural and divinely ordained process for the development of private property and – more importantly for our purposes – the category of "nobody's" property, through which everyone has a right to pass. Inseparable from this proposal is his theological effort to identify the free will and reason that persist even after the Fall, so that a human being (although he has a specific type of human being in mind) can act for the sake of good. The catch is that all of this was developed for a specific purpose.

Grotius came into the international spotlight after a notorious international incident. On February 25 in the year 1603, the Dutch captain Jakob van Heemskerck seized the Portuguese carrack *Santa Catarina*. After escorting the aforesaid ship back to Amsterdam, he was able to sell its contents for three million Dutch guilders. An act of piracy on the high seas? The Portuguese – then under the control of Spain, as the Netherlands had been only a generation earlier – certainly thought so. The Dutch had a different idea, for Heemskerck was a captain of the VOC. He had acted on behalf of the company, challenging the Portuguese-Spanish claim to exclusive possession of the ocean on which the carrack was sailing.

So the VOC called upon none other than Grotius to provide a well-reasoned argument as to why the Dutch were perfectly justified in their act against the prevailing maritime orthodoxy. Deploying all of his extensive knowledge of the Bible, as well as ancient Greek and Roman texts, Grotius wrote the extraordinary *De jure Praedae*, a lengthy work that was not actually published at the time.[1] The hard-headed managers of the VOC found the whole work rather obtuse and not immediately relevant to their commercial interests. Instead, they selected a section and published it as *Mare Liberum*, or *The Freedom of the Seas*, in March 1609.[2] The publication served its purpose, for the directors of the VOC were able to conclude the Ibero-Dutch negotiations by April 9, 1609.[3]

Who was Grotius and what did he argue? Grotius was a lawyer, a Renaissance man, enmeshed with the VOC, an escapee from prison, an exile, a Swedish ambassador, and a passionate theologically inspired champion of the free will and rationality of the individual.[4] The last item would have far-reaching implications for the development of liberal ideology. But I am interested in this particular case, especially why he argued that all human

1 Hugo Grotius, *Commentary on the Law of Prize and Booty*, ed. Martine Julia van Ittersum, trans. John Clarke (Indianapolis: Liberty Fund, 2006 [1868]).

2 Hugo Grotius, *The Freedom of the Seas* (Kitchener: Batoche Books, 2000 [1609]).

3 The full text of *De jure Praedae commentarius* was published only 260 years later, having been placed in a box and discovered when his descendants auctioned (through the bookseller and printer Martinus Nijhoff) some of his papers in 1864. The manuscript was eventually acquired by the University of Leiden Library and the first edition appeared in 1868 under the editorship H. G. Hamaker.

4 Henk Nellen, *Hugo de Groot: Een Leven in Strijd om de Vrede 1583–1645* (Amsterdam: Balans, 2007).

beings are rational, free-willing actors (even though, as we will see, he had a relatively limited sense of who counted as a "human being"). The Portuguese, he argued, had erred by claiming that they had exclusive possession of the seas in question. Such an evil act required some form of punishment. At this point, Captain Heemskerck enters the scene as an equally rational and free-willing agent, except that he acted as an agent of the good, which here meant the inherent "freedom of the seas." So, he was perfectly within his rights to punish the Portuguese for their willful act, setting wrong to right. He had enacted "freedom of navigation," the Portuguese had tried to prevent him, so he had captured the ship and its crew. These positions may seem relatively commonplace in our time, but they were not so then. Grotius found that he had to develop elaborate arguments to establish these points.

7.1 REDEFINING PROPERTY

Two parts of Grotius's argument are important, the first concerning the idea of private property and the second concerning free will and reason. Both of them turn on a significant reinterpretation of the biblical myth of the Fall.[5] This process takes place in the twelfth chapter of *De jure Praedae*, precisely the section published at the time as *Mare Liberum*.[6] Here Grotius is at his creative best, producing the outlines of a new myth that enables him to account for the origins of property, as well as the law, international commerce, states – all for the purpose of identifying large parts of the world that are neither private nor public property. I am particularly interested in the way in which Grotius reinterprets the biblical myth in order to produce his own alternative.

In doing so, Grotius must deal with two exegetical assumptions with a long history: a primal and paradisal state of common property, and the emergence of private property as a result of the Fall. The idea of communal property goes back to "Church Fathers" such as Basil and Ambrose, who also observed that salvation would eventually entail a return to such a state – as with the early Christians in Acts 2:44–5 and 4:32–5.[7] Grotius agrees, pointing out that there

5 Gen. 2–3.

6 Grotius, *Freedom of the Seas*.

7 Martin Schermaier, "Res Communes Omnium: The History of an Idea from Greek Philosophy to Grotian Jurisprudence," *Grotiana* 30, no. 1 (2009): 20–48, at 30–1. Elsewhere, Grotius observes that early Christian communism is characteristic of the "primitive" age of human existence. Hugo Grotius, *The Rights of War and Peace*, ed. Richard Tuck, trans. John Clarke (Indianapolis: Liberty Fund, 2005 [1625]), II.2.6.

was "no private property under the primary law of nations," for "God had given all things, not to this or that individual, but to the human race; and there was nothing to prevent a number of persons from being joint owners, in this fashion, of one and the same possession."[8]

However, this is not the situation in which private property exists today. How did the transition take place? Here Grotius faces a problem, for he must challenge the dominant interpretation deriving from the "Church Fathers" that the move from common ownership to private property was a result of the Fall. As the biblical text puts it, the earth itself was cursed after the act of disobedience by the human beings, and the man who is banished from the garden is told: "[I]n toil you shall eat of it all the days of your life ... By the sweat of your brow you shall eat bread."[9] The account is one of rupture and break, which Grotius counters with an alternative narrative of gradual evolution: "It is evident, however, that the present-day concept of distinctions in ownership was the result, not of any sudden transition, but of a gradual process whose initial steps were taken under the guidance of nature herself."[10]

The key to this gradual transition is use. Once a person uses something, it becomes private property: "[S]ome things ... are consumed by use, either in the sense that they are converted into the very substance of the user and therefore admit of no further use, or else in the sense that they are rendered less fit for additional service by the fact that they have once been made to serve."[11] Grotius's primary example is food – exactly the same as in the biblical text. If we eat and swallow some food, it becomes part of our bodies and cannot belong to another. He describes food and drink as "first class" articles, but now he makes a crucial move to "second class" objects, immovables such as fields and orchards, for these are necessary for the production of food and clothing and thus become private property as well. In light of all this, Grotius defines private property as that which "belongs to a given individual in such a way as to be incapable of belonging to any other individual."[12]

I am less interested here in the obvious criticism that may be leveled against this argument: its Eurocentrism; the dubious deployment of "use"; the ignoring of the history of private property from the ancient Roman definition in the

8 Grotius, *Commentary on the Law*, 316–17.

9 Gen. 3:17, 19.

10 Grotius, *Commentary on the Law*, 317.

11 Grotius, *Commentary on the Law*, 317. Elsewhere, Grotius deploys the theme of the fortuitous Fall, which was necessary not merely for the history of salvation but also for the development of knowledge and the arts. However, this means that he must displace the rupture moment of the Fall to later points in the biblical narrative, especially Cain and Abel, the Flood, and Babel. Grotius, *Rights of War*, II.2.2.

12 Grotius, *Commentary on the Law*, 317.

context of slavery; and the initial framework for a new myth of capitalism, one that would be developed further by subsequent thinkers (from John Locke to Adam Smith).[13] Instead, my concern is how this novel approach relates to the seas. In this case, the issue concerns occupation (*occupatio*) and seizure (*apprehensio*). How do these acts – constitutive of private property based on the defining role of use – relate to movable and immovable items? For movables, an actual act of seizure is more straightforward (for which purpose law comes into play), but for immovables it requires "some activity involving construction or the definition of boundaries."[14] It may be a building, boundary posts, working the land to a certain limit, or indeed the mutual agreement among states for defined borders with their obligatory checkpoints. We can already see how this approach will enable him to suggest that with the oceans it is somewhat difficult to provide evidence of having constructed anything or having imposed clear boundaries – beyond wharves and ports on the shoreline.[15]

With this in mind, Grotius produces a distinction between three types of property: public property, which is "owned by the people"; private property, which belongs to individuals; and "lands that did not fall into the possession of any nation in the process of apportionment, are called by Thucydides *aoriston*, that is to say, 'undefined' regions, marked by no fixed limits."[16] If we assume all of his previous points – and it is a big "if" – then we come to this point. Even in the long process of human appropriation, use, seizure, and law, some areas of the world have not been occupied or apportioned, simply because it is impossible to do so. They are "undefined" and without limitation. Do they remain part of the communal property, everyone's property, which he assumes was the primal and indeed paradisal state?

> From the foregoing discussion, two inferences may be drawn. The first runs as follows: those things which are incapable of being occupied, or which never have been occupied, cannot be the private property of any owner, since all property has its origin as such in occupancy. The second inference may be stated thus: all those things which have been so constituted by nature that, even when used by a specific individual, they nevertheless suffice for general

[13] This is indeed the concern of *Idols of Nations*. Roland Boer and Christina Petterson, *Idols of Nations: Biblical Myth at the Origins of Capitalism* (Philadelphia: Augsburg Fortress Publishers, 2014). The primary research for the current chapter was undertaken as background to this former work. I would like to thank Christina Petterson for her joint work on the earlier project and for permission to make use of that material here.

[14] Grotius, *Commentary on the Law*, 319.

[15] It is worth noting that this is precisely what China has done on some islands in the South China Sea, while Vietnam and the Philippines have constructions on some of the other islands.

[16] Grotius, *Commentary on the Law*, 319–20.

> use by other persons without discrimination, retain today and should retain for all time that status which characterized them when first they sprang from nature.[17]

The first part of the quotation follows from his earlier argument: what cannot or has not been occupied is not the private property of anyone. Note carefully what he has done: the state that springs from nature is not the property of everyone, not "the common," but instead it "cannot be the private property of any owner." Now it is nobody's property. No one owns it, which for Grotius also means that no one is excluded – since private property means the use which one person has to the exclusion of all others.[18] The conclusion should by now be clear: wastelands and wilds, the air, and the seas and oceans are precisely those areas of the world that have not or cannot be seized and claimed.[19] Anyone may make a passage through, on foot, on ship, or – for the future – in flying machines.

We have not yet addressed the second point in the quotation: although someone may pass through such an area, to the point of using it for one or another purpose (recall that use is a defining feature of property), the nature of the area in question precludes any claim to ownership. Such usage does not entail a claim to property, which leaves the area free for others to use as well. Thus, sailing across a sea or ocean does not entitle anyone to assert that the body of water in question has become public or private property. No matter whether a former pope had divided the world's oceans between Spain and Portugal, no matter whether the Portuguese assumed that the seas they sailed were theirs by right of primary passage: these decisions and claims were, for Grotius, not merely arbitrary but also spurious. The Dutch too, especially captains of VOC ships, were perfectly entitled to sail those seas.

7.2 THE FREE-WILLING INDIVIDUAL

The second plank of Grotius's argument is perhaps even more theological and biblical[20] for it deals directly with the question of human nature through the Fall (with an eye on the actions of our Captain Heemskerck). In a Dutch

17 Grotius, *Commentary on the Law*, 320–1.

18 Schermaier, "Res Communes Omnium," 35.

19 See also Grotius, *Rights of War*, II.2.3, II.3.8 18.

20 The deeply theological nature of Grotius's thought is emphasized by a number of scholars. A. H. Haentjes, *Hugo de Groot als godsdienstig Denker* (Amsterdam: Ploegsma, 1946); Henk J. M. Nellen and Edwin Rabbie, eds., *Hugo Grotius, Theologian: Essays in Honour of G.H.M. Posthumus Meyjes* (Leiden: Brill, 1994).

theological context, Grotius's preferences fell clearly on the Remonstrant (or Arminian) side, which gave relatively more scope to free will in fallen human nature than the more orthodox Calvinists. To put it this way risks simplifying what was an extraordinarily complex debate, in which – to add to the complexity – class lines added a whole new dimension. I will come back to the question of class later; for now, a brief summary of Jacobus Arminius's (1560–1609) approach to these questions is needed.[21]

Like Jean Calvin, Arminius argued that we are all depraved and corrupted through the Fall, but he also argued that prevenient grace (the preparatory work of the Holy Spirit) enables the removal of our first sin's guilt and thereby the possibility of actually responding through our own effort to the call of grace. By contrast, Calvin held that since we are unable to do anything remotely good through our own efforts, prevenient grace simple means that our response to God's call can only be God's own work through the Holy Spirit. In response, Arminius was careful indeed, feeling that he differed relatively little from Calvin. Thus, he argues that "we always and on all occasions make this grace to precede, to accompany and follow; and without which, we constantly assert, no good action whatever can be produced by man." He went so far as to argue that the power of free will could not be imagined "without the help of Divine Grace both infused and assisting."[22] The distinctions may seem extremely fine, but the crucial words here are "infused" and "assisting." Through infusing us with the Holy Spirit, God does not act through us but *assists* us. We too have a role to play, through the free will granted to us. The implications are far-reaching: grace is not irresistible but resistible; grace may be accepted or rejected; accepting the call of grace enables one to become part of the elect, but rejecting it means that one's election is annulled.[23]

What does Grotius make of these positions? Let us focus on three items that are relevant for the question of international law in relation to seas and oceans.

[21] Arminius (Harmenzoon) was erstwhile minister in an Amsterdam church and subsequently professor of theology at the University of Leiden (1603–9). Soon after his death, a number of followers published the "five articles of Remonstrance," from which the proper name of the movement arose.

[22] Jacobus Arminius, *The Complete Works of James Arminius* (Grand Rapids, MI: Baker Book House, 1956 [1853]), II, 19.

[23] Again, matters are subtler than they first appear. For Arminius, predestination means: "God decreed to save and damn certain particular persons. This decree has its foundation in the foreknowledge of God, by which he knew from all eternity those individuals who *would*, through his preventing [prevenient] grace, believe, and, through his subsequent grace *would* persevere by which foreknowledge, he likewise knew those who *would not believe and persevere*." Arminius, *Complete Works*, I: 248.

The first question concerns the origins of evil. Grotius followed Arminius in refusing to attribute (even implicitly) evil to God. The initial objection was to Calvin's strong doctrine of predestination. If one assents to this doctrine, they argued, God not only becomes a monstrous tyrant in condemning some to hell, with no possibility of redemption, but also a source of evil if human beings have no free will. If we are unable to choose between good and evil, if all our acts are inherently evil, then – they argued – God must be the source of evil.

This approach leads Grotius into further problems concerning the nature of evil. In short, evil is a "defect," an absence of good, a negative. It does not have a real existence.[24] By contrast, God is the creator of "all such things as have a real existence."[25] The problem here is that he is developing what may be called a weak doctrine of evil, for it struggles to account for sheer pervasiveness of evil in the world. To deal with this problem, Grotius makes a number of moves. To begin with, God provides ample promises, laws, warnings, and threats, which are reinforced with punishment or reward after death.[26] Further, God has given states the role of keeping social order so as to prevent the spread of evil acts. And – in line with his Arminian position – he argues that the knowledge of God's law was not completely extinguished even for those who have never heard of the Christian religion or refuse to believe in it. On this matter, he distinguishes between the specific law for ancient Israel, given to Moses, and the universal law first given at creation, then to Noah, and finally through Jesus Christ. The latter can be known in and of itself by all peoples.[27] At this point, Grotius's effort to develop a theory of natural law emerges, a law that is indeed known by all, irrespective of religious conviction or none. Indeed, "[t]he Law of Nature is so unalterable, that God himself cannot change it."[28]

Options for the cause of the Fall have been limited to the exercise of free will by human beings. The various texts of the Bible offer three distinct possibilities: that evil is the result of actions by an evil being, who became

24 Hugo Grotius, *The Truth of the Christian Religion*, trans. John Clarke (Indianapolis: Liberty Fund, 2012 [1627]), 1.9.

25 Grotius, *Christian Religion*, 1.8.

26 Grotius, *Christian Religion*, 1.19–25.

27 Christoph A. Stumpf, *The Grotian Theology of International Law: Hugo Grotius and the Moral Foundations of International Relations* (Berlin: Walter de Gruyter, 2006), 71–100; Matthijs De Blois, "Blessed [Are] the Peacemakers … Grotius on the Just War and Christian Pacifism," *Grotiana* 32, no. 1 (2011): 20–39, at 23–4.

28 Grotius, *Rights of War*, I.1.10. It is beyond my remit here to tackle the question of natural law in Grotius's thought. Stephen Buckle, *Natural Law and the Theory of Property: Grotius to Hume* (Oxford: Clarendon Press, 1991); Blois, "Blessed [Are] the Peacemakers …."

personified as the Devil or Satan by the New Testament (the appearance in the Hebrew Bible's book of Job of a "*satan*" refers to a quasi-legal "adversary"); that God is responsible for both good and evil, whether plagues, famine, or even – in Ezekiel – laws that could only lead to evil; that free-willing individuals are able to choose to do evil. Only the third option is available for Grotius in light of the larger theological framework of his thought. But he is careful: free will is inherently good, since it is bequeathed to human beings by God. But when human beings exercise this free will, the result may not quite be what was expected: "Liberty of acting is not in itself evil, but may be the cause of something that is evil."[29] This position has, of course, a long history in Christian theology, articulated clearly by Pelagius in his struggles with Augustine,[30] let alone Desiderius Erasmus in his debates with Martin Luther many centuries later.[31] Indeed, Grotius's (and Arminius') emphasis on free will also has many affinities with the theological humanism of Erasmus of Rotterdam.[32]

The free-willing individual was only one dimension of human nature emphasized by Grotius. To it he adds reason, which is – he argues – a gift that resembles God's own rational faculties. This emphasis on the reasoning and logically inclined individual not only reflects his training as a lawyer and love of legal argumentation but would also set in train a crucial development that would end with the mythical creature known later as *home oeconomicus* (so beloved of the myth-makers of a capitalist market economy).

In two important sections of *De jure Praedae* and *De jure Belli*, he notes a tension in human nature: on the one hand, human beings pursue a self-love that seeks good for oneself; on the other, human beings also have "an exquisite desire of society."[33] While Grotius tends to see the former as the more dominant, to the point at which human beings opt to become part of a society due to self-interest,[34] the crucial point for my purposes is that both forces are driven not by animal passions but by the

29 Grotius, *Christian Religion*, 1.8.

30 Pelagius, *Pelagius' Commentary on St Paul's Epistle to the Romans*, trans. Theodore De Bruyn (Oxford: Clarendon Press, 1993); Brinley Roderick Rees, *Pelagius: Life and Letters* (Martlesham: Boydell Press, 1998).

31 Martin Luther and Desiderius Erasmus, *Luther and Erasmus: On the Bondage of the Will and on the Freedom of the Will*, ed. E. G. Rupp and P. S. Watson (London: SCM 1969).

32 Johannes Trapman, "Grotius and Erasmus," in *Hugo Grotius, Theologian: Essays in Honour of G.H.M. Posthumus Meyjes*, ed. Henk J. M. Nellen and Edwin Rabbie (Leiden: Brill, 1994), 77–98.

33 Grotius, *Rights of War*, I.Prol.7.

34 Grotius, *Rights of War*, I.Prol.17.

"sovereign attribute of reason."[35] This divinely implanted faculty may be overshadowed by vice and sin, but these failings cannot extinguish the "divine light" of reason.[36] The reason – to recall an earlier point – is the working of prevenient grace.

The outcome of linking free will with reason, both divinely given and not completely effaced by the Fall, is an individual of significant power. It is not merely the case that "God made man a free agent, and at liberty to do ill or well,"[37] but even more that "[a]bsolute power every man has over his own actions."[38] Or, as *De jure Praedae* puts it in more detail:

> God created man αὐτεξούσιον, "free and *sui iuris*," so that the actions of each individual and the use of his possessions were made subject not to another's will but to his own. Moreover, this view is sanctioned by the common consent of all nations. For what is that well-known concept, "natural liberty," other than the power of the individual to act in accordance with his own will? And liberty in regard to actions is equivalent to ownership in regard to property. Hence the saying: "every man is the governor and arbiter of affairs relative to his own property."[39]

Thus, Captain Heemskerck had acted – according to Grotius – not on behalf of a sovereign power or even a growing company but as a free-willing and rational individual, able to discern and act according to the mandates of good and evil. The Portuguese had acted on the same premises, except that they had erred and deserved to be punished by Heemskerck. Evil deeds must be punished and good deeds rewarded.[40] This reality is not merely the preserve of states and their judiciaries, for it also applies to individuals outside the scope of aforesaid states – especially on the high seas that remain nobody's property.

7.3 ALL FOR THE VOC?

I have studiously left aside questions of class until this point, for the sake of focusing on the development of Grotius's ideas in response to a particular situation, if not a specific event itself. From this context, Grotius developed the first real outlines – inspired by theology – of what would become known as modern "international law," initially with regard to the majority of the earth's

35 Grotius, *Commentary on the Law*, 24.
36 Grotius, *Commentary on the Law*, 25.
37 Grotius, *Christian Religion*, 1.19.
38 Grotius, *Christian Religion*, 1.24.
39 Grotius, *Commentary on the Law*, 33–4; see also Grotius, *Rights of War*, I.3.8.
40 Grotius, *Commentary on the Law*, 29–30.

surface (seas and oceans) but with wider implications.[41] This claim to universality raises the philosophical question to which I return at the close: is it a genuine, false, or "rooted" universal?

Before I come to that point, let me say more about the class location in which Grotius was at home, along with most of the Remonstrants whose theology he championed. His family was among the regents of the town of Delft, a status that gave him access to the best humanist education that was available. He studied rhetoric and the classical texts of Greece and Rome, took on a Latinized form of his name, and conversed in Latin with his fellow humanists. This class location was less due to a faded aristocratic lineage than to the familial oligarchy that rose to power in the first commercial empire of the capitalist market economy.[42] The Dutch commercial families did so initially through taking over the Baltic trade and then through the more well-known VOC. Here indeed was the first global company, enmeshed with the ruling class and the newly independent state, which had itself shaken off Spanish colonial dominance not so long before. Internally, the small territory of the Netherlands had transformed itself through intensive farming methods and new manufacturing methods, so that it could buy raw materials from elsewhere, produce goods, and sell them in the same place from which it had obtained the raw materials at a far lower price. As for the VOC, it was the outcome of merging a number of smaller companies in 1602, with the result that in its first year, the VOC produced more revenue than the English government as a whole. The De Groots were company shareholders and male members of the family sat on the board of the Delft "chamber." In this light, it should be no surprise that most of Grotius's work as a lawyer and scholar was at the service of the VOC, often stimulated by new questions that arose. The best example is, of course, *Commentary on the Law of Prize and Booty*, or *De jure Praedae*.[43]

Therefore, the question arises as to what type of human being is designated by the free-willing and rational individual, able both to make mistakes but also to act for the good on his own initiative. I have used the masculine pronoun deliberately, for Grotius makes it clear that he speaks of "men of good

41 Stumpf, *Grotian Theology*; Benedict Kingsbury and Benjamin Straumann, "The State of Nature and Commercial Sociability in Early Modern International Legal Thought," *Grotiana* 31, no. 1 (2010): 22–43.

42 Immanuel Wallerstein, *The Modern World-System I: Capitalist Agriculture and the Origins of the European World-Economy in the Sixteenth Century* (Berkeley: University of California Press, 2011 [1974]).

43 Martine Julia van Ittersum, *Profit and Principle: Hugo Grotius, Natural Rights Theories and the Rise of Dutch Power in the East Indies 1595–1615* (Leiden: Brill, 2006).

judgment, and of no small learning."[44] Clearly, men with such abilities come from the same commercial ruling-class background as Grotius, with access to all of the privileges available to a family with members on the board of the VOC. This means that the human nature he seeks, the individual human being who has free will and reason, is a rather restricted category: it applies to the ideal man of his own class.

With these points in mind, I would like to close with the philosophical question of universals, which underlies the very notion of the international law to which Grotius was an early and significant contributor. He developed his positions in a very specific situation: a commercial ruling class with extensive privileges; Dutch imperialist and colonial claims; an international company bent on profit; and, indeed, a very European project, not merely in terms of political and economic aspirations but also in terms of the theological and biblical tenor of his thought. How is it possible that a universal principle may arise from such specificity? Is it a real universal that rises above its particular location so as to be applicable to all situations, irrespective of their different histories, cultures, political formations, and philosophies? The common assumption that this is so should give rise to a healthy dose of ideological suspicion. In this case, the old question of *cui bono* – for whose benefit – needs to be asked. Clearly, the benefit in this case was for the Dutch, the VOC, their militantly commercial interests, as well as later European colonialism. A similar suspicion should apply to "freedom of navigation" claims today, whether in the South China Sea or elsewhere.

However, this suspicion may lead to the position that Grotius's arguments constitute a false universal: the claim to universality is based on a dubious particular, so much so that the claim itself seeks to advance that particular interest. It is also a universal by exclusion, or a zero-sum assumption. In other words, if you agree to my universal, then you can be part of it; if not, you are excluded. The history of Christian factional struggles is an excellent case in point. Perhaps the answer can be found in another dimension of Grotius's thought, namely, his very liberal version of tolerance and understanding, seeking common ground rather than fostering division and conflict. For example, he observes that, like the early Christians, "there was no one sect that had discovered all truth, nor any but what held something that was true."[45] Another example is the whole project embodied in *The Truth of the Christian Religion*, where he sought to find common ground based on putting aside factional struggles between Protestants and Roman Catholics. This approach to tolerance

44 Grotius, *Rights of War*, I.Prol.43.
45 Grotius, *Rights of War*, I.Prol.43.

may at first seem like a contradiction with his universal claims based on the specific interests of the VOC, until we recall that liberal tolerance is based on a commercial ruling-class advantage: it is largely for the sake of leaving the current system in place, with men of privilege like him safe and secure.

In contrast with the opposition between real and false universal, I would like to propose a third option, which actually comes out of the complex and long tradition of Chinese approaches to human rights.[46] It concerns what may be called a "rooted" universal. Such a universal arises from a particular situation, but it remains genuine only as long as the context in question is always kept in mind, with its attendant promises and limitations.[47] Further, if rooted universals can arise in one situation, they can also arise in others. Or, further contributions to and emphases of an existing universal may arise in other contexts, thereby enriching the universal in question. And if such "rooted" universals are possible, they also entail that while common ground can be agreed upon by all, the emphases within such a universal vary depending on the context.

Is Grotius's idea of the freedom of the seas, upon which a free-willing and rational individual may act in the name of good, such a rooted universal? Perhaps in this case we need to separate these items from one another, for the deliberations on human nature are too specific to a European theological traditional to make a claim to universal status, no matter how much subsequent thinkers may have tried. But the freedom of the seas is another matter. It may indeed be a rooted universal to which others can contribute, as long as the specific context and interests of its initial articulation, as well as the uses to which it may be put, are always kept in mind and – if necessary – challenged. When naval dominance is couched in such terms, it slips into the category of a false universal. But when an agreement is reached through negotiation and mutual reinforcement, it may well be a rooted universal.

RECOMMENDED READING

Buckle, Stephen. *Natural Law and the Theory of Property: Grotius to Hume*. Oxford: Clarendon Press, 1991.

Grotius, Hugo. *The Truth of the Christian Religion*. Translated by John Clarke. Indianapolis: Liberty Fund, 2012 [1627].

46 Pinghua Sun, *Human Rights Protection System in China* (Heidelberg: Springer, 2014).

47 Thus, "human rights" is a term that arose in a specific European context but can be counted as a genuine universal. However, the limitation is that its European formulation focuses on civil and political rights, whereas its transformation in a Chinese context (for example) contributes to the universal an emphasis on economic and social rights. Indeed, the rights to economic well-being, work, and development become the primary human rights. This focus too is a rooted universal.

Ittersum, Martine Julia van. *Profit and Principle: Hugo Grotius, Natural Rights Theories and the Rise of Dutch Power in the East Indies 1595–1615*. Leiden: Brill, 2006.
Nellen, Henk, and Edwin Rabbie. *Hugo Grotius, Theologian: Essays in Honour of G.H. M. Posthumus Meyjes*. Leiden: Brill, 1994.
Stumpf, Christoph A. *The Grotian Theology of International Law: Hugo Grotius and the Moral Foundations of International Relations*. Berlin: Walter de Gruyter, 2006.
Sun, Pinghua. *Human Rights Protection System in China*. Heidelberg: Springer, 2014.
Wallerstein, Immanuel. *The Modern World-System I: Capitalist Agriculture and the Origins of the European World-Economy in the Sixteenth Century*. Berkeley: University of California Press, 2011 [1974].

8

Ius gentium et naturae: The Human Conscience and Early Modern International Law

Janne E. Nijman

8.1 INTRODUCTION

What to focus on in an intellectual history of *ius gentium et naturae* for a volume on the relations between international law and Christianities? For centuries, (international) law and Christian theology maintained intensive and complex relations, which it is impossible to do justice to within the scope of this chapter.[1] With the more recent "turn to history" in international legal scholarship, discussions of the relationship between *ius gentium et naturae* and Christianity generally center on secularization and/or empire.[2] For obvious reasons both sets of histories deal with early modernity – the time that the so-called *Respublica Christiana* or Holy Roman Empire was profoundly affected by Reformations, gradually fragmented, and religious and theological fights were part of the politics of the newly emerging European nation-states.[3] These states started to maintain relations, wage (religious) wars, compete over overseas trade and occupation, and engage in violent relations with peoples in Africa, Asia and the Americas. Both sets of histories build on the idea that early modern European scholars were looking for a solid and common basis for universal law applicable to relations among sovereigns and peoples from different Christian denominations, as well as among Christian and non-Christian sovereigns and

[1] Cf. Martti Koskenniemi, Mónica García-Salmones Rovira, and Paolo Amorosa, eds., *International Law and Religion: Historical and Contemporary Perspectives* (Oxford: Oxford University Press, 2017).

[2] Cf. Martti Koskenniemi, Walter Rech, and Manuel Jimenez Fonseca, eds., *International Law and Empire: Historical Explorations* (Oxford: Oxford University Press, 2017).

[3] Cf. Sarah Mortimer, "Law, Justice, and Charity in a Divided Christendom: 1500–1625," in *International Law and Religion*, ed. Martti Koskenniemi, Mónica García-Salmones Rovira, and Paolo Amorosa (Oxford: Oxford University Press, 2017), 25–42. Also, Richard Tuck, *The Rights of War and Peace: Political Thought and the International Order from Grotius to Kant* (New York: Oxford University Press, 1999), 28.

peoples. Since international law became defined by (the model of) the "modern state" as developed in Christian Europe, international law's historical narratives have been overwhelmingly Eurocentric.[4] Since this chapter aims to contribute a history of *ius gentium et naturae* in the context of international law and Christianities, it cannot escape the focus on early modern Europe either.

In early modernity, the influence of Christianities on the development of (international) law revolved around the concepts of reason and conscience. Christian natural law theory dominated this (trans)formative era of *ius gentium et naturae*: it was a deeply Christian Europe that rediscovered ancient Roman law (a *ratio scripta*) in the eleventh century. The conceptions of *ius gentium et naturae* which developed in medieval jurisprudence, both civil and canon, were pervaded with Christian theology.[5] Both legal systems, individually and conjoined as *ius commune*, were applied and enforced by secular and ecclesiastical courts (*forum externum*). Reason and human conscience became foundational to moral and legal thought and legal reform: "[i]t was generally believed that human law derived ultimately from, and was to be tested by, reason and conscience."[6] Roman Catholic doctrines of reason and conscience gave way to the medieval conception of (all) law. In the twelfth century, "the canonists and Romanists of western Europe deepened the earlier concepts of reason and equity by adding to them the Judaic and Christian concept of conscience, which they related to mercy and love."[7]

During the Middle Ages, reason and conscience were obvious moral and legal philosophical notions without which law and justice in this world (and "hereafter") were simply impossible. Together, reason and conscience were reforming custom (a predominant source of law) and constitutive of the Christianized Graeco-Roman conception of equity as justice.[8] Conscience of humans *and* communities had to give prevalence to the (Christian) moral

4 See Martti Koskenniemi, "Histories of International Law: Dealing with Eurocentrism," *Rechtsgeschichte* 19 (2011): 152–76; Arnulf Becker Lorca, "Eurocentrism in the History of International Law," *The Oxford Handbook History of International Law*, ed. Bardo Fassbender and Anne Peters (Oxford: Oxford University Press, 2012), 1034.

5 Wim Decock, *Theologians and Contract Law: The Moral Transformation of the Ius Commune (ca. 1500–1650)* (Leiden: Martinus Nijhoff Publishers, 2013); Randall Lesaffer, "Roman Law and the Intellectual History of International Law," in *The Oxford Handbook of the Theory of International Law*, ed. Anne Orford and Florian Hoffmann (Oxford: Oxford University Press, 2016), 50.

6 Harold J. Berman, *Law and Revolution: The Formation of the Western Legal Tradition*, vol. 1 (Cambridge, MA: Harvard University Press, 1983), 12.

7 Berman, *Law and Revolution*, 146, 196: "mercy asserted itself as a principle under the Graeco-Roman name of *aequitas* ('equity')", 253, 518–19.

8 Berman, *Law and Revolution*, 11–12, 111.

principles of natural law at all times. The Protestant Reformations turned against the Roman Catholic Church's rule of conscience. Sixteenth- and seventeenth-century theological, legal and political philosophical debates often came to center on the human conscience and its relationship with reason, law and God. "The seventeenth century can justly be called the Age of Conscience. … For much of the century it was generally believed that conscience, not force of habit or self-interest, was what held together the social and political order."[9]

The present chapter zooms in on the development of "modern" *ius gentium et naturae* amidst this fight over the human conscience and examines how conceptions of human conscience underpinned early modern *ius gentium et naturae* thinking, in particular through the work of Hugo Grotius (1583–1645). Section 8.2 introduces the Thomist conception of conscience as "*forum internum*," which is free to err and thus needs the Church to provide direct guidance and correction. Subsequently, we analyze the role that this judicial conception of conscience plays in the work of Spanish scholastic Francisco de Vitoria when he reconceives *ius gentium et naturae* as a body of law applicable to Christian and non-Christian peoples. *Ius gentium et naturae* is thus born within the Roman Catholic tradition and entangled in the institution of confession – or, as Michel Foucault coined it, in "the power of the pastorate." Section 8.3 then starts by briefly examining how the Reformations spurred a revisit of the relation between conscience and reason, in the sense of natural law. Tables were turned and reason or natural law was argued to be inferior to conscience and faith. The core of Section 8.3, however, discusses how Grotius's conception of the human conscience, which drew on both Thomism and Erasmian humanism, led to a *ius gentium et naturae* disentangled from Roman Catholic moral theology, doctrine and practice. Reason and conscience underpinned a universal law of nature backed up by a decentralized – internal – court system, which was equally operated by Christian, Catholic and Protestant, *Gewissener* and non-Christian sovereigns and peoples alike. Section 8.4 concludes this chapter.

8.2 HUMAN CONSCIENCE IN SPANISH SCHOLASTICS

In the early sixteenth century, moral theologians reworked the concept of *ius gentium et naturae* mostly by engaging with Thomas Aquinas's (c.1225–74) work. Reason and conscience were crucial to this move. In early modern

[9] Keith Thomas, "Cases of Conscience in Seventeenth-Century England," in *Public Duty and Private Conscience in Seventeenth-Century England: Essays Presented to G.E. Aylmer*, ed. John Morrill, Paul Slack, and Daniel Woolf (Oxford: Clarendon Press, 1993), 29.

Christian theology and jurisprudence, conceptions of conscience were at the heart of heated debates on free will, predestination, salvation, redemption and ultimately on the moral quality of the human soul after the Fall from Grace. A full history of the concept of conscience is outside the purpose and scope of this chapter. Here it suffices to point out that the concept of "conscience" was subject to (doctrinal) discussions in Christian theology ever since the writings of Church Fathers such as Jerome, Chrysostom and Augustine, and subsequently was a key concept in the writings of those medieval philosophers who engaged with patristic literature. Yet, only with scholastic theologian Peter Lombard (c.1095–1160) did the human conscience become a "standard topic of later medieval philosophy."[10] Here, I pick up the discussion with Aquinas's conception of conscience as a "court." This section briefly discusses the "court of conscience" conception in Aquinas, Vitoria and Francisco Suarez, and the politics that came with it, before I then turn to Grotius in the remainder of this chapter.

8.2.1 *Thomist Conception of* forum conscientiae *Presided Over by the Church*

Medieval scholastic theology discussed human conscience (*conscientia*) in relation to *synderesis* (the innate principle of reason, which directs humans to do good and avoid evil) and natural law.[11] In the *Summa theologiae*, "Aquinas occasionally replaces the word *synderesis* by the term understanding (*intellectus*), the intellectual virtue of grasping the first principles of reason."[12] Aquinas conceived of *conscientia* as the *act* of *applying* this moral knowledge to a specific case (*ex ante* and *ex post*), for which "one can take counsel."[13] He distinguished between *forum conscientiae* or *internum*, the domain of confession and penance, and *forum externum*, the ecclesiastical and secular courts. The *forum conscientiae* was to apply moral knowledge also when it interacted with the human legal sphere. In *Summa theologiae* I-II q. 96 art. 4 Aquinas asks "whether human law binds a man in the court of conscience."[14] Here, we also find the famous adagium "*lex injusta non est lex*." Human law is binding in

10 Timothy C. Potts, *Conscience in Medieval Philosophy* (Cambridge: Cambridge University Press, 1980), 1–2, 5ff.

11 Potts, *Conscience in Medieval Philosophy*, 10–11.

12 Tobias Hoffmann, "Conscience and Synderesis," *The Oxford Handbook of Aquinas*, ed. Brian Davies and Eleonore Stump (Oxford: Oxford University Press, 2012), 255.

13 Hoffmann, "Conscience and Synderesis," 257; Thomas Aquinas, "*Debated Questions on Truth* (De Veritate) 16–17," in Potts, *Conscience in Medieval Philosophy*, 130–6, at 132.

14 R. W. Dyson, ed., *Aquinas Political Writings* (Cambridge: Cambridge University Press, 2002), 143–5.

the "court of conscience" provided that the human conscience does not judge it unjust. That is, unjust because it is not "directed to the common good" or because "it inflicts unjust harm on its subjects" (the evil that needs to be avoided). One "is not obliged to obey the law in [the latter] cases, if [one] can resist [*resistere*] doing so without scandal or worse harm."[15] Human obedience to authority and law is not unlimited; it involves individual moral judgment.

Aquinas distinguished sharply between temporal and spiritual power, between imperial and papal jurisdiction. Within the confrontation between these powers, Pia Valenzuela argues, Aristotelian conceptions of *ius gentium* served Aquinas to reject the papal theocratic theory of government argued by thirteenth-century canonists.[16] His conception of *ius gentium* as human law emanating from – yet not the same as – natural law supported the legitimacy of the authority and autonomy of temporal or secular government and the declericalization of legal institutions. Secular government, he argued, was instituted by *ius gentium*.[17]

The spiritual jurisdiction of the Church of Rome remained undisputed. Moral theologians, as the Church's experts, gave authoritative interpretations of natural law applicable in the "court of conscience." They educated the clergy on giving guidance to prevent erring of conscience and to relieve the erroneous conscience by the sacrament of confession and penance. Hence, the famous "cases of conscience"[18] literature developed by this practice, which was in turn used to equip the future clergy in their function of confessors. In that role they were the judges of the "court of conscience," the superior in moral judgment. A "culture of counsel of conscience" emerged,[19] in which the individual moral agent examined his or her conscience in confession to then be guided or judged and unburdened by the confessor and the sacrament of penance. The conscience was thus both free and bound. It was free in its judgment, yet bound by natural law and justice interpreted and applied authoritatively by the Church.

15 Dyson, *Aquinas Political Writings* (14), I-II Qu. 96 "On the power of human law," 137–45.

16 Pia Valenzuela, "Between Scylla and Charybdis," in *International Law and Religion*, ed. Martti Koskenniemi, Mónica García-Salmones Rovira, and Paolo Amorosa (Oxford: Oxford University Press, 2017), 43.

17 Valenzuela, "Between Scylla and Charybdis," 51.

18 Grotius refers to this body of literature in both *Mare Liberum* and *DIBP* (*Prolegomena*).

19 Nicole Reinhardt, "How Individual Was Conscience in the Early-Modern Period? Observations on the Development of Catholic Moral Theology," *Religion* 45, no. 3 (2015): 409–28.

8.2.2 *Spanish Scholastics: Moral Theologian Francisco de Vitoria (c.1480–1546)*

For sixteenth-century Roman Catholic scholastics, the conscience was the dominion of God, and the Church provided the judges to exercise jurisdiction in the "court of conscience" and judge whether general natural law principles were applied correctly in a specific case. The moral theologians of the School of Salamanca, so significant and prominent in the history of international law, continued in the Aristotelian-Thomistic tradition well through the European Reformations. Vitoria belonged to the Dominican Order, which was founded in Bologna in 1216 and from there led a revival of Aquinas's moral theology. He was one of the most prominent moral theologians of his time. In his classroom in Salamanca, Vitoria taught the future pastors of the Spanish Crown and royals, the royal ministers and advisors, *Conquistatores*, financiers and merchants, and soldiers, some of whom would also travel to the Americas themselves.

This is the context of what we have come to know as *The First* Relectio *On the Indians Lately Discovered*, which Vitoria gave around 1537–9.[20] He did not hide his task or his troubles:[21] there was no peace of mind – "sovereigns and their advisors could not attain security and certitude of conscience" – regarding the title of Spanish rule in the Americas.[22] In the opening part of this *Relectio*, Vitoria cited from Deuteronomy where the Levitian priests are the experts, the judges, who provide authoritative opinions binding in conscience.[23] Similarly, he argued that whenever in doubt about an action being good or bad, the contemporary experts, "those whom the Church has appointed for that purpose," had to be consulted in and out of confession.[24]

In a preliminary argument, Vitoria argued that in any controversial matter there existed a "duty to consult" the Church's experts and to follow their interpretation of natural law and judgment, which then would provide security in conscience. The conscience of the flock might be mistaken; hence, there was a duty "to follow th[e] [experts'] opinion" in order to avoid sin.[25]

[20] Francisco de Vitoria, *De Indis et De jure belli relectiones*, ed. Ernest Nys, trans. John Pawley Bate (Washington, DC: Carnegie Institution of Washington, 1917), 115–62.

[21] Privately, in a letter to Miguel de Arcos of 8 November 1534, Vitoria wrote: "[N]o business shocks me or embarrasses me more than the corrupt profits and affairs of the Indies."

[22] Vitoria, *De Indis et De jure belli relectiones*, 116, 119.

[23] Vitoria, *De Indis et De jure belli relectiones*, 118.

[24] Vitoria, *De Indis et De jure belli relectiones*, 118.

[25] Vitoria, *De Indis et De jure belli relectiones*, 119.

> For in those matters which belong to his salvation a man is bound to yield credence to the teachers appointed by the Church, and in a doubtful matter their ruling is law. For just as in the contentious forum the judge is bound to judge in accordance with what is alleged and proved, so in *the forum of conscience a man is bound to base his judgment, not on his own sentiments, but on demonstrable reason or on the authority of the wise*; else his judgment is presumptuous and exposes him to the risk of going wrong, and indeed he does err in the very fact.[26]

The rest is history, told by many.[27] Victoria examined divine, natural and human law whereas all law, including civil laws, "bind in the forum of conscience, as St. Thomas teaches (*Prima Secundae*, qu. 96, art. 4)."[28] Ultimately, he had his opinion: there were no legitimate titles in divine law, yet he developed and interpreted natural law and applied it to the case at hand. He recalled Gaius's definition of *ius gentium* – what natural reason established among all nations – and redefined it as *ius gentium et naturae*, applicable to relations between all sovereigns and peoples, Christian and non-Christian.[29] Through this authoritative interpretation of the law of nature and nations, he gave birth to early modern *ius gentium et naturae*.

The Thomist conception of conscience as *forum conscientiae*, presided over by a confessor-judge outside the human person and ruled by natural law authoritatively developed and interpreted by the Church, allowed Vitoria to provide peace of mind to merchant and *conquistador*, king and soldier, all those subjects involved in the Spanish conquest of the Americas.

Later on, with Suarez (1548–1617), such juridification of the human conscience persisted. He contributed to the confessional literature. Handbooks for confessors – the aforementioned "cases of conscience" – became legal treatises in this Catholic tradition. The human conscience or rational soul was subject to natural law and the confessor was to judge within the "court of conscience" whether conscience correctly applied natural law. If a person erred, the

26 Vitoria, *De Indis et De jure belli relectiones*, 117–18.

27 See, e.g., Antony Anghie, "Francisco De Vitoria and the Colonial Origins of International Law," *Social & Legal Studies* 5, no. 3 (1996): 321–36; Martti Koskenniemi, "Vitoria and Us: Thoughts on Critical Histories of International Law," *Rechtsgeschichte* 22 (2014): 119–38.

28 Vitoria, *De Indis et De jure belli relectiones*, 124; see Vitoria's teaching on Aquinas's Summa Theologia I-II Qu 96.4 "What obliges in the court of conscience" as part of his lectures "On Laws," in *Vitoria: Political Writings*, ed. Anthony Pagden and Jeremy Lawrance (Cambridge: Cambridge University Press, 1991), 173–9.

29 Vitoria, *De Indis et De jure belli relectiones*, 151. In line with the Thomist tradition, for Vitoria, natural law knowledge and the faculty to apply it were at work in European as well as non-European peoples since all human beings were *in imagine Dei* – whether they realized it or not. Vitoria teaching on ST I-II Qu 94, in Pagden and Lawrence, "On Laws," 171.

Church's sacraments assisted the flock in relieving the soul and saving it for "eternal life." Suarez, too, was interested in the potential of the conscience for universal law and cites from Paul's letter to the Romans: "The Gentiles, who have not the law, do by nature those things that are of the law ... their conscience bearing witness to them."[30]

8.2.3 *Human Conscience and Confession as a "Technology of the Self"*

Foucault has done brilliant work on the sacraments of confession and penance. In a number of *Lectures at the Collège de France*, he examined the Christian institution of the pastorate and the spiritual direction – "*direction de conscience*" – enforced by the Church of Rome through these sacraments.[31] Vast was the power that came with the complex, mutually dependent spiritual relation between pastor and flock.[32] While Foucault did not deal with Vitoria specifically, the lectures of Salamanca's star-theologian testify to pastoral authority to "prescrib[e] the law," "teac[h] the truth" and give way to the salvation of the individual's soul, and as such what we would call "expert governance" operated on the human conscience. Foucault unraveled how this Christian examination of conscience, and thus of human action evaluated or anticipated in confession, created a "new form of power."[33]

In "Technologies of the Self," Foucault discusses the obligatory practice of confession and penance extensively in the context of what he called "technologies" through which humans produce knowledge (and power/domination).[34] Confession and penance were the practices that reinforced the Christian pastorate and the expert rule by the institutions of the Church of Rome. Through these practices, Foucault argued, the Church was involved in "governmentality" and produced domination. The practice of confession

30 Francisco Suarez, *Selections from Three Works of Francisco Suarez* (Oxford: Clarendon Press; London: Humphrey Milford, 1944), Book II: On the Eternal Law, the Natural Law, and the Ius Gentium, Ch. IX: "Is the Natural Law Binding in Conscience", 223–4.

31 Michel Foucault, *Security, Territory, Population: Lectures at the Collège de France*, 1977–1978, ed. Michel Senellart, François Ewald, and Alessandro Fontana, trans. Graham Burchell (Basingstoke: Palgrave Macmillan, 2009), 163ff.; see also Michel Foucault, *Abnormal: Lectures at the Collège de France* 1974–1975, ed. Graham Burchell (London: Verso 2016), Lecture Seven 19 February 1975.

32 Foucault, *Security, Territory, Population*, 169–77.

33 Foucault, *Security, Territory, Population*, 169–77. See also Reut Yael Paz, "Religion, Secularism and International Law," in *The Oxford Handbook of the Theory of International Law*, ed. Anne Orford and Florian Hoffmann (Oxford: Oxford University Press, 2016), 923–38.

34 Michel Foucault, "Technologies of the Self," in *Technologies of the Self: A Seminar with Michel Foucault*, ed. Luther H. Martin, Huck Gutman, and Patrick H. Hutton (London: Tavistock, 1988), 18.

became one of the issues at stake during the Reformations and a decisive step in the move from medieval to modern legal and political thought.

8.3 HUMAN CONSCIENCE IN GROTIUS'S *IUS GENTIUM ET NATURAE*

8.3.1 *Protestant Reformations and Christian Humanism: Luther and Calvin – Seneca and Erasmus*

Protestant reformers such as Martin Luther (1483–1546) and Jean Calvin (1509–64) turned ardently against involvement of clerical intermediaries in the self-examination of the human soul and against the (abuse of) power and domination that came with the law and institutions governing human conscience.[35] Luther famously burned the manual for confessors, *Summa Angelica* (1486), in 1520 in Wittenberg. He argued that "consciences are bound by the law of God alone," not by the interpretations of natural law given by the clergy ("what is written in Scriptures is plain to all").[36] Postlapsarian human nature had to be guided by God's law and grace otherwise no good could emanate from humans.[37] This affected the relation between reason and conscience: God was the highest authority for the free conscience. Conscience reconceived as "will and intent" then employed reason. The politics of this conception of Christian conscience lies in the "sanctity" it gave to property and contract rights, crucial to mercantile societies.[38]

For Calvin, too, conscience in its morally depraved state had to be guided directly by God's love and grace. Calvin conceived of the liberty of conscience as a "first and most essential right."[39] Jennifer Herdt explains how for Calvin, natural law was "linked emphatically with judicial conscience, and in particular with awareness of divine judgement."[40] Conscience creates a state of

35 Cf. Decock, *Theologians and Contract Law*, 46: on how *ius commune* was diffused into the smallest arteries of societies by confessional practice.

36 Martin Luther, "Bondage of the Free Will," in *Discourse on the Will*, trans. and ed. Ernst Winter (London: Continuum, 2002), 107–9.

37 Janne E. Nijman, "Grotius' *Imago Dei* Anthropology: Grounding *Ius Naturae et Gentium*," in *International Law and Religion*, ed. Martti Koskenniemi, Mónica García-Salmones Rovira, and Paolo Amorosa (Oxford: Oxford University Press, 2017), 87–110.

38 Berman, *Law and Revolution*, 30.

39 John Witte, Jr., *The Reformation of Rights: Law, Religion, and Human Rights in Early Modern Calvinism* (Cambridge: Cambridge University Press, 2007), 2, 45–7. John Witte also shows how therewith Calvin laid the foundation for the development of fundamental rights and freedoms.

40 Jennifer A. Herdt, "Calvin's Legacy for Contemporary Reformed Natural Law," *Scottish Journal of Theology* 67, no. 4 (2014): 414–35, at 419. Cf. Berman, *Law and Revolution*, 529–30, for Aquinas's theology of judgement.

continuous self-judgment as it "brings [humans] before the judgement seat of God." This judicial conception of conscience is entirely *internal*: the human individual's *free* conscience applies natural law in accordance with God's judgment.[41] In other words, the Protestant Reformations impacted the relation among conscience and natural reason and natural law. Not the Church official but individual conscience – being where God resides and speaks to humans – knows, interprets and applies natural law. Calvin had a keen eye for how humans often "blind" themselves to "the deliverances of conscience."[42]

Luther's antagonist, Desiderius Erasmus (c.1469–1536) was a Renaissance humanist who advocated religious toleration. He was educated in the "*devotio moderna*" and lived as an Augustianian monk for a short period of time before he became a freely traveling scholar and European citizen. Erasmus (as well-known, later greatly admired by Grotius) became known for his anti-clericalism, egalitarianism, social reformism and his attack on ecclesiastical corruption – for which he in turn came under attack from the Roman Catholic Church. His writings, as much of the Northern humanist's work, centered on the human conscience in general and the conscience of political leaders in particular.

Here it may be helpful to bring to mind Erasmus's admiration for Seneca's moral integrity and the "holiness of Seneca's teachings."[43] Apart from the Bible and Patristic literature, Erasmus drew on Seneca, other Stoics and Ancient philosophers, for his *philosophia Christi*, which entailed "the restoration of human nature originally well formed."[44] Such "rebirth" required moral instruction and a nurturing of "the love of what is good" innate in humans. To that end, Erasmus – following the Stoics – prescribed the practice of "daily self-examination,"[45] a practice to tell the truth to oneself about oneself to gain self-knowledge and self-mastery.

Erasmus's conception of conscience is less Thomist and more Stoic in nature. He undercut the power of the pastorate in the "court of confession" with emphasis on the discipline of self-examination without too much involvement of clerical intermediaries between the individual and God. Examination *of the self, by the self* could overcome sinful, vicious thoughts and inclinations and liberate right reasoning – that is, reasoning directed at the realization of

[41] Herdt, "Calvin's Legacy," 420.
[42] Herdt, "Calvin's Legacy," 417.
[43] Margo Todd, *Christian Humanism and the Puritan Social Order* (Cambridge: Cambridge University Press, 2002), 27–8.
[44] Todd, *Christian Humanism*, 29.
[45] Todd, *Christian Humanism*, 31.

the common good. The latter, incidentally, was also a precondition for Erasmus's "consensual model of lawful government."[46]

Rather than a courtroom, Erasmus's conception of human conscience thus reflects a classroom – to stay with spatial metaphors. It was first and foremost a space of learning for life on earth, a receptacle of moral instruction set to bring about social reform through moral (self-)reform.

8.3.2 *Grotius's Turn Inwards: The Concept of the* Free *Human Conscience and* forum conscientiae *Guided by* caritas

The Council of Trent (1545–63), the Peace of Augsburg (1555) and the Edict of Nantes (1598) are moments in the history of the Protestant Reformations and Counter-Reformation that testify to the controversies around the liberty of conscience. They were also conceptual and theological drivers of the Dutch Revolt against the Netherlands' Spanish sovereign. The revolting provinces laid down the principle of freedom of conscience in the Union of Utrecht (1579) and then in 1581 in the Act of Abjuration with which they liberated themselves from the allegiances to their sovereign, Philip II.[47]

Grotius, while actively engaged with the legal affairs in and of the Dutch Republic, was also a dedicated theologian. The free conscience was central to Grotius's theological, political and legal thought and to much that he wrote on peace and toleration, as both a practitioner and a scholar.[48]

Grotius can count as an epitome of the transition away from the outside clerical authority to the individual conscience *itself* as interpreter of the (natural) law to be applied by the human *forum conscientiae* pointed to in previous sections. Grotius liberated human conscience (and thus human agency) from the jurisdiction of the Roman Catholic Church. It was a political move of the highest importance for a Protestant member of the governing elite of the revolting Republic. Grotius thus secured a solid basis for *ius gentium et naturae* governing the free conscience of sovereigns.

46 Erasmus, *The Education of a Christian Prince*, ed. Lisa Jardine (Cambridge: Cambridge University Press, 1997), vii.

47 An English translation of the text of the Union of Utrecht is in E. H. Kossman and A. F. Mellink, eds., *Texts Concerning the Revolt of the Netherlands* (Cambridge: Cambridge University Press, 1974), 165–73; article 13 states that "each person shall remain free, especially in his religion, and that no one shall be persecuted or investigated because of their religion."

48 Grotius's draft Amsterdam *Jodenreglement* testifies to the individual freedom of conscience yet also to the limits on the exercise of *public* worship of non-Christian faiths. See Marc de Wilde, "Offering Hospitality to Strangers: Hugo Grotius's Draft Regulations for the Jews," *Tijdschrift voor Rechtsgeschiedenis* 85, no. 3–4 (2017): 391–433.

In *Enlightenment Contested*, Jonathan Israel explains how, in the second half of the seventeenth century, Holland was "identified as a prime sourc[e] of denial of God, flagrantly defying *consensus gentium*."[49] Israel points to an "organized movement" of "atheism" at German universities led by Matthias Knutzen.

> He named his "sect" the *Gewissener* [Conscientiaries] because, he said, there exists no other true God, Religion, or Magistracy than Man's Conscience, the medium by which all men are taught "the three precepts of justice," as Bayle puts it, precisely recording Knutzen's formula as given in his tracts: "to do no injury to anyone, to live honestly and give everyone his due."[50]

More than Knutzen's formula, this formula was of course central to natural law theorists, including Grotius and Gottfried Wilhelm Leibniz,[51] ever since discussed by the Roman lawyer Cicero in *De Officiis*. Earlier in the seventeenth century, Grotius had been accused of deism and Socinianism, and his famous *etiami daremus* disclaimer in *De jure belli ac pacis* (DJBP) had added to the controversies, while it actually seemed to have meant to provide stable ground underlying all theological differences: the universality of a free conscience as inner judge. Neo-Stoic philosopher and Erasmian humanist Justus Lipsius (Joost Lips) (1547–1606), whom Grotius admired, wrote, for example, in his 1598 *Politica*: "[E]ven where there is no religion or fear of the Divine at all, there is still a tiny sprig of conscience, in danger, so to speak, from the bad soil. Conscience, then, is THE SMALL SPARK OR RIGHT REASON LEFT IN MAN, THE JUDGE AND INDICATOR OF GOOD AND EVIL DEEDS."[52]

In *Adamus Exul* (1601), a biblical drama he personally sent to Lipsius,[53] Grotius examines the human conscience of Adam and Eve – and therewith of all humanity – before and after the Fall from Grace. The Thomist distinction between the abstract principles of natural law (*synderesis*) and their

[49] Jonathan I. Israel, *Enlightenment Contested: Philosophy, Modernity, and the Emancipation of Man 1670–1752* (Oxford: Oxford University Press, 2008), 166.

[50] Israel, *Enlightenment Contested*, 166.

[51] Gottfried Wilhelm Leibniz, "Codex Iuris Gentium," in *Leibniz: Political Writings*, 2nd ed., ed. Patrick Riley (Cambridge: Cambridge University Press, 1988), 171–3.

[52] Justus Lipsius, *Politica: Six Books of Politics Or Political Instruction*, ed. and trans. Jan Waszink (Assen: Van Gorcum, 2004), Book I Ch. 5, p. 277. Lipsius provided many citations from the classics on conscience, such as Stobaeus's "A good conscience is always free from fear", Cicero's "Nothing is more blissful than tranquillity of conscience", and Seneca's "A bad conscience ... is distressed and restless even in solitude." The last's more juristic language is there with "Miserable you are, if you ignore this witness!" Whether Grotius drew on these requires more research. (Caps in original.)

[53] Henk J. M. Nellen, *Hugo Grotius: A Lifelong Struggle for Peace in Church and State, 1583–1645* (Leiden: Brill, 2014), 58.

application by conscience (*conscientia*) shines through when the Angel speaks to Adam[54] and when God reveals Himself to be residing "within [Eve's] kindling conscience."[55]

In *Meletius* (1611), the human conscience features within an irenistic argument aimed at bringing peace to both the church and the state, in the Republic and beyond.[56] The argument has often been summed up as "*Necessariis Unitas, in Non Necessariis Libertas, in Utrisque Caritas*" ("unity in necessary things; liberty in uncertain things; charity in all things").[57] It was the same argument of freedom of conscience and the minimalist Christian creed that carried *De Veritate* (1622/47).

Distinguishing between theoretical (doctrines (*decreta*) or principles) and practical (ethical precepts (*praecepta*) or rules),[58] Grotius underscored the importance of the latter, the ethics and political philosophy in *Meletius*. This was also where his interest lay: how to live one's life well and how to develop a good social order.[59] Created *in imagine Dei*, the human is capable of doing "good" and capable of making "an effort" to improve after God's likeness and live in "mutual love and friendship."[60] He or she is sufficiently *un*corrupted to know natural law and apply it, yet corrupted by vice to a degree that conscience may err.[61] This should, however, not lead to too harsh a verdict on humans.[62] Humans can learn and return to virtue and virtuous judgment.[63]

The work that human conscience does in *Meletius* is fourfold. First, it testifies empirically (*ex post*) to humans' innate moral knowledge (natural law) and to humans' free choice as it may act on this knowledge or err (consciously or unconsciously). It testifies to humans as free moral agents, who may then freely become subject to law and authority.[64] "The repeated warnings of each individual conscience" when erring point to human moral

54 Hugo Grotius, "Adamus Exul," in *The Celestial Cycle*, ed. Watson Kirkconnell (Toronto: University of Toronto Press, 1952), 16: "Behold | Thy gifts of conscience, reason, active power | Of self-producing, self-combining all | Innate ideas of intellectual truth, | Intelligible abstract principles, | Illimitably applicable."

55 Grotius, 'Adamus Exul', 50.

56 Hugo Grotius, *Meletius, Sive De Iis quae inter Christianos Conveniunt Epistola*, ed. and trans. G. H. M. Posthumus Meyjes (Leiden: Brill, 1988), 10.47–50; 28.113–15.

57 Cf. Grotius, *Meletius*, 91.

58 Grotius, *Meletius*, 19.1–9.

59 Grotius, *Meletius*, 34–5.

60 Grotius, *Meletius*, 30.

61 Grotius, *Meletius*, 30–6.

62 Grotius, *Meletius*, 34–9, 89–91.

63 Grotius, *Meletius*, 43, 56–7.

64 Grotius, *Meletius*, 10, 35–6.

depravity – with the Fall, "nature became no longer 'mother' but 'step-mother'" – as well as to human "answerab[ility]" for ethical failures.[65]

Second, human conscience thus features as humans' internal self-judge that applies the standards of natural law and justice to the self. It "accuses us more or less severely according to the magnitude of our sins."[66] A bad conscience thus also functions as internal judge and executor of punishment for the self. These self-accusations become harder to live with when the sins become heavier. Grotius referred a few times to the Stoic philosopher of self-control and self-mastery, Seneca, on whom Erasmus also drew. "One of the frailties of the human condition is the obfuscation of the mind, which gives rise not only to inevitable error but even to an attachment to errors."[67] Therefore Seneca propagated rigorous self-examination of the human conscience and self-education. After all, as Grotius cites Seneca again, "[i]f we want to be just judges of everything, we would first convince ourselves that none of us is without guilt."[68] Self-examination had to assist people in taking up "responsib-[ility] for their deeds" and stimulate virtues such as modesty.[69]

Third, conscience plays an important role in Grotius's theory of ethics. It provides ground for four categories of "duties of love": toward (i) God (e.g. prayer), (ii) humanity (e.g. duty of friendship or charity "on the ground of natural kinship in the image of God"), (iii) society or the state (e.g. to be "good citizens" and to subject to governmental authority) and (iv) oneself (e.g. "to preserve as best as he can his own life, safety and health" and thus not to "commit suicide").[70] As the bottom-line, Grotius understood "that brief and famous rule, highly recommended by the emperor Hadrian: 'Do not do unto someone else what you do not want done to yourself.'"[71] Grotius harped on the natural duty of all humans to care for their neighbor (*caritas*) and take their interests into account.[72] Throughout *Meletius*, Grotius's Christian-humanist conception of human conscience conjoins "knowing" and "caring." Human conscience is the best counselor of justice; it applies natural law and justice to specific cases, including the duties of love (duties required by assignative justice).

65 Grotius, *Meletius*, 36.
66 Grotius, *Meletius*, 37.
67 Grotius, *Meletius*, 39.
68 Grotius, *Meletius*, 41.
69 Grotius, *Meletius*, 41–3. Here, the examination of the self takes the form of the duty to prayer and is conjoined with the "certain[ty] of foregiveness". Cf. Foucault's "Technology of the Self," 2.3.
70 Grotius, *Meletius*, ch. IV.
71 Grotius, *Meletius*, 68.
72 Grotius, *Meletius*, 82, 77–87.

Finally, conscience enables humanity to agree, to *consensus gentium*: "[as] ethical precepts are mostly plainer and less complicated, it stands to reason that most people readily agree on precepts."[73] Practical reason and virtuous judgment prevail over theoretical doctrines. Grotius's theory of natural religion and free conscience blends perfectly with his theory of natural law.

8.3.3 *The Human Conscience in Grotius's Thought on* ius gentium et naturae

Grotius was well aware of the "court of conscience" tradition within the Church of Rome – in particular, the handbooks of its moral theologians (Vitoria and Suarez) and the "cases of conscience."[74] An Arminian Protestant, he broke with the confessional court version of the "court of conscience" and reconceived *conscientia* as itself the *internal* judge and punisher of the self (these responsibilities were not executed by the confessor). Grotius thus disentangled universal natural law – *ius gentium et naturae* – from the spiritual jurisdiction of the Roman Catholic Church. If human conscience errs, punishment consists in internal turmoil over the violation of one's obligations. In the internal court, natural law and justice, that is, expletive (strict) and attributive (distributive) justice, applied.[75] As such, the human conscience came to underpin an international order in which *ius gentium et naturae* was backed up by punishment – and, thus, true law – and in which both strict justice (perfect rights and duties) and distributive justice (duties of love) applied. The latter requires virtuous or "well-tempered judgment" of all sovereigns.[76]

8.3.3.1 Mare Liberum

In *Mare Liberum*, *conscientia* features as a court. Grotius appealed directly to the "upright conscience and fidelity" of "the Rulers and Free Nations of the Christian World."[77] Right at the beginning, Grotius makes clear what is at stake: who determines right and wrong? The rich and powerful would suggest,

73 Grotius, *Meletius*, 89.

74 See, e.g., *Mare Liberum*, ch. 13, and *De Jure Belli ac Pacis, Prolegomena*, 36, Hugo Grotius, *De Jure Belli ac Pacis Libri Tres* (1646 edition), *The Classics of International Law*, ed. James Brown Scott, trans. Francis Kelsey (Oxford: Oxford Clarendon Press, 1925), hereinafter *DJBP*, where he shows to be well aware of the subject matters discussed: promises, oaths, reprisals, warfare and so on. Also, Grotius refers to the "courts of conscience" in Book II Ch. X: "internum animi tribunal".

75 Hugo Grotius, *Mare Liberum 1609–2009*, ed. Robert Feenstra (Leiden: Brill, 2009), Book I.I. VIII, at 36.

76 Grotius, *DJBP*, *Prolegomena*, 9.

77 Grotius, *Mare Liberum*, 5.

Grotius argues, "that justice and injustice are distinguished . . . merely by the opinion and custom of mankind."[78] This is "absurd and unnatural" to Grotius. Clearly it would put the normative standard too low. Law is more than social facts; it is more than what in DJBP Grotius called "might makes right."[79] If, however, it is not the rich and the powerful who determine what law and justice entail, who does? What is the independent source of law and authority? Grotius builds his argument through the theological language of God as father of the "one [human] race" and where this one humanity is governed by laws "written in the minds and on the hearts of every individual, where even the unwilling and the refractory must read them."[80] Natural law is known to humans and conscience testifies to this knowledge and applies it.

Grotius repeated later in his "Defence of Chapter V of *Mare Liberum*": the human conscience "bear[s] witness to" the law of nations written in the kings' hearts.[81] Without a doubt, Grotius argued, *ius gentium et naturae* then is binding upon kings like decrees are binding upon "the common people."[82] So, when Grotius asked rhetorically what Christian kings and nations ought to think and do, he presented the principles of natural law as "necessary to uphold the social structure of the whole human race and to maintain harmony thereof."[83] How then was this natural law of nations enforced? God, "the king of the universe," would give "the final punishment," yet, until then,

> he delegates to intervene in human affairs two judges whom the luckiest of sinners does not escape, namely, every man's own conscience and his fame (or other men's estimation). These two tribunals are open to those who are debarred from all others; to these the powerless appeal; in them are defeated those who are wont to win by might . . . .[84]

Conscientia as court and judge then is equivalent to what king and magistrate are to their subjects: judge and law enforcer. For kings upon whom *ius gentium et naturae* is binding, the human conscience fulfills the judiciary function, the *forum internum*, where *forum externum* is absent. *Conscientia* is the inescapable tribunal of sovereigns, the seat of judgment that stands open to those to whom other tribunals are debarred. And so, Grotius brought the natural law claim of the free sea against the Portuguese, not to the clergy

78 Grotius, *Mare Liberum*, 5.
79 Grotius, *DJBP*, *Prolegomena*, 3.
80 Grotius, *Mare Liberum*, 8–9.
81 Grotius, *Mare Liberum*, Ch. 13.
82 Grotius, *Mare Liberum*, 9.
83 Grotius, *Mare Liberum*, 11.
84 Grotius, *Mare Liberum*, 13.

and the moral theologians of the Church of Rome[85] but to the court of conscience within every Christian king, Catholic or Protestant. These *fora interna* were to interpret the principles of natural law and apply them to the case at hand, to prove the claim right.

It is important to mention here that *Mare Liberum* was originally written as a chapter of *De Iure Praedae*, an extensive opinion on the seizure of the Santa Catarina together with an extravagant prize by the Dutch East India Company (VOC). Some of the shareholders had a "*crise de conscience*" over the affair, but, as Martine van Ittersum points out, Grotius did not side with them; he supported the VOC.[86]

8.3.3.2 De jure belli ac pacis (DJBP)

The dedication of DJBP also explicitly addresses the free conscience of the respective sovereigns of Europe. In DJBP, Grotius argues that the natural law of nations exists and is binding upon sovereigns and nations. Engaging with natural law and justice in their conscience would tell these sovereigns that much of the warfare in which they were involved was in violation of this body of norms. In DJBP, the free human conscience provides ground to three important political moves.

First, the concept of human conscience enabled Grotius to establish a universal natural law applicable upon disputes within Christianity and between Christian and non-Christian peoples and sovereigns. Second, the free human conscience provided *ius gentium et naturae* with a decentralized system of law interpretation, application and enforcement in the *forum internum*, this being crucial for his answer to contemporary skepticism about natural law and justice as applicable to sovereigns and their nations. Third, the judge in the court of conscience was to apply natural law springing from both commutative and distributive justice. The latter was thus kept within the *ius gentium et naturae*.

As to the first point, Grotius articulated a rationalist take on natural law: humans have "been endowed with the faculty of knowing and of acting in accordance with general principles [of natural law]."[87] The human faculties of reason, free will and

85 Grotius, *Mare Liberum*, opening of ch. 12 – Grotius referred to them and the fact that their "reasons" cannot "pacify the conscience".

86 See on the "Fruin Thesis", which speculates about the "pangs of conscience" of VOC shareholders, Martine Julia van Ittersum, *Profit and Principle: Hugo Grotius, Natural Rights Theories and the Rise of Dutch Power in the East Indies* 1595–1615 (Leiden: Brill, 2006), ch. 3, 113. See also Chapter 7 in this volume.

87 Grotius, *DJBP, Prolegomena*, 7.

sociability (*appetitus societatis*)[88] ensure that natural law is knowable and applicable to a situation at hand. Human nature itself then is the source of *ius gentium et naturae* – "the source of law properly so called."[89] Human intelligence and sociability enable humans to exercise "well-tempered judgment." This exercise of judgment – that is, the application of *ius gentium et naturae* – then takes place *in foro interno* and may lead to right action.[90]

In DJBP Book I.I., Grotius famously continues: "The law of nature is a dictate of right reason" and he refers to Philo and John Chrysostom to foreground reason and conscience.[91] It goes to show how natural law is not dependent on revealed religion and law (e.g. divine law) yet is universally knowable and binding upon every human individual: "When Gentiles that have not the [divine] law do by nature . . . the things of the law, these, not having the law, are the law unto themselves, in that they show the work of the law written in their hearts, their conscience bearing witness therewith, and their thoughts one with another accusing or else excusing them."[92] Or, from Chrysostom: "In place of the law conscience and the use of reason suffice."[93] In other words, *ius gentium et naturae* is known by every ruler and can be applied directly and freely in their *forum conscientiae*. Here, too, *conscientia* bears witness to the existence of (universal) natural law, binding upon the sovereigns of all peoples.

Having the sources of *ius gentium et naturae* in place, Grotius addresses another skeptic argument, that law is only law if it is effective and backed up by force. In *Prolegomena* 19–20, Grotius argues that law is also law without an external court system to impose sanctions:

> Nevertheless law, even though without a sanction, is not entirely void of effect. For justice brings peace of conscience [*conscientia*], while injustice causes torments and anguish, such as Plato describes, in the breast of tyrants. Justice is approved, and injustice condemned, by the common agreement of good men. But, most important of all, in God injustice finds an enemy, justice a protector. He reserves His judgements for the life after this, yet in such a way that He often causes their effects to become manifest even in this life, as history teaches by numerous examples.[94]

As in *Mare Liberum*, *conscientia* here fulfills the court function and punishes the self. Violation of natural law and justice explicitly sanctions the

88 Grotius, *DJBP*, *Prolegomena*, 6.
89 Grotius, *DJBP*, *Prolegomena*, 8 (fn omitted).
90 Grotius, *DJBP*, *Prolegomena*, 9.
91 Grotius, *DJBP*, Book I Ch. 1.10, p. 38.
92 Grotius, *DJBP*, Book I Ch. 1.16, p. 47.
93 Grotius, *DJBP*, Book I Ch. 1.16, p. 47.
94 Grotius, *Prolegomena*, 20.

punishment of a tormenting conscience terrorizing the self. In other words, in the absence of an external court system such as in a domestic legal order, *ius gentium et naturae* had in fact a *forum internum* to rely on. It was backed up by a decentralized network of "courts of conscience" capable of punishment.[95]

At the end of the final chapter of DJBP Book III, we find a variation of what Grotius wrote in the Dedication of *Mare Liberum* on the two tribunals for sovereigns: "the duty of kings to cherish good faith scrupulously, first for conscience's sake and then also for the sake of the reputation by which the authority of the royal power is supported."[96] Also, in the previous quote from Book I.I.16, the human conscience features as the internal judge who accuses and excuses the self of violating natural law.[97] While the law that is to be applied by *conscientia* is universal, Grotius expects more from the individual free conscience that maintains an immediate relationship with God.[98] In Book III, ch. xxv, Grotius indicates that without faith the human conscience derails (more easily) and sovereigns become "like wild beasts." For "the sake of [a well-functioning] Conscience" (*conscientia*) and a good reputation, "on which depends the Authority of their Government," the sovereign's practice of faith is crucial. This is especially true in situations of military conflict; when in war, this "quiet [as in good] Conscience" can only exist if "we aim at Peace in every Thing we do throughout the whole Course of war."[99] An immediate conversation with God in prayer facilitates the sovereign soul scrutinizing itself in anticipation of God's judgment and thus, in any situation, allows for a well-tempered – peace-oriented – judgment in this life.

Grotius also conceived of *conscientia* as a corrective authority when there is any lack of clarity about law and justice in a strict sense.[100] Judgment gives direction to human action *ex ante*. If this guidance is taken lightly or ignored, humans "degenerate and become brutish."[101] The human conscience thus functions to ensure that natural law and justice – including both strict and

95 Through the text, we find such references to the punishment of a bad conscience tormenting the sovereign who violates *ius gentium et naturae*.
96 Grotius, *DJBP*, Book III.xxv.i, 860–1.
97 Grotius, *DJBP*, Book I Ch. 1.16, p. 47.
98 "Conscience itself, which, properly speaking, is under the Dominion of God only." Grotius, *DJBP*, Book I Ch. II. 7.2, ed. 1632, Liberty translation (Hugo Grotius, *The Rights of War and Peace*, ed. Richard Tuck, trans. John Clarke (Indianapolis: Liberty Fund, 2005[1625])), p. 200; the explicit mentioning of conscience is absent in the Kelsey translation. See also Book III.
99 Grotius, *DJBP*, Liberty translation, Book III, 1639.
100 In Book II Ch. XXIII.II on the "Dubious causes of war": "*Nihil faciendum contra animi dictamen quamvis errans.*" Hugo de Groot, *De iure belli ac pacis*, ed. B. J. A. de Kanter-van Hettinga Tromp (Leiden: Brill, 1939), 566.
101 Grotius, *DJBP*, Liberty translation, 1116.

distributive justice – find implementation and application in relations among sovereigns. Distributive justice or virtue (e.g. moderation) should assist in the application of strict justice. For example, earlier in Book III.II, one of the chapters on "moderation," that is, the chapter on "Moderation Concerning the Right of Killing Men in a Just War," section 2, discusses "who may be killed with a safe Conscience."[102] Here, moderation is explicated (like any virtue) to be a requirement of *iustitia interna*. Grotius refers back to Book I. I. in which he distinguished "Justice strictly taken" from wider justice, which springs from charity. In the *forum internum*, which is the judge that applies *iustitia interna*, killing is justified when the victim is "culpable" in "so heinous a Manner" that death is proportionate.[103] External judgment, or the application of strict law and justice, requires guidance by virtue and distributive justice. Conscience has to assure that external judgment is applied with moderation and care.[104]

This brings me to the third point. As the above shows, in order to have "peace of conscience," sovereigns have to apply the law springing from both expletive and distributive justice; that is, sovereigns must abide by both perfect and imperfect duties. Grotius keeps the latter – the duties constituted by distributive justice – within the *ius gentium et naturae* system by conceiving the human conscience as a court monitoring obedience of the self. Thereby, what he called in *Meletius* the "duties of love" are supported by this court system too. Grotius may perhaps be drawing on Erasmian thinking about conscience as a space for learning and caring for the self and the good of society. The good of society has to be kept in mind for justice to be done.[105] Also, when strict justice is enforced it should be guided by attributive justice to assure proportionate punishment.[106] Caring for the self – as a social being – is caring for others and for the good of society; from human nature springs the duty to obey natural law and justice: "deny[ing]" the fundamental principle of natural law would entail "doing violence to [one]self."[107] Conscience is where this is enforced, where humans interpret and apply the law and make

102 Grotius *DJBP*, Liberty translation, Book III.II, 1422.

103 Grotius *DJBP*, Liberty translation, 1422, 1481. See also Grotius, *DJBP*, Book III.X, sections 2–3; Book III.XIV; Book III.XVI.

104 Cf. Koskenniemi on the internal and external obligations binding in conscience; Martti Koskenniemi, "Imagining the Rule of Law: Rereading the Grotian 'Tradition'," *European Journal of International Law* 30, no. 1 (2019): 17–52, at 30–1.

105 Grotius, *DJBP*, Book III.XXV.

106 Grotius, *DJBP*, Book II.XX.40 on Punishments, e.g., the notion of excessiveness or disproportionate plays a crucial role.

107 Grotius, *DJBP*, *Prolegomena*, 39.

decisions. It demands humans to apply it virtuously, respecting others and taking their interests into account.

To sum up, in both *Mare Liberum* and *De jure belli ac pacis*, the human conscience bears witness to the existence of *ius gentium et naturae*. It provides ground for a decentralized court system, alternative to the confessional court system, and fills the gap of the nonexistent external courts for sovereign and nations. For Grotius, the stakes were high: skeptics argued that law without a system of enforcement could not be law. Once liberated from the jurisdiction of the Roman Catholic Church, *ius gentium et naturae* needed to be backed up by another court system. Grotius proceeded with the "court of conscience" to provide *ius gentium et naturae* with an alternative judge and punisher. With an alternative system in place, modern *ius gentium et naturae* was indisputably binding on its subjects. This internal judge was bound to apply strict and distributive justice.

8.4 CONCLUSION

In the Age of Conscience, "modern" *ius gentium et naturae* emerged. This chapter has examined how various early modern conceptions of *conscientia* related to this emergence of *ius gentium et naturae*. The Thomist conception of conscience as an internal court or judge was central to the work of Vitoria and his development of *ius gentium et naturae* to provide "safety of conscience" for the Spanish Court. In Grotius's work, the judicial function of *conscientia* was mobilized to support his argument that *ius gentium et naturae* was true and universal law, backed up by a type of court system. *Conscientia* underpinned this *ius gentium et naturae*, consisting in something more than strict law and justice or perfect rights and duties. Disregarding imperfect duties or distributive justice would be punished by the *forum internum*, too. Grotius argued that any European sovereign was obliged to apply and implement perfect rights and duties *in conjunction with* this broader conception of law and justice and the imperfect rights and duties that sprang from it. Moreover, without the free conscience, legal institutions as oath and promise could not play their foundational role in law and justice could not be done.

Unfortunately, Foucault never turned to the Protestant technologies of the self. Bringing Foucault's research question – "How have certain kinds of interdictions required the price of certain kinds of knowledge about oneself?"[108] – to Protestant international law thinkers and thought

108 Foucault, "Technologies of the Self," 16.

will make for great further research. Arguably, the rule of conscience became "democratized" with the withdrawal of the Church as its ruler. Yet with the self-examination and guidance of conscience in an unmediated relation with God (in prayer) and without externally administered unburdening practices, other power/knowledge production arose. Foucault's point that the classical "technology of the self" as care for the self and for others (including the *polis*) was lost in the Christian (Roman Catholic) tradition surely deserves research from an Erasmian humanist perspective.

The "technology of the self" operational in Grotius's work may be understood as predominantly Erasmian in nature. The practice of the internal judge requires self-examination against the standards of both strict and distributive justice – or: the duties of strict justice and those of love or *caritas*. *Conscientia* then is the space where humans exercise self-examination and thereby self-cultivation and self-mastery. Since the human is a social being, the care for the self includes care for others and for the good of society. And conscience also infuses mercy and *caritas* to direct human actions in the relations among sovereigns and states, both in peace and in war. This is the role of conscience that we find in Grotius's work. Equally, the often mentioned "bad conscience" bears witness to how frequently humans err. Grotius's court of conscience is a space where knowledge is applied and where judgment is formed and cultivated. It is here that one (individual or sovereign) may apply *ius gentium et naturae* to achieve a "well-tempered judgment" guided especially by the virtue of moderation (*temperantia*).

The early modern development in theological and legal thought that made every sovereign his or her own interpretative authority in the court of conscience was eminently suitable to the emerging European system of sovereign states and the ensuing "horizontal" system of international law. Scholarly scrutiny of Grotius's peace-through-law project has pointed to the weakness of his conception of *ius gentium et naturae*. *Conscientia* as the court for sovereigns in international relations ... Is that not very close to Thomas Hobbes's argument that there exists no international law as there is no external legislature and court? Who decides over the sovereign self and who judges their actions? Does this not lead exactly to the ideas of the nineteenth-century scholars who conceive of international law as merely *Selbstverpflichtung*?

In the course of the next centuries, *conscientia* (and surely its intermediate role in the relation with God) gradually faded into the background of international law and international legal thought; but it never disappeared completely. It featured prominently in the work of Hobbes[109] and Emer de Vattel[110] and later surfaced with scholars like Lassa Oppenheim[111] and Nicolas Politis.[112] Martti Koskenniemi has brilliantly shown how the "Men of 1873" haughtily understood themselves as "the legal conscience of the civilized world."[113] Today's international criminal law includes "the conscience of humanity," which can be "deeply shock[ed]."[114] Similarly, it features in the Preamble of the Universal Declaration of Human Rights (UDHR, 1948): the "outraged" conscience of humankind gave birth to the UDHR. Its first article has a long pedigree, some of which we discussed above: "All human beings are born free and equal in dignity and rights. They are endowed with *reason and conscience* and should act towards one another in a spirit of brotherhood [*sic*]."[115]

Generally, "conscience" is assumed or used uncritically in international law as a natural place of morality and justice. With the human conscience explicitly or implicitly carrying international law, however, comes a space for politics. As we have seen time and again, while it is the space for humans to apply moral knowledge, it is also the space to err profoundly. While law presupposes its application by the human conscience, without the latter the law becomes unimaginable. The politics that comes with the interpretations of the court of conscience, like with any court, requires our scrutinizing attention.

RECOMMENDED READING

Koskenniemi, Martti, Mónica García-Salmones Rovira, and Paolo Amorosa, eds. *International Law and Religion: Historical and Contemporary Perspectives.* Oxford: Oxford University Press, 2017.

109 Thomas Hobbes, *Leviathan*, ed. Richard Tuck (Cambridge: Cambridge University Press, 1991 [1651]), Ch. 30 "The office of soveraign Representative", 244: "there being no Court of Naturall Justice, but in the conscience onely; where not Man, but God raigneth".

110 Emer de Vattel, *Le droit des gens ou Principes de loi naturelle [Law of Nations or the Principles of Natural Law]* (Washington, DC: Carnegie Institution of Washington, 1916), e.g. at 10a and 11a: "the rules which by reason of man's free nature may govern *external* right do not destroy the obligation that the *internal* right imposes on the conscience of each individual" and "the necessary Law of Nations, which is the inner law of conscience".

111 Lassa Oppenheim, "The Science of International Law: Its Task and Method," *American Journal of International Law* 2, no. 2 (1908): 313–56, at 331.

112 Nicolas Politis, "The Status of the Individual in International Law," in *The New Aspects of International Law* (Washington, DC: Carnegie Endowment for International Peace, 1928), 20: "the legal conscience of nations".

113 Martti Koskenniemi, *The Gentle Civilizer of Nations: The Rise and Fall of International Law 1870–1960* (Cambridge: Cambridge University Press, 2001), 41ff.

114 Rome Statute 1998, Preamble.

115 Universal Declaration of Human Rights, GA Res. 217 A, 10 December 1948.

Neff, Stephen C. *Justice among Nations: A History of International Law*. Cambridge, MA: Harvard University Press, 2014.
Stumpf, Christoph A. *The Grotian Theology of International Law: Hugo Grotius and the Moral Foundations of International Relations*. Berlin: Walter de Gruyter, 2006.
Tierney, Brian. *The Idea of Natural Rights: Studies on Natural Rights, Natural Law and Church Law*. Grand Rapids, MI: Wm. B. Eerdmans Publishing, 1997.
Witte, John, Jr. *The Reformation of Rights: Law, Religion, and Human Rights in Early Modern Calvinism*. Cambridge: Cambridge University Press, 2007.

9

Legalizing Antisemitism? The Legacy of Savigny's Roman(tic) Law

Reut Yael Paz

This chapter focuses on an often-forgotten aspect in the story of Christianity and international law, namely, Judaism, Jews, and the Jew. More specifically, it discusses how Christian antisemitic sentiments – often serving as a precursor to further exclusion of the socially different "Other" – found their way into the doctrines and histories of international law. Antisemitism is a living legacy within Christianity and within the discipline of international law. The text explores this theme by revisiting one of the most famous "fathers" of international legal thought, Friedrich Carl von Savigny (1779–1861).

9.1 INTRODUCTION: IN THE BEGINNING THERE WAS *RECHTSWISSENSCHAFT*

The way in which Savigny is described posthumously is impressive, with its overbearing nineteenth-century romantic clichés and superlatives.[1] His impact on German jurisprudence is compared with Immanuel Kant's impact on philosophy and with Beethoven's influence on music. In German poetry and literature, his name is on a par with Johann Wolfgang von Goethe.[2] And in jurisprudence (*Rechtswissenschaft*), his legacy can be traced back to the very belief in Germany that law is a science – an independent, objective, and

[1] Benjamin Lahusen, *Alles Recht geht vom Volksgeist aus: Friedrich Carl v. Savigny und die moderne Rechtswissenschaft* (Berlin: Nicolaische Verlagsbuchhandlung, 2013), 8. Please note that all translations in this chapter are done by the author.

[2] Among other descriptions it is said of Savigny that he was "Darwinian before Darwin"; the "most shining star which the German jurisprudence [*sic*]"; "the most accomplished academic teacher of the 19th century" and "an Olympian who walked among mortals." Some even go so far as to describe his physical appearance by "aristocratic delicacy down to his dainty hands" and "the long brown hairs that surged down"; he was "anointed by the Heaven"; an "Apostle of Power and Consecration"; the "Crown of the Human Race" and "the Prince of German Law Teachers." These quotes are taken from Lahusen, *Alles Recht*, 140–1.

separate field from all other social sciences.[3] Indeed, however conservative, Savigny's historical need to legally root a people within a Christian state offered a progressive modern-day nationalistic alternative that reacted against and reversed the French Revolution. Naturally, this begs a serious return to history; and indeed, the excavation of the past for the sake of the legal present became the main characteristic of Savigny's scholarship.

Together with Karl Friedrich Eichhorn (1781–1854) and Johann Friedrich Ludwig Göschen (1778–1837), Savigny established the Historical School (*Historische Rechtsschule*) – in fact more a political movement than a school – that stressed its lineage with the works of Gustav Hugo (1764–1844).[4] For Savigny and the Historical School, the law is grounded in a romantic legacy that harkens back to Rome, which is often revisited in times of unrest as the idealized birthplace of European legal culture.[5] Exactly how historically scientific such an approach is remains debatable, especially if history's purpose is determined by the here and now. To scholars within the Historical School, the driver of legal development was the *Kulturnation*: the expression of a given people's convictions, language, customs, practices, and religion.[6] The law is the concrete representation of this popular consciousness, of the *Volksgeist* (people's spirit). The ultimate task of the jurist – according to Savigny – is to channel, profess, personify, and radiate the nation's *Volksrecht* and its underlying *Volksgeist*.[7] Although Savigny's ideal image

3 Lahusen, *Alles Recht*, 8.

4 Hugo and the Historical School were ridiculed and criticized by Karl Marx for their frivolous arbitrary legalization of power. See Karl Marx, "The Philosophical Manifesto of the Historical School of Law," first published (without "The Chapter on Marriage" which was cut by the censor) in the Supplement to the *Rheiniche Zeitung* No. 221, August 9, 1842; "The Chapter on Marriage" was first published in MECW 1927, https://marxists.catbull.com/archive/marx/works/1842/08/09.htm.

5 For instance, see how the sixteenth-century Catholic School of Salamanca reshaped the Roman law of *ius gentium*. See more in Reut Yael Paz, "Religion, Secularism and International Law," in *The Oxford Handbook of International Legal Theory*, ed. Anne Orford and Florian Hoffmann (Oxford: Oxford University Press, 2016), 923–38 and Martti Koskenniemi, "Empire and International Law: The Real Spanish Contribution," *The University of Toronto Law Journal* 61, no. 1 (2011): 1–36. Similarly, Savigny titled his 1840 magnum opus *System of Modern Roman Law* (das System des heutigen römischen Rechts). This work, which attempts to modernize Roman law for the present day, is the most dogmatic of his works.

6 This usually goes back to Johann Gottfried Herder's *Sturm und Drang* movement. See more in Hans Adler and Wulf Köpke, eds., *A Companion to the Works of Johann Gottfried Herder* (Rochester, NY: Camden House, 2009).

7 As Benjamin Lahusen explains, unlike other disciplines, in the case of the law it cannot be the "polyphonic murmuring in the countryside that is bundled into professional vernacular. What traditions the common man actually cultivates is of no consequence to popular law; instead it is the hands of the governing bodies of the learned inhabitants of the higher educational institutions." For Savigny it is in the work of the legal scholars to interpret that which only appears to be (Roman and hence) foreign law so that the (German) local order has merged into an indissoluble unity. The historical signposts therefore do not lead into the far-flung traditions

of the jurist was of a Christian, German, and Prussian man, his *Rechtswissenschaft* has impacted international law too.[8] As Martti Koskenniemi argues:

> [M]uch of the way we speak about international law has been received from German Public law as it developed from constitutional commentaries about the nature of the Holy Roman Empire in the seventeenth century to the natural law of the eighteenth and public law formalism of the nineteenth centuries. No legal tradition in this period compares with the German in the depth, complexity, or sense of urgency of its questions.[9]

The profound impact of Savigny's German legal approach on private international law exceeds the limits of this chapter.[10] Suffice it to note that for Savigny, unlike public law that is explicitly subjective and political, private law personified everything that law, or rather *Rechtswissenschaft*, ought to be: tangible, objective, and empirical. Most of his concepts are designed from and for the private. It is therefore only through private law (i.e. *Geschäftsfähigkeit*/contractual capability; *Rechtsfähigkeit*/capacity to be the subject of legal rights) that he "tames" public law and the state altogether.[11] It is exactly because he sees

of the country and its people, but back into general antiquity. "It is precisely in the connection between law and Rome that the connection between the soul of the people and popular law is revealed. In other words: The German national spirit has produced Roman law" (my translation); Lahusen, *Alles Recht geht*, 69–70.

8 As Roaxana Banu argues, "Savigny's PrIL [private international law] theory is considered one of the most important, if not the most important PrIL theory of the nineteenth century, having influenced an impressive number of scholars, national courts and codifications." Roxana Banu, *Nineteenth-Century Perspectives on Private International Law* (Oxford: Oxford University Press, 2018), 72. Moreover, Savigny was quick to detect the significance of juridical legal consciousness. This is a leading precept in international law that was integrated into the discipline by the first institute of international lawyers, *Institut de Droit International*, which held its first session in Geneva in 1874. Article 1 of the Institute's Statute proclaims: "It's [the institute's] purpose to promote the progress of international law by striving to formulate the general principles of the subject, in such a way as to correspond to the legal consciousness of the civilised world." As Martti Koskenniemi argues, it was then that eleven European men defined themselves as "the juridical conscience of the civilized world." Evidently, the idea of legal consciousness goes further back to early-nineteenth-century Prussia. Martti Koskenniemi, *From Apology to Utopia: The Structure of International Legal Argument* (Cambridge: Cambridge University Press, 2006), 113–24.

9 Martti Koskenniemi, "Introduction" to *The Function of Law in the International Community*, by Hersch Lauterpacht (Oxford: Oxford University Press, 2011), xxxiv.

10 See, e.g., Banu, *Nineteenth-Century Perspectives on Private International Law*; Ralf Michaels, "Globalizing Savigny? The State in Savigny's Private International Law and the Challenge from Europeanization and Globalization," in *Aktuelle Fragen zu politischer und rechtlicher Steuerung im Kontext der Globalisierung*, ed. Michael Stolleis and Wolfgang Streeck (Baden-Baden: Nomos, 2007), 119–44.

11 As Ralf Michael argues, "Savigny does not distinguish between state as government and people, as Anglo-American theories would do. Quite to the contrary, he argues explicitly that every people appears as state. Consequently, a state of nature – where there is private law without a state – is inconceivable . . .." Michaels, "Globalizing Savigny," 11.

no distinction between German private law, the state, and the church that the tensions implicated in international law's burdened relationship with German law are made all the more visible in German Christian antisemitism.[12]

Savigny's Christian-based antisemitism and/or anti-Judaism[13] energized his legal practice.[14] For Savigny, the jurist's intuitive accessibility to the people's spirit becomes a useful pseudoscientific "tool" with which to create legal generalities, distinctions, and exceptions that appear apolitical. However premeditated, these distinctions enabled the exclusion of numerous social groups from the field of classical private law.[15]

Just how intentional and political Savigny's *völkische* tendencies were is personified by his obsessive marginalization of Jews from German law as both citizens and practicing jurists. His view of the Jew, who is the embodiment that "remains alien to us," an uprooted existence of "badly applied humanity,"[16] is more central than often remembered.[17] Phrased differently, Savigny's antisemitism should stop being trivialized or footnoted,[18] and instead be taken as a symptom or representation of a deeper pathology within the development of international law and the state.[19]

Antisemitism, which reached one of its peaks during the Holocaust, is a form of hatred with a deeply sacral metaphysical quality that transcends its

12 For more on this relationship, see Reut Yael Paz, *A Gateway between a Distant God and a Cruel World: The Contribution of Jewish German-Speaking Scholars to International Law* (Leiden: Martinus Nijhoff, 2012).

13 Whereas a distinction is often made between antisemitism and anti-Judaism – the former signifying a modern and biological version of the latter which is about religious-based antagonism. Importantly, this contribution uses anti-Jewish and antisemitic interchangeably.

14 As Thomas Henne and Castern Kretschmann phrased it: "Savignys christlich fundierter antijudaismus war ebenfalls zugleich Mentalität und Bestandteil seiner (Rechts-)Praxis." See more in Thomas Henne and Carsten Kretschmann, "Der Christlich Fundierte Antijudaismus Savignys und Seine Umsetzung in Der Rechtspraxis," *Zeitschrift der Savigny-Stiftung für Rechtsgeschichte: Germanistische Abteilung* 119, no. 1 (2002): 250–315, at 254.

15 Lahusen, *Alles Recht*, 138.

16 Friedrich Carl von Savigny, "Stimmen für und wider neue Gesetzbücher," *Zeitschrift für geschichtliche Rechtswissenschaft* 3, no. 1 (1816), reprinted in Jacques Stern, ed., *A.F.J. Thibaut und F.C. von Savigny: zum hundertjährigen Gedächtnis des Kampfes um ein einheitliches bürgerliches Recht für Deutschland* (Berlin 1914, 2nd ed. Darmstadt, 1959), quoted in Lahusen, *Alles Recht*, 122.

17 The one exception to this is Henne and Kretschmann, "Der Christlich Fundierte Antijudaismus."

18 See, e.g., Duncan Kennedy, "Savigny's Family/Patrimony Distinction and Its Place in the Global Genealogy of Classical Legal Thought," *American Journal of Comparative Law* 58, no. 4 (2010): 811–42, at 821 n. 29.

19 As Max Horkheimer argued, "the elimination of anti-Semitism is identical with the struggle against the authoritarian state." Max Horkheimer, "The Jews and Europe," *Zeitschrift für Sozialforschung* 7, no. 1–2 (1939): 115–37, at 136–7

ontological manifestation and runs through the Western experience of Christianity and law.[20] As David Patterson argues, because antisemitism arises "from the depth of the human subjectivity, beyond all ontological categories and contingencies, probing the depths of antisemitism entails probing the depths of the human soul."[21] Considering Savigny's Roman(tic) Christian legal approach and the vicinity between law and religion – both are resorted to interchangeably in search of dictates of consciousness – the question here is more about how Savigny's antisemitism infiltrated and motivated his legal approach and how it mirrors broader tendencies within the worlds of the law.

More specifically, I examine how Savigny's Roman(tic) legal legacy excluded the Jew from German law and represented the threat of turning the law "non-Christian as well as non-German and non-Prussian."[22] The idea of an infiltrating "Other" became, in turn, a way to define what would come to be understood as Christian, German, and Prussian law at the beginning of the nineteenth century: in short, Savigny's *Rechtswissenschaft*.

To begin, it is useful to examine Savigny's participation as a founding member of the *Deutsche Tischgesellschaft* (German Table Society), an exclusive reactionary club with influential reach through Prussia and affinities to arguments of Christian state and a general antisemitic sensibility.[23] As we will see, Savigny's legal approach is strongly influenced by these antisemitic inclinations that took hold in the Romantic era and were reflected in his public writing and his personal relationships. Outward facing, Savigny's Romantic concept of *Volksgeist* established certain useful legal distinctions between Christians and their Others, allowing him to "legalize" antisemitism. In his private dealings, Savigny's antisemitism translated into an obsessive and vengeful hate-relationship toward Eduard Gans (1798–1839), the first lawyer of Jewish origins who reached professorship in Germany, which is discussed elsewhere.[24]

20 As Ernst Bloch argues, the aim behind such metaphysical antisemitism is often to eliminate the Hebrew Scriptures from the Christian canon, sustaining instead that the revealed truth in Christianity far transcends anything in Judaism. Ernst Bloch, *The Spirit of Utopia*, trans. Anthony A. Nassar (California: Stanford University Press, 2000), 30.

21 David Patterson, *Anti-Semitism and Its Metaphysical Origins* (New York: Cambridge University Press, 2015), 5.

22 Terry Pinkard, *Hegel: A Biography* (Cambridge: Cambridge University Press, 2000), 532.

23 *The Deutsche Tischgesellschaft* should not be confused with the *Christlich-Deutsche Tischgesellschaft*. It has taken a long time to establish that these two societies are different. For more on this, see Stefan Nienhaus, *Geschichte der deutschen Tischgesellschaft* (Tübingen: Niemeyer, 2003).

24 Johann Braun, "Eduard Gans (1797–1839): Ein homo Politicus zwischen Hegel und Savigny," in *Deutsche Juristen Jüdischer Herkunft*, ed. Helmut Heinrichs et al. (Munich: Beck Verlag, 1993), 45–57. See more on Savigny's relationship with Gans in Paz, *Gateway between a Distant God*, 98–105.

9.2 SETTING THE STAGE: GERMAN ROMANTICISM AND *DEUTSCHE TISCHGESELLSCHAFT*

The ambivalences within German Romanticism's antisemitism implied a simultaneous revulsion and attraction to the Jew.[25] Such antisemitism was well represented by the *Deutsche Tischgesellschaft* inaugurated on January 18, 1811 in Berlin. The date was deliberately chosen as it was the day of the royal coronation of Frederick I in 1701, when the Kingdom of Prussia was founded. The glorious beginnings of Prussia had to loom large in the background in times of great threats to its continued existence.[26] German unity was the goal, especially when the ramifications of the French Revolution – as the child of the Enlightenment – and the French presence were still reckoned with. The elected banner *Freiheit christlich-deutscher Treue* (liberty of Christian German fidelity) contrasted with the French *liberté, égalité, fraternité* and unified the Society under a romantic and heroic image of the thirteenth-century crusaders who conquered, converted, and created Prussia.[27] The rules of the Dining Society were clear: a confraternity of German, Christian, like-minded noblemen who were firmly convinced reactionaries met every two weeks in *Casino-Local* on Friedrichstrasse for lunch.[28] Members were the crème de la crème of nineteenth-century Berlin – an elite mix of civil servants, officers, academics, intellectuals, and artists.[29] The main authors of the association were the German Romantic poets, also known as the *Heidelberg Romantiker,* Achim von Arnim (1781–1831) and Clemens Brentano (1778–1842).[30] Savigny was an honorary founding member of the Society and

25 As Katja Garloff argues, the "difficulty arises because the hallmarks of Romantic antisemitism are inconsistency and ambivalence, a simultaneous attraction to, and revulsion from, Jews and Judaism." Katja Garloff, "Figures of Love in Romantic Antisemitism: Achim von Arnim," *The German Quarterly* 80, no. 4 (2007): 427–48, at 427.

26 Nienhaus, *Geschichte der deutschen Tischgesellschaft*, 12.

27 Achim von Arnim, the main founder of the Society, has proclaimed in his opening poetic remark: "Freiheit christlich-deutscher Treue Uns mit deinem Segen Weihe!" (Liberty of Christian German fidelity, Consecrate us with your blessing!). Nienhaus, *Geschichte der deutschen Tischgesellschaft*, 13.

28 See more in Ludwig Achim von Arnim, *Werke und Briefwechsel: Historisch-kritische Ausgabe*, vol. 11, *Texte der deutschen Tischgesellschaft*, ed. Stefan Nienhaus (Tübingen: Niemeyer, 2008), 4.

29 Apart from these three, suffice it to mention the Generals Carl von Clausewitz and August Friedrich Wilhelm von Bülow, Johann Gottlieb Fichte, Friedrich Schleiermacher, Wilhelm Müller, Ernst Moritz Arndt and Karl Friedrich Schinkel. For the full list of the members, see von Arnim, *Texte der deutschen Tischgesellschaft*, 5.

30 The Heidelberg Romantiker got their name due to the time spent publishing in the city of Heidelberg. For more on the group, see Urs Büttner, *Poiesis des 'Sozialen': Achim von Arnims frühe Poetik bis zur Heidelberger Romantik (1800–1808)* (Berlin: De Gruyter, 2015).

its "Legislative Committee."[31] After all, Brentano and Arnim both were his brothers-in-law.[32] The familial and religious ties and crossovers were inspirational in numerous ways,[33] some more romantic than others.[34] This is also felt when it is considered that the *Deutsche Tischgesellschaft* worked as a counter-model to earlier Romantic salons, formed and hosted by educated Jewish women and functioning as sites of Jewish-Christian rapprochement.[35]

Its politics followed instructions that were as straightforward as its format: hermetic exclusion of women, Jews, and *Philistern* (philistins).[36] Members must have been born Christian and *wohlanständig* (well-off/bred).[37] Even

[31] Savigny was one of the four-member "Legislative Committee" that formulated the Society's "Basic Constitution." Henne and Kretschmann, "Der Christlich Fundierte Antijudaismus," 263–5.

[32] Kunigunde (Gunda) Brentano married Savigny in 1804. Significantly, the wedding took place in a Protestant church (in Meerholz) although the wife was Catholic. Following the religious precepts of such mixed marriages, their children were raised as Catholics. Bettine von Brentano married Armin in 1811. Although their banns were announced in Berlin's Catholic Hedwigskirche, they too married in a Protestant church (in Weisenhauskirche). In their case, the household remained Protestant and not Catholic. See more in Allen W. Porterfield, "Some Popular Misconceptions Concerning German Romanticism," *Journal of English and Germanic Philology* 15, no. 4 (1916): 479–511, at 497.

[33] Most German Romanticists were Protestants. The common belief that most German Romantics were actually Catholics originates in their admiration of the "Catholic Church temporal priority, aestheticism in all of its phases and as a product of the time when the church was a power; mysticism that is attractive to all men and that is much more common than many men suppose; symbolism that stood sponsor to so many things; the inexplicability of the Madonna and her Child; and chronology." Porterfield, "Some Popular Misconceptions," 499.

[34] One revealing story is how Clemens Brentano, Wilhelm Müller and the composer Ludwig Berger were all in love with Luise Hensel, who was the sister of the painter Wilhelm Hensel and sister-in-law of the composer Fanny Hensel, née Mendelssohn. Luise, who, like several prominent Romanticists, converted out of Protestantism and into Catholicism, loved Ernst Ludwig von Gerlach, who later enjoyed a high reputation as Bismarck's teacher and friend. Yet when she turned twenty-two, Luise took the vow of virginity. Significantly, Brentano entrusted Luise with the task of sifting through his literary estate, with the aim of bringing his work to the public after his death. For more on this, see Susan Youens, *Schubert, Müller, and Die schöne Müllerin* (Cambridge: Cambridge University Press, 1997).

[35] Bettine von Brentano, who married Arnim in 1811, was a frequent visitor in these Jewish Salons. See more in Garloff, "Figures of Love." And in Deborah Hertz, "Dueling for Emancipation: Jewish Masculinity in the Era of Napoleon," in *Jüdische Welten: Juden in Deutschland vom 18. Jahrhundert bis in die Gegenwart*, ed. Marion A. Kaplan and Beate Meyer (Göttingen: Wallstein Verlag, 2005), 69–85.

[36] As von Armin wrote in 1810: "The wisest of the laws determines that every empty Philistine is excluded." Quoted in Henne and Kretschmann, "Der Christlich Fundierte Antijudaismus," 264.

[37] The exclusiveness of *Wohlanständige* crowds helped the society define its members as men of honor, good manners born into Christianity ("Die Gesellschaft versteht unter dieser Wohlanständigkeit, daß es ein Mann von Ehre und guten Sitten und in christlicher Religion geboren sei"). See more in Nienhaus, *Geschichte der deutschen Tischgesellschaft*, 10.

third-generation convert Jews could not join the Society.[38] That Jews and women were innately excluded implied the complete negation of their civil and political emancipation. It also infers the clandestine operation of the Society in terms of the political topics and information that might transpire during its meetings.[39] It remains unclear how exactly the Society conceived the Jew (i.e. were the Jews a collective nation? Or individuals who can be "healed" through conversion over time?). Mostly, it seems that the difficulty lay with the Jews as a nation that personified "a state within a state" threat.[40]

With the benefit of Savigny's close relationship to "the patriarch of German-national-Bavarian Romanticism" Bishop Johann Michael Sailer (1751–1832),[41] the Society put into practice the need to return to the ecumenical "Christian State," especially that of the Middle Ages.[42] As Thomas Henne and Carsten Kretschmann argue, "ecumenism was initially concerned with bringing together the Christian as a value in itself, but at the same time it was also concerned with the foundation of a 'Christian State' from which all those who did not subscribe to its principles – and this was particularly true of the Jews – were to be excluded."[43]

The exclusion of third-generation Jewish converts is curious for it symbolizes a transition from religious to racial – even if not biological – discrimination that is often assumed to have come later as a consequence of modernity.[44] In fact, racial antisemitism is always grounded in religion.[45] It certainly goes back to the sixteenth-century institution of the "pure blood laws"

38 Hertz, "Dueling for Emancipation," 69–85.

39 Hertz, "Dueling for Emancipation," 35–6.

40 See more in Henne and Kretschmann, "Der Christlich Fundierte Antijudaismus," 282–90.

41 Savigny's two-year stay in Southern German Landshut had a lifelong impact due to his meeting Sailer, "the man who was called and capable of bringing the separated confessions into balance and to reconnect them into one Christianity." Henne and Kretschmann, "Der Christlich Fundierte Antijudaismus," 257. Sailer, who was given charge of Savigny's children's religious education, also helped Savigny conceive of a "spiritually religious Christianism" that was based on the idea of a restorative ecumenism, "a secret church that pervades all centuries of Christianity." Henne and Kretschmann, "Der Christlich Fundierte Antijudaismus," 257. See also Konrad Baumgartner, "Die Familie Friedrich Carl von Savigny und Sailer," *Zeitschrift der Savigny-Stiftung für Rechtsgeschichte: Germanistische Abteilung* 135, no. 1 (2018): 359–80.

42 Henne and Kretschmann, "Der Christlich Fundierte Antijudaismus," 257–63.

43 Henne and Kretschmann, "Der Christlich Fundierte Antijudaismus," 257–63.

44 Otto D. Kulka, "The Critique of Judaism in Modern European Thought: Genuine Factors and Demonic Perceptions," in *Demonizing the Other: Antisemitism, Racism and Xenophobia*, ed. Robert S. Wistrich (London: Routledge, 1999), 197–209.

45 As Otto D. Kulka, for instance, argues, the roots of modern antisemitism go back to late-seventeenth-century English Deism. It was "the first philosophical current to express the crisis of faith in Christianity and to offer a rationalist concept of 'natural religion' as a radical alternative." Its critique of Christianity led them to Christianity's roots in Judaism, which was

legislated by the Spanish courts of Inquisition, only abolished during the nineteenth century with the Napoleonic wars.[46] The Society's aversion to the Enlightenment was in part an alliance with this earlier racial/religious blend of anxieties from Jewish infiltration, and partly a call for an ecumenist Christianity which synthesized all aspects of life into a common artistic, poetic, political, and spiritual aesthetic[47] – one which demands universal adherence, a type of internalized missionary project.[48]

The inability to bridge dissent among Christian sects (as the Thirty Years' War proved in the seventeenth century), antisemitism was more often than not a common unifying denominator. Engaging anew with religion (including Judaism) as a reaction to the French Revolution was high on everyone's agenda.[49] German Catholics and Protestants alike – no matter how Romantic and/or Enlightened – saw Judaism as an inadequate and inferior religion. Yet, while the *Aufklärer* (people of the Enlightenment) reduced Judaism to theocracy, the German Romanticists added a twist in historicizing Judaism,[50] implying a particular contextualization and even suspension of nineteenth-century Orthodox Judaism as a "curse" of a nonspiritual, overly rational and overly legalized *Weltanschauung*.[51] This became a necessary negative mirror image to the aesthetic Christianity that the Romanticists embraced.

easily made to be the physical embodiment for all things gone wrong with Christianity. Kulka, "Critique of Judaism," 199.

46 The Spanish Tribunal of the Holy Office of the Inquisition, which was governed by imperial civil servants, supplemented the earlier version that was led by *the Christian Church Inquisition* primarily against Catharism and Waldensian heretics. Significantly, all forms of Christian inquisitions – which often worked simultaneously – adapted legal and political elements from the original *Roman Inquisitorial procedure*. See more in Edward Peters, *Inquisition* (Berkeley: University of California Press, 1989), 1.

47 Here the Romantic movement welcomed Schleiermacher's attempt to bridge Christianities with a shared feeling dependent on the infinite (*Anschauung des Universum*), "the intuition of the universe," as he wrote in 1799. See more in William Alexander Johnson, *On Religion: A Study of the Theological Method in Schleiermacher and Nygren* (Leiden: Brill 1963), 33.

48 All Christianities share a common missionary impulse. And have done their best to colonize, internally as well as externally, not only the lives of their followers but also the lives of Others. Yet, however unifying missionarism is, it remains impossible to unite Christianities on its basis alone. See more in Paz, "Religion, Secularism and International Law," 923–38.

49 Wolf-Daniel Hartwick, *Romantischer Antisemitismus: Von Klopstock bis Richard Wagner* (Göttingen: Vandenhoeck & Ruprecht, 2005), 27.

50 Hartwick, *Romantischer Antisemitismus*, 27. See also Garloff, "Figures of Love," 428.

51 True enough, as Brentano presented the Society in 1811 and Savigny was the first to order its printed version, "the Jews were the people of promise before Christ's crucifixion. After the betrayal of the Son of God, the curse weighed on the Jews . . . by each of their Twelve Tribes." Henne and Kretschmann, "Der Christlich Fundierte Antijudaismus," 267.

Relying on such a negative mirror image of Judaism was not tension-free. Indeed, no matter how universal, the roots of all Christianities go back to the Old Testament. Whatever the Romantic idealized ecumenist vision of Christianity was, it could not really be reborn without going back to the Old Testament. Not even if it reread "the original ideas of the Old Testament and incorporated them into a secularized and aestheticized version of Christian *Heilsgeschichte*."[52] Ergo, for salvation to have only a Christian history, it had to be made as non-Jewish as possible. Otherwise, apart from acknowledging Christian schism, there is a need to recognize Judaism's impact on Christianity and the repetitive trope of demonizing or suppressing the Jew in the service of defining and unifying Christendom. The exclusion of the Jew serves to sanction and perhaps even consecrate a presumptuous Christian unity which expresses its power through the formalization of the law.[53]

That such racial antisemitism reappears in the predominantly Protestant Prussia only proves the depths of the fusion between religious and racially based antisemitism.[54] Possible "infiltration" of the invisible Jew – that is, the

52 Garloff, "Figures of Love," 428. Note that modern secularism and modern religious thought are essentially religious phenomena "derived from – and yet ... cut off from – a common political and religious heritage, an intellectual tradition born of the struggle to reconcile the idea of divinity with the practical needs and limitations of the mortal world." See Nomi Stolzenberg, "The Profanity of Law," in *Law and the Sacred*, ed. Austin Sarat et al. (Stanford: Stanford University Press, 2007), 3.

53 As I argue elsewhere, it is often forgotten, for instance, that the right to free exercise of religion granted *only* to Lutherans and Calvinists in the Holy Roman Empire– after the intra-Christian denominational war that ended with the Peace of Westphalia (1648) – was a rule of expediency. It cannot be stressed enough that religious tolerance – even within Western European Christendom, civilization, and/or culture – is nothing but a fragile and pragmatic acceptance that social stability has a price. According to its preamble, the Treaty of Münster, signed in Catholic Münster and Protestant Osnabrück, introduced a separation between the state and the church in Europe. This modified the political map of Europe, and influenced the present structure and configuration of international law, or at least this is how the story is traditionally told. Notably, the Treaty of Münster, which restructured Europe's politics of religion, lacks any reference to Judaism, although both Catholics and Protestants relied on the Jews and their money to finance the Thirty Years' War and peace. See more in Paz, *Gateway between a Distant God*, 7–8.

54 One could also argue that Christian credo held by civilized societies, such as the *Deutsche Tischgesellschaft*, symbolizes both the internalization and the universalization of Christianity that Michel Foucault terms "Christianization-in-depth." Importantly, Foucault characterized the Renaissance "not by the beginning of a dechristianization but by the beginning of a Christianization-in-depth." À la Foucault, the religious Christian missionary effort that keeps us all still locked in the dark ages came together with early modernity due to the "vast interiorization" of the Christian experience. While this took place through both the internal and the external expansion of Catholicism to the "new-world," especially since the Council of Trent (1545–63), it grew only in the period after the crisis of the Reformation and Counter-Reformation. See Michel Foucault, "19 February 1975," in *Abnormal: Lectures at the Collège*

"new Christian" – represents the potential loss of the significance in the attachment of an "original people" to a nation state.[55] Lest it be forgotten, the complete and successful admission of the new Christian-Jew might also challenge land ownership by the *wohlanständige* elites.[56] Such antisemitism grounded in land with a specific racial interpretation could be seen as a forerunner to the infamous Nazi "blood and soil" slogan. It is less than coincidental that Ernst Moritz Arndt (1769–1860) – a virulent antisemite and an earlier proponent of the German agrarian society as the climatic representation of German nationhood – was also a member of the Society.[57]

In sum, the German Romanticists' goal of a "universal" Christian state excluded the Jew on theological, economical, and, most importantly, racial grounds. The *Deutsche Tischgesellschaft* was neither "convivial" nor "open to many cultural manifestations."[58] And, in contrast to what some scholars argue, this antisemitism should not be ignored[59] (even if it did not always legitimize anti-Jewish violence per se); to the contrary, it is a core dynamic in understanding the shape of Christian faith, law, and the state. The dissolution of the Society occurred in tandem with the weakening of Prussian conservativism. The 11th of March 1812 edict (that under the first article declared all legally

de France, 1974–1975, ed. Valerio Marchetti and Antonella Salomoni, trans. Graham Burchell (London: Verso, 2003), 167–99; Michel Foucault, *The History of Sexuality: An Introduction* (New York: Pantheon, 1978), 61. For more on the importance of this to international law, see Paz, "Religion, Secularism and International Law."

55 Importantly, the fear from the invisible converted Jew was one that Martin Luther helped in spreading too. Jerome Friedman, "Jewish Conversion, the Spanish Pure Blood Laws and Reformation: A Revisionist View of Racial and Religious Antisemitism," *The Sixteenth Century Journal* 18, no. 1 (1987): 3–30.

56 The dual challenge to Arnim by Moritz Itzig (1787–1813) exemplifies the *Deutsche Tischgesellschaft* fear that Jews manage to avoid their background by "ancestry by purchase" but also by noble characteristics and social mores. See more in Hertz, "Dueling for Emancipation."

57 As Gesine Gerhard argues, Arndt "linked peasant romanticism with nationalism when he called for the state to protect peasants as the foundation of the German people." The Nazis inaugurated "blood and soil" as a leading slogan only after Richard Walther Darré (1895–1953) gave the idea new connotations of blood and race. Gesine Gerhard, "Change in European Countryside: Peasants and Democracy in Germany 1935–1955," in *War, Agriculture, and Food: Rural Europe from the 1930s to the 1950s*, ed. Paul Brassley et al. (New York: Routledge, 2012), 195–209, at 197.

58 As Roger Paulin phrases it: "The society's anti-Jewish, anti-French, anti-Philistine, xenophobic, and patriotic sentiment provided a heady mix for coming generations. It would[,] however, be a pity to lose sight of the better traits of the 'Deutsche Tischgesellschaft', its conviviality, its free causerie, its openness to many cultural manifestations." Roger Paulin, "Review of Stefan Nienhaus, *Geschichte der deutschen Tischgesellschaft*," *Modern Language Review* 100, no. 1 (2005): 251–3, at 253.

59 Paulin, in his review of Stefan Nienhaus's *Geschichte der deutschen Tischgesellschaft*, twice laments the reduction of the Society's to his exclusive politics. See Paulin, "Review," 251–3.

resident Jews of Prussia to be citizens), for instance, formally permitted Jews to actively participate in the Prussian legal administration.[60] These changes did not mean the end of Jewish exclusion, but they signaled a shift in the existing power constellations. While earlier antisemitic policies were governed solely by the Prussian administration, now the jurisdiction was shared with the universities, where the production of future administrators took place. Either way, Savigny remains central. In fact, just a day before the 1812 edict came into force, he became the rector of Friedrich Wilhelm University of Berlin after Johann Gottlieb Fichte (1762–1814) resigned due to the university's "first serious crisis" over attacks on a Jewish student in Berlin.[61] This crisis was as symbolic as Savigny's approach to Gans.[62] Apart for Savigny's clear antisemitism in practice, it is important to examine how his antisemitism interacts with his theoretical contributions.

9.3 SAVIGNY'S *VOLKSGEIST*: (A)POLITICAL LEGALIZATION OF "BLOOD/SOIL"?

Even if Savigny's scholarship shows slight changes in his views of Christianity,[63] it remains loyal to the Christian ecumenism promoted by the *Deutsche Tischgesellschaft*. It exemplifies, moreover, how his complex Christian background, which is often oversimplified with "Huguenot Protestant," is rooted in his legal methodology.[64] Whereas being a Protestant

60 Henne and Kretschmann, "Der Christlich Fundierte Antijudaismus," 269.

61 The incident goes back to the several attacks on a Jewish medicine student, Joseph Brogy. Although Brogy was the victim of several antisemitic attacks by fellow students, the Ehrengericht/Honorary Court, headed by Savigny himself, expelled Brogy. In Savigny's indictment, Brogy's Judaism is never even mentioned. Instead Savigny argues against Brogy's manners (*Sitte*), which did not match "the moral determination of human nature" that was identical with the "Christian view of life." Fichte did not accept these sentences, refused the execution of the student's sentences, and handed in his resignation. See more detail about this incident in Henne and Kretschmann, "Der Christlich Fundierte Antijudaismus," 270–6.

62 Paz, *Gateway between a Distant God*, 98–105.

63 As John E. Toews argues, Savigny's earlier historical works (1814–16) differ from his "great synthetic work of the 1840s, the *System des heutigen Römischen Rechts*." Whereas in the latter he strives toward "the universal spirit that reveals itself in the people in an individual way," in his earlier works he barely admits the universal tendencies of the law. In fact, the closest he gets to it is when he accepts "uniform tendencies (Richtungen) that could be defined as the philosophical element in all positive law." See more in John E. Toews, "The Immanent Genesis and Transcendent Goal of Law: Savigny, Stahl, and the Ideology of the Christian German State," *American Journal of Comparative Law* 37, no. 1 (1989): 139–69, at 142.

64 While there seems to be an acceptance that Christianity was central to his approach, there is still much to be excavated about what that Christianity means. See, e.g., Baumgartner, "Die Familie Friedrich Carl von Savigny und Sailer," 359–80; Henne and Kretschmann, "Der

antisemite in Prussia's Romantic circles was a conventional necessity, his increasingly adamant expression, wrapped up in the legal exclusion of the Jew, deserves closer attention. Savigny performs this eradication through a twofold Roman(tic) paradigm. First, he submerged his Christian background and erudition – a marriage of Lutheran/Calvinist parental heritage with a mixture of close communion with German Pietists, the German Free Church, and Catholicism – under the phenomena of an imagined (highly Germanic) Roman law.[65] The return to Rome, in his account, is to circumvent the Enlightenment and insinuate a certain desire to go further back to a pre-monotheistic/Jewish moment in Europe.[66] Second, he relied on a theoretical and abstract conception of *Volksgeist* to create legal theoretical conceptions, categories, and distinctions that are then used in theory and practice to legally exclude the Jew. Both these interrelated aspects are discussed in this section.

Drawing from the Romanticists' arch-enemy, the French Revolution, Savigny sought to avert civil codification at any cost. To do so, he focused on an incessant systematization and fortification of private law. More specifically, in order to entrench the separation of the public from the private, Savigny pushed for a pseudo objective "political-free science of private law."[67] Without unpacking all of Savigny's *Pandektenwissenschaft* (Pandect Science), let alone his eight volumes of the System of Modern Roman Law (*Das System des heutigen römischen Rechts*) published from 1840 to 1849, it is enough to say

Christlich Fundierte Antijudaismus"; Bernd Mertens, *Gönner, Feuerbach, Savigny: Über Deutungshoheit und Legendenbildung in der Rechtsgeschichte* (Tübingen: Mohr Siebeck, 2018), 15; Margaret Barber Crosby, *The Making of a German Constitution: A Slow Revolution* (Oxford: Berg Publishers, 2008), 62; and Lahusen, *Alles Recht*, 15.

65 Savigny's father was a Lutheran Jurist while his mother was a zealous Calvinist. This was a mixed marriage par excellence: Calvinists were forbidden to worship in the city, so every Sunday the son would join his mother for services in a nearby village, Bockenheim. At the age of thirteen, Savigny was orphaned by both parents and remained the only heir to their estate. Savigny then moved to Wetzlar where a family friend and colleague of his father, the jurist Constantin von Neurath (1739–1816), became his guardian. In 1795 Savigny began his legal studies in Marburg. It was during this time that he was acquainted with Roman law and met the influential philologist Friedrich Creuzer (1771–1858); received his doctorate (1800); became a professor (1801) who taught and befriended the Grimm brothers, Jacob Ludwig Karl (1785–1863) and Wilhelm Carl (1786–1859); published his famous *Das Recht des Besitzes*; and became the brother-in-law of the Catholic Romantic poet Clemens Bretano (1778–1842) after his marriage to Kunigunde (Gunda) during the same year (1804). See more in Baumgartner, "Die Familie Friedrich Carl von Savigny," 361.

66 One could here argue that Savigny draws from Roman legal patriarchy the idea of permanent divinely created institutions of personality and patriarchy. It is clear that Savigny's approach to patriarchy and blood stems from his nineteenth-century Romanticist context.

67 Lahusen, *Alles Recht*, 131.

that the very essence of law à la Savigny lies in the way it regulates a person's belonging to a *Volk*/people.

Relationships between individuals and their *Volk*/*Kulturvolk*/nation (words that Savigny uses interchangeably) are restrained by a legal system that is historically grounded in customary laws. According to Savigny, the *Volksgeist* had an almost chemical chain reaction that starts with a legal norm that is worked out through the people's unconsciousness until it develops into customs that, with time and the right rituals, conventions, and institutions, shape the jurist's consciousness and, in turn, the law (*Recht*). Law is different from and superior to positive statutes (*Gesetz*). Positive enacted legislation always follows the law that is "spiritual" and hence invisible until made visible by the jurist and possibly his legislations.[68] As long as the *Volksgeist* emerges from specialized jurists who translate it back to the people as law, the nation's future is safe. This works on the basis of a universalistic and abstract concept of law that keeps man at the center: The most important element to him in his surrounding is the contact with those "*who are like him* by their *nature* and *destination*."[69] Savigny's creation of a scientific gatekeeping professional class that is institutionalized in each single living jurist – whose task is to decipher the idea of "inexhaustible fertility" behind the people's spirit[70] – is entirely in sync with the German Romantic philosophy that at least since the sixteen century onwards repeatedly referenced the peculiarities of individual peoples, reflected in their respective legislations.[71] These just become more precise together with Savigny's infamous *Spezialistendogma* (specialist's dogma).[72]

Recalling that the law has to be Christian, German, and Prussian, there is no confusion about who this person is (German-speaker, Prussian national, Christian man) or what are his nature/destination/goals (law-abiding, Prussian nobility, whose destiny is in the Christian heavens). The law that develops over time from custom and is rationalized by national jurists and legal science is

68 Roger Berkowitz, "From Justice to Justification: An Alternative Genealogy of Positive Law," *UC Irvine Law Review* 1, no. 3 (2011): 611–30.

69 Friedrich Carl von Savigny, *System of the Modern Roman Law*, trans. William Holloway (Westport, CT: Hyperion Press, 1979 [1867]), 269–71 (emphasis added).

70 Hermann Klenner, "Savigny's Research Program of the Historical School of Law and Its Intellectual Impact in 19th Century Berlin," *American Journal of Comparative Law* 37, no. 1 (1989): 67–80, at 67.

71 Especially in the works of Herder, Friedrich Wilhelm Joseph Schelling, and Georg Wilhelm Friedrich Hegel, the "people" with all their peculiarities, detours, and achievements became the bearers of their own culture. These ideas quickly found their way into a historically well-versed legal doctrine, linked to the grown individuality of the people, that was thus entirely in keeping with the spirit of the time. Lahusen, *Alles Recht*, 69.

72 See more in Jan Schröder, "Savignys Spezialistendogma und die 'soziologische' Jurisprudenz," *Rechtstheorie* 7 (1976): 23–52.

given at times "concrete form and compulsory effect in legislation,"[73] but ideally legislation of civil law should be deferred for a later time[74] when the German national legal consciousness is mature enough.[75]

Savigny's ability to establish legal consciousness as an essential component of the legal form has impacted both German and international law. Indeed, the notion of "civilized consciousness," as inserted by the first professional international lawyers, has found its way into Article 38 of the International Court of Justice (ICJ) Statute (and that goes back to Article 38 of the 1920 Statute of the Permanent Court of International Justice). Article 38 provides that, in arriving at its decisions, the Court shall apply international conventions, international custom, and the "general principles of law recognized by civilized nations."[76] Or in more unlikely places; for instance, in the work of the progressive late-twentieth-century, left-of-center, Anglo-American legal theorist Duncan Kennedy. In his view, echoing Savigny, (international) law is "a vocabulary, of concepts and typical arguments, as a *langue*, or language, and to [*sic*] the specific, positively enacted rules," that is, determined by the drives and characteristics of the legal actors involved.[77] Unlike Savigny, Kennedy voices awareness that this consciousness can all-too-easily exclude others, but the notion remains that the law is somehow the manifestation of an already existing community's consciousness.

This needs to be contextualized together with Savigny's construction of *Volksgeist* because of its implicated generalities, distinctions, and exceptions. First, the jurist must be the right kind of participant (Christian, German, and Prussian noblemen) to be able to express "who is a people" (and who is not). Second, the jurist must have direct accessibility to the people's

73 Kennedy, "Savigny's Family/Patrimony Distinction," 812.

74 This leads us to the heart of the famous debate between Savigny and Anton Friedrich Justus Thibaut about Germany's future, discussed later.

75 As Lahusen is quoted as saying in *Die Locomotive*, a popular nineteenth-century newspaper, the paradox of a Savigny "'whose entire merit for Prussia is the drafting of laws' but who has drafted none because they have not 'matured to be implemented' did not escape his contemporaries." Lahusen, *Alles Recht*, 128.

76 See ICJ Statute, Article 38, 1(c): "The Statute of the International Court of Justice," Chapter II, www.icjcij.org/documents/index.php?p1=4&p2=2&p3=0. For a critique of the still existing religious and European bias in international law, see Paz, "Religion, Secularism and International Law."

77 Kennedy defines these legal professionals as "actors with privileged access to the legal apparatus – lawyers for economic actors, lawyers working as legislators, judges and legal academics – [who] have a professionally legitimated role to play, a role that parallels and overlaps that of economic power holders." Duncan Kennedy, "Three Globalizations of Law and Legal Thought: 1850–2000," in *The New Law and Economic Development: A Critical Appraisal*, ed. David Trubek and Alvaro Santos (Cambridge: Cambridge University Press, 2006), 20–6.

subconsciousness and popular tendencies (and what are not) and hence how the people are to be governed by law. More specifically, there is a law that governs regular instances (of "our" people) just as there is a key exception that may be claimed by the jurist for cases that deal with foreign law and courts. Whereas the former may rely on legal statutes (positive law), exceptional cases allow room for moral interpretation. Note that, with time, Savigny's morality is invoked through "reasons of public interests."[78] Only juridically recognized men have rights to those (specific legal) relationships that keep society free, secure and eternal.[79] For Savigny, the ethical character of the law that forever balances liberty and order is embedded in patriarchy and blood: "progressive development towards ethical community from the ethnic bonding among sons of a common maternal nationality [can] be achieved only through the submission to the law of a transcendent father."[80]

In his 1840 magnum opus, *System*, Savigny writes: "[T]he universal task of all law (*Recht*) is to simply let itself be led back to the ethical determination of human nature as the latter is presented in the Christian view of life."[81] The law is subordinated to the ethical and the ethical to Christianity. And if the law bows to a Christian orientation of ethics, it also acts as a companion to theology in that it "stands in an immediate relation with the history and unique characteristics of our nation."[82] Only two years after writing that Christianity has, "in fact, transformed the world," Savigny would be appointed Prussia's Minister of Justice by his personal friend and former tutee Frederick William IV. Savigny's feelings reflected the dominant ethos of the time – a deeply Christian sentiment but one which could be found most often outside traditional religious sources (e.g., in ancient Roman law). "The Christian ethos that Savigny reveres as the ultimate source of law is found not in religious texts or doctrines but rather in the actually existing social conditions of Christian life."[83]

78 By the time of the publication of his last System volume in 1848, that which previously was openly admitted to be "morality" becomes "reasons of public interest/welfare." Henne and Kretschmann, "Der Christlich Fundierte Antijudaismus," 310.

79 Or, in Savigny's terms, such contact assisting as long as there is recognition of "an invisible boundary within which the existence and activity of each individual gains a secure, free space. The rule, by which those boundaries and that free space are determined, is the law . . .." Kennedy, "Savigny's Family/Patrimony Distinction," 812.

80 John Edward Toews, *Becoming Historical: Cultural Reformation and Public Memory in Early Nineteenth-Century Berlin* (Cambridge: Cambridge University Press, 2004), 317.

81 Lahusen, *Alles Recht*, 53.

82 Pinkard, *Hegel*, 532.

83 Savigny continues to argue "that all of our thoughts, no matter how strange or even antagonistic they might seem to Christianity, are nevertheless governed and infused by it." Roger Berkowitz, *The Gift of Science Leibniz and the Modern Legal Tradition* (Cambridge, MA: Harvard University Press, 2009), 130.

The two legal exceptions here intimate the importance of Savigny's Berlin Romantic context: the issue of marriages and "the Jewish question" (before it even began to be called "the Jewish question").[84] In his 1816 review of "a typical representative of the Enlightenment" – Burkhard Pfeiffer (1777–1852) – Savigny attacks Pfeiffer's ideas for a new civil law. He begins by defining the essence of marriage in order to place the coexistence of man and woman in God's hands and to prevent the introduction of civil marriage.[85] In the same article, he arrives at the "concept of the citizen" with the insight that "the Jews . . . are and remain strangers to us in their inner nature"; emancipation may be meant "in a philanthropic way," but it only cements the "unfortunate national existence of the Jews."[86] Jews cannot be accepted as equal citizens considering that, for Savigny, the "aspiration of every human being" is "for the state or the true church, in which one can be a citizen interchangeably."[87]

As a cabinet member in Prussia's Ministry of Justice, Savigny intensifies this verdict and claims that the Jews are "annoying and harmful, but certainly dispensable."[88] Conceding to civil marriages might permit marriages between Jews and Christians, whereby the soilless-ness of the Jew contaminates the pure-blooded Christian Prussian. This must be prevented and,

84 The "Jewish question" is less a concept than a historical dynamic that arguably goes back to Imperial Germany (1850–90). It is, in very brief terms, constructed on and within the tension between two principal aspects of Jewish history, namely, Jewish Emancipation on the one hand and modern antisemitism on the other. Jewish Emancipation goes back to the "civic embitterment"/granting of equal rights to the Jews "when conscious efforts had been launched for the first time in Central Europe to hasten the process of transformation and transition from a corporate-feudal to a bourgeois-capitalist society." Given, however, that the emancipation of the Jews remains part and parcel of the so-called nationalist age – a climate of social aggression – it also implied modern antisemitism. It is in other words hardly surprising that the precarious position for the Jews in Germany as a minority group that was not completely integrated, particularly given being the target of age-old prejudices, gave "birth to modern antisemitism which sought to explain the crisis of society as the outcome of Jewish activities and wanted the emancipation of the Jews to be revoked." See more in Reinhard Rürup, "Emancipation and Crisis: The 'Jewish Question' in Germany 1850–1890," *The Leo Baeck Institute Yearbook* 20, no. 1 (1975): 13–25, at 14.

85 Savigny, "Stimmen für und wider neue Gesetzbücher," as quoted in Lahusen *Alles Recht*, 121–2. As Kennedy also argues, the distinction Savigny makes with marriage law works on the basis of an a priori understanding that each state has its own completely separate and distinct laws. Alas, if the "law of our state forbids polygamy, our judges must refuse the protection of the law to the polygamous marriages of foreigners, to whom they are permitted by the law of their own country." Ergo, "the family/patrimony distinction first establishes a basic principle as to the law that governs, and then a key exception when a foreign court is asked to enforce that law." Quoted in Kennedy, "Savigny's Family/Patrimony Distinction," 821.

86 Savigny, "Stimmen für und wider neue Gesetzbücher," quoted in Lahusen, *Alles Recht*, 122.

87 Henne and Kretschmann, "Der Christlich Fundierte Antijudaismus," 261.

88 Lahusen, *Alles Recht*, 122.

where it has already taken place, must be reversed. It is hardly surprising that Savigny continues this line of thought with his second class of exceptional "reasons of *public interest/welfare*" (earlier admitted to be moral issues) that establish "laws which restrict the acquisition of immoveable property by Jews."[89]

The invisible legal distinction between the "included" and the "excluded" is made visible with marriages and immovable property. For Savigny, the Jew ought to be kept outside the institutions of marriage and property by the apolitical jurist/translator. Such juridical gatekeeping favors and sustains an invisible economic status quo of the upper classes, itself entrenched in racially charged arguments,[90] and we should see Savigny's construction of the *Volksgeist* – essentializing national belonging through marriage and property – as anything but apolitical or liberal.[91] His distinctions carry an international legal dynamic as well:

> [S]everal independent states may voluntarily apply that which in each resides as law so far as it is suitable and as they find it convenient; but still no law arises in this way. Nevertheless[,] among different peoples a community of legal consciousness may arise like that which generates positive law in a people. The basis of this intellectual communion consists partly of a community of race, partly and principally in common religious convictions. Thereon grounds itself the international law which exists especially among the Christian states of Europe.[92]

Given that an idealized ecumenist Christianity is enough to unify Germany, it must be enough to unify Europe as well. And just as religious antisemitism was useful for German unity, so was the Jew important for a united Christian Europe. The Jews (together with the Turks and the Pagans) remained the adversary foreigners of all Christian Europeans into the nineteenth century.[93] The allusion here again is Rome. In a classic Savigny move, he argues that there is much to be learnt from the Peregrines' humane treatment of foreigners in Rome. However, "there can be no question of direct imitation" (of the Peregrines) because the "relationship of the Christian European States to each other is already quite unique."[94] Yet, in the relationship between the Christian

89 Henne and Kretschmann, "Der Christlich Fundierte Antijudaismus," 283.

90 See more in Lahusen, *Alles Recht*, 132.

91 Lahusen, *Alles Recht*, 121.

92 Savigny, *System of the Modern Roman Law*, 27–8.

93 Still, in his 1816 response to Pfeiffer, Savigny categorizes the Jews together with the Turks and Pagans – even if there were neither Turks nor Pagans in Germany at this time – as "foreigners" in order to create the nexus with the civilized Romans. See more in Henne and Kretschmann, "Der Christlich Fundierte Antijudaismus," 282.

94 Savigny, "Stimmen für und wider neue Gesetzbücher," 1. See also Henne and Kretschmann, "Der Christlich Fundierte Antijudaismus," 282–4.

European states, "the destruction of all borders is quite unnatural." Such a destruction of borders together with the civil and political equality of the Jews, "however well-intentioned it may be, is nothing less than benevolent in terms of its success, can only serve to preserve the unfortunate national existence of the Jews and, where possible, to expand it."[95] In brief, however exceptional the relationships between Christian European states are, sustaining national distinctions is important for the protection of Christianity because it stalls the infiltration of the Jew through the expansion of universal egalitarianism to all European citizens. For Savigny, Christianity remains the very source of all Roman(tic) law. However abstract such Christianity is in Europe, as long as it remains grounded in the jurist's Christian blood and the European soil, it will be eternal and secure.

9.4 CONCLUSION: PRUSSIA, THE UTOPIAN LAND OF THE *RECHTSWISSENSCHAFT*

Savignty's legacy is many things, much like the relationship between Christianity, the state and international law. An uncomfortable and often overlooked corner of this legacy in the discipline of international law is its long-standing, far too intimate relationship with antisemitism. That Savigny sought law to be grounded in *das gemeinsame Bewußtsein des Volkes* (the common consciousness of the people),[96] the *Nationalgeist* (national spirit), and eventually *Volksgeist* – instead of the king, the parliament, or even the community of sovereigns – obviously does not imply antisemitism. That he was considered a "Greater German" by the Nazis,[97] who later used his work to flesh out *Volksempfinden* (people/popular tendencies), also cannot implicate him in the Nazi death machinery of the Jews.[98] His promotion of an ecumenist Christian state, however, remains dangerously antisemitic both in theory and in practice.

95 "Aber auch hier ist die Vernichtung aller Gränze ganz unnatürlich. Vollends die Juden sind und bleiben uns ihrem innem Wesen nach Fremdlinge, und dieses zu verkennen konnte uns nur die unglückseligste Verwirrung politischer Begriffe verleiten; nicht zu gedenken, daß diese bürgerliche und politische Gleichstellung, so menschenfreundlich sie gemeynt seyn mag, dem Erfolg nach nichts weniger als wohlthätig ist, indem sie nur dazu dienen kann, die unglückselige Nationalexistenz der Juden zu erhalten und wo möglich noch auszubreiten." Savigny, "Stimmen für und wider neue Gesetzbücher," 215 n. 171.

96 Friedrich Carl von Savigny, *Vom Beruf unsrer Zeit für Gesetzgebung und Rechtswissenschaft* (Heidelberg: Mohr und Zimmer, 1814), 14.

97 Joachim Rückert, *Unrecht durch Recht: Zur Rechtsgeschichte der NS-Zeit* (Tübingen: Mohr Siebeck, 2018), 92.

98 Lahusen, *Alles Recht*, 68–9.

Contextualizing Savigny's scholarship in his Romanticist-*Deutsche Tischgesellschaft* milieu displays important parallels and similarities. Whereas the *Deutsche Tischgesellschaft* openly disqualified the membership of third-generation Jewish converts, Savigny legalizes their veneration for purity of Christian blood and soil in the way he exceptionalizes and links civil marriages and private property ownership to the emancipation of the Jew. This link attests to the beauty and danger of his *System*: while it was extremely strict and formal with its Roman/German legal distinctions and differences (e.g., legal generalities versus key exceptions, civil versus private law, *Recht* versus *Gesetz*), it remained in the hands of pseudo apolitical jurists who miraculously translated the people's spirit through and into law.[99]

The construction of the *Volksgeist* as a meta-juridical phenomenon that is both open to and protected by a specific Prussian, German, and Christian juridical consciousness in fact idealizes and institutionalizes a specific elitist class that represents German-nationhood. For Savigny, as for most other Romanticists, the creation of a *Volk*, *Volksrecht*, *Volksgeist*, and *Volkskultur* was a means to an end, namely the creation of an ecumenist Christian state. Given that such a state was defined through an act of negation, as a reaction to an unrealistic Other – be it the French, the Jews, the feminine, the *Philistern*, and so on – it was full of inner contradictions and tensions. Savigny attempted to solve these by keeping the Christian state on a pedestal while his "military" of jurists served as the gatekeepers of morality/public welfare.

Mostly, Savigny's German-Prussian-Christian jurists – who are rooted in blood and soil – safeguarded the Christian state against the Jewish ("state within a state") subversive, even if and especially because the Jews are the original owners of the Bible. That he showed no interest, not even anthropologically, in the possibility of the Jews sharing or at least possessing their own *Volksgeist* remains theoretically curious. Here, too, he keeps up with the Romantic Movement and, instead of facing such theoretical difficulties – on religious, philosophical, and legal levels – embraces the physical exclusion of the Jew.

This is certainly substantiated by Savigny's persistent effort to block the admission of (the Jewish jurist) Gans to the Berlin law faculty. Gans, an

99 Importantly, the notorious legal historian Franz Wieacker (1908–94), who was also a national socialist of the *Kieler Schule*, argues that Savigny's scholarly contributions are often distorted because too much attention is being paid to his *Volksgeist* and his involvement with German Romanticism. À la Wieacker, this focus diminishes from the administrative importance that Savigny's approach has precisely because of its formal and dry legalization. See more in Franz Wieacker, *Privatrechtsgeschichte der Neuzeit unter besonderer Berücksichtigung der deutschen Entwicklung* (Göttingen: Vandenhoeck & Ruprecht Verlag, 1967), 360–2.

educated Jew willing to convert for sociopolitical reasons, embodied everything that the *Deutsche Tischgesellschaft* feared and wished to nullify.[100] A few years later, Savigny wrote a very positive recommendation on the behalf of another Jewish convert, Julius Stahl (1802–61) – born Joel Golson (or Jolson) – to replace Gans.[101] Whereas this may reflect how he remained in line with the German Romantic inconsistencies, it could also show a growing moderation in his antisemitic zeal. Such decline in commitment could have been, as Henne and Kretschmann argue, a relaxation of anxiety in the wake of Friedrich Wilhelm IV's robust efforts to build a Christian state.[102]

Savigny's legacy is triumphant. After all, it was through his progressive private legal agenda that he succeeded in postponing the enactment of the Civil Code (*Bürgerliches Gesetzbuch* or BGB) for almost a hundred years after that of the French Civil Code (1804). However, even after its belated birth, Savigny looms in its background: it is still that which is outside the BGB's frame that determines its content.[103] In more than one way, Savigny placed *Rechtswissenschaft* upon its "unique scientific abstraction and formal rigour," as the gatekeeper to any social change in Germany.[104] It is precisely within the abstraction embedded in *Rechtswissenschaft* that the law sustains a normativity to deal with the existing social differences in a way that perpetuates them in the new codification.[105]

Similarly, in international law we still get a reminder of Savigny's juridical consciousness of "general principles of law" as specified by Article 38(1)c of the ICJ Statute. This too – especially as Hersch Lauterpacht (1897–1960) read it – serves as a blank check and even a duty requiring the legal actor to rely on his/her "natural built-in ethical ability" to solve any possible gaps in the law before

100 Only in 1826, after many years of seeking a position at the Berlin law faculty, and upon conversion, did Gans finally achieve this goal.

101 This is not to say that Savigny really "forgave" Stahl's Jewish roots. It was apparently more important to have someone outside the Hegelian School than to discriminate against Stahl's Jewish origins – evidence that nineteenth-century conversions were not the only acts of opportunism. Antisemitism seems to have been just as opportunistic. Savigny may have secured Stahl a position but he in no way made his life easy in Berlin. See more in Paz, *Gateway between a Distant God*, 105–7.

102 Henne and Kretschmann, "Der Christlich Fundierte Antijudaismus," 303.

103 As Lahusen terms it, the German "civil law is always only as good as legislation outside its frame. This makes the BGB as a whole a fragile entity." Not to mention that the same BGB "paragraphs were patient enough to serve under the Empire, the Weimar Republic, the Third Reich, two and a half decades of GDR and [the] Federal Republic equally." Lauhsen, *Alles Recht*, 135.

104 Lauhsen, *Alles Recht*, 132.

105 Lauhsen, *Alles Recht*, 132.

they become *non liquets*.[106] That Lauterpacht's legal actor was a liberal normative-based internationalist – who stands in a diametrical opposition to Savigny's Prussian, Christian German – only illustrates the necessarily empty basis for "the juridical consciousness."

It remains fascinating, even if counterintuitive, to note that it was Savigny's Christian view of life and the Prussian blood and soil narrative that became Europeanized and then internationalized. Such a Christian and antisemitic legacy upon its historical Eurocentrism characterizes international law and "remains a tool of subjugation and liberation of the 'Other' to date and hence, albeit historical and circumstantial differences, continues to be the discipline's Achilles' heel."[107] From his nineteenth-century Romantic and antisemitic milieu in Berlin, Savigny – who conceived the church and the modern Prussian state identically – understood the importance of political theology. He definitely did his best to legalize it both in theory and in practice. Be that as it may, one has to wonder how Savigny would have reacted to the political theology of Carl Schmitt (1888–1985). Whereas for Schmitt the "sovereign is he who decides on the exception,"[108] for Savigny the sovereign is a Prussian, Christian, German, and antisemitic jurist. Today, Savigny's views throughout Western Europe and the Anglophone world would be condemned. But many of our doctrines, institutions, and background imagination – especially at the interface of Christianity and international law – continue to be haunted by the demon of antisemitism.

RECOMMENDED READING

Henne, Thomas, and Carsten Kretschmann, "Der Christlich Fundierte Antijudaismus Savignys Und Seine Umsetzung in Der Rechtspraxis." *Zeitschrift der Savigny-Stiftung für Rechtsgeschichte: Germanistische Abteilung* 119, no. 1 (2002): 250–315.

Lahusen, Benjamin. *Alles Recht geht vom Volksgeist aus: Friedrich Carl v. Savigny und die moderne Rechtswissenschaft*. Berlin: Nicolaische Verlagsbuchhandlung, 2013.

Nienhaus, Stefan. *Geschichte der deutschen Tischgesellschaft*. Tübingen: Niemeyer, 2003.

von Savigny, Friedrich Carl. "Stimmen für und wider neue Gesetzbücher." *Zeitschrift für geschichtliche Rechtswissenschaft* 3 (1816): 1–52.

Vom Beruf unsrer Zeit für Gesetzgebung und Rechtswissenschaft (Heidelberg: Mohr und Zimmer, 1814).

106 See more in Paz, *Gateway between a Distant God*, 335.

107 Paz, *Gateway between a Distant God*, 225.

108 Carl Schmitt, *Political Theology: Four Chapters on the Concept of Sovereignty*, 2nd ed., trans. Georg Schwab (Chicago: University of Chicago Press, 2005).

10

Missionary Knowledge and the Empirical Foundations of Modern International Legal Thought

Jedidiah J. Kroncke

It is now near conventional wisdom that the nineteenth century witnessed a fundamental shift in the conceptual foundations of international law, and that this change was intertwined with a coordinate shift in the geography of Western international legal institutions beyond Europe.[1] At the same time, these shifts are commonly described as also involving a general process of secularization which decentered religiously inspired notions of natural law for positivist legal science which helped facilitate the progressive inclusion of non-Christian nations in the Middle East and Asia.[2] As generally follows such grand narratives of break and rupture, more granular histories have produced nuanced and ambivalent explorations of the myriad ways in which social change unfolds in muddier path-dependent genealogies. For international law, below the surface of the great nineteenth-century break are numerous instances of how religious imaginations and concepts still impacted basic notions about the aims and meaning of international legal practice.

This continuity amid transformation between the secular and the religious is now often evoked through citation of Carl Schmitt's concept of political theology. Yet, simply asserting that secularization is not a clear disjuncture from the past then begs a number of questions about the scope and consequence of such continuities. For international law, one clear site of this complicated inheritance is how teleology and evolution intermixed to ground

[1] Many now seminal texts have been writing on the movement of European international law into other parts of the world. For an updated overview and new synthesis, see Jennifer Pitts, *Boundaries of the International: Law and Empire* (Cambridge, MA: Harvard University Press, 2018).

[2] Many now seminal texts have also been written on this transition, e.g., Gerrit Gong, *The Standard of "Civilization" in International Society* (Oxford: Clarendon Press, 1984); Alexander Orakhelashvili, "The Idea of European, International Law," *European Journal of International Law* 17, no. 2 (2006): 315–47.

the notion that international law had a sort of inherent agency that could act upon nations to move them toward some ideal form of civilization.[3] Whether it be bringing peace to the globe through religious homogenization or post-millennial notions of perfecting the human world to induce the second coming of Christ, the nineteenth century was rife with notions of human development which sought active reconciliation with the emergent paradigms of natural and social sciences.[4] At the forefront in early debates about potential agents of social transformation in "foreign" contexts, international legal thinking of the era was suffused with diverse claims about secularization that were highly inconsistent even in professional legal discourse, where overt religious motivations were still forefront in public discourse. This presumed progressive agency abroad often led to quite blurred lines between the descriptive and the normative in accounts of international law's past and present.

Especially when the geographical scope of nineteenth-century international law is contemplated – narrowly understood as the global expansion of a particular set of European practices – this blurriness is acute as the potential agency of international law moved from Martti Koskenniemi's gentle civilizer to the asserted vessel of wholesale foreign transformation. At the transition from the nineteenth to the twentieth century, a whole host of secular practices took on an evangelical character which was openly acknowledged at the time but often retrospectively glossed over by modern perspectives convinced of their more secular lineages. Law is perhaps the field most plagued by this backwards-looking reinvention.[5] For in relatively short order, the once popular argument for the culturally particular grounds of law epitomized in the eighteenth century by Montesquieu gave way to the notion that law and religion could be exported to stimulate countries both non-Christian and deemed socially backward. The nineteenth-century intermingling of territory and peoples enabled by mutually reinforcing changes in trade and technology may have forced a rejection of strong cultural essentialism by necessity, but it also provided fertile ground for recasting what was considered universal and particular in law without fully severing law's religious meanings.

[3] Martti Koskenniemi, *The Gentle Civilizer of Nations: The Rise and Fall of International Law, 1870–1960* (Cambridge: Cambridge University Press, 2001).

[4] The tumultuous nineteenth century gave rise to classic theories of social change that inspired the foundations of modern sociology. However, in cross-cultural context this explanation often veered toward rationalization of existing power inequalities. Chloe Campbell, *Race and Empire* (New York: Manchester University Press, 2007).

[5] This lament motivated Harold Berman's now classic treatises on the subject. Harold J. Berman, *Law and Revolution*, 2 vols. (Cambridge, MA: Harvard University Press, 1983).

Herein, international law's place in and between nations and cultures, as well as in and between legal practices, displayed the traditionally evocative qualities of law for cross-cultural comparison and reasoning.[6] Law's existence as a form of institutionalized normative reasoning, never truly extant as Max Weber's disenchanted formally rational ideal type, has always enabled it to make claims to both moral expression and pragmatic efficiency. Such duality lends itself to smuggling the cultural particular into the universally productive. The coincidence of moral and pragmatic justifications is the subject of numerous studies of the role of law in empire and colonialism, where "good" law can be championed as sourced in one national tradition but justified on the terms of transcultural notions of efficacy.[7] The turn from colonial to neocolonial domination, of particular relevance to the emergence of American legal internationalism, doubled-down on this joint-assertion while often openly splicing religious sentiment into its claims about international law's promise in foreign contexts.

Within these broad strokes, the metaphorical coherence between evangelical notions of the salvation of the soul through religious conversion and the salvation of foreign nations through legal conversion was central. While professional discourses on international law may have publicly secularized various notions and practices, in popular discourse such metaphor was still dominant – an unfortunate elision in many traditional studies of international law's transformation to date. And an omission that provides one reason for why extant histories have often pushed the agency of foreign jurists and actors to the margins of international legal history.[8]

One thread of inquiry that reveals the pathways through which evangelical agency was transmitted to international legal thinking, and continues to be central to the popular life of international law, is the incredible impact of religious missionaries in providing and shaping the empirical representations of foreign legal and social practice upon which even countervailing positions in European and American international legal debates drew. More specifically, the very notion of foreign transformation through international legal practice was rendered plausible by the absorption of the proselytizing

[6] The use of law in cross-cultural understanding is a classic concern of legal anthropology. Laura Nader, "Promise or Plunder? A Past and Future Look at Law and Development," *Global Jurist* 7, no. 2 (2007): 1–21.

[7] This duality of domestic law assumed to be averse to foreign influences because of its cultural characteristics but still cast as exportable to improve the operational efficiency of foreign law is the core concern of Jedidiah Kroncke, "Law and Development as Anti-Comparative Law," *Vanderbilt Journal of Transnational Law* 40, no. 2 (2012): 477–555.

[8] Arnulf Becker Lorca, "Universal International Law: Nineteenth-Century, Histories of Imposition and Appropriation," *Harvard Journal of International Law* 51, no. 2 (2010): 475–522.

intentions of religious missionaries who fashioned many of the proto-concepts of modern development thinking. Moreover, this preoccupation with conversion suffused the very institutions of Western internationalism by acquiring, collectively disciplining, and disseminating cross-cultural knowledge and authority. Through a range of formal and informal mechanisms, missionaries transmitted evangelical presumptions into spaces presumed to be thoroughly secular. Simply considering the empirical sources on which claims about foreign law were made, or who formally secular agents relied on to form their opinions, during the nineteenth century reveals the formative impact of missionaries on international law long after their centrality to professional Western internationalism had faded.

Moreover, missionary's naturalization of the moral imperatives of foreign transformation never retreated from popular discourse, where even critiques of empire and exploitation were couched as interference with the proper transformation of foreign peoples.[9] Even those global actors motivated by sheer profit often retained private religious rationalizations regarding their work, and regardless of private sentiment had to negotiate the public terms of international legitimacy deeply impacted by a century of the active dissemination of missionary representations of foreign cultures and law across all spectrums of Western civil society.

The ideal type of this model of missionary impact is the relationship of Protestant missionaries to American understandings of China.[10] Invocations of China's regeneration through international law were critical to nineteenth-century international legal thinking more generally, and were an important intermediate step in asserted notions of legal evolution between "savage" and "civilized" law. The American relationship to China is especially instructive as it was here that missionaries retained near absolute control over how elite and non-elite Americans understood China and Chinese law well into the mid-twentieth century. Even quite conservative notions of American participation in international legal institutions were cast as the best method for redeeming China, a fallen empire, in the mold of American modernity – framed as a secular modernity but suffused with aspirational religious sentiment. The rest of this chapter will explore the historical impact of missionaries on the empirical grounds of international legal thinking, with reference to this ideal

9 Geneviève Dorais, "Missionary Critiques of Empire, 1920–1932: Between Interventionism and Anti-Imperialism," *The International History Review* 39, no. 3 (2017): 377–403; Ruth Slade, "English Missionaries and the Beginning of the Anti-Congolese Campaign in England," *Revue belge de Philologie et d'Histoire* 33, no.1 (1955): 37–73.

10 Exploring this historical relationship is a key preoccupation of Jedidiah Kroncke, *The Futility of Law and Development* (New York: Oxford University Press, 2016).

type and its implications for the still active but retreating dream of international law's civilizing potential.

10.1 THE TRANSFORMATIVE ETHER OF MISSIONARY REPRESENTATIONS

Almost all social reasoning, no matter how abstract, has some sort of anthropological predicate. The classic works of political philosophy presupposed varied states of nature from which the modern evolved; contemporary social scientists find themselves betwixt notions of culture and genetics in modeling how humans reason. Disagreements recur to the defense of such basic assumptions, much as moral philosophy does to first principles. In the history of international law, the how and why of the expansion of the basic Westphalian system beyond Europe similarly turned on arguments about the qualities and character of foreign peoples. Much has been written about the idea of the noble savage, and the various civilizing rationales of wholesale colonial usurpation of sovereignty in lands judged empty of proper legal regimes.[11] For lands considered more organized or, perhaps most crucially, more capable of resisting colonial expansion, such usurpation was less certain, even if desired. Still, judgments about foreign peoples were premised on available representations of their values and practices repatriated for domestic consumption and initially not by actors from those lands.

For European international law, the traditional criteria of national Christian religious practice for inclusion increasingly confronted the unassailable fact that the majority of the world was non-Christian. Many writers have explored how notions of "civilization" were developed as a facially neutral term with which to argue over whether nations with Islamic or polytheistic religious traditions were compatible with this new standard.[12] Less explored is how these judgments were formed, and whether secularized intellectual formulations were the actual drivers of the politics of legitimacy in which international law operated.

The basic frame of "cross-cultural" representation depends on some sort of spatial geography of discrete cultures. In premodern context, the cultural

11 The interrelationship of evolutionary theories of law and negative judgments of foreign legal systems is unfortunately central to the early history of comparative law. Peter Stein, *Legal Evolution* (New York: Cambridge University Press, 1980).

12 Contrast Lassa Oppenheim, "The Science of International Law: Its Task and Method," *The American Journal of International Law* 2, no. 2 (1908): 313–56; Gong, *The Standard of "Civilization" in International Society*.

other was powerfully shaped by access and transportation – the next village over could be the entire feasible world of otherness by which one's cultural identity was contrasted.[13] Over time, as technologies narrowed the effective distances between peoples, the average human still had to rely on a variety of exceptional intermediaries who moved between cultures and transmitted their impressions home. A new wave of histories has reshaped the timeline and content of the earliest exchanges between what may be considered nations, some arguing for important scientific links between Europe and Asia as early as the Roman Empire. It is little coincidence that some of the earliest "bestselling" novels of the printing press era were European travelogues of traders and well-heeled explorers who claimed to have traveled to the farthest logistical limits of their eras.[14] Their observations routinely included descriptions of the law of foreign peoples, commonly portrayed through the spectacle of criminal trials. Military expeditions also generated tales of foreign locales or, such in the exceptional case of the Mongols, brought the "foreign" to Europe's doorstep.

As such travel became less exceptional, traders were joined by religious missionaries as the most strongly motivated parties to move across cultures. Yet more than simply seeking to extract value from such relationships, the missionary was motivated by the very prospect of changing aspects of the foreign into the familiar. The particularly evangelical quality of Christian, and later Islamic, theology made missionary work one of the most consistent institutional pathways through which Europeans after the sixteenth century became familiar with far-flung nations. For missionaries, representing Europe to foreign nations and foreign nations to Europe were two sides of the same coin of legitimacy through which they sought to gain support for their endeavors.

As others have argued, missionaries thus became the first institutionalized source for empirical knowledge about foreign cultures. Primary to this influence was their acquisition of exceptional linguistic competences, perhaps an even more essential requirement of their enterprise than that of merchants. The very act of translating the Bible into foreign languages demanded a great deal of effort and interaction with local peoples willing

13 The increasing speed of maritime travel initiated entire new worlds of cross-cultural representation in law. Renisa Mawani, "Law, Settler Colonialism, and 'the Forgotten Space' of Maritime Worlds," *Annual Review of Law and Social Science* 12 (2016): 107–31.

14 While Marco Polo's fabled travel writings are the most famous, most every part of the world that became accessible to new writers attracted very broad audiences. For a less explored context, see Elizabeth Horodowich, *The Venetian Discovery of America* (Melbourne: Cambridge University Press, 2018).

to inform such translation.[15] Reciprocally, expertise about foreign religions was almost exclusively established by missionaries seeking to define that which they sought to overcome.[16] The transactional chains of international commerce also rarely required the sustained and engaged presence that missionary work demanded, nor did they necessarily motivate merchants to explore foreign cultures beyond those spaces incident to their own exchanges.[17]

This broader field of missionary expertise was not the only comparative advantage that missionaries developed, as the very nature of their longitudinal presence gave them a privileged claim to representing change over time in foreign nations.[18] Such advantage was also incident to the fact that their ultimate aim of religious conversion was a form of moral change at the individual level which was consistently claimed to be a catalytic force for large social transformation. Few missionary writings which discussed individual conversions refrained from the hopeful leap to beneficial transformations in law, commerce, and other realms of culture. For Europeans of varied cultural backgrounds, missionaries, though clearly sectarian, spoke this language of change in terms familiar to elite and non-elite audiences about the redemptive force of Christian conviction. The solvency of Christianity as a universal basis for social transformation required often creative intellectual work, reconciling seemingly alien peoples and their cultures within biblical historical narratives.[19]

It is thus not surprising that these missionary representations migrated to nonreligious forms of thinking by virtue of their descriptive quality but also by their active attempt to reconcile difference and social change in an increasingly tumultuous Europe. Numerous studies have been made of how Enlightenment thinkers drew on notions of foreign cultures to assert their proto-anthropological

15 It is difficult to overstate the centrality of missionaries not only to linguistic knowledge about non-Western legal cultures but also to their long-term impacts by creating many of the systems of transliteration still at work in the world today. Alastair Pennycook, "The Modern Mission: The Language Effects of Christianity," *Journal of Language Identity and Education* 4, no. 2 (2005): 137–55; Derek Peterson, "Colonizing Language? Missionaries and Gikuyu Dictionaries, 1904 to 1914," *History in Africa* 24, (1997): 257–72.

16 Geoffrey Oddie, *Imagined Hinduism: British Protestant Missionary Constructions of Hinduism, 1793–1900* (London: Sage Publications, 2006).

17 "British traders did not flock to the new inland trading centres and the consulates remained somewhat lonely 'outposts' with a small handful of British subjects – usually missionaries – as the only residents and sojourners." P. D. Coates, *The China Consuls* (Hong Kong: Cambridge University Press, 1988), 255.

18 Guido Abbattista, "Chinese Law and Justice: George Thomas Staunton and the European Discourses on China in the Eighteenth and Nineteenth Centuries," in *Law, Justice and Codification in Qing China*, ed. Guido Abbattista (Trieste: Edizioni Università di Trieste, 2017), 68.

19 Albert Wu, *From Christ to Confucius: German Missionaries, Chinese Christians and the Globalization of Christianity, 1860–1950* (New Haven: Yale University Press, 2016).

claims about human nature and various institutions. The most powerful example of this impact was the role of Jesuit missionaries in producing representations of China starting in the sixteenth century.[20] The investment of the Jesuit order in sending missionaries to China led to a dual representative authority. To a chaotic Europe, where the Catholic Church had been challenged by the Protestant Reformation, the Jesuits leveraged their access to China as a wealthy and stable empire to enhance their intellectual authority at home. Simultaneously, the Jesuits represented a dynamic Europe to China to argue for the type of social benefit that Christian faith offered/produced. The institutional presence of the Jesuits in China led to a set of disciplined practices for producing and disseminating their writings on China in Europe, subordinating private disagreement and criticisms for the greater good of the mission. As a result, their image of China became key to secularized notions of a modern rational state advanced by thinkers such as Gottfried Wilhelm Leibniz or Voltaire.[21]

In time, the Jesuit monopoly over representations of China weakened, in large part due to the growing confidence of European nations now looking to assert themselves internationally. The Sinophilism of the Enlightenment gave way to a new Sinophobic discourse where China was recast as a stagnant and oppressive empire. Subsequent missionaries, especially in eras of greater Chinese political turmoil, produced quite different images of China and, with increasing frequency, Chinese law. As such, if one looks carefully into the basis of Sinophobic ideas promoted by thinkers as diverse in sentiment and time as Georg Wilhelm Friedrich Hegel and John Stuart Mill, missionaries' representations are still frequent and authoritative.[22]

In fact, even as European nations began to spread their influence across the globe as the range of colonial engagement expanded, this same dynamic of missionary representation reveals itself again to varying degrees. While Edward Said's claims about Middle Eastern Orientalism do not foreground missionaries, empirical claims about Islamic law have clear missionary roots,[23] or at the

[20] The history of the Jesuits in China is a recurrent subject of study, in large part given this pioneering impact. Liam Brockey, *Journey to the East* (London: Harvard University Press, 2007).

[21] Some have gone as far as to say that Confucius was the patron saint of Enlightenment thinkers. Adolf Reichwein, *China and Europe* (New York: Barnes & Noble, 1925), 19.

[22] Teshale Tibebu, *Hegel and the Third World: The Making of Eurocentrism in World History* (Syracuse, NY: Syracuse University Press, 2011), 178; Jennifer Pitts, *A Turn to Empire: The Rise of Imperial Liberalism in Britain and France* (Princeton: Princeton University Press, 2005), 299 n. 65.

[23] The classic modern study on the role of missionaries in American foreign policy is Joseph Grabill, *Protestant Diplomacy and the Near East* (Minneapolis: University of Minnesota Press, 1971). For an update, see Emrah Sahin, *Faithful Encounters: Authorities*

very least missionaries were able to frame claims about the infirmities of Islamic law in the most evocative terms.[24] While not singularly attached to as directed a political agenda as the Jesuit project in China, the comparative advantages of missionaries were increasingly relevant as cross-cultural reasoning became core to international relations when even the rawest exercises of military domination abroad were legitimated by notions of noble empire and civilizing process dependent on descriptions produced almost exclusively by missionaries.

In parallel, the foundations of modern social science in the eighteenth to nineteenth centuries were driven by the desire to explain the rapid pace of change within Euro-American society and the differences among nations. As posited in Norbert Elias's work, many of the tropes of foreign difference and civilization were propounded intranationally before they were applied internationally.[25] It is similarly again not coincidental that domestic religious revival led to greater investments in missionary work abroad, and such revivals were stimulated by social anxiety.[26] While many modern social thinkers publicly eschewed religious reasoning in their work, the world of empirical reference in which they operated was still one dominated by missionary writings, and many histories of anthropological science grapple with the formative influence of missionary writings that often were the only written representations of "traditional" legal practices available, which in some cases holds true even today.[27] For what were called "savage" societies, these representations, however humane in intention, made it difficult to disentangle the idea that foreign people needed Western institutions as much as they needed Christianity. Missionaries were often quite adept at making the argument that the two were interrelated and in doing so advanced the earliest arguments about the discrete determinants of modern social progress.

Key to tying together these representations of foreign peoples to emerging notions of scientific reasoning was evolutionary thinking. Beyond cultural particularists like Montesquieu, almost every key social theorist of the

and American Missionaries in the Ottoman Empire (Montreal: McGill-Queen's University Press, 2018).

24 Jedidiah Kroncke, "The Flexible Orientalism of Islamic Law," *UCLA Journal of Islamic and Near Eastern Law* 4, no. 1 (2005): 41–73.

25 Norbert Elias, *The Civilizing Process* (Oxford: Blackwell, 1969).

26 William McLoughlin, *Revivals, Awakenings and Reform* (Chicago: University of Chicago Press, 1978).

27 The powerful contemporary effect of missionary representation on traditional legal practices is classically explored in Martin Chanock, *Law, Custom, and Social Order* (London: Cambridge University Press, 1985). For a broader take on the impact of missionaries on African history, see David Maxwell, "The Missionary Movement in African and World History," *The Historical Journal* 58, no. 4 (2015): 901–30.

nineteenth century onward advanced some sort of evolutionary scheme to classify foreign difference and explain European advances.[28] Legal practice increasingly took a central place as indicia for such schemes, with Henry Maine and Henry Morgan but two of the many thinkers who used missionary sources in their attempts to work out the relationship between legal change and social development.[29] If one looks closely at even less empirically oriented theorists, missionary writings are still the ultimate sources for their claims, even if not directly cited. Weber's typology of legal reasoning drew on then entrenched representations of foreign law produced by missionary authors, and has had perhaps the most lasting impact on modern comparative reasoning across the globe.[30] And even as late as the 1940s, Weber's influential American interpreter Talcott Parsons expounded modernization theory by drawing on missionary informants from China to frame his thinking about Asian development.[31]

In recent decades, there has been a revival in recognizing and outlining this missionary imprint,[32] where the relationship between missionaries and colonialism is explored through the role of missionary ethnological writings on academic traditions across Europe and the United States.[33] Consistent with

28 Even Montesquieu, who was central to shifting views of Chinese law toward the modern trope of "despotism," devoted a great deal of time to learning about Chinese culture and made friends with a Chinese citizen Hoange who was accompanied by a French missionary. Ming Dong Gu, "Sinologism, the Western World View, and the Chinese Perspective," *Comparative Literature and Culture* 15, no. 2 (2013): 2. https://doi.org/10.7771/1481–4374.2213.

29 Maine's place and impact in this discourse are explored in Roslyn Jolly, "Robert Louis Stevenson, Henry Maine and the Anthropology of Comparative Law," *Journal of British Studies* 45, no. 3 (2006): 556–80. Morgan's writing was far more humane but, by virtue of its subject, i.e., Native American populations in the United States, was heavily impacted by and in discourse with missionary writings. Lewis Henry Morgan, *Ancient Society* (Chicago: Charles H. Kerr, 1910).

30 The negative impact of Weber's categorization of Islamic and China law is a recurrent subject of critique, even though Weber himself presented them only as ideal types. Robert Marsh, "Weber's Misunderstanding of Traditional Chinese Law," *American Journal of Sociology* 106, no. 2 (2000): 281–302; Bryan Turner, "Revisiting Weber and Islam," *The British Journal of Sociology* 61, no. 1 (2010): 161–6.

31 William Buxton and Lawrence Nichols, "Talcott Parsons and the 'Far East' at Harvard," *American Sociologist* 31, no. 2 (2000): 5–17.

32 Sjaak van der Geest and Jon Kirby, "The Absence of the Missionary in African Ethnography, 1930–65," *African Studies Review* 35, no. 3 (1992): 59–103.

33 It would take a study of its own to bring together that now rapid proliferation of research across countries and time that illustrates the foundational impact of missionaries on the production and interpretation of knowledge about foreign cultures, often dubbed "ethnology." Representatively, see Walter Veit, "Missionaries and Their Ethnographic Instructions," *The Royal Society of Victoria* 127, no. 1 (2015): 73–82; Didier Aubert, "Surveys and Romance: Methodist Missionaries' Photographs of the South American 'Field' in the Early 20th Century," *IdeAs* 6 (2015): 1; Timothy Man-kong Wong, "Printing, Evangelism, and

each national or academic variation is that, whatever the varying political sensibilities or theological differences among missionary authors, they all produced their work under the basic assumption that they were themselves vectors of change in the broader context of the redemption of the societies in which they worked. Change was afoot, and they made aggressive claims as to the already demonstrated role of Western influence therein. Again, missionary writings were frequently edited and molded by institutional actors who actively circulated these representations to the home audiences who were the essential drivers for missionary financial support and political legitimacy.[34] If one looks to the first Western historians of various parts of the world, or sociologists, it is not uncommon for their motivation to be shaped by personal and familial experience with missionary work.[35]

Even this dividing line between missionary empirical representations and legal theorization was blurry as many missionaries of the nineteenth century were formally trained in law well before it was common to take on other forms of secular expertise. Returning to China, we can see that the two most internationally influential nineteenth-century representations of Chinese law were contained in the multivolume *Journey through the Chinese Empire* by French Lazarist missionary Evarist Régis Huc's and *The Middle Kingdom* by American lawyer-missionary Samuel Williams.[36] Huc epitomized a form of representation more closely tied to traditional colonial thought – that Chinese society was corrupt and its legal practice barbaric and thus in need of wholesale transformation from the outside.[37] Williams, though originally of this tradition, progressively shifted to the more modern representation that it was simply Chinese institutions that were corrupt, and that its people would

Sinology: A Historical Appraisal of the Sinological Publications by Protestant Missionaries in South China," *Journal of the History of Christianity in Modern China* 8 (2009): 47–64; Nicolas Peterson and Anna Kenny, eds., *German Ethnography in Australia* (Acton: Australian National University Press, 2017).

34 The development of missionary public relations methods often had them at the forefront of using novel multimedia technologies and refunding their use in domestic deputation work. Maud Michaud, "The Missionary and the Anthropologist," *Studies in World Christianity* 22, no. 1 (2016): 57–74; Cecile Fromont, "Collecting and Translating Knowledge Across Cultures: Capuchin Missionary Images of Early Modern Central Africa," in *Collecting Across Cultures: Material Exchanges in the Early Modern Atlantic World*, ed. Daniela Bleichmar and Peter Mancall (Philadelphia: University of Pennsylvania Press, 2011), 134–54.

35 Notable early examples are Samuel Kidd at University College London, James Legge at Oxford, Samuel Williams at Yale, and Kenneth LaTourette at Yale.

36 Evariste Huc, *A Journey through the Chinese Empire* (New York: Harper, 1856); Samuel Williams, *The Middle Kingdom* (New York: Wiley & Putnam, 1848).

37 Lauren Pfister, "Rethinking Mission in China: James Hudson Taylor and Timothy Richard," in *The Imperial Horizons of British Protestant Missions, 1880–1914*, ed. Andrew Porter (Grand Rapids, MI: William B. Eerdmans Publishing Co., 2003), 183–212.

welcome foreign (in this case American) legal and political institutions to give true expression to their genuine values. This turn in representation was crucial for noncolonial conceptualizations of foreign engagement as they allowed criticism and distance from formal colonialism by giving symbolic prominence to the value of missionary work to build consensual foreign converts. And while missionaries often supported outright military interventions to advance their cause, they were restrained by the still essentially consensual nature of individual religious conversion.[38]

What now may be called the transformative ether of missionary representations of foreign law thus became naturalized in international legal thinking and was one powerful arena in which to reconcile the aims of formally religious and secular objectives at the heart of international law's putative nineteenth-century turn to a more scientific self-conceptualization – while retaining its theoretical agency in favor of foreign transformation. While "civilization" could be advanced as an objective social metric for measuring who was in and who outside the proper purview of international law, international law's evangelical character, even for those formally admitted to its ambit, was rendered plausible and practical by an empirical foundation laid by missionaries who posited social transformation as a natural outgrowth of consensual interaction with Western law.

A telling example of this dynamic is the well-studied life of American Presbyterian missionary William Martin.[39] As discussed shortly, the development of the United States as a global power in the late nineteenth and early twentieth centuries was intimately connected to American missionaries' rise to global prominence after the American Civil War. Martin's tenure in China partially predated this rise, but his career demonstrates the growing power of lawyer-missionaries as key intermediaries in the international legal system, as he served both as a diplomatic interpreter in treaty negotiations and as a key player in domestic Chinese educational reform. Martin saw his evangelical calling as crucially enabled by, and in his case primarily sourced in, his ability to facilitate China's introduction into the Western international legal system. His long tenure in China granted him the rare linguistic facility to translate seminal international law texts into Chinese, driven by the faith that their technical terms embodied Christian values that could revive the progressively disintegrating Qing dynasty regime. Close readings of Martin's translations

[38] For an avid collection of public/private hypocrisy in the context of China, Hugh Deane, *Good Deeds and Gunboats* (San Francisco: China Books & Periodicals, 1990), 9.

[39] Mary Boggs, "William Alexander Parsons Martin, Missionary to China, 1850–1916" (MA thesis, McCormick Theological Seminary, 1949).

show how he used his cultural knowledge to inform his translations, giving texts with positivist orientations natural law reworkings more amenable to elite Chinese sensibilities. His most widely read book was entitled *The Awakening of China* and its third section is aptly titled "China in Transformation."[40]

Like the Jesuits, Martin spoke to two audiences over which he worked to represent international law derived from the West as a universal good: by representing Chinese culture to the Western world as compatible with international law and to Chinese audiences as an important arena in which to invest for China's future. He presented international law as a tool for the realization of Chinese independence, and presented Chinese actions as influenced by his legal work to American audiences looking for evidence of Chinese emulation. Martin saw no tension between his religious motivations and his international legal work, and, while he may not have been cited by later international legal thinkers about China directly, his work helped to set a lasting hermeneutical tone for the encounter.

10.2 FROM INTELLECTUAL ETHER TO INSTITUTIONALIZED ETHOS

The influence of missionaries on, or participation with, those engaged in cross-national legal comparison and reasoning should be the grounds of any complete intellectual history of international law. Yet, while this was an important context for the secularization of the missionary's transformative ethos, it was just once facet of the larger process of normalizing this perspective among actors not actively engaged in foreign relations. As mentioned earlier, a key comparative advantage for the circulation of missionary representations was their development of disciplined institutional practices for collecting and disseminating materials throughout their home societies and elsewhere in the West. Moreover, their specific linguistic capabilities did not just mediate specific acts of formal translation or interpretation but granted them positions of authority in a whole host of professional and informal spaces of foreign expertise. While sectarian differences were still quite real, the missionary

[40] Several recent studies have detailed the impact of Martin's missionary intent on his translation work. Li Zhaojie, "The Impact of International Law on the Transformation of China's Perception of the World: A Lesson from History," *Maryland Journal of International Law* 27, no. 1 (2012): 128–53; Junnan Lai, "Sovereignty and 'Civilization': International Law and East Asia in the Nineteenth Century," *Modern China* 40, no. 3 (2014): 282–314; Zhiguang Yin, "Heavenly Principles? The Translation of International Law in 19th-Century China and the Constitution of Universality," *The European Journal of International Law* 27, no. 4 (2016): 1005–23. This work also emphasizes how Martin's representations were less than critically imbibed by Western diplomatic audiences.

movement also benefited from numerous transnational collaborations which coordinated the global circulation of missionaries and their representations in the larger effort to save foreign souls.[41]

The expansion of international contact over the nineteenth century did allow for the production of alternative sources of foreign representation, such as the increasingly formal institutions of commerce and diplomacy which, at least in assertion, were secular in character. For some countries, notably England, the extensivity of their commercial empire generated interests and perspectives distinct from the missionary enterprise, if still codependent in practice. This expansion was matched by the professionalization of English diplomatic and colonial agencies who were often beset by nonreligious political and military imperatives. For many countries these expansions were less robust, and in some cases, such as the United States, the tangible infrastructure of the international missionary movement would outweigh commercial and diplomatic investments decades into the twentieth century.

Take for example the rise of overseas journalism and print mediums such as the modern newspaper or periodical. Here we can see that, even in formally secular institutions, missionary actors were key to the early organization of many foreign offices and editions, if not their founders, and were commonly the sources for overseas reporters.[42] Investment in producing and translating the Bible overlapped with the capability to translate and disseminate secular texts abroad, while making how missionaries reported foreign developments at home one of the original practices of interest journalism.[43] As mentioned earlier, the great sensitivity of missionaries to the financial bases of their support at home made public relations an inherent part of their institutional development.[44] The active role of missionaries in the rise of foreign print

[41] Walter Mead, *Special Providence* (New York: Routledge, 2002), 146.

[42] China was a key site for attracting overseas investments in journalism. Beyond Marx's well-known stint as a journalist covering the subject, it was during the Taiping Rebellion in China that disciplined missionary representations were used to strongly shape European perceptions of an event otherwise quite adverse to the missionary effort. Wong Ching Him Felix, "The Images of the Taiping Heavenly Kingdom as Shown in the Publications in France, Germany, and Italy during the Second Half of the Nineteenth Century," *Journal of Chinese Studies* 55 (2012): 139–74, at 140 nn. 2, 6.

[43] Donald Alban Jr., Robert H. Woods Jr., and Marsha Daigle-Williamson, "The Writings of William Carey: Journalism as Mission in a Modern Age," *Mission Studies* 22, no. 1 (2005): 85–113 and Robert Stevens, "J. B. Powell and the Missouri-China Connection," *Missouri Historical Review* 82, no. 3 (1988): 267–79.

[44] For histories of this relationship in different eras across the Atlantic, see Anna Johnston, *Missionary Writing and Empire, 1800–1860* (New York: Cambridge University Press, 2003); Lawrence Kessler, "Foreign Missions and Home Support," in *United States Attitudes and Policies toward China*, ed. Patricia Neils (Armonk, NY: M. E. Sharpe, 1990), 78–96, 82;

journalism was often the sole personal mission of many missionary institutions or their private beneficiaries. Thus, while diplomatic representatives produced texts about their activities, again to the limited extent that they did not rely on or were unconnected to missionaries, they could rarely claim the extensive circulation of missionary perspectives, especially to popular audiences at home and certainly abroad. Furthermore, while mercantile interests were well-funded, once again to the extent that they even wanted to challenge missionary perspectives, they often lacked the longitudinal authority of missionary writers or missionaries' first mover advantage in setting up foreign offices.[45]

The penetration of missionary sensibilities similarly traveled along a whole host of proactive engagements with the development of international institutions and the international-facing aspects of domestic institutions. This meant that missionary influence was not limited to the specific actions of individual missionaries but was most robust in their formative impact on those who relied on their expertise, who they trained, and for whom they provided private religious meaning for public secular engagements.[46]

Consider now the educational impact that missionaries had on the production of domestic and foreign international lawyers alike. The education investment of missionaries is still on open display across the world in various religiously affiliated universities, and it was a common quality of many nineteenth-century non-Western international elites that they had passed through missionary educational institutions, even sometimes explicitly missionary-oriented law schools.[47] While some of this history is more widely acknowledged, less explored is the impact that missionaries had on the

Murray Rubinstein, "American Board Missionaries and the Formation of American Opinion towards China," in *America Views China: American Images of China Now and Then*, ed. Jonathan Goldstein, Jerry Israel, and Hilary Conroy (Bethlehem, PA: Lehigh University Press; London: Associated University Press, 1991), 67–79.

45 Ian Welch, "Missionaries, Murder and Diplomacy in Late 19th Century China: A Case Study," Paper for 2nd ANU Missionary History Conference (2006): 14. At one point, merchants in England did try to have missionary activities in China banned as it disrupted trade. John Nevius, *China and the Chinese* (New York: Harper, 1869), 287. They failed spectacularly and never again tried to raise the issue.

46 Again, the training of other professional elites overseas by missionaries is still an obscured fact given their often non-official employment. Take Robert Morrison, the first Protestant missionary in China. Despite its customary proscription against directly hiring missionaries, the East India Company paid him a significant sum to instruct junior officers. S. P. Ong, "Jurisdictional Politics in Canton and the First English Translation of the Qing Penal Code," *Journal of the Royal Asiatic Society* 20, no. 2 (2010): 141–65.

47 While many books have been written about the historical impact of missionaries on education across the globe, less attention has been paid to the impact of missionary law schools and their role in promoting ideals of joint religious/legal conversion. See, e.g., Robert Bryan, "The

formation of Western universities at home. The sustained linguistic and cultural expertise that missionaries developed made them natural fits for staffing new area studies departments that emerged as regular components of modern universities. Many original university faculty positions with foreign orientation were filled by former missionaries, again near complete in the instance of American universities. The overt religious character of missionaries' experiences was far from dissonant with the early development of social science, where many new departments of political science, economics, and other disciplines welcomed the civilizing ethos inflected with religious meaning.[48] In some instances, the formalist and domestic orientation of professional legal education may have left specific law departments with fewer public markers of missionary impact. Yet evangelical presumptions were rearticulated when facing foreign contexts through notions of legal evolution. This rearticulation naturalized the presumption of comparative superiority and became a defining feature of professional identity as foreign service increasingly became a standardized part of academic and professional legal careers.

Just as with claims of secularization writ large, a great deal of the influence of missionary sensibilities has thus been retrospectively masked by the fact that the common reconciliation of religious and scientific commitments during and after the nineteenth century led many international actors to take on what would be now considered to be purely scientific roles but with ingrained missionary sensibilities or motivations. Law was but one of many technical fields where foreign missions were originally undertaken as explicit representations of the mutuality of Christianity and Western progress. While generally associated with North American Protestantism, the Social Gospel movement typified open arguments for, in postmillennial fashion, the religious duty to carry out social service as core to the missionary effort.[49] As a result, there were agricultural economist missionaries, educational missionaries, medical

Legal Profession," in *American University Men in China* (Shanghai: Comacrib Press, 1936), 89–111. Also see Alison Conner, "Anglo-American Law at Soochow," in *China's Christian Colleges*, ed. Daniel Bays and Ellen Widmer (Stanford: Stanford University Press, 2009), 147–72.

48 The strong modern presumption that religious and scientific authority clash was far from a universal sentiment in the nineteenth century. Many early professional academic societies welcomed religious mission in their discourse, as well as focus on overseas applications. Thomas Leonard, "Evolutionary Science and Christian Belief in Progressive Era Political Economy: Adversaries or Allies?," *History of Economics Society Meetings, York University* 4 (2008), https://ssrn.com/abstract=1166622.

49 Ronald White and Charles Hopkins, *The Social Gospel* (Philadelphia: Temple University Press, 1976).

missionaries, and every possible combination of technical expertise and mission. Such work was also mutually supportive of domestic reform work, where control over representations of foreign technical work became tied to reformist authority at home in much the same way as missionary success sustained arguments about the need for Western religious revival. In law this meant that extraterritorial judges could proclaim the religious effect of their adjudication sometimes openly in public, and consistently so in more private settings.[50] It also meant that recasting law as a tool of liberation, rather than domination, in foreign contexts began to seem more and more plausible even to those who sharply derided non-Western law as uncivilized.

Moreover, if we trace the foreign careers of many international lawyers, we can see the informal and associative influence of missionaries, especially when we consider the networks they relied on when overseas. If an international secular institution desired a foreign fact-finding mission, it was often as reliant on missionary interlocutors as any other.[51] Moreover, if formally secular actors had any formal or informal educational training, they were just as likely to have had missionary contact. George Staunton, the famed translator of the Qing Code for Europe, may appear at first glance to have had a secular British diplomatic career, but he learned Mandarin from missionary tutors and actively worked to bring missionaries into diplomatic affairs.[52]

This prompts the question of the formative influences on diplomatic institutions which would later move to insulate themselves from explicit affiliation with religious practices.[53] As late as World War II, we can see numerous examples of missionary interlocutors as local informants shaping the representations of foreign developments for public agents and agencies.[54] Similarly, the early international life of most every international philanthropic institution was reliant on missionaries. New histories of disaster relief showcase how dependent foreign actors were on missionary infrastructure, a dependence that still lives on until the present moment. Hybrid public-private institutions such as the American Carnegie Endowment for International Peace again relied on

50 Eileen Scully, *Bargaining from Afar* (New York: Columbia University Press, 2001), 140.

51 Casper Sylvest, "'Our Passion for Legality': International Law and Imperialism in Late 19th Century Britain," *Review of International Studies* 34, no. 3 (2008): 403–23.

52 Ong, "Jurisdictional Politics in Canton," 147.

53 See also Chapter 3 in this volume.

54 Missionaries served as key informants for governments during World Wars I and II. For American examples, see George Creel, *How We Advertised America* (New York: Arno Press, 1972); Margaret Denning, "The American Missionary and U.S. China Policy during World War II," in *United States Attitudes and Policies toward China*, ed. Patricia Neils (Armonk, NY: M. E. Sharpe, 1990), 211–18.

missionaries for their non-European work, and the perspectives of this institution have been remarkable over its continued century of operation.[55]

The impact of missionaries on these international institutions is more lasting if we analyze individual actors from a multigenerational perspective. Missionary work was commonly a family affair, with children born and raised overseas. Beyond the particular experience of individual missionaries, these family traditions often informed and inspired secular international careers. The American media empire of missionary child Henry Luce is a famous international example, but the impact of missionary family history on the staffing of foreign diplomatic corps was also a recurrent aspect of their earlier histories.[56] The Sino-American ideal type here is instructive as 50 percent of all American State Department officials were the immediate children of missionaries through World War II.[57] Again, if we apply this analysis to academic institutions, we can see similar patterns of familial motivations for foreign engagement. Especially in eras when international careers were still highly circumscribed for any national working population, both access and motivation to engage in international work required more than random interest and desire.

The cumulative force of this institutionalization of missionary representations and perspectives helps to explain how later histories could see cleavages and breaks when in fact there were so many continuities between missionary dreams of foreign social transformation and the aspirations of secular modernization. Just as others have argued for bringing to light the generally submerged influence of religious thought in legal history more broadly, it was the legal thinking of missionaries that in many ways had greater impact on the international life of the law than those who later claimed to have distanced themselves from explicit religious reference.

10.3 MISSIONARIES AND THE POPULAR LIFE OF INTERNATIONAL LAW

If histories of international law have become more granular in recent years, they can still suffer from the same malady that often infects diplomatic history – the presumption that elite interests and perspectives are more strongly determinative of popular opinion than the reverse.[58] Legal history itself has similarly

55 Kroncke, *Futility*, 126.

56 Alan Brinkley, *The Publisher* (Toronto: Penguin Random House, 2010).

57 Mead, *Special Providence*, 154.

58 In foreign affairs, a powerful intervention to this effect has been achieved in Andrew Preston, *Sword of the Spirit, Shield of Faith: Religion in American War and Diplomacy* (New York: Alfred A. Knopf, 2012).

struggled to look outside the consciously articulate materials of cases and judges – a struggle born from both professional ideology and ready accessibility.[59] Beyond professional or evidentiary rationales, the all-too-common excision of religion from diplomatic and legal history alike in many ways speaks to the great success with which religious sensibilities were naturalized within secular institutions. The domestic political grounds of foreign relations have always been the prime constraints on the legitimacy of international institutions, and the overdetermined focus on the particular decisions of individual diplomatic or legal agents can obscure as much as does their own sequestering of religious sentiment from public documents. Moreover, recognizing the popular life of foreign relations and law outside professional discourses clearly demonstrates that the missionary dream of simultaneous foreign legal and religious transformation has maintained vigorous popular expression.

For all the impact that missionary representations may have had on academic and governmental institutions, their historical force in the popular sphere is indelible. Rather than being mere propaganda sponsored by elite public and private interests, the proactive dissemination of missionary representations of foreign nations throughout civil society provides a key explanatory vector for shifts in legitimacy of international law – and far more so than its technical or pragmatic coherence as a body of law itself. Not only did missionaries have natural legitimacy in relating foreign developments to domestic constituencies but they were also able to provide meaning to such developments in arenas far removed from debates over legal evolution or trade policy. The immediacy of the vast number of souls being lost to damnation lent a sense of temporal urgency to even far-flung geographies – with numerous national missionary traditions constructing the image of the great masses of unreached foreign populations. Missionaries provided the interface through which most Western citizens experienced direct contact with foreign travelers well into the twentieth century, and such interface is still quite prevalent in nonurban settings in the contemporary world.

As missionaries were very rarely directly sponsored by state actors, their primary beneficiaries and audiences were always domestic religious ones. The often-triangular relationship among merchants, state aegis, and missionary activity was one grounded in the ability of missionaries to represent themselves as the truest avatars of Western altruism. The idea of international

59 The proper empirical sources of legal history have been a recurrent modern methodological concern, even among critical legal historians themselves. Robert Gordon, "J. Willard Hurst and the Common Law Tradition in American Legal Historiography," *Law and Society Review* 10, no. 1 (1975): 9–56, at 31.

humanitarianism through religious conversion was core to popular concern with overseas affairs even when sounded as route nationalism.[60] Modern histories of empire and colonialism have worked to uncover reconciliation of domination and salvation redolent in ideological articulations of foreign mission, trying to move beyond earlier narratives which too often took public justifications as purely derivative from military or economic interests.[61]

It is instructive to remember how important missionaries were to the earliest forms of European intervention abroad, especially in more cognizable nation-states. The abilities of missionaries to proselytize freely and to hold legitimate title to foreign property were the most common popular justifications for military campaigns which may have had otherwise economic motivations.[62] The Opium Wars in China are a key example where descriptions of the plight of missionaries were the main asserted basis for the legitimacy of military intervention, which missionaries themselves helped to promote through their representations of suppression and martyrdom. The extension of extraterritorial jurisdiction may have played upon racist caricatures of foreign legal practice, but it was the image of the unfairly imprisoned missionary that was energizing for home audiences – and far more so than any argument about contractual efficiency. Moreover, the plight of foreign Christian converts was also quite commonly summoned up as a rationale for intervention and legal protection, especially as they were asserted to be the first causal links in the eventual transformation of their home societies long promised by missionary efforts.

This form of legitimacy placed both missionaries and their competitors in a mutualistic bind. Diplomatic interests were often annoyed by missionary agitations of foreign governments, but such interests were always restrained from direct criticism of missionary actions in the public arena given their popularity back home. Some merchants were critical of missionary activity but

60 Even today, countries that are held up as more cosmopolitan still draw on transformative understandings of international law in their professional and popular discourses. Nico Schrijver, "A Missionary Burden or Enlightened Self-Interest? International Law in Dutch Foreign Policy," *Netherlands International Law Review* 57, no. 2 (2010): 209–44.

61 Amy Kaplan, *The Anarchy of Empire in the Making of US Culture* (Cambridge: Harvard University Press, 2005); Jean D'Aspremont, *The Critical Attitude and the History of International Law* (Boston: Brill, 2019).

62 Foreign governmental attempts to ban missionaries outright were in most cases eventually met with military force. Part of this deployment was the circulation of images of repression and persecution produced by missionaries themselves. Roger Thompson, "Reporting the Taiyuan Massacre: Culture and Politics in the China War of 1900," in *The Boxers, China, and the World*, ed. Robert Bickers and R. G. Tiedemann (Lantham: Rowman & Littlefield, 2007), 65–92.

were similarly constrained by the desire to spur support for any direct interest in greater access to foreign markets. Missionaries were similarly bound by claims that Christianity, international law, and commerce were all mutualistic,[63] and much intramissionary discourse confronted the pragmatic concessions to the less savory motivations of Western actors that facilitated their work.[64] Even when decolonization was still decades away, the language of social transformation through law was perhaps the easiest and the most immediate realm through which varied interests could reconcile their objectives in domestically legitimate secular terms. Thus, while formal debates over international law could take on a more scientific rationale for judging inclusion and exclusion, the very reason why it was a salient domestic concern was because of the missionary imprint on popular understanding.

While on readier display later during the Cold War, the popular religious life of international law also played a role in how foreign nations' legal actions were interpreted.[65] While China remained ever hopeful as a site of legal redemption up until 1949, the thin veneer of the legal rationality extended was much less secure for the Islamic world. After the fall of the Ottoman Empire, the specter of religious animus both drove support for greater missionary activity and gave new impetus to the notion that extending international legal institutions would have a civilizing force.[66] Japan stands out in large part because its successful effort to exclude foreign missionaries led to an active dissonance in acknowledging its adoption and redeployment of international legal thinking as justification for its imperial ambitions in Asia.[67] That more cynical views of international law did not immediately dominate after Japan's militaristic rise speaks in large part to the fact that Japan existed outside of the transnational networks of representation and meaning which the missionary movement had constructed. Japan's rejection of Christianity did help to facilitate Western demonization of Japan, but it did so

63 "Freedom of navigation upon the high seas and of sojourn within each and every country of the international community is requisite for industry and for commerce and for that highest branch of commerce – the traffic of ideas – embraced within the single word 'missionaries.'" James Brown Scott, *The Spanish Origin of International Law* (Oxford: Clarendon Press, 1934), 11.

64 Jon Miller and Gregory Stanczak, "Redeeming, Ruling, and Reaping: British Missionary Societies, the East India Company, and the India-to-China Opium Trade," *Journal for the Scientific Study of Religion* 48, no. 2 (2009): 332–52.

65 For a history that repeatedly touches on the religious context of popular understandings of international law, see Anna Su, *Exporting Freedom: Religious Liberty and American Power* (Cambridge, MA: Harvard University Press, 2018).

66 Umut Özsu, "The Ottoman Empire, the Origins of Extraterritoriality, and International Legal Theory," in *The Oxford Handbook of the Theory of International Law*, ed. Anne Orford and Florian Hoffman (Oxford: Oxford University Press, 2016), 123.

67 Donald Howland, *International Law and Japanese Sovereignty* (London: Palgrave Macmillan, 2016).

while speaking directly to how the formal inclusion of Japan in international law did not resolve its overt counterevidence to claims of civilizing influence.

As the missionary ethos became institutionalized in secular institutions and practices, this type of empirical example became less and less effective at undermining hopes for international law's transformative potential. As ideas of civilizational progress were articulated anew through concepts such as democracy or capitalism, international law continued to hover above the growing machinery of global integration as a reservoir of legitimacy seemingly immune to moments of raw self-interest or exploitation. Missionaries often became critics of the excesses of colonial or neocolonial exploitation but were fundamentally committed to continuing the popular frame of foreign transformation which economic and military interests became increasingly adroit at deploying – if again reconciled through private religious sentiment by individual actors. Most starkly, missionary criticism of domestic racial animus could never overcome the type of implicit paternalism that their dream of transforming their cultural particular into a global universal required.[68] The successful secularization of original missionary representations of cultural difference and teleology increasingly grew beyond their collective control.

While this chapter necessarily speaks in broad strokes, the centrality of missionaries to the popular life of international law in the nineteenth century and beyond provides answers and new questions as to why it had any domestic political relevance or how it could so easily persuade across domestic partisan differences. While it may seem to some to have been purely cynical, the testimony of missionaries in the Cold War era as to the evils of communism and its legal barbarism was no mere opportunistic tactic but reflected the continued power of religious thinking to claims about international law's popular legitimacy and aims. While the recent fall of communism may have ushered in a renewal of secular professional discourse, the persistence of religion in the popular life of international law continues to bear this missionary legacy.

10.4 DISENCHANTMENT AND THE END OF THE TRANSFORMATIVE ERA

In the contemporary moment, the halcyon days of international law's global legitimacy appear to be rapidly fading. There is certainly no lack of private

[68] A more optimistic interpretation of the missionary form of cosmopolitan is explored in David Hollinger, *Protestants Abroad: How Missionaries Tried to Change the World but Changed America* (Princeton: Princeton University Press, 2017). Hollinger details how the experience of missionaries abroad spilled over into a wide range of progressive social politics in the United States domestically.

international legal transactions which structure modern life operating beyond daily perception, but the once grand hopes that international legal institutions would themselves be agents of social change are now thoroughly drowned out by doubts about global social progress and the anxieties of national populist backlash.[69] It would be difficult to claim that international legal theory or international legal practice has grown less coherent or defined over time, but such procedural refinement seems far less relevant than deep cynicism about the type of disenchanted technocratic cosmopolitanism in which international lawyers increasingly partook in recent decades. The rise of authoritarian China as an influential actor reshaping international institutions has given many academics pause.[70] Yet, these events simply speak to the fact that the perhaps too successful disenchantment of international legal discourse has severed its tie to popular legitimacy – the terms of which for too long have been ignored.

Recovering the centrality of missionaries to the grounds of international law's modern history provides clarity as to how its claims to scientific reconceptualization were very much achieved through the naturalization of missionary presumptions about the promise of foreign legal transformation. But we can also see more clearly that many of its critics similarly embraced its conflation of the parochial as universal by doubling down on the promise of transformative redemption. Adherence to its ideals, rather than reconsideration of its presumed terms, is offered up by some as necessary for its relegitimization. Yet, this position takes for granted international law's secular terms as its functional components, and elides the fact that its aspirational universalism is rarely persuasive on purely technical terms for audiences set in more local moral communities. Similarly, criticisms of the international legal order that cast its ideological underpinnings as mere charades for the exertion of power and chauvinism risk parallel obfuscation of the sources of any alternative conception to be substituted in their stead.

It is perhaps then unsurprising that religious proselytization has increasingly set itself at odds with scientific authority and often carries with it far less of the ecumenical spirit of earlier generations. The popular conjoining of religious

69 Janne E. Nijman and Wouter Werner, "Populism and International Law: What Backlash and Which Rubicon?" *Netherlands Yearbook of International Law* 49 (2018): 3–17. This piece introduces an entire volume on the subject.

70 China's impact on the future of international law and its non-socialization by international legal practice are currently subjects of nonstop academic production. For a useful overview of approaches, see the contributions in Jacques deLisle and Avery Goldstein, eds., *China's Global Engagement: Cooperation, Competition, and Influence in the Twenty-First Century* (Washington, DC: The Brookings Institution, 2017).

and legal sentiment is resurgent in new forms of nationalistic nostalgia, but these sentiments are more often used to criticize international law as a false, if not hostile, ground for religious universalism. Moreover, while funding for missionary work still draws predominately from Western nations, missionaries' networks have become dominated by peoples from the Global South.[71]

However one normatively judges these observations, they do foreground the requirement that adding a cultural turn to the histories of international law means taking more seriously the dynamic relationship between elite and popular understandings of its meaning and their intimate links to religious sentiment. Can there be any legitimate supranational legal order that is not premised on more enchanted forms of universalism? And where else might we look to trace the impact of this transformative ethos in the development of other forms of secular reasoning on which global legal and other forms of social analysis have depended? Answering these questions, if they can be answered, requires a far greater appreciation of international law's missionary past.

RECOMMENDED READING

Chanock, Martin. *Law, Custom, and Social Order*. London: Cambridge University Press, 1985.

Johnston, Anna. *Missionary Writing and Empire, 1800–1860*. New York: Cambridge University Press, 2003.

Mead, Walter. *Special Providence*. New York: Routledge, 2002.

Oddie, Geoffrey. *Imagined Hinduism: British Protestant Missionary Constructions of Hinduism, 1793–1900*. London: Sage, 2006.

Pitts, Jennifer. *Boundaries of the International: Law and Empire*. Cambridge, MA: Harvard University Press, 2018.

Preston, Andrew. *Sword of the Spirit, Shield of Faith: Religion in American War and Diplomacy*. New York: Alfred A. Knopf, 2012.

Sahin, Emrah. *Faithful Encounters: Authorities and American Missionaries in the Ottoman Empire*. Montreal: McGill-Queen's University Press, 2018.

[71] The Gordon Conwell Theological Seminary produces an annual report that includes one synthesis of the empirical state of global missionary activity: Status of Global Christianity, gordonconwell.edu/center-for-global-christianity/resources/status-of-global-christianity/.

11

Standards for a Righteous and Civilized World: Religion and America's Emergence as a Global Power

Andrew Preston

In the era of the two world wars, internationally minded American statesmen turned their attention to meeting two objectives. The first was to engage the United States more with the wider world; more particularly to embed the United States within an international system dominated by European states but, with the inclusion of Japan, becoming increasingly pluralistic. The second was to use this new American global consciousness to reform the international system so that it accorded with the standards of civilization and operated along commonly regarded civilized norms. The codification and promotion of international law was one of the key methods of achieving these objectives; not coincidentally, many, if not most, of the key American internationalists of the era were lawyers.

All this was in keeping with much of the internationalist thought emanating from Europe around the same time. Yet American statesmen added another element to this emerging transatlantic body of internationalism and international law: religious faith. Just as most American internationalists were lawyers, they were also personally devout Protestants who were active in their churches and other religious institutions.

The onrush of globalization between the US Civil War and World War I transformed the way in which major institutions operated – this was no less true for churches than it was for nation-states. In confronting the challenges of globalization, American statesmen turned to their culture of faith for answers. Just as the increasing pluralism of empires and nation-states, represented by the emergence of the United States and Japan as great powers, meant that the international system had to find better ways of managing international cooperation and confrontation, increasing awareness of global religious pluralism forced them to innovate new ways of managing religious difference. Their vision, then, was one which combined secular internationalism and sacred ecumenism. And yet, just as their internationalism combined pluralism and

Anglo-American supremacy, their ecumenism was invariably, indelibly shaped by a heavily American-inflected strain of Protestantism, one that emphasized the sanctity of individual rights/conscience, the separation of church and state, a suspicion of Roman Catholicism, and the inviolability of a supposedly universal right to religious liberty.

The main challenge that Western statesmen had, then, was to reconcile increasing pluralism and interconnectedness with the sustainability of empire, both the formal kind expressed through direct rule over territory and the informal kind expressed through the maintenance of hegemonic networks of trade and political authority. International law was perfectly suited to the task. The past half-century has seen international law aspire to serve as an antidote to war and imperialism, but before then law was the handmaiden to empire. The political ethos and legal architecture of the League of Nations were designed to preserve Western imperial rule; later on, despite a global wave of decolonization, the founders of the United Nations (UN) did their best to follow suit.[1] Law provided rules for the proper establishment of empires and the inter-imperial relations that followed, a legal-imperial tradition that dated back centuries to the founding of the first overseas European empires.[2]

As the historian Benjamin Allen Coates has shown, it was no coincidence that some of America's most ardent international legalists were also the most ardent imperialists. "The exercise of American power abroad in the early twentieth century," writes Coates, "is thus better conceptualized not as a disregard for law, but as the implementation of a particular form of it." American international lawyers "were simultaneously idealists and imperialists, dreamers of world order and participants in imperial politics and administration." This was because empire was seen as a force for good, establishing order in a chaotic and violent world.[3] The Progressive movement, the context in which most American internationalists and legalists of the time are best

[1] On the League's accommodations to imperialism, see Erez Manela, *The Wilsonian Moment: Self-Determination and the International Origins of Anticolonial Nationalism* (New York: Oxford University Press, 2007); and Susan Pedersen, *The Guardians: The League of Nations and the Crisis of Empire* (New York: Oxford University Press, 2015). On the UN's, see Mark Mazower, *No Enchanted Palace: The End of Empire and the Ideological Origins of the United Nations* (Princeton: Princeton University Press, 2009).

[2] Lauren Benton, *Law and Colonial Cultures: Legal Regimes in World History, 1400–1900* (New York: Cambridge University Press, 2002); Lauren Benton and Richard J. Ross, eds., *Legal Pluralism and Empires, 1500–1850* (New York: New York University Press, 2013); Jennifer Pitts, *Boundaries of the International: Law and Empire* (Cambridge, MA: Harvard University Press, 2018).

[3] Benjamin Allen Coates, *Legalist Empire: International Law and American Foreign Relations in the Early Twentieth Century* (New York: Oxford University Press, 2016), 5.

situated, sought to reconcile justice with stability, both of which were thought to be necessary for modern development. Whether it was a "search for order" or a "rage for order," Western political and legal thought in the nineteenth and early twentieth centuries used self-styled progressivist and reformist laws to spread their purportedly civilizing influence throughout the world.[4] For American internationalists who wanted to export justice and order, a foreign policy we might think of as "progressive imperialism," the law was an ideal solution. But what animated this body of law? What was the spirit that drove it forward? To understand how internationalists "made sense of law's meaning," Coates enjoins us to "interpret it through the cultural and ideological prisms of their time and place." Coates suggests that "a particular vision of civilized modernity" is the most important prism that historians must consider, and this chapter follows his suggestion.[5] Law, Martti Koskenniemi has illustrated, was seen as a civilizing force, an antidote to global anarchy that provided the justification for proper international and transnational relations in the modern age.[6] This ideology of civilization coursed through the internationalism of American statesmen and strategists of the time.[7]

But what provided the foundation for civilization? What provided the basis for the civilized international laws that would underpin world order? Coates and Koskenniemi explore these issues with depth and sensitivity, but largely missing from their accounts on the conjunction between international law and international norms in the late nineteenth and early twentieth centuries is religion.[8] In the American case – an important one given the centrality of Americans to international law, international relations, and the creation of international organizations – religion meant particularly Christianity, and even more particularly Protestantism.[9] Even when they were not formally codified in law, the norms of Protestant morality and politics were, in the eyes of many American internationalists, the glue that held everything together.

4 Robert H. Wiebe, *The Search for Order, 1877–1920* (New York: Hill and Wang, 1967); Lauren Benton and Lisa Ford, *Rage for Order: The British Empire and the Origins of International Law, 1800–1850* (Cambridge, MA: Harvard University Press, 2016).

5 Coates, *Legalist Empire*, 7, 10.

6 Martti Koskenniemi, *The Gentle Civilizer of Nations: The Rise and Fall of International Law 1870–1960* (Cambridge: Cambridge University Press, 2001).

7 Frank Ninkovich, "Theodore Roosevelt: Civilization as Ideology," *Diplomatic History* 10, no. 3 (July 1986), 221–45.

8 A brilliant exception, which analyzes the influence of Christianity on the development of international law in this era, is Paolo Amorosa, *Rewriting the History of the Law of Nations: How James Brown Scott Made Francisco de Vitoria the Founder of International Law* (Oxford: Oxford University Press, 2019).

9 Although some international lawyers in the United States also drew on Roman Catholicism for inspiration: Amorosa, *Rewriting the History of the Law of Nations*, 186–244.

This chapter explores these paradoxes between norms, identities, and power, the resolution of which provided the normative basis for a new world order emanating from Washington in the wake of World War I and eventually covering much of the world by the early Cold War.

11.1 FAITH IN AMERICAN INTERNATIONALISM

While it is a common misconception that the United States was "isolationist" before the twentieth century, the period between 1898 and 1945 undoubtedly marked a new threshold for America's engagement with the rest of the world. Before the 1890s, the United States had been restlessly, sometimes relentlessly, active in world affairs, but always on its own terms. Americans not only waged frequent warfare on the North American continent, they also thrust themselves into regional and national affairs in Europe and Asia. The most famous example remains Commodore Matthew Perry's coerced opening of Japan in 1854, which ended centuries of Japanese self-imposed isolation, but it was not unusual. Over the course of the entire nineteenth century, from North Africa to Europe to East Asia, the United States was an active participant in the world even if it did not establish overseas colonial empires as did its European peers.

Perry forcibly opened Japan to the outside world in pursuit of the American national interest, particularly commercial interests, but he also did so in keeping with an American ideology of expansive conquest: manifest destiny. This worldview, common to nationalisms with a sense of chosenness at their core, deemed that Americans had a right of conquest, but with that right came a self-appointed responsibility to civilize and uplift those who had been conquered. In other words, with great power came great responsibility. Manifest destiny was coined by John L. O'Sullivan, a New York-based writer and Democratic Party activist, at the height of expansionist fever in 1845, but the idea long predated him – indeed, the concept of responsible power, and of conquest as a civilizational, developmental, and providential imperative, motivated the very first English transplantations of the seventeenth century.[10] Thus by the time Texas joined the United States in 1845, US troops occupied Mexico City in 1847, and Perry landed in Japan, two ideas had become embedded in the American worldview: first, America's presence in world affairs was beneficial for everyone; and second, the nature of that presence would be determined by Americans themselves, on their own, and

[10] The literature on manifest destiny is voluminous, but for an excellent concise overview of these themes, see Anders Stephanson, *Manifest Destiny: American Expansionism and the Empire of Right* (New York: Hill & Wang, 1995).

with little regard for others. A sense of mission – both figurative and, in a deeply religious sense, literal – fueled manifest destiny.[11]

For these reasons, historians have tried to retire the term "isolationism" and replace it with ones, such as "unilateralism," that more accurately define a globally active nation that acted on its own terms and not in concert with others.[12] And, until the early twentieth century, it was this assumptive ideology of unilateralism that defined American engagement with the rest of the world. Three major developments, which catalyzed and shaped each other, changed this relationship between the United States and the world. The first was the nation's spectacular economic growth between the American Civil War and World War I, which not only deepened America's trading networks around the world but also exponentially increased the nation's potential military power and diplomatic reach. The second was the technological revolution in communications and transportation – undersea international telegraph cables, the telephone, automobiles, aviation, and so on – which made the era the modern period's first era of globalization. The third was a product, perhaps inevitably, of the first two: increasingly close rivalries and frequent collisions among the great powers, and a concomitant sense of greater international insecurity.[13] The same processes of economic globalization allowed for the advancement of technological innovation in military weaponry and transport, which in turn allowed states to project greater amounts of power farther than ever from their own shores. The world was shrinking economically, but it was also shrinking militarily. Foreign controversies which the United States may once have ignored – in Cuba and the Philippines in 1898, for instance, or in China in 1900 – now triggered American intervention. When the "scramble for Africa" broke out

11 Andrew Preston, *Sword of the Spirit, Shield of Faith: Religion in American War and Diplomacy* (New York: Alfred A. Knopf, 2012), 135–59.

12 "Unilateralism" is probably the most common substitute: see Walter A. McDougall, *Promised Land, Crusader State: The American Encounter with the World Since 1776* (Boston: Houghton Mifflin, 1997). But "neutrality" is another: see Brooke L. Blower, "From Isolationism to Neutrality: A New Framework for Understanding American Political Culture, 1919–1941," *Diplomatic History* 38, no. 2 (April 2014), 345–76. For a good analysis of the development of the concepts of "isolationism" and "internationalism," see Andrew Johnstone, "Isolationism and Internationalism in American Foreign Relations," *Journal of Transatlantic Studies* 9, no. 1 (March 2011), 7–20. But for a thoughtful defense of the term and analysis of its history, see Christopher McKnight Nichols, *Promise and Peril: America at the Dawn of a Global Age* (Cambridge, MA: Harvard University Press, 2011).

13 On these developments and what they meant for the United States in the world, see Michael Mann, *The Sources of Social Power*, vol. 3: *Global Empires and Revolution, 1890–1945* (Cambridge: Cambridge University Press, 2012); and Walter LaFeber, *The New Cambridge History of American Foreign Relations*, vol. 2: *The American Search for Opportunity, 1865–1913* (Cambridge: Cambridge University Press, 2013).

among European empires in the 1870s, culminating in the Berlin Conference of 1884, the United States stood aside as an observer. But when a scramble for China erupted in the late 1890s, Americans were at the forefront and drafted the Open Door Notes as a way to regulate foreign involvement in China.[14]

Still, as the historian John A. Thompson has pointed out, throughout this entire period the United States remained almost completely economically self-sufficient and immune to foreign attack. International insecurity, be it economic or military, was not all that pressing a problem for American statesmen between the Civil War and the outbreak of World War I in Europe. Instead of it being a case of Americans responding to external threats, Thompson has offered a persuasive alternative explanation for the rise of American internationalism: choice. Americans, he argues, developed an appreciation of their own potential power just as they were perceiving their country as a guardian of Western civilization.[15] American internationalism arose, in other words, not as a reaction to external threats but as a proactive initiative to reorder the world along certain liberal lines of individual rights, private property, free markets, freedom of movement, and capitalist development. There were significant exceptions to these liberal norms, of course, especially when a nativist backlash impinged upon the freedom of movement through a variety of anti-immigrant measures beginning with the 1882 Chinese Exclusion Act and culminating with the 1924 National Origins Act. But, overall, Americans chose to use their growing national power to intervene in world affairs on terms conducive to the norms and values as well as the interests of the United States.

The new internationalist sensibility in turn created the need for a body of international law. Liberal norms, particularly those regarding capitalist political economy and interstate relations, could only function when protected by the rule of law – this was as true internationally as it was domestically. Otherwise, anarchy would predominate and prevent the establishment of stability that was essential for capitalism to function. While the United States often expanded its reach into foreign societies at the barrel of a gun, Americans always made sure to coordinate their actions through laws and treaties.[16] When Perry forced Japan to open up, for instance, he began

[14] On the United States, see Michael H. Hunt, *The Making of a Special Relationship: The United States and China to 1914* (New York: Columbia University Press, 1983). More generally, and for the concept, see Robert Bickers, *The Scramble for China: Foreign Devils in the Qing Empire, 1832–1914* (London: Allen Lane, 2011).

[15] John A. Thompson, *A Sense of Power: The Roots of America's Global Role* (Ithaca: Cornell University Press, 2015).

[16] See especially Coates, *Legalist Empire*. But see also Noel Maurer, *The Empire Trap: The Rise and Fall of U.S. Intervention to Protect American Property Overseas, 1893–2013* (Princeton: Princeton University Press, 2013).

a decades-long process of codifying new laws in Japan, the United States, and beyond.[17]

But the emerging body of international law was not only designed to protect the needs of industry, trade, and capital. Individual rights, not just property rights, were also American priorities, especially the rights of foreigners (i.e., Americans) traveling and living abroad. This was true for all Americans, but most Americans did not travel abroad then. Often, the test cases for the international viability of liberal norms were provided by America's veritable army of Protestant foreign missions. Missionaries were almost uniquely suited to test the functionality of international liberalism. For one thing, they were almost always nonviolent, and so could not be deported or imprisoned for committing, or even advocating, violent acts. For another, missionaries' main purpose was predicated on fundamental individual rights – the freedoms of conscience, expression, and especially religion – which were enshrined in the First Amendment of the Bill of Rights in the US Constitution but which were also presumed to be universal and ideally inviolable the world over. Those freedoms spurred Protestant missionaries to live in foreign countries and preach the gospel as an inviolable human right. Moreover, missionaries engaged in what would now be called development projects, such as the building of schools and medical clinics, the teaching of children, and the improvement of agricultural techniques. The schools and institutions of higher education that American missionaries established were of very high quality and usually found favor among local and imperial elites. The institutions which later became the American universities in Cairo and Beirut, as well as Robert College in Istanbul, were renowned in the Ottoman Empire, and missionary schools in China were held in similarly high esteem. Overall, then, as Chapter 10 in this volume shows, missionaries sought not only to spread the gospel but also to build a global empire of paternalistic moral reform.[18]

Preaching the twin gospels of Christian religion and Western development brought missionaries into conflict with local authorities even when their avowed purpose had little or nothing to do with politics. But whether they

17 Michael R. Auslin, *Negotiating with Imperialism: The Unequal Treaties and the Culture of Japanese Diplomacy* (Cambridge, MA: Harvard University Press, 2004).

18 See also William R. Hutchison, *Errand to the World: American Protestant Thought and Foreign Missions* (Chicago: University of Chicago Press, 1987); Ian Tyrrell, *Reforming the World: The Creation of America's Moral Empire* (Princeton: Princeton University Press, 2010); Preston, *Sword of the Spirit*, 122–34, 175–97; and Jedidiah J. Kroncke, *The Futility of Law and Development: China and the Dangers of Exporting American Law* (New York: Oxford University Press, 2016), esp. 47–70, 110–31.

realized it (sometimes they did, but often they did not), their inculcation of foreign values, systems, and doctrines through education often represented a fundamental challenge to the reigning political order. The very simple act of teaching literacy, for instance, would allow children to read the Bible, but it would also allow them to read and write political tracts that challenged the political order. Literacy would also empower local communities by bolstering their own ethnic identity that was often subsumed by a higher imperial sovereign; the teaching of subjects such as history and politics often had the same effect. For example, education could empower Koreans living under Japanese rule or Arabs living under Turkish Ottoman rule and even embolden them to resist their imperial rulers.

Even more common was the resistance missionaries faced to what was ostensibly their main objective: evangelism. American missionaries believed in the universal applicability of religious liberty as an individual's natural right that transcended and superseded the affairs of state. This, even more than education or medicine, brought missionaries into conflict with local authorities. Education and health care could be provided, in theory, without political or religious content, and even when political or spiritual subthemes were unavoidable in the teaching of history or economics they could at least be muted and mitigated by non-missionaries. But there was virtually no way to compromise or dilute the message of evangelism. Even the deliberately generic spiritual message spread by modernist Protestant missionaries represented a fundamental threat to local faiths and traditions. More assertive missionaries who refused to water-down their proselytism or tailor their message to suit local cultures faced open backlash that sometimes became violent. The Boxer Rebellion was the most notorious of such episodes, but it was far from unique. Methodist missionaries in Bolivia and Ecuador were harassed for presiding over marriages and burials. Non-Protestant Christian missionaries who simply preached their faith to win converts faced persecution for being religious eccentrics or nonconformists. For example, from French Polynesia to major European cities such as Paris and Copenhagen, Mormons (for whom going on mission was not a choice but a fundamental tenet of faith) found themselves arrested and jailed simply for being Mormon.[19]

American Jews who had been born in Russia but had emigrated to the United States and become US citizens faced a similar problem. They still had family and business connections in Russia, and needed to travel back to Russia from time to time. Russian immigration in the United States surged in the last three decades of the nineteenth century, which meant that increasing

[19] Preston, *Sword of the Spirit*, 188–97.

numbers of Russian-American Jews were traveling back and forth across the Atlantic. When they did, they were not respected as US citizens but found themselves persecuted – imprisoned or impressed into the Russian army, their property and money seized – as Jews and as deserters. By the 1880s, thanks to the attention in the press given to persecuted Russian-American Jews traveling on US passports, religious liberty became a major flashpoint in relations between Washington and Moscow.[20]

The US State Department was not altogether receptive to the needs of these faith communities. Diplomats, by nature technocratic and secular even in the days before the reforms of 1888 that professionalized the foreign service, found the plight of Methodists, let alone Mormons and Jews, bewildering. This is because they found these religious actors strange and unsympathetic. There was also a high degree of anti-Mormonism and antisemitism within the US State Department and other federal agencies. Nonetheless, Washington supported these religious communities for the simple reason that they were US citizens abroad, in distress and in need of their government's assistance. More to the point, in none of the cases above – missionaries, Mormons, or Russian-American Jews – were the religious actors accused of committing acts of violence, crime, or insurrection. They had been targeted purely because of their faith, the protection of which is enshrined in the first two clauses of the First Amendment, and so the State Department had little choice but to mobilize its resources in support of US citizens under duress overseas.

In every case, the US government mobilized its power not simply in support of its citizens' physical safety but also, even more importantly, in support of its citizens' right to religious liberty anywhere in the world. The radical implications of this policy cannot be overestimated, for it meant that Washington was insisting that a right ensconced in American jurisprudence and political thought was not national but universal. And by insisting that other countries respect the universal right of US citizens to religious liberty, Washington's policy was not just a theoretical statement of intent but an attempt to effect actual change in the legal and political regimes of other countries. For instance, the case of the Methodist missionaries in South America resulted in the governments of Bolivia, Peru, and Ecuador revising their laws to

20 Three such cases involved Henry Pinkos, Marx Wilczynski, and Isaac Goldner. Their stories have not been given attention by historians, but for the Pinkos case, see Documents 558–9, 561–2, 564–8, May 7–September 16, 1880, *Foreign Relations of the United States, 1880–1881*, vol. 1 (Washington, DC: Government Printing Office, 1880), 873–82 (hereafter *FRUS*). For Wilczynski, see Andrew D. White (Berlin) to John W. Foster (St. Petersburg), October 15, 1800, *FRUS, 1881–1882* (Washington, DC: Government Printing Office, 1882), 991. And for Goldner, see Foster to James G. Blaine (Washington), July 23, 1881, *FRUS, 1881–1882*, 1028.

accommodate foreign missionaries. European governments acceded to American Mormons' right to be, well, Mormons and left in peace to speak their minds and preach in public. The case of Russian-American Jews was harder to solve because Moscow was less susceptible to American pressure, and Washington and Moscow had already been locked in a low-level cold war for decades. Moreover, Russia's treatment of its own substantial Jewish population was appalling – the period witnessed some of the worst pogroms on record, such as in Kishinev and Odessa – and so Moscow was not likely to be swayed by arguments about natural law and human rights in an age of interdependence. But still, the US State Department's effort, even just as an effort, was remarkable in itself.[21]

The US government's response to all these instances of religious persecution in the late nineteenth and early twentieth centuries is not simply an interesting case study of the influence that religion can have over US foreign policy – it was also indicative of the normative ways in which American power would be deployed over the next century. It initiated a wave of foreign-policy decisions that exported American values on the assumption that these values were not simply American, and provided the muscle for enforcing, as much as possible, their implementation and protection. This was a critical development in the rise of the United States to global hegemony later in the twentieth century, based as it was on the spread of political and economic value systems, which in turn provided the foundation for a working liberal international order. The religious test cases were not the only source of this normative hegemony, but they were one of the first; and, being almost entirely unconnected to economic or military gain, they illustrate that the power of normative universalism was not solely aimed at securing immediate tangible benefits for the United States.

11.2 THE SPIRIT OF THE LAW

By the turn of the twentieth century, American statesmen found themselves managing several developments that were unfolding at once and which were not necessarily theirs to control: the industrial boom of the Machine Age, the revolution in transportation and communication technologies, the new immigration, and the shrinkage of geopolitical space. Their response, a new internationalist sensibility based on the international promotion and protection of liberalism, aimed to harmonize as many of these disparate developments as possible, not just with each other but with rising American

[21] Preston, *Sword of the Spirit*, 188–91.

power as well.[22] The key to doing so, successfully, was evident in the US response to the confrontations in which religious actors found themselves unwittingly involved: the protection of supposedly universal liberal norms. By the first two decades of the twentieth century, American statesmen looked to the norms of the civilized world as a foundation for a new kind of world order.

This foundation was in turn predicated on two realms, the legal and the religious. This was not a coincidence, for three reasons. One, religious liberty, via the First Amendment's separation of church and state, was enshrined in the Constitution and thereby provided a bedrock for other aspects of American political values and constitutional rights. Two, in a broader sense, religion and the law sat at the heart of American political culture; both were touchstones on what it meant to be a US citizen, and therefore what it meant to be a citizen of the world. Third, in the American political imaginary, religion and law were seen as both the source and the product of civilization itself; without religion, and without law, there could be no civilized order.

Belief in the interrelationship between religion and law, and in their importance to civilization, was particularly strongly held in the years between the Civil War and World War I – the same era in which the United States rose to become a global power of the first rank. Thus, when American statesmen tried to make sense of the world as it changed around them, and figured out how to adapt their nation's rapidly growing power to the world, they turned to the tenets of religion and the codification of law.

Perhaps not coincidentally, then, many of the key architects of American internationalism in the early twentieth century were lawyers. In fact, between 1898 and 1919, every single secretary of state was a lawyer, and most of them had been founding members of the American Society of International Law (ASIL), while three of the four presidents had trained as lawyers.[23] These legalist-internationalist statesmen were keen supporters of the establishment of an international court at the Hague, and many had been participants in the two Hague peace conferences of 1899 and 1907.[24]

Most of these figures were also personally religious or had intimate connections to religious institutions (John Hay, Secretary of State from 1898 to 1905, was a notable exception). This was also true of some of the major international thinkers of the time, such as the naval strategist Alfred Thayer Mahan, a close

22 Frank Ninkovich, *Global Dawn: The Cultural Foundation of American Internationalism, 1865–1890* (Cambridge, MA: Harvard University Press, 2009).

23 Coates, *Legalist Empire*, 2.

24 Coates, *Legalist Empire*, 86–95.

adviser to presidents and other statesmen as well as a passionately devout Episcopalian, and the missionary leader John R. Mott, who declined ambassadorships so he could focus on his mission work but who helped lead the national relief effort during World War I.[25] It was also true of major American efforts to promote international law: the international jurist James Brown Scott was a founder of the ASIL, a legal adviser in the US State Department, and a lifelong committed Presbyterian.[26] More specifically, these figures were, almost to a person, liberal Protestants – "mainline" or "modernist" Protestants, to use the terms of their day, but we should also think of them, as the historian David Hollinger has enjoined historians, as "ecumenical" Protestants, for ecumenism was at the very heart of their politics as well as their faith.[27] Liberal Protestants earned their various monikers through their pluralist vision of faith as well as of society, for their eagerness to adapt religion to science (and vice versa), and for their place at the very heart of the nation's intellectual and political establishment. Active liberal Protestants were found at the highest reaches of America's key educational, political, cultural, and philanthropic institutions, and were in the leadership of both political parties. They stood in contrast to, and often in conflict with, the more conservative Protestants who later came to call themselves "fundamentalist" or "evangelical." For the most part, with a few exceptions, liberal Protestants predominated among the elite, while conservatives were nowhere to be found. The implications of this quirk of American political culture were profoundly important for US foreign policy, and, given the growing importance of the United States, by extension for the evolution of the international system as a whole.

Setting the overall tone was William McKinley, an Ohio lawyer who steadily rose through the ranks of the Republican Party to become president in 1897. McKinley was a pro-business, fiscally conservative, gold-standard Republican, but many of his formative experiences as a lawyer came from representing trade unions. He was also an activist campaigner for various causes of benevolent reform, such as abolitionism and temperance. His devout evangelical Methodism explains this mix of reformism and nationalism, tempered by economic conservatism. Above all, one might say that

[25] On Mahan and Mott and their role in crafting a Christian-inflected foreign policy, see Preston, *Sword of the Spirit*, 184–5, 208–11, 224–5, 230–1, 242–3, 261–7, 280–3.

[26] Amorosa, *Rewriting the History of the Law of Nations*, esp. 22, 29 for Scott's Presbyterianism. Coates, *Legalist Empire*, also has an extensive analysis of Scott's career as an international lawyer but has nothing on his religious beliefs.

[27] David A. Hollinger, *Protestants Abroad: How Missionaries Tried to Change the World but Changed America* (Princeton: Princeton University Press, 2017), 10–12.

McKinley was a cautious progressive who feared radicalism and anarchy above all else.[28] In 1898, shortly after the United States had routed Spain, McKinley famously sought divine inspiration over whether to annex the Philippines as a formal American colony. Once he concluded that Filipinos were "unfit for self-government" and susceptible to "anarchy and misrule," he concluded that "there was nothing left for us to do but to take them all, and to educate the Filipinos, and uplift and civilize and Christianize them, and by God's grace do the very best we could by them, as our fellow-men for whom Christ also died."[29] This foreign policy of faith-based "progressive imperialism," as one historian has dubbed it, set the tone for America's mission in the world for the next two decades.[30]

McKinley was assassinated in 1901, which thrust his young vice president, Theodore Roosevelt, into the White House. Roosevelt's faith was wholly unlike McKinley's: eclectic, even eccentric, simultaneously profound in its inquisitiveness and shallow in its devotion, and historians would be hard-pressed to find a direct link between Roosevelt's religious views and his foreign policy. Still, the similarities between his religious background and his worldview are close enough to draw logical if still only suggestive conclusions about the tone he set for US foreign policy overall, especially as it was in many ways in keeping with his predecessor's worldview. Roosevelt's father, Theodore Sr., was a Calvinist stalwart of the Dutch Reformed Church and avid follower of Dwight L. Moody, the evangelical revivalist who traveled the country and preached to thousands of Americans in the decades after the Civil War. Roosevelt absorbed his father's religious lessons, and, though his faith cooled once he left home, he never shook the fierce righteousness inherent to Calvinist theology. Roosevelt has gone down in history as an arch-realist, a grand strategist who believed in power and little else. But while he was indeed a shrewd statesman, his worldview was not at all that of an amoral realist. "The state must be practical and efficient," he wrote to Mott, "but the state should ever show its fealty to lofty ideals."[31] As the historian Frank Ninkovich has shown, Roosevelt saw himself first and foremost as a custodian of civilization.[32]

28 Preston, *Sword of the Spirit*, 157–8.

29 Quoted in Charles S. Olcott, *The Life of William McKinley*, vol. 2 (Boston: Houghton Mifflin, 1916), 109–11.

30 See Preston, *Sword of the Spirit*, 155–9, 223–32.

31 Theodore Roosevelt to John R. Mott, October 12, 1908, John R. Mott papers, Box 76, Folder 1383, Special Collections, Yale Divinity School Library.

32 Ninkovich, "Theodore Roosevelt."

McKinley made a tentative first step to base US foreign policy on principles of Western civilization, but it was Roosevelt who did the most to make it run. Roosevelt responded to international crises with the instincts of a moralist. To be sure, he did not deliberately take measures in keeping with morality that would harm the American national interest. Instead he believed, in keeping with the traditions of the Monroe Doctrine and manifest destiny, that power and responsibility were mutually constitutive. Might and right were inseparable, and because America was always in the right it was therefore also permitted to use its might. The Roosevelt Corollary of 1904 and the building of the Panama Canal were both instances in which Roosevelt justified the use of raw power in service to a higher, nobler good. But Roosevelt was also critical of other states when he felt they abused their power, when their use of might was very much not as a furtherance of right. This humanist, even humanitarian sensibility was as much a part of Roosevelt's worldview as the realist appreciation of power.[33]

In his 1904 Annual Message to Congress (now known as the State of the Union address), Roosevelt committed a major breach of diplomatic protocol to single out great powers who violated the norms of the civilized world even though those violations posed no threat to the United States or its people. "A great free people," Roosevelt explained in reference to his fellow Americans, "owes it to itself and to all mankind not to sink into helplessness before the powers of evil." The United States "shows by its consistent practice its belief in the principles of civil and religious liberty and of orderly freedom," without which international peace and stability could not endure. Roosevelt expressed his "horror on an occasion like that of the massacre of the Jews" in Russia's pogroms, and he also chastised the Ottomans for the persecution of their Armenian population. This was, not coincidentally, the same speech in which Roosevelt laid out his eponymous corollary to the Monroe Doctrine, which self-appointed the United States as an "international police power" to ensure that other states, starting in the Caribbean Sea, would "obey the primary laws of civilized society." "It is a mere truism," Roosevelt concluded, "to say that every nation, whether in America or anywhere else, which desires to maintain its freedom, its independence, must ultimately realize that the right of such independence can not be separated from the responsibility of making good use of it."[34] As Coates observes, Roosevelt "shared important legalist assumptions about civilization and order."[35]

[33] See Charlie Laderman, *Sharing the Burden: The Armenian Question, Humanitarian Intervention, and Anglo-American Visions of Global Order* (New York: Oxford University Press, 2019).

[34] Theodore Roosevelt, "Fourth Annual Message," December 6, 1904, *The American Presidency Project*, www.presidency.ucsb.edu/node/206208.

[35] Coates, *Legalist Empire*, 4.

Roosevelt, though, was not a lawyer – he was the only major American statesman of the era not to receive legal training – and his appreciation of the law, while deep and abiding, was not grounded in formal training or even informed amateurism. His legalism was thus like his religious faith: powerful but raw, insightful but instinctual. None of this should dilute the importance of both the law and religion to his worldview, but they are necessarily difficult to pin down. Yet he did surround himself with advisers who had been formally trained as lawyers and (with the exception of Hay) were also men of faith. They took the grand ideas forwarded by Roosevelt and applied them to the functioning of US foreign policy. All, not coincidentally, were loyal but moderate Republicans who possessed a strong American nationalism tempered by a cosmopolitan outlook. However paradoxical this may seem, their Americanism and internationalism were both deeply felt, and they combined to form a potent American worldview.

Elihu Root served in Roosevelt's Cabinet for almost his entire presidency, with his time split between being Secretary of War and, later, Secretary of State (where his chief legal counsel was Scott). Root had been born into a devout Presbyterian family in a heavily revivalist region of upstate New York known as "the burned-over district" for the intensity of its religious fervor and political radicalism.[36] He was active in the YMCA as a boy and, later, as an undergraduate at Hamilton College, and when he moved to study law at New York University he taught Sunday school at his local church. His career as a Manhattan corporate lawyer was distinguished and lucrative, and for two years he served as the US Attorney for the Southern District of New York (a powerful post once held by Roosevelt's great-uncle James). But Root only really made his mark as a Washington statesman. As Secretary of War, he oversaw the Spanish-American War in 1898 and the Philippine War to deny the Filipinos national independence that began a year later. Progressive imperialism, which saw empire as a moral duty to uplift the uncivilized peoples of the world, was in keeping with his Christian faith. "We give ourselves to Christ – little enough, surely, in return for what He has done," he explained. "Should not each one strive to make this the gift of as perfect and fully developed a man as possible?"[37]

Root's protégé, Henry L. Stimson, carried this mission forward. A graduate of Harvard Law School and associate of the prestigious New York firm of Root

36 Michael Barkun, *Crucible of the Millennium: The Burned-Over District of New York in the 1840s* (Syracuse, NY: Syracuse University Press, 1986).

37 Quoted in Philip C. Jessup, *Elihu Root*, vol. 1 (New York: Dodd, Mead, 1938), 58. Amazingly, there is only one other biography of Root, published more than sixty-five years ago: Richard William Leopold, *Elihu Root and the Conservative Tradition* (Boston: Little, Brown, 1954).

& Clarke (later becoming the powerhouse law firm Winthrop, Stimson, Putnam and Roberts), he entered the public arena through an appointment by President Roosevelt to US Attorney of the Southern District of New York. While Stimson lacked Root's intensely devout faith, he did consider a career in the ministry before turning to the law. It was a natural choice: his uncle, also named Henry, was the reverend of Manhattan Congregational Church and a formative influence on his nephew, and several of their Stimson ancestors before them had been Protestant ministers.[38]

After two years at the helm of the Southern District, Stimson continued to follow in Root's footsteps by becoming Secretary of War in 1911, before returning to private practice two years later. But in 1927, Stimson was called back into public service, first as colonial Governor-General of the Philippines and then, in 1929, as Secretary of State to President Herbert Hoover. As Secretary of State, Stimson oversaw implementation of the Pact of Paris, an international agreement officially known as the General Treaty for Renunciation of War as an Instrument of National Policy. This idealistic attempt to outlaw war by declaring it illegal except in cases of self-defense lacked an enforcement mechanism and was therefore wholly ineffective, but it signaled the ambitions of American statesmen of the era. It also provided Stimson with the legal wherewithal to announce the Stimson Doctrine of nonrecognition, by which the United States refused to approve of Japan's conquest of Manchuria and establishment of a new state known as Manchukuo. He stepped down from his duties in 1933, but was reappointed as Secretary of War in 1940. For the next five years, he oversaw US preparations for, and then prosecution of, a global conflict against Nazi Germany and Imperial Japan.

Stimson's boss during his first tenure as Secretary of War, William Howard Taft, was also steeped in the traditions of the legal and religious realms. His Unitarian faith, however, was more unorthodox than the Protestantism of Root, Stimson, and even Roosevelt. Unitarians were theologically further to the left than most other Protestants, and this often meant that their politics were more progressive too. Though he was a Republican, Taft was a reformer (albeit a moderate) in keeping with the Unitarian and Republican political traditions that both dated back to the abolitionist movement before the Civil War. But Taft was better known for his glittering career as a lawyer: he was only thirty-three when he was appointed as the Solicitor General of the United

38 Elting Elmore Morison, *Turmoil and Tradition: A Study of the Life and Times of Henry L. Stimson* (Boston: Houghton Mifflin, 1960), 40–1; Godfrey Hodgson, *The Colonel: The Life and Wars of Henry Stimson, 1867–1950* (New York: Knopf, 1990), 27.

States, and he subsequently served as a federal appeals-court judge and a professor at the University of Cincinnati's law school. Like Root and Stimson, Taft served as Secretary of War (in fact, he succeeded Root as Roosevelt's only other secretary of war), and, like Stimson, Taft also spent three years as Governor-General of the Philippines. He served one term as President, succeeding Roosevelt. Taft's foreign policy applied the McKinley administration's Open Door policy toward China to foreign affairs more broadly; the result, Dollar Diplomacy, was a template for a more informal type of empire that wedded capitalism to empire, not simply in the pursuit of profits or markets but as a kind of civilizational paternalism that would spread economic liberalism.[39] During World War I, Taft, now back in private practice, became a member of the League to Enforce Peace and a staunch advocate of the League of Nations. He capped his career by serving for a decade as the Chief Justice of the Supreme Court.[40]

Taft's successor as president, Woodrow Wilson, revolutionized the basis of US foreign relations more than anyone before him. But Wilson also embodied the intertwining of norms and faith more than most of his peers. Though most famous as an educator and a politician, Wilson had actually first trained as a lawyer at the University of Virginia, and he practiced law in Atlanta for a few years before deciding it was not the career for him. Still, his legal training instilled in him a reverence for norms – one of his actual hobbies was drawing up constitutions for imaginary organizations – even if he also believed that those norms must evolve as society evolved. He was, in other words, a conservative progressive who believed in change but only the most gradual and organic change that society would tolerate.[41] Instead of pursuing a career as a lawyer, Wilson became a political scientist specializing in democratic theory and practice, earning a PhD from Johns Hopkins and culminating his academic career as president of his alma mater, Princeton University. But the most consistent force throughout his life was Christianity – more specifically, Presbyterianism. His grandfather, father, and uncle had all been Presbyterian ministers and educators, and Wilson himself carried his Calvinistic faith with him all the way to the White House. Various biographers have shown how Presbyterianism suffused his upbringing, education, political thought, and

39 Emily S. Rosenberg, *Financial Missionaries to the World: The Politics and Culture of Dollar Diplomacy* (Cambridge, MA: Harvard University Press, 1999); Cyrus Veeser, *A World Safe for Capitalism: Dollar Diplomacy and America's Rise to Global Power* (New York: Columbia University Press, 2002).

40 Judith Icke Anderson, *William Howard Taft: An Intimate History* (New York: Norton, 1981).

41 John A. Thompson, "Woodrow Wilson and a World Governed by Evolving Law," *Journal of Policy History* 20 (January 2008): 113–25, at 113–19.

moral principles.[42] As he told his aide Cary T. Grayson during his fight with the Senate over the ratification of the Treaty of Versailles, "If I were not a Christian, I think I should go mad, but my faith in God holds me to the belief that He is in some way working out His own plans through human perversities and mistakes."[43]

Both of Wilson's secretaries of state were men of deep faith, and both were lawyers. His first chief diplomat, William Jennings Bryan, had unsuccessfully run for president three times, each time on a platform of economic populism. Bryan was also an early Protestant fundamentalist and was later one of several prosecutors to represent the state of Tennessee in the famous 1925 Scopes trial over whether the teaching of Darwinian evolution could be banned (Bryan's side won: it could). Unlike other internationalists of the time, Bryan was a theologically conservative fundamentalist. But he was also a staunch peace crusader and resigned in protest over Wilson's ultimatum to the Germans to stop submarine warfare against neutral shipping, or else (Bryan feared that this put America's fate in the hands of the Germans: it did, and the United States entered the war with the resumption of submarine attacks in 1917).[44]

Bryan was replaced by Robert Lansing, an esteemed international lawyer who had represented the United States before international arbitration panels at the Hague. Lansing, too, was personally devout, professing a hard-shell Presbyterianism that in many ways resembled Bryan's theological fundamentalism, albeit without the populist radicalism. "I consider myself," Lansing once explained, "of the orthodox school which look[s] upon the Bible as containing the history of the true religion, and of God's relation to man, and which consider[s] repentance toward God and belief in Jesus Christ to be the only means of salvation." Lansing was also a member of the ASIL, but he was a moderate who felt that international law could be a civilizing force in its potential to stabilize the interactions of sovereign states rather than transcend and possibly end interstate conflict altogether.[45]

42 See, e.g., John M. Mulder, *Woodrow Wilson: The Years of Preparation* (Princeton: Princeton University Press, 1978); and Cara Lea Burnidge, *A Peaceful Conquest: Woodrow Wilson, Religion, and the New World Order* (Chicago: University of Chicago Press, 2016).

43 Cary T. Grayson, *Woodrow Wilson: An Intimate Memoir* (New York: Holt, Rinehart, and Winston, 1960), 106.

44 The best overview of Bryan's ideas and values, especially his religion, and how they shaped his politics is Michael Kazin, *A Godly Hero: The Life of William Jennings Bryan* (New York: Knopf, 2007).

45 Coates, *Legalist Empire*, 142; Lansing quoted in James Reed, *The Missionary Mind and American East Asia Policy, 1911–1915* (Cambridge, MA: Council on East Asian Studies, Harvard University, 1983), 195.

Wilson's principal internationalist innovation was American membership in the League of Nations. But within this innovation lay another that is far more subtle, yet still quintessential to American foreign policy and the source of its flexible yet hegemonic power after 1945. Root, Taft, and other legal-minded internationalists called for the League to be grounded in a codified body of positive law. Wilson saw things differently; law should be a servant to politics, not the other way around.[46] Wilson claimed, in a 1914 speech to the American Bar Association to which many lawyers in the audience would undoubtedly have objected, that the "opinion of the world is the mistress of the world, and the processes of international law are the slow processes by which opinion works its will."[47] He had a passion for constitutionalism, but as a legal realist; constitutions provided a set of common rules, but those rules could and should change as circumstances changed. As his most perceptive biographer has noted, "[r]ather than as a fixed contract between sovereign states, Wilson envisaged the Covenant as a framework within which what is nowadays called 'the international community' could develop its norms and authority."[48] He oversaw the drafting of a "covenant" – not coincidentally, a term that was both sacred and legalistic – for the League of Nations that would adapt as the organization and its members grew. "My own conviction," he said to a trusted adviser, "is that the administrative constitution of the League must grow and not be made; that we must begin with solemn covenants . . . but that the method of carrying those mutual pledges out should be left to develop of itself, case by case."[49] What was instead enduring were values, norms that were respected and inspirational but not as a rigidly formal body of law with formal mechanisms of enforcement. American federalism was one of the sources of these values, Christianity another.

11.3 ECUMENICAL INTERNATIONALISM

The Depression and the failure of internationalist solutions to stop endemic conflict, such as the League of Nations and the Kellogg-Briand Pact, could easily have spelled an end to American legalist-internationalism. However, the

46 See Stephen Wertheim, "The League That Wasn't: American Designs for a Legalist-Sanctionist League of Nations and the Intellectual Origins of International Organization, 1914–1920," *Diplomatic History* 35, no. 5 (2011), 797–836; and Stephen Wertheim, "The League of Nations: A Retreat from International Law?," *Journal of Global History* 7, no. 2 (2012), 210–32.

47 Quoted in Thompson, "Woodrow Wilson," 123.

48 Thompson, "Woodrow Wilson," 122.

49 Quoted in Thompson, "Woodrow Wilson," 121.

opposite occurred.[50] Halfway through World War II, when it started becoming clear that the Allies would win, President Franklin D. Roosevelt (FDR) encouraged the US State Department to begin planning for a postwar world order based on the combined authority of American liberal norms and US military power.[51] This new order would be built upon the settlement following World War I, albeit with some significant alterations that gave the United States and its wartime allies more control over the protection of their own sovereignty. In constructing the UN to replace the defunct and discredited League, FDR believed that, as one historian has noted, "Wilsonianism had to be practical."[52] Once again internationalist lawyers were at the heart of this planning process, not least Stimson in his second stint as Secretary of War, but also Secretary of State Cordell Hull, a Tennessee lawyer who was a passionate internationalist and a committed free trader.[53]

And once again, religious sensibilities played a significant role in shaping the norms that would in turn undergird the architecture of the new internationalism. Even before the United States had entered the war, Roosevelt used countless speeches, ranging from his famously informal "fireside chats" over the radio to the 1939 and 1941 State of the Union addresses, to frame the world crisis as a conflict not simply between good and evil but also between religiously based peace and freedom and irreligious aggression and tyranny.[54] He did this not simply as a matter of political expediency but because he was a deeply religious person – Roosevelt was active as a layman in the Episcopal Church, even during his tumultuous presidency – whose faith and politics had an instinctively ecumenical cast.[55] Roosevelt's successor, Harry Truman, was a dedicated Southern Baptist who, similar to FDR despite the very different

50 Robert A. Divine, *Second Chance: The Triumph of Internationalism in America during World War II* (New York: Atheneum, 1967); Andrew Johnstone, *Against Immediate Evil: American Internationalists and the Four Freedoms on the Eve of World War II* (Ithaca: Cornell University Press, 2014).

51 For liberal norms, see Elizabeth Borgwardt, *A New Deal for the World: America's Vision for Human Rights* (Cambridge, MA: Harvard University Press, 2005). For military power, see Stephen Wertheim, *Tomorrow, the World: The Birth of U.S. Global Supremacy* (Cambridge, MA: Harvard University Press, 2020).

52 Warren F. Kimball, *The Juggler: Franklin Roosevelt as Wartime Statesman* (Princeton: Princeton University Press, 1991), 102.

53 Hull's influence is regularly underestimated, but for a more balanced assessment, see Kimball, *The Juggler*, 44–5, 93–6, 187–90.

54 See, e.g., Franklin D. Roosevelt, "Annual Message to Congress," January 4, 1939, *The American Presidency Project*, www.presidency.ucsb.edu/node/209128; "Annual Message to Congress on the State of the Union," January 6, 1941, *The American Presidency Project*, www.presidency.ucsb.edu/node/209473; "Address for Navy and Total Defense Day," October 27, 1941, *The American Presidency Project*, www.presidency.ucsb.edu/node/210207.

55 Preston, *Sword of the Spirit*, 315–26.

social character of their respective denominations, had a strongly ecumenical outlook on both religion and politics.[56]

This ecumenism, indelibly shaped by liberal American Protestantism, helped to provide the foundation for world order following World War II. In the United States, Protestant ecumenists had formed effective networks of social power working through the Federal Council of Churches (FCC), founded in 1908, and they extended their mission globally with the founding of the World Council of Churches in 1938. In 1914, moreover, Andrew Carnegie, a Presbyterian of little doctrinal rigor but a firm belief in ecumenism's potential to inspire international peace, endowed the founding of Church Peace Union, which later evolved into the Carnegie Council for Ethics in International Affairs.[57] Meanwhile, Church Peace Union's sister organization, the Carnegie Endowment for International Peace, promoted international law under the direction of Root, after he became its director in 1910, and his legal adjutant from the State Department, James Brown Scott.[58]

Protestant ecumenists had been stalwart supporters of the League of Nations, but their vision was actually better suited to the more realistic version that FDR launched during World War II. In the UN, Roosevelt wanted to safeguard a measure of national sovereignty for the great powers. Protestant ecumenism did this for religious denominations by allowing them to preserve their own identities and rituals even as they came together on common grounds of cooperation. The purpose of ecumenism, as practiced by the FCC, was not to dilute denominational identity completely but to facilitate cooperation so as to foster religious peace. But not peace at any price – Protestant ecumenists, for example, refused to work with the Catholic Church so long as Catholics rejected basic liberal norms that Protestants saw as indivisible and nonnegotiable. The ecumenical community, in other words, was based on a realist belief that common ideals and norms were a necessary precondition: to become a member of the community, one had to subscribe to the ideals and live by the norms.[59]

56 Elizabeth Edwards Spalding, *The First Cold Warrior: Harry Truman, Containment, and the Remaking of Liberal Internationalism* (Lexington: University Press of Kentucky, 2006); William Inboden, *Religion and American Foreign Policy, 1945–1960: The Soul of Containment* (New York: Cambridge University Press, 2008); Preston, *Sword of the Spirit*, 417–22, 427–39.

57 Preston, *Sword of the Spirit*, 266–8, 276–8.

58 Coates, *Legalist Empire*, 95–8; Amorosa, *Rewriting the History of the Law of Nations*.

59 In 1950, the FCC was reformed and renamed the National Council of Churches. On the realism of American ecumenism as it evolved during the war years, see Heather A. Warren, *Theologians of a New World Order: Reinhold Niebuhr and the Christian Realists, 1920–1948* (New York: Oxford University Press, 1997); and David A. Hollinger, *After Cloven Tongues of*

American ecumenism provided part of the inspiration for the construction of the UN, founded in 1945 – two of the UN's many planners made sure of it. One was Frederick Nolde, a Pennsylvania Lutheran, missionary official, seminary educator, and FCC leader who helped enshrine a particular vision of human rights in the UN Charter oriented to a liberal Protestant notion of the supreme dignity of the individual.[60] Nolde furthered the ecumenical agenda, first proposed by missionary leaders like John R. Mott, in promoting liberal, individualist human rights around the world. Not coincidentally, Mott received the Nobel Peace Prize in 1946.

The other key UN planner was John Foster Dulles, the very embodiment of faith-based legalist internationalism. One of Dulles's grandfathers had been secretary of state, and his uncle was Robert Lansing. Dulles's father was a Presbyterian minister, and Dulles himself was heavily involved in church activities. After an undergraduate career at Princeton (Wilson's alma mater), Dulles became an international lawyer at a major Wall Street firm, but he also saved time to represent the Presbyterian Church. During World War II he headed up the FCC's Commission on a Just and Durable Peace, which laid out a vision for a world order based on the principles of ecumenical internationalism. Dulles led an FCC delegation to the White House to consult with Roosevelt and Hull, and FDR later appointed him to be a delegate to the founding conference in San Francisco that established the UN. In San Francisco, Dulles was instrumental in encouraging broad international participation while also bolstering safeguards for US national sovereignty. He sought to work with the Soviet Union and other communist states at the UN, but when he felt that they did not respect the liberal norms that were supposed to be the lifeblood of the institution, he pivoted toward a rather harsh anticommunist stance. Truman later named Dulles as a delegate to the founding conference of the North Atlantic Treaty Organization (NATO), where he helped to promote the ecumenical vision of cooperating toward a common cause, within the same community, so long as the community was bound by common norms. Truman's Secretary of State Dean Acheson, a Harvard-trained international lawyer and the son of an Episcopalian Bishop, fulfilled this mandate with the launch of NATO in April 1949. In 1953, Dulles himself became Secretary of State.[61]

Fire: Protestant Liberalism in Modern American History (Princeton: Princeton University Press, 2013), 18–81.

60 John S. Nurser, *For All Peoples and All Nations: The Ecumenical Church and Human Rights* (Washington, DC: Georgetown University Press, 2005).

61 Preston, *Sword of the Spirit*, 384–409, 450–64.

The American internationalists examined in this chapter may have represented different political parties and religious denominations, and they often differed on the means of implementing internationalism. But they all agreed that the United States had to play an integral part in international affairs, that legal norms needed to be established for the functioning of world order, and that religious values and traditions, namely those associated with liberal, modernist, ecumenical Protestantism, would provide the normative guideposts. Despite their political and temperamental differences, then, they all shared a worldview grounded in a set of basic principles that were shaped, in part, by Christianity and the law. With the perspectival advantage of history, we can see that worldview in action in the conduct of US foreign policy in the first half of the twentieth century. These were the policies that established a normative international order based on a liberal ideology that was itself inescapably grounded in the mainline Protestant liberalism common among American elites. In tandem, law and religion provided the normative glue that would transform the world for the better, while the functioning of the system itself was underwritten by US military power.

RECOMMENDED READING

Amorosa, Paolo. *Rewriting the History of the Law of Nations: How James Brown Scott Made Francisco de Vitoria the Founder of International Law*. Oxford: Oxford University Press, 2019.

Coates, Benjamin Allen. *Legalist Empire: International Law and American Foreign Relations in the Early Twentieth Century*. New York: Oxford University Press, 2016.

Laderman, Charlie. *Sharing the Burden: The Armenian Question, Humanitarian Intervention, and Anglo-American Visions of Global Order*. New York: Oxford University Press, 2019.

Preston, Andrew. *Sword of the Spirit, Shield of Faith: Religion in American War and Diplomacy*. New York: Alfred A. Knopf, 2012.

Thompson, John A. *A Sense of Power: The Roots of America's Global Role*. Ithaca: Cornell University Press, 2015.

Tyrrell, Ian. *Reforming the World: The Creation of America's Moral Empire*. Princeton: Princeton University Press, 2010.

12

International Protestantism and Its Changing Religious Freedoms

Udi Greenberg

The enshrining of religious freedom in international law has long been an important Protestant project. Whether as theoreticians, advocates, or policy-makers, Protestants played a significant role in securing the right for religious worship's inclusion in major international treaties and conventions, and in explaining why it could trump national sovereignty. This was true in the era of "high imperialism" and brutal European expansion, most notably in the 1885 Berlin Final Act, which divided Africa between the leading colonial powers. Representatives of Protestant missions from Britain and Germany and Protestant scholars of international law were important in drafting a clause that guaranteed "freedom of consciousness and religious toleration" to both Africans and Europeans, and which allowed missionaries of all denominations to freely preach without state restriction. Protestant visions were also central to the establishment of the League of Nations' minority right treaties from 1919 to 1923, which allowed religious minorities in Eastern Europe to appeal against their governments' discrimination. US President Woodrow Wilson, a devout Presbyterian, in particular insisted that the right for free worship was integral to the formation of a peaceful world order. Perhaps most famously, Protestant organizations such as the World Council of Churches (WCC) – a broad umbrella organ that brought together hundreds of Protestant churches – were important advocates in religious freedom's elevation to the status of a universal right. Its representative, American Lutheran scholar Frederick Nolde, helped draft the United Nations Universal Declaration of Human Rights (UDHR, 1948), and especially Article 18, which endowed all humans with the "freedom of thought, conscience, and religion."[1]

[1] The quote is from Arthur Berriedale Keith, ed., *The Belgian Congo and the Berlin Act* (Oxford: Clarendon Press, 1919), 304. On Wilson and religious freedom, see Anna Su, *Exporting Freedom: Religious Liberty and American Power* (Cambridge, MA: Harvard University Press,

Historians have become increasingly aware of Protestants' important role in religious freedom's legal proliferation, but they have hardly agreed on its implication. What does it mean for our understanding of religious freedom that its inclusion in international law stemmed not from growing religious indifference or from liberal humanistic universalism but from Protestantism's specific theologies and visions? For some, this entanglement helped reveal Protestantism's revolutionary nature. Historian John Witte, in particular, suggested that it was Luther's message about *sola scriptura* and believers' ability to access the Gospel that ultimately paved the way to modern understanding of human autonomy and rights, including for religious worship. Others, such as Helena Rosenblatt, have instead focused on the nineteenth century. It was then, she claimed, when European thinkers debated the virtues and limits of the French Revolution, that Protestants firmly embraced the notion of universal rights and spiritual freedom. Others still have focused on the twentieth century, and in particular on American mainline liberals. The project of religious liberty, they suggested, was integral to their reimagining of Christianity as equal to other faiths, and their vision of a universal brotherhood without oppression.[2]

A different group of scholars, in contrast, have taken a much grimmer interpretation of the historical record. If Protestants were so central to religious liberty's evolution, they claimed, it showed how deeply the term, for all its universal pretense, was entangled in the hierarchies of power and exclusion. For anthropologists Talal Asad and Saba Mahmood, for example, the legacy of Protestant missionaries and thinkers was not to overthrow religious oppression as such but to replace it with a Western-centric religious regulation. Protestants, they claimed, inscribed their own conception of individualized, faith-based religious identification into constitutions and treaties, thus deeming other religious behavior (such as collective public rites) illegitimate. This, in turn, allowed regimes that claim to be religiously neutral, such as Britain or Egypt, to regulate religious behavior ever more tightly, fostering harsh

2016). On Nolde, see John S. Nurser, *For All People and All Nations: The Ecumenical Church and Human Rights* (Washington, DC: Georgetown University Press, 2005). More broadly on the writing of the UDHR, see Linde Lindkvist, *Religious Freedom and the Universal Declaration of Human Rights* (New York: Cambridge University Press, 2017). The quote is from the UN General Assembly, "Universal Declaration of Human Rights," 217 (III) A (Paris, 1948), www.un.org/en/universal-declaration-human-rights/.

2 John Witte, Jr., *Law and Protestantism: The Legal Teachings of the Lutheran Reformation* (New York: Cambridge University Press, 2002); Helena Rosenblatt, *Liberal Values: Benjamin Constant and the Politics of Religion* (New York: Cambridge University Press, 2008); David A. Hollinger, *Protestants Abroad: How Missionaries Tried to Change the World but Changed America* (Princeton: Princeton University Press, 2017).

discrimination (against Muslims or Copts, respectively). Others similarly pointed out that European and American Protestants' celebrations of religious freedom were always mired in imperial imposition. Like international law more broadly, the term was a tool used by great powers to legitimize their foreign interventions on behalf of allegedly oppressed minorities and thus to solidify, rather than diminish, inequalities and domination.[3]

What has sometimes been missing from these illuminating observations, however, is the ways in which Protestant thinking about religious freedom changed from the nineteenth to the middle of the twentieth century. Even as they remained entangled in the hierarchies of international politics, Protestants after the 1940s expanded what they considered "legitimate" religious practice worthy of defending. Few examples demonstrate this change more potently than Protestants' approach to Catholicism. As several scholars have noted, many Protestant thinkers in the late nineteenth century preserved a long-standing view of Catholicism as a primitive and collectivist creed that was antagonistic to modern freedoms. As a result, even many who claimed to believe in religious freedom argued that the Catholic Church could occasionally be excluded from its protection. This was also true for key founders of international law, many of whom were practicing Protestants and who insisted that some Catholic organizations, like colonial subjects, were unworthy of free worship. This approach, however, substantially shifted in the middle of the twentieth century, when Protestants began to join Catholics in new social and political alliances. Even before the Second Vatican Council (1962–5) formally updated Catholic teachings, many Protestant writers came to see Catholics as friendly allies that deserved to be protected. As part of this shift, Protestants also abandoned their view of Catholicism as an enemy of religious freedom. Just like Protestants, several commentators began to argue, Catholics should be defended from religious oppression.

Elsewhere I suggested that this shift can perhaps help us rethink the utility of religious freedom today. Unlike scholars who argue that the concept is irredeemably oppressive, I wondered if its malleability over time means that it could be updated to promote egalitarian goals.[4] This history, however, can also

[3] See, e.g., Talal Asad, *Formations of the Secular: Christianity, Islam, Modernity* (Stanford: Stanford University Press, 2003); Saba Mahmood, *Religious Freedom in a Secular Age: A Minority Report* (Princeton: Princeton University Press, 2015); Elizabeth Shakman Hurd, *Beyond Religious Freedom: The New Global Politics of Religion* (Princeton: Princeton University Press, 2015); David Chidester, *Empire of Religion* (Chicago: University of Chicago Press, 2014).

[4] Udi Greenberg, "Is Secularism Protestant? A Genealogy of a Critical Idea," *Journal of the American Academy of Religion* 88, no. 1 (2020): 74–91.

highlight how flexible Protestantism's impact on international law itself has been. Rather than adhering to a timeless and rigid conception of "religion," Protestants occasionally demonstrated their ability to expand their horizons and to view new religious traditions as worthy of protection.[5] To outline this change, this chapter progresses in two steps. The first section charts how early efforts to craft international law in the nineteenth century were deeply soaked in anti-Catholic exclusion. It demonstrates how the first theoreticians of international law shared many of their contemporaries' belief that Catholics could and should be denied the right for free religious practice. The second section then explores how Protestants changed their mind in the 1940s. It traces how shifting political calculations – especially the belief that inter-confessional cooperation was needed against global Communism – led Protestants to observe Catholics not only as religious brethren, but also as partners in the mission to establish religious freedom. This expansion, to be sure, had its harsh limits. Even after they made peace with Catholics, for example, some American and European Protestants saw no problem to talk of religious liberty while supporting restrictions on Muslims' choice of clothing (such as banning women's *burkas*) or freedom of movement (such as the United States' 2017 restrictions on travels from Muslim-majority countries). In the late nineteenth century, similar restrictions would have seemed perfectly normal to Protestant theorists of international law if they were applied to Catholics. To see how this changed so quickly can therefore shed light on surprising transformations in religious law and politics.

Because it declined so quickly in the twentieth century, it is easy to forget how integral anti-Catholicism was for Protestant writers throughout the nineteenth century. Across countries and languages, a vast array of Protestant writers attributed an astounding list of evils to the Catholic Church. Indeed, like anti-Semites, anti-Catholics proved capacious in their ability to update older theological traditions to contemporary circumstances, seeing their enemy's fingerprints in a wide variety of social interactions. Some, like Canadian Charles Chiniquy, blamed Catholic priests for destroying heterosexual marriages. Enclosed during the confessional with married women, he argued in his blockbuster *The Priest, the Woman, and the Confessional* (1874), they encouraged women to indulge in sexual fantasies, dismantle the "citadel of womanly self-respect," and lead to "secret orgies." Others bemoaned Catholicism's alleged opposition to scientific progress. If the

5 For similar transformation in Protestants' approach to Confucianism, see Albert Monshan Wu, *From Christ to Confucius: German Missionaries, Chinese Christians, and the Globalization of Christianity, 1860–1950* (New Haven: Yale University Press, 2016).

Church once persecuted Galileo and Copernicus, French writer Edgar Quinet argued in *The Roman Church and Modern Society* (1845), it was not as a result of a temporary failure but due to an inherent theological backwardness and hostility to knowledge. Others still lamented the Church's alleged opposition to industrialism and capitalism, which they saw as the essence of modernity. Books like French pastor Napoleon Roussel's *Catholic and Protestant Nations Compared in their Threefold Relations to Wealth, Knowledge, and Morality* (1854) explained that Catholics were mentally incapable of understanding the logic of competition and investment. While Protestants were not alone in their anti-Catholicism, which was also shared by liberal agnostics and Jewish writers, they often insisted that Protestantism alone was the antidote to Catholicism's deficiencies. The Reformation, many explained, instilled in its followers self-control, reason, and industrious creativity, and was thus the force behind modernity's greatest achievements.[6]

Few things alarmed anti-Catholic writers more than the Catholic Church's formal opposition to freedom of religion (which it would formally abandon only in the 1960s). This disposition, many insisted, revealed the Vatican's intention to foster in its flock spiritual obedience, sentiment that received further boost after the First Vatican Council (1870–1871) formally embraced the principle of papal infallibility. Some writers in fact viewed anti-Catholicism as a cause analogous to abolitionism. In cringe-inducing comparisons, they insisted that membership in the Catholic Church was more harmful than slavery, because it destroyed one's soul, not merely one's body. The British writers Mortimer O'Sullivan and Robert James M'Ghee, for example, explained in their *Romanism As It Rules in Ireland* (1840) that "slavery is of two kinds: one bodily, and one mental." While African slaves were at least capable of imagining freedom and striving for it, "the victim of Popery is bound with a mental chain. The iron enters his soul; his heart turns cold; and he sits down in darkness and the shadow of death." Robert Benton Seeley, in his *Essays on Romanism* (1839), added that Rome's demand for "absolute, unconditional submission to the teaching of the church" was akin only to the mental passivity and weakness he claimed defined the non-Western world. In his orientalist take, it was "neither more respectable or more safe

6 Charles Chiniquy, *The Priest, the Woman, and the Confessional* (London: Gibson, 1874); Edgar Quinet, *Ultramontanism, or, the Roman Church and Modern Society* (New York: Gates & Stedman, 1845); Napoleon Roussel, *Catholic and Protestant Nations Compared in Their Threefold Relations to Wealth, Knowledge, and Morality* (London: Ward, 1855). Scholarship on anti-Catholicism is vast. For a good overview, see, e.g., Manuel Borutta, *Antikatholizismus: Deutschland und Italien in Zeitalter der europäishen Kulturkämpfen* (Göttingen: Vandenhoeck & Ruprecht, 2011).

than the same kind of mental slavery as it exists in Ceylon, in Hindustan, or in Madagascar."[7]

Such sentiments meant that Catholicism was sometimes pushed beyond the borders of religious freedom. Following the long tradition established with John Locke and his classic *Letter Concerning Toleration* (1689), Protestant and liberal commentators claimed that even religiously-neutral states had the right to discriminate against Catholics, who, as freedom's anti-thesis, were an existential threat. As the German theologian Theodor Häring put it in *The Ethics of the Christian Life* (1902), "it would be absurd if the state, on the ground of quality and fairness, treat both [Catholics and Protestants] alike. Such equality of treatment," he explained, "is, in fact, inequality, since the relation of the two Churches to the state is not alike." Fighting words of this kind also had real legal consequences. While they rarely accompanied large-scale violence of the kind wrought by antisemitism, anti-Catholic ideas helped inspire multiple political campaigns, as government from Switzerland to Germany shut down Catholic monasteries, imposed special restrictions on Catholic schools, and put Catholic missionaries under surveillance. Of special concern were the Catholic orders, especially the Jesuits, who many contemporaries decried as the vanguard of Catholic subversion. One government after another expelled it from its territories, whether Austro-Hungary (1848), Sicily (1860), Germany (1872), or France (1880). Norway went so far to ban the Jesuits in Article 2 of its constitution.[8]

These religious animosities also provided crucial backdrop for the emergence of international law's first modern theories. The discipline's leading figures, whose work picked up steam 1860s onward, were liberal Protestants, whose theory of freedom, laws, and their limits had an important religious dimension. An indicative example is the Swiss Johann Caspar Bluntschli, who was co-founder of the International Association for the Advancement of the Social Sciences (1862), the field's first scholarly organ, and of the *Journal of International Law and Comparative Legislation* (1868), its first academic journal. Like many of his associates in those endeavors, Bluntschli claimed that the emergence of modern international law was a symptom of humanity's progress and improvement. The rules that determine international conduct

7 Mortimer O'Sullivan and Robert James M'Ghee, *Romanism As It Rules in Ireland* (London: Seeley and Burnside, 1840), 388; Robert Benton Seeley, *Essays on Romanism* (London: Seeley and Ditton, 1839), 92.

8 Theodor Häring, *The Ethics of the Christian Life*, trans. James S. Hill (New York: G. P. Putnam's Sons, 1909), 226. There is no comprehensive and comparative study of government policies against Catholics. For a helpful series of case studies, see Christopher Clark and Wolfram Kaiser, eds., *Culture Wars* (Cambridge: Cambridge University Press, 2003).

emerged not from legislation (there was after all no international parliament) or even international pacts, but an organic process, in which humans rationally and voluntarily put limits on sovereigns' authority; it was then up to lawyers to articulate these emerging norms for statesmen. In Bluntschli's eyes, freedom of religion was integral to this enlightened international order. Part of humanity's path toward modernity was religion's relegation to the private sphere, where citizens could worship as they saw fit, and the "liberation" of the state to run the economy, education, and other public from church supervision; it was therefore natural that international treaties would go on to make it a universal arrangement. For Bluntschli and others who shared his view, like the British legal historian Henry Sumner Maine, freedom of religion was one of the distinguishing elements between "dynamic" and modern societies and "stationary" and backward ones. While the first were "civilized" enough to help shape international law, the latter were not yet modern enough, and thus could not enjoy the protections international law ostensibly provided from foreign intervention.[9]

Scholars have rightfully noted how deeply these ideas were implicated by Europe's colonial expansion. Such taxonomy that separated "modern" from "barbarian" societies fed into the notion of Europe's "civilizing mission," which legitimized the occupation and subjugation of Asia and Africa.[10] What has gone less noted, however, is how this distinction was also designed to legitimize anti-Catholic sentiments and arrangements. Bluntschli, for example, developed his theories while leading anti-Catholic campaigns in Switzerland and Germany, where he served as liberal legislator and writer. Because the Catholic Church was the enemy of progress and agent of foreign subversion, he wrote in lengthy essays, the suppression of its monasteries and banning of the Jesuits by governments was very much in line with international law. It was even permissible for the German government to break its treaties with the Vatican (which secured Catholic autonomy in education and other fields), since the Catholic Church, as non-sovereign, did not come

9 Johann Caspar Bluntschli, "Geschichte des Rechtes der religiösen Bekenntnisfreihet," in *Gesammelte kleine Schriften*, vol 1. (Nördlingen: C. H. Beck, 1879), 101–33. Henry Sumner Maine's distinction appears in his *Ancient Law: Its Connection with the Early History of Society and Its Relation to Modern Ideas* (London: Oxford University Press, 1861), 352.

10 On international law and colonialism, see Jennifer Pitts, *Boundaries of the International: Law and Empire* (Cambridge: Harvard University Press, 2018); Jörg Fisch, *The Right of Self-Determination of Peoples: The Domestication of an Illusion* (New York: Cambridge University Press, 2015); and Martti Koskenniemi, *The Gentle Civilizer of Nations: The Rise and Fall of International Law, 1870–1960* (New York: Cambridge University Press, 2001). Koskenniemi also briefly remarks on the anti-Catholicism of the field's founders on p. 65.

under the protection of international law. Indeed, Bluntschli explained that freedom of religion's main obstacle has not been state oppression, but Catholic persecution. It was the popes, he bemoaned while conveniently overlooking cases of anti-Catholic persecutions, who claimed that freedom of religious was a "heresy" and thus fostered Europe's worst religious discrimination. Similar sentiments were expressed by the British legal scholar James Lorimer, who pointed to the Irish population's Catholic devotion when explaining why it should remain under British rule and denied an independent status in international law. "In Roman Catholic countries," he explained in his influential *The Institutes of the Law of Nations* (1872), "men become materialists, whilst the women continue to be idolaters," possessed by irrational desires and impulses akin to those prevalent among "barbarians," and thus still required foreign tutelage and control.[11]

Indeed, anti-Catholic considerations permeated the typologies of early international law theories. Like colonial hierarchies, confessional animosities loomed large in the effort of making religious freedom a universal principle, and occupied the minds of many of international law's founding figures. Belgian lawyers Gustave Rolin-Jaequemyns, who was the *Journal of International Law and Comparative Legislation*'s first editor, saw the shrinking of Catholicism's influence as an urgent priority. During the 1880s, as the minister of the interior, he led the liberals' crusade to limit Catholic influence in public education, the so-called "school wars." John Westlake, a liberal politician, Cambridge professor of international law, and Bluntschli's partner in finding the Association, similarly agreed that Catholicism was a danger to international law. This was in part why in the 1880s he voted as a member of parliament against self-rule for Ireland, and claimed in his *Chapters on the Principles of International Law* (1894) that freedom of religion was a gift of the Reformation. Perhaps most extreme was Belgian economists Emile de Laveley, who was among the co-founder of the Institute of International Law in Ghent in 1873 and a close collaborator of Bluntschli and Lorimer. Alongside reflections on international law, he published a stream of anti-Catholic texts, darkly warning that Catholic-dominated countries will "fall into anarchy." The implications of this

[11] Johann Caspar Bluntschli, "Das römische Papstthum und das Völkerrecht," in *Gesammelte kleine Schriften*, vol. 2 (Nördlingen: C. H. Beck 1881), 236–55; James Lorimer, *The Institutes of the Laws of Nations* (Edinburgh: T. & T. Clark, 1872), 115. On Bluntschli's role in running political anti-Catholic organizations, see Matthew P. Fitzpatrick, *Purging the Empire: Mass Expulsions in Germany, 1871–1914* (New York: Oxford University Press, 2015), 45–51; and Betsy Baker Röben, *Johann Caspar Bluntschli, Francis Lieber und das moderne Völkerrecht 1861–1881* (Baden-Baden: Nomos, 2003), 191–3.

thinking for the status of Catholic-majority countries was not always as consistent or sweeping as in the case of colonial subjects. Lorimer, for example, argued that Catholicism was "moribund" enough in Italy and France to be included in the list of "civilized" countries, a generosity he did not extend to non-Europeans. Still, what all these figures agreed that part of international law's mission was breaking Catholicism's stronghold on its believers, even if that entailed limiting the Church's autonomy of action.[12]

To be sure, these visions did not go uncontested. During the nineteenth century's closing decades and after, Catholics scholars retorted that it was in fact the Holy See that provided the foundations for legal relations between nations and peoples. According to this line of argument, modern international law emerged organically from medieval Christendom and the Catholic conception of universal brotherhood. The popes and their teachings on natural law were the most effective limits on excessive state sovereignty, since they brought together leaders under peaceful authority. Few articulated this notion as clearly as the influential Catholic legal scholars from Germany Joseph Adam Gustav Hergenröther, whose *Catholic Church and Christian State* (1873) was widely read and translated. "The perfection of international law," he explained, was nurtured by Catholicism's international nature. Since the fall of the Roman Empire, "Christendom created amongst the new States common interests and an international law, which, founded upon the principles and laws of the Church, was administered by her and her Head as an international tribunal." Such ideas became especially popular after World War I, when Vatican officials used them in their efforts to craft new legal treaties (concordats) with Europe's national governments. Because the Catholic Church had a unique position in the international sphere, they claimed, its teachings should enjoy a privileged status in schooling and marriage laws.[13] Most Protestants, however, remained cool to these efforts, and saw the Vatican's diplomacy as a challenge to religious tolerance. When Protestant thinkers, politicians, and church leaders from across Europe and North American gathered in Stockholm in 1925 for a conference on the

12 For Gustave Rolin-Jaequemyns's approach to Catholicism, see, e.g., his *Rétablissement des relations diplomatiques entre la Belgique & le Vatican* (Brussels: Weissenbruch, 1884); John Westlake, *Chapters on the Principles of International Law* (Cambridge: Cambridge University Press, 1894). For Emile de Laveley, see, e.g., his "The Clerical Party in Belgium," *The Fortnightly Review* 18 (1872): 503–18; the quote is from p. 515.

13 Joseph Adam Gustav Hergenröther, *Catholic Church and Christian State* (London: Burns and Oates, 1873), 369. On the Vatican's campaign after World War I, see Giuliana Chamedes, *A Twentieth Century Crusade: The Vatican's Battle to Remake Christian Europe* (Cambridge: Harvard University Press, 2019). Hergenröther's significance to the ideological mission is discussed in 27–32.

churches and global politics, one speaker scoffed that "the conduct of Romanism" in international treaties "recalls the action of a rich and cunning landlord, who strives to get as much as possible of the goods of his sick and disheartened neighbor into his own hands."[14]

Like anti-Catholicism more broadly, Protestant anxieties about Catholicism's resistance to religious freedom's universalization remained powerful deep into the twentieth century. Indeed, even after Hitler's genocidal assault on Europe's Jews and other religious minorities and Stalin's campaign against Christian churches unfolded, Protestant activists and writers continued to describe Catholicism as an urgent (though certainly no longer the main) problem for free worship. The influential Swiss Lutheran Adolf Keller, for example, lamented in the midst of World War II that religious freedom was facing a three-headed challenge. Alongside Nazi Germany and the Soviet Union, he pointed to Spain and Italy, where Catholicism was formal state religion and Protestant missionaries were prohibited from working, as similar in their menace. Parallel sentiments were apparent when the International Missionary Council, an umbrella organization that coordinated the work of all Protestant missionary organizations in the world, began to chart its advocacy efforts for the postwar world, and commissioned from the American scholar M. Searle Bates a survey of religious freedom's status around the globe. The tome he published, *Religious Liberty* (1945), which became the era's most important text on the topic, similarly decried Catholicism as equal to Communism in its oppression and second only to Nazism. Such convictions remained common even into the 1950s. Influential surveys such as Italian Lutheran Giovanni Miegge's *Religious Liberty* (1957) claimed that Catholic-majority countries, alongside Communist regimes and Muslims states in the Middle East, should be the targets of international pressure to institute freedom of worship.[15]

All of this meant that when Protestants activists mobilized in the postwar years to promote religious freedom in international treaties and constitutions, their vision remained selective. Rather than opposing anti-Catholic measures that remained in place in Norway and other Nordic countries, which were never even mentioned in their publications and correspondence, Protestants continued to focus on restrictions to Protestant evangelization efforts.

[14] Cited in G. K. A. Bell, ed., *The Stockholm Conference 1925: The Official Report of the Universal Christian Conference on Life and Work Held in Stockholm, 19–30 August, 1925* (London: Oxford University Press, 1926), 655.

[15] Adolf Keller, *Christian Europe Today* (New York: Harper, 1942); M. Serle Bates, *Religious Liberty* (New York: International Missionary Council, 1945); Giovanni Miegge, *Religious Liberty* (New York: Associated Press, 1957).

Alongside Communist and Middle Eastern countries, of special attention was Catholic-majority Italy. Throughout the 1950s, for example, the International Protestant organizations such as the WCC, sought to pressure the Italian and Spanish governments. Together with the pan-Protestant American National Council of Churches, it organized petitions and demonstrations that demanded the liberalization of these countries' restrictions on Protestant marriages and rites. Indeed, when the Word Council of Churches decided to establish a special Secretariat for religious freedom, whose main goal was to coordinate Protestant advocacy around the globe, Catholicism was clearly among its top priorities. To lead it, the WCC appointed an ex-Jesuit from Spain, Angel Francisco Carrillo de Albornoz, whose *Roman Catholicism and Religious Liberty* (1959) lamented Catholicism as the world's worst oppressor in religious matters. It seems as if only a radical change would dislodge Catholicism from its position in the Protestant imagination.[16]

In many ways, the Protestant approach to religious freedom during international law's formative decades confirms the claims of critical scholars. It seems undeniable that when Protestants promoted the right for free worship, they had only very certain creeds in mind, and that their vision could easily exclude faiths that did not fit their conceptions of modernity. Yet even as Protestant speakers lamented Spain and Italy's intransigence, things began to shift. From the 1930s onward, Protestant thinkers and organizations boldly rethought earlier convictions, and claimed that Catholics were allies in the churches' struggle against their enemies. As part of this transformation, Protestants also rethought their definition of religious freedom's application in international law. While they remained adamant that this principle must undergird international treaties and be superior to sovereign restrictions, they now argued that Catholicism, too, should come under its protection.

Why this *rapprochement* took place has only recently begun to draw scholarly attention. And while many of its reasons are yet to be fully uncovered, historians agree that it was at least in part powered by political considerations. The first systematic efforts to overcome confessional animosities took place in Germany, and in response to the Nazi vision of an interconfessional and unified racial body. Both Nazi-sympathizers and anti-Nazi thinkers began to wonder if Catholics were indeed so different from Protestants, and began to

16 Baastian Bouwman, "From Religious Freedom to Social Justice: The Human Rights Engagement of the Ecumenical Movement from the 1940s to the 1970s," *Journal of Global History* 13, no. 2 (2018): 252–73. Angel Francisco Carrillo de Albornoz, *Roman Catholicism and Religious Liberty* (Geneva: World Council of Churches, 1959).

argue that both shared common future. This reconciliation continued after World War II and with the flaring of the Cold War, when prominent Protestant thinkers viewed Catholics as essential allies in the struggle against Marxist "materialism." Compared to moderate Socialists and radical Communists, which many commentators conflated as similarly "totalitarian," Catholics seemed natural comrades, equally committed to traditional sexuality, the sanctity of private property, and autonomy of religious education. For some, especially in the missionary world, the unfolding of decolonization in the 1950s and early 1960s also played a role. As postcolonial states encroached on churches' traditional control of education and health services, some writers wondered if an interconfessional cooperation could help protect both churches' interests.[17]

Whatever the immediate trigger, the postwar era witnessed a sea change in Protestant thinking about Catholicism. A growing chorus began to depict the Catholic Church as a source of spiritual energy, a natural ally in the struggle against atheist or non-Christian challenges. The Swiss Protestant writer Walter Nigg, for example, sought to uproot long-standing Protestant suspicion of Catholic habits, such as celebration of saints or monastic life. Those traditions, he argued in the widely-read *Great Saints* (1946) and *Warriors of God* (1953), were rooted in spiritual resilience, which Protestants had every reason to respect. In fact, they could enrich and rejuvenate Protestants who Nigg worried had become not sufficiently devout. The followers of Martin Luther, he explained, would do well to celebrate the spirit of monastic devotion as they sought to resist Communist "materialism." Religious leaders similarly argued that the differences between the creeds have been overly exaggerated, and that the confessions instead shared similar convictions. The German theologian and bishop Wilhelm Stählin, for example, maintained in 1952 that both Western churches were one in their recognition of human sin, which helped them curtail hubristic efforts to construct political utopias (such as Communism) and establish societies that aspired peace. Writers went out of their way to explain the inter-confessional bond as more than a tactical cease-fire or begrudging toleration. Catholics, many now argued, were spiritual brethren.[18]

Following the anti-Catholic precedent, religious thought both echoed and helped shape legal and political realities. This was especially the case in West

17 For an overview of those dynamics, see Udi Greenberg, "Catholics, Protestants, and the Violent Birth of European Religious Pluralism," *The American Historical Review* 124, no. 2 (2019): 511–38.

18 Walter Nigg, *Great Saints* (London: Siders, 1948) and Walter Nigg, *Warriors of God: The Great Religious Orders and Their Founders* (New York: Knopf, 1959). Stählin is cited in Felix Dirsch, *Authentischer Konservatismus* (Berlin: LIT, 2012), 275.

Germany, where Nazi-era experiences, new demographic realities (the country's partition and massive migration flow at the war's end transformed Catholics from minority to equal in size to Protestants), and a joint opposition to Socialism and Communism made inter-confessional cooperation the order of the day. Protestants, who until then congregated in largely confessional political bodies, joined hands with veterans of the Catholic Center party. Under the leadership of Catholic former mayor of Bonn, Konrad Adenauer, they joined the new and interconfessional Christian-Democratic Union, which won elections and ruled the country for more than a decade. While this cooperation was never free of tensions – Catholics and Protestants could occasionally disagree on family law legislation or the conduct of international relations – it also brought about the removal of the country's last standing legal restrictions on Catholicism. The so-called pulpit law, which was legislated in 1872 as part of the government's assault on Catholicism and which banned priests from discussing politics (then a common Catholic practice), was formally removed from the country's criminal code in 1953.[19]

As was the case with anti-Catholicism before, these new sentiments also shaped contemporaries' approach to international matters. Especially among Protestant advocates of early European integration, which began in the postwar years and slowly progressed in the 1950s, it seemed evident that pan-European cooperation that would transcend national sovereignty went hand in hand with confessional cooperation. An indicative example is the renowned British historian Arnold Toynbee. According to Toynbee, Europe's future depended on its ability to resist the "toxic" notion of unlimited national sovereignty, which in his eyes unified fascism and Communism. Alongside economic cooperation, the nations of Western Europe had to submit themselves to a new set of laws and a new court, which would guarantee basic freedoms to all. Even though Toynbee's writing during the interwar period sometimes echoed the belief that the Catholic Church fostered authoritarian submission, by the 1950s he became convinced that the Pope and his flock were integral to his vision of a postwar Europe. It was the Church, he explained in publications and speeches, which was the first to limit state sovereignty in modern Europe, and thus could once again provide the tools for anti-fascist and anti-Communist reconstruction. Indeed, Toynbee was convinced that Protestant and Catholic cooperation was necessary to create a new and free Europe. As he explained it to a group of Christian thinkers and

19 Maria Mitchell, *The Origins of Christian Democracy* (Ann Arbor: University of Michigan Press, 2012). On persistent tensions, see Mark Edward Ruff, *The Battle for the Catholic Past in Germany, 1945–1980* (New York: Cambridge University Press, 2017).

politicians in a 1953 seminar in Rome, "we Europeans must re-unite on the cultural and spiritual planes" and this goal will require "the cooperation of all the living branches of the Western Christian Church."[20]

Indeed, the effort to promote European integration through international law reflected these shifting Protestant visions. One can detect them among many of the key figures who helped draft the European Convention of Human Rights (the Convention, which was ratified in 1953) and establish the European Court of Human Rights (which opened in 1959). Few represented this fact more clearly than Winston Churchill, who spent the immediate postwar years (while being out of office as Britain's prime minister) leading the international movement for European legal integration. Like the earliest theoreticians of international law, Churchill was adamant that freedom of religion was necessary to secure a "civilized" order (which he understood as anti-fascist and anti-Communist). Integration, in his mind, and the restriction of national sovereignty through international law were supposed to lead to Europe's spiritual and ethical rebirth, and that required that its people would be able to freely worship. Churchill, however, often insisted that the Catholic Church was an integral part of guaranteeing this freedom. As he told a gathering of Dutch parliamentarians in 1946, "since the bygone struggles between Protestants and Catholics of the sixteenth centuries, there is at least one profound and beneficent new fact of which all should take account. The Church of Rome has ranged itself with those who defend the rights and dignity of the individual, and the cause of personal freedom throughout the world." For Churchill, Christian credentials (and their implied anti-Communist convictions) seemed often even more important than adherence to democratic norms. He insisted, for example, that Spain's deep ties to the Catholic Church made it a natural member for the Convention, an idea that others rejected in light of Francisco Franco's brutal dictatorship.[21]

Scholars have correctly noted that such understanding of religious freedom was glaringly limited, conflating as it did religion and Christianity. Churchill mused that the Convention's goal was to defend "the health of ... Christendom" against its secular Marxist opponents, and so did other major figures in its creation, such as British conservative politician David Maxwell-Fyfe, who described its provisions as bringing

20 Arnold Toynbee, *Christianity and Civilization* (London: CMS, 1940). The quote is from his "The Idea of Europe and the Unity of Europe – Europeans' Common Destiny," in *The European Round Table Discussion in Rome, October 1953* (Strasbourg: Council of Europe, 1953), 21.

21 As cited in Marco Duranti, *The Conservative Human Rights Revolution: European Identity, Transnational Politics, and the Origins of the European Convention* (New York: Oxford University Press, 2017), 171, which also uncovers Churchill's approach to Spain in 108.

together "the great family of Western European and Christian civilization," never mentioning Judaism, Islam, or other creeds. Indeed, when the European Convention, in Article 9, guaranteed freedom of religion, its clear goal first and foremost was to secure Christian rights. It is also significant, however, that the Convention signaled a new sensibility to Catholic demands. As historian Marco Duranti has shown, Protestants were hardly alone in shaping the Convention's clauses on religion. In their work, they rather joined hands with conservative Catholics from France, such as Christian Democratic politician Pierre-Henri Teitgen, who hoped that the convention would secure Catholics' right to run their own schools (preferably with public funding), and thus foil renewed efforts to separate religion from education. The Convention's understanding of religious freedom, then, reflected a substantial change in Protestant legal thinking. What was once clearly beyond freedom was now integral to international protection.[22]

Given this context, it is perhaps not surprising that a consequential impact of the Convention was in dismantling some legal remnants of anti-Catholicism. In one Nordic country after another, the Convention's ratification was followed by removal of restrictions on Catholic worship and education. The most notable case was Norway, whose constitutional ban on the Jesuit order was still in place in the 1950s. Despite its government's formal note of concern during the Convention's writing, in 1956 it ultimately revised Article 2 and, for the first time in a century and a half, allowed members of the order to enter the country. Similar dynamics unfolded in Finland, whose 1922 Act of Religious Freedom guaranteed free worship but allowed Catholic schools to be banned from public funding (Lutheran-run institutions did not face similar restrictions) and put severe restrictions on Catholic orders and monasteries (for example by allowing them to accept only Finnish citizens). After a prolonged parliamentary debate, the country embraced the Convention's inter-confessional spirit and removed those qualifications. The last was Sweden, whose sweeping legal restrictions prohibited all Catholic orders from operating. Following the Convention's approval, its parliament removed those restrictions, and a group of Carmelite women arrived in Stockholm to establish a small monastery and health center.[23]

[22] The most important scholarly works in this school are Samuel Moyn, *Christian Human Rights* (Philadelphia: University of Pennsylvania Press, 2015) and Duranti, *The Conservative*. Churchill's quote is from Winston Churchill, "Foreword," in *Europe Unites* (London: United Europe Movement, 1948), viii. Maxwell-Fyfe is cited in Duranti, *The Conservative*, 195.

[23] See Carolyn Evans, *Freedom of Religion under the European Convention of Human Rights* (Oxford: Oxford University Press, 2001), 49, and Yvonne Maria Werner, "The Catholic Danger: The Changing Patterns of Swedish Anti-Catholicism 1850–1965," in *European Anti-Catholicism in a Comparative and Transnational Perspective*, ed. Yvonne Maria Werner and Jonas Harvard (Amsterdam: Rodpi, 2013), 13–24.

Finally, the WCC, which for years mobilized against Catholicism's alleged oppression, embraced the new spirit. Especially after the Catholic bishops who gathered in Rome formally embraced *Dignitatis Humanae* (1965), the declaration on religious freedom, Protestant thinkers and activists now joined hands with Catholics to promote a broad vision of Christian action. That year, the WCC's President, the Dutch Lutheran Willem Adolph Visser 't Hooft, met for a series of meetings with the head of the Vatican's newly established Secretariat for the Promotion of Christian Unity, German Cardinal Augustin Bea. After the two agreed to cooperate, a series of joint Catholic-Protestant conferences followed, in which directors of charities and missions discussed how to work together on Bible translation in Asia, medical assistance in Africa, and education advocacy in Europe. These initiatives would soon become permanent, as standing working groups would continue them in the following decades. From that point on, it would be only non-Christian majority regimes that would draw protestations over the freedom of evangelization and Christian education.[24]

The recent expansion in Protestants' understanding of religious freedom is hardly a cause for uncritical celebration. If writers, politicians, and jurists abandoned their anti-Catholic vision of international law and came to include Catholicism as worthy of protection, it was at least in part because many redrew the borders of exclusion and became much more anxious about other groups. In the early Cold War, as historian Samuel Moyn has shown, the main objects of these fears were "godless" Marxists. The European Court's first judgment on Article 9's scope, after all, was an approval of the West German government's ban of the Communist party, which the Court justified by claiming that Communism was an ideology so dangerous that it could not be defended by freedom of conscience. More recently, the Court invoked Article 9 to explain why it must allow restriction on Muslim clothes to proceed in France, Belgium, and elsewhere. Muslim beliefs, the justices implied, can occasionally pose a threat to the democratic order; restricting them is therefore hardly contradictory to the Convention's spirit. Even in its new meaning, then, religious freedom has not fostered universal pluralism, and remains mired in power struggles and religious hierarchies.[25]

[24] Margaret Nash, *The Ecumenical Movement in the 1960s* (Johannesburg: Ravan, 1975).

[25] Moyn, *Christian Human Rights*; on Islam, see Peter G. Danchin, "Islam in the Secular *Nomos* of the European Court of Human Rights," *Michigan Journal of International Law* 32, no. 4 (2011): 663–747.

What this historical record does show, however, is how malleable Protestantism's engagement with law has been. Rather than inaugurating a conception of right that unfolded through the centuries, and that (even if inadvertently) ultimately flowered in liberal or republican politics, Protestantism proved open to multiple interpretations, inspiring both anti-Catholic and inter-confessional approaches. Those, in turn, produced profoundly different visions of international law. Both those who in the nineteenth century viewed Catholicism as beyond the pale of religious law's protections and those who later saw it as a partner in the fight for Christianity equally rooted their convictions in the history of the Reformation. Protestantism, in short, had many religious freedoms. What its future iterations will look like is yet to be seen.

RECOMMENDED READING

Chappel, James. *Catholic Modern: The Challenge of Totalitarianism and the Remaking of the Church*. Cambridge, MA: Harvard University Press, 2018.

Lindkvist, Linde. *Religious Freedom and the Universal Declaration of Human Rights*. New York: Cambridge University Press, 2017.

Scott, Joan. *The Politics of the Veil*. Princeton: Princeton University Press, 2007.

Sullivan, Winnifred F., Elizabeth Shakman Hurd, and Saba Mahmood, eds. *The Politics of Religious Freedom*. Chicago: University of Chicago Press, 2015.

13

Beyond the Freedom of Worship: The Contested Meaning of Religious Freedom in International Human Rights Law and Politics, 1945–1967

Linde Lindkvist

This chapter offers a brief history of how religious freedom has been conceptualized in international human rights law and politics after 1945, starting with the drafting of the Universal Declaration of Human Rights (UDHR, 1948) Article 18 on the freedom of conscience, religion or belief, and ending with the aborted attempts in the 1960s to craft an international treaty on religious intolerance and discrimination. The chapter highlights how religious freedom over time became linked to a wider human rights discourse centered on combating different forms of structural injustice. It concludes with a set of critical reflections on recent attempts, including by the Donald J. Trump administration in the United States, to return to the "moral landscape" of the 1940s in order to salvage an allegedly natural right to religious freedom from the more comprehensive framework of human rights.

13.1 A CHRISTIAN AND AMERICAN HUMAN RIGHT?

The recent surge of interest in the history of human rights has sparked spirited debates among professional historians, human rights scholars, and members of the wider human rights community on the emancipatory potential of rights-based politics. Behind the often-hair-splitting discussions on chronology – on when and in what settings the idea of human rights originated and later moved to become a salient feature of transnational discourse – lurk more fundamental moral and political questions: To what extent can the discourse of human rights function as a resource for wider struggles of social justice and equality? And to what extent is it a discourse that instead tends to privilege the status quo, merely humanizing fundamentally unequal and unjust structures of power?[1]

[1] For three recent interventions exploring the links between the histories and the potential futures of human rights, see Samuel Moyn, *Not Enough: Human Rights in an Unequal*

Much of the scholarly debate still revolves around the origins, as well as the historical and present uses, of the UDHR. True, some historians have tried their best to shift our attention away from the declaration to developments of later decades, including the international campaigns against racial discrimination and colonialism in the 1960s or the crisis of Western socialism in the 1970s, suggesting that it is in such processes that we ought to search for the origins of our contemporary understandings of human rights. Yet even these accounts tend to involve more or less thorough attempts to come to grips with the legacy of the UDHR, at the very least by highlighting the ideological and political rifts separating the human rights diplomacy of the 1940s from, say, the transnational human rights movements of the 1970s.[2]

One of the central discontinuities that historians like Samuel Moyn have discerned in the twentieth-century history of human rights has to do with the concept's relationship to Christianity. In his 2015 book *Christian Human Rights*, Moyn suggests that if we want to grasp the ideological and cultural context of early human rights declarations and treaties, we must appreciate how in the thirties and forties the cause of human rights was predominantly carried forward by self-consciously Christian thinkers and actors, especially on the European continent. Moyn highlights the intellectual trajectory of the prominent Catholic philosopher Jacques Maritain, who in the transwar period metamorphosed from a fierce critic to a staunch defender of personal human rights, simultaneously claiming them as fruits of a scholastic natural law tradition as opposed to enlightenment philosophy and revolutionary politics. Moyn shows how variants of Christian personalism shaped the ways in which human rights were articulated and wielded in local and international settings, repeatedly drawing contrasts with the developments in the 1970s when human rights, he says, re-emerged as "a secular doctrine of the left."[3]

In the wake of *Christian Human Rights*, scholars have sought to flesh out, nuance, or dispute many of Moyn's findings and interpretations. This includes Sarah Shortall's textured work on the internal frictions among Catholic

World (Cambridge, MA: Harvard University Press, 2018); Justine Lacroix and Jean-Yves Pranchère, *Human Rights on Trial: A Genealogy of the Critique of Human Rights* (New York: Cambridge University Press, 2018); Jessica Whyte, *The Morals of the Market: Human Rights and the Rise of Neoliberalism* (London: Verso, 2019).

2 For a balanced discussion of these debates, see Jan Eckel, *The Ambivalence of Good: Human Rights in International Politics Since the 1940s* (New York: Oxford University Press, 2019), 3–13.

3 Samuel Moyn, *Christian Human Rights* (Philadelphia: University of Pennsylvania Press, 2015), 100. For a parallel account showcasing the significance of personalist and conservative conceptions in the constitution of European human rights law, see Marco Duranti, *The Conservative Human Rights Revolution: European Identity, Transnational Politics, and the Origins of the European Convention* (Oxford: Oxford University Press, 2016).

intellectuals who embraced human rights in the 1930s and 1940s, effectively questioning the view that this was a straightforwardly conservative enterprise.[4] In a similar vein, Gene Zubovich has carried out groundbreaking empirical work that showcases the generally anti-racist, anti-colonial, and economically progressive human rights politics of mid-century American Protestants.[5] Moreover, the scholarly reactions to *Christian Human Rights* include significant attempts to make sense of one specific right that became central to international human rights discourse in the 1940s: the right to religious freedom.

There is much evidence pointing to the significance of religious freedom in the human rights activism and diplomacy of the 1940s. Clauses on the freedom of conscience and belief and the rights of religious practice were featured in all of the early human rights instruments, including the American Declaration of the Rights and Duties of Man (1948), the UDHR, and the European Convention on Human Rights (1950). Moreover, religious freedom informed the very first country-specific United Nations (UN) resolutions on human rights of 1949, which targeted the crackdown on organized religion in Eastern Europe, epitomized by the internment of the anti-communist Hungarian Cardinal Jószef Mindszenty.[6] Finally, one estimate suggests that 7,850 of a total of 9,524 individual human rights petitions submitted to the UN Secretariat in 1950 (a body which at the time could only defer them to the states in question) involved violations of the freedom of religion.[7]

To be sure, scholars have long recognized the prominence of religious freedom in the formative years of the international human rights enterprise.[8] Yet, it is only in the past decade that they have come to appreciate the political and ideological contexts in which this work unfolded. Herein lies the principal contribution of human rights historians like Moyn, who includes a chapter on religious freedom in *Christian Human Rights*. They encourage us to shift our

4 Sarah Shortall, "Theology and Politics of Christian Human Rights," *Journal of the History of Ideas* 79, no. 3 (2018): 445–60.

5 Gene Zubovich, "American Protestants and the Era of Anti-racist Human Rights," *Journal of the History of Ideas* 79, no. 3 (2018): 427–43; Gene Zubovich, "For Human Rights Abroad, Against Jim Crow at Home: The Political Mobilization of American Ecumenical Protestants in the World War II Era," *The Journal of American History* 105, no. 2 (2018): 267–90.

6 UN General Assembly Resolutions 272 (III) (1949); 294 (IV) (1950) and 385 (V) (1950).

7 Howard Tolley, *The U.N. Commission on Human Rights* (Boulder: Westview Press, 1987).

8 See, e.g., John Nurser, *For All Peoples and All Nations: The Ecumenical Church and Human Rights* (Washington, DC: Georgetown University Press, 2005); Carl-Gustaf Andrén, "De mänskliga rättigheternas religiösa och rättsliga bakgrund: Debatten inom Förenta nationerna och Europarådet i slutet på 1940-talet," *Svensk teologisk kvartalskrift* 51, no. 4 (1975): 158–66.

attention away from the ideational roots of the idea, whether medieval or early-modern, to the external factors causing individual thinkers, nongovernmental organizations (NGOs), and states to embrace it as a tool of their causes.

Partly building on Moyn's account, historian and legal scholar Anna Su locates the birth of international religious freedom protection in a twentieth-century history of American foreign policy. In *Exporting Freedom*, she stitches together both familiar and obscure chapters of American religious freedom promotion: starting off with President William McKinley's Instructions to the Philippine Commission of 1900 and Woodrow Wilson's outlines for the Covenant of the League of Nations and taking us all the way up to the International Religious Freedom Act of 1998 and the 2004 Transitional Administrative Law for Iraq. Through an exemplary work of serial contextualism, Su reveals how religious freedom has repeatedly functioned not only as a means for more or less idealistic efforts to export American values but also as "a handmaiden for [the United States'] rise to world power."[9]

The emergence of the UN framework for human rights forms a central part of this story. Su sees religious freedom's role in the early international human rights project as flowing from the "diplomatic thought" of President Franklin D. Roosevelt (FDR). She reveals how FDR – who carefully cultivated the public persona of a "simple Christian" – was drawn to the concept "not only as an ideological weapon in the war against totalitarian Nazi Germany, but as a pillar of enduring peace."[10] Tapping into a tradition of Christian republicanism, Roosevelt viewed religious freedom both as an inviolable human right and as an instrument in the creation of a future world-order, premised on the peaceful coexistence of democratic nations.[11] "Where democracy has been overthrown," Roosevelt declared in his 1939 State of the Union address, "the spirit of free worship has disappeared. And where religion and democracy have vanished, good faith and reason in international affairs have given way to strident ambition and brute force."[12] In this way, the freedom of religion worked as a tool for framing the ongoing world-crisis as a struggle between democracy and totalitarianism.

Perhaps surprisingly, Roosevelt made use of the freedom of worship in justifying the wartime alliance with the Soviet Union. To the dismay of both Catholic and Protestant critics who viewed the Soviet Union as the greatest

9 Anna Su, *Exporting Freedom: Religious Liberty and American Power* (Cambridge, MA: Harvard University Press, 2016), 10.

10 Su, *Exporting Freedom*, 62.

11 Andrew Preston, *Sword of the Spirit, Shield of Faith: Religion in American War and Diplomacy* (New York: Alfred A. Knopf, 2012), 320–7.

12 Su, *Exporting Freedom*, 66.

planetary threat to religion and religious rights, FDR stressed how Article 124 of the USSR constitution provided legal protection for the freedom of worship.[13] "The President arguably knew full well the lack of such freedom in the Soviet Union," Su argues, "but … he was more concerned about the bigger picture he was painting for his fellow Americans to help them sign on to the case for the country's likely involvement in the war: the contrast between Nazi totalitarianism and Anglo-American freedom. Thus, he wanted to place the Russians in the latter camp."[14] Consequently, the 1942 Declaration of the United Nations announced that the Allied powers were pulled together not only by common enemies but also by a set of shared values, including "life, liberty, independence and religious freedom."[15]

After 1945, religious freedom transformed from a war-slogan to a vital component of international human rights law and politics. FDR's postwar vision, centered as it was on individual freedom of worship, paved the way for the "contemporary human rights regime through the UN Charter and the UDHR," Su says.[16] She points to the ways in which FDR's mantle was claimed by leading figures within the American ecumenical movement, such as John Foster Dulles and O. Frederick Nolde, who were actively present in the process of setting up the UN and in crafting its framework for human rights. "Although the exact degree of hegemony of the United States by the end of the war could be debated," she concludes, "it exercised an overwhelming influence in the drafting processes of these foundational documents."[17]

13.2 THE UNIVERSAL DECLARATION AND THE MOVE BEYOND FREE WORSHIP

Su is undoubtedly correct in asserting that any international history of religious freedom must appreciate the concept's intimate ties to American power. Indeed, the rise of the UN human rights framework, including its emphasis on individual conscience and religious practice, was largely propelled by Washington's efforts to create a world institution that would ratify American values as universal, while exempting itself from external scrutiny. Yet, her

[13] 1936 Constitution of the Soviet Union, Article 124, www.departments.bucknell.edu/russian/const/36cons04.html#chap10.

[14] Su, *Exporting Freedom*, 71.

[15] Declaration by the United Nations, January 1, 1942, https://avalon.law.yale.edu/20th century/decade03.asp.

[16] Su, *Exporting Freedom*, 63.

[17] Su, *Exporting Freedom*, 87.

account also reveals the limitations of this perspective if we seek to grasp the changing *content* of religious freedom at the international level. The problem is not just that she exaggerates the role of the US government in crafting religious freedom as a human right, overlooking the significant contributions of other state and nonstate actors. Her account also tends to present religious freedom as a relatively stable idea, albeit one that is activated for different purposes in different times and places. This glosses over how the main debates on religious freedom have not been on whether it should enjoy protection by international law and institutions but on what it actually means.[18]

As I have argued elsewhere, the drafting of the UDHR's Article 18 on the freedom of thought, conscience, and religion[19] can be construed as a window onto such broader debates on human rights and religion that took place in, and in connection to, the UN in the late 1940s. Even though this clause was cast in a highly abstract form, its structure and emphases mirrored the concerns of a relatively small circle of individual diplomats and lobbyists. What united these actors, most notably Charles H. Malik of Lebanon and Nolde of the World Council of Churches (WCC), was not just the realization that religious freedom was central to the formation of a just and durable world-order but that the precise conceptualization of this freedom was of outmost importance. They argued that unless the Commission got the wording right, the UDHR would not work as an effective antidote to current and emerging forces threatening both personal conscience as well as individual and collective religious life.[20]

What made this a pressing concern was partly the nascent Cold War, which loaded the talks on an international bill of human rights with sharply conflicting visions. On paper, the Soviet Union supported the "freedom of religious worship" through the Stalin Constitution of 1936. But such constitutional provisions had done little to counteract the state's clampdown on organized religion, including large-scale incarcerations of Orthodox clergy and severe restrictions on religious education.[21] To leading members of the ecumenical movement, such as Dulles, it was essential to move beyond the freedom of

18 Malcolm D. Evans, *Religious Liberty and International Law in Europe* (New York: Cambridge University Press, 1997), 192–3.

19 Article 18 reads: "Everyone has the right to freedom of thought, conscience and religion; this right includes freedom to change his religion or belief, and freedom, either alone or in community with others and in public or private, to manifest his religion or belief in teaching, practice, worship and observance."

20 This summarizes the main argument in Linde Lindkvist, *Religious Freedom and the Universal Declaration of Human Rights* (New York: Cambridge University Press, 2017).

21 M. Searle Bates, *Religious Liberty: An Inquiry* (New York: International Missionary Council, 1945), 7–9.

worship for the simple reason of avoiding a human rights framework that harmonized with Soviet laws and policies. Moreover, a framework that restricted religious freedom to the dimension of worship would fail to capture the depth of individual religiosity and organized religion.[22]

In the drafting of the UDHR, Malik and Nolde were pulled together by a shared commitment to an understanding of religious freedom that went beyond protection of worship. Yet they approached the task from fundamentally different angles. Malik treated the UN negotiations as a process of resurrecting an authentic understanding of the human person in response to what he, like other personalists, viewed as a profound crisis of humanity.[23] Having received his doctorate from Harvard's philosophy department in 1937, Malik had gone on to teach a fairly conventional Western philosophical canon at the American University of Beirut, before being appointed as the country's ambassador to the UN and the United States. During his doctoral studies he studied before Martin Heidegger in Germany, embracing his diagnosis of the predicaments of modern man, while reaching for an idiosyncratic Christian existentialism as a more constructive response to it.[24] Malik viewed the UN activities in the field of human rights as an extension of a wider ideological struggle against materialist conceptions of man, whether liberal or communist in appearance: "We are trying in effect, knowingly or unknowingly, to go back to the Platonic-Christian tradition which affirms man's original, integral dignity and immortality."[25]

For Malik, in short, the project was much more about the figure of the *human* than it was of *rights*. With close to no instructions from Beirut, Malik used his membership in the drafting group to advance clauses that revolved around the inner freedoms of man. This was most visible in the debates on the UDHR's Article 1, where Malik insisted on including a phrase specifying that human beings are endowed with reason and conscience.[26] But he also engaged actively in the debates on Article 18 on the freedom of religion,

22 Matti Peiponen, "Ecumenical Action in World Politics: The Creation of the Commission of the Churches on International Affairs (CCIA), 1945–1949" (PhD dissertation, University of Helsinki, 2014), 214.

23 Terence Renaud, "Human Rights as Radical Anthropology: Protestant Theology and Ecumenism in the Transwar Era," *The Historical Journal* 60, no. 2 (2016): 493–518, at 494.

24 For more on Malik, see Glenn Mitoma, "Charles H. Malik and Human Rights: Notes on a Biography," *Biography* 33, no. 1 (2010): 222–41; Alexandre Lefebvre, *Human Rights and the Care of the Self* (Durham, NC: Duke University Press, 2018), 143–52.

25 Charles H. Malik, "Human Rights and Religious Liberty," *The Ecumenical Review* 1, no. 4 (1949): 404–9, at 404.

26 For more on the negotiations on Article 1, see Mitoma, "Charles H. Malik and Human Rights," 226; Lydia H. Liu, "Shadows of Universalism: The Untold Story of Human Rights around 1948," *Critical Inquiry* 40, no. 4 (2014): 385–417, at 408–11.

arguing that it was essential to draw a line between the absolute inner freedoms of thought and conscience, on the one hand, and the rights of religious practice, on the other.[27] This is not to suggest that he considered the tangible rights of worship, practice, and observance as insignificant. The point was rather to have the declaration echo a certain understanding of man as a person; and of human freedom as a process of acquiring ever deeper acquaintance with a divine truth. The problem of reducing the right to religious freedom to the freedom of worship was that it glossed over how religion was essentially a matter of man's evolving relationship with God.[28]

In connection to the drafting process, Malik worked in close cooperation with Nolde, who represented the Commission of the Churches on International Affairs (CCIA).[29] The two shared positions on most topics. Most notably, they were adamant that an international statement on human rights must provide recognition of the right to change religion or belief.[30] But while Malik focused on the declaration's underlying anthropology, Nolde ran an intense campaign to make sure that the structure of Article 18 provided protection for a broad range of religious practices, including missionary activities and charitable work. Critically, and following the policies adopted by the international ecumenical conferences in the 1930s and 1940s, he held that religious freedom was not merely an individual human right but applied to corporate bodies as well.[31] A key concern in the context of writing the UDHR was to recognize that religion had collective and institutional dimensions and that individual beliefs often involved a sense of discipleship, expressing itself

27 UN Doc. E/CN.4/SR.14 (1947), 3–4.

28 Charles H. Malik, "Asia and Africa Ask Searching Questions," *Presbyterian Life* 5, no. 24 (1954): 7–9, 36.

29 The CCIA was established as a joint venture by the WCC and the International Missionary Council. For more on its early history, see Peiponen, "Ecumenical Action in World Politics." For more on the ways in which the ecumenical movement later evolved into a champion of a broad range of human rights connected to visions of social justice, see Bastiaan Bouwman, "From Religious Freedom to Social Justice: The Human Rights Engagement of the Ecumenical Movement from the 1940s to the 1970s," *Journal of Global History* 13, no. 2 (2018): 252–73; Patrick William Kelley, "Human Rights and Christian Responsibility: Transnational Christian Activism, Human Rights, and State Violence in Brazil and Chile in the 1970s," in *Religious Responses to Violence: Human Rights in Latin America Past and Present*, ed. Alexander Wilde (Notre Dame, IN: University of Notre Dame Press, 2015), 95–122.

30 O. Frederick Nolde, *Free and Equal: Human Rights in Ecumenical Perspective* (Geneva: World Council of Churches, 1968), 45–6.

31 Nolde frequently stressed the significance of the Oxford Conference in 1937; see Nolde, *Free and Equal*, 16–20. See also Resolution on Religious Liberty, adopted by the World Council of Churches and the International Missionary Council in August and September, 1948, Papers of Charles Habib Malik, Library of Congress, Washington D.C., Box 193, Folder 6.

not just in acts of worship but in social and political action as well.[32] "So long as freedom of religion is denied," Nolde asserted, "man's conscience cannot operate adequately in criticism or in condemnation of national and international policies."[33]

In his 1946 book *Power for Peace*, Nolde elaborated on the rationales behind the ecumenical movement's deep attachment to religious freedom as a universal human right. He did not shy away from asserting that religious freedom was essential for the Christian mission to "preach the Gospel of Jesus Christ to the uttermost part of the world." "Because we believe that all men should have the opportunity to hear and accept the Gospel," he stated, "we seek to promote religious liberty." Yet religious freedom was not merely about the rights of proselytism and conversion. Nolde held out as Christian ideals the alleviation of those "in suffering or distress" and the creation of a "brotherhood of nations, co-operating for their mutual well-being and advancement."[34] The latter point is worth underscoring because it points to a recurrent theme in the human rights discourse of the 1940s: religious freedom was not just about providing protection for individual and organized religion, it was also linked to wider visions of democracy, the free-exchange of ideas, and international law as paths to peace.[35]

13.3 THE 1960s AND THE TURN TO NONDISCRIMINATION

In spite of dogged efforts by actors like Malik and Nolde, the UDHR did not provide a definite statement on the meaning of religious freedom as a human right. In fact, the ink had barely dried on the document adopted in Paris in 1948 before the question resurfaced in the UN Commission on Human Rights, which turned its attention to the creation of a binding human rights covenant. One of the many questions at hand was whether a future UN covenant should follow the example of the European Convention on Human Rights and simply reproduce the UDHR's statement on religious

32 Peiponen, "Ecumenical Action in World Politics," 248–9. For more on the link between the ideal of discipleship and protestant human rights activism, see Pamela Slotte, "Whose Justice? What Political Theology? On Christian and Theological Approaches to Human Rights in the Twentieth and Twenty-First Centuries," in *International Law and Religion: Historical and Contemporary Perspectives*, ed. Martti Koskenniemi, Mónica García-Salmones Rovira, and Paolo Amorosa (New York: Oxford University Press, 2017), 196–216.

33 O. Frederick Nolde, *Power for Peace: The Way of the United Nations and the Will of Christian People* (Philadelphia: Muhlenberg Press, 1946), 62.

34 Nolde, *Power for Peace*, 62.

35 See also Jay Winter and Antoine Prost, *René Cassin and Human Rights: From the Great War to the Universal Declaration* (New York: Cambridge University Press, 2013), 347–8.

freedom with an additional clause on the legitimate grounds for state restrictions. While states agreed to retain the statement's basic structure in what later became the religious freedom clause of the International Covenant on Civil and Political Rights (1966), they once again clashed on certain aspects, and especially on the right to change religion or belief.[36]

Scholars have been quick to note that the most vocal critics of the right to change religion came from Muslim majority states, including Egypt and Saudi Arabia, concluding that the main stumbling block was Islamic doctrine, and more specifically the ban on apostasy in Islamic law.[37] But the states opposing the right to change religion or belief were, at least rhetorically, more concerned with politics than theology. Speaking before the Third Committee of the General Assembly in 1950, the Egyptian delegate expressed principled support for the right to change religion, but suggested that it "might make it difficult for many governments to secure ratification" of a human rights covenant, given that "attitudes in national legislatures varied from extreme liberalism to extreme reaction."[38] The Saudi delegate Jamil Baroody concurred. Again, the problem was not the right to change religion as a principle, "which was implicit" in the freedom of conscience and belief. Instead, he suggested that those campaigning for an express recognition of the right to change religion acted on dubious grounds. By way of analogy he cited the medieval crusades, which had "concealed undeniable economic and political ambitions under the cloak of religion."[39]

As in the drafting of the UDHR, the right to change religion was defended by the WCC and its CCIA – both as an integral aspect of individual freedom and as a key to a new world order in which "conflicting ideologies can compete peacefully."[40] But the churches also realized that it was a more profound challenge to draft an international treaty than a non-binding declaration. Nolde stated that it was most essential to find a statement that would "pave the way for ratification without reservation."[41] He also realized that support for the churches' position was waning, since many Western states had become convinced by the

36 UN Doc. E/CN.4/SR.117 (1949).
37 See, e.g., Paul M. Taylor, *Freedom of Religion: UN and European Human Rights Law and Practice* (Cambridge: Cambridge University Press, 2005), 28–30.
38 UN Doc. A/C.3/SR.288 (1950), § 26.
39 UN Doc. A/C.3/SR.289 (1950), § 40–7.
40 O. Frederick Nolde, Supplementary Memorandum: Freedom to Change Religion or Belief, July, 1951. Papers of Charles H. Malik, Box 80, Folder 2.
41 O. Frederick Nolde to Charles H. Malik, May 26, 1952. Papers of Charles H. Malik, Box 138, Folder 6.

argument that the right to change religion was implied in the general freedom of thought, conscience, and belief.[42]

A settlement was reached in 1960 when Brazil and the Philippines presented an amendment replacing the right to change with the right "to have a religion or belief of [one's] choice." This received widespread support, especially after the United Kingdom proposed changing the wording to "have *or adopt* a religion or belief," making the treatment of religious choice less static.[43] Though this successfully solved the diplomatic dispute, the wording of this clause has continued to generate concern among international lawyers, some of whom see the International Covenant on Civil and Political Rights as the beginning of a downward trend in the human rights protection of the right to religious choice.[44]

But the watering down of the right to change religion was not all that happened to religious freedom in UN human rights politics in the decades after 1948. In the 1960s, religious freedom also became juxtaposed with the overlapping but somewhat different concepts of religious discrimination and intolerance. "After a brief flourishing as an autonomous concept," Malcolm D. Evans notes somewhat lamentingly, religious freedom was now ever more frequently approached "from the perspective of non-discrimination."[45] In fact, in the mid-1960s, the UN came close to adopting a full-blown international treaty on the elimination of religious intolerance, a treaty which would have provided an elaborate international standard on human rights and religion.

As Steven L. B. Jensen reveals in his landmark study of UN human rights politics in the 1960s, the central context for this transformation was that of decolonization. In the course of the decade, the UN membership increased by forty-four states, mainly in the shape of newly independent nations from Africa, Asia and the Caribbean. In the same period, the UN Commission on Human Rights grew from an original eighteen members to twenty-eight in 1967. This "tectonic shift" in international politics profoundly impacted the orientation of the human rights project. States from the Global South, Jensen writes, "explored and used this global transformation to reform the norms of international society and create a platform for human rights in international politics."[46] He goes on to point out how southern human rights activism, spearheaded by Liberia and Jamaica, went beyond efforts to guard the right to

42 See, e.g., statement by Canada in A/C.3/SR.1024 (1960), § 1–4.
43 Evans, *Religious Liberty*, 199.
44 See, e.g., Natan Lerner, "Proselytism, Change of Religion, and International Human Rights," *Emory International Law Review* 12, no. 2 (1998): 477–561, at 560.
45 Evans, *Religious Liberty*, 366.
46 Steven L. B. Jensen, *The Making of International Human Rights: The 1960s, Decolonization, and the Reconstruction of Global Values* (New York: Cambridge University Press, 2016), 2.

national self-determination to also involve the creation of new standards on racial and religious discrimination.

At the beginning of the decade, race and religion – "political Achilles' heels for the two superpowers" – were treated as intertwined concepts. A 1960 General Assembly resolution – which came about in response to the mushrooming of anti-Semitic hate crimes in Europe – denounced all forms of "racial, religious, and national hatred" as affronts to human rights and the principles of the UN Charter.[47] Yet following the Sharpeville massacre in South Africa in 1960, race emerged as the principal concern for post-colonial states in the UN Commission on Human Rights. In a fascinating episode of UN human rights diplomacy, an alliance of mainly African, Arab and Asian states managed to create widespread support behind both a declaration and a binding treaty on the Elimination of all Forms of Racial Discrimination (CERD). The treaty was approved by the General Assembly in 1965 and became the starting point for an intense twenty-five-year period of UN human rights treaty-making.[48]

Apart from offering a detailed account of the negotiations on race, Jensen includes a chapter on the parallel but ultimately aborted attempt to craft a corresponding framework on religion. This project was preceded by Arcot Krishnaswami's influential 1960 report on "Discrimination in the Matter of Religious Rights and Practices," which was prepared under the auspices of the UN Sub-Commission on Prevention of Discrimination and Protection of Minorities (the Sub-Commission). The report provided a broad-brush global assessment of the status of religious freedom, both de jure and de facto, drawing on an extensive body of reports by states and various UN bodies, and using the UDHR's Article 18 as its normative framework. Though generally upbeat, the report noted residual patterns of discrimination of racial and religious minorities. Hence, it suggested that the discussion on religion and human rights should become more focused on equality among faiths: "Each religion or belief makes different demands on its followers," Krishnaswami explained. "A mechanical application of the principle of equality which does not take into account these various demands will often lead to injustice and in some cases even to discrimination."[49]

At the back of his report, Krishnaswami inserted a draft list of principles with regard to religious freedom and religious discrimination to complement the

[47] Jensen, *Making of International Human Rights*, 138; UN GA Res. 1510 (XV), December 12, 1960.

[48] For more on the evolution of CERD in the context of UN human rights politics of the 1960s, see Eckel, *Ambivalence of Good*, 131–41.

[49] Arcot Krishnaswami, *Study of Discrimination in the Matter of Religious Rights and Practices* (New York: United Nations, 1960), 15.

UDHR and the future covenant on civil and political rights. Jensen notes this, but goes on to downplay the report's significance, arguing that it was "completely overtaken" by a Liberian initiative of 1962, to produce both a declaration and a convention on the topic. While offering few clues as to the political rationales behind this initiative, he notes how Liberia (one of the UN's founding members) had long established itself as a spokesperson for individual freedom of religious choice and worship, echoing the provisions of the country's 1847 constitution.[50]

A central factor for the growing attention to racial and religious discrimination in UN diplomacy of the 1960s was the surge of antisemitism. In 1959–1960, a wave of antisemitic hate crimes – known as the "Swastika Epidemic" – swept through Western Germany, inspiring copycats in scattered locations like Buenos Aires, Oslo, London, Vancouver, and Hong Kong. Meanwhile, Jewish rights activists sought to bring international attention to the anti-Semitic policies of the USSR. This included more or less overt attacks on specific religious practices like the baking of the Passover matzah. But there was also brewing concern over the Soviet regime's severe restrictions on emigration, which inhibited the rights of Jews seeking to leave the country except in certain cases of family reunification.[51]

During the negotiations on CERD, antisemitism also emerged as a central bone of contention. The United States pushed for a clause that singled out antisemitism, along with Nazism, apartheid, and colonialism as affronts to human rights. This led to reactions from Arab and Communist states, who questioned the problem's universal relevance. They even went so far as to propose the specific mentioning of Zionism as a form of racial discrimination. The solution, not uncommon in the making of a UN human rights instrument, was to go for silence. As a result, the final version of CERD retains references only to colonialism and apartheid.[52]

What begun "as a response to the Swastika Epidemic," historian James Loeffler argues, "morphed into a larger legal convention on racism that did not even mention antisemitism." Loeffler further suggests that the talks on treaties on racial and religious intolerance foreshadowed the infamous General

[50] Jensen, *Making of International Human Rights*, 141 n. 9, 142.

[51] For more on the context, see James Loeffler, *Rooted Cosmopolitans: Jews and Human Rights in the Twentieth Century* (New Haven: Yale University Press, 2018), 230–60; Nathan Kurz, "'A Sphere above the Nations?' The Rise and Fall of International Jewish Human Rights Politics, 1945–1975" (PhD dissertation, Yale University, 2015), 265–85.

[52] Eckel, *Ambivalence of Good*, 136. For more detail, see Ofra Friesel, "Race versus Religion in the Making of the International Convention Against Racial Discrimination, 1965," *Law and History Review* 32, no. 2 (2014): 351–83.

Assembly Resolution of 1975 denouncing Zionism as a form of racism.[53] That said, it is clear that the 1960s debates on racism and religious intolerance – triggered as they were by the "return" of antisemitism – transformed the international discourse on religious freedom. If that discourse had previously centered on individual belief and worship, it now came to take issue with different forms of structural inequality and became more attuned to the intersection among religion, race, and ethnicity. This tendency was visible in Krishnaswami's 1960 report, which held out the Nazi regime's persecution and subsequent genocide of Jews as the paradigmatic violation of religious freedom and the most clear-cut case of religious and racial discrimination in recent history, showcasing how "forward advance of humanity in this field, as in other fields of human rights, is not in a straight line."[54]

These transformations, and the specific project of creating a treaty on religious discrimination, acquired further steam from the opening of the Second Vatican Council in 1962. Pope John XXIII's 1963 encyclical *Pacem in Terris* suggested that Catholic natural law doctrine was compatible with the modern human rights idea and referred to the UDHR as "an assertion of everyone's right to be free to seek out the truth, to follow moral principles, discharge the duties imposed by justice, and lead a fully human life."[55] A similar endorsement of human rights principles was contained in the Declaration on Religious Freedom, *Dignitatis Humane*, which was approved by the Bishops gathered in Rome in 1965. Apart from recognizing rights of individual worship and religious choice, the declaration rejected the idea that religious belief could ever be instilled by means of political power: "The truth cannot impose itself except by virtue of its own truth."[56]

These developments in Rome became frequent points of reference in the UN negotiations on religious freedom and nondiscrimination. In 1963, the French delegate and human rights veteran René Cassin argued that it was imperative for the UN Commission on Human Rights to keep pace with

53 Loeffler, *Rooted Cosmopolitans*, 231–2.

54 Krishnaswami, *Study of Discrimination*, 10.

55 *Pacem in Terris*, April 11, 1963, http://w2.vatican.va/content/john-xxiii/en/encyclicals/documents/hf_j-xxiii_enc_11041963_pacem.html. For a recent assessment, see Carlo Invernizzi-Accetti, "Catholic Social Doctrine and Human Rights: From Rejection to Endorsement?," *Humanity: An International Journal of Human Rights, Humanitarianism, and Development* 9, no. 2 (2018): 271–95.

56 *Dignitatis Humane*, December 7, 1965, www.vatican.va/archive/hist_councils/ii_vatican_council/documents/vat-ii_decl_19651207_dignitatis-humanae_en.html. For a recent study, stressing how the Catholic turn to religious freedom was inspired by changing perceptions of Protestantism, see Udi Greenberg, "Catholics, Protestants, and the Tortured Path to Religious Liberty," *Journal of the History of Ideas* 79, no. 3 (2018): 461–79.

"world public opinion," reminding delegates that "for the past year or more leaders of religious movements with hundreds of millions of members had been protesting against religious intolerance."[57] Occasionally, such references were fused with Cold War rhetoric. The US delegate Morris Abram, for instance, saw a sharp contrast between Vatican progress and sustained Soviet oppression: "At a time when religions were becoming more tolerant of the rights and freedoms of others," he said in 1965, "attacks against religions by public bodies were becoming more frequent. Acts of intolerance in the name of scientific atheism were as reprehensible as religious persecution."[58]

Given the then recent UN contestations on the right to religious choice, the sharp Cold War tensions, and the disputes on antisemitism, it was evident that a binding human rights treaty on religion would be difficult to pursue. One UN report suggested that the "subject of religious intolerance was more delicate" than that of race, not least because it "impinged upon the area where the State touched upon the most intimate emotions of human beings."[59] Still, the talks on a convention on religious intolerance made surprising headway in the UN Commission on Human Rights. In 1965, the Sub-Commission prepared an elaborate draft that generated some enthusiasm among states. John Humphrey, the senior Canadian UN official who had been instrumental in the making of the UDHR, marveled at these developments: "I began to think that my early skepticism ... that the United Nations would never agree on standards in a matter like religion had been unwarranted."[60]

According to Jensen, all such optimism vanished with the diplomatic turmoil caused by the outbreak of the Six Day War in 1967. In the UN records, this is mainly reflected in what Jensen refers to as a "shift in geographical reference." After 1967, the allusions to Rome and Vatican II were replaced by references to the Israeli occupation of eastern Jerusalem. "Israel's religious fanaticism," a Bulgarian delegate lambasted in a UN General Assembly, "was supported by precisely those who claimed to favor the elimination of religious intolerance." Then other political conflicts with religious overtones entered into the debates, including Northern Ireland and discrimination against Muslim minorities in India.[61] "War was clearly a determinant for human rights," Jensen concludes, suggesting that religion had now become

57 Cited in Jensen, *Making of International Human Rights*, 147.

58 Cited in Jensen, *Making of International Human Rights*, 156.

59 Report of the 17th Session of the Sub-Commission on Prevention of Discrimination and Protection of Minorities to the Commission on Human Rights, UN Doc. E/CN.4/882 (1965).

60 John Humphrey, *Human Rights and the United Nations: A Great Adventure* (New York: Transnational Publishers, 1984), 323.

61 Jensen, *Making of International Human Rights*, 165–6.

considered more a source of conflict and human rights violations than an object of individual purpose and responsibility, let alone a source of democratic advancement and international peace as had been the case in the drafting of the UDHR. "At the moment when human rights became international law in the mid-1960s, religion experienced its fall."[62]

Jensen may be right, as long as we take the creation of human rights treaties as our measure. It was not until 1981 that the talks on a UN instrument on religious intolerance and discrimination were to bear fruit as the UN approved the Declaration on the Elimination of All Forms of Intolerance and of Discrimination Based on Religion or Belief. And the final result was a far cry from what the initiators of the project had originally hoped for. The most obvious feature is that it was cast as a nonbinding declaration of principle, which is yet to be followed by an actual treaty. But the substance was also far from the principles discussed in the 1960s. For instance, the text includes no references to positive discrimination of marginalized minorities and does not address incitement to hatred, or religious intolerance.[63]

Still, the 1981 text echoed the conceptual shift that had taken place in the way that religion was approached in UN human rights circles after 1948. Albeit in hollowed-out form, the text made clear that religious freedom was a right with a much wider purpose than the protection of individual beliefs and acts of worship: "Freedom of religion or belief," the preamble announced, "should also contribute to the attainment of the goals of world peace, social justice and friendship among peoples and to the elimination of ideologies or practices of colonialism and racial discrimination."[64]

13.4 CONCLUSION: IS RELIGIOUS FREEDOM POSSIBLE?

This chapter has outlined some of the political and ideological developments that shaped the content of religious freedom as an international human right. It has also charted some of the subsequent efforts to realign this concept with a broader vision of human rights as a project of combating structural discrimination and intolerance. All of this could be read as a partial historical backdrop to more present-day studies on the ways in which religion and religious rights are

[62] Jensen, *Making of International Human Rights*, 173.

[63] Nazila Ghanea, "The 1981 UN Declaration on the Elimination of All Forms of Intolerance and of Discrimination Based on Religion or Belief: Some Observations," in *The Challenge of Religious Discrimination at the Dawn of the New Millennium*, ed. Nazila Ghanea (Dordrecht: Springer, 2004), 9–31.

[64] United Nations Declaration on the Elimination of All Forms of Intolerance and of Discrimination Based on Religion or Belief, UNGA Res. 36/55 of November 25, 1981.

construed by states, international experts, and NGOs within the frame of UN human rights politics and law. Helge Årsheim, for instance, has recently revealed how the UN human rights committees, largely due to the normative tensions between the instruments they are set up to monitor, tend to construe religion in different ways, including as a matter of personal choice and belief, as an individual and collective identity marker, and as a social force with uneven effects on the implementation of different categories of rights.[65] What this suggests is that the normative layers enshrined in international human rights law, including its provisions on religious freedom and nondiscrimination, frequently pull in different directions, creating ever new grounds for ideological conflict concerning the purpose and reach of human rights norms.

Our current moment overflows with attempts to exploit such tensions for political ends. Internationally, the most blatant example of late is the Trump administration's campaign to play out religious freedom against other human rights norms, such as gender equality and LGBT rights. In his 2019 address to the UN General Assembly, Trump announced his plans to set up a new international body called the International Religious Freedom Alliance, effectively launching a new chapter in the long history of US religious freedom promotion.[66] Trump himself did not invoke the UDHR, instead stating that "the United States is founded on the principle that our rights do not come from government; they come from God."[67] Yet some of his aides – including Secretary of State Michael R. Pompeo – spoke publicly on the UDHR's continued relevance, citing its Article 18 as a reaffirmation of American values.[68] In July 2019, Pompeo announced the creation of a US Commission on Unalienable Rights, to be headed by human rights historian Mary Ann Glendon. The project, Pompeo explained in a press briefing, was partly one of returning to the "moral landscape" of the 1940s, before "international institutions designed and built to protect human rights ... drifted from their original mission." The stated goal was to salvage certain natural human rights, including that of individual religious freedom, from a purportedly unrestrained "human

65 Helge Årsheim, *Making Religion and Human Rights at the United Nations* (Boston: Walter de Gruyter, 2018).

66 For more on American foreign policy and its influence on the wider global politics of religious freedom, see Pasquale Annicchino, *Law and Religious Freedom: The Rise and Decline of the American Model* (London: Routledge, 2018).

67 Remarks by President Trump at the United Nations Event on Religious Freedom, September 23, 2019, www.whitehouse.gov/briefings-statements/remarks-president-trump-united-nations-event-religious-freedom-new-york-ny/.

68 Press statement by Michael R. Pompeo: U.S. Commitment to Religious Freedom, January 16, 2019, www.state.gov/u-s-commitment-to-religious-freedom/.

rights discourse" that was too often being "corrupted or hijacked or used for dubious or malignant purposes."[69]

My point is essentially that we ought to resist such efforts to break out religious freedom from the broader idea of human rights as this has evolved, largely due to the wave of international treaty-making that began in the 1960s. This framework may not amount to a comprehensive and sufficiently progressive political project for our time. Yet, at its best, it allows us to discern and begin to dismantle structures of inequality, discrimination, and intolerance. Some scholars suggest that the concept of religious freedom is essentially too burdened by its historical association with belief-based ideas of religion and particular structures of power to be of any use in such endeavors.[70] Yet the international history of this norm suggests a more complex picture, reminding us of the multiple ideological and political visions in which religious freedom has played a part, from the hopes for a peaceful world order in the 1940s to the campaigns to combat antisemitism in the 1960s. The political challenge, then, is perhaps not so much to forgo religious freedom as it is about employing it for better ends, though with a constant awareness that it will necessarily intersect (and occasionally clash) with other and equally important principles of human rights.

RECOMMENDED READING

Bouwman, Bastiaan. "From Religious Freedom to Social Justice: The Human Rights Engagement of the Ecumenical Movement from the 1940s to the 1970s." *Journal of Global History* 13, no. 2 (2018): 252–73.

Jensen, Steven L. B. *The Making of International Human Rights: The 1960s, Decolonization, and the Reconstruction of Global Values*. New York: Cambridge University Press, 2016.

Lindkvist, Linde. *Religious Freedom and the Universal Declaration of Human Rights*. New York: Cambridge University Press, 2017.

Shortall, Sarah. "Theology and Politics of Christian Human Rights." *Journal of the History of Ideas* 79, no. 3 (2018): 445–60.

Su, Anna. *Exporting Freedom: Religious Liberty and American Power*. Cambridge: Harvard University Press, 2018.

Zubovich, Gene. "American Protestants and the Era of Anti-racist Human Rights." *Journal of the History of Ideas* 79, no. 3 (2018): 427–43.

69 Secretary of State Michael R. Pompeo Remarks to the Press, July 8, 2019, https://translations.state.gov/2019/07/08/secretary-of-state-michael-r-pompeo-remarks-to-the-press-7/.

70 See, e.g., Winnifred Fallers Sullivan, *The Impossibility of Religious Freedom*, new ed. (Princeton: Princeton University Press, 2018).

14

Process Theology and a Pluralistic Foundation for Human Rights

Mark C. Modak-Truran

14.1 INTRODUCTION

Historical accounts of human rights in the West readily acknowledge a deep indebtedness to the conceptions of human dignity found in religious traditions – particularly Christianity and Judaism. Modern conceptions of human rights, however, usually avoid religious justifications and implicitly or explicitly rely on a secular justification. For example, most scholars mark the beginning of modern human rights law with the United Nations Universal Declaration of Human Rights (UDHR) in 1948. The UDHR sets forth an extensive list of rights including the "right to life, liberty and the security of person," the "right to marry and to found a family," the "right to own property," and the "freedom of thought, conscience and association." While the Preamble of the UDHR maintains that "recognition of the inherent dignity and of the equal and inalienable rights of all members of the human family is the foundation of freedom, justice and peace in the world," the UDHR does not posit a justification for its claim of inherent human dignity or for its list of rights. The same approach was followed when the rights recognized in the UDHR were incorporated into two international conventions – the International Convention on Civil and Political Rights (ICCPR, 1976) and the International Covenant on Economic, Social and Cultural Rights (ICESCR, 1976). These Conventions made the rights recognized in the UDHR binding on the signatories as part of positive international law.

The United Nations Commission on Human Rights (the "Commission") was responsible for drafting the UDHR. The Commission and its drafting committee had diverse representation "from countries with majoritarian Atheist, Buddhist, Christian, Confucian, Hindu, and Muslim populations, including India, China, the Philippines, the U.S.S.R., Iran, Egypt, Lebanon,

Austria, France, the United States Panama, and Chile."[1] Jacques Maritain, a prominent French Roman Catholic philosopher and France's ambassador to the Vatican, represented France on the Commission. With respect to this diverse support for the UDHR, Maritain was asked how "proponents of violently opposed ideologies had agreed on the draft of a list of rights." He replied that "we agree on these rights, *providing we are not asked why*."[2] Maritain was not suggesting, however, that a justification or foundation for human rights is not important. To the contrary, he stressed that this gave rise to a "paradox" because "rational justifications are *indispensable* and at the same time *powerless* to create agreement."[3] These justifications or foundations were "indispensable" because consent by the representatives to the list of rights in the UDHR depended on them. At the same time, these justifications were powerless to create agreement because the representatives belonged to different religions, cultures, and civilizations that were often opposed to one another. The UDHR, the ICCPR, and the ICESCR thus represented an agreement "not on common speculative notions, but on common practical notions, not on the affirmation of the same conception of the world, man, and knowledge, but on the affirmation of the same set of convictions concerning action."[4]

Does the absence of a justification or foundation in the UDHR mean that its legitimacy is self-evident or needs no foundation? If not, what is its foundation? Does the incorporation of the rights in the UDHR into positive international law – the ICCPR and the ICESCR – provide a sufficient foundation or legitimation for these rights? Alternatively, can there be a plurality of justifications or foundations for the UDHR and other international human rights treaties and conventions? Can these foundations be both secular and religious?

Human rights scholars have debated these questions ever since the UDHR was adopted by the United Nations. Some scholars argue that human rights law in general and UDHR in particular are based on a Christian moral foundation. For example, in *Christian Human Rights*, Samuel Moyn challenges the consensus that the annunciation of human rights in the UDHR was an "uncomplicated triumph of liberal democracy." He argues to the contrary that the human rights movement has its roots in the Christian right. In particular, he highlights the importance of Pope Pius XII's Christmas message

1 John Witte, Jr., and M. Christian Green, "Introduction," in *Religion and Human Rights: An Introduction*, ed. John Witte, Jr. and M. Christian Green (Oxford: Oxford University Press, 2012), 3–24, 6. See also Chapter 13 in this volume.

2 Jacques Maritain, *Man and the State* (Chicago: University of Chicago Press 1951, repr., 1998), 77 (emphasis in original).

3 Maritain, *Man and the State*, 77.

4 Maritain, *Man and the State*, 77.

in 1942, which lifted up the God-given "Dignity of the Human Person" and advocated "a juridical order resting on the supreme dominion of God" that protects "*the unforgettable rights of man*."[5] Moyn further emphasizes that this Christian notion of human rights aimed at moral constraint and countering totalitarianism rather than celebrating individual liberation, which later became the liberal mantra for the purpose of human rights.

Secular theories of human rights, however, reject religious foundations for human rights but maintain the universality of human rights on secular and pragmatic moral grounds. For instance, Johannes Morsink argues that the human rights recognized in the UDHR "are not man-made, but inherent in the human person from the moment of birth."[6] To this Enlightenment-based metaphysical universality he adds an epistemological universality (moral intuitionism) that maintains that all humans can discern these inherent human rights through their conscience. By contrast, Michael Ignatieff rejects both religious and secular foundational claims for human rights and cautions against viewing human rights as "a secular religion." Human rights are "not a creed" or "a metaphysics" and to treat them as such is "a species of idolatry: humanism worshiping itself."[7] Based on "prudential grounds" rather than "intrinsically contestable" metaphysical claims about human nature, Ignatieff argues that "human rights are essentially designed to validate and enhance human agency."[8] History tells us, according to Ignatieff, "that human beings are at risk of their lives if they lack a basic measure of free agency; that agency itself requires protection through internationally agreed standards."[9] Consequently, for Ignatieff, "human rights is a secular humanism: an ethics ungrounded in divine or ultimate sanction and based only in human prudence."[10]

These three types of human rights theory (religious foundational, secular foundational, and secular non-foundational), however, are now under attack for promoting parochial notions of human rights. In other words, the charge of cultural relativism maintains that the notions of human rights proposed as universal derive their meaning and legitimacy from a Western cultural context that has been shaped by Christianity and the Enlightenment. Christian human rights theory is unacceptable to secularists and those of other faith traditions as

5 Samuel Moyn, *Christian Human Rights* (Philadelphia: University of Pennsylvania Press, 2015), 2 (emphasis in original).
6 Johannes Morsink, *Inherent Human Rights* (Philadelphia: University of Pennsylvania Press, 2015), 17.
7 Michael Ignatieff, *Human Rights as Politics and Idolatry*, ed. Amy Gutmann (Princeton: Princeton University Press, 2001), 53.
8 Ignatieff, *Human Rights as Politics and Idolatry*, 164.
9 Ignatieff, *Human Rights as Politics and Idolatry*, 55.
10 Ignatieff, *Human Rights as Politics and Idolatry*, 81.

well as to those colonized by Western Christian countries. Similarly, Morsink and Ignatieff promote Western Enlightenment–inspired accounts of human rights, not universal ones. Linda Hogan argues that these critiques have resulted in a crisis of legitimacy and a crisis of meaning in human rights discourse. These fundamentally ethnocentric Western accounts of human rights are no longer viewed as neutral or universal because they have displaced "local, customary or traditional moralities and all forms of transcendental faiths" in the name of a "universal" critical or rational morality that is binding on all humans. These critiques have come from communitarian, feminist, and postcolonial theorists who maintain that the governing norms of rationality are connected to their historical and cultural contexts rather than a universal form of rationality. To revitalize faith in human rights politics, Hogan proposes "a genuinely inclusive, deliberative, cross-cultural conversation through which agreement on contested issues can be pursued."[11]

Similarly, Ignatieff identifies two crises for human rights – *a cultural crisis* and *a spiritual crisis* – that together raise substantial questions about the legitimacy of human rights norms. The cultural crisis concerns "the inter-cultural validity of human rights norms" while "the spiritual crisis concerns the ultimate metaphysical grounds for these norms."[12] With respect to the cultural crises, he identifies three challenges to the universality of human rights. Summarily, these include the Islamic challenge to rights such as free choice in marriage and religious freedom, the Asian communitarian challenge to Western individualism, and the challenge to Western individualism and its imperialistic legacy by Western defenders of human rights. The spiritual crisis worries about the "deliberate silence at the heart of human rights culture" regarding what aspect of human nature (e.g., conscience) or ultimate reality (e.g., God) provides a bulwark against human horrors like the Holocaust. Ignatieff counters that this "pragmatic silence on ultimate questions" in the UDHR has helped, rather than hindered, the development of a global human rights culture that aims to stem the tide of human abuses.

This chapter will address the crisis of legitimacy currently threatening foundational and nonfoundational theories of human rights. Section 14.2, after sorting out the moral, political, and legal aspects of human rights (Section 14.2.1), will provide an overview of changes in international human rights law since the UDHR in 1948 (Section 14.2.2). It will then analyze the legal, moral, and sociological dimensions of the legitimacy of international law and human rights

[11] Linda Hogan, *Keeping Faith with Human Rights* (Washington, DC: Georgetown University Press, 2015), 9.

[12] Ignatieff, *Human Rights as Politics and Idolatry*, 77.

(Section 14.2.3). Moral legitimacy is the most important dimension at the international level because the legal dimension is weakened by the lack of enforcement through international legal institutions and by the lack of international democracy to support human rights conventions and treaties.

Section 14.3 will introduce the key concepts of process theology, which is a "theological movement based primarily on the 'process philosophy' of Alfred North Whitehead (1861–1947) and Charles Hartshorne (1897–2000)."[13] Most process theologians have been Christian, but process theology has begun to influence other traditions including Judaism, Buddhism, Islam, and Hinduism.[14] Unlike most Christian theology, process theology is "grounded in a metaphysical position in which theism is defended philosophically, and science and religion are included within the same scheme of thought."[15] Process theology provides abundant resources for understanding how religious convictions relate to international law and human rights. First, process theology provides an account of religion that shows how religious beliefs are connected to moral, political, and legal claims because religious convictions constitute the comprehensive condition of validity for all normative claims. In addition, process theology provides two theories of religious pluralism that explain how Christians can embrace the uniqueness of Christianity while at the same time gain insights from other religious and secular traditions.

Section 14.4 will argue for a pluralistic foundation for international human rights law. My thesis is that there is a plurality of comprehensive religious and secular convictions about authentic human existence that legitimate and ground international human rights law. I will then show that this pluralistic foundation for human rights can meet the challenges posed by the spiritual and the cultural crises already mentioned.

14.2 LEGITIMATION OF INTERNATIONAL LAW AND HUMAN RIGHTS

14.2.1 *Moral, Political, and Legal Aspects of Human Rights*

Discussions of human rights are often confusing because they conflate claims about what rights persons have because they are human (the morality of human rights), political advocacy for the recognition of human rights, and

[13] David Ray Griffin, *Process Theology: On Postmodernism, Morality, Pluralism, Eschatology, and Demonic Evil* (Anoka, MN: Process Century Press, 2017), 1.

[14] See David Ray Griffin, ed., *Deep Religious Pluralism* (Louisville, KY: Westminster John Knox Press, 2005).

[15] Griffin, *Process Theology*, 2.

the legal protection of human rights. For reasons of brevity, the preceding discussion of human rights theories did not demarcate the moral, political, and legal aspects of human rights. In the discussion of legitimating international human rights law, however, these distinctions are very important and will be discussed in this section.

Michael Perry has helpfully clarified the moral, political, and legal aspects of human rights. He first emphasizes that many scholars in various disciplines discuss the morality of human rights or "*the morality that supports the law of human rights.*"[16] When discussing the morality that supports the law of human rights, I will sometimes refer to this as part of the foundation, justification, or legitimation of human rights law. Section 14.2.3 will also refer to this as the moral justifiability of human rights law and clarify how this relates to two other aspects of legitimation – legality and social acceptance.

Many kinds of moral theory can be used to justify human rights – natural law theory, moral rights theory, consequentialist theory, and others. In most cases, there are also both religious and secular versions of these types of moral theory. For example, Jeremy Waldron argues that the *imago Dei* – the theological claim that humans are created in the image of God – is a religious foundation for human rights that appeals to followers of the Abrahamic religions (Judaism, Christianity, and Islam) and possibly to others open to a religious foundation for human rights. While noting several objections to the idea, he concludes "that *imago Dei* is above all an empowering idea, validating and affirming our powers of reason when they are oriented not just to discerning God's order in the world, but participating with others in its realization."[17] The discussion in Section 14.1 noted a similar secular foundation proposed by Morsink. He argues that human rights "are not man-made, but inherent in the human person from the moment of birth," and that all humans can discern these inherent human rights through their conscience.[18] In both of these cases, the morality that supports human rights is not a moral rights theory. The *imago Dei* is a theological doctrine of creation establishing the status of humans, which supports a moral claim about the human rights relating to that status. Similarly, Morsink's theory of human rights is based on a metaphysical claim about human rights being inherent in humans and an epistemological claim (moral intuitionism) about how they know those rights through their

[16] Michael J. Perry, *Toward a Theory of Human Rights: Religion, Law, Courts* (Cambridge: Cambridge University Press, 2007), xiii (emphasis in original).

[17] Jeremy Waldron, "The Image of God: Rights, Reasons, and Order," in *Religion and Human Rights: An Introduction*, ed. John Witte, Jr. and M. Christian Green (Oxford: Oxford University Press, 2012), 234.

[18] Morsink, *Inherent Human Rights*, 17.

conscience. Process theology will likewise justify human rights based on a theological ethics that is not a moral rights theory of morality.

With moral rights theories of morality, however, the morality justifying human rights and the human rights themselves overlap to a large extent. This makes separating out the morality justifying human rights and the human rights being justified difficult and often confusing. For example, in Immanuel Kant's moral theory of rights, he argues that one should "[a]ct only on that maxim through which you can at the same time will that it should become a universal law."[19] The individual, in her autonomy, creates the moral law, but she is also subject to its principles because it universally applies to all rational creatures. In other words, the content of the moral law is determined by the process of universalization. Ignatieff also focuses on human autonomy and agency. He makes a prudential argument "that human rights are essentially designed to validate and enhance human agency," which he sometimes refers to as "dignity as agency."[20] Not surprisingly, most scholars who subscribe to moral rights theories of morality, like Kant and Ignatieff, also subscribe to liberal political theory. Furthermore, many human rights scholars consider liberal political theory as primarily responsible for the advent of the human rights tradition in the political history of the West. As a result, those who support the legal protection of human rights have too often been assumed to embrace a moral rights theory of morality, but this is often not the case, as will be shown by the process theory of human rights expounded in this chapter.

Perry similarly challenges this assumption and maintains that a secular or nonreligious ground for human rights has not been clearly established by John Finnis, Ronald Dworkin, Martha Nussbaum, or any other philosopher. To the contrary, he argues "[t]hat there is a religious ground for the morality of human rights – indeed, more than one – is clear."[21] He then concludes that those rejecting a religious ground may have "no ground for the morality of human rights, no warrant for the claim that every human being has inherent dignity and is inviolable."[22]

In addition, Perry differentiates the political aspect of human rights. The political aspect considers the question "What laws should we who affirm the morality of human rights, because we affirm it, press our government – our

19 Immanuel Kant, *Groundwork of the Metaphysics of Morals*, trans. H. J. Paton (New York: Harper & Row Publishers, 1964 [1785]), 88.
20 Ignatieff, *Human Rights as Politics and Idolatry*, 164.
21 Perry, *Toward a Theory of Human Rights*, xi.
22 Perry, *Toward a Theory of Human Rights*, 26.

elected representatives – to enact?"[23] In other words, the political aspect of human rights focuses on advocating for which human rights norms should become legal rights. This includes the protection of human rights in domestic constitutions, statutes, and case law, as well as international treaties and conventions.[24]

14.2.2 *International Law and Human Rights*

Before moving on to the legitimation of international human rights law, it is important to clarify my descriptive assumptions about the nature of international law and the legal protection of human rights. International law has traditionally been conceived as the law governing the relations between sovereign states. The core principles include "[t]erritorial sovereignty, equality of states, non-intervention in domestic affairs and state consent as the basis of international legal obligation."[25] Some refer to this as the Westphalian model of international law because they date its origin from the treaties signed to achieve the Peace of Westphalia in 1648.[26] Under this model, domestic affairs, including human rights, are governed by domestic law. Independent states may hold each other to the terms of their treaties, but they do not have the right to meddle in one another's internal affairs.

Many theorists have argued, however, that since World War II, a new model of international law has emerged. This model provides that sovereignty over domestic affairs is no longer absolute. For example, in 1945, the Nuremberg Charter established that individuals could be punished for "Crimes Against Peace," "War Crimes," and "Crimes Against Humanity" even if the individuals committing those crimes were acting in accordance with domestic law or orders of a superior.

[23] Perry, *Toward a Theory of Human Rights*, xiii.

[24] Perry further notes that the legal aspect of human rights focuses on how legal rights should be interpreted by the courts. For example, does the protection of fundamental liberties and equality support recognizing a fundamental right to marry a person of the same sex? For reasons discussed in Section 14.2.2, this aspect of human rights law will not be covered in this chapter. However, in a previous article entitled *Reenchanting International Law*, I addressed quite extensively the role of comprehensive religious convictions in the interpretation of indeterminate international legal norms in hard cases. See Mark C. Modak-Truran, "Reenchanting International Law," *Mississippi College Law Review* 22, no.2 (2003): 263–301.

[25] James Crawford and Susan Marks, "The Global Democracy Deficit: An Essay in International Law and Its Limits," in *Re-imagining Political Community: Studies in Cosmopolitan Democracy*, ed. Daniele Archibugi, David Held, and Martin Köhler (Stanford: Stanford University Press, 1998), 72.

[26] David Held and Anthony McGrew, "The Great Globalization Debate: An Introduction," in *The Global Transformations Reader: An Introduction to the Globalization Debate*, ed. David Held and Anthony McGrew (Cambridge: Polity Press, 2000), 37.

As discussed in Section 14.1, the Preamble to the UDHR also proclaims itself "a *common standard* of achievement for all peoples and all nations." The UDHR and its subsequent corporation into the ICCPR and the ICESCR further suggest that the human rights recognized in its text are "universal," at least in the sense that they are superior to any contrary rights protected by domestic law.

In 1950, the European Convention for the Protection of Human Rights and Fundamental Freedoms (ECHR) established a radical innovation in international law by allowing citizens to initiate claims against their own governments for failing to protect the human rights recognized by the ECHR.[27] This innovation meant that individuals, rather than only states, had standing to bring charges for violations of human rights. More recently, the United Nations took the unprecedented step of establishing the International Criminal Court (ICC) in 1998, to provide a permanent institution for prosecuting "the most serious crimes of concern to the international community" including crimes of aggression, crimes against humanity, genocide, and war crimes. The ICC has the authority to try individuals for these international crimes even if the accused complied with domestic laws or the orders of their military or civilian superiors. International criminal law, however, has not been universally enforced and has been deeply divisive as to its selective enforcement and the specific content of its rules.

Some commentators argue that these developments indicate a shift toward a "universal constitutional order." Others, like David Held, have referred to these changes in international law "as an emerging framework of cosmopolitan law . . . which circumscribes and delimits the political power of individual states."[28] In other words, there is a sense in which international law has become more global or cosmopolitan so that it provides an autonomous set of legal norms that can protect individual rights and adjudicate conflicts among countries on an objective basis. On the other hand, scholars such as Christine Schwöbel-Patel have pointed out that there are many problematic assumptions about global constitutionalism including a presupposed "unity or homogeneity of the international sphere" that result in a hegemony in international law relating to "cultural, economic, and political domination of certain states" and to "male gender domination."[29]

[27] See David Held, "International Law," in *The Global Transformations Reader: An Introduction to the Globalization Debate*, ed. David Held and Anthony McGrew (Cambridge: Polity Press, 2000), 168.

[28] David Held, "Regulating Globalization?," in *The Global Transformations Reader: An Introduction to the Globalization Debate*, ed. David Held and Anthony McGrew (Cambridge: Polity Press, 2000), 426.

[29] Christine E. J. Schwöbel, "Organic Global Constitutionalism," *Leiden Journal of International Law* 23, no. 3 (2010): 529–53, at 534.

14.2.3 *Legitimation of International Human Rights Law*

One of the most challenging aspects of the debates about the legitimation of the law is that they implicate multiple disciplines including political theory, legal theory, constitutional theory, international affairs, social theory, empirical sociology, social psychology, political theology, and law and religion. These disciplines and the differing positions within them have very different understandings of the process of legitimation and the relevant criteria – normative and/or descriptive – for measuring legitimacy (e.g., legal validity, societal acceptance, principles of justice, theories of democracy).[30] There are also more fundamental disagreements among these approaches about the nature of rationality, about the nature of existence, and even about what counts as knowledge. Still other approaches claim that legitimation does not justify the social order but is a form of ideology that masks and perpetuates forms of hierarchy within it. Consequently, these multiple layers of disagreement make it difficult to define legitimation without unduly privileging the parochial assumptions of one of these approaches.

Despite this disagreement, theories about the legitimation of the law tend to have three dimensions – legal, moral or normative, and sociological. David Beetham identifies and clarifies these three dimensions. First, the legal dimension (legal legitimacy) views legitimacy as "equivalent to legal validity." The second dimension looks at legitimacy from the perspective of moral and political philosophy (moral or normative legitimacy) so that "legitimacy entails the moral justifiability of power relations." Finally, the third dimension is the social scientific perspective (sociological legitimacy) that looks at legitimacy as "belief in legitimacy on the part of the relevant social agents."[31]

According to Beetham, however, legitimacy is substantially different at the international level from the level of nation-states. At the international level, the legal dimension of legitimacy plays a less significant role because the power of enforcement rarely exists, and the international human rights norms are not democratically created. Beetham quotes Thomas Franck's famous conclusion that "'[t]he *international society* should be the best social system in which to observe a "normative" (i.e., legitimated) social order in its pure form precisely because of the absence of an international government to enforce international law and contracts.'"[32] Beetham further maintains that

[30] See David Beetham, *The Legitimation of Power*, 2nd ed. (New York: Palgrave Macmillan, 2013), 3–41; R. H. Fallon, "Legitimacy and the Constitution," *Harvard Law Review* 118, no. 6 (2005): 1787–835, at 1789–802.

[31] Beetham, *The Legitimation of Power*, 4–6.

[32] Beetham, *The Legitimation of Power*, 270 (emphasis added) (quoting Thomas Franck, *The Power of Legitimacy among Nations* (Oxford: Oxford University Press, 1990)).

the power or influence of international institutions thus "depends almost wholly on a recognition of its legitimacy to be effective." In other words, the effectiveness of international human rights law depends more on persuasion than on coercion because the moral dimension of legitimacy takes on a more significant role in the international context.

Two additional issues complicate the discussion of the moral legitimacy of international human rights law. The first issue concerns the lack of democratic decision making in adopting human rights treaties and conventions. In constitutional democracies, the prevailing conceptions of legitimation stem from the "consent of the governed." The "people" are sovereign and made up of free and equal citizens who legitimate the form of government by a voluntary agreement – a constitution (social contract). The constitution creates binding obligations and restrictions on their conduct and establishes political and legal institutions to enforce those constitutional commitments on the community. In other words, the "consent of the governed" includes two principles of legitimation – the principle of democracy (or popular sovereignty) and the principle of constitutionalism (or the rule of law).[33] Conversely, "international human rights have not been deliberated and adopted by highly inclusive international democratic procedures the way constitutional rights have."[34] Rather, both democratic and nondemocratic states negotiate and sign international human rights treaties through a process that is not inclusive, egalitarian, or transparent. In the case of democratic states, indirect democratic consent occurs through the domestic democratic decision-making process, but this is still far short of a robust deliberation about the rights in question.

In addition, the second issue concerns who constitutes the audience for moral legitimacy at the international level. In the context of nation-states, "it is the citizens who constitute the ultimate audience for, and judge of, legitimacy claims."[35] Initially, the states may seem to be the relevant audience. The parties to the international conventions recognizing the rights in question and creating the institutions of enforcement should be amenable to requests to comply with the relevant legal rights. Beetham emphasizes, however, that

33 Jürgen Habermas, "Constitutional Democracy: A Paradoxical Union of Contradictory Principles?," *Political Theory* 29, no. 6 (2001): 766–81, at 766–8.

34 Samatha Besson, "The Legitimate Authority of International Human Rights: On the Reciprocal Legitimation of Domestic and International Human Rights," in *The Legitimacy of International Human Rights Regimes: Legal, Political and Philosophical Perspectives*, ed. Andreas Follesdal, Johan Karlssson Schaffer, and Geir Ulfstein (Cambridge: Cambridge University Press, 2014), 37.

35 Beetham, *The Legitimation of Power*, 271.

"over the past two decades, non-governmental actors, whether NGOs, bodies of experts or representatives of economic interests, have played an increasingly significant role in the development of international treaties and the monitoring of their implementation at national level." This has been particularly the case for international human rights conventions. Beetham concludes that "[t]hese non-governmental actors, working across national boundaries, now constitute a kind of *global civil society*, which constitutes both an audience for, and an adjudicator of, the legitimacy claims of international institutions."[36] While some scholars have argued that this makes the international level closer to the national level, "there exists no identifiable global public which corresponds to the citizens body of the nation-state, and the global civil society remains largely an elite phenomenon."[37]

Even if the process of making international human rights covenants included all the characteristics of decision-making typical of constitutional democracies, the moral and sociological aspects of legitimacy still would have a role to play. Scholars in sociology, political theory, and even legal theory now readily acknowledge that legal systems depend upon nonlegal foundations. For example, legal theorists Larry Alexander and Frederick Schauer astutely argue that there is an "unavoidable dependence of law on the nonlegal environment in which it exists."[38] This dependence is "not simply to decide how law should be interpreted" or "to evaluate the extent to which law will be effective" but "to determine just what is to count as law and what is not." They emphasize that "the unavoidable and dizzying fragility of a legal system's nonlegal foundations" means "that the security and stability that constitutionalism is alleged to bring depends less on constitutionalism itself than on the preconstitutional understandings that make constitutionalism possible."[39]

In the international context, this would present a larger concern because the legal legitimacy of international law is much weaker than the legal legitimacy of a domestic constitution. The comments by Alexander and Schauer also suggest that legitimacy goes beyond just moral and sociological legitimacy. They seem to be referring to what some scholars call an ethos of sovereignty, which is the highest level of legitimation. In this respect, Peter Berger and Thomas

36 Beetham, *The Legitimation of Power*, 271 (emphasis added).

37 Beetham, *The Legitimation of Power*, 271.

38 Lawrence Alexander and Frederick Schauer, "Rules of Recognition, Constitutional Controversies, and the Dizzying Dependence of Law on Acceptance," in *The Rule of Recognition and the U.S. Constitution*, ed. Matthew Adler and Kenneth Einar Himma (New York: Oxford University Press, 2009), 192.

39 Alexander and Schauer, "Rules of Recognition," 192 (emphasis added).

Luckmann have argued that there are four levels of legitimation with the final level being "the most comprehensive level of legitimation." These four levels of legitimation are: (1) the "pretheoretical" acceptance of existing institutions; (2) "rudimentary" theory based on "proverbs, moral maxims and wise sayings"; (3) "explicit theories by which an institutional sector is legitimated in terms of a differentiated body of knowledge"; and (4) "the most comprehensive level of legitimation," involving "symbolic universes," where "all the sectors of the institutional order are integrated in an all-embracing frame of reference."[40] In this final level of legitimation, institutional roles as well as subjective experiences participate in "a universe that transcends and includes the institutional order," and "the symbolic universe provides a comprehensive integration of all discrete institutional processes," including those relating to law and politics.[41]

Any normative order is thus dependent on a significant degree of legitimacy, and legitimacy is wrapped up in specific moral commitments and perspectives. This moral character is also what legitimation and universalizing arguments find most difficult to face and exactly where we now turn. I will argue that this normative legitimacy depends upon comprehensive religious and secular convictions that constitute the most comprehensive level of legitimation identified by Berger and Luckmann.

14.3 DEFINING RELIGION AND RELIGIOUS PLURALISM

For Christians, it is essential to understand how claims about human rights relate to the Christian tradition. Some scholars jump to a discussion of passages of the Christian Bible and others focus on the role of natural law and natural rights in the Christian tradition. While these are important discussions, they often overlook the importance of thinking through how Christian theology relates to human rights principles. To analyze how Christianity and Christian theology are related to the foundation of human rights, I will draw on the insights of process theology and process philosophy. This section will start with a very short introduction to the key concepts of process theology and process philosophy before setting forth a process understanding of religion (including theology) (Section 14.3.2) and two normative process theories of religious pluralism (Section 14.3.3).

40 Peter Berger and Thomas Luckmann, *The Social Construction of Reality: A Treatise in the Sociology of Knowledge* (New York: Anchor Books, 1967), 94–6.

41 Berger and Luckmann, *Social Construction of Reality*, 96–7, 103.

14.3.1 *Process Theology: An Introduction*

Unlike classical Western metaphysics, process philosophy makes process or becoming ultimate rather than substance or being. In classical metaphysics, the universe is constituted by one or more substances, which are the basic building blocks of the universe. For example, the essence of Baruch Spinoza's metaphysics can be summarized with a few key propositions about God. God is the eternal and infinite substance and cause of the universe, "the efficient cause of all things that can come within the scope of infinite intellect."[42] Once we understand God's nature, everything else flows from it as a matter of logical necessity. Thus, God or Nature is presupposed by or is the condition of conceiving of everything else.

Conversely, process metaphysics (the philosophy of organism) maintains that the final real things of the universe are actual occasions or entities, which are units of process (or processes of becoming) rather than substances (being) in the traditional sense. Process metaphysics rejects the "substance-quality concept" in the Spinoza example and replaces it with a "description of dynamic process." This dynamic process – the philosophy of organism – can be summarized as "The many become one and are increased by one."[43] Process metaphysics, like all other philosophical schemes, is an abstraction from concrete experience. Whitehead tries to avoid the "fallacy of misplaced concreteness," which is "the accidental error of mistaking the abstract for the concrete,"[44] by grounding the philosophy of organism in the most concrete elements of our experience, which he refers to as actual entities. The Whiteheadian world is a microcosmic multitude of actual entities (the many); it is atomistic. The becoming, the being, and the relatedness of actual entities – "The many become one and are increased by one" – are shorthand for Whitehead's process philosophy.

Whitehead's metaphysics or speculative philosophy shows that atomic physics and Darwinian evolution are not inconsistent with a religious ontology. John Cobb emphasizes that Whitehead's speculative philosophy blends together the new insights in physics (e.g., "relativity and quantum theory") with William James's new philosophical insights (e.g., radical empiricism) to challenge the pervasive "scientific materialism and the

42 Baruch Spinoza, *Ethics: Treatise on the Emendation of the Intellect and Selected Letters*, ed. Seymour Feldman, trans. Samuel Shirley (Indianapolis: Hackett Publishing Company, 1992), 39, 43.

43 Alfred North Whitehead, *Process and Reality*, ed. David Ray Griffin and Donald W. Sherburn, corrected ed. (New York: The Free Press, 1978 [1929]), 21.

44 Alfred North Whitehead, *Science and the Modern World* (New York: The Free Press, 1967 [1925]), 51.

Cartesian Ego."[45] Similarly, David Ray Griffin clarifies that Whitehead's philosophy is part of "constructive or revisionary postmodernism" that "rejects not science as such but only that scientism in which the data of the modern natural sciences are alone allowed to contribute to the construction of our worldview."[46] At the same time, Whitehead maintains that God is a necessary part of his metaphysics because God "shares with every new creation its actual world; and the concrescent creature is objectified in God as a novel element in God's objectification of that actual world."[47] God is crucial for the creative advance of the universe because God lures the world toward the categorical imperative of maximizing beauty or the "intensity of feeling ... in the immediate subject, and ... in the relevant future."[48]

Furthermore, Whitehead maintains that maximizing beauty is categorical or universal because "[t]he teleology of the Universe is directed to the production of Beauty."[49] Beauty or unity-in-diversity entails achieving both a sense of order (harmony or an absence of mutual inhibition among various prehensions) and a raised intensity of feelings (complexity or a synthesis of contrasting feelings). Because this transcendent (a priori) telos is universally applicable to all experience (human and nonhuman), humans as self-conscious experiencing agents should direct their actions to maximize beauty. Consequently, normative legal claims should maximize beauty (unity-in-diversity) no less than moral claims and, as I will argue in Section 14.4.3, Whitehead's metaphysics requires a theory of human rights based on the telos of beauty.

Despite his focus on theoretical or speculative reasoning, Whitehead argues that the "function of Reason" "is to promote the art of life." Whitehead clarifies that practical reasoning is the enlightenment of purpose which renders purpose effective. More specifically, he states that it has "a three-fold urge: (i) to live, (ii) to live well, (iii) to live better. In fact, the art of life is *first* to be alive, *secondly* to be alive in a satisfactory way, and *thirdly* to acquire an increase in satisfaction."[50] In other words, Whitehead maintains that the telos of beauty leads to a different form for practical reasoning. Unlike the Greeks

45 John B. Cobb, Jr., "Alfred North Whitehead," in *Founders of Constructive Postmodern Philosophy: Peirce, James, Bergson, Whitehead, and Hartshorne*, ed. David Ray Griffin et al. (Albany: State University of New York Press, 1993), 165–6.

46 David Ray Griffin, "Introduction to SUNY Series in Constructive Postmodern Thought," in *Founders of Constructive Postmodern Philosophy: Peirce, James, Bergson, Whitehead, and Hartshorne*, ed. David Ray Griffin et al. (Albany: State University of New York Press, 1993), viii.

47 Whitehead, *Process and Reality*, 345.

48 Whitehead, *Process and Reality*, 27.

49 Alfred North Whitehead, *Adventures of Ideas* (New York: The Free Press, 1933), 265.

50 Whitehead, *Adventures of Ideas*, 8.

who thought the final ends for humans were fixed, the end is not just to live well. There is also an imperative toward the creative advance of a higher form of perfection – "the adventure of living better." This pragmatic function of reason presupposes a notion of final causation and seeks to make that end effective. In a process perspective, the end is never finally realized because there are always higher levels of perfection to be realized in the future.

In the *Adventures of Ideas*, Whitehead gives the example of the "growth of the idea of the essential rights of human beings, arising from their sheer humanity" or the humanitarian ideal to demonstrate how the aspiration to live better can surpass the aspiration to live well.[51] He points out that "Freedom and Equality constitute an inevitable presupposition for modern political thought . . . while Slavery was a corresponding presupposition for the ancients."[52] For the ancients, slavery was a presupposition consistent with democracy while modern political thought presupposes freedom and equality. While certain technological advances weakened the necessity for slavery, its eradication required the combined influence of philosophy, law, and religion. In the West, Whitehead credits the moral energy of "the impracticable ethics of Christianity," the philosophical generality of outlook Platonic philosophy, and the "constructive ability" of law for "the evolution from the notion of society based upon servitude to that of society based upon individual freedom."[53] Social reform thus requires an "alliance of philosophy, law, and religion."[54]

14.3.2 *Defining Religion*

Religion is not a natural thing about which there are clear-cut characteristics. Rather, the concept of religion has been the subject of much debate and disagreement and has often been linked to the particular challenges arising from the divisions within Christianity following the Protestant Reformation in Europe. For example, Paul Griffiths emphasizes that despite substantial disagreement, "[t]he desire to philosophize about religion and to think of religion as a type with tokens is very much a product of a particular European history."[55] During the Protestant Reformation, theological differences resulted in dramatic differences in how to understand the requirements of the Christian life and whether the state could be held to Christian standards.

51 Whitehead, *Adventures of Ideas*, 13.
52 Whitehead, *Adventures of Ideas*, 13.
53 Whitehead, *Adventures of Ideas*, 42, 26.
54 Whitehead, *Adventures of Ideas*, 19.
55 Paul J. Griffiths, *Problems of Religious Diversity* (Oxford: Blackwell Publishing, 2001), 6.

These theological differences helped fuel the wars of religion that ravaged Europe and England in the seventeenth century. Partly in response to these religious wars, Wilfred Cantwell Smith notes that scholars in the seventeenth and eighteenth centuries began developing the concept of religion as something with generic characteristics which many religions exhibit.[56]

This development of the concept of religion had several important consequences. First, it helped move beyond the pejorative use of the term religion as a label to distinguish "religions" (i.e., a false faith) from your personal piety or true faith.[57] Prior to this change, the term "faith" was used as a positive reference to one's own personal piety while others with different beliefs merely had "religion." In addition, it allowed reference to "a generic 'religion' . . . as an external entity the total system or sum of all systems of beliefs, or simply the generalization that they are there."[58] This facilitated referring to all faiths by the plural "religions" so that no particular religion had a prima facie preference to other religions. Finally, this concept of religion meant that "religion is something that one believes or does not believe, something whose propositions are true or are not true, something whose *locus* is in the realm of the intelligible, is up for inspection by the speculative mind."[59]

Given this history, some scholars have noted a pronounced Protestant Christian influence on defining religion as something that is individual, chosen, and private. In response to these criticisms, religion scholars have broadened definitions of religion to include many forms of life: collective and individual, doctrinal and mystical, scriptural and liturgical, a way of life and an aspect of it, etcetera. Griffiths, for instance, has argued that religion is "a form of life that seems to those who inhabit it to be comprehensive, incapable of abandonment, and of central importance to the ordering of their lives."[60] Religion is comprehensive in that it seems to those engaged in the form of life to explicitly take into account everything, such as marriage practices, forms of dress, forms of worship, forms of body art, and all forms of communal organization. Griffiths maintains that religion is "incapable of abandonment" in that "it is sufficiently constitutive or definitive of who they are that leaving it is impossible without also leaving themselves."[61] Finally, it is "of central importance" in that it seems "for those who belong to it to say that it seems

[56] Wilfred Cantwell Smith, *The Meaning and End of Religion: A New Approach to the Religious Traditions of Mankind* (New York: Macmillan, 1962), 43.
[57] Cantwell Smith, *Meaning and End of Religion*, 42–3.
[58] Cantwell Smith, *Meaning and End of Religion*, 43.
[59] Cantwell Smith, *Meaning and End of Religion*, 40.
[60] Griffiths, *Problems of Religious Diversity*, 12.
[61] Griffiths, *Problems of Religious Diversity*, 10.

to them to address the questions of paramount importance to the ordering of their lives."[62]

Furthermore, rather than assuming that everyone knows what counts as "religion," the academic study of religion proceeds by various methods of analyzing religion. Religion scholar John Hick maintains that "[r]eligion is one thing to the anthropologist, another to the sociologist, another to the psychologist," another to the theologian, and another to the philosopher.[63] This results, in part, from the different disciplinary orientations and purposes involved in analyzing the nature of religion. Despite these advances, no generally accepted definition of religion exists and probably never will exist.

For the purposes of this chapter, however, the central concern is to understand the role of religious convictions or claims in legitimating the law. The primary concern is with the kinds of claims that religion makes and how religious claims are related to other types of claims such as legal and moral claims. In contrast to the other approaches to understanding religion, the philosophy of religion has typically focused on these questions. Therefore, I will adopt the philosophy of religion approach taken by process theologian Schubert Ogden and define religion in such a way as to outline the relationship between religious claims and legal and moral claims.

Regarding the definition of religion, Ogden defines religion as "the primary form of culture in terms of which we human beings *explicitly* ask and answer the existential question of the meaning of ultimate reality for us."[64] According to this account, religion *explicitly* asks "What is authentic human existence?" (the ethical aspect of religion) or "How we are to understand ourselves and others in relation to the whole?" (the metaphysical aspect of religion). The existential question, the question of meaning, is the question which is presupposed by all other questions. It is the comprehensive question concerning "What is the valid comprehensive self-understanding" or "comprehensive human purpose?"[65] Religion *explicitly* answers the existential or comprehensive question by providing the "concepts and symbols whose express function is to mediate authentic self-understanding."[66] In other words, religion includes a comprehensive evaluation of human activity to determine how

62 Griffiths, *Problems of Religious Diversity*, 11.

63 John Hick, *Philosophy of Religion*, 2nd ed. (Englewood Cliffs, NJ: Prentice-Hall, 1973), 3.

64 Schubert M. Ogden, *Is There Only One True Religion or Are There Many?* (Dallas: SMU Press, 1992), 5 (emphasis added).

65 Franklin I. Gamwell, *The Meaning of Religious Freedom: Modern Politics and Democratic Resolution* (Albany: State University of New York Press, 1995), 22–3.

66 Ogden, *Is There Only One*, 8.

the human activity in question should relate to the larger reality of which it is a part.

If the existential or comprehensive question is presupposed by all other questions, does that mean that answering any question (such as which party should win a lawsuit) presupposes an answer to the existential question? Yes and no. Ogden argues that "everything that we think, say, or do, insofar, at least, as it makes or implies a claim to validity, necessarily presupposes that ultimate reality is such as to authorize some understanding of ourselves as authentic and that, conversely, some understanding of our existence is authentic because it is authorized by ultimate reality."[67] Consequently, in a sense, answering any question implies an understanding of what constitutes authentic human existence or an answer to the comprehensive or existential question. However, Franklin Gamwell notes that this does not mean that all human activity is religious but that "the character of human activity as such implies the possibility of religion, in the sense that it implies the comprehensive question and, therefore, the possibility that this question is asked and answered explicitly."[68] Human activity is thus religious only to the extent that the existential or comprehensive question has been *explicitly* asked and answered.

To differentiate between explicitly answering and implicitly "answering" the comprehensive question, Ogden refers to the former as religion and the latter as a "basic faith in the meaning of life." Ogden argues that this basic faith is presupposed by all human activity. It involves "accepting the larger setting of one's life and adjusting oneself to it."[69] It implicitly answers the existential or comprehensive question because it involves a self-conscious adjustment to these conditions. Unlike other animals, human animals not only "live by faith" but also "seek understanding." Humans are "instinct poor"; "[n]ot only the details of our lives but even their overall pattern as authentically human remain undecided by our membership in the human species and are left to our own freedom and responsibility to decide."[70] In other words, humans do not live by merely accepting their setting and adjusting to it (basic faith); they seek a reflective self-understanding of reality (the whole) and their place in it (authentic human existence). Religion provides the concepts and symbols for human reflective self-understanding; it attempts to make sense "of our basic faith in the meaning of life, given the facts of life as

67 Ogden, *Is There Only One*, 7.
68 Gamwell, *Meaning of Religious Freedom*, 23 n. 5.
69 Shubert M. Ogden, *On Theology* (New York: Harper & Row, 1986), 70.
70 Ogden, *Is There Only One*, 6.

we actually experience it."[71] To the extent that humans act with reflective self-understanding or have an explicit comprehensive understanding of authentic human existence, they are religious. On occasion, however, people act with a self-awareness of their comprehensive understanding of authentic human existence, but they will not express that to others. In those cases, I refer to an implicit comprehensive conviction. Consequently, for the purposes of this discussion, "religion" will be equated with an explicit "comprehensive claim or conviction about authentic human existence."

Accordingly, religion includes not only the recognized world religions of Christianity, Judaism, Islam, Hinduism, and Buddhism but also humanism, capitalism (when proposed as a normative rather than as a positive theory), communism, and other so-called secular answers to the existential question. For this reason, I sometimes refer to "comprehensive religious and secular convictions" to make it clear that I am referring both to traditional religious convictions and to secular convictions about authentic human existence. This means that there is and always has been a plurality of religions or comprehensive self-understandings. As a result, all human activity (including theories of human rights) is either explicitly informed by a plurality of religious convictions or implicitly informed by a basic faith in the meaningfulness of existence. In the latter case, I will sometimes refer to implicit comprehensive convictions even though this is not technically correct.

Ogden also maintains that reason plays an essential role in the articulation and evaluation of religious convictions. He rejects two common assumptions about theology that preclude critical reflection on religious convictions: "(1) that theology as such has to appeal to special criteria of truth for some if not all of its assertions; and (2) that the theologian as such has to be a believer already committed to the truth of the assertions that theological reflection seeks to establish."[72] To the contrary, he argues that religious convictions are subject to critical validation. Religious convictions are different in the sense that they are comprehensive, but that does not mean that they are beyond critical or rational validation. In fact, he maintains that "it is the very nature of a religion to make or imply the claim to formal religious truth."[73] In other words, religious convictions, like any cognitive claim, suggest that they can be validated in a nonquestion-begging way.

Philosophy and theology are also forms of culture, but they are secondary forms of culture which reflect on the validity of the claims made by religion.

[71] Ogden, *Is There Only One*, 18.
[72] Ogden, *On Theology*, 103.
[73] Ogden, *Is There Only One*, 13.

Theology consists in "critical reflection on the validity claims of some specific religion." Similarly, philosophy "involves critically reflecting on the claims of religion, along with those of so-called secular forms of praxis and culture."[74] What distinguishes theology and philosophy, however, is that theology is critical reflection on the validity claims of a specific religion while philosophy may critically reflect on the claims of many different religions or on the possibility of the claims of religion in general. In this respect, Christian theology critically reflects on two distinctive validity claims: (1) that the Christian witness is "adequate to its content" (appropriate to the earliest Christian witness and credible to reason and common human experience) and (2) "fitting to its situation."[75] Despite this critical role of philosophy and theology, religion claims to be formally true "not only for all other true religion, but also for any other existential truth whatever, including that of philosophy."[76] As a result, all of philosophy, even that not specifically concerning the validity of the claims of religion, presupposes the answers given to the existential question by religion. Religion is primary while philosophy and theology are secondary.

Despite the assumptions of many human rights scholars, Ogden's claim that reason plays an essential role in the articulation and evaluation of religious claims is not uncommon in theology. Many theologians and philosophers have argued that religious convictions depend, at least in part, on rational reflection for their articulation and evaluation. This does not mean that they have agreed upon the definition of reason, its role in critical reflection, or its priority with respect to revelation. Differences about these issues should not take away from the important role reason has played in formulating and critiquing religious convictions. For example, reason has been central to systematic theology and philosophical theology even though there has not been agreement on how the role of reason should be defined. At one extreme, Kant argues that philosophical theology depends on pure reason to understand the possibility and the attributes of the concept of God.[77] At the other extreme, Paul Tillich claims that reason alone cannot give answers to the ultimate questions about life because in the existential situation, reason contradicts itself.[78] Philosophy facilitates defining the questions raised by the existential situation in which we live, but "[r]evelation is the answer to the questions

74 Ogden, *Is There Only One*, 34.

75 Ogden, *Is There Only One*, 34–5.

76 Ogden, *Is There Only One*, 71.

77 Immanuel Kant, *Lectures on Philosophical Theology*, trans. Allen W. Wood and Gertrude M. Clark (Ithaca: Cornell University Press, 1978).

78 Paul Tillich, *Systematic Theology*, vol. 1 (Chicago: University of Chicago Press, 1951), 18–28.

implied in the existential conflicts of reason."[79] Somewhere in between, David Tracy maintains that "contemporary Christian theology is best understood as philosophical reflection upon the meanings present in common human experience and the meanings present in the Christian tradition."[80] Although these approaches incorporate philosophy (reason) into theology in different ways, they all support the necessary role of reason for theological reflection about religious convictions. Religious convictions are not exempt from critical reflection; they are the product of it.

14.3.3 *Two Process Theories of Religious Pluralism*

Process theology has made noteworthy contributions to the contemporary debates about religious pluralism, and Whitehead's process philosophy supports different accounts of religious pluralism. This section will discuss two of those accounts – one by Ogden (Section 14.3.3.1) and the other by Cobb (Section 14.3.3.2). In addition, while the following discussion of religious pluralism will cover other traditions, many of its starting points are within the Christian tradition because most of the discussion of religious pluralism has occurred in that context and because of the intended audience for this chapter.

There are several important questions to keep in mind when considering the process theories of religious pluralism in this section and their relevance for grounding human rights in the last part of the chapter. How should Christians view other comprehensive groundings for human rights? Is there only one true foundation for human rights? Is there only one true religion? Can Christians recognize the validity of other foundations for human rights and learn from dialogue with those who embrace those foundations?

14.3.3.1 Ogden's Pluralistic Inclusivism

Given that religious convictions can be critically validated, Ogden could be read to suggest that there is only one true religion that can be arrived at by critical reflection. If this were the case, the state could establish this religion as the official legitimation of the law and the state. To the contrary, Ogden maintains that the debate about religious pluralism has been mistaken because it has proceeded from the assumption that there is either one true religion (*monism*) or that there are many equally true religions (*pluralism*). He

79 Tillich, *Systematic Theology*, 147.

80 David Tracy, *Blessed Rage for Order: The New Pluralism in Theology* (New York: Seabury Press, 1975), 34.

argues that religious monism comes in two varieties: exclusivism and inclusivism. For example, some Christian exclusivists claim that there is "no salvation outside of the Church" or "no salvation outside of Christianity." By contrast, Christian inclusivists argue that

> the possibility of salvation uniquely constituted by the event of Jesus Christ is somehow made available to each and every human being without exception [usually through the fragmentary explication of the true religion (Christianity) by other religions] and, therefore, is exclusive of no one unless she or he excludes her- or himself from its effect by a free and responsible decision to reject it.[81]

The alternative usually proposed to these two forms of monism is pluralism. Pluralists maintain "not only that there *can be* many true religions but [that] there actually *are*."[82] On this account, all religions are equally true, and one religion cannot be shown to be true and another false. Like liberal political theory, most secular theories of human rights appear to assume pluralism in this sense. Treating religious convictions as equally true (or equally false) means that they can be relegated to the private or subjective realm which is consistent with the conventional understanding of secularizing the law.

Conversely, Ogden contends that religious convictions are capable of critical validation. Some religious convictions are capable of critical validation by theology and philosophy and others are not. This seems to suggest religious monism, but Ogden argues for another option, which he calls "pluralistic inclusivism." He maintains that the logical contradictory to religious monism "is not that there actually *are* many true religions, but only that there *can be*."[83] In other words, more than one religion may be capable of critical validation. More than one religion may be the true reflective understanding of our basic existential faith. Also, as a product of critical reflection, religious convictions can be modified and corrected based on further reflection and based on what is learned from dialogue with other religions. The pursuit of religious truth is never complete. Through ongoing reflection and encounters with other religions, the possibility for improvement is ever present. Consequently, even if a religion could be shown to be truer than others, Ogden would oppose the establishment of an official religion. Establishing an official religion would cut off the opportunity for further improvement and refinement of religious truth. It would stifle the pursuit of religious truth and

81 Tracy, *Blessed Rage for Order*, 31.
82 Tracy, *Blessed Rage for Order*, 27.
83 Ogden, *Is There Only One*, 83.

jeopardize further progress from subsequent rational reflection and dialogue among those holding a plurality of religious convictions.

14.3.3.2 Cobb's Complementary Pluralism

In contrast to Ogden's pluralistic inclusivism, process theologian Cobb interprets process philosophy to support what he refers to as "complementary pluralism." Cobb's insights come both from his experiences with interreligious dialogue and from process philosophy. With respect to religious dialogue, he maintains that one should enter dialogue with a duality of attitudes. "One enters dialogue both as a believer convinced of the claims of one religious tradition and as a human being open to the possibility that one has something to learn from representatives of another religious tradition."[84] The belief that guides the dialogue is "that there is more truth and wisdom than one's own tradition." Cobb emphasizes repeatedly that approaching dialogue this way does not compromise his affirmation of Christianity. Rather, he argues that being Christocentric – centering oneself on Christ – "provides the deepest and fullest reason for openness to others." Cobb affirms the universality and the uniqueness of Christianity, but he also affirms the uniqueness of the universal claims of other religions.

Cobb further points out that the dialogue often begins with what seems to be conflict between two incompatible religious claims. He recommends that we keep in mind "that the totality of what is, is very complex, far exceeding all that we can ever hope to know or think."[85] He further recommends that we keep in mind that the religious traditions may be addressing different questions. In the dialogue, the "goal is to transform contradictory statements into different but not contradictory ones." He illustrates this by reconciling the seeming contradiction between Christian theism and Buddhist atheism.

> When a Buddhist says that no God exists, the main point is that there is nothing in reality to which one should be attached. When a Christian says that God exists, the meaning may be that there is that in reality that is worthy of trust and worship. *If* those translations are correct …, then it is not impossible that both be correct. … [T]he Buddhist could in principle acknowledge the reality of something worthy of trust and worship without abandoning the central insight that attachment blocks the way to enlightenment. And the Christian could come to see that real trust is not attachment in the Buddhist sense.[86]

84 John B. Cobb, *Transforming Christianity and the World: A Way beyond Absolutism and Relativism* (Maryknoll: Orbis Books, 1999), 66.
85 Cobb, *Transforming Christianity and the World*, 135.
86 Cobb, *Transforming Christianity and the World*, 74.

Whitehead's process philosophy further supports the complementary pluralism that Cobb has experienced in interreligious dialogue. Cobb rejects the assumption that "what is approached as 'ultimate reality' must be one and the same." Based on Whitehead's metaphysics, Cobb maintains that there are three ultimates – God (the Supreme Being), creativity (Being Itself), and the cosmos (the totality of finite things). These three ultimates have been very helpful to Cobb in explaining "how theistic Christianity and nontheistic Buddhism could both be oriented toward something ultimate in the nature of things."[87] Cobb argues that creativity (the formless ultimate) is the ultimate that some Buddhists point to with the term "Emptiness." Similarly, God or the Supreme Being is "the source of forms (such as truth, beauty, and justice)" that shapes creativity and is similar to what Jews refer to as "Yahweh" and Muslims refer to as "Allah."[88] Finally, the cosmos (the totality of finite things) is the ultimate that is referred to by forms of Taoism and many Native American religions that consider the cosmos as sacred. Process theologians have also argued that the reverence for the cosmos is crucial for dealing with climate change and moving toward a sustainable way of life on Earth.[89] While time will not permit discussing his arguments, Cobb responds to criticisms that these three ultimates are not consistent with Christian theology.[90] Moreover, Cobb's notion of three ultimates and his view that traditions can focus on some or all of these ultimates provide grounds for recognizing a wide array of religious experiences and for concluding that the insights of these diverse traditions are complementary.

14.4 COMPREHENSIVE CONVICTIONS AND HUMAN RIGHTS

14.4.1 A *Pluralistic Foundation for Human Rights*

Recall from the beginning of the chapter that the legitimacy of international human rights law depends mainly on the moral or normative dimension of legitimacy. At the international level, the legal dimension is weakened by the lack of enforcement through international legal institutions and the lack of international democracy to support human rights conventions and treaties.

87 David Ray Griffin, "John Cobb's Whiteheadian Complementary Pluralism," in *Deep Religious Pluralism*, ed. David Ray Griffin (Louisville: Westminster John Knox Press, 2005), 49.

88 Griffin, "John Cobb's Whiteheadian Complementary Pluralism," 47.

89 David Ray Griffin, *Process Theology: On Postmodernism, Morality, Pluralism, Eschatology, and Demonic Evil* (Anoka: Process Century Press, 2017), 113–37 (ch. 6).

90 Cobb, *Transforming Christianity and the World*, 184–6.

While it is not clear whose comprehensive convictions (e.g., world citizens', states', NGOs') constitute the normative legitimation, there is a plurality of comprehensive convictions that legitimate international human rights law rather than one foundation (based on some form of consensus) or no foundation at all.

Ogden's definition of religion also made it clear that religious convictions are the comprehensive condition of validity presupposed by any normative judgment. Recall that religious or comprehensive convictions include both an ethical aspect (a notion of authentic human existence) and a metaphysical aspect (the meaning of ultimate reality for us). The comprehensive religious and secular convictions supporting an international human rights convention thus are the morality that supports human rights law. To be clear, the comprehensive convictions about authentic human existence will not likely be moral rights theories. Moral rights theories proposed by liberal political theories typically exclude conceptions of the good and metaphysical principles as a justification for political morality and the law. As Perry emphasized in Section 14.2.1, however, the morality justifying or providing a foundation for the law does not need to be a moral rights theory.

Given that religious convictions are the comprehensive condition of normative validity, it should not be surprising that many religious traditions have posited justifications for human rights from within their traditions. Theories of human rights are now proposed by Jewish, Christian, Islamic, Hindu, Confucian, Buddhist, and indigenous religious traditions.[91] Within each of these religious traditions, there are also multiple theories of human rights. For example, human rights conceptions have been developed within the three main branches of Christianity – Roman Catholicism, Orthodox Christianity, and Protestant Christianity – and within the many denominations of each branch.[92] Protestant Christians, for instance, have generated theories of human rights from the perspectives of the Lutheran, Episcopalian, Methodist, Presbyterian, and Baptist denominations.[93] This broad array of comprehensive religious convictions can contribute to the pluralistic foundation for human rights laws when those laws are consistent with their religious convictions about authentic human existence.

[91] John Witte, Jr. and M. Christian Green, "Introduction," in *Religion and Human Rights: An Introduction*, ed. John Witte, Jr. and M. Christian Green (Oxford: Oxford University Press, 2012).

[92] John Witte, Jr., "Introduction," in *Christianity and Human Rights: An Introduction*, ed. John Witte, Jr. and Frank S. Alexander (Cambridge: Cambridge University Press, 2010), 20–37.

[93] See also Chapter 15 in this volume.

Both Ogden's pluralistic inclusivism and Cobb's complementary pluralism counter the claims by some human rights scholars like Ignatieff that religious convictions are nonrational, dogmatic, naïve, and intolerant. They also call into question Ignatieff's assumptions that foundations are incontestable and that "[f]oundational beliefs of all kinds have been a long-standing menace to the human rights of ordinary individuals."[94] While this may be true of dogmatic comprehensive religious convictions, it is likewise true of dogmatic comprehensive secular convictions. The refusal to entertain dialogue about the foundations of human rights, however, is much more problematic. In fact, based on Ogden's definition, Ignatieff's prudential theory of human rights at least implicitly relies on a comprehensive conviction about authentic human existence. At the very least, Ignatieff views human agency and reasoning as key aspects of authentic human existence. Ignatieff, however, refuses to acknowledge that his theory of human rights has a foundation, which makes it very difficult for those critical of his theory of human rights to identify many of the important areas of disagreement. In other words, Ogden's account of religion calls into question the possibility of nonfoundational theories of human rights. Scholars may refuse to articulate their foundation, but any implicit or explicit claims about authentic human existence will depend on a comprehensive religious or secular conviction.

14.4.2 *Responding to the Spiritual Crisis*

As noted in Section 14.1, Ignatieff identifies two crises for human rights – *a cultural crisis* and *a spiritual crisis* – that together raise substantial questions about the legitimacy of human rights norms. I will address the spiritual crisis first because I think it is related to the cultural crisis in ways not addressed by Ignatieff. Ignatieff argues that the spiritual crisis stems from a "deliberate silence at the heart of human rights culture" regarding what aspect of human nature (e.g., conscience) or ultimate reality (e.g., God) provides a bulwark against human horrors like the Holocaust. He counters that this "pragmatic silence on ultimate questions" in the UDHR has helped, rather than hindered, the development of a global human rights culture that aims to stem the tide of human abuses.

I concur with Ignatieff's argument for a "deliberate silence" in the text of the UDHR and international human rights covenants, but for very different reasons. Both Ogden's and Cobb's understandings of religious pluralism provide a normative justification for keeping religious justifications of

[94] Ignatieff, *Human Rights as Politics and Idolatry*, 86.

human dignity or human rights out of the text of international human rights conventions. Putting religious convictions (e.g., the *imago Dei*) into international human rights treaties cuts off the debate for religious truth. When the text is secularized, the participants in a debate can bring their comprehensive religious or secular convictions into the debate without having to challenge or reconcile these beliefs with the religious conviction in the text of the law. The text of the law should remain secularized so that it includes only noncomprehensive rules and principles.

Nevertheless, the secularized text of the law does not mean that a treaty or convention does not have a foundation based on a plurality of comprehensive religious and secular convictions. In *Democracy and Tradition*, religion scholar Jeffrey Stout argues that "[t]here is a sense in which the ethical discourse of most modern democracies is *secularized*, for such discourse is not 'framed by a theological perspective' taken for granted by all those who participate in it."[95] Secularized discourse, however, "is not a reflection of commitment to secularism."[96] Stout further emphasizes that a secularized modern democratic discourse does not "involve endorsement of the 'secular state' as a realm entirely insulated from the effects of religious convictions, let alone removed from God's ultimate authority. It is simply a matter of what can be presupposed in a discussion with other people who happen to have different theological commitments and interpretive dispositions."[97]

Stout's argument is further supported by Maritain's observation (noted in Section 14.1) that the rights recognized in the UDHR were based on agreement about "common practical notions" but not on common speculative notions. In other words, the practical agreement was about what rights to protect but not why. Similarly, in Cass Sunstein's terms, agreement on what rights to protect in a human rights law are "incompletely theorized agreements on practical outcomes."[98] Sunstein argues that law is basically composed of "incompletely theorized agreements on particular outcomes, accompanied by agreements on the narrow or low-level principles that account for them." This allows for substantial disagreement on more general theoretical principles that attempt to explain and legitimize the law, such as comprehensive convictions about authentic human existence.

95 Jeffrey Stout, *Democracy and Tradition* (Princeton: Princeton University Press, 2004), 93.

96 Stout, *Democracy and Tradition*, 93. Like Ogden, Stout considers secularism an ideology that competes with religious traditions for ultimate commitment. Stout, *Democracy and Tradition*, 97.

97 Stout, *Democracy and Tradition*, 93.

98 Cass Sunstein, *Legal Reasoning and Political Conflict* (Oxford: Oxford University Press, 1996), 37.

On the other hand, the international human rights convention in question implies comprehensive religious or secular convictions about authentic human existence. The legitimation of a convention is provided by a plurality of religious and comprehensive convictions which must always remain implicit. Parties can put forward their comprehensive convictions in the debate about the terms of the convention, but the convention must include only a noncomprehensive justification. For example, many religious or comprehensive convictions support the legal prohibition of sex trafficking, but the text of the conventions prohibiting sex trafficking do not explicitly adopt any of these religious justifications. In other words, the text of the law does not provide religious or comprehensive justifications for prohibiting sex trafficking; it only implies them. Both Ogden's pluralistic inclusivism and Cobb's complementary pluralism require this normative theory of secularization.

This addresses the spiritual crisis by recognizing that a plurality of comprehensive convictions provides the bulwark against parties becoming complacent about human rights law. This results in a human rights ethos or culture that supports the conventions and treaties protecting human rights. John Witte emphasizes "that human rights norms need a human rights culture to be effective."[99] Human rights norms, according to Witte, "have little cogency in communities that lack the ethos and ethic to render human rights violations a source of shame and regret, restraint and respect, confession and responsibility, reconciliation and restitution."[100] The plurality of comprehensive religious and secular convictions thus provides the motivation for passing human rights conventions, holding violators accountable through enforcement or moral persuasion, and keeping the public debate focused on the importance of human rights. Arguably, this human rights culture based on a plurality of comprehensive convictions about authentic human existence provides a more durable foundation for the human rights law in question. This follows from the fact that inevitably some comprehensive convictions are undermined by arguments, experiences (e.g., world wars or natural disasters), or changes in international society. If the comprehensive conviction in questions was the only foundation for the human rights law, the law would likely lose its effectiveness because of the lack of a human rights ethos supporting it. Similarly, if there were no foundations for the human rights law, the support for it would depend on the pragmatic reasons supporting the law. If those pragmatic reasons were no longer persuasive, the human rights law would lose

99 Witte, "Introduction," 11.

100 Witte, "Introduction," 11.

its support and become ineffective. Consequently, a human rights ethos based on a plurality of comprehensive convictions provides a formidable response to the spiritual crisis identified by Ignatieff.

14.4.3 *Responding to the Cultural Crisis*

With respect to the cultural crisis, Ignatieff identified three challenges to the universality of human rights including the Islamic challenge, the Asian communitarian challenge, and the challenge to Western individualism by Western defenders of human rights. Together, these challenges constitute a relativist critique of a liberal oriented human rights regime. In her comments on Ignatieff's cultural crisis argument, Diane Orentlicher identified four strategies used to address the relativist critique: "(1) substantive accommodation; (2) moral anthropology; (3) procedural inclusiveness; and its close relation, (4) transnational collaboration."[101] The following discussion will focus on procedural inclusiveness, which Orentlicher argues is one of the most effective against the relativist critique. The procedural inclusiveness strategy "recognizes that the human rights idea faces a crisis of legitimacy principally because the *process* by which key international treaties were drafted was highly exclusionary."[102] Her recommendation is to make the transcultural process of constructing human rights "truly inclusive." The prescription is straightforward in theory but much more complicated in practice. Orentlicher points out that one of the key problems for Ignatieff is how he engages with religion. As indicated in Section 14.1, Ignatieff wants to forgo debating claims attempting to ground human rights in religious or other ultimate terms. Orentlicher recognizes that "universal acceptance of the human rights idea depends upon its legitimation *within* diverse religious traditions, not just *alongside* them."[103]

As discussed in Section 14.3.3.2, Cobb's complementary pluralism seems to fulfill Orentlicher's recommendation for procedural inclusiveness with regards to religion. Unlike Ignatieff, Cobb welcomes dialogue with other religious traditions that at first blush appear to propose religious claims incompatible with his own. He enters the dialogue, however, with an openness to those religious claims and seeks "to transform contradictory statements into different but not contradictory ones." This strategy could be effectively adopted in the context of debate about the universality of human rights law.

[101] Diane F. Orentlicher, "Relativism and Religion," in *Human Rights as Politics and Idolatry*, ed. Amy Gutmann (Princeton: Princeton University Press, 2001), 142.

[102] Orentlicher, "Relativism and Religion," 151.

[103] Orentlicher, "Relativism and Religion," 155 (emphasis in original).

To demonstrate the potential of this strategy, the following will apply Cobb's approach to the Asian communitarian challenge and the challenge to Western individualism by Western defenders of human rights. For purposes of this discussion, these challenges will not be explicitly demarcated because the challenge to individualism will be similar in both cases.

Drawing on the extensive work by David Hall and Roger Ames, Wang Shik Jang argues that "Whitehead's philosophy points the way" to integrating the "aesthetic way of thinking" characteristic of Eastern civilization with the "rational way of thinking" characteristic of Western civilization.[104] Hall and Ames maintain that different forms of social organization flow from these different ways of thinking. Further, they hold that "rational or logical order consists in a pattern of relatedness which is, in principle, indifferent to the elements whose mutual relatedness comprise the order."[105] Rational ordering occurs in accordance with conforming actions to "habits, customs, rules, or laws determinate of our conduct" and moves "away from the concrete particular toward the universal" and "tends toward uniformity and pattern regularity."[106]

Roberto Unger unpacks many of the presuppositions of the rational ordering achieved by the typical Western conception of the rule of law offered by liberal legalism. Unger argues that in legal liberalism, "[t]he main task of the theory of adjudication is to say when a decision can truly be said to stand 'under a rule'" because "[o]nly decisions 'under a rule' are consistent with freedom; others constitute arbitrary exercises of judicial power."[107] Unger further points out that liberal political theory adopts the principle of individualism; a concept which asserts that "[g]roups are artificial because all values are individual and subjective."[108] Society must be constructed and "held together by rules." Legislation and constitutions must be based on the will of the people (an aggregation of subjective wills) because there are no "natural" or rational social bonds. The rule of law ideal attempts to ensure that the legislative process is done according to fair procedures and requires that the laws are "general, impersonal, or neutral." While Unger's characterization of liberal legalism is somewhat exaggerated, it poignantly identifies the rational

104 Wang Shik Jang, "A Philosophical Evaluation of Western and Eastern Civilization from a Whiteheadian Perspective," *Process Studies* 33, no. 1 (2004): 135–48, at 135.

105 David L. Hall and Roger T. Ames, *Thinking Through Confucius* (Albany: State University of New York Press, 1987), 135.

106 Hall and Ames, *Thinking Through Confucius*, 134–6.

107 Roberto Mangabeira Unger, *Knowledge and Politics* (New York: The Free Press, 1975), 89.

108 Unger, *Knowledge and Politics*, 83.

or logical ordering at the root of legal liberalism's conception of the "rule of law."

In contrast to Western philosophy, Hall and Ames argue that "Confucius' social and political philosophy gives priority to aesthetic over rational ordering."[109] The "[a]esthetic order begins with the uniqueness of the one thing and assesses this particular as contributing to the balanced complexity of its context."[110] It is "constituted by just those particularities . . . those features that distinguish one ordering perspective from another."[111] Hall and Ames argue that Confucius's ideal society does not require the application of laws. For Confucius, both rulers and people should participate voluntarily in "an emergent harmony defined by the personal display of meaning and value in the performance of ritual action" so that the aesthetic "order is effected by a modeling process in which personal cultivation above inspires emulation below."[112] In this process, the participants *become the sociopolitical order* based on the emergent harmony from their voluntary participation. Julia Ching adds that "[t]he evolution of law in China may be described as the *devolution* of ritual (*li*) into law (*fa*) and of law into punishment (*xing*)."[113] This devolution resulted in the term "law" being associated mainly with penal law in Chinese society. Thus, in the Chinese context, the "rule of law" (as the negative sense of *cheng*) signals the failure of spontaneous voluntary ordering based on ritual and targets merely "a minimum standard of orderly conduct" for "the sake of general harmony."[114]

Not surprisingly, Ching notes "that human rights are not historically a Chinese concept, but a Western import."[115] The word "rights" does not have an exact Chinese equivalent and is usually translated as "power." To incorporate these Western notions, "the Chinese language had to coin a word for 'freedom' (*ziyou,* literally, self-determination). The closest classical term was *ziran* (literally, the natural), connoting more a Taoist sense of harmony with nature than of Promethean self-assertion."[116] Consequently, "the concept of freedom as a *right* – such as the right to freedom of thought and religion, to

109 Hall and Ames, *Thinking Through Confucius*, 158.
110 Hall and Ames, *Thinking Through Confucius*, 158.
111 Hall and Ames, *Thinking Through Confucius*, 138.
112 Hall and Ames, *Thinking Through Confucius*, 157.
113 Julia Ching, "Human Rights: A Valid Chinese Concept?," in *Confucianism and Human Rights*, ed. Wm. Theodore de Bary and Tu Weiming (New York: Columbia University Press, 1998), 67, 74.
114 Hall and Ames, *Thinking Through Confucius*, 157–8.
115 Ching, "Human Rights," 70.
116 Ching, "Human Rights," 73.

freedom of speech and assembly – was never clearly articulated until modern times, and under Western influence."[117]

Can a process view of human rights aim at a balance between the rational and the aesthetic notions of social ordering? Recall that the realization of the universal telos of maximizing beauty is always relative to the particular circumstances. For example, Whitehead claims that the details of all moral codes "are relative to the social circumstances of the immediate environment" and that there is a transcendent "aim of social perfection" (i.e., "beauty") for all these moral codes.[118] Conduct in one environment produces a measure of harmony, but in another environment it is destructively degrading. "Each society has its own type of perfection."[119] Similarly, the substantive laws in any country should embody legal norms which are relevant to its particular environment and which aim at promoting the evolution of that environment toward its proper perfection. Consequently, we must continually seek for some highly general principles underlying all such codes. Such generalities should reflect the very notions of the harmonizing of harmonies, and of individual actualities as the sole authentic reality. These are the principles of the generality of harmony (i.e., "order") "and of the importance of the individual" (i.e., "increased intensity of feeling"), which together constitute beauty.

The telos of beauty, however, is never fully realized, which means that substantive laws and "[m]orals consist in the aim at the ideal."[120] Aiming at the ideal does not mean achieving a static state of affairs but instead striving for creative advance. While the telos of beauty is universal, the unique circumstances of each society in question determine which state of affairs will maximize beauty in that particular legal system. Except for the telos of beauty and the formative and substantive rights it implies, the ends of the law do not include any fixed and unchanging substantive rights or state of affairs as they would in classical natural law and natural rights theory. Thus, the substantive rights and regulations must be continually modified to facilitate the ideal social perfection that is relevant to the current societal circumstances.

With respect to human rights, Douglas Sturm has set forth relational or process perspectives on property rights.[121] He replaces the individualistic ontology of "classical western liberalism" with a process-based

117 Ching, "Human Rights," 73.

118 Whitehead, *Adventures of Ideas*, 269, 290–1.

119 Whitehead, *Adventures of Ideas*, 291.

120 Whitehead, *Adventures of Ideas*, 269.

121 Douglas Sturm, "Property: A Relational Perspective," in *Economic Life: Process Interpretations and Critical Responses*, ed. W. Widick Schroeder and Franklin I. Gamwell (Chicago: Center for the Scientific Study of Religion, 1988), 29.

"communitarian political ontology" which "is more relational and ecological, even organic, in character."[122] Sturm further advocates a "jurisprudence of solidarity" rather than a "jurisprudence of individuality." In a jurisprudence of solidarity, "the driving passion of law is not so much to protect the individual against trespass as it is to create a quality of social interaction conducive to the flourishing of a vibrant community of life across the world."[123] In other words, Sturm argues that "human rights are of greatest importance as a form of empowerment, enabling people, as individuals and in their associations, to participate effectively in and through political community."[124]

In addition, Sturm argues that the "right to subsistence" is a fundamental human right that should be given constitutional protection. He argues that the right to subsistence (which includes economic and social rights) is inextricably interdependent with the "right to participation." Sturm clarifies that "[w]ithout a guarantee of effective participation in the public forum, one's economic condition is likely to suffer," and "[w]ithout the economic wherewithal to provide for at least minimal sustenance, basic education, and some degree of social mobility, one's participation in public life is likely to be minimalized, if not marginalized."[125] This debate highlights that a process theory of human rights may support more than one interpretation of fundamental rights. Rather than imperialistically imposing a Western conception of the rule of law, a process-oriented conception of the rule of law takes into account the important cultural differences among countries like the United States and China. For example, in China's "socialist democracy" and "socialist legal system," one possibility would be to emphasize the social welfare requirements mentioned by Sturm in addition to, or more strongly than, Western notions of individual rights.

On the other hand, this process-oriented notion of the rule of law should not be interpreted as a form of cultural relativism. For example, some women may be concerned that the renewed emphasis on the Confucian tradition will mean that the advances for women in China will succumb to the reinstitution of Confucius's (551–479 BC) feudal notion of the place of women in society. In addressing current concerns that "Confucianism spells authority and discipline, limiting individual freedom, and strengthening the state," Wm. Theodore de Bary notes the feminist critique of Confucian thought in the

122 Douglas Sturm, *Solidarity and Suffering: Toward a Politics of Relationality* (Albany: State University of New York Press, 1998), 19–20.

123 Sturm, *Solidarity and Suffering*, 11.

124 Sturm, *Solidarity and Suffering*, 18.

125 Douglas Sturm, "Taking Human Rights Seriously: Relationality and Subjectivity," *Process Studies* 33, no. 2 (2004): 237–57, at 253.

early 1900s by Ho Shen. Ho Shen maintained that "Confucian learning is marked by its devotion to honoring men and denigrating women" so that "women have duties but no rights."[126] She further argues that Confucianism venerated "men like gods while condemning women to the hells" and that "Confucianism marks the beginning of justifications for polygamy [for men] and chastity [for women]."[127] While I am not suggesting that this is the only way to interpret Confucian thought on the role of women, this feminist critique raises valid concerns that tailoring the rule of law to Confucian cultural traditions may diminish the equality of women in China. A process theory of human rights would share these concerns and would not support such retrogression in women's equality.

14.5 CONCLUSION

Heeding Maritain's admonition that rational justifications for international human rights are *indispensable*, this chapter argued that there is a plurality of comprehensive religious and secular convictions about authentic human existence that legitimates and grounds international human rights law. It also responded to the crisis of legitimacy posed by the spiritual and the cultural crises identified by Ignatieff. The pluralistic foundation for human rights law is part of the human rights culture that is necessary to support human rights institutions and law in a way that responds to this spiritual crisis. To support this argument, this chapter analyzed the legal, moral, and sociological dimensions of the legitimacy of international law and human rights. It argued that moral legitimacy was the most important dimension at the international level because the legal dimension is weakened by the lack of enforcement through international legal institutions and the lack of international democracy to support human rights conventions and treaties. Consequently, the pluralistic foundation of comprehensive religious and secular convictions constitutes the morality that supports the law of human rights.

The resources of process theology prove invaluable for defining religion and religious pluralism and providing insights to help Christians understand how they can embrace the uniqueness of Christianity while at the same time gaining insights from other religious and secular traditions. In addressing the cultural crisis, process philosophy also mediates the tension created by the cultural differences between the East and the West. The telos of beauty (unity-

126 Wm. Theodore de Bary, "Introduction," in *Confucianism and Human Rights*, ed. Wm. Theodore de Bary and Tu Weiming (New York: Columbia University Press, 1998), 3 (quoting Ho Chen, "Nuzi Fuchou Iun," *Tianyi Bao*, no. 3 (10): 7–13 (trans. Peter Zarrow)).

127 de Bary, "Introduction," 2 (quoting Chen, *Tianyi Bao*, 7–13).

in-diversity) entails maximizing both an Eastern aesthetic sense of order (emergent harmony or spontaneous order) and a Western rational sense of order (complexity arising from diverse individual orderings). Social order arises from diverse and harmonious individual and collective human choices that partially construct the internal relatedness of all things in the universe. This constitutes an ongoing process of "imaging the real" that will never reach a final or fixed state. The "ideal civilization" and the ideal human rights law will constantly change as society and the larger universe continue changing.

While the UDHR continues to be "a global ethic," it is more than ever in need of support. The Covid-19 pandemic has pushed the world apart rather than brought it together. In a book chapter entitled "The Final Word: Can Christianity Contribute to a Global Civil Religion?,"[128] the late Robert Bellah asked whether the world's religions could "mobilize their commitments so that they can at last have genuine institutional force" for a global civil society. While not naïve about religion's capacity to separate us, he also hopes that the world's religions "have capacities to strengthen and generalize a sense of solidarity so that it reaches truly global proportions."[129] In the same breath, he calls for "a religious war against selfishness, ignorance, and sinfulness in each of us according to our own faith." He closes by saying that "I am convinced that religious motivation is a necessary factor if we are to transform the growing global moral consensus and the significant beginnings of world law into an effective form of global solidarity and global governance."[130] Amen.

RECOMMENDED READING

Griffin, David Ray, ed. *Deep Religious Pluralism*. Louisville, KY: Westminster John Knox Press, 2005.

Griffin, David Ray. *Process Theology: On Postmodernism, Morality, Pluralism, Eschatology, and Demonic Evil*. Anoka, MN: Process Century Press, 2017.

Modak-Truran, Mark C. "A Process Theory of Natural Law and the Rule of Law in China." *Penn State International Law Review* 26, no. 3 (2008): 607–52.

Whitehead, Alfred North. *Adventures of Ideas*. New York: The Free Press, 1933.

Whitehead, Alfred North. *Process and Reality*, corrected ed., edited by David Ray Griffin and Donald W. Sherburn. New York: The Free Press 1978 (1929).

Witte, John, Jr., and Frank S. Alexander, eds. *Christianity and Human Rights: An Introduction*. Cambridge: Cambridge University Press, 2010.

128 Robert N. Bellah, "The Final Word: Can Christianity Contribute to a Global Civil Religion?," in *Christianity and Human Rights: An Introduction*, ed. John Witte, Jr. and Frank S. Alexander (Cambridge: Cambridge University Press, 2010), 361.

129 Bellah, "The Final Word," 362.

130 Bellah, "The Final Word," 364.

15

Christianity and Human Rights Law: Orthodox Perspectives

Elena Namli

As stated by the editors, this volume addresses the topic of Christianity and international law within the broader conversation about the relevance of religion in the dynamics of global governance. Human rights law is one of the most important elements of international law and there are several dimensions of its relation to Christianity – historically, institutionally, and theologically – that generate theoretical concern. One such dimension is that of Christian agencies within the genealogy and historical developments of human rights law. As demonstrated in several chapters of this volume, an analysis of Christian agencies brings new insights into the research field of international human rights law.

Another dimension of the relationship between Christianity and human rights law is the issue of Christianity as a resource for critique of the contemporary human rights law. Such a critique might have impact on legitimacy as well as on efficiency of the human rights instruments, and it cannot but be framed in particular settings of various Christian traditions and communities. Therefore, the goal of this chapter is to offer an analysis of one particular Christian context, namely that of the Russian Orthodox Church.[1] What are the theological resources for a constructive critique of human rights? Is it possible to ground such a critique in a development of Orthodox theology and its social potential?

The chapter begins (Section 15.1) with a presentation and a critique of the official position of the Russian Orthodox Church regarding human rights. The focus of the analysis is on those understandings of morality and of the relationship between morality and law that are important for the current discourse on

[1] The Russian Orthodox Church is one of many autocephalic (independent) churches of the Eastern Orthodox Church. Although unity is a proclaimed theological ideal, there are significant differences between various Orthodox traditions – on the level of doctrine as well as politically.

"traditional values" and human rights law. The Russian Orthodox Church defends an alternative to the liberal human rights paradigm, arguing that values such as traditional family and traditional sexual morality should be protected by human rights law. What is the logic of interpreting traditional values as a human rights issue? The official position of the Moscow Patriarchate as well as critical theological reflections by contemporary Russian theologians are discussed.

In Section 15.2, the current Orthodox skepticism toward the legitimacy of international human rights law is related to what some theologians and philosophers describe as a radical critique of law. It is demonstrated that although this critique is valuable, it often overlooks the fundamental social dimension of law – that is, social justice – and thus tends to legitimize patriarchal structures. Christian theology can and should develop critical approaches to the liberal understanding of human rights. However, if "traditional values" are reduced to a conservation of conventional norms of private morality, it is not a plausible alternative to the liberal human rights discourse.

In Section 15.3, an alternative position is outlined. This position – critical Orthodox theology – is informed by an Orthodox critique of the liberal discourse on human rights. However, critical theology seeks to overcome the current tendency to reduce theological ethics to issues of personal morality. The goal is to develop an eschatological Orthodox perspective on social justice that would be relevant for a constructive critique of international and domestic law. In the context of human rights law, this implies that Critical Orthodox theology recognizes global inequalities, but it does not use such inequalities and injustices as a legitimization of the uncritical acceptance of the dominant domestic discourse.

15.1 THE RUSSIAN ORTHODOX CHURCH AND UNIVERSAL HUMAN RIGHTS

In her monograph *The Russian Orthodox Church and Human Rights* (2014), Kristina Stoeckl offers a most clarifying analysis of the dynamics of the Russian Church's perspective on human rights. The Moscow Patriarchate had not regarded human rights as an issue of theological concern until 2000 when the department of foreign relations initiated a theological discussion about human rights. This work resulted in the 2008 document *The Russian Orthodox Church's Basic Teaching on Human Dignity, Freedom and Rights*.[2] According to Stoeckl,

[2] The Russian Orthodox Church, "The Russian Orthodox Church's Basic Teaching on Human Dignity, Freedom and Rights" (n.d.), https://mospat.ru/en/documents/dignity-freedom-rights/.

there are several internal, external, and explicitly political reasons that explain "why the Church decided to engage with the idea of human rights (instead of simply rejecting it as a Western, secular concept, or ignoring it as a matter that does not pertain to the world of the Church)."[3] Among the most important of these reasons is pressure from Russian civil society as well as from the European Court of Human Rights. If Stoeckl is right, and I believe that she is, the Russian Church's position has been, and still is, a reaction to legal, political, and moral discourses outside the Church. In this reactive mode, the Church defines its task as the defense of traditional morality, working against what it perceives as a "moral decline."[4] Therefore, the Russian Church engages in the discussion about human rights and international human rights law with the explicit agenda of defending morality.

Some radical Orthodox critics of human rights law reject the authority of the international legal regime, or parts of it. Roman Silantyev, the director of the Human Rights Center of the World Russian People's Council, states, for example, that the European Court of Human Rights is "biased and anti-Russian."[5] Others engage themselves in coalitions that attempt to influence international human rights bodies. One recent example of this engagement is Russia's leading role in the international coalition promoting the anti-liberal agenda of "traditional values" in the United Nations Human Rights Council (UNHRC).[6] As a result of these efforts, traditional values have been framed as an important dimension of human rights and human dignity in a number of UN resolutions. Official representatives of the Russian Church justify this particular strategy by claiming a right to interpret human rights in the light of traditions, and they engage in a dialogue with and a criticism of different human rights bodies.[7]

The Russian Orthodox Church opposes the individualism of human rights in their liberal interpretations and claims that human dignity should be protected by means of legislation and policies that secure the institutions of

3 Kristina Stoeckl, *The Russian Orthodox Church and Human Rights* (London: Routledge, 2014), 67.

4 Stoeckl, *Russian Orthodox Church*, 67.

5 Roman Silantyev, "Rossiya ni v chem ne obyazana oriyentirovat'sya na Yevropeyskiy sud po pravam cheloveka" [Russia Should Not Be Guided by the European Court of Human Rights], *Gosudarstvo, Religiia, Tserkov' v Rossii i za Rubezhom* [State, Religion and Church in Russia and Worldwide] 31, no. 2 (2013): 286–90, at 288.

6 Kristina Stoeckl and Kseniya Medvedeva, "Double Bind at the UN: Western Actors, Russia and the Traditionalist Agenda," *Global Constitutionalism* 7, no. 3 (2018): 383–421.

7 Stoeckl together with other researchers in the "Postsecular conflicts" project demonstrate convincingly that the Russian Church is now trying to claim a particular set of "traditional values" as *universal* human rights. See, e.g., Stoeckl and Medvedeva, "Double Bind at the UN."

the traditional family, traditional sexuality, and traditional religious morality. Human rights are not understood as a means to scrutinize different traditions in order to defend individual freedom. Instead, human rights are interpreted as an instrument to protect traditions that, according to the Church, guarantee dignified human life. This position, here in the context of the right to life, is explained as follows: "The Church, by virtue of her basic calling, suggests considering rights and freedoms in the perspective of their possible role in creating favorable external conditions for the improvement of personality on its way to salvation."[8]

How should these strategies and positions that explicitly aim at counteracting liberal human rights culture be evaluated? Are they just an expression of an unwillingness to take human rights seriously?

I believe that a sustainable human rights regime must acknowledge that all traditions – liberal, that is, cultures focusing on individual autonomy as the ultimate value, as well as non-liberal – are equally entitled to be subjects of human rights law. It is also plausible to bring different moral perspectives into the discussion. As I have argued elsewhere, to claim a liberal (or potentially any other) monopoly on human rights is wrong and counterproductive.[9] If human rights are expected to protect humans in different cultures and under different political conditions, it is crucial that they are interpreted, prioritized, and implemented in concrete contextual settings. I find the position of Jürgen Habermas and, more recently, of Rainer Forst reasonable. Generally, they highlight the importance of political constructivism in the field of human rights. Human rights become functional legal and institutional norms only when they are constructed through democratic[10] political processes.[11] To view human rights as primarily, or even exclusively, a *positive* law to be uniformly implemented in all countries is to put the very liberating potential of human rights at risk.

Therefore, I believe that an understanding of international human rights law as a set of guiding principles intended to become positive law in different political and contextual settings is more productive than an understanding of international human rights law as a set of positive legal norms. Does this mean

8 "The Russian Orthodox Church's Basic Teaching on Human Dignity, Freedom and Rights."

9 Elena Namli, *Human Rights as Ethics, Politics, and Law* (Uppsala: Acta Universitatis Upsaliensis, 2014), 35–62.

10 Democratic process is not limited to liberal democracy in this context.

11 Jürgen Habermas, "The Concept of Human Dignity and the Realistic Utopia of Human Rights," *Metaphilosophy* 41, no. 4 (2010): 464–80, at 464; Rainer Forst, *The Right to Justification: Elements of a Constructivist Theory of Justice*, trans. Jeffrey Flynn (New York: Columbia University Press, 2012), 218–21.

that contextualistic and traditionalist approaches put proponents of universal human rights in a position described by Stoeckl and Medvedeva as double bind:[12] either rejecting others' right to influence the content of human rights law or giving up on human rights as a project of human liberation? Is it impossible to be critical of tradition-related arguments and simultaneously defend the equality of subjectivity within the human rights field?

I do not think so. A recognition of the equal subjectivity of different traditions in human rights matters can and must be combined with instruments that counteract the risk of human rights losing their potential to be a tool for human liberation and the protection of human dignity. In the case of the Russian Orthodox Church, it is reasonable to claim that it has a right to question the individualism of the liberal human rights discourse. At the same time, a position on human rights that reduces them to "traditional values" in terms of personal morality, and/or aspires to be universally valid, is not acceptable. Let me elaborate further on this thesis.

Like many other religions, Orthodox traditions view the moral dimensions of human rights as crucial when human rights law is discussed, interpreted, and implemented. This in itself does not present a novel challenge to international human rights law. However, what is important is the fact that in a tradition such as the Orthodox Christian, morality is understood not just as the conventional regulations of relationships between human individuals and groups. It is also, and fundamentally, about the ontological relationship between humans and God. A human person's, or a community's, moral choices are therefore never exclusively about his or her (or its) independent vision of a good life; they always concern God and the whole of creation. This means that "traditional values" are understood by the Church in a theocentric perspective; they secure the proper relationship between humans and God. Neither the well-being nor the freedom of humans is the ultimate criterion of theocentric morality.

The nonanthropocentric character of this position is both an advantage and a serious challenge. On the one hand, Orthodox theocentrism may contribute to the environmental movement and its politics. As stated in the Church's document on human rights: "The recognition of human rights does not mean that people can squander natural resources in favour of their egoistic interests. Human dignity is inseparable from the calling of the human beings to take care of God's world (cf. Gen. 2:15), to be moderate in meeting their needs, to preserve the richness, variety and beauty of nature."[13] Additionally, Christian

12 Stoeckl and Medvedeva, "Double Bind at the UN," 387.

13 "The Russian Orthodox Church's Basic Teaching on Human Dignity, Freedom and Rights," III: 5.

theocentrism has the resources to question the utilitarian ethic that, in many cases, is in conflict with the deontological ethic of justice and rights. On the other hand, there is an obvious risk that human rights in a theocentric perspective can be transformed into a discourse that, in practice, legitimizes violations of the human dignity of persons. In my view, this happens when the ontological dimension of morality as the relationship between humans and God becomes a moralism, that is, a rigid scheme for personal (or even private) morality and conventional behavior, thus suppressing any possibility of vital and critical social ethics.

Let us recall the "Pussy Riot" case and the position of the Russian Orthodox Church on the matter. A sufficient part of the discussion in Russia was devoted to the issue of the personal morality and character of the members of Pussy Riot, and only a few voices acknowledged the social and political dimension of the case.

On February 21, 2012, in the middle of the presidential election campaign, the group Pussy Riot performed a feminist "punk prayer" in the Cathedral of Christ the Savior in Moscow. According to the members of the group, their aim was to protest against what they experienced as the support that the Moscow Patriarchate gave President Putin during the election campaign. In Pussy Riot's blog post on March 4, they claimed that the performance was a prayer to Maria "to banish Putin" (*Bogoroditca, Putina progoni*).[14] On August 17, 2012, the three members of the group were convicted of "hooliganism motivated by religious hatred."

As is well known, Justice Marina Syrova rejected the claim of the members of the group that their performance had political character and was a critique of the leadership of the Church. In the court's final verdict, it was found that Pussy Riot's performance was a case of hooliganism motivated by "hatred against religion." Interestingly, the transparently feminist position of the group members was described by the justice in apolitical terms: "Although feminism is not a religious doctrine, its proponents invade such social domains as morals, norms of decency, family relations, and sexuality, non-traditional sexuality included . . . ."[15] The court accepted the interpretation of the Russian Church in its view of the performance as an aggressive offense against Orthodox believers rather than a radical critique of the leadership of

14 Dmitry Uzlaner, "Delo 'Pussi raiot' i osobennosti rossiiskogo postsekuliarizma" [The Pussy Riot Case and the Peculiarities of Russian Post-Secularism], *Gosudarstvo, Religiia, Tserkov' v Rossii i za Rubezhom* [State, Religion and Church in Russia and Worldwide] 31, no. 2 (2013): 93–133, at 93.

15 Quoted from Case 1–170/12 (informally known as the Pussy Riot Case), decided in the Khamovnichesky Court, Moscow. My translation.

the Church. This official position was articulated by Vsevolod Chaplin, head of the department of Church-society relations at the Moscow Patriarchate at the time, who called the performance "a case of blasphemy."[16]

It is beyond the scope of this chapter to offer an analysis of the complex character of the Pussy Riot case.[17] The performance was obviously provocative and offensive. However, what is of interest here is the fact that the official position of the Russian Church ignored the very existence of a critical and political dimension of the performance. Instead, the representatives of the Church depicted the members of the group as simple violators of traditional morality. Their feminism was described, and still is described, as a negative part of personal character rather than an ideological position. In such a framing, there was no need of balancing freedom of religion on one side and freedom of expression on the other.

Internal as well as external critics of the official position of the Church highlighted that the representation of feminist women as violent persons could be and actually was used as a legitimization of different forms of violence on behalf of the proponents of freedom of religion.[18] Many Orthodox critics of the official line of the Church in the Pussy Riot case were concerned about the lack of humanity and mercy. In his analysis of the case, Dmitry Uzlaner cites the Orthodox priest Igor Gagarin who openly encouraged Christians to recall the commandment to love one's enemies (Matt. 5:40) instead of becoming a part of the violent discourse of condemnation and revenge.[19] However, the logic of forgiveness and mercy of "enemies" does not allow Orthodox participants in the controversy to transcend the very confrontational framing of the discussion. Overcoming the nonproductive mode of discourse would require focusing on the social and political messages of the parties rather than on responses to "the enemy."

Different in most regards, Pussy Riot and the Church had the same kind of vision of moral society: a vision focusing on persons and personal characters, rather than on competing understandings of justice and just social relations. While Pussy Riot presented President Putin and Patriarch Kirill as enemies to get rid of, the leadership of the Church depicted the young women in Pussy Riot as simply unstable and violent individuals that should be punished.

16 Quoted from Uzlaner, "Delo 'Pussi raiot' i osobennosti rossiiskogo postsekuliarizma," 100.

17 I also leave aside the ECHR decision on the case. See ECHR 261 (2018).

18 Unfortunately, violence has become a significant part of the discourse on Pussy Riot. Both opponents and supporters of the group use different forms of violence. The group itself does accept symbolic violence as a crucial tool for political critique.

19 Uzlaner, "The Pussy Riot Case and the Peculiarities of Russian Postsecularism," 106–7.

In my view, the Pussy Riot case is significant as a symptom of a situation in which many actors, albeit for different reasons, reduce morality to personal morality. When the Russian Church involves itself in human rights issues and when it brings into the discussion the moral dimensions of human rights, it tends to reduce Christian morality to traditional moral conventions on a personal, or even private, level. Human rights are interpreted as a matter of personal behavior rather than a matter of the quality of social relations. The Pussy Riot case is just one example of the general logic of "traditional values" as conventions of personal morality. Although personal morality might be regulated by law, such regulation is never the main concern of human rights. Therefore, every plausible claim on agency within human rights law demands a transparent articulation of its perspective on social ethics.

15.2 RUSSIAN ORTHODOX THEOLOGY, LAW, AND THE LACK OF SOCIAL ETHICS

In the Russian case, I argue, there is a deficit of theological reflection on social morality – of theological social ethics – that makes it difficult to use "traditional values" as an instrument for critique of injustice. This deficit is relatively easy to explain by means of political and historical analysis. The Church that for centuries accepted, or was forced to accept, the role of ideological supporter of state power has very little experience of critical theological reflection. To be more precise, there have been some cases of critique of abuse of power by individual tsars and members of the aristocracy, but almost no critique of unjust political structures.[20] Even today, the Church remains in a symbolic symbiosis with state power. In the document entitled "Basis of the Social Concept of the Russian Orthodox Church," the ideological position of the Church becomes clear when patriotism is presented as an important Christian virtue:

> The patriotism of the Orthodox Christian should be active. It is manifested when he defends his fatherland against an enemy, works for the good of the motherland, cares for the good order of people's life through, among other things, participation in the affairs of government. The Christian is called to preserve and develop national culture and people's self-awareness.[21]

[20] Antonov Konstantin, "Politicheskoe izmerenie russkoy religioznoy filosofii" [The Political Dimension of Russian Religious Philosophy], *Gosudarstvo, Religiia, Tserkov' v Rossii i za Rubezhom* [State, Religion and Church in Russia and Worldwide] 32, no. 3 (2014): 265–94, at 268.

[21] The Russian Orthodox Church, "The Basis of the Social Concept," II:3 (n.d.), https://mospat.ru/en/documents/social-concepts/.

However, there are voices within the Church that expect or even demand a change. One proposal, in the context of this chapter the most important, is to build up the institution of academic theology, that is, to create theological departments at universities in order to promote free and critical theological work.[22] An important task of such a theology would be to explore the theological resources for Orthodox *social* ethics.

What, then, are the theological elements of Orthodox theology that currently constrain a development of critical theological reflection in general and on human rights law and morality in particular? What resources that might promote a socially relevant critique are there? Let me introduce some preliminary reflections.[23]

In my understanding, the main weakness of Russian Orthodox theology in its current form is a deficit of methodological reflection on the Tradition. The Orthodox Tradition (*Predanie*) is viewed as the main source of Orthodox theology and the most important element of Orthodox theological identity: "The principle of the Tradition is a work of memory, a trust into the path of those before us and, simultaneously, a development of this path. However, the development is not understood here as a movement onto a higher stage, but rather as a return to the very source."[24] What does this mean? How do we determine whether a concrete theological view or a position of the Church is in accordance with the Tradition? Metropolitan Hilarion (Alfeyev) states that, in practice, an Orthodox theologian should look for *consensus patrum*, although this agreement between the Church Fathers must be an agreement on fundamental issues – or even basic principles – rather than on contextual particularities.[25]

However, it is unclear how to find out what these fundamental issues and principles are. The risk is obvious that it is precisely those issues on which the

22 See, e.g., Alexander Kyrlezhev, Andrey Shishkov, and Vladimir Shmaliy, "Dialog religii i nauki: novye podhody (itogi diskussii)" [The Dialogue of Religion and Science: New Approaches (An Overview)], *Gosudarstvo, Religiia, Tserkov' v Rossii i za Rubezhom* [State, Religion and Church in Russia and Worldwide] 33, no. 1 (2015): 164–83, at 178–9.

23 See also Elena Namli, "Orthodox Theology, Politics, and Power," in *Political Theologies in Orthodox Christianity: Common Challenges, Divergent Positions*, ed. Kristina Stoeckl, Gabriel Ingeborg, and Aristotle Papanikolaou (London: Bloomsbury T&T Clark, 2017).

24 Vladimir Zelinsky, "Predaniye, pamyat' i sokrytoye 'Ya'" [Tradition, Memory and the Hidden "I"], in *Materialy mezhdunarodnoi bogoslovskoi konferentsii "Zhivoye Predaniye"* [Materials of the International Theological Conference "Living Tradition"], ed. Yevgeni Krest'yaninov and Sergei Minov (Moscow: Svyato-Filaretovskaya moskovskaya vysshaya pravoslavno-khristianskaya shkola, 1999), 14. My translation.

25 Metropolitan Hilarion (Alfeyev), *Tainstvo very: vvedeniye v pravoslavnoye dogmaticheskoye bogosloviye* [Sacrament of Faith: Introduction to Orthodox Dogmatic Theology] (Moscow: Izdatel'stvo bratstva svyatitelya Tikhona, 1996), 9–10.

Church Fathers happen to agree that are understood as the most important elements of the Tradition. Obviously, many such agreements were of a conventional nature – such as, for example, the traditional model of legitimate sexuality – and they merely reflected the patriarchal structures of ancient societies. Similar to sources of other historical traditions, Orthodox patristics lacks the experience of a public political space and, therefore, of a transparent social ethics. Some Orthodox critics of the Russian focus on the patristics as the source of theology claim that a monolithic understanding of the "return to the Fathers" prevents "Orthodoxy from developing a progressive or radical political theology."[26] I agree with this critique; Orthodox theology does need a transparent method for selection between particular traditional conventions and the Tradition. In our case, there is an obvious need for distinguishing the core social ethics of the Orthodox Tradition beyond the *consensus patrum*.

What, then, are the candidates for interpretative methods for theological inquiry in social morality? Natural law theory with its rationalism is one such candidate used in other Christian traditions, even inspiring some current Muslim reflection on the relationship between the moral basis of Islam and human rights law.[27]

Officially, natural law is not rejected in Orthodox ethics and therefore, at least in theory, it could be a tool for dealing with the heritage of the Church. In his textbook on *Orthodox Moral Theology*, archimandrite Platon introduces natural law as a part of Orthodox ethics: "[T]he patristic tradition views natural law as the universal foundation of moral life of humans and societies."[28] He defines natural law as a universal law of reason that reflects the natural order of creation, that is, the law given by God.[29] However, in his presentation of natural law, Platon plays down its rationalism and mostly reduces the content of natural law to the Ten Commandments. Platon goes as far as claiming that Christians have no need for natural law because they already have "a completely perfect morality of the gospel."[30]

On the one hand, Platon does recognize the authority of natural law. On the other hand, he states that in practice it is not needed. In my view, this self-

[26] Pantelis Kalaizidis, "Towards an Orthodox Political Theology: The Churches' Theological Foundations and Public Role in the Context of the Greek Economic Crisis," in *Political Theologies in Orthodox Christianity: Common Challenges, Divergent Positions*, ed. Kristina Stoeckl, Gabriel Ingeborg, and Aristotle Papanikolaou (London: Bloomsbury T&T Clark, 2017), 155.

[27] See Anver M. Emon, *Islamic Natural Law Theories* (New York: Oxford University Press, 2010).

[28] Archimandrite Platon (Igumnov), *Pravoslavnoye nravstvennoye bogosloviye* (Sergiyev Posad: Izdaniye Svyato-Troitse-Sergiyevoy Lavry, 1994), 37.

[29] Platon, *Pravoslavnoye nravstvennoye bogosloviye*, 34.

[30] Platon, *Pravoslavnoye nravstvennoye bogosloviye*, 43.

contradiction in Platon's writings is just one expression of the systematic skepticism toward the rationalism of the natural law in the Russian context. Reason as a universal instrument of moral inquiry is mentioned and then immediately put under suspicion. What remains of natural law is a rigid ontological idea about the given universal order of creation.

As several Catholic theologians have convincingly demonstrated, critical reason is crucial when natural law is used as an instrument for dealing with moral and legal norms.[31] The belief that there is an order in the creation can easily become an instrument with which to declare that some particular conventions of a culture represent such an order. Critical reasoning is, therefore, central in order to minimize the risk of elevating power-sensitive contextual norms and structures to the level of God's given law.

It is not beyond any doubt that the rationalism of natural law can efficiently counteract sufficiently conservative elements of the natural law tradition. However, in Russia the theological skepticism against the rationalism of natural law is very often a reaction against any rationalism. Interestingly, there seems to be a connection between the skepticism against rationalism of natural law on the one hand and the skepticism against law on the other. Recall the famous sentence from *The Brothers Karamazov* that Fyodor Dostoevsky puts into the mouth of the Grand Inquisitor:

> Instead of the firm ancient law, man had henceforth to decide for himself, with a free hart, what is good and what is evil, having only your image before him as a guide – but did it not occur to you that he would eventually reject and dispute even your image and your truth if he was oppressed by so terrible a burden as freedom of choice?[32]

Dostoevsky's critique of the law as an opposition to genuine freedom is radical and it has strong philosophical potential. Many theologians and philosophers in various traditions have been inspired by this critique. However, I claim that this radical critique of law is easily transformed into an instrument of power and domination when law is contrasted with freedom on an entirely personal level. In the case of Dostoevsky himself, the critique of law is always articulated from a position of individuals: those who either realize the existence of a higher, transrational truth (Sonya, Raskolnikov, Dmitry Karamazov) or reject it, just playing legal games of "justice." The trial in *The Brothers Karamazov* is most interesting in this regard. The defense attorney, a liberal lawyer from Petersburg,

31 Jean Porter, *Ministers of the Law: A Natural-Law Theory of Legal Authority* (Grand Rapids, MI: Eerdmans, 2010), 74–6.

32 Fyodor Dostoyevsky, *The Brothers Karamazov*, trans. Richard Pevear and Larissa Volokhonsky (New York: Vintage, 1990), 255.

is depicted as both talented and attractive but alienated from the people. Dostoevsky builds up a sharp contrast between this liberal attorney and "the ladies" who admire him on the one hand, and Orthodox peasants in the jury on the other. When the attorney was about to finish his speech, "the orator was interrupted by unrestrained, almost frenzied applause. Of course, the whole room did not applaud, but still about half of the room applauded. ... From above, where the ladies were sitting, shrieks and cries could be heard. Handkerchiefs were waved."[33] The jury, on the contrary, was not impressed by the logic of the attorney and found Dmitry guilty. Someone in the audience commented on the verdict: "[O]ur peasants stood up for themselves."[34]

The reader of this episode in the novel already knows that Dmitry is not guilty of the murder. Why, then, is the wrong decision of the court related to a higher truth, while the attorney's argumentation is mocked? In my interpretation, the ambivalence of Dostoevsky's critique of law appears here. To begin with, the ideal of radical personal responsibility, which inspired a lot of philosophical and theological critique of rationalism, is constructed by Dostoevsky as a contrast to the law. Dmitry, who did not kill his father, came to realize his moral responsibility for the crime as well as for his other selfish deeds. Very much echoing Raskolnikov in *Crime and Punishment* (who indeed was guilty of two murders), Dmitry looked forward to a kind of purifying suffering in Siberia. An even more radical perspective appears in the characters of Alyosha and Zosima, who defend the idea that each of us is *personally* responsible for all.

Simultaneously, Dostoevsky turns a personal and anti-rationalistic perspective of radical responsibility into the most important dimension of the critique of law. He firmly rejects any possibility of social and legal justice that can be harmonized with this critique. In the later writings of Dostoevsky, there are no positive images of rational social engagement – on behalf of neither state employers nor revolutionaries. Radical responsibility on a personal level is therefore associated with a nihilistic approach toward social and legal justice.

Orthodox philosopher Boris Vysheslavtsev (1877–1954) gave a pregnant theoretical framing of Dostoevsky's rejection of the rationalism of law. Vysheslavtsev argues that the law is transcended by Christian eschatology, that is, the promise of God's kingdom. He therefore rejects the possibility of liberating law because any law necessarily demands a submission to power.[35] In Vysheslavtsev, as in Dostoevsky, there is an obvious dimension of antisemitism. Both view

33 Dostoyevsky, *Brothers Karamazov*, 746.

34 Dostoyevsky, *Brothers Karamazov*, 753.

35 Boris Vysheslavtsev, *Etika preobrazhennogo Erosa* (Moscow: Biblioteka eticheskoy mysli, 1994), 20–1. My translation.

Christianity as the genuine religion of freedom in contrast to Judaism as a religion of law. Both are convinced that only Christianity brings about universal moral truth and universal freedom, while the law is always contextual and particular. They cannot think of law and freedom beyond this Christian narrative of freedom *from* the law.

Antisemitism is still a challenge in Russian theology. However, an equally important challenge is to find ways to approach social dimensions of law – instead of reducing the analysis of law to its phenomenology. The latter seeks to understand the law by means of a philosophical analysis of human experience of the law. In most cases, phenomenological investigation reduces law to some general features of personal experience leaving aside social and structural dimensions of legal justice. Such a reduction is salient in Vysheslavtsev, who consequently depicts the law on the phenomenological level of personal experience. Vysheslavtsev believes that he is following Paul when he claims: "Law as an imperative regulating external deeds, as a commandment directed to bodily human is contrasted with a free transformation of the heart that . . . is a result of faith – that is the direct intuition of God and God's grace."[36] Such a phenomenology of law, although valuable in many regards, reduces the critique of law to an analysis of the personal experiences of positive regulations and, therefore, has little to contribute to further developments of human rights. Human rights law regulates, or should regulate, the exercise of power and social structures. A relevant critique of this law must include a clearly articulated perspective on social justice. Moreover, a reduction to personal phenomenology can counteract the developments of human rights by transforming social issues into issues of personal morality. Fundamental injustices are not matters of personal behavior; they are structural and demand an institutional approach. Even the most radical elements of Christian tradition, such as eschatology, become socially harmless when reduced to matters of exclusively personal morality and personal faith.

The abovementioned combination of radical skepticism toward the rationalism of natural law and the tendency to discuss law and morality in a personal, rather than social, perspective are serious obstacles to a progressive development of social ethics in the Orthodox Tradition. Such ethics, in turn, are needed if the Church wants to constructively influence the human rights discourse. Should the Russian Orthodox Church, then, refrain from human rights discussions and, generally, leave politics and focus instead on matters of liturgy and personal salvation? I believe that such a retreat is an option, but not a good one. In what follows, I will argue that there are potent recourses for social ethics and

[36] Vysheslavtsev, *Etika preobrazhennogo Erosa*, 25.

constructive critiques of human rights law within the Russian Orthodox tradition.

15.3 RECOURSES FOR SOCIAL ETHICS WITHIN RUSSIAN THEOLOGY

There is an emerging discussion on the social impact of Orthodox theology in Russia. I have already mentioned the Moscow-based *State, Religion, and Church*, one of the most important platforms of the discussion. In 2013, the second issue of the journal was devoted to the theme of "religion in courts," and the contributors offered different critical perspectives on the relationship among law, religion, and theology.[37] The editorial board is generally very active and relates challenges in Russia to international scholarship on religion and society.

Russian theologians such as Alexander Kyrlezhev, Andrey Shishkov, and Vladimir Shmaliy work intensively to promote a transparent public and academic dialogue. Theories of communicative ethics and deliberative democracy are used and are even becoming common elements in the discourse on the social positioning of the Church. Both liberal and conservative theologians use the concept of public reason.

Yet another, related development is the struggle to strengthen local Orthodox communities. These communities are often critical of the Moscow Patriarchate, which cares very little about their everyday life and opinions. Moral conservatism is strong even on the ground, but the social framing of the discussion is changing: new voices are included, not least as the consequence of many university programs offering theological education for both men and women. Women cannot be ordained as priests in the Russian Orthodox Church, which makes the field of academic theology even more attractive for Orthodox women looking for a platform for agency.

Most importantly, there are voices claiming that the Church must develop a theologically coherent and relevant position toward politics and society. In one of his publications, theologian Shishkov argues that in Russia there is an obvious and urgent need for "a constructive program for a theological reflection on the contemporary world."[38] Such a program demands, according to Shishkov, a new approach to

37 *Gosudarstvo, Religiia, Tserkov' v Rossii i za Rubezhom* 31, no. 2 (2013).

38 A. V. Shishkov, "Dva ponimaniya traditsii v russkom pravoslavnom bogoslovii" [Two Understandings of Tradition in Russian Orthodox Theology], *Vestnik russkoy khristianskoy gumanitarnoy akademii* [Review of the Russian Christian Academy for the Humanities] 18, no. 3 (2017): 22–9, at 27.

the Tradition. Similar to the abovementioned Greek theologian Pantelis Kalaizidis, Shishkov believes that the dominant interpretative paradigm, with its focus on *consensus patrum*, in fact prevents any socially relevant theological work. In his view, the theology of "traditional values" (that is, the main strategy of the Church in response to human rights law) is empty of *theological* substance. What Shishkov means here is that the preservation of "traditional values" in practice is about the preservation of social conventions (moral as well as liturgical) that in most cases are not related to any theological elements of the Christian faith.[39]

According to Shishkov, a liberal approach to the Tradition is much more promising in that it encourages individual theologians and the Church to address relevant social challenges by means of theological components of the Tradition, rather than focusing on nontheological conventions on private morality and particular liturgical practices. "Liberal" does not indicate any particular ideological position here. Instead, it signifies a broad normative position of free theological critique of the Tradition. This "liberal approach" is defined by Shishkov in the following words (emphasis in the original, my translation): "A liberal approach presupposes *free* critical reinterpretation of the Church Tradition: first, a distinguishing and an articulation of the core meaning of the Christian faith; secondly, a purification of this meaning from shadow elements; thirdly, a return to the genuine fundaments of the faith through their actuality in the current situation."[40] What are then these "genuine fundaments" that are expected to actualize the challenges of the current situation? This question is not easy to answer. It is hard to believe that any contemporary religious tradition can offer unanimous answers. Moreover, posing this question already presupposes a theological climate that tolerates, or even embraces, a plurality of theological positions. My hope is that this climate, emerging in some parts of the Russian Orthodoxy, will prevail and enable theological creativity for the sake of both the Church and the society.

Let me elaborate on one candidate for socially relevant theological elements of Christian faith acknowledged by several Russian theologians. In my view, it can function as an efficient tool for the critique and development of human rights law.

Many theologians argue that eschatology is the most crucial dimension of Christian faith. When it is not reduced to a private expectation of life after death, it offers a powerful tool for the social critique of different forms of

39 Shishkov, "Dva ponimaniya traditsii v russkom pravoslavnom bogoslovii," 28.
40 Shishkov, "Dva ponimaniya traditsii v russkom pravoslavnom bogoslovii," 24.

injustice. Eschatology radicalizes social ethics in Christian and other religious traditions. From Thomas Müntzer to current forms of political theology within Christianity, Judaism, and Islam, eschatological perspectives – visions of God's kingdom and the promise of justice – offer a horizon for the critique of power as well as for hope for the oppressed; that is, a horizon of justice.

On a local Moscow parish website, one can find the archive of the émigré journal *Novy Grad*.[41] Contributors to the journal included Orthodox theologians such as Nikolai Berdyaev and Mother Maria Scobtsova. The electronic archive seems to be an attempt to make the political theology of these Orthodox thinkers and activists accessible for the public audience. It is of importance that Mother Maria, who was killed by Nazis, is canonized by the Constantinople Patriarchate. The canonization makes her heritage a recognized part of the Tradition.

The title *Novy Grad* (New City) is an allusion to Augustine, and the editors had the explicit ambition of making Christian eschatology politically relevant at a time when Europe had failed to mobilize against growing fascism and Nazism (the fourteen issues of the journal were published between 1931 and 1939). In the thirteenth issue of the journal, the reader finds an article by Georgy Fedotov entitled "Eschatology and Culture." The author of the article aims to articulate what he defines as an eschatological tension of the Russian Orthodox tradition. Fedotov highlights that this tension has different variations within the tradition, and he defends a political theology that utilizes eschatology for the purpose of political liberation. He writes about the position of the journal:

> It wants to contribute to the creation of a new city here on Earth, a new society that should come instead of the dying capitalism. Our city is not the one anticipated in the Apocalypses. Those who refuse to take part in the work of development and construction of the earthly city with the excuse of awaiting the New City in Heaven are not with us, they are not with *Novy Grad*.[42]

In my reading of the article, the eschatology of *Novy Grad* is neither about personal salvation nor about awaiting the mystical end of history. Rather, it is a horizon for social acts that are both radical and conscious of their

[41] I would like to thank Andrey Shishkov for bringing my attention to this resource and to the article by Fedotov. See "Novy Grad Electronic Archive," Orthodox Digital Library of Odintsovo Deanery of the Moscow Diocese of the Russian Orthodox Church, www.odinblago.ru/noviy_grad/.

[42] Georgy Petrovich Fedotov, "Eskhatologiya i kul'tura" [Eschatology and Culture], *Novy Grad* [New City] 13 (1938): 45–56, at 46. www.odinblago.ru/noviy_grad/13/3. My translation.

incompleteness. Inspired by the promise of God's Kingdom, the contributors to the journal were fighting against Nazism and stayed critical of the Soviet totalitarianism: "[E]schatology defines a particular spiritual mode: the understanding of relativity, vulnerability, finiteness of every human dead and, [simultaneously,] the longing for absolute perfection, never saturated by human culture."[43] This kind of prophetic eschatology that, in the name of God's Kingdom, both condemns injustices and inspires political action for and within the society is a potent instrument for constructive social critique and political agency. It is also relevant when the task is to evaluate positive law, including human rights law. Instead of focusing on traditional conventions of private morality, the eschatological critique of law focuses on injustices and violations of human dignity in order to reclaim a Christian dimension of the human rights project. Critiques of liberalism become more concrete and nuanced when they are conducted for the sake of more, not less, freedom and justice.

A prophetic, eschatological position – is it too radical for the Russian Church, which has served political power for centuries? Many theologians and sociologists would say so, and they would never mention theologians such as Berdyaev or Scobtsova when discussing the Orthodox tradition. However, any attempt to marginalize eschatology would, in fact, contradict the Russian Orthodox tradition. The Russian tradition (as well as most interpretations of the Tradition) is focused on the liturgy, which, in turn, demands a clear eschatological perspective. As Alexander Shmeman puts it when he describes a relationship between theology and liturgical images of God's kingdom, "the main liturgical aim is to bring eschatology back into theology."[44] The theological challenge in the Russian context is, therefore, not reclaiming eschatology as such but finding the courage to articulate the social consequences of Christian eschatology.

This challenge is not unique to the Russian context. As already mentioned, eschatology as a tool for social critique radicalizes the scrutiny of contextual injustices and, therefore, is put under suspicion by political and discursive power. In Lutheran theology, eschatology and Christology are played down by the idea of two kingdoms; in Roman Catholicism, the official doctrine of natural law tends to make the eschatological perspective harmless.

How, then, can eschatology be used for a constructive critique of human rights? Is it not a transcendent perspective that is difficult to apply to positive

43 Fedotov, "Eskhatologiya i kul'tura," 51.

44 Alexander Shmeman, *Sobraniye statey* 1947–1983 [Collection of Articles 1947–1983] (Moscow: Russkiy put', 2009), 230.

law and institutional justice? I believe that a plausible eschatological critique of human rights law should be framed as an analysis of concrete forms of injustice – powerlessness, domination, nonrecognition – that, for different reasons, are not addressed by the liberal framing of human rights law. As already stated, I believe that it is justified for a religious actor to question the limitations of the liberal interpretation of human rights, and eschatology might help the development of such a critique. The individualism of the liberal paradigm of human rights is insensitive to several forms of injustice and oppression that can be unveiled by more radical visions of human dignity and freedom.

For the time being, the Russian Church mostly follows the old imperialist tactics of the West by trying to use the power of alliances in order to get a monopoly on the interpretation of human rights: conservative instead of liberal. This is highly problematic because it risks identifying positive human rights law, which is always imperfect and power sensitive, with the very ideal of human rights and justice. As early as 1934, Reinhold Niebuhr highlighted such a risk and argued that precisely eschatology should counteract it.[45]

Further, the Russian Church promotes an understanding of human rights that prioritizes the dimension of rights as a matter of the state's power and obligations. The Church demonstrates strong solidarity with the Russian state in both international and domestic issues. An eschatological perspective questions this position and reclaims the centrality of principles of justice for implementations and developments of human rights. In this view, Pussy Riot's claim to free speech should be recognized and transparently balanced with other rights. Although in an unfortunately aggressive way, the group did try to put an eschatological perspective on the Russian situation by evoking Maria as a sovereign. As already stated, the young women, like the representatives of the Church, reduced the critique to the level of individual abuse of power.

15.4 TOWARD A CRITICAL THEOLOGY OF LAW

Let me summarize my preliminary suggestion for a potent Orthodox theology of relevance for human rights law. Such a theology is critical theology based on a clearly articulated eschatological position. An eschatologically informed position focuses on human rights as the justified demand for every person to be respected as *equally dignified.* Such an egalitarian position can be used for critiquing liberal

[45] Reinhold Niebuhr, *An Interpretation of Christian Ethics* (San Francisco: Harper & Row, 1935), 9.

understandings of human rights without becoming an instrument for the legitimization of nationalism, racism, or other forms of anti-humanism, religious or secular. The main objective of an eschatological theology of human rights is a critique of human rights when they are corrupted by social structures of domination. However, it recognizes that any alternative solution is also an approximation that is open to abuse of power and corruption.

In order for an Orthodox critical theology of human rights to develop, there is a need for social ethics and a theological discussion on social justice. Human rights – as morals, politics, and law – are not about individual morality. They should regulate social relations, and, when these relations are unjust, inspire either the democratic development of the law or social revolution. This means that a potent eschatological perspective on human rights law is fundamentally mediated by social ethics. Only then would a radical critique of human rights law not lead to irrational rejections of the law as such.

A transparent social ethics in Orthodox theology is needed for the Russian critique of liberal understandings of human rights to become more nuanced and just. Currently, the risk is obvious that an aggressive rejection of liberal positions on human rights contributes to populism and nationalism rather than to a Christian personalism in its humanistic forms. This has to do with the focus on the identity of a position, the Orthodox in our case, rather than on its content. A critical theology does recognize the freedom to define one's own identity for both individuals and cultures. However, this right aims to counteract domination and nonrecognition, not to conserve traditional conventions in the name of cultural identity.

The current official position of the Russian Church on human rights is far from such a critical theology. Instead of looking for a nuanced critique of liberalism for the sake of a more radical vision of human rights and justice, the Church focuses on the defense of a number of particular conventions of patriarchal nature. Do we have reason to believe that the Russian Orthodox Church will develop a more plausible approach to human rights law? I think that we do. However, such developments are time- and energy-consuming. For many proponents of human rights who are, rightly, worried about the impact that the defense of "traditional values" has on human rights law, it is tempting to dismiss the whole project and to look for instruments to stop all non-liberal initiatives on human rights. This temptation should be questioned in principle as well as for pragmatic reasons. As a matter of principle, defending human rights by rejecting the other's right to be an equal subject of international law is a self-contradiction. Pragmatically, progressive developments of a tradition must relate to it, not suppress its very existence. As many defeated liberationist projects all over the world have demonstrated, aggressive attempt to liberate the other from their traditions results in rejection of foreign "enlightenment," and legitimizes the most rigid fundamentalism.[46] This means that proponents of international human rights law must engage themselves in dialogues on theological issues; it is a demanding but genuine strategy for the further development of human rights law.

RECOMMENDED READING

Callewaert, Teresa. *Theologies Speak of Justice: A Study of Islamic and Christian Social Ethics*. Uppsala: Acta Universitatis Upsaliensis, 2017.

Kalaitzidis, Pantelis. *Orthodoxy and Political Theology*. Geneva: World Council of Churches, 2012.

Namli, Elena. *Human Rights as Ethics, Politics, and Law*. Uppsala: Acta Universitatis Upsaliensis, 2014.

Stoeckl, Kristina. *The Russian Orthodox Church and Human Rights*. London: Routledge, 2014.

Stoeckl, Kristina, Gabriel Ingeborg, and Aristotle Papanikolaou, eds. *Political Theologies in Orthodox Christianity: Common Challenges, Divergent Positions*. London: Bloomsbury T&T Clark, 2017.

[46] I find the position of Michael Walzer, who argues that the main paradox of liberation projects is related to the liberators' inability to engage with the religious traditions of those they are trying to liberate, most reasonable. In this particular context Walzer is engaged in a discussion on national liberation, but I believe his reasoning is applicable to international agency as well: Michael Walzer, *The Paradox of Liberation: Secular Revolutions and Religious Counterrevolutions* (New Haven: Yale University Press, 2015), 125. See also Teresa Callewaert's pioneering work on comparative political ethics within Christianity and Islam: Teresa Callewaert, "Theologies Speak of Justice: A Study of Islamic and Christian Social Ethics" (PhD dissertation, Uppsala University, 2017).

16

Conquest, Sacred Sites, and "Religion" in a Time of Crisis

Nathaniel Berman

But if you say to me, "We trust in the Lord our God," is it not He whose high places and whose altars Hezekiah has taken away, and said to Judah and Jerusalem, "You shall worship only before this altar in Jerusalem?"

– Rabshakeh, Assyrian emissary, 2 KINGS 18:22

[During the Crusades], the Christian world received a second time the response given to the disciples when they sought the body of the Lord [at the Holy Sepulchre]: "Why seek ye the living among the dead? He is not here, but is risen." *You must not look for the principle of your religion in the Sensuous, in the grave among the dead, but in the living Spirit in yourselves. .... Christendom found the empty Sepulchre, but not the union of the Worldly and the Eternal – and so it lost the Holy Land.*

– G. W. F. Hegel, LECTURES ON THE PHILOSOPHY OF HISTORY (1822–30)

16.1 A TIME OF CRISIS

After a generation of academic critique and legal and political transformation, the field of law-and-religion stands in the midst of a crisis. Theorists in disciplines ranging from religious studies and anthropology to international relations and law have problematized the category of "religion" from a variety of perspectives. To be sure, these theorists have rarely, if ever, sought to do away with the category, either as an empirical descriptor or as a tool of analysis. Rather, they have shown its historically contingent, politically constructed, and perennially contested nature.

Post-colonial theorists, for example, have argued for the Eurocentric genealogy of "religion" and its global diffusion through colonialism and its aftermath. Legal critics have undermined the perennial protestations of theological agnosticism by courts in the West; in the United States, such criticism has revealed an implicit strand of "low-church" Protestant presuppositions.[1] Transposing the basic lessons of Legal Realism to law-and-religion, other critics have shown the ways courts *construct* "religion," as well as particular religions, while purporting merely to *apply* legal rules to them. J. Z. Smith, Talal Asad, Saba Mahmood, Ashis Nandy, Dipesh Chakrabarty, and Winnifred Sullivan are only some of the more well-known of the scholars who have engaged in this critical work spanning several disciplines.

Meanwhile, political pressures around the world on religion/state separation have grown in ways too numerous to rehearse fully here. In the United States, a number of high-profile cases have exerted such pressures, perhaps most famously *Hobby Lobby* v. *Burwell*[2] and *Town of Greece* v. *Galloway*.[3] Elsewhere, these pressures are leading to what may equally be described as the nationalization of religion or the sacralization of the nation, in places as disparate as Israel and India.

It has become urgent to take stock of the cumulative effect of a generation of such developments: in particular, of the light they shed on the conceptual bedrock of law-and-religion. In this chapter, I suggest that conflicts over "sacred sites" provide a crucial vantage-point from which to undertake this stocktaking. Such conflicts have gained renewed prominence over the past generation in divergent settings, from Medicine Bluffs, Oklahoma, to Ayodhya, India, to that eternal cauldron, Jerusalem. I propose that one genealogy of law-and-religion lies in the circumstances attending the birth of modern legal ideas about such sites: the geographical and temporal ruptures wrought by the aftermath of conquest.

Such a genealogy must be understood in an international frame, if only due to the very nature of conquest. The entry on "Holy Places" in the *Max Planck Encyclopedia of Public International Law* begins with a symptomatic expression of the nature of this frame: "The term holy or sacred places refers *largo sensu* to sites which are of special meaning to the followers of one or more particular religion(s). *Stricto sensu* it is used in connection with certain sites in

[1] The phrases "low church" and "high church" originated in seventeenth- and eighteenth-century Anglican polemics about the place of ritual, and more generally about the degree of rejection of Catholic-like forms. "Low church" designates those de-emphasizing or even denigrating ritual. Over time, the term was generalized to describe difference among and within many Protestant denominations.

[2] 573 U.S. 682 (2014). The Supreme Court here upheld the claim of a for-profit corporation for exemption from a federal requirement to provide insurance coverage for certain contraceptive methods to which it objected on religious grounds.

[3] 572 U.S. 565 (2014). The Supreme Court here upheld a town board's practice of beginning each meeting with a sectarian Christian prayer.

the Holy Land . . . ."[4] This seemingly innocuous preface to a systematic overview of the topic implies that the legal idea of "holy places" originates in Western preoccupations with the biblical "Holy Land" – and that its generalization has come about only through imperfect analogies. Indeed, although one might say that this "*stricto sensu*" meaning of "Holy Places" points to a Judeo-Islamo-Christian genealogy, close examination of the legal conceptualization suggests that it stems from a particular strand of specifically Christian thought and practice. It is also significant that there is no general international legal regime governing such sacred sites, but only piecemeal, indirect, and episodic schemes of protection. What is the connection between these features: the Christian origin, the obstacles to legal protection, and the nonetheless quintessentially international topic of "Holy Places?"

I argue that a link between these heterogeneous features emerges when we trace a genealogy of law-and-religion generally in the vicissitudes of "sacred sites." Before proceeding to some familiar legal texts, I begin, perhaps unexpectedly, with Georg Wilhelm Friedrich Hegel's interpretation of the Crusades, those quintessential Western symbols of a hyperbolic focus on the sacredness of place. I then turn to two case-studies: conflicts over Native American sacred land in the United States and the conflict over a site sacred to Hindus and Muslims in Ayodhya.

16.2 THE CRUSADES, "TRUE RELIGION," AND THE "FAREWELL" TO SACRED SITES

In both the *Phenomenology of Spirit* (1807) and the *Philosophy of History* (1822–30), Hegel identifies the Crusades as a crucial turning-point in the history of Christianity and, consequently, of the World-Spirit. As with every stage in his dialectical historiography, Hegel portrays the Crusades as necessary to the World-Spirit's unfolding, not *in spite of* but precisely *because* they revealed the limitations of their guiding principle. For Hegel, the Crusades were driven by an acute sense of the insufficiency of celebrating Mass in randomly located churches and, consequently, of the vital importance of physical presence at the intrinsically sacred "Holy Places" in Jerusalem. This sense derived from a particular understanding of the path to finding the Eternal in the Worldly, the sacred in this-world, the divine in the mundane:

> The Host, the supreme manifestation [of the divine], is to be found indeed in innumerable churches; Christ is therein transubstantiated into a present

[4] Heribert Franz Koeck, "Holy Places," in *Max Planck Encyclopedia of Public International Law*, ed. Rüdiger Wolfrum (London: Oxford University Press, 2008).

> particularity. But this itself is only of a general character [that is, it can be done, and re-done, anywhere] – not a truly particularized presence in *Space.* That presence [i.e., the physical being of Jesus] has passed away in *Time;* but as spatial and in concrete *Space* it has an enduring this-worldly presence in *this* particular spot, *this* particular village, etc. It is then this this-worldly presence [that is, the Holy Places in Jerusalem] that Christendom goes in quest of, that it must attain.[5]

Hegel here articulates what he sees as true in the Crusades' principle, the desire for the presence of the infinite in the finite world. However, the *means* by which the Crusades sought this goal, the physical possession of the Holy Places, was fundamentally flawed. This defect could only be revealed after conquest had brought the Holy Places within the Crusaders' grasp.

> Thus did Christendom come into the possession of its highest good. Jerusalem was made a kingdom .... Christendom, therefore, had appeased its religious craving; it could now veritably walk unobstructed in the footsteps of the Saviour. ... But in the Grave [the Holy Sepulchre] is found the real point of retro-version; it is in the grave that all the vanity of the Sensuous perishes. ... At this sepulchre the Christian world received a second time the response given to the disciples when they sought the body of the Lord there: "*Why seek ye the living among the dead? He is not here, but is risen*" [Matt. 28:6].[6]

Through its very failure to achieve its ultimate goal, conquest was necessary to teach the World-Spirit the irrelevance of sacred sites to the true religious quest. Religion would henceforth be sought in subjectivity, not in a contingent external embodiment.

> You must not look for the principle of your religion in the Sensuous, in the grave among the dead, but in the living Spirit in yourselves. ... Christendom found the empty Sepulchre, but not the union of the Worldly and the Eternal; and so it lost the Holy Land. ... [T]he "*This*" [the presence of the Eternal in the Worldly] that it was seeking, was to be looked for in *Subjective Consciousness alone*, and in no external object ....[7]

Hegel even declares that the disillusionment with sacred sites wrought by the Crusades was a decisive turning-point on the road to the Enlightenment and human emancipation.

5 G. W. F. Hegel, *The Philosophy of History*, trans. J. Sibree (Kitchner, ON: Batoche Books, 2001 [1824]), 409 (translation modified).

6 Hegel, *Philosophy of History*, 411.

7 Hegel, *Philosophy of History*, 411–12.

> Thus the world gained the consciousness that the human being must look within himself for the "*This*" which is of a divine nature. Subjectivity thereby receives absolute authorization, and arrogates to itself the determination of the relationship to the divine. This then was the absolute result of the Crusades, and thenceforth begins the era of self-reliance and spontaneous activity.[8]

Most importantly for my argument, this post-conquest turning away from sacred sites also effected a geographical and temporal reconfiguration of world history: "The West bade *an eternal farewell to the East* at the Holy Sepulchre, and gained a comprehension of its own principle of subjective infinite Freedom. Christendom never appeared again on the scene of history as *one* body."[9] Hegel here identifies the "West" with the principle of subjectivity, attained only through conquest – or, rather, through the bitter lesson, taught by the *futility* of conquest, of the "vanity" of the sacred sites in the "East." We would remain well within the Hegelian spirit if we sharpened this formulation by declaring that the West *becomes itself* precisely *through* this "farewell" to the East. The "farewell" to the East is also a farewell to "Christendom" and its succession by the "West." Moreover, through this same "farewell," the "East" itself also comes into being, as that which has been transcended, that which lies in the transcended past of the World-Spirit.[10]

The Crusades thereby effected what I call a "geo-temporal reconfiguration" of the world: an opposition between "West" and "East" in which the latter embodies a transcended past. This "farewell to the East" is, of course, not incompatible with physical control over the territory so denominated. It is, rather, a cognitive moment, a coming to awareness by the World-Spirit of the irrelevance of physical sites to the quest for the sacred in this-world. Instead of "Christendom" facing a world of infidels, a "West" of nascent modernity now faces an "East" as a land of the past – and hence available for a different kind of subordination than that achieved by Holy War.

Hegel also declares that the Crusades, or, rather, their failure, initiated a reconfiguration of the relationship between religious and worldly power: "Through the Crusades the Church arrived at the end of its authority: it had achieved the perversion of religion and of the divine Spirit; it had distorted the principle of Christian Freedom .... In the Crusades the Pope stood at the head

8 Hegel, *Philosophy of History*, 412.
9 Hegel, *Philosophy of History*, 412.
10 My analysis here rejoins some of the major theses in Edward Said, *Orientalism* (New York: Vintage Books, 1979).

of worldly power: the Emperor appeared only in a subordinate position . . . ."[11] For Hegel, the post-Crusades abandonment of sacred sites, with its consequent turn to subjectivity, thus lies at the origin of the entire problematics of modern Western thought – theological, psychological, political, legal. It foreshadows the end of "Christendom" as a unified theological/political entity and the beginning of the separation of religion and state. It also marks the end of religion as a quest for truth divorced from the subject and the beginning of religion as a subjective, even privatized, affair. It is thus also at the origin of international legal order in the nineteenth-century sense: a system of sovereign states coordinated not through a common religious allegiance but through a notion of "civilization" coterminous with the "West."[12] To be sure, as I shall discuss, Hegel's own work seeks to respond to these problematics: dialectically sublimating all dichotomies, theological/political, subjective/objective, and so on.

Hegel's distinctive identification of the Crusades' failure with the beginning of modern Western thought finds strong confirmation if we re-read him in light of John Locke's 1689 *Letter Concerning Toleration* – that text so central to all modern Western constructions of the law/religion relationship.[13] Locke famously declared that "true religion" lies in "the inner persuasion of the mind,"[14] rather than in any "external pomp,"[15] or, indeed, anything external at all. Indeed, Hegel may very well have written his proclamations about the post-Crusades' turn to subjectivity with Locke as his key reference.

Locke refers twice to sacred sites in the *Letter*. In the first, clearly writing metaphorically, Locke discusses the "way which, according to the sacred geography, leads straight to Jerusalem."[16] The "way to Jerusalem" here is simply a trope for the path to spiritual salvation, in which the physical Jerusalem has no importance. Indeed, Locke makes this reference precisely in a passage mocking attachment to external ritual practices.

The second reference, however, concerns a literal concern with "place":

> [I]n religious worship we must distinguish between what is part of the worship itself and what is but a circumstance. That is a part of the worship which is believed to be appointed by God and to be well-pleasing to Him, and

[11] Hegel, *Philosophy of History*, 413.

[12] See, generally, Martti Koskenniemi, *The Gentle Civilizer of Nations* (Cambridge: Cambridge University Press, 2001).

[13] John Locke, *A Letter Concerning Toleration*, ed. Mario Montuori (The Hague: Martinus Nijhoff, 1963 [1689]).

[14] Locke, *Letter Concerning Toleration*, 19.

[15] Locke, *Letter Concerning Toleration*, 7.

[16] Locke, *Letter Concerning Toleration*, 47.

> therefore that is necessary. Circumstances are such things which, though in general they cannot be separated from worship, yet the particular instances or modifications of them are . . . indifferent. Of this sort are the time and place of worship . . . . These are circumstances, and perfectly indifferent, where God has not given any express command about them.[17]

Locke's declaration that the "place of worship" is a "perfectly indifferent" matter is almost logically entailed in his notion that "true religion" is "inner persuasion." Locke here implicitly embraces the moral of the Crusades as it would be later formulated by Hegel.

Locke's decisively influential *Letter* thus roots the modern separation of the religious and the secular spheres in a theological conception that takes the rejection of intrinsically sacred sites as axiomatic. Locke's notion of "true religion," which he presents as the outcome of a political-theological inquiry, converges with the lesson taught, according to Hegel, by the historical event of the Crusades.[18]

Like Hegel, Locke explicitly links his conception of "true religion" to an invidious judgment of other religious conceptions. This judgment entails a rejection, indeed a mockery, of most ritual practices, thereby condemning a good deal of the activity of most actually existing religions. In his *Letter*, Locke's low-church judgment falls on Islam, Catholicism, and Judaism, as well as on any ritual-minded versions of Protestantism. However, it is primarily in relation to Judaism that this judgment concerns the sacredness of place.

> [A]mongst the Jews the time and place of their worship . . . were not mere circumstances, but a part of the worship itself, in which, if anything were defective, or different from the institution, they could not hope that it would be accepted by God. But these, to Christians under the liberty of the Gospel, are mere circumstances of worship . . . .[19]

In relation to sacred sites, Judaism thus serves as a crucial foil: Jews consider "time and place," those "perfectly indifferent" matters, to be essential to worship, in contrast with those who live "under the liberty of the Gospel."

The conundrum bequeathed by Locke and Hegel to our own time is a variant of the question posed by a generation of critical thinkers: can a framework founded on a particular conception of law-and-religion fully respect cultures founded on other conceptions? My discussion here shows the extent of the particularity of the Western conception, particularly in light

17 Locke, *Letter Concerning Toleration*, 19.

18 I leave aside here the complex topic of Locke's theoretical justification for the colonization of the Americas and his practical involvement in that colonization.

19 Locke, *Letter Concerning Toleration*, 63–4.

of Hegel's narrative. No doubt there remain few, if any, orthodox Hegelians who adhere to the notion of history as the necessary unfolding, and education, of the World-Spirit. Nonetheless, Hegel's key point retains its power, even if in a slightly modified version: the de-valorization of sacred sites in the aftermath of conquest, whether by the Crusaders or the European colonizers more generally, as genealogical turning-points marking the foundation, and continual re-foundation, of the modern West.

I note that I have been employing "genealogy" here in its familiar Nietzschean/Foucauldian usage: the notion (*pace* Hegel) that history, including intellectual history, does not develop through any kind of necessary unfolding but, rather, by the contingent, periodic reconfigurations of power-relations. This notion tends to emphasize discontinuities, rather than smooth, or even dialectical, progress. It also tends to emphasize violent ruptures rather than logically necessary developments – all traits key to the theme of sacred sites, as we shall continue to see.

Before proceeding, I note that Hegel sees the "truth" of Locke's "true religion" in a rather different way from Locke himself. For Hegel, the subjectivization of religion is indeed the truth of religion – but that truth, indeed "religion" itself, has only a relative validity.

> Religion is a relation to the Absolute, a relation which takes the form of feeling, representative thinking, faith .... In contrast with the truth thus veiled behind subjective ideas and feelings, the genuine truth is the prodigious transfer of the inner into the outer, the building of reason into the real world, and this has been the task of the world during the whole course of its history. It is by working at this task that civilised man has actually given reason an embodiment in law and government and achieved consciousness of the fact.[20]

This passage prepares us for Hegel's otherwise startling justification for the supremacy of the state over religion. In reading this justification, remember that, for Hegel, "Spirit" is an "inter-subjective self-conscious process,"[21] embodied at every cultural-historical stage in a greater or lesser degree of articulation and collective self-awareness.

> *The state is the divine will, in the sense that it is Spirit present on earth,* unfolding itself to be the actual shape and organisation of a world. Those who insist on stopping at the form of *religion,* as opposed to the State, are acting

[20] G. W. F. Hegel, *Hegel's Philosophy of Right,* trans. T. M. Knox (Oxford: Clarendon Press, 1942 [1820]), 167–8 (sec. 270, Remark).

[21] Thomas A. Lewis, "Cultivating Our Intuitions: Hegel on Religion, Politics, and Public Discourse," *Journal of the Society of Christian Ethics* 27, no.1 (2007): 205–24, at 207.

> like those logicians who think they are right if they continually stop at the essence and refuse to advance beyond that abstraction to existence, or like those moralists . . . who will only good in the abstract and leave it to caprice to decide *what* is good.[22]

The present chapter is obviously not the place for a full (or even adequate!) exploration of Hegel's notion of Spirit. However, I do wish to highlight the distinctiveness of Hegel's argument for the general supremacy of state law over religious dictates: not a jurisdictional-style separation of spheres, as in Locke, but a consequence of the state's embodiment of a higher truth of Spirit. A bit metaphysical for some tastes, to be sure, but a powerful (though hardly uncontestable) philosophical argument for the supremacy of secular law and courts over religious dictates, including over putatively inviolable sacred sites. A juxtaposition of this Hegelian terminology with its more familiar legal kin, such as "public interest" or "general applicability," could well yield crucial insights into both. Indeed, this range of legal/philosophical/theological ideas will be central to judicial discussions of sacred sites, to which I now turn.

16.3 CONQUEST AND ADJUDICATION: FROM THE HIGH COUNTRY TO AYODHYA

The divergences between the two thinkers notwithstanding, the "perfect indifference" of sacred sites is a feature of true religiosity both for Locke (due to the essence of religion) and for Hegel (due to transcendence of a less developed historical phase in the unfolding of Spirit). This philosophical heritage illuminates the phenomenon that some of the US law-and-religion cases that most defy principled resolution involve sacred sites. That these cases often involve Native Americans, the quintessential objects of conquest in American history, further confirms this link. Nor is it surprising that this defiance of principled resolution also appears in quite different contexts, but in which conflicts between dominant groups and those they perceive as religious Others are also at their sharpest, such as Hindu-Muslim conflict in India – in which claims and counter-claims of conquest feature prominently.

I preface this discussion with some well-known and yet symptomatic differentiations among "sacred sites." Such sites may be natural terrains or human constructions such as buildings, ruins, wells, and so forth. They may be sacred due to the unique access to the divine they afford or due to historical or mythical events that have transpired there. The religions in question may view

22 Hegel, *Philosophy of Right*, 167 (emphasis added).

the sacredness of such sites as permanent or as enduring only so long as rituals continued to be performed there. And so on.

Even this brief catalogue suggests that the "sacredness" of sites may differ from religion to religion. The entire range of critiques that have been brought to bear upon a homogenized category of "religion" may also be deployed upon a homogenized category of "sacred sites." Above all, the notion of the "sacred" here implies an absolute differentiation from the "profane" that may be quite alien to some, indeed most, religious traditions, Émile Durkheim notwithstanding. If a homogenized notion of sacred sites is, like "religion," an artifact of the global diffusion of Western modernity due to colonial and post-colonial hegemony, what power-relations does it codify? How would departing from that homogenized notion affect particular disputes? For example, divergences in the sources of the sacredness (intrinsic, human, experiential, permanence, provisionality, etc.) may well have decisive implications in specific conflicts.

With these caveats, I proceed to two high-profile sacred sites disputes, from widely divergent contexts: the US case of *Lyng* v. *Northwest Indian Cemetery Protective Association*[23] and three decisions from Indian courts in the Ayodhya conflict. Despite their numerous differences, they share crucial elements: religious alterity, conquest, property issues, and problematic claims of the state to embody a religiously neutral public interest.

16.3.1 Lyng, *Marshall, and Hegel (Again)*

Lyng is perhaps the most well-known, indeed notorious, American sacred sites case. The dispute arose from a federal government plan to build a road through the "High Country," an area in Northern California of supreme spiritual significance to three Native American nations. The Supreme Court rejected constitutional and statutory challenges to this plan. Among other things, it ruled that the Native American claimants had *no cognizable First Amendment interest* in a road built on federal land – despite accepting, at least *arguendo*, that the road would "destroy" their "ability to practice their religion."[24]

In his dissenting opinion, Justice Brennan valiantly sought to explain the incommensurability of Western and Native American "religions," occasionally referring to the latter as "Native American faith." Brennan's 1988 opinion should come as no surprise to those familiar with the critique of the category of "religion" by Asad and others in more recent decades. If "religion" must be

[23] 485 U.S. 439 (1988).
[24] *Lyng*, at 451.

understood, as such writers have taught us, as a modern Western construct, arising in perennial struggle with "secularity," then it is not applicable, in Brennan's words, where "religion is not a discrete sphere of activity separate from all others."[25] For Brennan, as for recent critics, "any attempt to isolate the religious aspects of Indian life 'is in reality an exercise which forces Indian concepts into non-Indian categories.'"[26] I note that this problem also applies to many (if not most) religious traditions, Western and otherwise – and, for example, underpinned the US Supreme Court's decision in *Wisconsin v. Yoder*.[27]

I note, though, that Brennan's language of "faith" reminds us of the stubborn persistence in American legal thought of a particular strand of post-Reformation theology. "Faith," at least in modern English, denotes a subjective state, a belief in some proposition or set of propositions. The word clashes with Brennan's description of Native American culture, which does not "rely on doctrines, creeds, or dogmas."[28] This linguistic symptom highlights the incompatibility of Native American culture and US legal language, diagnosed as well as reenacted by Brennan (and which my use of "culture" does not even begin to resolve).

The sacred site dimension of this case further accentuated this incompatibility, for, as Brennan explained, it thereby presented "yet another stress point in the longstanding conflict between two disparate cultures – the dominant Western culture, which views land in terms of ownership and use, and that of Native Americans, in which concepts of private property are not only alien, but contrary to a belief system that holds land sacred."[29] Brennan concluded that "the competing claims that both the Government and Native Americans assert in federal land are fundamentally incompatible, and unless they are tempered by compromise, mutual accommodation will remain impossible."[30] Such a "compromise" thus could not consist in a principled synthesis. Rather, it would demand practical concessions by both sides, leaving intact the incommensurability of the two "cultures."

It is remarkable, therefore, that Brennan's portrayal of the incommensurability is less than persuasive. As I have hinted, almost all of the distinguishing characteristics of "Native American faith" listed by Brennan feature in various

25 *Lyng*, at 459.

26 *Lyng*, at 459.

27 406 U.S. 205 (1972). *Yoder* granted an exemption, under the Free Exercise Clause, to Amish parents who objected to a statute requiring school attendance through age 16.

28 *Lyng*, at 460.

29 *Lyng*, at 473.

30 *Lyng*, at 474.

strands of both Christianity and Judaism: the notion that "religion is not a discrete sphere of activity separate from all others"; the notion of "creation as an ongoing process" in which human beings are "morally and religiously obligated to participate"; the performance of "rituals designed to preserve and stabilize the earth"; the de-emphasizing of "doctrines, creeds, or dogmas."[31] Most importantly here, this is also true of the "site-specific nature" of "religious practice," as any casual visitor to Jerusalem knows – and was a powerful enough force within Christianity to launch the Crusades, regardless of their outcome. It would take a volume or two to portray all the prominent strands in Judaism and Christianity that share these characteristics or at least very similar ones.[32] The conflict would thus not lie *between* "cultures" but *within* each, at least within all "Western religions."

I am not claiming, of course, that Native American traditions, despite the great diversity that exists among them, do not contain features that decisively differentiate them from "Western religions" – but, rather, that attempts like Brennan's are inadequate. Such attempts tend primarily to present as "non-Western" the opposite of the imagined characteristics of "Western religion" – an opposite that also tends to apply to many (or most) strands of "Western religions" themselves. (I leave aside here the inaccuracy of Brennan's broad claim of the absence of any notion of property among Native Americans.)

The kind of incommensurability to which Brennan points thus derives not from "Western religion" but from a very particular strand of the modern West: that which envisions "true religion" as "inner persuasion" (Locke) or which locates it "in *Subjective Consciousness alone*, and in no external object" (Hegel). While the exact nature of Locke's theological views remains a matter of debate, his sharp articulation of the "inner persuasion" criterion left a deep mark on modern legal discourse. But it is by reading Hegel that we can see the full implications of this conception in relationship to *Lyng*.

Hegel's comments about the Crusades suggest a different explanation for the view of both the *Lyng* majority and the dissent that the Native American claims were incommensurable with American law – and, indeed, seemed to lie even beyond the simple comprehension, let alone the empathy, of the majority. If Hegel's account is correct, or even partially insightful, the strand of Western thought that subtends this area of law views the sacredness of place as intrinsically premodern and non-Western – due to the geo-temporal

[31] *Lyng*, at 460–1.

[32] In a study of Paul Tillich and his relationship to law, I described his very Western theological critique of religion as a "discrete sphere." See Nathaniel Berman, "'In a Place Parallel to God': The Draft, the Demonic, and the Conscientious Cubist," *Journal of Law and Religion* 32, no. 2 (2017): 311–39.

reconfiguration described in Section 16.2. Moreover, just as significant here is Hegel's proclamation that the devalorization of sacred sites founding Western modernity was inextricably, though dialectically, linked with conquest.

This Hegelian framework sheds light on the otherwise startling fact that nowhere in *Lyng* does either the majority or the dissent even mention Native American dispossession. This absence is, of course, particularly galling in the majority's infamous statement that "[w]hatever rights the Indians may have to the use of the area, . . . those rights do not divest the Government of its right to use what is, after all, *its* land."[33] However, even the dissent does not mention the harsh fact that the clash here is not simply between property and religion but between dispossessed nations and their dispossessors. Conquest, by 1988, seemed to have become something of an unmentionable, perhaps even unconsciously repressed, specter that nonetheless founded American law – rather than its loudly proclaimed basis, as it had been in John Marshall's seminal judicial opinions in the early nineteenth century.

In an intriguing coincidence, Marshall (1755–1835) and Hegel (1770–1831) were contemporaries – with Hegel's *Lectures on the Philosophy of History* (1822–30) spanning almost the same years as Marshall's decisions in the so-called "Indian law trilogy" (1823–31). Hegel's portrayal of the Crusaders' conquests shares some crucial features with Marshall's portrayal of the conquest of North America, or, more precisely, conquest's metonymical substitute, "discovery." In *Johnson* v. *M'Intosh*, Marshall proclaimed that discovery by Europeans bestows upon them "ultimate dominion" over non-European lands[34] – a principle "confined to countries 'then unknown to all Christian people.'"[35] Marshall repeatedly emphasized throughout his opinion that this transfer of "dominion" requires no actual displacement of the inhabitants. In fact, the latter need not even know that they had been discovered by Europeans. But once the Christian European gaze alights upon "heathen" land, Native "dominion" is already a thing of the past. History has turned a page, with physical dispossession merely a matter of time and effort.

The "original fundamental principle," Marshall declared, was that "discovery gave exclusive title to those who made it."[36] Therefore, while the natives

33 *Lyng*, at 453. For an overview of the process by which the High Country came to be the property of the US government, see Amy Bowers and Kristin Carpenter, "Challenging the Narrative of Conquest: The Story of *Lyng v. Northwest Indian Cemetery Protective Association*," in *Indian Law Stories*, ed. Carole E. Goldberg, Kevin K. Washburn, and Philip P. Frickey (New York: Foundation Press, 2010), 497–504.

34 *Johnson* v. *M'Intosh*, 21 U.S. (8 Wheat.) 543, at 574 (1823).

35 *Johnson*, at 576.

36 *Johnson*, at 574.

"were admitted to be the rightful occupants of the soil,"[37] this "occupation" was henceforth only at the pleasure of the discovering Europeans. Discovery rendered the entire Native political, cultural, and religious order obsolete in principle, a transcended stage of history. In principle, Native America no longer existed. It had been replaced by Euro-America – even though, empirically, nothing at all need have changed.

Marshall's insistence on this geo-temporal reconfiguration through the cognitive act of discovery, not physical possession, takes up most of his *Johnson* decision. France, for example, "asserted her right of dominion over a great extent of country not actually settled by Frenchmen and her exclusive right to acquire and dispose of the soil which remained in the occupation of Indians."[38] This claim extended to vast regions, including "all Canada and Acadie," as well as "Louisiana, comprehending the immense territories watered by the Mississippi."[39] As to the territory of the future United States, "our whole country had been granted by the crown while in the occupation of the Indians."[40]

Upon a first reading, Hegel and Marshall seem to differ on the role of literal conquest. Hegel proclaimed that actual conquest – or, rather, its failure – was necessary for the education of the World-Spirit in the vanity of sacred sites. No stage of world history can be transcended, for Hegel, without an arduous struggle. Marshall, by contrast, even if in rather ironic tones, endorsed the "extravagant . . . pretension of converting the discovery of an inhabited country into conquest."[41]

Closer examination, however, attenuates this difference. For Marshall, while actual conquest was irrelevant to the transfer of "dominion," it made possible literal dispossession which could occur at any time. For Hegel, actual conquest was important precisely due to its futility in achieving its stated goals. Nonetheless, Hegel implicitly shows us that it is this abandonment that makes colonization in the modern sense possible – for the devalorization of sacred sites enables secular conquest of the land. Thus, for both Hegel and Marshall, the decisive rupture effected by a cognitive shift entailed real-world as well as normative consequences.

Hegel and Marshall thus share the notion of a geo-temporal rupture effected by a pivotal Christian European cognitive shift, founding the West and its modernity (Hegel) and the United States and its legal system

37 *Johnson*, at 574.
38 *Johnson*, at 575.
39 *Johnson*, at 575.
40 *Johnson*, at 579.
41 *Johnson*, at 591.

(Marshall). In both discourses, the historically transcended culture continues to exist in the physical world, at least temporarily: the Crusaders withdrew from Palestine; the Native Americans continued, for a time, to occupy some of their lands. Yet, the power of the cognitive shift is such that Marshall's famous *normative* dictum that the "courts of the conqueror cannot deny" the title given by "conquest" (i.e., "discovery")[42] becomes, by 1988, a taken-for-granted *empirical* fact of legal consciousness (or, perhaps, subconsciousness): the repression by both the *Lyng* majority and the dissent of Native dispossession. That both *Lyng* opinions viewed the case as turning on the question of property rights makes particularly striking this amnesia about the vast land theft upon which the United States was founded.[43]

The vastness of the geo-temporal reconfiguration portrayed by Marshall is underscored by the way he frames the entire discussion in *international* legal terms. Marshall proves his notion that discovery alone transfers sovereignty by engaging in a masterful, indeed textbook exercise in proving a rule of customary international law: adducing state practice from a broad array of contexts, citing a large number of treaties with diverse settings and parties, quoting pronouncements of leaders of a wide variety of polities, and so on. This demonstration of the international legal basis for first British then US sovereignty over a vast land mass thus founds the entire US legal system upon international law.

I caution that I am not attributing any absolute necessity to the defeat of Native claims in cases such as *Lyng*, even if the principle of discovery has never been overturned. I note that, despite Hegel (!), Marshall, and Brennan's own proclamation of the incommensurability of the Native claim with Western culture, the dissent in *Lyng* was vociferous. For Brennan, the incommensurability of perspectives did not leave courts in a hopeless position but rather mandated that they seek a practical compromise. I also note that, in 1996, President Clinton issued an Executive Order to "accommodate access to and ceremonial use of Indian sacred sites."[44] Even if qualifying language rendered that order somewhat aspirational, it retains a bit more influence than Brennan's dissent.

42 *Johnson*, at 588.

43 I note that my understanding of the relationship of US law and Native American dispossession has been influenced by, among others, Walter R. Echo-Hawk, *In the Courts of the Conqueror: The 10 Worst Indian Law Cases Ever Decided* (Golden, CO: Fulcrum Publishing, 2010); Joseph Singer, "Sovereignty and Property," *Northwestern University Law Review* 86, no. 1 (1991): 1–56; and Robert A. Williams, *The American Indian in Western Legal Thought* (Oxford: Oxford University Press, 1990).

44 Executive Order 13,007, 61 Fed. Reg. 26,771 (May 29, 1996).

Moreover, nothing absolutely prevents US federal courts from issuing decisions in seeming opposition to the spirit of *Lyng*. In 2008, a US District Court issued a very straightforward decision granting an injunction to stop military construction that would interfere with the "Medicine Bluffs," land sacred to the Comanche Nation in Oklahoma.[45] One could debate whether the statutory (RFRA)[46] basis of the *Comanche* case suffices to distinguish it from *Lyng*'s constitutional inquiry, though that seems dubious. In any case, such subtle legal argumentation would not affect my point here, which is to register an anti-necessitarian caveat to my broader historical claim. It is notable, nonetheless, that the "unreported" Western Oklahoma District Court decision granting the *Comanche* injunction has found little, if any, echo in other decisions.

16.3.2 *Ayodhya: Legal-Theological Pluralism ... or Another Tale of Effaced Conquest (Re-)Founding the State?*

What would be the consequence of a secular court acknowledging a diversity of religious stances to the sacredness of place? What if a court fully embraced incommensurate cultures' temporal coexistence, rejecting the Hegel/Marshall/*Lyng* projection of certain cultures into an obsolete past? I note that the *Yoder* decision rested in large part on the notion that Amish culture did not recognize the modern secular/religious divide – and that interfering with the Amish vision of the proper activities of adolescents would do violence to that culture. A close reading of that decision, however, shows that the Court did, indeed, view the Amish as relics of the past, but valorized them precisely on that basis. The Court's nostalgic romanticization of the Amish as living fossils of Thomas Jefferson's "sturdy yeomen"[47] allowed it to vindicate the Amish claims without relinquishing a conventional modernization narrative. In any event, *Yoder* presented issues quite different from those of sacred sites.

Striking, and sobering, examples of nonuniform evaluations of different religions' relationship to sacred sites may be found in Indian court decisions in the aftermath of the 1992 destruction of the Ayodhya mosque by Hindu extremists. The three decisions – 1995, 2010, and 2019 – concerned the post-destruction acquisition and disposition by the state of the land upon which the

45 *Comanche Nation* v. *United States*, No. CIV-08–849-D, 2008 WL 4426621 (W.D. Okla. September 23, 2008).

46 Religious Freedom Restoration Act, 42 U.S.C. §§2000bb to 2000bb-4 (Supp. V 1993). RFRA restored, as a matter of statutory law, the test for the free exercise of religion developed in the constitutional context in cases such as *Yoder*.

47 *Yoder*, 406 U.S. at 225.

mosque stood. The last of these decisions, issued on November 9, 2019, ordered that the entire area be rendered to Hindus and that a Hindu temple be constructed upon it.

I will not here give a comprehensive overview of the decisions' extremely complex factual and legal dimensions. Rather, I will limit myself to key features of the decisions that implicate the central issues of this chapter: sacred sites, conquest, property, the power of cognitive shifts, and the construction of both the state and divergent conceptions of "religion." The 1995 and 2010 cases have been systematically analyzed in indispensable studies by Ratna Kapur, to whom I am greatly indebted.[48]

The Ayodhya mosque, the "Babri Masjid," was built in the sixteenth century. By the mid-nineteenth century, Hindu activists were claiming that it had been constructed on the site of a Hindu temple – and was thus a crowning symbol of the Muslim emperor Babur's conquest of India. Even more crucially, they claimed that the central part of the mosque was located on the birthplace of the Hindu god Ram. In the mid-1850s, after Hindu-Muslim riots, the British colonial authorities built a "grill-brick wall" dividing "the premises into two parts: the inner portion [the area under the dome of the mosque] which would be used by the Muslim community and the outer portion or courtyard, which would be used by the Hindu community."[49]

The following decades saw a series of sometimes violent Hindu encroachments on the mosque and Muslim access to it. In 1949, in a crucial turning-point, Hindu activists broke into the mosque and placed idols under its dome. This act forced the end of Muslim prayer when the authorities declined to remove the idols, rendering it unfit for Muslim worship. Instead, they barred Muslims and most, but not all, Hindus from the site. The complete destruction of the mosque in December 1992 brought this process to its devastating conclusion. Competing claims of conquest thus structure this dispute: the conquest that Hindus alleged was entailed in the construction of the mosque *versus* the gradual Hindu encroachment upon the mosque and its ultimate destruction.

After the destruction, the central government acted to acquire the land upon and around which the mosque had stood.[50] In the 1995 *M. Ismail*

48 See, especially, Ratna Kapur, "The 'Ayodhya' Case: Hindu Majoritarianism and the Right to Religious Liberty," *Maryland Journal of International Law* 29, no. 1 (2014): 305–65.

49 *M Siddiq, Thr Lrs, v. Mahant Durash Das, & Ors.* (Supreme Court of India, 2019), www.sci.gov.in/pdf/JUD_2.pdf, at 9.

50 See The Acquisition of Certain Area at Ayodhya Act, 1993 Act No. 33 of 1993, https://indiacode.nic.in/bitstream/123456789/1915/3/A1993-33.pdf.

Faruqui v. *Union of India*, Muslim petitioners challenged this acquisition on the ground that

> a mosque enjoys a particular position in Muslim Law and once a mosque is established and prayers are offered in such a mosque, the same remains for all time to come a property of Allah . . .. [A]ny person professing Islamic faith can offer prayer in such a mosque . . . even if the structure is demolished . . ..[51]

The Indian Supreme Court interpreted this challenge as a Muslim claim for special legal protection not granted to other religions. It understood the plaintiffs to be arguing for the mosque's exemption, due to its intrinsic sacredness, from the state's general power to exercise eminent domain in the public interest. In rejecting this contention, the Court opined on the role of mosques within Islam.

> [T]here can be no reason to hold that a mosque has a unique or special status, higher than that of the places of worship of other religions in secular India to make it immune from acquisition by exercise of the sovereign or prerogative power of the State. A *mosque is not an essential part of the practice of the religion of Islam*[,] and *Namaz* (prayer) by Muslims can be offered anywhere, even in [the] open. Accordingly, its acquisition is not prohibited by the provisions in the Constitution of India.[52]

The Court's position here is congruent with the Lockean/Hegelian disdain for the intrinsic sacredness of place, especially vis-à-vis an act of state power purportedly in the public interest.

In its reliance on the notion that a "mosque is not an essential part of the practice of the religion of Islam," the decision evoked the Indian Supreme Court's "essential practices" doctrine. This doctrine plays a role functionally similar to that of the belief/action distinction in American legal discourse – distinguishing those elements of religion that enjoy absolute protection from those that may be subordinated to a superior public interest. The two doctrines are far from identical, as their names indicate: the Indian doctrine grants absolute protection to certain *practices*, while the American doctrine does so only to *beliefs*. Both doctrines, however, purport to provide a theologically neutral criterion for drawing the line between state power and a protected religious sphere.

Theorists like Asad have taught us to detect the constructive effect of such purportedly neutral line-drawing. In distinguishing the features of religion

[51] *M. Ismail Faruqui* v. *Union of India*, AIR 1995 SC 605, at par. 83, https://indiankanoon.org/doc/37494799/. See Kapur, "The 'Ayodhya' Case," 322.

[52] *Faruqui*, at para. 85 (emphasis added).

shielded from state regulation from those subject to that regulation, courts construct the contours of "religion" itself as well as of particular religions. Indeed, Asad would argue, such line-drawing constructs both "the secular" and "the religious" in the very act of distinguishing between them. If we consider, in a Legal Realist vein, that every case requires a court to redraw this line anew, we see that the religious/secular divide continually undergoes construction and reconstruction. While this constructive quality is more obvious in the jurisprudence of Indian courts, which often have not shied away from theological discussions, it is no less true of American courts, which almost always deny engaging in such discussions. Nonetheless, the oft-repeated American judicial declaration that "belief" is absolutely protected, while "action" is not, effectively enshrines a radically low-church, Lockean-style subordination of practice to faith. This subordination of practice found one of its most extreme expressions in *Lyng* – where the Court failed to find a cognizable First Amendment interest, despite acknowledging, *arguendo*, that interfering with Native American practices could destroy their religion.

To return to *Faruqui*: a ruling that all religious sites are equally subject to acquisition by the state in the name of the public interest would impose the inessentiality of place on all religions in India. The passage cited above does seem, at first, to lay down such a general rule, a theological position reminiscent of Locke, as well as a legal position reminiscent of *Lyng*. The Court continued, however, with a hint that religions might have different conceptions of place, a theological pluralism with potentially decisive consequences for state power:

> [T]he acquisition of any religious place is to be made only in unusual and extraordinary situations for a larger national purpose, keeping in view that *such acquisition should not result in extinction of the right to practice the religion*, if the significance of that place be such. ... The right to worship is not at any and every place, so long as it can be practised effectively, unless the right to worship at a particular place is itself an integral part of that right.[53]

The Court, however, did not suggest any circumstance in which its caveat – "that such acquisition should not result in extinction of the right to practice the religion" – might affect a ruling concerning an *Indian Muslim* sacred site.

Nonetheless, in the middle of the very paragraph just quoted (where I placed an ellipsis), the Court alluded to possible limitations on its broad pronouncement about the inessentiality of place in Islam. In the first clause of the following passage, the Court seemed to suggest not only that the

[53] *Faruqui*, at para. 85 (emphasis added).

"essentiality" of mosques in Islam varied from region to region but that that variance was imbricated in differences in state law:

> *Irrespective of the status of a mosque in an Islamic country* for the purpose of immunity from acquisition by the State in exercise of the sovereign power, its status and immunity from acquisition in the secular ethos of India under the Constitution is the same and equal to that of the places of worship of the other religions, namely, church, temple etc.[54]

This passage lends itself to several interpretations, each with a different stance on the law/religion relationship. One may read it as leaving open the possibility that mosques may indeed be an essential part of Islam elsewhere. This interpretation would bypass a unitary "Islam" in favor of local "Islams," with state law deferring to each variant. By contrast, one may read the passage as positing a rupture between the internal theological meaning of sacred sites and their status in secular law. Each state would be free to determine that status in accordance with its own interests and values. Finally, the passage may amount to a frank acknowledgment of the role of the secular state in constructing "religion," even the contours of specific religions. Under this view, local differences in "Islam" would be due to its divergent constructions by different state legal systems.

In any case, as the *Faruqui* dissent pointed out, the Court's initial proclamation of the equality of religions vis-à-vis the state was dubious in the post-1992 context: the conquest of a minority religion's sacred site by those purporting to act on behalf of the majority religion. This conquest created the conditions, indeed the motivation, for the state's acquisition of the land. The Court's ratification of this acquisition, the dissent argued, thus constituted ratification of that conquest.

By separating the destruction of the mosque, which it explicitly condemned, from the legitimacy of the state acquisition of the property, which it upheld, the Court engaged in a sort of self-conscious amnesia, what Sigmund Freud might call "avoidance through confession." No less than Hegel and Marshall, the Indian Supreme Court placed conquest in a transcended past, however empirically recent – a past nonetheless indispensable to the current legitimacy of the state seizure of the conquered land. The neutrality and the legitimacy of state power thus rested on a conquest effaced through its very acknowledgment.

Although *Lyng* and *Faruqui* emerged from vastly different historical contexts, they share certain crucial features for my purposes here. The US

[54] *Faruqui*, at para. 85 (emphasis added).

government's ownership of the High Country, no less than the Indian government's acquisition of the Ayodhya site, depended on prior acts of violent dispossession. In both cases, that violent dispossession was perpetrated against a minority group. In both cases, the government was dominated by the majority group whose members perpetrated the dispossession. In both cases, the Courts projected that dispossession into a transcended past, either explicitly (*Faruqui*) or implicitly (*Lyng*). In both, the Courts portrayed the government as acting in the neutral public interest, ignoring the de facto ethnoreligious affiliation of the government with the agents of the dispossession.

While the "avoidance through confession" effacement of conquest in *Faruqui* differed from its complete suppression in *Lyng*, both Courts created a rupture between conquest and the purportedly neutral action of the government. In both cases, conquest became a fait accompli not relevant to current adjudication – a similarity between the decisions only highlighted by the difference in the respective amounts of time elapsed since the violent dispossession. In both cases, the explicit or implicit projection of the dispossession into a transcended past made possible the portrayal of the current acts of the state as in the neutral public interest.

Such an establishment of legal neutrality by projecting conquest into a transcended past resonates very strongly with Hegel's discussion of the Crusades, as well as Marshall's contemporaneous discussion of the doctrine of "discovery" – the latter, of course, closely related to the historical background of the *Lyng* case. Projection of conquest of sacred sites into a transcended past desacralizes the land, making possible a secular property (or sovereignty) relationship in the present. It thus constructs the separate domains of property and religion, making possible, and urgent, the question of their interrelationship – indeed the very discipline of "law-and-religion."

The *Faruqui* dissent rejected this entire framework. For the dissent, the Court's proclamation of facial equality among religions in India made it complicit in the most egregious kind of de facto inequality. Indeed, "[t]o condone the acquisition of a place of worship in such circumstances," justified by supposedly secular and neutral principles, "is to efface the principle of secularism from the Constitution."

This de facto inequality in the *Faruqui* case was, however, displaced by overtly disparate treatment in the 2010 Ayodhya decision of the Allahabad High Court, *Visharad* v. *Ahmad*.[55] This decision concerned the *disposition* of

55 *Visharad and Ors.* v. *Ahmad and Ors.*, O.S.Nos. 1/1989, 3/1989, 4/1989, 5/1989, All. H.C., at para. 4 (2010), http://elegalix.allahabadhighcourt.in/elegalix/WebShowJudgment.do. See Kapur, "The 'Ayodhya' Case," 341–51.

the land whose *acquisition* concerned *Faruqui*. Writing for the Court, Justice Agarwal flipped the issue allegedly raised by the *Faruqui* case and declared that *it was the Hindu claim that was entitled to special treatment*. First, relying on *Faruqui*, he declared that the acquisition of the mosque does not impinge on the religious practices of Muslims, for they may "offer prayer at any other place like they could have done here ...."[56] In stark contrast,

> Hindus are not placed on similar footing. According to Hindus, this is a place of birth of lord Rama .... [T]here cannot be any other place for which such belief persists since time immemorial. Once this land is allowed to be lost due to the acts of persons other than Hindus, the very right of this section of people ... shall stand destroyed.[57]

Indeed, as Kapur states, Agarwal was arguing here that excluding Hindus from prayer at the site would "extinguish a core feature of the religion and hence the religion itself."[58] The Hindu claim of the site's non-fungibility – and its vital importance to the Hindu religion's very existence – again recalls the claims by the Native Americans in the *Lyng* case.

The *Faruqui* decision and Justice Agarwal's *Visharad* opinion highlight several important points. First, the stance of various traditions toward the sacredness of place can be the subject of reasoned debate – whether or not those learned in the Hindu and Muslim traditions would agree with Agarwal's characterizations (and I am certainly incompetent to take a substantive position here). To be sure, Agarwal may well have been utterly wrong (depending on highly contested judgments about the two traditions, each containing many divergent subtraditions). Nevertheless, his attempt to justify his position makes it available for factual and textual contestation. Second, such deliberations will often be imbricated with state law and power. The *Faruqui* case came very close to conflating the status of mosques in Islamic law with their status under the secular law of India and even their status under British colonial law. One might try to purify the intrareligious debate from this imbrication, but this goal would probably be elusive at best. Third, and perhaps most importantly here: it is not obvious a priori which theological position favors majority or minority, or dispossessing or dispossessed, groups. While the notion of the intrinsic sacredness of land would have favored the dispossessed Native Americans in *Lyng*, it favored the dispossessing Hindus in *Visharad*. It is only by taking into account the entire array of contextual

56 *Visharad*, at para. 2725 (all commas added).
57 *Visharad*, at para. 2725.
58 Kapur, "The 'Ayodhya' Case," 344.

factors – possession, power, relationship of the state to the competing groups, and so on – that the implications of the theological positions for justice emerge.

On November 9, 2019, the Indian Supreme Court issued its final Ayodhya decision, *M Siddiq, Thr Lrs,* v. *Mahant Durash Das, & Ors.* This decision departed from *Visharad* in a number of crucial ways, in both reasoning and result. Most strikingly, while *Visharad* ordered the division of the disputed area into three parts, two for Hindus and one for Muslims, *Siddiq* awarded the entire area to Hindus and ordered that a Hindu temple be built on the site of the destroyed mosque. Nonetheless, for all these differences, *Siddiq* operates within the same broad framework I have outlined here, if anything resonating even more strongly than *Lyng* with Marshall and Hegel. In what follows, I will again not describe this entire complex decision but only those elements directly relevant here.

Rather than focusing on the comparative degree of essentiality of the site to the two religions, the *Siddiq* Court inquired into the "preponderance of probabilities" as to which religion has most continuously maintained its claim to the entire area. Despite the division of the area by the "grill-brick wall" in the 1850s, the Court treated the entire area as "one composite property"[59] whose disposition must be determined as a whole. The Court found that Hindus maintained exclusive possession over the outer courtyard since the construction of the wall. Moreover, they continued to maintain their claims over the inner portion, most spectacularly by the 1949 placing of the idols. By contrast, the Court found that Muslims seemed to have resigned themselves to the loss of the outer courtyard and were compelled to struggle over possession of the inner portion.[60] From this unequal situation, the Court concluded that the "preponderance of probabilities" test favored Hindus and mandated rendering the entire area to them.

Two features of this decision particularly bear upon my discussion here. First, the Court sought to prove the persistence of the Hindu claim to the inner portion by citing, among other things, the "acts of individuals in trying to set up idols and perform puja" there. Yet the Court seemed to feel unease about the legal weight of such actions, since one could easily construe them merely as illicit trespass. Perhaps as a result, the Court continually stressed that there was a "continuum of faith and belief of the Hindus" that the inner courtyard was Lord Ram's birthplace.[61] One proof of this "faith and belief" was that

[59] E.g., *Siddiq*, at 909.
[60] E.g., *Siddiq*, at 910.
[61] *Siddiq*, at 885.

Hindu "pilgrims offered prayer at the railing by *looking* towards the sanctum sanctorum"[62] (employing the Christian Latin phrase to characterize the Hindu attitude toward the inner portion).

"Looking" as evidence of "faith and belief," as well as according that "faith and belief" decisive legal weight, is strikingly reminiscent of Marshall's notion that "discovery" provides title. While Muslims remained in physical possession of the inner portion, the Hindu gaze rendered it a disputed area – and, ultimately, in *Siddiq*, provided the basis for total Muslim dispossession. Despite all the vast differences between the cases, the religious gaze functions in strikingly similar ways in *Siddiq* and *Johnson*. The *Siddiq* Court invested the Hindu gaze with the power to legally dispossess the Muslims despite their physical possession of the inner portion; Marshall invested the Christian European gaze with the power to legally dispossess Native Americans despite their physical possession of North America.

The importance accorded to this cognitive dispossession allowed the *Siddiq* Court to treat as secondary the *physical actions*, sometimes violent, usually illegal, by which Hindus encroached on the inner part of the mosque. While the Court insisted that it was basing its decision on "evidence," not on "faith and belief," that "evidence" mostly concerned evidence precisely of the *persistence of Hindu belief* in the sanctity of the entire site. A certain rhetorical ambiguity consequently marks the entire decision. We saw earlier that Marshall maintained a certain rhetorical distance from his seminal decision by ironically evoking the "extravagant ... pretension of converting ... discovery ... into conquest." In a related manner, the Indian Supreme Court maintained a rhetorical distance by disclaiming that it founded its decision on the *truth* of Hindu "faith and belief," rather than on the *fact of its persistence*. It was by such rhetorical stratagems that both Courts sought to construct their religious neutrality even as they upheld religiously based claims. In both cases, nevertheless, it was precisely the religious cognitive acts that proved decisive in the establishment of title.

The *Siddiq* Court's stance toward the illegal acts of Hindus, including the mosque's destruction in 1992, thus resembled the confession-and-avoidance of the *Faruqui* Court. Despite its unequivocal condemnation of these actions, the Court proceeded to render the entire site to Hindus – a rendering predicated on the very destruction it condemned. The Court thus placed the final conquest of the site in 1992 in a different timeline, indeed a different normative universe, from the disposition of the territory in 2019. In ordering that Muslims be given a 5-acre site elsewhere as compensation for the 1992

[62] *Siddiq*, at 884 (emphasis added).

destruction, the Court placed Muslims in a different spatial continuum as well.

Conquest, indispensable factually and legally to making the mosque area subject to the Court's power, was thus thoroughly effaced from its disposition of that area. This effacement also constructed a crucial religion/secularity line here, just as it did in *Johnson*. Dispossession, effected by the religious gaze, provided the precondition for the two courts to present themselves as the voice of neutral, secular reason through their respective techniques of effacing those dispossessions.

In sum, in the Ayodhya cases, as in Hegel, Marshall, and *Lyng*, conquest – or, rather, the *effacement* of conquest – becomes the basis for the legitimation of state power. This effacement may be effected through temporal rupture (Hegel and Marshall), confession-and-avoidance (the Ayodhya cases), or psychological repression (*Lyng*). All these texts set conquest in a legally irrelevant past, explicitly or implicitly – and this effaced conquest, by virtue of the cognitive shift it effects, both gives rise to the legal dispute and establishes the authority of the secular, putatively neutral state and Court to decide it.

This framework makes sense of the otherwise striking fact that the *Siddiq* Court granted the entire Ayodhya site to Hindus, even while rejecting one of their major factual contentions: that the construction of the mosque was a wrongful consequence of Babur's conquest, above all that it required the destruction of a Hindu temple.[63] The Court found it unproven that a Hindu temple had, in fact, been destroyed. Moreover, the Court declared that, in any case, it "cannot compel a subsequent sovereign to recognize and remedy historical wrongs."[64] It is conquest effaced – projected into the past, suppressed, or avoided-through-confession – that provided these courts with their implicit basis, not conquest condemned (or celebrated, for that matter).

16.4 CONCLUSION

I have offered here a genealogy of law-and-religion, situating one of its birthplaces in an intricate "farewell" to the sacredness of place. In this genealogy, the modern state constructs its neutral status, above the fray of competing religious claims, through a dialectical effacement of conquest of sacred sites. This process became diffused globally through colonialism and its aftermath, though not without intercultural complexity. The Indian court decisions, with their mixture of Western and Indian frameworks, provide intriguing examples

63 *Siddiq*, at 906.
64 *Siddiq*, at 766.

of this complexity. However, even within Western legal systems, the coexistence of incompatible perspectives, contradictory concepts, and multiple legal and religious traditions yields divergent and sometimes unpredictable results.

In this conclusion, I note some limitations of my argument, as well as some of its broader implications. First, I am offering only *one* genealogy. Genealogies, in the Nietzschean/Foucauldian sense, devote themselves to showing the birth of the new through contingent reconfigurations of diverse power-relations – power-relations with often unrelated histories that contingently converge in ways that are neither logically nor causally necessary. The current patchwork status of sacred sites in modern legal systems, as well as in international law, could well be the result of converging genealogies that may have only tangential relations among themselves.[65]

Second, the genealogy I am proposing primarily concerns conflicts among religious groups who perceive each other as fundamentally alien, as "Other" – particularly where one of these groups is subordinated. I believe that this genealogy illuminates the legitimation of secular state power generally, though I have only broached that demonstration here. The establishment of state territorial control against the power of religious authority has been a key feature of the legitimation of Western-style sovereignty, both within Europe and elsewhere – and struggles over sacred sites have played a key role in that process. Expropriations of church property, for example, were crucial in the establishment of modern European states in widely varying contexts (compare, for example, the very different contexts of Henry VIII's expropriations and those of the French revolutionaries 250 years later). Indeed, early post-Reformation uses of the very word "secularization" denoted the expropriation of church property by the state.[66]

The legitimation of international law as a system of territorial states coordinated within a Western-oriented international community has also been marked by similar dynamics. Consider, for example, the French justification in 1923 for its colonial "protectorates" in North Africa (even though it was not

65 Compare, e.g., Christopher Serkin and Nelson Tebbe, "Condemning Religion: RLUIPA and the Politics of Eminent Domain," *Notre Dame Law Review* 85, no. 1 (2009): 1–54. The political, cultural, and religious contexts that Serkin and Tebbe envision are markedly different from those under consideration here. Whether the contexts they discuss demand a different genealogy for eminent domain over sacred sites is an open question.

66 Talal Asad, *Formations of the Secular: Christianity, Islam, Modernity* (Stanford: Stanford University Press, 2003), 192. Referring to such expropriations, an anonymous German pamphlet in 1798 was entitled "*Reason Requires Secularizations*." See Hans Blumenberg, *The Legitimacy of the Modern Age*, trans. Robert M. Wallace (Cambridge, MA: MIT Press, 1983), 20. In medieval usage, by contrast, "secularization" denoted the "legal transition from monastic life (*regularis*) to the life of canons (*saecularis*)." Asad, *Formations of the Secular*, 192.

made in the context of sacred sites "*stricto sensu*"). France proclaimed that the goal of these protectorates was to establish Tunisia and Morocco as truly sovereign territorial states, by detaching them from a putatively transnational Islam. In the words of a French brief to the Permanent Court of International Justice:

> Called upon by the treaties [of protectorate] into Tunisia and Morocco to guide them in the paths of civilization and progress, France has taken from this mission a duty to help them to establish, on the foundation of territory, the firm basis of a homogeneous, coherent population, attached by a direct tie to the Prince . . ., by awakening in these States who were completely penetrated by the principles of a theocratic civilization, the free, independent, stronger, and more durable idea of nationality which would evolve in the broader framework of Western conceptions, freed from all religious contingencies.[67]

This justification seems quintessentially "republican" in the French sense: breaking the power of any institutions intermediate between the individual and the state. Locke's *Letter*, however, also vehemently expresses this underlying ideology. This ideology particularly comes to the fore when such intermediate institutions are perceived to have transnational affiliations. It has thus been variously pressed into the service of anti-Catholic, anti-Muslim, and anti-Jewish hostility.

In the 1923 case, the French were arguing for the extraction of the entirety of Tunisia and Morocco from a putatively nonterritorialized religion, in order to place them under territorial sovereigns that could be integrated into the Western state system. The territory of Tunisia and Morocco, conceived as part of the *Dar al-Islam*, plays a role here similar to the sacred sites in my entire foregoing discussion. The process envisioned by the French demanded a transformation of "religion," no less than that of the "state."[68]

In a context more directly related to sacred sites "*stricto sensu*," European powers, including France, long asserted their authority over the Holy Places and Christian populations in the Middle East – in derogation, even if nominally consensual, from Ottoman sovereignty. The "Capitulations" granting this

67 *Nationality Decrees Issued in Tunis and Morocco (French Zone), French Mémoire*, PCIJ Rep. (1923) Series C No. 2, Additional Volume, at 3. See my discussion in "'The Sacred Conspiracy': Religion, Nationalism, and the Crisis of Internationalism," *Leiden Journal of International Law* 25, no. 1 (2012): 9–54, at 9.

68 See, generally, my discussion in "The Nationality Decrees Case, or, of Intimacy and Consent," *Leiden Journal of International Law* 13, no. 2 (2000): 265–95, at 265.

authority came to an end in 1922 with the establishment of the Western-style Turkish Republic in the place of the Ottoman Empire. As a secular, territorial nation-state, the new Turkey could be allowed Western-style sovereign supremacy over sacred sites and religious populations.

There have, nonetheless, always been countervailing forces. As I have argued, the subordination of sacred sites emerged from a very particular strand of Protestantism. This subordination has always stood in contrast to many other forms of Protestantism, let alone Catholicism, Judaism, and Islam. The Capitulations are long gone, but international protection of sacred sites has taken a variety of piecemeal and episodic modern forms, including bilateral agreements and "cultural heritage of mankind" protection. Perhaps the most audacious example, even if not motivated solely by the protection of sacred sites, was the proposal to establish Jerusalem as a "*corpus separatum*" in the 1947 Palestine Partition Plan. Moreover, many proposals to resolve the Israeli-Palestinian conflict continue to include some form of internationalization of the Holy Places, even the Old City as a whole. Such proposals implicitly acknowledge the impasse between modern sovereignty and sacred sites, whose genealogy I have broached here, and seek to bypass it in favor of *international* legal and political authority.

By contrast, Adnan Abu Odeh, a former Jordanian UN Ambassador, offered a quite different exit from this impasse, a new construction of the separation of "religion" and *all* "political" authority. Abu Odeh proposed administration of the Old City of Jerusalem (about one square mile) by a joint council of religious authorities, extracting it from both national sovereignty and international authority.[69] Such a proposal would, indeed, effect a "farewell" to the Holy Places by the world's political authorities, both national and international. That "farewell" would be nearly the opposite of the one I have diagnosed here. In stark contrast to Abu Odeh's proposal, the "farewell" envisioned by Hegel and elaborated by Western courts is a cognitive farewell to intrinsic sacredness – not only compatible with sovereign supremacy but underpinning it. That proposals such as Abu Odeh's seem utopian in the literal sense – feasible only "no-place" – suggests the enduring power of the Hegelian "farewell." That some of today's most daring prophets of a peaceful future can only envision the sacredness of place in a future of no-place: this is my sobering concluding thought for a time of crisis.

[69] Adnan Abu Odeh, "Two Capitals in an Undivided Jerusalem," *Foreign Affairs* 71, no. 2 (Spring 1992): 183–8, at 187. See my discussion in "Legalizing Jerusalem, or, Of Law, Fantasy, and Faith," *Catholic University Law Review* 45 (1996): 823–35, at 823.

RECOMMENDED READING

Asad, Talal. *Formations of the Secular: Christianity, Islam, Modernity*. Stanford: Stanford University Press, 2003.

Hyppolite, Jean. *Genesis and Structure of Hegel's Phenomenology of Spirit*. Evanston: Northwestern University Press, 1974.

Nandy, Ashis, Shikha Trivedy, Shail Mayaram, and Achyut Yagnik. *Creating a Nationality: Ramjanmabhumi Movement and the Fear of the Self*. Oxford: Oxford University Press, 1998.

Tillich, Paul. *The Interpretation of History*, translated by Elsa L. Tamley. New York: C. Scribner's Sons, 1936 [1926].

Williams, Robert A. *The American Indian in Western Legal Thought: The Discourses of Conquest*. New York: Oxford University Press, 1992.

17

Constantine's Legacy: Preserving Empire While Undermining International Law

Craig B. Mousin

Thou shall not return a refugee to persecution. Nation-states declared they had learned that critical lesson from the tragedy of the Holocaust by enacting international refugee conventions and protocols. Today, as refugees seek safety, they find fortress-like liberal democracies building walls of steel interlaced with legal strategies that undermine the international protections forged from the fires of the Holocaust. Consequently, refugees drown in the Mediterranean, die in the Mexico-United States desert, become detained in overcrowded refugee camps and unofficial street shelters, or become victims of criminal gangs. Nation-states have all too often abdicated their responsibility to refugees. This chapter explores this interlocking struggle between Christian hospitality toward the outsider and Christian refusal to offer that hospitality in support of national security. Christian beliefs that encourage submission to governing authorities and prioritize the nation undermine international law to the detriment of not just refugees but also citizens and the world community.

Constantine thought that by establishing Christianity as the religion of the Roman Empire, peace and prosperity would reign forever. Since Constantine linked power between the secular and the religious, the West has experienced multiple models of government under empire, loss of empire, and religious wars. The Treaty of Westphalia in 1648 commenced a three-century experiment with the nation-state system of law that established the sovereign state's duty to protect all its residents. In the twentieth century, Hannah Arendt exposed the fragility and broken promise of Westphalia due to its failure to protect individuals who fled persecution when no other nation offered protection.[1] Since 1951, the international community has sought to address that breach of responsibility toward refugees through law as well as informal

[1] Hannah Arendt, *The Origins of Totalitarianism* (New York: Harcourt, 1976), 280, 290.

agreements. Mass refugee flows early in the twenty-first century, however, have raised questions as to whether international law has solved Arendt's dilemma. Moreover, the seeds of Christian establishment within the nation-state, first planted by Constantine, have sprouted through bans on non-Christian immigration and restrictions on refugees, regardless of religion.

Section 17.1 of this chapter explores Christianity's transition from persecution to establishment after Constantine's conversion to Christianity. It then links the imperial church to the nation-states that formed after 1648. Section 17.2 reviews Arendt's twentieth-century critique of the nation-state and identifies its actions that resemble current treatment of refugees and immigrants. It then summarizes the waxing and waning of international law since World War II. Section 17.3 deals with some of the United States's Executive Orders, federal policies, and political rhetoric that undermine international law. It addresses four concerns: deterring applicants for asylum, detention, untrammeled police enforcement, and the evisceration of the rule of law. Section 17.4 contrasts Christian nationalist rhetoric and arguments that deter asylum, encourage detention, and expedite deportation with a biblical theology to welcome the stranger.

17.1 CONSTANTINE'S LEGACY: THE IMPERIAL STATE ADOPTS RELIGION AND THE RISE OF THE NATION-STATE

Christianity, born in the midst of empire, began in crisis when that empire executed Jesus. It later experienced growth and persecution. Paul transformed religion by evangelizing in the empire's urban centers and, eventually, in Rome itself. With growth came controversy over its principles and understandings of Jesus's ministry. Expansion in the midst of significant disunity and periodic persecution within the empire characterized the first three centuries. The most significant transformation, however, came not through internal discernment but rather from Constantine's conversion to Christianity and his designation of Christianity as the imperial religion in the fourth century. Scholars debate whether Rome saved Christianity or Christianity saved Rome, but recognize that two partners entered a mutually beneficial relationship sparking the ongoing dance between establishment of a church/state partnership or two autonomous disputing sovereigns. Although his personal motives for accepting Christ are lost in time, Constantine saw in Christianity a way to preserve his empire.[2] Constantine adopted this particular faith, eventually

[2] William C. Placher, *A History of Christian Theology: An Introduction* (Louisville, KY: Westminster John Knox Press, 1983), 74. See also Jaroslav Pelikan, *The Excellent Empire:*

even using state control to eliminate competing faiths.[3] Constantine paid clergy salaries, built residences for bishops, constructed new churches, and called councils to determine doctrine. He even waived municipal taxes for clergy.[4] The bishops welcomed the support and built the church on the scaffolding of the empire. Constantine's biographer Eusebius reported:

> He made [the Bishops] also his companions in travel, believing that He whose servants they were would thus help him. Besides this, he gave from his own private resources costly benefactions to the churches of God, both enlarging and heightening the sacred edifices, and embellishing the august sanctuaries of the church with abundant offerings.[5]

The emperor, with the concurrence of the bishops, established the *canon* as the approved writings of the Hebrew Scriptures and the New Testament.[6] David Dungan further notes:

> In general, the Catholic church adopted the geographical divisions (dioceses) of Roman administration, and Catholic clergy took on the official titles of Roman government. They began to think and act like Roman officials. Living in stately villas and conducting public worship services, not in the little house-churches they were previously accustomed to, but in huge new temples or basilicas, packed with masses of half-converted parishioners.[7]

These developments transformed both empire and church. Constantine saw his prosperity and security based upon his faith in the Christian God, reporting to the bishops that to Christ "I ascribe the cause of my own prosperity, and of all that I now possess. To this truth the happy issue of all my endeavors bears testimony: brave deeds, victories in war, and triumphs over conquered foes."[8] With the change in structure came important differences in theology and practice. A paid clergy looked to the empire, not the early community's model of voluntary contributions, for sustenance or for charity. The church became more established, maintaining its basilicas and interlocking relationships with

The Fall of Rome and the Triumph of the Church (San Francisco: Harper & Row, 1987), 26 (Constantine's conversion led to "a new form of Christian empire").

[3] David Dungan, *Constantine's Bible: Politics and the Making of the New Testament* (Minneapolis: Fortress Press, 2007), 115.

[4] Edward J. Watts, *The Final Pagan Generation* (Oakland: University of California Press, 2015), 46.

[5] Eusebius, "Oration of Eusebius in Praise of Constantine," in *Church History; Life of Constantine the Great, and Oration in Praise of Constantine*, trans. Ernest Cushing Richardson et al. (New York: Christian Literature Co., 1890), 1196.

[6] Dungan, *Constantine's Bible*, 122.

[7] Dungan, *Constantine's Bible*, 96.

[8] Eusebius, "Oration of Eusebius," 1475.

secular government. As Luke Timothy Johnson said: "The radical nature of the Christian mission was thereby weakened. Even the ideas it incorporated of a right created from the perspective of the weak were adapted to the prevailing power structure."[9]

As Robin Lovin finds, however: "These powers were not conceived on either side as antagonist. They were complementary parts of a large system of authority established by God," yet "the concept of two powers representing different sources of authority and legitimacy in a single social and political order proved surprisingly durable."[10] Indeed, it proved so durable that it led to various forms of Christendom, not always identical but most claiming roots in this established Christian state until the twentieth century.[11]

That linkage began on May 20, AD 325 when Constantine called 230 bishops together at Nicaea with his goal to engage Christianity to forge unity within the empire.[12] Dungan found no evidence that any of the bishops protested Constantine's significant leadership in the internal affairs of the Christian Church.[13] At its conclusion, however, the only two bishops who failed to agree on the Council's decisions were exiled, both an irony of a church founded in exile (now cooperating with the imperial power to exile those considered objectionable) and a portent of the negative consequences of linking too closely with any governmental power.[14] But one theme emerges when both civil and religious power unite in harmony: the religious leaders concur as they believe the civil leader has been chosen and given authority by God.

Despite his conversion, Constantine ruled over an empire with many non-Christians, and, therefore, pragmatically kept many of the trappings and mores of imperial leadership. Many non-Christians still saw Constantine as a traditional Roman pagan emperor.[15] His chameleon ability to entice loyalty from both communities demonstrated his practical skill in ruling over such a diverse

9 Luke Timothy Johnson, "Religious Rights and Christian Texts," in *Religious Human Rights in Global Perspective, Religious Perspectives*, ed. John Witte, Jr. and Johan D. van der Vyver (Kluwer Law International, 1996), 49. See also David Joseph Wellman, "Trump, the Cross and the Lynching Tree: White Christian Nationalists and the Future of American Political Identity," in *Gender-Nation-Religion: Ein internationaler Vergleigh von Akteursstrategien und Diskursverflechtungen*, ed. Maren Behrensen et al. (Frankfurt: Campus Verlag, 2018), 93.

10 Robin Lovin, "Authority, Legitimacy and Sovereignty: Religion and Politics in the Roman Empire before Constantine," *Studies in Christian Ethics* 29, no. 2 (2016): 177–89, at 187.

11 Diarmaid MacCulloch, *Christianity, the First Three Thousand Years* (New York: Viking, 2009), 188.

12 Mark Noll, *Turning Points: Decisive Moments in the History of Christianity*, 3rd ed. (Grand Rapids, MI: Baker Academic, 2012), 40.

13 Dungan, *Constantine's Bible*, 113.

14 Dungan, *Constantine's Bible*, 113.

15 Watts, *Pagan*, 50–1.

empire, and, right up to the present day, has provided a model for subsequent leaders who rule over sovereign nations consisting of competing creeds and nonbelievers while maintaining the claim of being chosen to lead by God.

This tension between secular and religious has modulated over the last two thousand years, but with each shift between secular and religious sovereigns, Western law developed.[16] The exile of the two bishops from Nicaea simply foreshadowed years of persecution, exclusion, and struggle between crown and altar, yet, at its best, the church continued to hold both together.[17] The Protestant Reformation incited new wars but also broke the universal political realm of the Catholic Church. Westphalia marked the emergence of sovereign states purportedly protecting their respective citizens. The two wars of the twentieth century, however, shattered the principle that the sovereign would protect all of its residents.

17.2 THE FAILURE OF THE NATION-STATE

Despite experiencing weakness and vulnerability, refugees have often exposed the fragility of the world's powers. Westphalia invoked two responsibilities: the sovereign protected a nation's borders without fear of foreign interference with the concomitant responsibility to protect all the members within the sovereign's jurisdiction. Historically, citizens possessed the right to leave a nation, but, given each sovereign's prerogative, no state was required to accept and protect any specific person appearing at their borders.[18] Arendt's insight revealed that the twentieth century's tragic response to refugees and stateless persons undermined that foundation of the nation-state. "[I]t turned out that the moment human beings lacked their own government and had to fall back upon their minimum rights, no authority was left to protect them and no institution was willing to guarantee them."[19]

16 See, generally, John Witte, Jr., *God's Joust, God's Justice: Law and Religion in the Western Tradition* (Grand Rapids, MI: Eerdmans Publishing Company, 2006). See also Walter Russell Meade, *God and Gold: Britain, America and the Making of the Modern World* (New York: Alfred A. Knopf, 2008); for an interesting discussion of this dance between the secular and the religious and its impact on history, see Frederick Mark Gedicks, "True Lies: Canossa as Myth," *Journal of Contemporary Legal Issues* 21, (2013): 133–44, at 133. See also Nehal Bhuta, "What Should Freedom of Religion Become?," in *Freedom of Religion, Secularism and Human Rights*, ed. Nehal Bhuta (Oxford: Oxford University Press, 2019), addressing the transformation from religious empire to sovereign states to secular republics.

17 See, e.g., Dungan, *Constantine's Bible*, 123.

18 Aristide R. Zolberg, "Why Not the Whole World? Ethical Dilemmas of Immigration Policy," *American Behavioral Scientist* 56, no. 9 (2012): 1204–22, at 1204.

19 Arendt, *Totalitarianism*, 293.

Arendt drew several lessons from these failures. First, rights based on the state were not inalienable, and therefore, the world needed to draw new political principles to guarantee human dignity for all humans, not just those a nation chose to protect.[20] Second, the nation itself faced new risks, for it "cannot exist once its principle of equality before the law has broken down."[21] Through the evisceration of rights, it abdicated its duty under the rule of law. "The modern nation state was being transformed from an organ which would execute the rule of law for all its citizens and residents into an instrument of the nation alone."[22]

Third, once this transformation occurred, both the refugee and anyone considered an outsider faced risk. The Holocaust provides the paramount example of a sovereign designating a group as outsiders and eliminating their rights, let alone lives, while at the same time restricting the rights of all citizens. Subsequently, during the Cold War both antagonists sacrificed individual rights in the name of security. US Supreme Court Justice Robert Jackson observed the weakness of the state fearing the lone individual, let alone thousands approaching a border, when he described a man "who seems to have led a life of unrelieved insignificance" who put

> . . . the Government of the United States in such fear that it was afraid to tell him why it was afraid of him . . .. Since we proclaimed him a Samson who might pull down the pillars of our temple, we should not be surprised if peoples less prosperous, less strongly established, and less stable feared to take him off our timorous hands.[23]

Jackson revealed the creeping restrictions on human rights in the name of national security and the contagious nature of such policy decisions among other nations. For example, within two months of 9/11, the United States detained over a thousand persons, mostly Muslims, many of whom were lawful permanent residents or citizens.[24] The current efforts to detain thousands and build a wall once again stem from a fear of the other.

Arendt had already posited that modern governments learned different mechanisms for denying people equal protection of the law. She noted that "society has discovered discrimination as the great social weapon by which one may kill men

20 Arendt, *Totalitarianism*, ix.

21 Arendt, *Totalitarianism*, 290.

22 Arendt, *Totalitarianism*, 275.

23 *Shaughnessy* v. *Mezei*, 345 U.S. 206, 219–20, Jackson, J., dissent (1953).

24 U.S. Department of Justice Special Report: "The September 11 Detainees," June 2003, https://oig.justice.gov/special/0306/full.pdf.

without any bloodshed; since passports or birth certificates, and sometimes even income tax receipts, are no longer formal papers but matters of social distinction."[25] More than ten million persons reside in the United States without the proper papers necessary for lawful presence. Hiroshi Motomura describes them as being "outside the law" without full constitutional or statutory protection, yet still many engage with families and communities in making the US nation stronger.[26] The political rhetoric names them illegal residents. Yet many have never been adjudicated as violating US immigration laws, although they still remain at great risk.[27] Seyla Benhabib summarized this problem, observing that the "nation-state system ... is based upon the tension, and at times outright contradiction, between human rights and the principle of national autonomy."[28]

17.2.1 *International Law and Refugees*

17.2.1.1 Development of International Law's Protection of Refugees after World War II

Arendt was not alone in recognizing the tension and danger of the sovereign state operating outside the bounds of law. As war devastated Europe, Justice Jackson foresaw the need for enhancing international law. Two months before Pearl Harbor, in predicting that this nation "will face a tough and fateful decision as to her attitude toward peace," he posed this compelling dilemma:

> At the end of this war we must either throw the full weight of American influence to the support of an international order based on law, or we must outstrip the world in naval and air, and perhaps in military, force .... The tragedy and irony of our present position is that we who would make no commitment to support world peace are making contributions a thousandfold greater to support a world war.[29]

After the war, the victors attempted to address some of those contradictions through international law. The 1951 Refugee Convention established a process

[25] Hannah Arendt, "We Refugees," in *Altogether Elsewhere: Writers on Exile*, ed. Marc Robinson (Boston: Faber and Faber, 1994), 118.

[26] Hiroshi Motomura, *Immigration Outside the Law* (New York: Oxford University Press, 2014), 4.

[27] See Craig B. Mousin, "Rights Disappear When US Policy Engages Children as Weapons of Deterrence," AMA *Journal of Ethics* 21, no. 1 (2019): E58–66, at 60.

[28] Seyla Benhabib, *The Rights of Others: Aliens, Residents and Citizens* (New York: Cambridge University Press, 2004), 61.

[29] Robert H. Jackson, "The Challenge of International Lawlessness," *American Bar Association Journal* 27, no. 11 (1941): 690–3, at 690, 693.

to address the refugees.[30] The drafters' optimism led them to conclude that the Convention would only address existing refugees through January 1, 1951. Although the United States had participated in the drafting of the Convention, it never ratified it, exercising its sovereign power to ameliorate refugee issues without sacrificing its power.

Refugees did not cease to exist. The Cold War and its proxy wars led to persecution within and beyond Europe, leading to the Protocol Relating to the Status of Refugees in 1967 which expanded the Convention's protections worldwide and without a sunset provision.[31] The Senate ratified the Protocol but did not transform it into domestic law until the Refugee Act of 1980.[32] Its major provisions of asylum and withholding of deportation (non-refoulement) accepted the lessons of World War II that the denial of entry left many refugees no recourse but to return home to face death and persecution. Refugees fleeing the targeted violence of their native lands could not be expected to patiently wait for consulates or to follow normal immigration procedures. Too many people had died in Europe while their visa applications sat in consulates. Therefore, the signatories agreed upon an almost biblical covenant to protect refugees: thou shall not return a refugee to face persecution. Instead, at the very minimum, each signatory agreed to offer a procedure to determine eligibility as a refugee. After significant debate, the Convention limited those eligible for asylum protection to persons who arrived at a border seeking safe haven and who had been persecuted or faced a well-founded fear of persecution on account of race, religion, nationality, political opinion, or membership in a particular social group.[33] The Refugee Act adopted that definition and also authorized an annual process to designate a number of refugees who would be processed overseas but would then be resettled as refugees.

The success of international law has resulted in safety for millions of refugees who have fled persecution. The United States since 1980 has led the world in accepting refugees. Through both overseas resettlement and the asylum process, over three million have found that safe haven within US borders.[34] Ongoing developments have also enhanced refugee protection. The United States negotiated the Convention on the Rights of the Child

30 Convention Relating to the Status of Refugees, July 28, 1951, 189 U.N.T.S. 150, www.ohchr.org/Documents/ProfessionalInterest/refugees.pdf.

31 Protocol Relating to the Status of Refugees, January 31, 1967, 606 U.N.T.S. 267, www.ohchr.org/Documents/ProfessionalInterest/protocolrefugees.pdf.

32 Refugee Act of 1980, Pub. L. No. 96–212, 94 Stat. 102.

33 See also Chapter 18 in this volume for a more expansive description of the asylum process.

34 Since the Refugee Act of 1980, the USA has taken in 3 million of the more than 4 million refugees worldwide. Phillip Connor and Jens Manuel Krogstad, "For the First Time, U.S. Resettles Fewer Refugees than the Rest of the World," Pew Research Center, July 5, 2018, www

(CRC) which included provisions on asylum and detention of refugee minors.[35] Most important, the CRC calls for governments to take the best interests of the child into account when ascertaining the eligibility of minors for asylum or relief from deportation or detention.[36] The United Nations adopted the CRC in 1989, but once again, fearful of a loss of sovereignty, the United States stood alone in abstaining from ratifying the CRC. In contrast, in 1994, the United States signed the Convention Against Torture (CAT), implementing it in 1998. CAT provided a definition of torture and withheld deportation for victims and also made work authorization available.[37]

Initially inspired by evangelical Christians, but subsequently supported by other faith traditions, Congress passed the International Religious Freedom Act of 1998 (IRFA) when studies demonstrated that asylum adjudicators did not fully understand religious persecution.[38] Under IRFA, Congress instructed immigration judges (IJs) and asylum officers to seek greater clarity about religious persecution and required them to follow international law's definition of religious persecution rather than domestic law.[39] The International Covenant on Civil and Political Rights (ICCPR), although not specifically addressed to refugees, asks each of its signatories to grant "all persons" equality within a nation.[40] Although it permits some citizenship distinctions, it recalls Arendt's failure of the nation-state to provide equal protection under the law.

Less formal developments have also advanced refugee protection. The crisis of genocide and persecution challenged the principle of the sovereign's

.pewresearch.org/fact-tank/2018/07/05/for-the-first-time-u-s-resettles-fewer-refugees-than-the-rest-of-the-world/.

35 Convention on the Rights of the Child, November 20, 1989, 1577 U.N.T.S. 3, www2.ohchr.org/english/law/pdf/crc.pdf.

36 Mousin, "Rights Disappear," 60. See also Carolus Grütters, "The Return of the Children," in *Law and Judicial Dialogue on the Return of Irregular Migrants from the European Union*, ed. Madalina Moraru, Galina Cornelisse, and Philippe De Bruycker (Oxford: Hart Publishing, 2020), 1.

37 Convention Against Torture and Other Cruel, Inhuman or Degrading Treatment or Punishment (CAT), December 10, 1984, 1465 U.N.T.S. 85, www.ohchr.org/Documents/ProfessionalInterest/cat.pdf.

38 International Religious Freedom Act of 1998, H.R. 2431, 105th Cong. (1997).

39 Craig B. Mousin, "Can One Still Call It Ignorance or Improper Bias?," in *Migration and Religious Freedom*, ed. Carolus Grütters and Dario Dzananovic (Nijmegen: Wolf Legal Publishers, 2018), 71–2.

40 International Covenant on Civil and Political Rights (ICCPR), December 16, 1966, 999 U.N.T.S. 171, www.ohchr.org/Documents/ProfessionalInterest/ccpr.pdf; T. Alexander Aleinikoff, "International Legal Norms and Migration, A Report," in *Migration and International Legal Norms*, ed. T. Alexander Aleinikoff and Vincent Chetail (The Hague: T.M.C. Asser Press, 2003), 14–15.

integrity and control over its territory, calling for intervention by the United Nations or alliances such as North Atlantic Treaty Organization (NATO). Daniel Philpott writes that "these interventions represent new conditions that the United Nations places on states' sovereignty, making them accountable to a higher authority for upholding certain standards of civilized behavior."[41] Alexander Aleinikoff adds that the current international legal regime through multilateral conventions and bilateral agreements "constrain and channel state authority over migration."[42] He sees much more cooperative efforts that serve the interests of not just migrants but the nation-states themselves.[43]

17.2.1.2 Refugee Protections Undermined When Challenged by National Security

Despite these advances, the threat to national security and the fear of diminished sovereignty from porous borders undercut federal commitment to refugees.[44] In the 1980s, thousands of Haitians fled persecution. With potentially unprecedented numbers seeking entry, the United States interdicted them at sea and returned them to Haiti. These boat people posed the question of whether non-refoulement (the "thou shall not return" principle) required an applicant to be at the border requesting admission or whether the law had extraterritoriality, requiring a hearing prior to a return to Haiti. The Supreme Court held that, in contrast to international law, non-refoulement under the Refugee Act held no extraterritoriality provisions. The United States was not bound to provide a hearing beyond the border.[45] Subsequently, the Court also narrowed US protection from international law by holding that the proof necessary to sustain a withholding of deportation claim was higher than the well-founded fear standard for asylum.[46]

Thus, the United States has carved out exceptions to what other nations in the world have followed under the Refugee Convention. Other steps taken to increase border control efficiency include implementing a credible fear

41 Daniel Philpott, *Revolutions in Sovereignty: How Modern Ideas Shaped Modern International Relations* (Princeton: Princeton University Press, 2001), 41.

42 Aleinikoff, "Legal Norms," 1.

43 Aleinikoff, "Legal Norms," 1.

44 Other nations have also escalated nationalism, often with Christian support, to exclude refugees. See Maryellen Fullerton, "Borders, Bans, and Courts in the European Union," *Roger Williams University Law Review* 23, no. 2 (2018): 393–418, at 393. Fullerton writes, "Victor Orbàn, the Prime Minister of Hungary . . . calls his nation the 'gatekeeper of Christian Europe'." Fullerton, "Borders," 404.

45 *Sale* v. *Haitian Centers Council*, 509 U.S 155, 173–4 (1993).

46 *I.N.S.* v. *Stevic*, 467 U.S. 407, 412–13 (1984); *I.N.S.* v. *Cardoza-Fonseca*, 480 U.S. 421, 423–4 (1987).

standard at an entry point enabling the government to decide the initial bona fides of the applicant, to determine whether he or she will be provided with the full protection of a hearing. Against the standard accepted by most of the signatories, the United States has also required mandatory detention for asylum seekers.

Increasingly harsh immigration laws starting in 1986 made unauthorized status more difficult. The 1986 Immigration Reform and Control Act (IRCA) limited work to citizens or others authorized by the federal government.[47] Although international law recommended that applicants receive work authorization upon filing for asylum, Congress delayed work authorization for at least six months, and often far longer, until the adjudication of the asylum request. Congress provided no explanation as to how applicants were to eat or pay for housing while awaiting authorization.[48]

As the political rhetoric paints refugees as criminals or terrorists, another of Arendt's observations proves prescient. She argued: "The more the number of rightless people increased, the greater became the temptation to pay less attention to the deeds of the persecuting governments than to the status of the persecuted."[49] President Trump's 2016 campaign proclaimed "Build the Wall" while categorizing refugees as criminals and terrorists. Little or no effort by any party sought to discover why persons would flee a home to come to a strange land. Three centuries of US exploitation in Central and South America have contributed to the decline of the rule of law and the corruption and gang violence that plague the homes of refugees.[50] These sovereigns have failed to protect their own citizens, forcing refugees to flee. But the campaign's priority on building the wall and detention facilities while increasing deportations has turned any focus away from the causes of exile. These concerns became a primary linchpin of the 2016 primary and election campaigns, and therefore intensified the incentive to build the wall and ignore the valuable principles of international law.[51]

47 Immigration Reform and Control Act of 1986, Pub. L. No. 99–603, 100 Stat. 3359.

48 Seton Hall Law Human Rights Watch Report, "At Least Let Them Work: The Denial of Work Authorization and Assistance for Asylum Seekers in the United States," November 12, 2013, www.hrw.org/report/2013/11/12/least-let-them-work/denial-work-authorization-and-assistance-asylum-seekers-united, 27–32.

49 Arendt, *Totalitarianism*, 293.

50 Craig B. Mousin, "You Were Told to Love the Immigrant, But What If the Story Never Happened? Hospitality and United States Immigration Law," *Vincentian Heritage* 33, no. 1 (2016), see text between footnotes 161–6.

51 Julie Hirschfeld Davis and Michael D. Shear, *Border Wars: Inside Trump's Assault on Immigration* (New York: Simon & Shuster, 2019), 12–14, 392.

17.3 SINCE 2016, EXECUTIVE ORDERS, FEDERAL POLICIES, AND POLITICAL RHETORIC UNDERMINE INTERNATIONAL LAW

As our amnesia hides the causes and consequences of the Holocaust, the US response to the appearance of refugees at its borders sows seeds similar to the ones that previously fractured protection. Arendt reminds that responses to refugees at borders not only built walls that excluded and confined but also changed domestic law reducing the rights of all within the sovereign's boundary. The inequality between persons within the nation did not just lead to treating people differently; it also undermined rule of law and due process for those targeted, and also for citizens. Arendt warned of the peril we face if we ignore the seeds sown in neglecting the rule of law in the name of security. Her careful observation of how those seeds germinated chillingly reveals current patterns.

Compiling all the litigation, new Executive Orders, Department of Justice (DOJ) policies, Department of Homeland Security (DHS) policies, and State Department policies would overwhelm the constraints of this chapter, but four major areas of concern reveal the evisceration of international law in the name of Christian morals and national security.[52] Taken together, they prove the validity of Supreme Court Justice Sonia Sotomayor's rueful conclusion: "Once again the Executive Branch has issued a rule that seeks to upend longstanding practices regarding refugees who seek shelter from persecution."[53]

17.3.1 *Reducing the Ability to Apply for Asylum*

Within days of taking office, President Trump issued several Executive Orders including "Border Security and Immigration Enforcement Improvements"[54] and "Enhancing Public Safety in the Interior of the United States."[55] Both accused the previous administration of failing "to discharge this basic

[52] See Sarah Pierce, "Immigration-Related Policy Changes in the First Two Years of the Trump Administration," Migration Policy Institute, 2019, listing over 140 changes in the law in less than three years, www.migrationpolicy.org/research/immigration-policy-changes-two-years-trump-administration. See also "Civil Rights Challenges to the Trump Refugee/Visa Order," Civil Rights Litigation Clearinghouse, University of Michigan Law School (2019), www.clearinghouse.net/results.php?searchSpecialCollection=44; "Civil Rights Challenges to Trump Immigration Enforcement Orders," Civil Rights Litigation Clearinghouse, University of Michigan Clearinghouse (2019), www.clearinghouse.net/featuredCase.php?id=40.

[53] *Barr* v. *E. Bay Sanctuary Covenant*, 140 S. Ct. 3, 4, 204 L. Ed. 2d 1189 (2019). (Sotomayor, J., dissenting).

[54] Exec. Order No. 13767, 82 F.R. 8793 (2017).

[55] Exec. Order No. 13768, 82 F.R. 8799 (2017).

sovereign responsibility" of securing the border. The first order gave the DHS new powers to implement security measures, to design and build a new wall, and to build new detention facilities on the southern border.[56] The second order aimed at interior enforcement and changed the prosecutorial enforcement against noncitizens within the interior including those with only alleged criminal acts that had not yet been adjudicated.[57] On January 27, he issued the first of the Travel Ban Executive Orders: "Protecting the Nation from Foreign Terrorist Entry into the United States."[58] Litigation necessitated amending and issuing subsequent orders and proclamations, but the Supreme Court upheld the ban in June 2018.[59]

In addition, then US Attorney General Jeff Sessions issued a "Zero Tolerance Policy for Criminal Illegal Entry" on April 6, 2018.[60] Notwithstanding the Refugee Act's promise that one could apply for asylum irrespective of status, Sessions ordered all who entered or attempted to enter without inspection to be prosecuted prior to applying for asylum. Sessions later defended this policy, when he "cited Romans 13, imploring his 'church friends' to remember the Bible passage that directs the faithful to obey the laws of the government" stressing that "it is very biblical to enforce the law."[61]

Although the Refugee Act provides a process for asylum applicants to determine their eligibility and adopts the Convention's requirement to not return refugees to persecution, zero tolerance contributed to this retreat from refugee protection. Three other orders soon followed that further abandoned these commitments.[62] The first banned applicants who entered either at

56 Shoba Sivaprasad Wahdia, "Summary of the Executive Order on 'The Wall' or 'Border Security and Immigration Enforcement Improvements'," Penn State Law (January 2017), https://pennstatelaw.psu.edu/sites/default/files/The%20Wall.PDF.

57 Shoba Sivaprasad Wahdia, "Summary of the Executive Order on 'Sanctuary' or Enhancing Public Safety in the Interior of the United States," Penn State Law (January 2017), https://pennstatelaw.psu.edu/sites/default/files/Public%20Safety%20Summary%201.27.17.pdf.

58 "President Trump's Executive Orders on Immigration and Refugees," Center for Migration Studies (2017), https://cmsny.org/trumps-executive-orders-immigration-refugees/.

59 *Trump* v. *Hawaii*, 138 S. Ct. 2392 (2018). See *Executive Order Entry Ban Litigation Updates*, NAFSA (2018), www.nafsa.org/Professional_Resources/Browse_by_Interest/International_Students_and_Scholars/Executive_Order_Entry_Ban_Litigation_Updates/.

60 Department of Justice, Office of Public Affairs, "Attorney General Announces Zero-Tolerance Policy for Criminal Illegal Entry," press release no. 18–417, April 6, 2018, www.justice.gov/opa/pr/attorney-general-announces-zero-tolerance-policy-criminal-illegal-entry.

61 John Fritze, "Citing Bible, Trump Administration Digs In on 'Zero Tolerance' Immigration Policy," *USA Today*, June 14, 2018. www.usatoday.com/story/news/politics/2018/06/14/jeff-sessions-sarah-sanders-defend-zero-tolerance-immigration-policy/703664002/.

62 In addition, the administration has cut back on all refugee resettlement. Although the USA has often resettled more than 100,000 per year, it processed only 22,491 in 2018 and in the first six months of 2019 only 12,154 were admitted. See Migration Policy Institute (MPI), "Analysis

a place other than a port of entry or without proper papers.[63] A nationwide injunction has held this order illegal, but it remains in litigation. The Migrant Protection Protocols (MPPs) order most asylum seekers who come to a port of entry in Mexico to remain in Mexico until their hearing.[64] No formal procedure exists in Mexico, nor is there sufficient food or housing while they wait. Thousands now face exploitation by criminals, corrupt police, and lack of facilities in Mexico.[65] The plan adds almost insurmountable impediments due to the difficulties of receiving notice, getting through the border, and getting to court.[66] Even those fortunate enough to get a hearing date must arrive at the border by four a.m. to process and get to the tent court for their hearing. They are given virtually no time to meet with an attorney if they are fortunate enough to have one. Of the 12,997 MPP cases pending at the end of June 2019, only 163 applicants were able to secure attorneys.[67] Lawyers are not permitted to observe hearings. Although the court falls within the jurisdiction of the DOJ, the DHS built the tent courts and retains control over all activity within even establishing procedures and instructions for immigration judges.[68] This policy grants law enforcement control over the judges and attorneys, precluding an independent judiciary and hindering zealous advocacy.

As these seeds of control germinate, they reveal similarities to the early stages in Germany before World War II, when the police were given full power over the courts. Arendt remarked:

> The nation-state, incapable of providing a law for those who had lost the protection of a national government, transferred the whole matter to the

of WRAPS Data from the State Department Bureau of Population, Refugees, and Migration," www.wrapsnet.org/admissions-and-arrivals/, at 18.

63 MPI, "WRAPS Data," 19–20. *East Bay* v. *Trump*, 932 F.3d 742 (9th Cir. 2018).

64 Department of Homeland Security, "Policy Guidance for Implementation of the Migrant Protection Protocols," January 25, 2019, www.dhs.gov/sites/default/files/publications/19_0129_OPA_migrant-protection-protocols-policy-guidance.pdf.

65 Leonard Cavise, "Immigration: Manufactured Misery at the Tijuana Border Crossing," *Truthout*, September 28, 2019, https://truthout.org/articles/manufactured-misery-at-the-tijuana-border-crossing/.

66 TRAC Immigration, "Access to Attorneys Difficult for Those Required to Remain in Mexico," July 29, 2019, https://trac.syr.edu/immigration/reports/568/.

67 Ibid.

68 *Policy Brief: Public Access to Tent Courts Not Allowed, but Meaningful Access Still Absent*, AILA Doc. No. 20011061 (January 2020), www.aila.org/File/DownloadEmbeddedFile/83330. Further demonstrating how these policies and acceptance by the courts undercuts the protection of refugees, the Board of Immigration Appeals has ordered IJs to enter in absentia orders of removal for any applicant returned to Mexico under MPP who misses the scheduled hearing perhaps because of a failure to navigate the labyrinthine procedures to appear at the hearing. This ruling precludes the applicant from presenting the facts that initially fostered the flight from persecution. *Matter of J.J. Rodriguez*, 27 I&N Dec. 762 (BIA 2020).

> police. This was the first time the police in Western Europe had received authority to act on its own, to rule directly over people, in one sphere of public life it was no longer an instrument to carry out and enforce the law ....[69]

Although not identical to Arendt's situation, police control of courts betrays a commitment to fairness and independence. The President of the American Bar Association has criticized the denial of access to lawyers and the lack of transparency, alleging that these policies "should concern anyone who believes that individuals who come before our courts should be afforded due process and that justice should be delivered."[70] All of these efforts weave together a policy of "extraterritoriality" and "remote control" – a direct affront to the rule of "thou shall not return." By pushing enforcement away from the border, the administration alleges that it is meeting the law's requirements, but in practice it is minimizing refugee protection.[71] As David Scott Fitzgerald argues, the "defining characteristic of modern remote control is that it has become a global system. The architecture of repulsion includes cages, domes, moats, buffers, and barbicans whose functions are all linked to one another."[72]

17.3.2 *Family Separation and Detention*

Within the interior, moreover, federal policies and actions linked detention to deterrence. Although international and domestic law disfavor detention, President Trump has used detention to deter asylum seekers from approaching US borders. In 2017, his administration intentionally separated detained families.[73] Although the official policy has been canceled, thousands of minors remain in detention. Parents were forced to decide whether to accept plea bargains in mass court hearings with fifty or seventy defendants charged simultaneously with improper entry, often without legal representation or information on the consequences of their choices. A guilty plea might allow family reunification sooner, but it also frequently led to deportation without

69 Arendt, *Totalitarianism*, 287. See also Arno A. Herzberg, "The Situation of the Lawyer in Germany," *American Bar Association Journal* 27, no. 5 (1941): 294–5, at 295.

70 ABA President Judy Perry Martinez, "ABA President: Due Process Concerns at US-Mexico Border," October www.americanbar.org/news/abanews/publications/youraba/2019/october-2019/aba-president–due-process-concerns-at-u-s-mexico-border/.

71 David Scott Fitzgerald, *Refuge Beyond Reach: How Rich Democracies Repel Asylum Seekers* (New York: Oxford University Press, 2019), 10, 14.

72 Fitzgerald, *Refuge Beyond Reach*, 14.

73 Pierce, "Immigration-Related Policy Changes," 2, 20.

an opportunity to apply for asylum.[74] Children suffer trauma when isolated in detention.[75] Some minor children as young as two have been required to appear in immigration hearings without an attorney or guardian to make their case for asylum.[76] International law calls for detention of children to be a last resort and for any decision regarding minors to take the best interests of the child into account.[77] Because US immigration law does not adopt international law's best interests of the child standard, IJs have been precluded from examining the child's best interests as a ground for relief.[78] In addition, the reliance on private for-profit detention centers has led to poor medical care and insufficient food, again in violation of international standards. The DHS frequently builds detention facilities far from metropolitan areas where legal services or other social services might otherwise be available, thus further reducing ability to avoid deportation.

17.3.3 *Impunity of the Border Enforcement Authorities*

Customs and Border Protection (CBP) often acts with impunity at the border and throughout much of the land. In its official capacity, it often provides wrong information or sends asylum applicants away from the border. One applicant reported that the agent told him he was not eligible because they were giving asylum only to Christians fleeing persecution.[79] Numerous deaths have been attributed to officers, even murders of Mexican citizens clearly on the Mexican side of the wall, but no agent has been found guilty for excessive use of force or murder. Although neither CBP nor Immigration and Customs Enforcement (ICE) has been given the carte blanche found within totalitarian governments, expanded enforcement practices create fear within immigrant communities.

74 Michael E. Miller, "'They Just Took Them?' Frantic Parents Separated from Their Kids Fill Courts on the Border," *Washington Post*, June 9, 2018, www.washingtonpost.com/local/they-just-took-them-frantic-parents-separated-from-their-kids-fill-courts-on-the-border/2018/06/09/e3f5170c-6aa9-11e8-bea7-c8eb28bc52b1_story.html.

75 U.S. Commission on Civil Rights, "Trauma at the Border: The Human Cost of Inhumane Immigration Policies," October 24, 2019, www.usccr.gov/pubs/2019/10–24-Trauma-at-the-Border.pdf.

76 Jennifer Anzardo Valdes, "Your Honor, Can I Play with That Gavel?," *New York Times*, August 22, 2018, www.nytimes.com/2018/08/26/opinion/zero-tolerance-separated-migrant-children-court-system.html.

77 Craig Mousin, "Rights Disappear," 60.

78 U.S. Department of Justice, Executive Office for Immigration Review (EIOR), "Operating Policies and Procedures Memorandum 17–03," December 20, 2017, www.justice.gov/eoir/file/oppm17-03/download.

79 Human Rights First, "Crossing the Line: U.S. Border Agents Illegally Reject Asylum Seekers," May 2017, www.humanrightsfirst.org/sites/default/files/hrf-crossing-the-line-report.pdf, 5.

Ongoing violations of civil rights and due process in ICE and CBP enforcement practices frighten both unauthorized persons and citizens from accessing health care, local police protection, courts, and public places.[80] Echoes of Arendt's critique of police powers reverberate throughout the land as ICE agents enter hospitals, interfere with state court proceedings, and engage in intensive electronic surveillance and research to isolate, detain, and deport alleged illegal aliens. Many US citizens have also been improperly detained and deported.

The US CBP constitutes the largest police force in the nation.[81] The Supreme Court has given it additional powers not held by local law enforcement up to 100 miles from the border. The largest urban areas in the United States mostly fall within those hundred miles. Moreover, ICE, which has enforcement responsibilities in the interior, has also expanded greatly. Arendt revealed that, as in this nation, the number of police officers charged with enforcing laws regarding stateless or refugees and their emancipation from legal standards "grew in direct proportion to the influx of refugees."[82]

Papers, whether a passport or a permanent residence card, delineate status. One of the first steps in pre-World War II Germany was the denaturalization of persons, removing them from the protection of the law.[83] In the United States, the administration has started a program to review past naturalization decisions and reopen cases alleging fraud or other minor mistakes, thus taking away citizenship and seeking deportation.[84] Delaying work authorization for asylum applicants makes it difficult for them to gain housing and food security while awaiting adjudication, which might take years. Arendt claimed: "The first loss which the rightless suffered was the loss of their homes, and this meant the loss of the entire social texture .... What is unprecedented is not the loss of a home but the impossibility of finding a new one."[85] The inability to

80 See Craig B. Mousin, "It is More Than Just the Dreamers" (Vincentian Heritage Podcast, 2018), https://soundcloud.com/bcicirel/it-is-more-than-just-the-dreamers, and the reports linked to this recording revealing the many ways in which ICE enforcement has threatened the security of our communities.

81 "Brief of Amici Curiae Former Officials of U.S Customs and Border Protection Agency in Support of Petitioners in U.S. Supreme Court Case *Jesus C. Hernandez v. Jesus Mesa, Jr.*, No. 17–1678," August 9, 2019, www.supremecourt.gov/DocketPDF/17/17–1678/111771/20190809110057092_Hernandez%20v.%20Mesa%20Amicus.pdf, 5.

82 Arendt, *Totalitarianism*, 287.

83 Arendt, *Totalitarianism*, 296. See also Philippe Sands, *East West Street: On the Origins of "Genocide" and "Crimes Against Humanity"* (New York: Alfred A. Knopf, 2016), 168–9.

84 Amanda Frost, "Alienating Citizens," *Northwestern University Law Review Online* 114, no. 1 (2019): 241–67.

85 Arendt, *Totalitarianism*, 293. See also Ori Z. Soltes, "Cultural Plunder and Restitution and Human Identity," *John Marshall Law School Review of Intellectual Property Law* 15, no. 3 (2016): 460–71, at 461.

access work authorization limits the ability to find a new home. Moreover, certain states and municipalities attempted to ban landlords from renting to persons who could not provide the proper immigration paperwork. Although many of these laws have been challenged and overturned through litigation, the local efforts have nonetheless increased the anti-immigrant animus, further heightening the separation of community. Moreover, many families consist of citizens, lawful permanent residents, and unauthorized, or persons in proceedings, thus complicating efforts to buy or rent housing as landlords may fear prosecution if any tenants are without papers.[86]

The use of big data offers new enforcement tools that make the daily interchange with government offices, banks, and insurance companies a new source of threat. Even when individuals try to follow the rules of this society, registration adds information to big data, giving the immigration police new ways of enforcement, causing the breakdown of families and communities. As the administration expands enforcement in all areas, big data and advanced technology heighten the division between those with papers and those without.[87]

17.3.4 *Disregard for the Rule of Law*

Many of these unilateral orders and policies have been stayed or found illegal under litigation. Indeed, President Trump has complained that "activist judges" have interfered with its unilateral actions to make the nation more secure.[88] If it cannot prevail in court, it attacks the legitimacy of the judicial system.

As Arendt warned, once a nation-state refuses to follow equal protection under the law for all residing within the nation, the nation commences losing its raison d'être, its very sovereignty. As ICE and CBP exercise expanded enforcement with impunity, democracy and its promises break down. In seeking arrests, ICE agents enter public court houses, which creates fear amongst citizens and lawful residents. State and federal judges have objected to such policies: "[F]or courts to effectively do justice, ensure public safety,

86 Marie Friedmann Marquardt et al., *Living "Illegal": The Human Face of Unauthorized Immigration* (New York: The New Press, 2011), 10, 147.

87 McKenzie Funk, "How ICE Picks Its Targets in the Surveillance Age," *New York Times*, October 2, 2019, www.nytimes.com/2019/10/02/magazine/ice-surveillance-deportation.html.

88 White House Office of the Press, "Activist Judicial Rulings Block the Administration from Enforcing Our Nation's Immigration Laws," Fact Sheets, October 11, 2019, www.whitehouse.gov/briefings-statements/activist-judicial-rulings-block-administration-enforcing-nations-immigration-laws/.

and serve their communities, the public must be able to access courthouses safely and without fear of retribution."[89] Civic places designed for public engagement and safety become less safe for families who might have unauthorized persons living with them, thus frightening them from enjoying the fruits of society.

IJs, as employees of the DOJ, lack judicial independence. Under the Trump administration, the Attorney General (AG) has limited the IJ's ability to seek justice by taking away many of the judicial tools of discretion and even the freedom to manage a court calendar to continue a case if a party might have an alternative immigration remedy available but only needs time for the process. Because the IJs do not operate as independent judges, the AG has authority to review cases and issue decisions that further limit asylum and eliminate judicial autonomy. Former Chief Judge of the Board of Immigration Appeals (BIA) Paul Schmidt recently wrote: "Thus, the BIA continues its downward spiral from a tribunal devoted to excellence, best practices, due process, and fundamental fairness to one whose primary function is to serve as a 'rubber stamp' for White Nationalist restrictionist enforcement initiatives by DHS."[90] From IJs to appeals courts, these policies further weaken the power of law to protect statutory remedies.

The cumulative impact of forcing asylum applicants farther from the border and detaining them within the border eviscerates legal protections for all unauthorized persons residing in the nation and violates the principle "thou shall not return refugees." The juxtaposition of the Trump administration's policies toward refugees and immigrants with its need to fulfill campaign promises, especially to white evangelical Christians and cultural Christians,[91] has accelerated the abdication of any responsibility toward international law.

89 "Letter from Former Judges-Courthouse Immigration Arrests," December 12, 2018, www.scribd.com/document/395488473/Letter-From-Former-Judges-Courthouse-Immigration-Arrests.

90 Paul Wickham Schmidt, "BIA News: Judge Garry D. Malphrus Leapfrogs into Acting Chair Job, as Two of the Remaining 'Voices of Reason' Bite the Dust at Barr's 'Newly Packed' Falls Church Station Stop on the 'Trump Deportation Express,'" November 7, 2019, https://immigrationcourtside.com/2019/11/07/bia-news-judge-garry-d-malphrus-leapfrogs-into-acting-chair-job-as-two-of-the-remaining-voices-of-reason-bite-the-dust-at-barrs-newly-packed-falls-churc/.

91 Scholars debate the specific definition of evangelical in the United States, but polls suggest that over 80 percent of white evangelicals supported President Trump in the 2016 election and they continue to support him three years later in significant numbers. See Thomas Kidd, *Who Is an Evangelical? The History of a Movement in Crisis* (New Haven: Yale University Press, 2019), 145, 154. Thomas Kidd compares evangelicals as biblically based born-again Christians who have "a personal relationship with Jesus Christ through the Holy Spirit" with those whom the media have labeled due to their political behavior based on their support of the

17.4 BIBLICAL INTERPRETATION: NATION-STATE VS. REFUGEES

17.4.1 *White Evangelical Support of the Nation-State*

Political tradition invites a newly elected president of the United States to attend a private church service on the morning of the inauguration. Southern Baptist pastor Robert Jeffress preached the sermon for the newly elected Trump entitled "When God Chooses a Leader."[92] Rev. Jeffress stressed three main points: First, God had elected the new president for the specific task of making America great again. Second, God wanted the president to build a wall to fulfill his campaign promises. Jeffress proclaimed: "And the first step of rebuilding the nation was the building of a great wall. God instructed Nehemiah to build a wall around Jerusalem to protect its citizens from enemy attack. You see, God is NOT against building walls!"[93] Third, God would support the president's efforts to fulfill his campaign pledge to make America great again. He cited Psalm 33:12 as providing "the starting point for making that happen: 'Blessed – great – is the nation whose God is the Lord.'"[94] Jeffress, the pastor of one of the largest congregations in the nation, subsequently preached a sermon "America as a Christian Nation"[95] in which he proclaimed that America was "founded as a predominantly Christian nation"[96] whose "founding document is the Bible[,] not the Constitution."[97]

The Trump administration heard the sermon as true believers. Just one week later, it issued its first Muslim ban precluding admission of Muslims

administration including its anti-immigrant policies. Kidd, *Who Is an Evangelical?*, 4, 151–4. In addition, many who support the restrictive immigration policies may include cultural Christians fitting into the latter category. For a discussion of cultural Christians, see Dean Inserra, "Why a Pastor Made the Bible Belt His Mission Field," *Religion News*, April 1, 2019, https://religionnews.com/2019/04/01/cultural-christianity-and-the-gospel-why-a-pastor-made-the-bible-belt-his-mission-field/.

92 Dr. Robert Jeffress, "When God Chooses a Leader," Inauguration Day Message, January 20, 2017, First Baptist Dallas, www.firstdallas.org/blog/when-god-chooses-a-leader-dr-jeffress-inauguration-day-message/ (emphasis in original). See also Sarah Pulliam Bailey, "'God Is Not Against Building Walls!' The Sermon Trump Heard from Robert Jeffress before His Inauguration," *The Washington Post*, January 20, 2017, www.washingtonpost.com/news/acts-of-faith/wp/2017/01/20/god-is-not-against-building-walls-the-sermon-donald-trump-heard-before-his-inauguration/.

93 Jeffress, "When God Chooses a Leader" (emphasis in original).

94 Jeffress, "When God Chooses a Leader," quoting Psalm 33:12.

95 Jeffress, "America Is a Christian Nation" sermon, June 24, 2018, www.firstdallas.org/day-one-worship-videos/america-is-a-christian-nation/.

96 Jeffress, "Christian Nation," at 8.33.

97 Jeffress, "Christian Nation," at 8.33.

from selected countries. The administration responded to its most loyal base. Christian supporters of such policies offer three main themes to link the Bible to these policies. First, in the Genesis (11:6–8) story of the Tower of Babel, God saw a united humanity as a threat to God's sovereignty. Thus, God has established nation-states as part of God's plan for humans. Biblical nations possess and defend borders.[98] Second, Romans 13:1–7 suggests that God has ordained the governors to defend the nation's sovereignty and protect the people. To maintain the sovereignty of the nation-state, its borders must be defended and immigration regulated. US AG Sessions had previously expressed support for building walls to deter immigrants, stating that the United States "has the right to secure its border" because Nehemiah left Babylon as "he went to build a wall in Jerusalem and it wasn't to keep the people in ...."[99] Mark R. Amstutz cites Paul's deference to the governing authorities because the "coercive power of the state has been a crucial role to ensure that justice is done."[100]

Third, the law designates noncitizens as aliens. Israel recognized different categories of persons residing with Israel. Those residing on the land who followed Israel's law were recognized as *ger* or the *gerim* who God commands the Israelites to welcome and treat as the native. Restrictionists argue, however, that the illegal alien should be compared instead to the *nekhar* or *zar*, the foreigner or the enemy who should not be welcome – who should be deported.[101] For instance, James R. Edwards argues: "[T]he government has the duty to defend the nation against foreign invaders" and "it safeguards the public good for a particular group of people, in a particular geographic location, who belong to a particular body politic."[102] The nationalists believe if we have open borders many, if not all, would seek admission, thus robbing the nation of its resources.

Ralph Drollinger, who leads Bible studies for members of Congress and the president's Cabinet, linked the biblical insight to the debate over the wall.[103]

98 James R. Edwards, Jr., "A Biblical Perspective on Immigration Policy," in *Debating Immigration*, ed. Carol Swain (New York: Cambridge University Press, 2007), 57.

99 Penny Star, "Sessions on Border Security: Nehemiah Built a Wall in Jerusalem and 'It Wasn't to Keep People In,'" *CSN News*, June 13, 2016, www.cnsnews.com/news/article/penny-starr/sessions-border-security-nehemiah-built-wall-jerusalem-and-it-wasnt-keep.

100 Mark R. Amstutz, "Two Theories of Immigration," *First Things*, December 2015, at 8, www.firstthings.com/article/2015/12/two-theories-of-immigration.

101 James K. Hoffmeier, *The Immigration Crisis* (Wheaton, IL: Crossway, 2009), 48–52.

102 Edwards, Jr., "Biblical Perspective," 47.

103 Ralph Drollinger, President and Founder of Capitol Ministries, Letter to the Cabinet, Senate, and House Bible Studies, January 26, 2019, https://capmin.org/wp-content/uploads/2019/01/The-Bible-and-The-Wall-by-Ralph-Drollinger-2019.pdf.

Affirming that the Bible "explicitly states we are to be submissive to governing authorities," he wrote:

> In specific regard to building a wall, is that a biblically justifiable objective: The answer is an unequivocal YES; God had Nehemiah build a wall to protect this people . . .. [In] God's eyes, our President has every biblical right to construct a wall in order to keep out **illegals.** And since he is our elected leader, we the people, including Congress, should submit to his authority as our President and all get behind building the wall.[104]

Drollinger concluded that the president "is pursuing a biblically justifiable objective."[105] Drollinger echoes the legacy of Constantine's empire, if not more recent examples of Christian submission to the state. Ernst Fraenkel recalls that in Germany, "Lutheranism preached unconditional obedience to every secular regime" and that the "Lutheran Church had not only failed to offer any resistance to the National-Socialist regime, but had actually assisted it during the first phase of the Third Reich."[106] Fraenkel noted that even the Confessional Church in Germany failed in resisting all Nazi doctrines when it was still possible, as its "resistance is limited to the defense of the Christian freedom of religious belief."[107] The Trump administration similarly argues, as it builds the wall, that it is assiduously defending religious freedom, to bolster white evangelical support of its policies.[108]

Although many Catholics[109] and mainline Protestants, in addition to many secularists, also support restrictive immigration policies, they may not cite the Bible as their main concern. But many remain silent bystanders, often stating that we cannot just have open borders and that illegal aliens must be deported. As it was a major linchpin of the 2016 primary and election campaign for white evangelicals, building a wall that will allegedly keep the nation safe from immigrants and refugees has remained of critical significance to the Trump

104 Drollinger, Letter to the Cabinet, Senate, and House Bible Studies, 1 (bold and emphasis in original).

105 Drollinger, Letter to the Cabinet, Senate, and House Bible Studies, 1.

106 Ernst Fraenkel, *The Dual State: A Contribution to the Theory of Dictatorship* (New York: Octagon Books, 1969), 116–17.

107 Fraenkel, *Dual State*, 118. See also Chapter 12 in this volume discussing Protestant advocacy for religious freedom in Germany.

108 Donald J. Trump, "Speech to the Center on Values," October 14, 2019, www.whitehouse.gov/briefings-statements/remarks-president-trump-values-voter-summit/.

109 See, e.g., the recent speech of Cardinal Burke where he stated: "To resist large-scale Muslim immigration in my judgment is to be responsible." Robert Duncan, "Cardinal Burke: Limiting Muslim Immigration Is Patriotic," *America: The Jesuit Review*, May 21, 2019, www.americamagazine.org/politics-society/2019/05/21/cardinal-burke-limiting-muslim-immigration-patriotic.

administration. Corroborating that view, the Pew Research Center's January 2019 survey reported that "nearly three-quarters of white evangelicals expressed support for substantially expanding the wall along the U.S. border with Mexico."[110] Robert Linder counters that these evangelical Christians "confuse civil religion with Christianity."[111]

17.4.2 *Biblical Narratives Supporting Welcoming the Stranger*

For many, Constantine's legacy continues to haunt interpretation of the Bible as unambiguously favoring the nation-state. Luke Timothy Johnson noted the losses that the church suffered when it merged with the Roman Empire, asserting that the virus of the imperial church continued to lurk within the body politic. Johnson warned: "It is not enough for Christians to forswear the sins of the past, or even embrace the collapse of the Constantinian era, for the virus that created the fevers of fanatic intolerance and that welcome the coercive power of the state remains dormant and potentially dangerous with the testimony of the Christian tradition."[112]

The Bible has been exploited since its inception to condone the murder and torture of humans.[113] The United States has engaged in its own sins relying on the Bible against Native peoples and slavery.[114] The biblical debate cannot escape this past without engaging in Johnson's call to end the virus of linking Christianity to the coercive state. The 2016 election campaign rekindled the virus that endangers millions of residents and refugees as well as all residents of this nation. Not only does the current debate need the new biblical exegesis that Johnson called for; it also needs a practical theology to engage the public square to uphold human dignity.

Part of the virus's cure might entail reexamining the faith connections not just to the nation-state but to the land that has fueled America's beliefs in its

110 Philip Schwadel and Gregory A. Smith, "Evangelical Approval of Trump Remains High, but Other Religious Groups Are Less Supportive," March 18, 2019, www.pewresearch.org/fact-tank/2019/03/18/evangelical-approval-of-trump-remains-high-but-other-religious-groups-are-less-supportive/?utm_source=Pew%20Research%20Center&utm_campaign=037c29d868-EMAIL_CAMPAIGN_2019_03_21_06_45&utm_medium=email&utm_term=0_3e953b9b70-037c29d868-399362653.

111 Robert Linder, "Changes in the Evangelical Protestant Understanding of Church and State During the Twentieth Century," unpublished paper on file with the author based on a talk presented at DePaul University College of Law, March 11, 1999.

112 Luke Timothy Johnson, in Witte, Jr., *Human Rights*, 71.

113 Michael Prior, "The Right to Expel: The Bible and Ethnic Cleansing," in *Palestinian Refugees: The Right to Return*, ed. Nasser Aruri (London: Pluto Press, 2001), 9.

114 Prior, "Right to Expel," 17. See also Wellman, "Lynching Tree," 85–6.

own exceptionalism. Walter Brueggemann, after reviewing much of the Old Testament scholarship, argues "that the core of faith, for Christians as for Jews, is situated in the matrix of exile."[115] That matrix involves understanding the fullness of the biblical message without proof texting one or two lines of Scripture. Much of the Hebrew Bible involves the Israelites wrestling with the covenant and the promise of land as the goal of the Exodus. For Brueggemann:

> The very land that promised to create space for human joy and freedom became the very source of dehumanizing exploitation and oppression. Land was indeed a problem in Israel. Time after time, Israel saw the land of promise become the land of problem. The very land that contained the sources of life drove kings to become agents of death. Society became the frantic effort of the landed to hold onto the turf, no matter what the cost.[116]

God promised the land, but Israel must fulfill the covenant. Land also seduced Israel to forget its commitments to justice. Israel, as both a migrating people and a host to migrants, understood both the perils of exile and the perils of the land.[117] God gave the land as a gift but the covenantal relationship required taking care of creation. In addition, the promise of a new land under the covenant meant taking care of those residing in the land, especially the vulnerable such as the widow, the orphan, and the stranger. According to Brueggemann, God gave the land with the warning not to succumb to a new form of slavery that entailed defense of the land by violating the rights of others. Instead, Yahweh required justice for the most vulnerable, the widow, the orphan, and the migrant.[118] We face that choice today as almost ten million unauthorized persons who reside in the United States, many for more than ten years, may more closely resemble the vulnerable *gerim* of the Hebrew Scriptures than the deportable enemy.

According to Mark Hamilton, contemporary interpreters seeking to impose a Westphalian concept of citizen or alien find no support in Israel's laws.[119] Too often, those who name the alien in the United States as an illegal alien invent modern categories that do not fit within the biblical narrative. Indeed, the very helplessness of the stranger, the one residing in the land, calls for

115 Walter Brueggemann, *Theology of the Old Testament: Testimony, Dispute, Advocacy* (Minneapolis: Fortress Press, 1997), 77.

116 Walter Brueggemann, *The Land: Place as Gift, Promise and Challenge in Biblical Faith* (Minneapolis: Fortress Press, 2002), 10.

117 Mark Hamilton, *Jesus, King of Strangers: What the Bible Really Says about Immigration* (Grand Rapids, MI: William B. Eerdmans Publishing, 2019), 15.

118 Brueggemann, *The Land*, 61.

119 Hamilton, *Jesus, King of Strangers*, 85.

protection. For Hamilton: "The migrant does not appear in law as a problem, but as a welcome guest that, if anything, gives the redeemed people opportunity to demonstrate their gratitude to Yahweh for the exodus and to each other their commitment to generous, ethical lives."[120]

The biblical conundrum – the promise of protecting land without succumbing to violating the rights of refugees and other unauthorized people – challenges all who count the Bible as authority.[121] US exceptionalism still lives. That exceptionalism, however, fuels the fear that security requires strong borders and denies entry. Dorothee Soelle reminds us, however: "The God of the prophets did not preach the nation-state, but community between strangers and natives. The apostle Paul did not base the justification of sinners on the Protestant work ethic, but on grace . . .!"[122]

Christianity has struggled since its inception with responding to the choice of whether to fortify the security of the nation-state or to seek the security of God, or to conflate the two by claiming that God blesses the nation's decisions to build a wall or exclude the stranger. André LaCocque offers a prime example of how Christians can interpret the Hebrew understanding of the law through Jesus's eyes to examine submission to this legal system. He calls the Parable of the Good Samaritan "preeminently *legal*"[123] naming the parable "pivotal in teaching how to interpret a text of the Hebrew Bible."[124] A lawyer, one well versed in understanding the biblical law, asks Jesus how to gain eternal life. Jesus compliments the lawyer for understanding that one must love both God and neighbor. The lawyer asks, "But who is my neighbor?" The lawyer today might ask, "What duty do we owe to the refugee at our border – is she my neighbor?" The parable identifies three persons seeing a stranger who has been mugged and tossed aside. Two walk by, but the Samaritan stops and seeks to heal. Nowhere in the parable do we learn of the identity of the wounded man. We know not if he is Jewish,

[120] Hamilton, *Jesus, King of Strangers*, 97.

[121] Placher, *History of Christian Theology*, 268: "Nothing symbolizes the unfulfilled character of the Puritan dream of America as the city on a hill, inspiring all the earth, so well as slavery. Yet in spite of slavery and much else, Americans have continued to think of themselves as a chosen people, set apart by God. Jonathan Edwards and other early Puritans, however, understood that God chooses without regard to merit, and the chosen should feel gratitude rather than pride . . . but that is a theological lesson Americans have found hard to remember."

[122] Dorothee Soelle, *The Window of Vulnerability: A Political Spirituality*, trans. Linda M. Maloney (Minneapolis: Fortress Press, 1990), 140.

[123] André LaCocque, "Jesus's Hermeneutics of the Law: Reading the Parable of the Good Samaritan," in *Creation, Life and Hope: Essays in Honor of Jacques Doukhan*, ed. Jiri Moskala (Berrien Springs, MI: Seventh Day Adventist Theological Seminary, 2000), 251 (emphasis in original).

[124] LaCocque, "Jesus's Hermeneutics," 252.

Samaritan, friend or enemy, known or unknown to any of those who fail to stop. He was in need – the Samaritan responded. National boundaries, law, constitutional status – none of these influenced the response. For LaCocque, this parable answers the question of who my neighbor is with "[A]nyone and everyone who is in need to be cared for, comforted, confirmed, shown mercy .... [O]nly mercy is not exclusive in its application, as it transcends all legal definitions."[125] When we ask whether we can assist a refugee if the law prohibits it, we tend, like the lawyer, to seek self-justification. "Jesus's agenda is to demonstrate that even one's enemy can become one's neighbor – or, ... – one's opportunity and invitation to be 'neighboring.'"[126] Because Jesus demonstrated great command of the Torah, his joust with the lawyer reveals both consistency with Jewish understandings and his claim upon the lawyer and his followers today. Mayer Gruber stresses that LaCocque's expansive reading of neighbor as anyone – friend or foe, Jew or Samaritan, citizen or undocumented resident – has a strong foundation in the Torah. Gruber links this parable to Exodus 11.2 where neighbors "include members of social and ethnic groups that are enemies."[127] The parable "transcends national boundaries."[128]

The question is not really "Who is my neighbor?" but "How do I be the neighbor?"[129] For those of us in the prosperous liberal democracies, the questions may be even more difficult. Sixty million people are either displaced or refugees: how do we respond? As the United States detains over 50,000 immigrants and refugees each night, as children are separated from families and placed in legal proceedings without legal assistance, and as thousands more are banned or turned away at our border, our goal may be to be the neighbor to one or more and to seek creative responses. Like Israel torn between the promise of the land as freedom and the seduction of the land as slavery, such choices seem impossible, especially if one is comfortable in our republic. We are called to go and do likewise. Faith calls us to become the neighbors to those who are hurting, not to build walls. The nation-state seduces us into believing that building walls excluding those fleeing persecution will make us safe. But that has been the seduction of the imperial call since Constantine.

125 LaCocque, "Jesus's Hermeneutics," 267–8.

126 André LaCocque, *Jesus, the Central Jew: His Times and His People* (Atlanta: SBL Press, 2015), 121.

127 Mayer I. Gruber, "André LaCocque, *Jesus the Central Jew*," *Review of Rabbinic Judaism* 22, no. 2 (2019): 277–307, at 294.

128 LaCocque, "Jesus's Hermeneutics," 259.

129 LaCocque, *Jesus, the Central Jew*, 127.

17.4.3 *The Interpretive Question*

In exploring public international law in light of refugees and immigrants, it behooves us to recall that God spoke first. After God spoke, the human interpretive experiment began. Multiple voices through thousands of years have replied. Christians debate immigration policy through the Bible. Submission to the state stifles that discourse. The temptation of American exceptionalism when combined with submission may silence biblical interpretation. To give priority to submission to governing authorities precludes other biblical responses. In exploring public international law in light of refugees and immigrants, a single story of submission to the state teaches us to forget why the nations agreed through international law to not return refugees. A single story says that the nation has enemies which must be subdued. Chimamanda Ngozi Adichie warns that a single story can do much harm.[130] We are all called to interpret the biblical narrative to hear multiple voices offering us the opportunity to be the neighbor. To base a political theology on one verse calling for submission to governing authorities and on a second verse that designates persons created in God's image to be stigmatized as illegal aliens even when most have never even been adjudicated as lawbreakers exposes the danger of the single story and provides the thinnest support for such draconian policies. Ironically, Jesus's conviction for sedition and execution by governing authorities, Peter's and Paul's martyrdom as political enemies of the government – these examples contradict Romans 13:1–7. Paul even brags of his criminality in 2 Timothy 2:8–10.[131] Jesus's response to the lawyer in the Parable of the Good Samaritan opens the way for multiple stories of the vulnerable: the widow, the orphan, and the stranger. We are called to heal and to see the vulnerable and to respond to the opportunity to be a neighbor.

Nor can we resolve the dilemma by extraterritoriality – pushing the control of the border far from our physical borders through control mechanisms that dilute the ability of refugees to properly present their stories of persecution and loss. As Justice Jackson predicted in 1941, if we do not work with the world community to address these issues, we will expend millions more in armaments and military expenditures seeking a vain effort to build security. We already spend billions on border securitization with mere millions spent on

[130] Chimamanda Ngozi Adichie, "The Danger of a Single Story," https:youtu.be/D9Ihs241zeg. I thank Georgina Leal for alerting me to this talk.

[131] See Mousin, "You Were Told," text from footnotes 65–105, where almost every major biblical protagonist would be guilty of an immigration violation had our laws been in effect then.

refugee resettlement and care.[132] As Brueggemann argues: "With the world-wide economic and environmental crisis that indicates no soon-to-come abatement and with frantic response of intensified militarism, the world political economy is actively engaged in the production of exiles, as was the old Babylonian empire."[133] Those who interpret the Bible as expressing God's blessing of the nation have permitted the state not only to weaken its international commitments to human rights but also to condone significant violations of domestic rights for both citizens and others residing within its boundaries.

17.5 CONCLUSION

The US Senate adopted the Refugee Act and accepted the responsibility to not deport refugees to their countries of origin to face persecution. Refugees approach the US border seeking safety, but the government turned them away. Although many Americans seek to restrict immigration, white evangelical Christians constitute the most significant group supporting the administration's policies to build the wall, increase deportation, and push refugees away from US borders. Urged on by biblical arguments that they must be submissive to the governing authorities who are ordained by God to enforce the law, they support policies undermining international law's protections.

In the interior, US law names the citizen as worthy of constitutional and statutory protection but offers far less protection to the alien – the very word itself suggests something less than human. When others define "illegal" prior to any adjudication of that mark, it permits the nation to abuse the vulnerable through detention and deportation. The very protections of international law are further denigrated when the policies and procedures attempt to move the physical border farther away, thus mitigating any sense of international law providing the protection envisioned by our failures during World War II. In the last edition of her work on totalitarianism, Arendt warned us that knowledge alone will not stop violations of international law. She argued: "[Germany] was remarkably well informed about all so-called secrets – massacres of Jews in Poland, preparation of the attack on Russia .... It is quite obvious that mass support for totalitarianism comes neither from ignorance nor from brainwashing."[134] Today, we too know much of how the US government is treating those we

132 Todd Miller, "More Than a Wall: Corporate Profiteering and the Militarization of US Borders," *Transnational Institute*, September 16, 2019, www.tni.org/en/morethanawall, 1–3.

133 Brueggemann, *Old Testament Theology*, 78.

134 Arendt, *Totalitarianism*, xxiii, n.1.

call illegal aliens or law-breakers (instead of refugees). We know that there are still thousands of children locked in detention centers. The crisis in US immigration courts, where results are dictated by the DHS or the AG rather than through judicial independence, suggests that the process has failed fairness or the minimum standard for the rule of law. We know that asylum seekers who have been turned away at the US-Mexico border have been murdered, raped, or assaulted while they waited for the chance to enter and begin the process of seeking asylum. We know that US border patrols and the ICE often enter homes and courtrooms with impunity.

To welcome the stranger or to ask how to be a neighbor for those seeking safety does not automatically make one an advocate for open borders. Indeed, international law does not call for open borders or solve all refugee problems. The world community still needs to resolve Arendt's question of what happens when a sovereign nation not only fails to protect but actively persecutes its own citizens.

International law is not a panacea for refugees. But in the days after the Holocaust, it gave hope that the issue of refugees was a nation-state problem, not just an issue of generosity. International law provided a process for nations to work together. By not working together, we also forgo the opportunity for Christians to be a neighbor. By eviscerating those protections and forcing refugees farther from our borders, we neglect both Jesus's answer about to whom we should be neighbors as well as our own commitment to the rule of law, both domestically and internationally. Let us instead follow the Samaritan and go and do likewise to be a neighbor.

RECOMMENDED READING

Heimburger, Robert W. *God and the Illegal Alien*. New York: Cambridge University Press, 2018.

Kanstroom, Daniel. *Deportation Nation: Outsiders in American History*. Cambridge, MA: Harvard University Press, 2010.

Motomura, Hiroshi. *Immigration Outside the Law*. New York: Oxford University Press, 2014.

Smith-Christopher, Daniel L. A *Biblical Theology of Exile*. Minneapolis: Augsburg Fortress, 2002.

18

Hopelessly Practicing Law: Asylum Seekers, Advocates, and Hostile Jurisdictions

Silas W. Allard

18.1 INTRODUCTION

What does it mean to *practice* public international law? This is a frequent topic of conversation for many of us who work with law students inspired to study the law and pursue legal vocations in the belief that peace, justice, and human rights may be best advanced through the international legal framework. But, as our students often discover, that framework can be deeply frustrating. From its heavily bureaucratic structure anchored in the United Nations (UN) system, to the unresolved tension between individuals and states as actors in and beneficiaries of international law, public international law can often seem as much an obstacle as a means to our virtue.

This chapter examines the ethic of praxis in public international law by examining an often-overlooked area of international legal practice: refugee and asylum law.[1] An ethic of praxis, as I discuss it in this chapter, is an ethic with attention to creatureliness, which is to say finitude. As imperfect actors in an imperfect world, how do we practice toward justice? How do we understand justice through our practices? An ethic of praxis, then, interrogates the possibilities and constraints of action, as well as how to act within those constraints. But it is also an ethic of discontent with the disembodied aspirations of international law divorced from the messiness and humanness of its implementation. By attending to the practices of refugees, asylum seekers, and their legal advocates, this chapter illuminates an ethic of practice that lives in the tension between the promise of international law and the reality of the people it intends to protect.

[1] Section 18.4 is adapted from Silas W. Allard, "Reimagining Asylum: Religious Narratives and the Moral Obligation to the Asylum Seeker," *Refuge: Canada's Journal on Refugees* 29, no. 1 (2013): 121–9. Section 18.5 is adapted from Silas W. Allard, "Global and Local Challenges to Refugee Protection," *International Journal of Legal Information* 46, no. 1 (2018): 45–52.

Refugee and asylum law is a particularly useful forum for such an inquiry. This body of law is fundamentally shaped by public international law, principally the 1951 Convention Relating to the Status of Refugees and its 1967 Protocol; however, unlike much public international law, it is practiced far from the centers of international law in New York, Geneva, and the Hague. Rather, refugee and asylum law is practiced in United Nations High Commissioner for Refugees (UNHCR) field offices and at asylum offices and immigration courts often found at the periphery of domestic court systems.

Unfortunately, the business of refugee and asylum law is booming. UNHCR estimates that in 2018, 1.7 million new claims for asylum were lodged by asylum seekers, and at year's end 3.5 million claims remained unresolved. Over 1.1 million decisions were made in asylum cases in 2018, meaning that just over 3,100 asylum decisions were made each day. Of these decisions, 6 percent were made by the UNHCR, with the remaining 94 percent made by domestic courts or asylum offices.[2]

There is little profit to be made by representing those fleeing violence, persecution, and economic deprivation, however, and the demand for attorneys has not generated a concomitant supply. In a comprehensive analysis of representation rates in US immigration courts from 2007 to 2012, Ingrid Eagly and Steven Shafer found that only 37 percent of immigrants were represented by counsel. Nor do the resources exist to fill the gap with nonprofit, pro bono representation; only 2 percent of all immigrants to the United States are represented pro bono.[3] There are profits to be made from the growth in asylum seekers and refugees, but those profits are reaped by those building walls, surveilling movement, and detaining immigrants.[4]

Lawyers and other advocates who do represent asylum seekers in refugee status adjudications undertake what are often difficult cases, as will be discussed throughout this chapter. For now, let me simply note the stakes. By definition, these claims are premised on the likelihood of harm befalling a person if returned to their country of origin. The consequences of denial can be dire; they are often life and death. Nonetheless, it is more likely than

2 These statistics are taken from UNHCR's Global Trends Report for 2018. United Nations High Commissioner for Refugees, *Global Trends: Forced Displacement in 2018* (Geneva: UNHCR, 2019), ch. 5.

3 See Ingrid V. Eagly and Steven Shafer, "A National Study of Access to Counsel in Immigration Court," *University of Pennsylvania Law Review* 164, no. 1 (2015): 1–91, at 7–8.

4 See John Washington, "The Amount of Money Being Made Ripping Migrant Families Apart Is Staggering," *The Nation*, October 28, 2019, www.thenation.com/article/immigration-ice-family-separation/, and the reports cited therein.

not that an asylum seeker will be denied any form of protection and returned to the harms, dangers, or difficulties that await them in their country of origin. The UNHCR reports that the total rate of protection for claimants in 2018 was 44 percent, with significant variation among jurisdictions.[5] Such challenges may lead many to ask, along with social ethicist Sharon Welch, "What does it mean to act ethically in a world of expediency, to stand for justice in a world of exploitation, to act with compassion in a world of indifference, cynicism, and despair?"[6]

Christian theology and ethics have long answered this question by turning to the virtue of hope. Among the three theological virtues (1 Corinthians 13:13), hope is deeply connected to Christian expectations of a coming reign of God's justice and peace.[7] As the Letter to the Hebrews states succinctly: "Let us hold unswervingly to the hope we profess, for he who promised is faithful."[8] For some Christian theologians, perhaps most powerfully and pointedly in the work of Jürgen Moltmann,[9] hope is a vital Christian virtue and the necessary condition of transformative action.

Like Christianity, public international law and its advocates have also had recourse to the virtue of hope. The vision of public international law is often a progressive vision of a perfected future where peace and human rights are the fruit of the rule of law. Both the preamble to the UN Charter and the preamble to the Universal Declaration of Human Rights (UDHR) recite a progressive vision of history moving from the chaos and violence of the world wars, through the founding of the postwar international legal order, and looking toward a future of order and peace under international law.[10] Furthermore, as

5 UNHCR, *Global Trends: Forced Displacement in 2018*, 46. The report states that "[t]he TPR [Total Protection Rate] varies greatly among countries of asylum. For example, Switzerland had a TPR of 75 per cent, compared with Australia and Sweden where only about a quarter of asylum decisions granted protection (27 per cent and 23 per cent respectively). Germany made the most substantive decisions (245,700) and had a TPR of 43 per cent." UNHCR, *Global Trends: Forced Displacement in 2018*, 47. In its 2017 *Global Trends Report*, UNHCR noted the following with regard to variation in scope of protection: "Among countries of asylum with more than 1,000 substantive decisions, protection rates vary greatly, and some countries had very low figures: Gabon, Israel, Japan, Pakistan, and Republic of Korea all had a TPR of below 10 per cent." United Nations High Commissioner for Refugees, *Global Trends: Forced Displacement in 2017* (Geneva: UNHCR, 2018), 45.

6 Sharon Welch, *A Feminist Ethic of Risk* (Minneapolis: Fortress Press, 2000), 13.

7 See Isa. 11:1–6; Rev. 21:1–7.

8 Heb. 10:23 [New International Version].

9 See Jürgen Moltmann, *Ethics of Hope* (Minneapolis: Fortress Press, 2012).

10 Charter of the United Nations (June 26, 1945), preamble; General Assembly Resolution 217 (III) A, Universal Declaration of Human Rights (December 10, 1948), preamble. See also Jenna Reinbold, *Seeing the Myth in Human Rights* (Philadelphia: University of Pennsylvania Press, 2017), especially 73–9.

Pamela Slotte has documented, the progressive hope of international law and the progressive hope of liberal Christianity were mutually informing and reinforcing, particularly in the first half of the twentieth century.[11] Hope, it seems, is both a legal and a theological virtue.[12] Miguel De La Torre has recently lodged a challenge to hope as the basis for a viable and liberative Christian ethic of praxis. "I have been wrestling with the realization that for many of the ultra-poor, hope seems to be mainly claimed by those with economic privilege as a means of distancing themselves from the unsolvable disenfranchisement most of the world's wretched are forced to face." In the light of this revelation, "*The first step toward liberation requires the crucifixion of hope* – for as long as hope exists, the world's wretched have something to lose, and thus will not risk all to change the social structures."[13] For De La Torre, hopelessness offers a better foundation for a liberative ethic of praxis: "Better to remain with one's feet planted in solidarity with the marginalized, sharing in their hopelessness, if we wish to contribute any praxis that might move beyond uplifting platitudes."[14] Hope distracts from the necessary work of imagining and acting to create new realities and only in hopelessness can new realities be imagined and pursued.[15]

What of those who wish to stand in solidarity with, for example, asylum seekers but who are also bound by their context and social position to the very legal structures that may demand radical reimagining? Can and should attorneys, who are actors bound to a system of law, "embrace hopelessness"?

To explore hope and the ethic of praxis in refugee and asylum law, this chapter will look first at the structure of the Refugee Convention and, in particular, its limitations in light of changes to forced migration patterns. The chapter will then take a look at a particular example of a "hopeless" situation by focusing on the immigration courts in the US state of Georgia, where asylum grant rates are exceptionally low. The chapter then engages more directly with the work of De La Torre and Welch to argue that De La Torre's framework is an important insight for an ethic of praxis in international

11 Pamela Slotte, "Whose Justice? What Political Theology? On Christian and Theological Approaches to Human Rights in the Twentieth and Twenty-First Centuries," in *International Law and Religion: Historical and Contemporary Perspectives*, ed. Martti Koskenniemi, Mónica García-Salmones Rovira, and Paolo Amorosa (Oxford: Oxford University Press, 2017), 196–216.

12 For a thorough examination of the eschatological in international law and state law, see John D. Haskell and Jessica Fish, "Law as Eschatology," *Journal of Catholic Legal Studies* 53, no. 2 (2014): 185–210.

13 Miguel A. De La Torre, *Embracing Hopelessness* (Minneapolis: Fortress Press, 2017), 5–6.

14 De La Torre, *Embracing Hopelessness*, 49.

15 De La Torre, *Embracing Hopelessness*, 52.

law that does not see the international legal system generally or the refugee protection system specifically as either a necessarily progressive or an irreversible move toward justice. Rather, the ethic of praxis called for in this situation is what Welch describes as an ethic of risk and De La Torre describes, somewhat differently, as an ethics *para joder*.

18.2 CAUSE FOR HOPE OR DESPAIR: REFUGEE AND ASYLUM LAW

Before turning to the insights of De La Torre's critique, it is important to take a careful look at the state of refugee and asylum law. It is, on one reading, easy to see refugee and asylum law as a beacon of hope. Here is a body of law, initiated by the 1951 Convention Relating to the Status of Refugees, that responds to persecution and displacement with an avenue for protection. Like its predecessor treaties, the UN Charter (1945) and the UDHR (1948), the 1951 Convention aspired to an international order that would guarantee human rights and advance international peace. As former High Commissioner for Refugees Sadako Ogata has written:

> It was, however, recognized already at that time [of drafting] that the standards defined in the Convention were of universal applicability, and the Conference which adopted the Convention therefore included in its Final Act, Recommendation E in which it "Expressed the hope that the Convention would have value as an example exceeding its contractual scope that all nations would be guided by it in granting as far as possible to persons in their territory as refugees and who would not be covered by the terms of the Convention the treatment for which it provides."[16]

The 1951 Convention is, undoubtedly, an important and vital development in refugee and asylum law. And yet many asylum seekers face overwhelming legal challenges in making their claim for asylum. In what follows, I will discuss the challenges inherent to the convention, to the process of claiming asylum, and to the adjudicatory contexts of asylum claims.

18.3 THE REFUGEE CONVENTION

The 1951 Convention was not the first effort to address refugee movements at the level of international law.[17] As Terje Einarsen has explained, the pre-1951

[16] Sadako Ogata, "Foreword," in *Refugee Convention 1951: The Travaux Preparatoires Analysed with a Commentary*, ed. Paul Weis (Geneva: UNHCR, 1990), 4.

[17] For a good discussion of the pre-1951 history of refugee protection, see Terje Einarsen, "Drafting History of the 1951 Convention and the 1967 Protocol," in *The 1951 Convention*

approach (most prominent during the League of Nations years) was "to tie protection to particular national groups in ad hoc instruments as new refugee situations arose . . . . With this type of definition 'by categories', interpretation was simple, but protection of new groups uncertain."[18] Prior to 1951, refugee protection was ad hoc and based on group identity; threatened minority communities were protected in response to a specific threat to the community on the basis of their minority status.

The 1951 Convention, by contrast, eschewed both ad hoc and group-based protection, establishing instead a general refugee definition that applied to persons unable to return to their country of origin for fear of persecution on the basis of race, religion, political opinion, national origin, or membership in a particular social group.[19] With this new definition, the 1951 Convention shifted the analysis from groups to individuals. Any person could be recognized as a refugee if that person met the criteria of the definition; refugee status determination would be made on an individual basis, not en masse.

In addition to shifting the focus of refugee protection to individualized determinations, the 1951 Convention created a comprehensive protection scheme through the principle of non-refoulement. The principle of non-refoulement forbids a state party to "expel or return ('refouler') a refugee in any manner whatsoever to the frontiers of territories where his life or freedom would be threatened on account of his race, religion, nationality, membership of a particular social group or political opinion."[20] Bolstering the comprehensiveness of the protection regime, several scholars have argued that the principle of non-refoulement has become a norm of customary international law – meaning

Relating to the Status of Refugees and Its 1967 Protocol: A Commentary, ed. Andreas Zimmermann, Felix Machts, and Jonas Dörschner (Oxford: Oxford University Press, 2011), ch. 2. For a social history of the modern refugee, see Peter Gatrell, *The Making of the Modern Refugee* (Oxford: Oxford University Press, 2013).

18 Einarsen, "Drafting History," para. 9; Gatrell, *Making of the Modern Refugee*, 53 and, generally, ch. 2; Guy S. Goodwin-Gill and Jane McAdam, *The Refugee in International Law* (Oxford: Oxford University Press, 2007), 16.

19 The full refugee definition is "any person who owing to a well-founded fear of being persecuted for reasons of race, religion, nationality, membership of a particular social group or political opinion, is outside the country of his nationality and is unable or, owing to such fear, is unwilling to avail himself of the protection of that country; or who, not having a nationality and being outside the country of his former habitual residence as a result of such events, is unable or, owing to such fear, is unwilling to return to it." "Convention Relating to the Status of Refugees," July 28, 1951, 189 *United Nations Treaty Series* no. 137, art. 1(A)(2), as modified by "Protocol Relating to the Status of Refugees," January 31, 1967, 606 *United Nations Treaty Series* no. 267, art. 1(2). The 1967 Protocol altered the definition by removing geographic and temporal restrictions in the original definition that limited its application to post-war Europe.

20 1951 Convention, art. 33.

that the principle is binding even on states that are not parties to the Convention.[21]

Despite the comprehensive protection offered to those who meet the definition of a refugee, there are important ways that the refugee definition itself is incomplete and undermined by states. First, the refugee definition is not comprehensive, and it limits protection to those fleeing *persecution* on the basis of *race, religion, nationality, political opinion, or membership in a particular social group*. Thus, many forms of survival migration – which may result from threats to human rights and human flourishing equivalent to the persecution recognized under the 1951 Convention – are neither recognized nor protected.[22]

Second, while the Refugee Convention may not be endlessly elastic, it does have the capacity to adapt to the necessity for new forms of protection, what Andrew Schoenholtz has termed its "evolutionary potential." Despite this capacity, however, "State Parties have tried for some time to minimize [the Refugee Convention's] relevance to today's forced migrants."[23] States have engaged a practice of reading the refugee definition narrowly, particularly the more open-ended "particular social group category," and weaponized the

21 T. Alexander Aleinikoff, *International Legal Norms and Migration: An Analysis* (Geneva: International Organization for Migration, 2002), 29 n. 36; Elihu Lauterpacht and Daniel Bethlehem, "The Scope and Content of the Principle of Non-refoulement: Opinion," in *Refugee Protection in International Law: UNHCR's Global Consultations on International Protection*, ed. Erika Feller, Volker Türk, and Frances Nicholson (Cambridge: Cambridge University Press, 2003); Goodwin-Gill and McAdam, *Refugee in International Law*, 345–54. For arguments that non-refoulement is a *jus cogens* norm and, therefore, non-derogable, see Cathryn Costello and Michelle Foster, "Non-refoulement as Custom and Jus Cogens? Putting the Prohibition to the Test," *Netherlands Yearbook of International Law* 46 (2015): 273–327; Jean Allain, "The Jus Cogens Nature of Non-refoulement," *International Journal of Refugee Law* 13, no. 4 (2001): 533–58.

22 The term "survival migration" was coined by Alexander Betts, *Survival Migration: Failed Governance and the Crisis of Displacement* (Ithaca: Cornell University Press, 2013). Some of these forms of survival migration are recognized in more limited international legal instruments, while other forms of survival migration, such as climate migration, have garnered little or no legal purchase. For regional agreements, see, e.g., Organization of African Unity (OAU), "Convention Governing the Specific Aspects of Refugee Problems in Africa," September 10, 1969, 1001 *United Nations Treaties Series* no. 45; Cartagena Declaration on Refugees, adopted by the Colloquium on the International Protection of Refugees in Central America, Mexico and Panama, held at Cartagena, Colombia, November 19–22, 1984. For international treaties, see, e.g., "International Convention on the Protection of the Rights of All Migrant Workers and Members of Their Families," December 18, 1990, 2220 *United Nations Treaties Series* no. 3.

23 Andrew I. Schoenholtz, "The New Refugees and the Old Treaty: Persecutors and Persecuted in the Twenty-First Century," *Chicago Journal of International Law* 16, no. 1 (2015): 81–126, at 83.

refugee definition to characterize those whose claims are at or beyond the edges of the definition as frauds and cheats looking to exploit the system.[24]

The 1951 Convention opened the door to individualized protection for refugees and asylum seekers, making it possible for persons experiencing persecution to claim protection in a new state on the basis of their personal experience. The range of experiences recognized as worthy of protection, however, is limited. As the nature of migration changes, the Convention is in some ways constrained by the refugee definition, and in other ways inhibited by states parties' interpretation of the definition in responding to those changes. This is one important way in which hope is cabined in refugee and asylum law. In the next section, I look at the process of claiming asylum in the United States, to explore some of the further impediments that are erected against asylum seekers.

18.4 THE ASYLUM PROCESS

By making refugee status individual and contingent on meeting the definition of a refugee, the 1951 Convention also changed the nature of the status determination process. Under the 1951 Convention, status is a matter of adjudication; a qualified decision-maker will determine if an asylum seeker qualifies as a refugee by meeting the refugee definition. Whether and how a person meets the definition of a refugee in the United States is the focus of Section 208 of the Immigration and Nationality Act (INA). According to INA § 208(b)(1)(A):

> The Secretary of Homeland Security or the Attorney General *may* grant asylum to an alien who has applied for asylum in accordance with the requirements and procedures established by the Secretary of Homeland Security or the Attorney General under this section *if* the Secretary of Homeland Security or the Attorney General *determines* that such alien is a refugee within the meaning of section 101(a)(42)(A).[25]

It is important to note two aspects of the text quoted above. First, the grant of asylum is entirely discretionary. The Secretary of Homeland Security and the Attorney General *may* grant asylum, but there is no positive obligation upon them to do so. Second, eligibility is determined by either the Secretary or the Attorney General, which means that an asylum seeker is evaluated for a status determination. Flipping the order of these two points, we realize that there are

[24] See Allard, "Global and Local Challenges."

[25] U.S. Code 8 (2018), § 1158(b)(1)(A) [emphasis added].

two critical questions facing every asylum seeker to the United States: (1) are you really a refugee, and (2) are you worthy of admission to the United States?

Are you really a refugee? The question itself is framed in skepticism because the asylum process must be vigilantly policed for fraud and merit.[26] This concern results in a presumption against the asylum seeker; the asylum seeker is presumed not to be a refugee. The burden of proof that an individual meets the definition of a refugee is placed upon the asylum seeker.[27] The asylum seeker's testimony alone may be sufficient if "the applicant satisfies the trier of fact that the applicant's testimony is credible, is persuasive, and refers to specific facts sufficient to demonstrate that the applicant is a refugee."[28] Thus, it can be assumed that the asylum seeker has a burden of credibility, a burden of persuasion, and a burden of fact. It is important to understand the implications created by the presumption that places the burden of proof on the asylum seeker. Unless the asylum seeker can meet the burdens of credibility, persuasion, and fact, his or her asylum claim will be denied.

The asylum seeker does not, however, receive a presumption of credibility. Rather, the trier of fact is free to determine that an asylum seeker is not credible based on any such indication or inconsistency. Any lapse in an asylum seeker's credibility "without regard to whether an inconsistency, inaccuracy, or falsehood goes to the heart of the applicant's claim" can be the basis for an adverse credibility determination.[29] The trier of fact may also demand evidence that the trier of fact determines is necessary to corroborate otherwise credible testimony.[30]

[26] See, e.g., Jeff Sessions, "Remarks to the Executive Office of Immigration Review," October 12, 2017, www.justice.gov/opa/speech/attorney-general-jeff-sessions-delivers-remarks-executive-office-immigration-review. Carol Bohmer and Amy Shuman's extensive treatment of which types of claim are recognized and which are excluded lead them to conclude: "Part of the problem with the system for granting asylum is that we're ambivalent about our moral obligation to the people who make claims. Increasingly, we go to greater and greater lengths to strengthen the barriers to entry and to make sure that only a few people slip through the net. . . . We let in people whose experiences are so horrifying that we're shocked; others don't get in." Carol Bohmer and Amy Shuman, *Rejecting Refugees: Political Asylum in the 21st Century* (London: Routledge, 2008), 263.

[27] U.S. Code 8, § 1158(b)(1)(B)(i).

[28] U.S. Code 8, § 1158(b)(1)(B)(ii).

[29] U.S. Code 8, § 1158(b)(1)(B)(iii).

[30] Any evidence demanded "must be provided unless the applicant does not have the evidence and cannot reasonably obtain the evidence." U.S. Code 8, § 1158(b)(1)(B)(ii). Unfortunately, there is frequently a disconnect between what the trier of fact determines to be "reasonably obtainable" and what is within the ability of the respondent to actually obtain, resulting in the irony that respondents are denied asylum because it is implausible for them to present reasonably obtainable evidence. See, e.g., Sarah R. Goodman, "Asking for Too Much? The

Thus, it can be seen how the burden of proof establishes a certain moral subjectivity of the asylum seeker. By placing the burden on the asylum seeker and denying a presumption of credibility, only certain narratives will be able to meet the established standard. As Jennifer Beard and Gregor Noll have written regarding refugee status determinations more broadly, “the conditions of the refugee’s speech are regulated in ways that bring forth the legal structures and credible testimonies of the [Refugee Convention]. … Under threat of being rejected, [the refugee] becomes aware of her extreme limitations in communication and apprehension.”[31] The most clear-cut, sympathetic cases of unambiguous persecution will be both the most persuasive and the easiest to prove. By placing such an overwhelming emphasis on credibility, and denying the asylum seeker a presumption of credibility, the statute assumes that any inconsistency is the mark of attempted fraud and that “true” victim narratives are marked by consistency and accuracy. These burdens place incredible power in the hands of the adjudicators and create the conditions for hostile jurisdictions and asylum-free zones, which I discuss further in the next section.

18.5 HOSTILE JURISDICTIONS AND ASYLUM-FREE ZONES

As the UNHCR’s Global Trends Reports make clear, protection rates vary significantly across the globe.[32] In federated states such as the United States, protection rates also vary across internal jurisdictions. For the fiscal year 2018, the nationwide grant rate for asylum in the United States was 21 percent, down significantly from the 2016 rate of 43 percent.[33] While this nationwide grant rate fell precipitously under the Trump administration, it is the case that asylum grant rates in the state of Georgia remain shockingly low compared to the national average. Georgia is home to two immigration courts: the Atlanta immigration court and the court at Stewart Detention Center in Lumpkin, Georgia. In both 2016 and 2018, the asylum grant rate for the Atlanta immigration court was 2 percent, and the grant rate at Stewart Detention Center was 7 percent.[34]

Role of Corroborating Evidence in Asylum Proceedings in the United States and United Kingdom,” *Fordham International Law Journal* 36, no. 6 (2013): 1733–66.

31 Jennifer Beard and Gregor Noll, “Parrhēsia and Credibility: The Sovereign of Refugee Status Determinations,” *Social & Legal Studies* 18, no. 4 (2009): 455–77, at 458.

32 See footnote 5 above.

33 Executive Office of Immigration Review, *FY 2018 Statistics Yearbook* (Falls Church, VA: U. S. Department of Justice, 2019), 28 tbl. 14; Executive Office of Immigration Review, *FY 2016 Statistics Yearbook* (Falls Church, VA: U. S. Department of Justice, March 2017), K12 fig. 16.

34 Executive Office of Immigration Review, *FY 2016*, K12 fig. 16; Executive Office of Immigration Review, *FY 2018*, 28 tbl. 14.

There is anecdotal evidence that the disparity in asylum grant rates is connected to a perspective among immigration judges in Georgia that there is a greater prevalence of meritless cases in their jurisdiction. In 2001, the *Los Angeles Times* published an article based on analysis of immigration judge decisions. The article highlighted an Atlanta immigration judge who had approved zero asylum requests from 807 Guatemalans who appeared before him over the course of 6 years, and who had approved only 80 of the nearly 2,400 requests filed by immigrants from other nations in the same time period. In a rare response provided through a court spokesperson, the judge argued that Atlanta does "not get the kind of cases that are easily granted."[35] In a 2016 article in *Vice Magazine*, a local nonprofit attorney "suggested local lawyers might be hesitant to take asylum cases because they expect to be stonewalled by an immigration judge."[36] And a 2016 *Huffington Post* article reported another attorney's account that "judges have told her they think granting asylum in certain instances would open the floodgates and make them bound to grant relief more often in general, going against an office culture of high skepticism of those claims."[37]

In the fall of 2016, the Southern Poverty Law Center (SPLC), in collaboration with Professor Hallie Ludsin's human rights practicum at Emory University School of Law, conducted court observation at the Atlanta immigration court. Based on information collected by students during their court watching, SPLC published a letter to the Director of the Executive Office of Immigration Review (the official name of the US immigration courts) detailing concerns about the operation of the Atlanta immigration court. In one of its findings, SPLC observed that "Immigration Judges made prejudicial statements and expressed significant disinterest or even hostility towards respondents in their courts."[38] Of particular interest for our discussion, the court observers reported examples of prejudice in its most literal sense – a prejudging – of the asylum claims before the court. In one example, observers reported that a judge stated in court that "individuals before [him]

35 Lisa Getter, "Few Applicants Succeed in Immigration Courts," *Los Angeles Times*, April 15, 2001, http://articles.latimes.com/2001/apr/15/news/mn-51336.

36 Ted Hesson, "Why It's Almost Impossible to Get Asylum in Atlanta," *Vice*, June 8, 2016, www.vice.com/en_us/article/bn38x5/why-its-almost-impossible-to-get-asylum-in-atlanta.

37 Elise Foley, "Here's Why Atlanta Is One of the Worst Places to Be an Undocumented Immigrant," *Huffington Post*, May 25, 2016, sec. Politics, www.huffingtonpost.com/entry/deportation-raids-immigration-courts_us_574378d9e4b0613b512b0f37.

38 Hallie Ludsin, Lisa Graybill, and Eunice Cho, "Letter to Juan P. Osuna, Director, Executive Office of Immigration Review: Observations of Atlanta Immigration Court," March 2, 2017, www.splcenter.org/sites/default/files/2017-atl_complaint_letter_final.pdf.

were economic migrants and that they do not pay taxes."[39] The judge then "concluded the hearing by stating that the credible fear standard is not a proper test for review of asylum seekers, wholly disregarding the established legal standard for such cases," and "[i]n a private conversation after this case, [the judge] told the observer that the cases that come before him involve individuals 'trying to scam the system' and that none of them want to be citizens."[40]

In a filing before the Inter-American Council on Human Rights (IACHR), advocates put the matter starkly. "Practically speaking, there is no asylum law within the 100,000 square miles that generally comprise the physical reach of the Atlanta, Georgia Immigration Court."[41] Beyond the limitations of the 1951 Convention and the legal impediments to claiming asylum, asylum seekers making their claim in a jurisdiction like Atlanta enter a truly desolate legal landscape where their chances of receiving protection approach a vanishing point.

18.6 WHENCE HOPE IN THIS WASTE LAND?

Viewed from the perspective of asylum seekers and their advocates, the landscape of international law is bleak. Perhaps it should not be surprising. Hannah Arendt eloquently articulated and prophesied the refugee's fundamental challenge to state-centered modernity at the dawn of the human rights era. "The world found nothing sacred," Arendt famously remarks, "in the abstract nakedness of being human."[42] She goes on to write:

> The paradox involved in the loss of human rights is that such loss coincides with the instant when a person becomes a human being in general – without a profession, without a citizenship, without an opinion, without a deed by which to identify and specify himself – and different in general, representing nothing but his own absolutely unique individuality which, deprived of expression within and action upon a common world, loses all significance.[43]

39 Ludsin, Graybill, and Cho, "Letter to Juan P. Osuna."

40 Ludsin, Graybill, and Cho, "Letter to Juan P. Osuna."

41 David Baluarte et al., "Submission to the Inter-American Commission on Human Rights Regarding a Special Interest Hearing on the Human Rights of Asylum Seekers in the United States," December 2, 2016, https://cgrs.uchastings.edu/sites/default/files/Human%20Rights%20of%20Asylum%20Seekers%20in%20US%20%5BPetitioners%5D_1.pdf.

42 Hannah Arendt, *The Origins of Totalitarianism* (Orlando: Houghton Mifflin Harcourt, 1994), 179.

43 Arendt, *Origins of Totalitarianism*, 182. For a more extended engagement with Arendt on refugees, see Chapter 17 in this volume; see also Allard, "Reimagining Asylum."

As the international community celebrates the seventieth anniversary of the UNHCR (founded in 1950) and the 1951 Convention, Arendt's critique continues to haunt refugee and asylum law. And recent efforts culminating in the Global Compact on Refugees appear to perpetuate these conditions.[44]

One response to this bleak landscape, a response with a long Christian genealogy, would be to look beyond this "heap of broken images, where the sun beats, and the dead tree gives no shelter, the cricket no relief, and the dry stone no sound of water,"[45] in hope for an alternate future. The preeminent theologian of hope Moltmann writes:

> We hope in so far as we can see into the sphere of future possibilities. We undertake what we think is possible. If, for example, we hope that the world will continue to be as it is now, we shall keep things as they are. If we hope for an alternative future, we shall already change things now as far as possible in accord with that. If the future is closed, then nothing more is possible; we cannot do anything more.[46]

On Moltmann's account, hope is the possibility of transformative action. Without hope and the resulting ability to imagine a future different from (and better than) the present, there is no reason or basis to act for the transformation of the present into that different future.

For Moltmann, hope for an alternate future is possible because the crucifixion and resurrection inaugurate the possibility of a radically transformed world. "The Christian ethics of hope is called to life through the recollection of the raising of the crucified Christ and therefore expects the dawn of God's new world in the passing away of the old one."[47] Scripture promises a redeemed and transformed future (Revelation 21:1–5, Isaiah 65:17–25). The resurrection inaugurates a movement toward that future. The Christian life of hope is lived in waiting for and hastening movement toward that future. "God's coming unfolds a transforming power in the present. In our tense expectation [of waiting] we are prepared for God's future, and that future acquires power in the present. … To 'hasten' in time means crossing the frontiers of present reality into the spheres of what is possible in the future. In crossing these frontiers we anticipate the future for which we hope."[48] Thus,

44 See James C. Hathaway, "The Global Cop-Out on Refugees," *International Journal of Refugee Law* 30, no. 4 (2018): 591–604.

45 T. S. Eliot, "The Waste Land," in *The Waste Land: Authoritative Text, Contexts, Criticism*, ed. Michael North (New York: W.W. Norton & Company, 2001), 5.

46 Moltmann, *Ethics of Hope*, 3.

47 Moltmann, *Ethics of Hope*, 5 (citing Rev. 21:1).

48 Moltmann, *Ethics of Hope*, 7–8.

for Moltmann, hope grounded in eschatological expectation is both the possibility of and the inspiration for transformative action in the present.

What if, however, hope is neither the possibility of nor the inspiration for transformative action? Christian ethicist De La Torre has made this claim in his biting critique of hope as a means to justice. For De La Torre, hope is not a universal possibility, even for the Christian. Rather, "[h]ope is possible when privilege allows for a future."[49] Drawing from his experience "[a]mong the disenfranchised, the dispossessed, the least of the least," De La Torre writes that he "discovered an ethos where hope is not apparent; rather, it is imposed by those who might be endangered if the marginalized were to instead act."[50] For De La Torre, hope is neither an empirical reality for many people living in conditions of oppression and deprivation, nor is it a sober assessment of the future. The coming of justice is far less likely than continued or worsening injustice and suffering for many; and those who lack the privilege of anticipating a better, more just future are fully aware of this reality.

I am reminded of James Hathaway's comments on the recently negotiated Global Compact on Refugees, arguably the most significant development in refugee and asylum policy since the 1967 Protocol. The Global Compact, writes Hathaway, "is all about process – a bureaucrat's dream perhaps, but nothing that comes even close to dependably addressing the operational deficits of the refugee regime." Hathaway, an international law advocate, goes on to question why the Global Compact fails to imagine an alternative future of effective global cooperation: "Why were we presented with such a tepid response when the need for decisive action is so clear? Why a 'thin' approach to protection reform when something robust is so obviously what both refugees and the poorer States that receive most of them need and deserve?"[51] A better future is not the promise of the present or its legal institutions.

Hope cannot, therefore, be the possibility of action because that would deny those without hope or cause for hope the possibility of acting. Making hope the possibility of action annuls the justice work of those who act not in the security of a better future but against the injustices of the present, whether the future means justice, the perpetuation of injustice, or a different species of injustice altogether. In response to Moltmann's claim

[49] De La Torre, *Embracing Hopelessness*, 5.

[50] De La Torre, *Embracing Hopelessness*, 5.

[51] Hathaway, "Global Cop-Out on Refugees," 594; see also, Silas W. Allard, "Christianity and a Global Law for Migration," in *Christianity and Global Law*, ed. Rafael Domingo and John Witte, Jr. (London: Routledge, 2020), 351–64.

that "[w]e undertake what we think is possible,"[52] De La Torre replies, "[t]o be hopeless is a desperation of refusing to give up, a recognition that even if carrying the cross leads to crucifixion, the struggle for justice is what defines the present and could plant seeds that might blossom in some future."[53] Those whose lot is unlikely to improve can still work for a different and better future, even if they are unassured by the hope that such a future is likely, imminent, or possible. De La Torre enjoins his readers to recognize and acknowledge that much of the world lives under conditions in which hope is nonsense; yet, struggles for justice are often the response of the hopeless to the conditions of hopelessness.

Hope, for De La Torre, is not only descriptively misguided when used to describe the possibility of action. It has a darker side. Rather than inspiration for transformative action, De La Torre sees hope as the inspiration for inaction because hope participates in a dialectical history that trusts in progress toward a better future. Where Moltmann understands the possibility of a different future to inspire action in the present to bring about that future, De La Torre sees the expected unfolding of a better future as the basis for acquiescing to the status quo. "Hope, as a middle-class privilege," writes De La Torre, "soothes the conscience of those complicit with oppressive structures, lulling them to do nothing except look forward to a salvific future where every wrong will be righted and every tear wiped away, while numbing themselves to the pain of those oppressed, lest that pain motivate them to take radical action."[54]

Hope as progressive dialectical history also tends to obfuscate actual histories of atrocity. De La Torre is specifically concerned that salvation history (transcendentalist or materialist; religious or secular) promises to make sense of past and ongoing atrocities, and thereby erase responsibility and the possibility of reparation for historic wrongs. Accountability and responsibility are washed away by the tide of history. The illusion of dialectical historical development can also serve to legitimate an appreciation for the present as an overcoming of the past. Sure, injustice still exists, *but we've come so far*. Or, in its more pernicious form, the claim that present formal equality obviates the need for historical redress. This "progress" limits or tempers the obligation for ongoing justice work.[55]

52 Moltmann, *Ethics of Hope*, 3.

53 De La Torre, *Embracing Hopelessness*, 155.

54 De La Torre, *Embracing Hopelessness*, 5.

55 The critique of salvation history is explored throughout De La Torre, *Embracing Hopelessness*, ch. 2.

Finally, for De La Torre, organizing the inspiration for action around hope fails to serve the justice work of those living under conditions of hopelessness. "For the world's disenfranchised to embrace a theology of hope, constructed independently of their real-life experiences, requires that they first deny their existential reality in exchange for the illusion of some dialectical movement toward a predominately white utopia that continues to exclude them in the here-and-now."[56] Privileging hope as the possibility of action makes action the province of the privileged and encourages savior narratives; privileging hope as the inspiration for action encourages the hopeless to collude in visions of justice that will often fail to address the injustices under which the hopeless live. Furthermore, "[f]or those without a future, eschatological visions of utopia have the potential of creating an apathy that steers the oppressed from rebelling and creating the possibility of new realities."[57]

The current landscape of asylum in the United States is not one that inspires hope. In addition to the significant structural barriers discussed in the first half of this chapter, the Trump administration engaged in a systematic and enduring effort to further limit asylum to the United States.[58] And, the United States is not alone in placing greater restrictions on refugee and asylum law.[59] Many asylum seekers live in conditions of hopelessness as De La Torre describes it; hopelessness resulting from the situations of both violence and deprivation that lead them to seek asylum, and hopelessness in a system of law more likely than not to deny them protection. A sober assessment of refugee and asylum law does not support hope in a progressive history of greater protection for refugees and asylum seekers. De La Torre helps advocates to reckon with this reality of hopelessness. Embracing hopelessness is not an abandonment of praxis.

56 De La Torre, *Embracing Hopelessness*, 49.

57 De La Torre, *Embracing Hopelessness*, 52.

58 See, e.g., Matter of A-R-C-G-, 26 I&N Dec. 388 (BIA 2014) (overturning case-law recognizing domestic violence as a grounds for asylum); Kirstjen M. Nielsen, "Memorandum: Policy Guidance for Implementation of the Migrant Protection Protocols," January 25, 2019 (requiring asylum seekers to remain in Mexico while their case is pending), www.dhs.gov/sites/default/files/publications/19_0129_OPA_migrant-protection-protocols-policy-guidance.pdf; Donald J. Trump, "Presidential Proclamation Addressing Mass Migration through the Southern Border of the United States," November 9, 2018 (requiring that asylum claims be made only at designated ports of entry), www.whitehouse.gov/presidential-actions/presidential-proclamation-addressing-mass-migration-southern-border-united-states/. For detailed analysis of these and other policies, see Chapter 17 in this volume.

59 Tania Karas, "US Leads Global 'Race to the Bottom' in Shutting Door on Refugees and Asylum-Seekers," *Public Radio International*, September 17, 2019, www.pri.org/stories/2019-09-17/us-leads-global-race-bottom-shutting-door-refugees-and-asylum-seekers.

18.7 GENEROSITY TOWARD THE FUTURE: AN ETHIC OF ASYLUM PRAXIS

"Real generosity towards the future," according to Albert Camus, "lies in giving all to the present."[60] An ethic of praxis under conditions of hopelessness demands a full investment in the present because the future does not determine the possibilities of the present – the present is the possibility of a future. As De La Torre argues: "Hopelessness is an act of courage to embrace reality and to act even when the odds are in favor of defeat. . . . [W]e can only and boldly engage in a liberative praxis within the now – and *hope* for the best."[61] For De La Torre, hopelessness is a liberative ethic because it liberates action from the constraints of an apathy that waits for the unfolding of a progressive future. Hopelessness liberates the privileged from the comfort of meaningful salvation histories and encourages an uncomfortable solidarity of instability with those living under conditions of hopelessness.[62]

Welch adds an additional dimension to the liberative ethic of praxis. Welch has written of the liberative potential of abandoning an ethic of control and embracing an ethic of risk. "In trading an ethic of control for an ethic of risk, and in living out this ethos, we can neither undo the past nor control the future. But we can learn from the past, and we can live creatively, responsibly, and compassionately in the present."[63] By an "ethic of control," Welch means an ethic that presumes that we can both know with assurance and achieve in fullness that which is just and right. But "[t]he drive of moral life," Welch points out, "is that we can never know the difference between that which we can change and that which we cannot."[64] An ethic of risk abandons the constraints of the progressive promise of perfect justice as action-confining and embraces creative, responsible, and compassionate action that risks imperfection and failure.

An ethic of asylum praxis that acknowledges the hopelessness of the situation and embraces an ethic of risk is an ethic of solidarity that begins with the risky, hopeless claims of asylum seekers themselves.

18.8 CLAIMING ASYLUM

As I detailed earlier, the asylum seeker is constrained by the limited legal definition of a refugee and the way that definition is deployed through the

60 Albert Camus, *The Rebel*, trans. Anthony Bower (New York: Alfred A. Knopf, 1954), 271.
61 De La Torre, *Embracing Hopelessness*, 140.
62 De La Torre, *Embracing Hopelessness*, 49.
63 Welch, *Feminist Ethic of Risk*, 37.
64 Welch, *Feminist Ethic of Risk*, 37.

expansive power of asylum adjudicators.[65] While the asylum seeker must navigate the established boundaries of the definition, the asylum seeker's claim is not contained by those boundaries. The claim is also a moral demand for recognition and protection that exceeds any simple categorization. Each asylum seeker's story is unique and, therefore, each claim asserts not only that the asylum's seeker's story does conform to the refugee definition but also that the definition should accommodate the asylum seeker's story. Thus, each new claim not only negotiates the existing boundaries of who counts as a refugee based on prior claims; each new claim renegotiates those boundaries.

The moral agency of the asylum seeker as claimant is essential to the legal process. It is the claim that initiates the possibility of recognition and protection. In making the claim, the asylum seeker negotiates the established boundaries of the refugee definition by attempting to conform to or fit within those boundaries, but the claim is also a demand that the boundaries be moved and the definition expanded if and when that is necessary for the recognition and protection of this person. The demand that the boundaries be negotiated is not aberrational; it is intrinsic to the process. The demand that the boundaries be negotiated is neither fraud nor abuse; it is the very possibility of asylum.

18.9 DEFENDING EVERY CLAIM

Lawyers play a vital role in this process. The professional skills and knowledge of the immigration attorney are often the difference between a claim's success and failure in the complicated, bureaucratic legal process.[66] If every asylum claim is a demand in the present that renegotiates the future of asylum, then advocates engaged in an ethic of praxis have the hopeless project of defending every claim, of walking in solidarity with asylum seekers by helping to realize the possibility of a more expansive future for asylum through the moral demands and legal arguments made in the claim to asylum.

De La Torre names an ethic of practice operating from hopelessness as an ethics *para joder*. An ethics *para joder*, as De La Torre describes it, is "an ethics

65 For a more detailed analysis of the argument in this section, see Silas W. Allard, "Asylum: The Constraint of a Definition and the Agency of a Claim," *Moral Agency under Constraint*, August 3, 2020, https://scholarblogs.emory.edu/moralagency2019/2020/08/03/claiming-asylum-as-moral-agency/.

66 Eagly and Shafer found that if represented, detained immigrants were twice as likely to be granted some form of relief from deportation, those released from detention were three times as likely to succeed, and those never detained were almost five times as likely to succeed. Eagly and Shafer, "National Study of Access to Counsel," 50–1.

that f*cks with the prevailing power structures," and the practitioner of such an ethics, the *joderon*, is a trickster who creates possibilities through disruption and making trouble.[67] De La Torre addresses an ethics *para joder* to immigration, specifically arguing that "the insurmountable task of creating justice-based immigration policies in our lifetime makes f*cking with the immigration system the only ethical response to the immigration dilemma in the *hope* of creating new opportunities through disorder and chaos."[68] Playing the role of the trickster by seeking disruption and making trouble for the law may seem beyond the capacity of attorneys whose professional role places them centrally within the legal system, but the professional responsibility of the attorney also includes an obligation to push at the boundaries of existing law and to ask how the law can better serve justice.[69] To take up every claim as a legitimate demand for protection is to risk the possibility of expanding refugee and asylum law – to risk an expansive refugee and asylum law.

There are projects that embody this ethic. The Innovation Law Lab in Portland, Oregon, is spearheading what its director Stephen Manning refers to as "big immigration law." Big immigration law is a collaborative representation approach that focuses "people, networks, data, and technology on a select immigration issue in a particular locality," with the goal of creating new forms of advocacy and "forms of resistance that go beyond opposing unbridled exercise of authority to take on a new role in shaping law around an imagined community."[70] One of Innovation Law Lab's projects are Centers of Excellence that seek to leverage collaborative representation of cases with low expectations of success in hostile jurisdictions to challenge and disrupt the ecosystem of denials that leads to asylum-free zones.[71] Other projects include universal representation models such as the New York Family Unity Project and immigrant defense projects within public defenders offices that aspire to represent everyone but, working with limited resources, begin by not testing cases for their likelihood of success.

67 De La Torre, *Embracing Hopelessness*, 150–1.

68 De La Torre, *Embracing Hopelessness*, 152.

69 "A lawyer shall not bring or defend a proceeding, or assert or controvert an issue therein, unless there is a basis in law and fact for doing so that is not frivolous, which includes a *good faith argument for an extension, modification or reversal of existing law*" [emphasis added]. American Bar Association, *Model Rules of Professional Conduct* (Chicago: ABA Book Publishing, 2019), Rule 3.1: Meritorious Claims & Contentions.

70 Stephen Manning and Juliet Stumpf, "Big Immigration Law," *UC Davis Law Review* 52, no. 1 (2018): 407–34, at 413.

71 Innovation Law Lab, "Building the Resistance: Innovation Law Lab Impact Report," 2018, https://innovationlawlab.org/reports/Impact-2018.pdf, 4–5.

None of these projects can actually defend every claim. But defending every claim is not, of course, a practical reality; it is a hopeless ethic of praxis.

18.10 CONCLUSION

I opened this chapter thinking about the law students with whom I work and their eagerness to become agents of justice as practitioners of public international law. In defense of that desire, this chapter joins De La Torre in looking skeptically at hoped for promises from the future, including the promises of public international law. The flawed and fallible Refugee Convention, like all public international law, guarantees no particular future of justice. But, the Refugee Convention, even with its limitations, does make possible certain kinds of action – claiming asylum and defending the claim – that imagine alternative, possible futures. Thus, this chapter is not intended as discouragement; quite the opposite. It is an invitation to those students who inspire it, as well as the practitioners they will become, not to trust in the promise of a better future but to think about how an ethic of praxis can risk the present for another possible future.

If hope is a virtue, it is so only if and when it imagines a future that makes demands on the present. Hope that defers justice is a vice. But risking the present for another possible future does not necessarily or always proceed from virtuous hope; it is sometimes and necessarily born of despair, desperation, survival, and the sheer stubborn refusal to acquiesce here, now. The Christian story attests to both: Bethlehem and Gethsemane, Golgotha and Emmaus.

RECOMMENDED READING

Betts, Alexander. *Survival Migration: Failed Governance and the Crisis of Displacement*. Ithaca: Cornell University Press, 2013.

De La Torre, Miguel A. *Embracing Hopelessness*. Minneapolis: Fortress Press, 2017.

Gatrell, Peter. *The Making of the Modern Refugee*. Oxford: Oxford University Press, 2013.

Goodwin-Gill, Guy S., and Jane McAdam. *The Refugee in International Law*. Oxford: Oxford University Press, 2007.

Snyder, Susanna. *Asylum-Seeking, Migration and Church*. Burlington, VT: Ashgate, 2012.

19

The Hidden Theology of International Legal Positivism

Akbar Rasulov*

19.1 INTRODUCTION

This chapter is a study in the critical deconstruction of one of the most popular theoretical paradigms in modern international law and its basic ideological impact on international law as a discipline.[1] The paradigm in question is *voluntarist positivism*, and the general thrust of its ideological impact on the discipline of international law, I am going to argue, has been to encourage within it the rise and spread of what one might call a theoretical culture of bad faith – a mix of false consciousness, self-censorship, and a "crooked attitude towards truth and knowledge"[2] – particularly, in what concerns international law's relationship with natural law and Christian theology.

The last two sentences use a lot of notoriously ambivalent concepts. For the prevention of doubt, let me explain briefly how I understand them in these pages.

* The argument set out in this chapter has spent a long time in gestation. Its development has benefited from numerous conversations I have had over the years with John Haskell, who has finally convinced me to write it down. I am grateful to him for his encouragement and support, without which this work would have never been completed. I am also thankful to Pierre Schlag, Pamela Slotte, and John for their generous comments and feedback on an earlier draft. As usual, the responsibility for all mistakes and errors is mine alone.

1 A note on influences: I think of this chapter as a continuation – adaptation, imitation – of the first-wave critical legal studies tradition as exemplified in Roberto Mangabeira Unger, *Knowledge and Politics* (New York: Free Press, 1975); Duncan Kennedy, "Form and Substance in Private Law Adjudication," *Harvard Law Review* 89, no. 8 (1976): 1685–778; Karl Klare, "Contracts Jurisprudence and the First-Year Casebook," *New York University Law Review* 54 (1979): 876–99; and Frances Olsen, "The Family and the Market: A Study of Ideology and Legal Reform," *Harvard Law Review* 96, no. 7 (1983): 1497–578. I have also drawn inspiration from Duncan Kennedy, A *Critique of Adjudication (fin de siècle)* (Cambridge, MA: Harvard University Press, 1997) and Pierre Schlag, "Law as the Continuation of God by Other Means," *California Law Review* 85, no. 2 (1997): 427–40.

2 Peter Sloterdijk, *Critique of Cynical Reason* (Minneapolis: University of Minnesota Press, 1987), 296.

International law is a discipline of legal studies that focuses on the study of rules, processes, institutions, and actors conventionally associated with the phenomenon of the international legal order. A *discipline* is a more or less established field of theoretical inquiry that has its own distinct object of study, history, set of orientating questions, and knowledge archive. *Theory* is that body of thought which relates to the interpretation of abstract concepts. It is a term that describes those protocols of reasoning and working assumptions about ontology, proof, causality, and so on, which we use to make sense of whatever objects, phenomena, or ideas we are reflecting on. A different way of thinking about theory is to think of it as a framework for the production of meaning. Marxism, psychoanalysis, and empiricism are all textbook examples of theories. So are neoclassical economics and second-wave feminism.

A *paradigm* is a synonym for a relatively well-established theoretical tradition or "school of thought." To be a school of thought in any given discipline or field is to have a relatively determinate, coherent, and stable position on those questions which are recognized within that discipline or field as among its central theoretical problems.[3] Hegelian Marxism is a distinct school of thought within Marxism. Lacanian psychoanalysis is a distinct school of thought within psychoanalysis. Constructivism is a relatively distinct school of thought within international relations.

Natural law is a school of thought that assumes the existence of an authoritative, non-human-defined "standard of justice . . . against which [all] existing laws can be measured,"[4] and which can thus serve as an objective criterion of legal truth in reference to which the positive legal order can be judged and evaluated. The specific strand of the natural law tradition that interests me in this chapter is the quasi-Providential theory which assumes that the positive legal order in a more or less spontaneous fashion will always gravitate toward the natural standard justice, that is, that, like Georg Wilhelm Friedrich Hegel's Reason or Richard Posner's allocative efficiency, natural justice is bound inevitably to surface from within the murky depths of the positive legal order, as if propelled by some unstoppable force. The thesis that I want to put forward in these pages, in a nutshell, states that (a) this is precisely the kind of theoretical orientation that the vast majority of international lawyers who otherwise believe themselves to be positivists actually take for granted; and (b) they may not always be conscious of this fact – and that is precisely why the question of bad faith is such an important

[3] David Kennedy, "When Renewal Repeats: Thinking against the Box," *NYU Journal of International Law & Politics* 32, no. 2 (2000): 335–500, at 373.

[4] Paul Sieghart, *The International Law of Human Rights* (Oxford: Oxford University Press, 1983), 7.

question to raise – but that ultimately does not matter: their theoretical culture and analytical reflexes are still dominated by this kind of quasi-Providential outlook, and the consequences of that, on the whole, are not insignificant.

Positivism is the great historical other of the natural law tradition. Its main starting premise is the idea that all laws and legal systems are man-made social artifacts and that somewhere behind these artifacts, if one only looks hard enough, one is always going to find the institutional apparatuses of the modern state. Or, as Georges Gurvitch puts it, "all law is … established in a given social milieu," and it so obtains because "of a superior and dominant will, generally of the State."[5] What distinguishes the different strands of the positivist tradition from one another is which particular species of socially embedded processes (forms of social life) they assume to be constitutive of the "legal reality," that is, legally relevant, and how one should be able, in practice, to determine "what is going on" within these processes.

Voluntarist positivism (VP) is the "classical" face of the positivist tradition in international law.[6] I will say a lot more about VP's underlying theory in a few pages. For now, let me just note that VP's single most important defining feature is that it aims, ultimately, to ground all international legal processes – lawmaking, law-ascertainment, law-enforcement – as well as all the different varieties of conceptual materials that are used in these processes – rules, principles, doctrines – in state consent. This does not mean that VP does not recognize the fact that many international law mechanisms today operate on a nonconsensual basis or that states are not the only relevant actors in the contemporary international legal system. But the reason why these mechanisms exist, and why nonstate actors can partake in the workings of international law in the first place, is because the community of states, expressly or tacitly, have willed it to be so. Everything that is a part of international law, in the final analysis is "an emanation of State will."[7] Conversely, "only that is … international law which has received the general assent of States"[8] and "nothing can be law unless [States] have consented to it."[9]

5 Georges Gurvitch, *Sociology of Law* (New York: Philosophical Library and Alliance Book Corporation, 1942), 4.

6 Jean d'Aspremont and Jörg Kammerhofer, "Introduction: The Future of International Legal Positivism," in *International Legal Positivism in a Post-Modern World*, ed. Jörg Kammerhofer and Jean d'Aspremont (Cambridge: Cambridge University Press, 2014), 4–7.

7 Bruno Simma and Andreas Paulus, "The Responsibility of Individuals for Human Rights Abuses in Internal Conflicts: A Positivist View," *American Journal of International Law* 93, no. 2 (1999): 302–16, at 303.

8 Percy Ellwood Corbett, "The Consent of States and the Sources of the Law of Nations," *British Yearbook of International Law* 6, (1925): 20–30, at 21–3.

9 Andrew Clapham, *Brierly's Law of Nations*, 7th ed. (Oxford: Oxford University Press, 2012), 49–50.

Theology is that field of inquiry which deals with the study of religious topics, or, as Richard Hooker put it, "the science of things divine."[10] For the purposes of this chapter, I will ignore the usual distinctions between natural and dogmatic theology and between negative and positive theology[11] – not because they are wrong or unwarranted but because they are not immediately relevant. In a similar fashion, the concept of *ideology* will not be given any special connotations but will be used instead in its most general, sociological sense, which is that changing people's perceptions of what is right, good, and true often pushes them to mobilize against or in support of certain political causes, agendas, and projects, the result of which may be to make the pursuit of these causes, agendas, and projects more or less politically costly.

Last but not least, the concept of *bad faith* comes from the French philosopher Jean-Paul Sartre. Here is how he defines it:

> [B]ad faith is a lie to oneself [but it is different] from lying in general. . . . The essence of the lie implies in fact that the liar actually is in complete possession of the truth which he is hiding. . . . The ideal description of the liar would be a cynical consciousness, affirming truth within himself, denying it in his words, and denying that negation as such. . . . The liar intends to deceive and he does not hide that intention from himself. . . .
>
> By the lie the consciousness affirms that it exists by nature as hidden from the Other; it utilizes for its own profit the ontological duality of myself and myself in the eyes of the Other. . . .
>
> The situation cannot be the same for bad faith. . . . Bad faith . . . has in appearance the structure of falsehood. Only what changes everything is the fact that *in bad faith it is from myself that I am hiding the truth.* Thus the duality of the deceiver and the deceived does not exist here[,] which means that I must know in my capacity as deceiver the truth which is hidden from me in my capacity as the one deceived. Better yet *I must know the truth very exactly in order to conceal it more carefully.*[12]

Note the two passages set off in italics. In bad faith, it is from ourselves that we seek to hide the truth. To hide it well, however, we must always already know the truth we are trying to hide.

What is that truth then which the VP tradition – by encouraging a culture of bad faith – has pushed the discipline of international law to learn to hide from itself even though deep inside the discipline still remains secretly aware of it?

10 Richard Hooker, *The Works of That Learned and Judicious Divine, Mr. Richard Hooker, in Eight Books of the Laws of Ecclesiastical Polity* (London: R. White, 1723), 69.

11 See Anthony Kenny, *Medieval Philosophy* (Oxford: Oxford University Press, 2005), 41, 285.

12 Jean-Paul Sartre, *Being and Nothingness*, trans. by Hazel E. Barnes (London: Routledge, 2006), 71–2 (italics added).

The answer to this question begins with what I call the *problem of international law's absent center*.

At the root of the VP paradigm lies a *fundamental paradox*, that is to say a formally unresolvable logical contradiction.[13] As a matter of its "official theory," VP persistently seeks to portray international law as an essentially horizontal, that is, decentralized, legal order. A systematic examination of the standard reasoning patterns that sustain the vast majority of its discursive output, however, indicates that "in reality" the VP theoretical framework actually tends to presume quite the contrary. Even though the international legal process is supposed to be decentralized, in practice the VP discourse typically tends to proceed *as though* international law were somehow permeated with the kind of internal dynamics that are normally associated with institutionally centralized systems. It is as if international law both has a structuring center and is free of any centralizing structures at the same time.

How can this paradox be made sense of? Note an important detail: the argument here is not that the VP tradition openly contradicts itself by saying one thing at one time and another thing at another time. The contradiction we have here is a performative one: the VP tradition states one thing at the level of its *official narrative* but signals something completely different through its *actual theoretical practice*. Which of these two "messages" ought we to believe, the official narrative or the apparent theoretical practice? The answer that I propose to give in this chapter can be thought of as an extension of what legal realists called the functionalist method:[14] the real theoretical identity of any given paradigm is revealed by how its discourse actually operates in practice, not by what that paradigm officially claims about itself; and the actual operative framework on the basis of which the VP discourse functions clearly seems to suggest that the international legal system is structured in a fundamentally centralized fashion.

The argument I am drawing on here in large part echoes the Derridean concept of "structurality," which can be defined as that abstract quality which characterizes any given field that, regardless of its official self-presentation, reveals itself in practice to be infused with the kind of *immanent organizing force* whose primary function is to bring to it a certain sense of order and balance and to ensure its basic stability throughout whatever changes may take

13 "Paradoxes are questions . . . that suspend us between too many good answers." Roy Sorensen, *A Brief History of the Paradox: Philosophy and the Labyrinths of the Mind* (Oxford: Oxford University Press, 2003), xii.

14 Felix S. Cohen, "Transcendental Nonsense and the Functional Approach," *Columbia Law Review* 35 (1935): 809–49.

place within or outside of it.[15] One of the central claims that I put forward in this chapter is that, despite what VP's official narrative states, the actual VP understanding of international law presumes international law to be a system thoroughly infused by precisely this kind of immanent organizing force: a hidden presence whose principal function is to balance it, integrate it, and ensure that it retains its basic coherence, stability, and predictability irrespective of whatever changes may take place within or outside its horizon.

The last three paragraphs may not be the easiest piece of text to wade through. If it helps, just think of what I am going to do in this chapter as a form of "logical reverse-engineering," or what Louis Althusser called an exercise in symptomatic reading.[16] By looking at how the VP tradition approaches a certain issue in practice, we can reconstruct, symptomatically, its actual operative theory about that issue. Based on that, we can then compare what the VP tradition really "thinks" with what it says it thinks and explore what may be the reason for any divergences between the two.

The argument that is developed below follows a relatively simple template. Analytically, it consists of three main parts. The *first* part (Section 19.2) states that a fundamental discrepancy appears to exist between the actual operative theory that underpins the VP tradition and its officially declared theoretical account. The *third* part (Section 19.4) aims to show that this discrepancy is neither accidental nor logically inevitable but is instead thoroughly ideological, that is to say that (i) its initial emergence and continuing persistence are ideologically motivated, and (ii) its consequences for the discipline of international law are not ideologically trivial. The *second* part (Section 19.3) serves as a bridge that connects the first and the third parts in that it offers a critical exploration of VP's broader theoretical genealogy. The main objective behind this exercise is to show, firstly, that the same basic theoretical conundrum that underlies the paradox of international law's absent center can also be found, structurally, in numerous other, broadly comparable theoretical contexts; and, secondly, that by reviewing what sorts of solution have been proposed to this conundrum in those other contexts, it may be possible to deduce what kind of conceptual content may in fact be "hiding" behind that apparent theoretical gap which in VP's theoretical structure corresponds to the problem of international law's absent center.

15 Jacques Derrida, *Writing and Difference* (Chicago: University of Chicago Press, 1978), 278–9.

16 Louis Althusser, "From *Capital* to Marx's Philosophy," in *Reading Capital*, ed. Louis Althusser and Etienne Balibar (London: New Left Books, 1970), 28–34.

A brief disclaimer: the chain of theoretical parallels that I explore in this chapter is not meant to be anything other than illustrative. I do not pretend to have worked out the entire genealogical tree behind the VP paradigm. Nor does my argument require me to claim that. There are two main stages in the particular genealogical sequence that I outline in Section 19.3. In the first stage (Section 19.3.1), I trace VP's problem of international law's absent center to two Enlightenment-period traditions: Immanuel Kant's moral theory (Section 19.3.1.1) and Adam Smith's theory of economics (Section 19.3.1.2). During the second stage (Section 19.3.2), extending the critical exercise a step further, I show how both the Kantian argument about personal autonomy and the Smithian concept of competitive markets reproduce the exact same theoretical structure and conceptual strategies that had been used previously to "resolve" the analytical paradox raised by the problem of free will in medieval Christian theology. For the purposes of the present study, I focus my discussion in this part of the chapter on the particular structures and strategies developed by the Franciscan scholar John Duns Scotus. For the avoidance of doubt, let me note, however, that one could as easily use in this context Thomas Aquinas, Desiderius Erasmus, Martin Luther, or Jean Calvin, all of whom essentially made use of the same *basic analytical framework*. The reason I went for Scotus is that, to my mind, he simply articulated things more elegantly and insightfully.

19.2 VOLUNTARIST POSITIVISM AS A PARADIGM

19.2.1 *The Importance of VP*

An intellectual tradition that first emerged at the end of the nineteenth century, VP occupies a rather peculiar place in international law's theoretical ecosystem. For starters, it is not just *a* theory or *a* school of thought – at least not in the same sense in which the Marxist theory of international law is a "theory" or the New Haven school of international law was a "school." The impact that VP's theoretical culture has had on the basic structures of international law's disciplinary consciousness has been enduring, pervasive, and totally without precedent. From the moment of its inception, one might say, VP has served, to borrow another famous concept from Sartre, as the discipline's ultimate unsurpassable theoretical horizon.[17] Fads and fashions came and went. But, like pigskin in Hans Christian Andersen's tale, VP has remained that simple irreducible core which survived long after all the gilding

[17] Jean-Paul Sartre, *Search for a Method*, trans. by Hazel E. Barnes (New York: Alfred A. Knopf, 1963), 7.

faded away. Every generation of international lawyers since the start of the twentieth century has declared its intention to bury VP and end its theoretical hegemony.[18] And yet, even as they attempted to do so at the level of their "official legal theory," they also at the same time continued to reproduce its broader theoretical framework, preserving and entrenching it at the level of their actual analytical practices, discursive conventions, and reasoning protocols.

From Gerald Fitzmaurice to Alain Pellet, from J. G. Starke to Andrew Clapham, from Rosalyn Higgins to Charles de Visscher, countless spokespersons of the disciplinary mainstream over the course of the last century have sought to denounce and repudiate the VP tradition, openly decrying its philosophical unsoundness,[19] its propensity for reductionism, and its lack of realism.[20] And yet, whatever one hand took, the other gave back. Even today, the vast majority of the disciplinary debate within international law, as Richard Collins observes, still continues to "move within [VP's] inherited frame."[21] The sun has risen and set over New Havenite policy jurisprudence, Tunkinian Marxist pandectism, Bedjaoui's *droit de finalité*, and countless other schools and traditions. But more than a century after Heinrich Triepel,[22] Dionisio Anzilotti,[23] and Lassa Oppenheim[24] first outlined its main theoretic parameters, international lawyers still comfortably inhabit the world of VP thought, debate classical VP topics, rehearse standard VP tropes, and measure one another's professional competence, above and before everything else, in terms of how well one has mastered the art of VP rhetoric and argument.

What are the principal defining features of VP? What does it believe as a school of thought? From the outside, the logical structure of the VP paradigm does not seem very sophisticated. In its standard formulation, it boils down to four general propositions:

18 See David Kennedy, "A New World Order: Yesterday, Today, and Tomorrow," *Transnational Law Contemporary Problems* 4, no. 2 (1994): 329–76.

19 Clapham, *Brierly's Law of Nations*, 50.

20 Alain Pellet, "The Normative Dilemma: Will and Consent in International Law-Making," *Australian Year Book of International Law* 12 (1989): 22–53, at 23.

21 Richard Collins, "Classical Legal Positivism in International Law Revisited," in *International Legal Positivism in a Post-Modern World*, ed. Jörg Kammerhofer and Jean d'Aspremont (Cambridge: Cambridge University Press, 2014), 48.

22 Heinrich Triepel, *Völkerrecht und Landesrecht* (Leipzig: C. L. Hirschfeld, 1899).

23 See, in particular, "Teoria generale della responsibilità dello Stato nel diritto internazionale," as reprinted in Dionisio Anzilotti, *Scritti di Diritto Internazionale Pubblico* 1 (Padova: Cedam, 1956).

24 Lassa Oppenheim, *International Law: A Treatise*, vol. 1, *Peace* (London: Longmans, Green, and Co., 1905).

(1) international law is a body of rules created by states;
(2) every state is free and sovereign in the sense that there exists no higher authority above it and it may determine its own future and pursue whichever course of political, economic, and social development it desires;
(3) all rules, processes, and institutions that make up the international legal system are a product of inter-state agreement; and
(4) the international legal order thus constituted is both *effective* as a mechanism of international governance and fully *sufficient* to bring the realization of the international community's overarching "first values" such as international peace, security, sustainable development, and so on.

At first glance, the picture does not seem very complex: international law is a law by, for, and between, not above, sovereign states, and everything that is international law is derived from agreements among states. So far, so good. But note now a curious logical jump that takes place between proposition (3) – the international legal system is a product of agreement among sovereign states – and proposition (4) – as a mechanism of international governance international law is not only effective but also sufficient when it comes to the protection and promotion of international stability, security, prosperity, and so on. How can a system of decision-making that is devoid of hierarchy, and in which every participating agent is free to choose what rules they will follow, give rise to a stable normative order that can meet the needs and demands of a decidedly communal character? Or, to put it in slightly different terms, how can harmony be expected to arise out of cacophony and, moreover, do so as a matter of course?

19.2.2 *The Basic Theoretical Structure of VP: A General Outline*

As most commentators agree,[25] the *locus classicus* for the statement of the VP creed in modern international law is typically found in the *Lotus* case:

> International law governs relations between independent States. The rules of law binding upon States, therefore, emanate from their own free will as expressed in conventions or usages generally accepted as expressing principles of law and established in order to regulate the relations between these co-existing independent communities or with a view to the achievement of

[25] See, e.g., Collins, "Classical Legal Positivism," 26; Simma and Paulus, "Responsibility of Individuals," 304.

> common aims. Restrictions upon the independence of States cannot, therefore, be presumed.[26]

Add to this statement the slightly more extended summary provided in the mid-1950s by the Italian jurist Roberto Ago and what emerges is commonly understood to be the basic outline of VP in its classical configuration:

> Positive law is … law which is laid down (*gesetzt*), and the character of positivity is always conferred on the legal norm by its being derived from some creative act which [is] historically perceptible. [A]ll those acts which are not direct or indirect manifestations of the will of the state are excluded …, for only the state has the power to lay down legal norms. … "Positive law" thus [is] a term applicable to all existing law, to any form of law which has been so created in history, as opposed to … ideal law, or law created only by thought. … Internally law is that which the state has willed, internationally it is that which several states have willed and established collectively.[27]

In more recent times, Bruno Simma and Andreas Paulus have sought to update the classical definition as follows:

> The main characteristic of [this paradigm] is the association of law with an emanation of state will (voluntarism). Voluntarism requires the deduction of all norms from acts of state will: states create international norms by reaching consent on the content of a rule. … This system of rules is an "objective" reality and needs to be distinguished from law "as it should be". Classic positivism demands rigorous tests for legal validity. Extralegal arguments … are deemed irrelevant to legal analysis; there is only hard law, no soft law. …
>
> For international law, this implies that all norms derive their pedigree from one of the traditional sources of international law, custom and treaty. Treaties embody the express consent of states, custom nothing but their tacit consent. The only relevant conduct is that of states seen as unitary actors. Treaties, including so-called lawmaking treaties – e.g., those creating new rules or changing old ones – are binding upon the contracting parties only. Whether habitual conduct of states amounts to legally binding custom is a question of objective determination of fact.[28]

A few years before that Louis Henkin captured the same sentiment from a slightly different angle:

[26] *SS Lotus* (1927), PCIJ Series A, No. 10, at 18.

[27] Roberto Ago, "Positive Law and International Law," *American Journal of International Law* 51, no. 4 (1957): 691–733, at 697–701.

[28] Simma and Paulus, "Responsibility of Individuals," 303–5.

> International law is made by the States themselves, not by a legislative body representing them. ... States make law by consent, by agreement. Inter-State law is made, or recognized, or accepted, by the "will" of States. Nothing becomes law for the international system from any other source. ... The principle that law is binding on a State only by its consent remains an axiom of the political system, an implication of State autonomy. ... International law is comprised of ... custom and treaty. ... Treaty law is made; customary law results. Treaties are made by an act of will, purposefully; custom grows. [B]oth are rooted in State consent.[29]

Note the main themes that run through each of these passages. International law is a body of rules each of which exists as an objective fact. It is a body of rules that have been "laid down" by states as opposed to being "created only by thought." All states are sovereign, and international law is created solely on the basis of state consent. Consent can be granted either expressly, through formal agreements (treaties), or tacitly, through regularly repeated common usages (customs). Unless a given rule can be traced to an objectively verifiable treaty provision or custom to which the state in question has consented, it will not bind that state, and the laudability or importance of whatever values and purposes it may otherwise seek to serve will be, in this context, entirely irrelevant. Even the most important ethical and political concerns, in the end, can only "constitute the inspirational basis for" but will never be "sufficient in themselves to generate" a binding rule of international law.[30]

Note also the persistent imagery of unmediated democratism: the international legal order, as depicted in the VP tradition, is essentially a system of "direct self-government."[31] Every state gets to have a say in what legal rules ultimately will bind it. "The international system is horizontal, consisting of over 190 independent States, all equal ... and recognizing no one in authority over them."[32] Every "governmental function" – legislation, interpretation, implementation, adjudication, and enforcement – in the international arena, thus, is reserved to the states themselves,[33] who exercise it collectively, all together, all at the same time:

29 Louis Henkin, *International Law: Politics, Values and Functions* (The Hague: The Hague Academy of International Law, 1989), 45–7.

30 *South West Africa (Second Phase)*, ICJ Reports (1966), 6, 34.

31 Henkin, *International Law*, 45.

32 Malcolm Shaw, *International Law*, 8th ed. (Cambridge: Cambridge University Press, 2017), 4–5.

33 Karl Zemanek, *The Legal Foundations of the International System* (The Hague: The Hague Academy of International Law, 1997), 40.

> It is for each State, acting together with other States . . ., to set new legal standards or to change them. . . . It is for each of them to decide how to settle disputes or to impel compliance with law [which means] that each State [also] has the power of "auto-interpretation" of legal rules, a power that necessarily follows from the absence of courts endowed with general and compulsory jurisdiction.[34]

And while some exceptions to the logic of unmediated democratism do exist, it is still a "true statement . . . of the law" that the consent of "the weakest and the smallest State has . . . as much weight as [that] of the largest and most powerful,"[35] and, however imperfect it may be, thus constituted, international law is, most certainly, "a system, not just a random collection of rules."[36]

Of course, in modern practice many rules that make up the body of international law appear to be generated not through the traditional mechanism of inter-state diplomacy but in a top-down fashion by various international organs or through the build-up of different bodies of international jurisprudence, often generated at the behest of nonstate actors.[37] But let there be no mistake about it: all of this is possible, according to the VP tradition, only because the community of states has so willed it, that is, because states have agreed to allow this state of affairs to take place.[38] It is the practice of this community that, in the final analysis, "rounds off the process" of rule-creation and provides these normative developments with the necessary degree of legal force.[39] When all is said and done, in short, it is still the "States [that] are the sole source of authority and law in the international system."[40]

Horizontality, democratism, decentralization – each of these themes has long been recognized in the international law literature as a defining feature of the VP sensibility. What has not enjoyed the same degree of recognition, however, is VP's underlying conception of regulatory sufficiency – proposition

34 Antonio Cassese, *International Law*, 2nd ed. (Oxford: Oxford University Press, 2005), 6.
35 Clapham, *Brierly's Law of Nations*, 147.
36 James Crawford, *Chance, Order, Change: The Course of International Law* (Leiden: Brill, 2014), 191.
37 See further, e.g., Robert Howse, "The World Trade Organization 20 Years On: Global Governance by Judiciary," *European Journal of International Law* 27, no. 1 (2016): 9–77; Nico Krisch, "The Decay of Consent: International Law in the Age of Global Public Goods," *American Journal of International Law* 108, no. 1 (2014): 1–40; Alan Boyle and Christine Chinkin, *The Making of International Law* (Oxford: Oxford University Press, 2007); Jose Alvarez, *International Organizations as Law-Makers* (Oxford: Oxford University Press, 2005).
38 Henkin, *International Law*, 35.
39 Bing Bing Jia, *International Case Law in the Development of International Law* (The Hague: The Hague Academy of International Law, 2015), 175, 209.
40 Henkin, *International Law*, 34.

(4) from our earlier summary – the idea that a positive legal order created as a result of a decentralized lawmaking process can turn out to be both effective and sufficient in terms of meeting those regulatory goals which international law is supposed to perform.

Let us go back briefly to the *Lotus* passage. Consider the sequence of the argument it puts forward: right off the bat, before we get to any other issue we are immediately presented with the claim that the process of international relations cannot simply be left to take its natural course, that is, that some form of *governance* and purposeful ordering is structurally essential.[41] This is then quickly followed by the suggestion that this process of *international ordering* should obviously involve the creation of *binding legal rules*[42] and the accompanying belief that there exists, in fact, no preexisting code of such rules that could be simply copied and pasted,[43] that is, that the international legal regime has to be *purpose-built* and cannot be just extrapolated from some external source.[44] The best way to build this regime, it is then proposed, is to have sovereign states legislate it by concluding a series of *voluntary agreements* inter se that take place "as if between equals." A normative order thus built, follows the conclusion, would then be able to meet the needs not only of *ensuring the coexistence* of "these ... independent communities" but also of *enabling* "the achievement of common aims."

Note the last two points: (i) the best way to build international law is to have states create it through a series of discrete voluntary transactions inter se; and (ii) international law's "job" is to ensure the stability (coexistence) and progressive development (cooperation with the view to realizing common goals) of the international community. Each of these propositions on its own seems perfectly straight and unexceptional. But put the two of them together into a single logical sequence and what emerges is a narrative whose underlying assumptions seem anything but self-evident.

41 Cf. Shaw, *International Law*, 1.

42 Cf. Percy Ellwood Corbett, *The Study of International Law* (New York: Doubleday, 1955), 45; Vaughan Lowe, *International Law* (Oxford: Oxford University Press, 2007), 1.

43 Even in the case of the so-called domestic law analogies, the long-established position among the adherents of VP has been to resist the view that any segment of any domestic legal system could be transposed into international law "lock, stock, and barrel." See, e.g., Arnold McNair, "So-Called State Servitudes," *British Yearbook of International Law* 6, (1925): 111–27; Albert-Geouffre de Lapradelle, *Les Principes Généraux du Droit International* (Paris: Centre Européen de la Dotation Carnegie, 1932), 6–8.

44 "International law is different [f]rom all other systems of law, which means in effect national systems of law." Hugh Thirlway, *Concepts, Principles, Rules and Analogies: International and Municipal Legal Reasoning* (The Hague: The Hague Academy of International Law, 2002), 265, 273.

19.2.3 *The Problem of the Absent Center: The Hidden "Immanent Force" at the Core of the VP Model*

Positivism, explains Starke in one of the most popular and influential textbooks on international law, is a theory that defines international law "as a system of rules depending for their validity only on the fact that States have consented to them," that is, "rules which [they] have accepted by a process of voluntary self-restriction."[45] Why would states want to accept this process of self-restriction? The answer given by the VP tradition is a combination of Parsonian functionalism – "it is not simply that where society is found, law is found, but that it must be so found"[46] – and Georg Jellinek's concept of *Selbstverpflichtungslehre* (auto-limitation):[47] "an accurate statement of the reason why a system of [such] binding rules is necessary and actually exists," writes Percy Corbett, is "the desire of states to have their necessary mutual relations regulated with the *greatest possible rationality and uniformity*."[48] There are many issues "which States cannot [address] efficiently unless they act together."[49]

But would not the causes of rationality and uniformity be better served by some other rule-generation procedure? Not at all, says VP: the only thing which keeps the international legal system working "is the consent of states . . . It is the *sine qua non* of every rule in the system, the 'sole' source of its 'legal authority'."[50] Could the international legal system be made more effective if it did not have to depend on this kind of decentralized consensualist dynamic? Highly unlikely, argues Eelco van Kleffens: "probability is against it."[51] Not a chance, confirms Ian Brownlie: even to put things in such terms would be to miss the point entirely – "international law is essentially a law *between* States"; the existing model of the international legal system categorically rejects the possibility of a "world State," any advancement toward which would, indeed, signal its termination.[52] At the same time, Brownlie adds immediately, the practical efficacy of this system continues to remain high and is "not to be

45 J. G. Starke, *Introduction to International Law*, 8th ed. (London: Butterworths, 1977), 26.
46 G. G. Fitzmaurice, *The General Principles of International Law Considered from the Standpoint of the Rule of Law* (The Hague: The Hague Academy of International Law, 1957), 38.
47 For background, see Collins, "Classical Legal Positivism," 39–41.
48 Corbett, "Consent of States," 22 (italics added).
49 Clapham, *Brierly's Law of Nations*, 108–9.
50 Corbett, "Consent of States," 23.
51 E. N. van Kleffens, *Sovereignty in International Law: Five Lectures* (The Hague: The Hague Academy of International Law, 1953), 1, 129.
52 Ian Brownlie, *International Law at the Fiftieth Anniversary of the United Nations* (The Hague: The Hague Academy of International Law, 1995), 33 (italics in the original).

questioned."[53] Why? Because, firstly, "[a]ll normal Governments . . . routinely use rules [of] international law . . . [and] define their relations with other States in terms of international law."[54] And, secondly, "both in the routine stewardship of State affairs and also in more strenuous political circumstances," even "on empirical grounds, . . . a good case can be made out for saying that public international law is more efficacious than public law within States."[55]

So far, so good. But note the hidden tension at the core of VP's concept of international lawmaking. From the VP standpoint, international law, as Vaughan Lowe puts it, cannot be understood as "a unified, manufactured system" that has been somehow "imposed upon the world of international . . . relations" from the outside.[56] Nor can it be understood as a construct that has been logically derived from some initial core concept. Neither its substance nor its form is preordained:

> [I]ts scope is [not] determined a priori. The rules of international law cover *whatever topics happen to have been regarded as appropriate for legal solution on the international plane*. It is simply a formalized account of practices and principles which spring spontaneously and inevitably from the coexistence . . . or from conscious efforts of States to cooperate in dealing with certain problems.[57]

Put differently, there exists no predetermined content or any essentialized substance behind the term "international law." Like metaphysical universals in William Ockham's philosophy, the idea of international law is just a useful epistemological tool, a formal abstraction that captures all that which the community of states has decided to designate as deserving of "legal solution on the international plane."

An interesting turn to nominalism, to be sure, but there is in fact nothing surprising about any of this. Exponents of the VP tradition have been rehearsing this line for more than a century. Oppenheim: international law is but a "name given to the body of such rules as . . . are considered legally binding by civilized States in their intercourse with each other."[58] The International Court of Justice: "in international law there are no rules, other than such rules as may be accepted by the State concerned."[59] Emmanuelle

53 Brownlie, *International Law*, 32.
54 Brownlie, *International Law*, 32.
55 Brownlie, *International Law*, 32–5.
56 Lowe, *International Law*, 8.
57 Lowe, *International Law*, 8 (emphasis added).
58 Oppenheim, *International Law*, 3.
59 *Nicaragua* v. *United States (merits)*, ICJ Reports (1986) 14, 135.

Tourme-Jouannet: "[I]nternational law consists of rules, practices, and discourses that emanate from [its] subjects . . . [and] is [thus] defined principally by its international origin, not its [purported] object."[60] There is nothing particularly original or unusual about Lowe's formulation. This is an archetypal positivist statement, however one looks at it. Except, of course, that only a few short paragraphs *before* he makes this statement, Lowe also addresses the question of international law's systemic role and function. And what he says there is highly curious indeed.

International law, Lowe argues, is a mechanism that has two primary functions: "to secure the conditions that allow sovereign States to co-exist and to enable each State to choose what kind of society will exist within its borders."[61] A few pages later he expands on this formula: international law's "job" also includes the protection and realization of universal human rights, the promotion of trade, and the preservation of the environment.[62] Neither of these characterizations – let us add immediately – is unique to Lowe's account; the same themes can be found all over the mainstream international law literature.[63] But put them alongside the nominalist-positivist argument Lowe rehearses above, and what emerges certainly seems thought-provoking.

For starters, notice how there are two rather different narratives unfolding within the same analytical space. On the one hand, international law is said to be a mechanism whose main function is to ensure the advancement of peace, security, human rights, trade, and environmental protection. On the other hand, it is also said to be a legal order that has no predetermined content and is entirely a product of what sovereign states decide to make of it. On its own, neither of these propositions seems particularly problematic: international law is a system that performs a certain function; the content and form of international law are determined by inter-state agreement. Both of these claims are relatively straightforward, and neither of these narratives seems convoluted. But notice now what happens when we combine these narratives into a single whole. Consider

60 Emmanuelle Tourme-Jouannet, *Le Droit International*, 2nd ed. (Paris: Presses universitaires de France, 2016), 31.
61 Lowe, *International Law*, 7.
62 Lowe, *International Law*, 15–18.
63 Corbett speaks of international law in terms of a structure ideally meant to "prevent World War III." Corbett, *Study of International Law*, 47. Shaw starts with a slightly less ambitious but similar set of objectives. Shaw, *International Law*, 34–5. Henkin goes further, positing an equivalence between international law and its domestic cousins. Henkin, *International Law*, 22. It is just that, alongside the more traditional "state values," such as territorial integrity and state "impermeability," international law has now also come to promote and protect "human values" and the "common good of mankind" and "world environment." Henkin, *International Law*, 127–9, 341.

the questions that immediately start popping up: in the absence of any central planning, how does the international lawmaking process manage to produce exactly those positive legal rules that are required to ensure the realization of the international community's first values? States are free to agree on whatever rules they want. What if the particular set of rules they agree on turns out not to be conducive to the achievement of peace, sustainable development, or the protection of human rights? If international law is supposed to be the royal road to international stability, justice, and prosperity, but the positive international legal order does not have any predetermined content or structure, since both of these are decided by states, what makes us think that states are going to do a good enough job of figuring out what the best structure and content of international law ought to be? What if they turn out not to be patient enough, impartial enough, or well-tempered enough? Even if we could assume that states will always come to the proverbial negotiating table in good faith, what makes us think that they would *actually know* what positive legal rules they ought to create to help the international legal system meet the demands of global governance? If we cannot know what those rules ought to be *ex ante*, what makes us think that states would ever be able to figure it out *in media res*?

Note the point we are moving toward: the argument here is not that Lowe – or any other VP scholar for that matter – has never noticed these possibilities or thought of any of these questions. Anyone familiar with his work will know just how deeply aware Lowe has been throughout his career of the fact that sovereign states and the people who act on their behalf far more often than not tend to act in crudely cynical, self-serving, and myopic ways, motivated as much by folly and ill-will as by greed and ignorance.[64] Neither he nor Corbett, Starke, or Brownlie was ever a naïve idealist, let alone a lazy thinker. The fact that each of them nevertheless has *ended up skipping over this entire body of questions*, when setting out the *theory* of how, according to the VP approach, the international legal system is supposed to work, thus certainly seems more than a little remarkable. At the very least, it appears to suggest that, from their point of view, none of these questions can be considered *theoretically relevant*. States being selfish, thinking myopically, and acting disruptively are all very real scenarios for Lowe, Brownlie, and others. But none of these bleak realities would appear to have any bearing on how one ought to understand the *concept of the international legal system*. Pause a second here because this is important: the real logical jump that is taking place in Lowe's argument is not that his theory of the international lawmaking process is utopian and fails to recognize

[64] See, e.g., Vaughan Lowe, "The Iraq Crisis: What Now?," *International and Comparative Law Quarterly* 52 (2003): 859–71.

the true reality of state behavior. The twist here, rather, lies in the implicit suggestion that all of those questions listed above are not in fact theoretically relevant – and, thus, do not deserve to be explored in the formal account of the international legal system – *because there is something within this system that cancels out their importance.*

It is a given truth, declares the VP tradition, that the decentralized process of international lawmaking can sustain a perfectly suitable mechanism for the production of normative output that will enable the international community to preserve peace, security, free trade, human dignity, sustainable development, and any number of equally ambitious goals. It is a given truth also that a plurality of self-determining sovereignties will do exactly what needs to be done to ensure the production of that kind of output.

Consider once more Brownlie's and Corbett's explanations and the broader logic behind the *Lotus* passage. The VP tradition does not say that we have no choice, in the end, but to use the decentralized Westphalian process of lawmaking because it is the only one that is presently available and operative. If it had said that, its theoretical setup would have had a very different complexion. What the VP tradition says instead is that: *the decentralized character of the international legal system is precisely what makes it so well suited to the performance of its task and purpose.* If the system had been built differently, it would not have worked nearly as well as it does. Consensualism and horizontalism are exactly what makes the system legitimate and rational (Corbett) as well as practical and efficacious (Brownlie). Put differently, knowing everything that we know about sovereign states and about how decentralized decision-making processes tend to work, the VP tradition essentially tells us that we should not worry about the threat of anarchy, that a stable, efficient, and just order will ultimately – inevitably – emerge in the international plane, harmony will arise out of cacophony, and the lion will lie down with the lamb.

19.3 THE THEORETICAL GENEALOGY OF THE VP PARADIGM: THE HIDDEN THEOLOGY BEHIND THE PROBLEM OF THE ABSENT CENTER

19.3.1 *The Enlightenment Roots of the VP Paradigm*

19.3.1.1 The Fundamental Paradox Restated: Kant's Moral Philosophy and the Categorical Imperative

The belief in the capacity of hierarchically decentralized social structures to generate fully coherent and thematically integrated normative orders has a long and illustrious pedigree in the history of Western philosophy. To a large extent, indeed, it can be considered one of the most important defining features of the entire tradition of Classical Liberal thought. In the field of political theory, some of its most well-known examples and illustrations can be found in Jean-Jacques Rousseau's theory of the social contract and John Locke's writings on constitutionalism. Analytically, however, the basic model that underpins this way of thinking finds its most consistent expression in the moral philosophy of Kant.

A chapter on the hidden genealogy of international legal positivism may not be the best place to attempt a general overview of Kant's broader philosophical legacy. The one defining theme, however, which passes like a red thread through his entire corpus of writings is his enduring preoccupation with the question of moral autonomy. For Kant, the central overarching aim of all human existence, from the moral standpoint, was the attainment of the state of personal autonomy.[65] Autonomy, in its Kantian understanding, constituted that kind of ethical condition which embodied simultaneously a relationship of freedom and responsibility, a state of being which Kant additionally defines as the "submission to laws which one has made for oneself."[66] To achieve full self-realization as a moral subject, a human being, on this view of things, would have to become the author of his own moral code. Only at that point when one comes to abide exclusively by those rules which originate in one's own ethical choices does one become truly autonomous and thus achieve the state of ethical self-fulfillment.

So far, so good, but taken to its logical conclusion, one is immediately tempted to ask, how is all of this different from outright anarchy? How is it possible for a community in which everyone follows their own moral code not to descend into complete chaos? Kant's answer is: because of something called the Categorical Imperative.

Contrary to the common assumption, when we achieve the state of full moral autonomy, argues Kant, we do not automatically turn into rampant anarchic monads randomly drifting across the ethical space without any structure or direction. On the contrary, precisely because of our autonomy – which, once again, is a state where freedom combines with responsibility – we inevitably develop a certain tendency whereby all of our ethical choices that

65 Further on Kant's theory of autonomy, see Immanuel Kant, *Groundwork of the Metaphysics of Morals*, trans. H. J. Paton (New York: Harper & Row Publishers, 1964 [1785]). See also Andrews Reath, "Autonomy, Ethical," in *Routledge Encyclopedia of Philosophy*, vol. 1, ed. Edward Craig (London: Routledge, 1998), 586.

66 Robert Paul Wolff, *In Defense of Anarchism* (New York: Harper, 1970), 14. See also Anthony Kenny, *The Rise of Modern Philosophy* (Oxford: Oxford University Press, 2006), 107.

we would be willing to turn into general norms of behavior applicable to others, from that point onwards, even though they remain entirely self-determined, *somehow* end up reflecting and channeling universal, eternally valid moral principles.[67] The name which Kant gives to the mysterious mechanism that guarantees this outcome is the Categorical Imperative.

"This [C]ategorical [I]mperative is present in every man without exception, even when it operates against him."[68] Like the laws of physics and chemistry, it is impossible for us to ignore it: it works on our ethical choices even when it is not invited, since when it does not do so, then by definition it can only mean that we are not at that point (yet) truly free. Conversely when we are free, it simply becomes impossible for us to make any ethical choices that we expect may turn into norms of general application and not at the same time channel the Categorical Imperative. And thus "the [C]ategorical [I]mperative unites all men in a formal whole. By it each man is bound, consciously or unconsciously, to other men in each of his own actions, as in the judgements he makes upon the actions of others."[69]

Expanded into a constitutional theory, Kant's moral philosophy thus turns, essentially, into a blueprint for fundamentalist libertarianism. In a society composed of fully autonomous subjects, there will be no need for any institutions of formal control or any centralization of the lawmaking or law-ascertainment processes, since every subject, so long as their autonomy is not tampered with, will always choose to postulate the same laws for themselves as everyone else because all of their moral and normative decisions are always already going to be expressions of some higher universal justice as mediated through the mechanics of the Categorical Imperative.[70]

Notice the strongly pronounced natural-legalist accent. Stripped to its basics, Kant's moral philosophy essentially comes down to a series of four claims: (i) when a subject becomes fully autonomous, it starts producing its own rules and moral values; (ii) the rules and values that will be produced under these conditions will be in consonance with some kind of universally valid morality thanks to the intervention of the Categorical Imperative; (iii) thus, even though the subject purports to act in a self-guided fashion, its

67 Why this should happen is not at all self-evident. Its paradoxical and opaque character is the first thing many commentators observe about Kant's theory of moral autonomy. See, e.g., Thomas E. Hill, "The Kantian Conception of Autonomy," in *The Inner Citadel: Essays on Individual Autonomy*, ed. John Christman (New York: Oxford University Press, 1989), 91–151; Robert Paul Wolff, *The Autonomy of Reason: A Commentary on Kant's Groundwork of the Metaphysics of Morals* (New York: Harper & Row, 1986), 178.

68 Lucien Goldmann, *Immanuel Kant* (New York: Verso, 2011), 166.

69 Goldmann, *Immanuel Kant*, 166.

70 Hill, "Kantian Conception of Autonomy," 93, 99.

actions and choices will channel some transcendental standard of justice; (iv) the shortest route to achieving a system of just and lasting social order is to ensure the attainment of the state of full personal autonomy by as many subjects as possible. So long as this prescription is followed, there is going to be no need for anything like the Hobbesian Leviathan or the Austinian commanding superior. Through the magic procedure of the automatic synchronization ensured by the Categorical Imperative, all ethical choices will come to embody the one true universal law.

The parallels between Kantian moral philosophy and the VP tradition are striking and uncanny. In both cases, the internal coherence and substantive rationality of the projected normative order are ensured not by the action of some hegemonic force but by a decentralized institutional structure designed to secure a state of full moral autonomy for each member of the respective community of actors. To the extent to which each of these actors retains its moral autonomy, whatever normative choices they end up then making in the exercise of their normative self-determination are somehow all magically imagined to become the conduit for the one true universal code, the repository of eternally valid transcendental wisdom capable of providing answer to every conceivable normative problem or question of social ordering.

19.3.1.2 Smith's Invisible Hand: Markets, Competition, Self-Interest, and the Alchemy of Market Adjustment

The idea that a state of spontaneous order will arise so long as each subject is left freely to decide for themselves what values and goals they ought to pursue was not, of course, the sole provenance of Liberal moral philosophers. In the history of modern social thought, the figure that is most commonly associated with this line of argument, indeed, is known more for his achievements as an economist. A complex and prolific thinker, Adam Smith over the course of his career had shown an interest in a wide variety of subjects. But it is primarily for his writings on what came to be known as political economy that he is most commonly remembered today.

At the center of Smith's vision lies a series of concepts that at first glance seems worlds away from anything used in Kant's moral philosophy: profit, competition, demand, supply, market adjustment. Scratch the surface, however, and what you find below this apparently specialist vocabulary is, in fact, a very familiar set of questions and problems: how can order and prosperity ensue from the naked pursuit of self-interest? How can social harmony and public virtue arise out of greed and private vice? Taking the sphere of trade and commerce as the microcosm of the larger society, Smith, confronted with the newly forming realities of capitalist production and exchange, unerringly zeroed in on the central conundrum of economic organization. The baffling combination of the apparent noncoerciveness of capitalist markets – merchants were free to trade with whomever they pleased – and their sheer impersonality – unlike in the earlier times, because of its tremendous scale, everyone in the market could now be assumed to be a complete stranger – raised the inevitable question: how can all of this hold together? In the absence of any central intelligence or coercive power, how can an ever-expanding group of completely disparate agents end up coexisting in a state of order rather than chaos?

The answer to this question, Smith quickly surmised, did not just have considerable theoretical value. It also had obvious normative and policy implications since it pointed the way to one of the most valuable prizes in the science of government. It promised to reveal the clue to "society's orderly provisioning":

> the mechanism by which society hangs together. How is it possible for a community in which everyone is busily following his self-interest not to fly apart from sheer centrifugal force? What is it that guides each individual's private business so that it conforms to the needs of the group? With no central planning ... how does society manage to get those tasks done which are necessary for its survival?[71]

The explanation Smith proposed drew on two closely related theoretical hypotheses – the concept of *market competition* and the idea of *market adjustment* – which combined together to show how, in principle, a decentralized social structure lacking any apparatus of "coercion or centralized direction"[72] could cause "people to produce what other members of society want, even when [as] individuals [they would] have no intention to do anything for anyone else."[73] The end-goal was to demonstrate the existence, within such structures, of something akin to a *spontaneous gravitational field*,[74] one that worked, like clockwork, independently of anyone's consciousness of it, and the effects of which were such as to make it possible that "the private interests and passions of men were led in the direction ... most agreeable to the interests of the whole society."[75]

71 Robert Heilbroner, *The Worldly Philosophers: The Lives, Times and Ideas of the Great Economic Thinkers* (New York: Simon & Schuster, 2000), 53–4.

72 Paul Samuelson, *Economics* (New York: McGraw-Hill, 1976), 42.

73 Roger Backhouse, *The Ordinary Business of Life* (Princeton: Princeton University Press, 2002), 126.

74 The gravitational analogy was, indeed, so central to Smith's theory that he returned to it over and over. See Alessandro Roncaglia, *A Brief History of Economic Thought* (Cambridge: Cambridge University Press, 2017), 72.

75 Heilbroner, *Worldly Philosophers*, 54.

The essence of this gravitational dynamics, Smith explained, lay in the close correlation between Man's inherent drive for self-interest and his equally inherent responsiveness to the promise or loss of profits, or what in the modern vocabulary is called "incentives." Conceived as quasi-mechanical automatons manipulable like so many levers, human subjects, on this view of things, were thus not only easily governable: if a correct system of arrangements was put in place, it was entirely conceivable that they would not need to be governed at all but could be left entirely to themselves, allowed to do whatever naturally came to their mind. The reason for this, Smith argued, lay in the magical effects of market competition. The concept of self-interest, the argument went, offered an important starting point in elucidating the logic of social gravitation. But it captured only half the picture. The other half came from the phenomenon of competitive pressures. "[E]ach man out to do his best for himself with no thought of social consequences is faced with a flock of similarly motivated individuals who are engaged in exactly the same pursuit."[76] As conflicting interests clash, each individual, while still trying to secure the greatest benefit for themselves, will attempt simultaneously to undercut their rivals by, inter alia, accepting a partial reduction of their profit margins, which potentially will continue up to that point beyond which their enterprise no longer appears profitable enough for them to persist with. Once that point is reached the individual in question, Smith postulated, responding to the negative incentives raised by the imminent loss of profits, would exit the given line of business in favor of another one.

Note the latent assumptions about "behavioral physics" running through this account: what makes subjective behavior predictable, for Smith, is our inherent propensity toward profit-maximization and the culture of reasoning that this inspires in us. Note also the quasi-alchemical powers assigned to the phenomenon of market competition: it is not just our inherent propensity toward selfishness but our *encounter* with other equally selfish subjects that magically transmutes us from simple profit-seeking monads into complex, aptitudinally nuanced economic entrepreneurs, so supremely adept at self-reinvention and structural (re-)integration into the different sectors of the economy.

This last point is important – and indeed has often been so acknowledged in the literature – but it has rarely been unpacked in terms of its radical theoretical implications. Unlike Kant, Smith is not just a student of the individual: his interest in "personal physics" here is but an opening chapter in his exploration of the "physics of the social." The key to the logic of his argument, in other

76 Heilbroner, *Worldly Philosophers*, 55.

words, lies not so much in what he has to say about Man's basically acquisitive nature but in the bold shift from what starts out as a *fundamentally psychological hypothesis* – all men pursue self-interest – to a *confident sociopolitical inference* – free markets ensure the best allocation of resources. As Thomas Sowell observes, Smith did not simply conflate the laws of individual behavior with societal regularities but rather argued that, under very specific institutional conditions, the grasp of the former can be used to master the latter.[77] Global prosperity – the optimum state of economic affairs – was not just a product of a mechanical adding-up of all individual-level profits and benefits. The whole was much greater than the sum of its parts – "the selfish motives of men are transmuted [into economic harmony] by [the fact of their] interaction" with one another[78] – and at the root of this alchemical-style transmutation lay the idea of market competition.

The rest of the theoretical sequence was quite predictable. Taking as his starting point this unyielding belief in the possibility of social physics, Smith in due course went on to postulate alongside the Classical Liberal concept of governance without a government – what after the French Physiocrats came to be known as laissez-faire – a new theoretical construct that, structurally, assumed within his economic theory a role essentially equivalent to Kant's Categorical Imperative. What this new construct represented, in essence, was the idea of a spontaneously existing principle or regularity that, like the Categorical Imperative, took the form of a *formal mediating mechanism* that, on the one hand, transmitted the impetus received from all the myriad individual agents' choices and decisions to the global level of "the system" and, on the other hand, channeled the response issuing from that global system into all the countless choices and decisions made by individual agents. The name that liberal economic theory gave to this process was *market adjustment*.

The basic structure behind the concept should be broadly familiar by now. Like the VP paradigm and Kant's moral theory, Smith's theory of market adjustment uses a conceptual framework that is built, fundamentally, around three basic ideas: a decentralized decisional process; something that looks very similar to Kant's concept of personal autonomy; and what is essentially a version of the idea of natural justice. The only distinct feature here is that what gets "naturalized" in this case is given a decidedly commercial appearance: prices, rents, profit, and wages.[79] As Alessandro Roncaglia explains, Smith's theory of

77 Thomas Sowell, *On Classical Economics* (New Haven: Yale University Press, 2006), 11.
78 Heilbroner, *Worldly Philosophers*, 56.
79 Backhouse, *Ordinary Business of Life*, 125.

the market adjustment mechanism is based, ultimately, on the presupposition of an inherent relationship between markets and natural prices: for every commodity there exists a natural level of demand; if production levels exceed it, competition will drive the market price down, producers will be unable to obtain the "natural" profits they need and will have to move from that sector elsewhere, production levels will then decrease, and excess supply will cease. Every market thus inclines toward equilibrium and so too do prices: "The natural price [is the price to which] the prices of all commodities are continually gravitating."[80]

Note an important metaphysical nuance: the natural price is never postulated or declared *ex ante* – like the laws of physics, it can only be discovered and measured, not changed or readjusted. And, like the laws of physics too, its demands are inexorable and brook no appeal. "Traders who inflate their prices" beyond the level of the natural price "will lose their customers to others . . . and so will go out of business. . . . Anyone charging more can always be undercut by their competitors."[81] And this, Smith concluded, was precisely the reason why competitive markets could succeed in "link[ing] up the productive units operating in the different sectors of the economy[82] . . . without [any] central direction or master plan . . . pooling the knowledge and actions of millions of diverse individuals" into a seamless system.[83]

By guaranteeing that all the relevant resources would end up "moved into those activities where they were most needed,"[84] Smith's market adjustment hypothesis thus explained not only how "every individual, in pursuing only his own selfish good," could still wind up working "to achieve the best good for all"[85] but also how "the provision of [exactly] those goods that society wants, in the quantities [it] desires, and at the prices [it] is prepared to pay" could become possible.[86] Like the Categorical Imperative in Kant's moral theory, the concept of market adjustment thus assumed, within the Smithian tradition, the role of that all-explaining, loose-ends-tying mediating category, the Derridean immanent organizing concept whose principal function, ultimately, was to ensure that every outstanding claim could be tidied up and every logical contradiction resolved.

In time, Smith's ideas about the alchemy of market competition received further development, nowhere more so than in the work of the so-called

80 Roncaglia, *Brief History of Economic Thought*, 72.
81 Philip Ball, *Critical Mass* (New York: Farrar, Straus and Giroux, 2006), 222.
82 Roncaglia, *Brief History of Economic Thought*, 71.
83 Samuelson, *Economics*, 42.
84 Backhouse, *Ordinary Business of Life*, 128.
85 Samuelson, *Economics*, 42.
86 Heilbroner, *Worldly Philosophers*, 55.

Austrian school economists, two of whom in particular deserve mention at this point: Carl Menger and Friedrich Hayek. A proponent of the subjective theory of value, Menger, taking Smith's ideas about the beneficence of allowing every producer and trader an unrestrained freedom of choice with regard to their economic decision-making, laid the foundations for what later became known as the doctrine of *consumer sovereignty*.[87] Hayek, the far more widely known "Austrian scholar," gave the traditional Smithian belief in the allocative superiority of decentralized market structures over centrally integrated economic systems a new philosophico-ideological grounding by contriving to show that not only did the market provide a far superior epistemological apparatus for determining what the society at large really needs and desires than any form of centralized planning, but that, in doing so, it also preserved the ideals of *democracy* and *freedom and equality* of consumer choice.[88]

The importance of these two contributions for our purposes should not be hard to spot. Even more so than the original Smithian concept of market freedom, the concept of consumer sovereignty drives home the fact of the fundamental homology between the Smithian version of economic liberalism and the VP tradition. Every state, explains VP, pursues its national interests which it understands entirely subjectively – what is valuable to one state may not necessarily be so to another – and that, at the end of the day, is not only perfectly fine from the international law point of view but is, in fact, the only correct way of doing things. The more subjective their choices are, the more logical it is, in fact, to insist that states, as international actors, are ascribed with the quality of sovereignty. For, the moment we establish that value is always subjective is also the moment we inevitably discover that the subject of these values constitutes that system's *primum movens*.[89] Thus, to be able to justify viewing states as the prime movers of international law – for what, in a positivist universe, does the concept of sovereignty describe if not being the prime mover? – it is logically indispensable that whatever interests one imagines states pursue in the international arena invariably have to be understood as *essentially subjective*. And the more subjective they turn out to be in practice, the better it is, from the standpoint of theory. For then it all adds up and comes together neatly: the more a state is moved by nothing more than its own sense of what is beneficial for it, the more assured becomes its ability to

87 See for further discussion Roncaglia, *Brief History of Economic Thought*, 154–5.

88 See Friedrich A. Hayek, "The Use of Knowledge in Society," *American Economic Review* 35 (1945): 519–30. See also, more generally, Friedrich A. Hayek, *The Road to Serfdom* (London: Routledge, 1944).

89 Roncaglia, *Brief History of Economic Thought*, 155.

contribute to what, in fact, is good for the international community. And since it is precisely their lack of preestablished assumptions as to what is good and valuable and the fundamental decentralization of their decisional structures that make markets so good at figuring out and responding to all of society's short-term and long-term needs, the more decentralized and content-wise unprejudiced the international legal process becomes, the more likely it is that a legal system set up along VP lines will be able to supply the international community precisely with the kind of normative structures and regimes that it needs and in the precise forms and quantities that it needs. Put differently, they may not have been necessarily aware of this, but the argument which the likes of Lowe and Brownlie make for and about international law is really, at its most basic level, deeply Hayekian both in terms of its intellectual aesthetics and its presumed metaphysics.

19.3.2 *The Shared Theological Roots of VP and Classical Liberalism: A Comparative Structure and a Genealogy*

That the discipline of international law owes a rather large theoretical debt to both Kant and Smith – and Classical Liberalism more generally – is a fact well-established among the students of international law.[90] What is less broadly appreciated, however, is how deeply this inheritance goes. It is not just a general predilection for a politics of individualism, consent, and non-intervention that the discipline, as it evolved within the framework of its dominant theoretical paradigm, has absorbed from its liberal source code. The entire ontological and epistemological apparatus around which it developed its basic analytical habits and reasoning protocols – its general theory of agency, causality, and capacity – has been copied from the founding figures of the Classical Liberal tradition as well.

The usefulness of the mapping exercises undertaken so far in explaining the deeper parallels between the VP paradigm and the Kantian and Smithian traditions can be summarized in the form of Table 19.1. Note the slightly different insights highlighted in each case. The exploration of the Kantian parallels helped lay bare the presence within VP's broader theory of rather

90 For further discussion, see, generally, Anthony Carty, *The Decay of International Law? A Reappraisal of the Limits of Legal Imagination in International Affairs* (Manchester: Manchester University Press, 1986); Philip Allott, *The Health of Nations* (Cambridge: Cambridge University Press, 2002); Martti Koskenniemi, *From Apology to Utopia: The Structure of International Legal Argument* (Cambridge: Cambridge University Press, 2006); Emmanuelle Jouannet, *Vattel and the Emergence of Classical International Law* (Oxford: Hart Publishing, 2017).

TABLE 19.1 *Parallels between the VP paradigm and the Kantian and Smithian traditions*

	Kantian moral theory	Smithian economics	VP
Units (constituent subjects)	Men as ethical actors	Men as economic actors	States
Optimal position for each subject at the individual level	Moral autonomy	Business freedom/ consumer sovereignty	State sovereignty
The iron law of individual behavior	Every subject, when making decisions they know may become laws applicable also to others, channels the Categorical Imperative	Every subject, when making any decisions, inevitably pursues naked self-interest (profit)	Every state always pursues its national interest
Optimal institutional policy (ground rule)	Political (moral) liberalism	Laissez-faire	Decentralization
Mediating mechanism that prevents anarchy	Categorical Imperative	Market adjustment	? [International law's absent center]
What the mediating mechanism channels	Universal morality	Natural prices	?

suspiciously placed blank spots corresponding, structurally, to the mechanism of the Categorical Imperative and universal morality which this mechanism helps to channel and express. The foray into the Smithian tradition, in turn, helped bring forward the idea that not only does it look as though the VP paradigm functionally presumes a certain model of behavioral physics on a par with Smith's idea of the inexorable drive for self-interest but that its faith in the quasi-alchemical powers of a decentralized institutional structure to transform the selfish interests of every individual state into the public good of the international community must also be fundamentally premised on some underlying belief in *supra-systemic adjustment* and a corresponding notion of *natural justice* to which, like all positively charged market prices in Smith's theory of natural prices, all positively undertaken attempts to articulate international law are inevitably supposed to gravitate.

The closer one looks at this table, the more evident become two points. Firstly, in all three of these traditions, the "system" – what the mediating mechanism allows the subjects to embody and give voice to – is understood to be both superior to and unaffected by the subjects' sovereign capacity for autonomous choice in the sense that it does not matter what the subjects may end up choosing, since the "system" will realize itself anyway. And, secondly, what we are looking at in each of these cases is, essentially, a theory of Natural Law. The only difference is that in the case of the VP tradition this fact appears to be systematically suppressed and covered up – hence the empty spaces and question marks in the bottom-right corner.

And yet, it does not take very much effort – even if one ignores the parallels indicated by the structural homologies already outlined – to uncover this fact. The "naturalism" of VP's theory of law is indeed rather glaring.

How can a decision-making process that lacks any formal hierarchy ensure that peace, justice, and sustainable development, rather than anarchy, violence, and the tragedy of the commons, should become the logical course of events in international relations? Sovereignty plus consensualism plus horizontality would normally look like a recipe for guaranteed fragmentation. How can anyone expect that instead of complete cacophony it will actually lead to harmony, yielding a normative framework capable of inducing a dynamic of cooperation as well as coexistence? Even the briefest scrutiny of the VP theory is enough to work out that things do not quite add up. The structure of the international lawmaking process is supposed to be decentralized. And yet the positive international legal regime that is meant to be created on its basis is still expected to turn out fundamentally non-self-contradictory and sufficiently devoid of gaps and blind-spots to be able to meet the demands imposed on the international legal system by its first values. How can this happen? It is as if, despite being decentralized at the surface, the international legal process were also at the same time permeated, deep within, by some invisible force-field that somehow enabled it to resolve all of the countless conflicts and contradictions that are guaranteed to arise under the conditions of legislative cacophony. But where would that sort of force-field come from? What would be its source?

In the history of modern legal thought, the answer that would have been most commonly given to this question is Natural Law. In the broader philosophical discourse, by comparison the more popular rubric would be "God." The two constructs, to be sure, are not entirely identical: the natural law tradition has many strands, not all of which are expressly theistic in their presentation. Still, the essential theoretical premise that underpins every species of the natural-legal argument is the assumption that somewhere out there an objective, non-human-made standard of justice exists whose normative validity does not depend on its formal endorsement by any socially embedded institution because it derives from some "higher source."[91] And that assumption, however one looks at it, is a product of a *fundamentally theological belief structure*.

Natural law, the Categorical Imperative, the natural order of things, the market adjustment mechanism – the labels change, but the basic theoretical function performed by the concept remains the same. In the Lacanian tradition, the heading under which it is known is the Name-of-the-Father; in deconstruction, the transcendental signified – that immanent organizing force that Jacques Derrida talked about. The universal morality which every autonomous moral agent inevitably ends up channeling, the natural price to which all real-world market prices inevitably tend to gravitate – the answer to the question of international law's absent center in the VP tradition, in the final analysis, has nothing particularly voluntarist or positivist about it. The requirements of the official decorum may prevent it from admitting this in the open, but, in the end, it is God's grace (or some undisclosed substance equivalent to it) and it alone, in the VP universe, holds the international legal system together. And the God in question here, very clearly, is the God of Christian theology.

19.3.2.1 VP's First Debt to Christian Theology: Sovereignty and Consent as the Problematic of Free Will – from the "Blessed in Heaven" to *firmitas* and Predestination

The structural parallels between the VP worldview and classical Christian theology are undeniable. What are less clear are their exact contours. For the purposes of our present argument, the debt – if one can talk of it in such terms – owed by the former to the latter can be said to have two different dimensions.

The first can be perceived most readily if we extend the excavation exercise that we started earlier with our forays into Kantian and Smithian traditions by tracing the genealogical influences behind *their* theoretical structures. Where did their models of ontology, agency, causality, and capacity come from?

Both Kant and Smith, it is no secret, were profoundly theologically minded thinkers.[92] Though neither of them was particularly orthodox in their religious practices, the degree to which the Christian theological worldview had

[91] See Michael D. A. Freeman, ed., *Lloyd's Introduction to Jurisprudence*, 6th ed. (London: Sweet & Maxwell, 1994), 79–86; Peter Malanczuk, ed., *Akehurst's Modern Introduction to International Law*, 7th rev. ed. (London: Routledge, 1997), 15.

[92] For general background, see Kenny, *Rise of Modern Philosophy*, 100–8; Goldmann, *Immanuel Kant*, 193–205; Heilbroner, *Worldly Philosophers*, 42–74.

pervaded their theoretical sensibilities is undeniable. Both devoted significant energies and mental resources to the exploration of classical theological topics (Kant perhaps more visibly so than Smith). Even more importantly, both of them had also absorbed and actively repurposed Christian theology's basic operative framework, categories, and master-plots.

One of these master-plots, as Alex Callinicos notes, was the narrative of *miraculous unintended consequences* – the logical end-product of combining the concepts of divine ineffability, omnipotence, benevolence, and predetermination, first worked out by medieval logicians and theological historians, that assumed in Kant's and Smith's writings the form of that paradoxical argument which purports to see the act of private self-ordering as the best conceivable source of public legislation and the naked pursuit of profit as the foundation of social harmony.[93] Indeed, it was Smith, notes Callinicos, who articulated one of the first clearly recognizable adaptations of this narrative in modern social thought, by developing a theoretical framework expressly constructed around the idea "that social structures [constitute] the unintended consequences of individual actions":

> Kant would later express the same idea more generally when he argued that the mechanism through which historical progress takes place is men's "unsocial sociability". [In doing so, he] more explicitly than Smith . . . reveals the theological roots of [this hypothesis, since it was originally] Christian thinkers such as St Augustine [who] had developed a philosophy of history in which the selfish actions of individual humans unwittingly serve the purposes of God's secret plan for the world.[94]

Both Kant and Smith, of course, were openly Protestant – not just in terms of their religious upbringing but also of their general ideological leanings. Smith, in particular, was notoriously anti-Catholic in his outlook, characterizing the Catholic Church and religion at one point as the enemy of liberty and reason and openly detrimental to all social and economic progress.[95] And yet the conventional division between Protestants and Catholics, though certainly not insignificant in other contexts, should not be allowed to obscure here the fact that, for all their opposition to the Catholic Church and the Catholic doctrine of their time, an overwhelmingly large part of the deeper theoretical structure on which Kant and Smith erected the edifice of their respective philosophies

93 Alex Callinicos, *Social Theory*, 2nd ed. (Cambridge: Polity, 2007), 17.

94 Callinicos, *Social Theory*, 17.

95 See further Barry R. Weingast, "*Adam Smith's Industrial Organization of Religion: Explaining the Medieval Church's Monopoly and Its Breakdown in the Reformation*," October 17, 2015, https://papers.ssrn.com/sol3/papers.cfm?abstract_id=2675590.

belonged, in fact, to that basic stratum of ideas and preconceptions that is shared equally by Protestant and Catholic thinkers. And like the narrative of miraculous unintended consequences, many of these ideas and preconceptions received their first full elaboration in the writings of pre-Reformation thinkers and scholars.

One of these thinkers who exerted a particularly lasting influence was the late-thirteenth-century Franciscan theologian, the *Doctor Subtilis*, Scotus. A rich and famously complex writer, Scotus in many ways, as Anthony Kenny puts it, can be considered "a philosopher's philosopher":[96] though he did not as such found any distinct movement or school of thought,

> many of his philosophical innovations came to be accepted as unquestioned principles by thinkers in later generations who had never read a word of his works. The Reformation debates between Luther and Calvin and their Catholic adversaries took place against a backcloth of fundamentally Scotist assumptions. The framework within which Descartes laid out the foundations of modern philosophy was in all its essentials a construction created in Oxford around the year 1300 [when Scotus was there].[97]

Moreover, just as it is commonly recognized now that it is with Scotus that the entire modern conception of *modality* – the theory of the relationship between necessity, actuality, and contingency – first began to emerge,[98] so too, notes Kenny, "[i]t is arguable that epistemology, as understood in modern times, [also made] its first appearance in [Scotus's] writings."[99]

What was the basic core of Scotus's legacy that found its way several centuries later into the shared theoretical structures of liberal social theory? The answer, as is so often the case in medieval Christian theology, begins with the question of death and salvation.

Like with most theological systems that incorporate the concept of afterlife, one of the fundamental issues at the heart of Christian philosophy, traditionally, has been the question of reward and punishment: on what grounds, following what criteria, are we to be rewarded and punished for what we do in this life, after we die? The official solution proposed by the Christian dogma

96 Kenny, *Medieval Philosophy*, 89.

97 Kenny, *Medieval Philosophy*, 89.

98 See Simo Knuuttila, "Duns Scotus and the Foundations of Logical Modalities," in *John Duns Scotus: Metaphysics and Ethics*, ed. Ludger Honnefelder, Rega Wood, and Mechthild Dreyer (New York: Oxford University Press, 1996), 129–30; Stephen Marrone, "Revisiting Duns Scotus and Henry of Ghent on Modality," in *John Duns Scotus: Metaphysics and Ethics*, ed. Ludger Honnefelder, Rega Wood, and Mechthild Dreyer (New York: Oxford University Press, 1996), 175–89.

99 Kenny, *Medieval Philosophy*, 171.

was given its formal articulation under the heading of the doctrine of *free will*: people are judged in their afterlife inasmuch as and because they possess a freedom of the will, that is to say, the power to choose what course of action to take in any given situation. Because of this freedom – which, as Bernardine Bonansea correctly notes, is essentially a form of "the power of self-determination"[100] – human beings enjoy a privilege unavailable to any other class of creatures such as, say, angels or animals.

Now, a large part of what the concept of free will covers is of course the ability to choose between sin and virtue. Precisely because "man in his earthly existence" has the power to turn away or toward sin, that is, to reject or follow God's prescriptions about what is right and wrong, he earns whatever reward or punishment he may receive in the afterlife. "For nothing is imputed to anyone as deserving reward or punishment," remarks Scotus, "and hence as praiseworthy or blameworthy, unless it lies in his power"; "nothing is accepted as meritorious unless it be freely in the power of the agent."[101]

The problem that arises at this point is, of course, the issue of God's axiomatic omnipotence and omniscience and, by extension, the question of the relationship between human will and God's will. Since God is the first cause of all that is, was, and will be, and since He is also, by definition, omnipotent and nothing happens without His knowledge of it, it follows logically that every action or choice that a person makes happens because God has so willed, which seems to suggest that none of us can be held responsible for any sins we commit since (i) all of these sins were, in fact, a part of God's plan, and so in committing them we were actually realizing God's design, so how can we be punished for doing God's work; and (ii) it was God who made us do what we did, and we ourselves did not have any say in it, since if it were actually possible for us not to sin in those situations where He wanted us to sin, He is either not really omnipotent (since we managed to resist His will) or not really omniscient (since He did not know we would object to His plans), both of which are blasphemous concepts.

However one looks at it, it seems that we are falling now into an irresolvable paradox: either God is omnipotent and omniscient, in which case all our actions and choices, including whether or not to sin, are already predetermined, which logically destroys all justification for posthumous reward and punishment since none of us really has any free will. Or we do have freedom of

100 Bernardine Bonansea, "Duns Scotus' Voluntarism," in *John Duns Scotus, 1265–1965*, ed. John Ryan and Bernardine Bonansea (Washington, DC: Catholic University of America Press, 1965), 94.

101 John Duns Scotus, *God and Creatures: The Quodlibetal Questions* (Princeton: Princeton University Press, 1975), 390.

will, which means that we do get to make our own choices and that God cannot change them or predetermine them for us, in which case God is not really God, or at least not in the way He is supposed to be.

In the hands of a less talented theologian, the answer to this paradox would probably have taken the route of invoking God's ineffability – it is a blasphemy to believe that the principle of free will can contradict divine determinism, for that would be precisely the kind of thing one would conclude as a matter of human logic, and who said that God's design is susceptible to human logic or understanding? An equally tempting solution would be to allude to the idea of divine perfection – the nuclear bomb of all theological arguments – namely that what is said to be a contradiction seems so only to our feeble human minds, but that to God, who has an infinitely more perfect mind, there is no real contradiction between freedom and determinism, a fact of which we can be reassured not least by the knowledge that His design is always perfect and He has evidently created this world exactly the way He designed it. Scotus, the consummate logician that he was, resisted both of these cheap moves.

Every will, begins Scotus's argument, is fundamentally a self-moving cause, and human will is not, in this regard, an exception. "When we do act rather than not, or act in one way rather than another, there is no cause of such a choice other than that [which] is [our] will."[102] It follows, thus, that to blame our bad decisions on the rigidity of God's plan or to abdicate any responsibility for them on grounds of His omnipotence is, everything else aside, analytically indefensible. The power to choose sin comes to us from God – "i.e. God is the source of that nature which enables its possessor to commit sin"[103] – but God himself does not ordain how exactly we exercise that power. Indeed, that is precisely what His divine will consists in: that each of us freely chooses where we stand vis-à-vis good and evil at any given point and what actions we take in that regard. Thus,

> the will is not acted upon, strictly speaking, by anything else [even though] the human will is, after all, a creature of . . . God as a higher-order cause. [But] higher-order . . . causes are typically not causes of the effects [but] are, rather, causes of the causing of those effects . . . Hence while God causes any given human will, God does not cause the willing of that will. Instead God causes it to be the case that the willing of that will is a production of what it does produce.[104]

102 Calvin G. Normore, "Duns Scotus's Modal Theory," in *The Cambridge Companion to Duns Scotus*, ed. Thomas Williams (Cambridge: Cambridge University Press, 2003), 129–60, 144.

103 William Frank, ed., *Duns Scotus on the Will and Morality* (Washington, DC: Catholic University of America Press, 1997), 294.

104 Normore, "Duns Scotus's Modal Theory," 144.

Put differently, God is not our personal co-author – and thus a moral co-owner of every bad decision we make – even if He is, ultimately, the author of our very ability to author and to decide.

So far, so good, but notice now that up till this point Scotus has addressed the problem of free will only in the case of *homo viator*, "man in his earthly existence." The power of free will, according to the Christian dogma, does not cease at the point of one's death. Indeed, if anything it becomes greater. But as the souls of those who, because of their virtuousness, receive the reward of heaven enter their heavenly existence – as they become the "blessed in heaven" – a new paradox quickly emerges. Being in heaven, the blessed of course still retain their capacity for free will. "Essentially, the will of the blessed remains the same as the will of the *homo viator*, for the attainment of the end does not change the nature of the faculty attaining it."[105] And yet at the same time "the blessed cannot possibly turn away from the supreme good" and choose sin "because of a positive decree of the divine will."[106] How can this make sense? Scotus's reasoning, as he himself acknowledges, comes at this point from St. Augustine:

> that text of Augustine from the Enchiridion [states]: "It was fitting that men should be made in the first place with the power to will both good and evil – if good, not without reward; if evil, not without impunity." ... And he continues: "In the afterlife he will not be able to will evil and yet he will not be deprived of his free will. In fact, his will will be much more free in that it will in no way be subject to sin."[107]

To say that the blessed in heaven still have freedom of will is to suggest that they retain the power to choose between good and evil. Because, however, they are now in heaven, it follows, logically, that though they have this power, they necessarily will not exercise it in favor of evil, which, predictably, raises the question: how can one be said to have a certain freedom (choose or reject sin) and at the same time be restricted to always having to act in a certain fashion (reject sin)?

The detour into Scotus's argument has been long – much longer than anything that was attempted with Smith or Kant – but hopefully by now it should become clear why it was necessary. The irresolvable paradox at the center of VP's theory of international law – the idea that states, though they are free to choose whatever rules and principles they want, will somehow necessarily end up choosing what is objectively best for the international community – is essentially nothing more than a latter-day adaptation of the concept of the blessed in heaven. Like the blessed in heaven, states, in the VP account,

105 Bonansea, "Duns Scotus' Voluntarism," 94–5.
106 Bonansea, "Duns Scotus' Voluntarism," 94.
107 Scotus, *God and Creatures*, 377.

are presumed to possess an untrammeled freedom of will – the sovereign power to determine one's duties and obligations. Like the blessed in heaven, this means, ultimately, that they are able to choose both what is "good," that is, conducive for the preservation of international peace, stability, human dignity, and sustainable development, and what is "evil," that is, detrimental to the achievement of all of these goals. Like the blessed in heaven, too, they are, however, also guaranteed, in the end, always to choose what is "good," which fact, however, not only does not diminish their sovereign status but, on the contrary, enhances and reinforces it. How can this state of affairs make any sense?

Scotus's answer to the paradox of the blessed's freedom was to introduce the following theoretical formula:

> [T]he blessed in heaven feel such an attraction towards God . . . that they love him by what may be called moral necessity or necessity *secundum quid*. This becomes for them like a second nature and is similar to the natural tendency by which stones and metals tend to the centre of the earth.[108]

Note that the moral necessity Scotus has in mind here is itself the product of the "positive decree of the divine will," not an actual intrinsic feature of the blessed in heaven, that is, it arises in them as a result of God's intervention and not spontaneously by itself. But what exactly is the nature of this new element that God adds to the blessed's psychological makeup? Scotus's answer is *firmitas*, a concept that can be most closely translated into English as "steadfastness." What happens, according to Scotus, essentially, is that God, through his wisdom, awards the blessed in heaven with a new additional power: He "ensures *firmitas* to [them], and so while they retain the power to refrain from loving God and so can [in fact] refrain [from doing so], they steadfastly (and in that sense necessarily) exercise their power to love God."[109]

What exactly does all of this mean concretely? What is this thing called *firmitas*, in what does it manifest itself, why is it imposed on or made available to the blessed in heaven but not the *homo viator*? The answer to that, alas, nobody seems to know. "How does God ensure *firmitas* to the blessed?" asks Calvin Normore in his study of Scotus's theory of necessity and freedom, before immediately adding: "Scotus does not say."[110]

"If you ask, how does freedom coexist with necessity," observes Scotus enigmatically in his *Quodlibet*, "I answer with [Aristotle]: 'Do not seek a reason for things for which no reason can be given: for there is no

108 Bonansea, "Duns Scotus' Voluntarism," 95.
109 Normore, "Duns Scotus's Modal Theory," 144–5.
110 Normore, "Duns Scotus's Modal Theory," 145.

demonstration of the starting point of demonstration.' And so I say here."[111] Even the *Doctor Subtilis*, it turns out, could not refrain, in the end, from embracing the "nuclear solution."

Scotus's treatment of the problem of freedom for the blessed in heaven did not, in the end, produce a conceptual vocabulary that survived the historically specific context of medieval scholasticism. But it provided the blueprint for all subsequent forays into this theoretical territory: both Kant's Categorical Imperative and Smith's mechanism of market adjustment can be counted among the direct intellectual descendants of Scotus's *firmitas*.

In the tradition of later Christian theologians, many of the nuances of Scotus's theoretical solution, including the distinction between effective causes and higher-order causes, were either flattened out or abandoned. The Augustinian dialectic of freedom and necessity in its Protestant rendition turned into the dialectic of personal and universal God. The "nuclear solution" in this context increasingly received the form of God's grace – a concept designed to perform the same structural role as *firmitas* (but somehow also applicable to the living) and to shift the main theoretical accent further away toward the ineffability end of the "nuclear" spectrum. Far less committed to the belief in Man's innate goodness, Luther and Calvin chose to assign to the category of grace the function of an all-organizing force with a much broader range of powers than Scotian *firmitas*, until, taken to its logical conclusion, it became a direct stand-in for the idea of the divine intervention itself and the whole question of how a necessitated outcome can arise in a context of apparently free and uncoerced action was dissolved in the acid of compulsory faith.[112]

19.3.2.2 VP's Second Debt to Christian Theology: The State as Christ

The second dimension of VP's debt to Christian theology has a slightly different theoretical complexion. It reveals itself most clearly when one considers the curious parallelism between VP's basic concept of states as international lawmakers and one of the oldest theological controversies in Christianity: the debate about Christ's "natures" and "essences." The idea that Christ, being the son of God – the Word (*Logos*) made Flesh, is one with God-the-Father and thus is equally as divine forms one of the central tenets of the Christian religion. But how exactly should one understand this idea in terms of what it says about Christ's "other" side? Was being human a part of

111 Scotus, *God and Creatures*, 379.

112 For further discussion, see Erich Fromm, *The Fear of Freedom* (London: Routledge, 2001 [1942]), 66–74.

Christ's essential nature or was it something more or less incidental? Was Christ, in other words, both a man and a God or was he, for theological purposes, "only" a God? Should Christ, as a matter of official dogma, be considered to have only one or two different natures?

Here is how Philip Jenkins summarizes the terms of this debate as it first took form in the early centuries of Christian history:

> At one extreme, a One Nature believer like [the fourth-century Alexandrian bishop] Appolinarius presented Christ as a kind of automaton controlled by a Logos from above, so that he could not in any real sense face temptation: he could not wrestle with moral dilemmas or overcome the seductions of evil. [At the other extreme,] Two Nature adherents, like the third-century Christian Paul of Samosata, ... taught that the man Jesus became Christ when the Spirit of God descended on him, so that the purity and sanctity of his life was a major factor in letting him become divine.[113]

It can be noticed immediately how closely the structure of this "one versus two natures" controversy maps onto the basic model of international law presumed under the VP paradigm. All that one needs to do is substitute "states" for "Christ" to see the parallels.

International law, argues the VP tradition, is essentially a product of states' choices. At the same time, international law is also a mechanism that delivers peace, justice, and developmental sustainability to international life. Bring these two claims together and the question arises: when states get down to the business of producing international law, do they automatically channel this universalist function or is there something else going on here? Put differently, can states do no wrong when it comes to choosing what norms to elevate into international law's *corpus juris* – because no matter what they do in this context, their actions at this point inevitably express some higher universal reason that acts through them as if they were "a kind of automaton"? A large part of what goes into the traditional theory of customary international law indicates a strong predisposition toward this quasi-Appolinarian view: inasmuch as every violation of a preexisting customary rule, in principle, can become the founding act of a new custom, on a long enough timeline states indeed can do no wrong.[114] Or is it the case, rather, that not every act performed by states automatically channels the universal reason, so that – to

[113] Philip Jenkins, *Jesus Wars: How Four Patriarchs, Three Queens, and Two Emperors Decided What Christians Would Believe for the Next 1,500 years* (New York: HarperOne, 2011), 7–8.

[114] For a rather insightful discussion, see Anthony D'Amato, "The Theory of Customary International Law," *Proceedings of the Annual Meeting (American Society of International Law)* 82 (1988): 242–60, at 246–7.

borrow the language of Paul of Samosata – only under a very particular set of circumstances will the "spirit" descend on their conduct? The formula commonly used to explain how *jus cogens* norms are created[115] as well as the *Nicaragua* theory of how to tell violations of customary law from new-custom-forming conduct indicate a certain predisposition toward this view.[116]

Despite at first sight coming across as hopelessly abstract and metaphysical, the "one or two natures" debate carried extremely significant stakes from the standpoint of the official Christian doctrine. In the first place, it touched directly on the question of salvation. On the one hand, the general consensus accepted that "[i]n order for redemptive doctrine to make any sense, Christ would have to be fully human" since it is the fact that "Christ shared humanity [that] allowed him to redeem humanity through his sacrificial death"[117] – or, as Gregory Nazianus wrote, "[T]hat which Christ has not assumed, He has not healed."[118] On the other hand, the argument went, "[u]nless Christ were fully divine, ... his death could not save us."[119] Depending on where one stood on the question of one versus two natures of Christ, humanity, thus, was presented with two fundamentally different routes to salvation: if Christ was nothing but wholly divine, one could only worship him and ask for redemption; if he was both human and divine, one was well-advised to study and emulate his good works.

In the second place, there was also the question of textual sources and their "ethical" reliability. As Jenkins puts is:

> how do we know how much weight to attach to the words of Christ recorded in the New Testament? Just who do we hear speaking? Assuming for the sake of argument that the scriptural text accurately records Jesus' sayings ... When Jesus tells a parable or utters a pronouncement, do those words come directly and literally from the mind of God, or are they the thoughts of an individual bound by the constraints of his time and place?[120]

Again, the parallels with the VP context are obvious and undeniable. When states "speak" through treaties and state practice, who exactly do we hear speaking? Is it states as the legislators of that law which will ensure the preservation and strengthening of international peace, security, sustainable development, and human dignity, or states as political entities that are

115 See Article 53 of the Vienna Convention on the Law of Treaties (1969): "[A] peremptory norm of general international law is a norm accepted and recognized by the international community of States as a whole as a norm from which no derogation is permitted."

116 *Nicaragua* v. *United States (merits)*, ICJ Reports (1986), 98.

117 Jenkins, *Jesus Wars*, 7.

118 Jenkins, *Jesus Wars*, 7.

119 Jenkins, *Jesus Wars*, 7.

120 Jenkins, *Jesus Wars*, 9.

themselves supposed to be the subjects of this law, bound and constrained by it? When states agree on, interpret, or enforce positive legal rules, how much weight are we meant to attach to these acts? Should we "worship" these acts and trust the norms they project to deliver us the "redemption" we hope for, or should we only study them with a view to extracting out of them a possible reflection of that redemptive truth? However one answers these questions, the fundamental paradox is clear: it is not just the case that for the VP theory to make sense, states must be simultaneously assumed to be both one-natured and two-natured; it is also the case that *in either event* states will consistently be expected to be *more than just themselves*, more than just states, more than just governments acting in their own national interest. The "one versus two natures" debate in Christian theology, lest we forget, was born out of a desire to establish that Jesus was either "fully divine" or "divine and human at the same time," not that he was only human.

There is another important lesson that we can learn from this early theological episode. As history shows, in the end, the philosophical tensions raised by the "one versus two natures" paradox did not present too much of an obstacle for Christian dogma. Again, the "nuclear solution" ultimately came to the rescue: God, by definition, was an ineffable being, His ways were mysterious, inscrutable, and beyond human reason. Whatever contradictions one might observe in Christ's ontological position, thus, could as easily be dismissed on the grounds that God, being omniscient and omnipotent, can always will them away whenever He wants as they could be explained away as ultimately nonproblematic on the grounds that God, being the first cause of everything, was not bound by the laws of logic any more than he was bound by the laws of physics.

A neat argument strategy by any measure, but not one – let us note – that could ever be made available in the context of the (supposedly secular) VP tradition.

19.3.3 *The Origins of International Law's Bad Faith*

Let us recap our findings so far. There exists a massive paradox at the heart of the VP tradition. The only logical way to solve this paradox would be to introduce into the VP theoretical framework something along the lines of a Natural Law construct or the idea of divine wisdom, *firmitas*, or God's grace. Any of these theoretical elements could immediately resolve the problem of international law's absent center. The difficulty with this strategy, however, is that it would also result in giving the VP tradition an immediately recognizable theological flavor. As even the first-year law students know, however, the entire raison d'être of legal positivism as a theoretical project, historically, has been its promise of secularism and its categorical rejection of every form of natural-legalist sensibility. Recall Simma and Paulus's argument: the foundation of the positivist tradition lies in the "strict separation of the law in force . . . from non-legal factors such as natural reason [and] moral principles." It is precisely because of this separation that positivism has been able to promise the discipline of international law a far more "rigorous [understanding of] legal validity" and a more "objective determination of fact[s]" than it could find elsewhere.[121]

Right from its very inception, the basic bargain offered by the VP tradition to the discipline of international law has hinged on this exact point: from the rejection of theology and natural law comes the promise of greater rigor and objectivity. The more the discipline of international law embraced the positivist outlook, the more it could liberate itself from the debilitating influences of theological superstition and natural-legalism, the more its thinking about law, consequently, would become rigorous and objective. The only problem, as it turned out, was that the particular species of the positivist theory which the VP tradition sold to international law was not actually all that positivist to begin with. Once this realization had sunk in, the dilemma it gave rise to at first glance must have seemed rather stark. Either one or the other thing needed to go: theoretical honesty with oneself or the highly desirable secular status.

Which of the two ambitions should the discipline of international law give up on? Should it accept that VP's theoretical premises are, in fact, logically unsustainable on their own terms or that they are, rather, deeply theological? Anyone familiar with the actual course of disciplinary history will know which of these options prevailed in the end. The discipline never found within itself the power to terminate its union with the VP tradition. The precise reasons for this are anyone's guess, but the argument that I want to put forward here is that they were, ultimately, a function of intra-disciplinary politics, ideology, and labor conditions.

An open acknowledgment of the fact that the VP paradigm could make sense only if it were given a distinctly theological foundation offered the discipline prospects that seemed unacceptable not (so much) because making such kind of acknowledgment would have hurt the discipline's intellectual pride or undermined its formal status as an aspiring social science but because it also risked exposing a dangerously large proportion of the international law profession to potential accusations of charlatanry and intellectual fraud, while at the same time threatening to blow an enormous hole through the entire

[121] Simma and Paulus, "Responsibility of Individuals," 304–5.

division of labor established within the discipline's internal and adjacent social spaces over the course of the last 120 years.

Changing a discipline's governing paradigm, as Pierre Schlag notes, is an expensive luxury.[122] Theoretical frameworks are not a free resource: they take time, effort, training, access to specialist instruction, and the commitment of various other expensive factors to learn, internalize, and master. The replacement of a dominant paradigm by a new theoretical framework is not a costless process, and its costs can never be spread evenly. The discipline of international law, at the end of the day, is a part of the capitalist economy. Knowledge products generated within it – be they policy proposals (knowledge of how to resolve a particular problem from a legal standpoint) or normative interpretations (knowledge of what the law means) – are configured as marketable commodities. The analytical skills one learns as a follower of a particular school or tradition are the capital assets with which these goods can be produced. It takes time to hone these skills, and the decision to do so, ultimately, is not dissimilar to an investment decision. Every economic community in which capital investment decisions are made without strict centralized coordination is vulnerable to the problem of capital overaccumulation.[123]

Like with every type of investment, decreasing the value of a theoretical framework by debunking its sales-pitch hurts most those who have invested in it most heavily, which, in this case, raises the question of unequal exposure and distributional impact not only across different subdisciplinary communities but also across different generations. Put differently, it may be all well and good for us to speak in the abstract of the need for the followers of the VP tradition to face up to the implications of its logical incoherence, but, seen from their end, the effects of such an adjustment would be equivalent to an act of expropriation, and many of those who would suffer from this expropriation the most are also, in relative terms, older and thus will have had more time to take over those positions of academic power that would allow them to block any such expropriatory actions. Notes Schlag: the more wide-ranging is expected to be a program of theoretical reforms proposed to a disciplinary community, the more expensive it will be to implement at the individual level, and the readiness of the vested interests to defend their position with grim determination and rage should never be underestimated.[124]

122 Pierre Schlag, "The Brilliant, the Curious, and the Wrong," *Stanford Law Review* 39, no. 4 (1987): 917–27.

123 Further on the problem of capital overaccumulation in capitalist economies, see David Harvey, *The Limits to Capital* (London: Verso, 2006), 190–203.

124 Harvey, *The Limits to Capital*, 925.

One of the ways in which the culture of bad faith begins is when the ethics of *parrhesia* is forced to give way to vulgar economic expediency. The endurance of the problem of international law's absent center in mainstream international law theory is a product of a fundamentally ideological dynamics. There is nothing inevitable at the level of logic or critical reasoning that prevents the discipline from accepting that, under the basic institutional conditions presumed by the VP paradigm, the only factor that could prevent the positive international law regime from descending into anarchy and cacophony is God's grace or direct divine intervention. Doing so, however, would almost certainly destroy the discipline's ideological image in the wider outside world.

And then there is also the question of the discipline's "external commitments." A hundred or so years ago, the hassle of having to rewire the entire disciplinary field around a new theoretical blueprint might have been the main politico-economic concern limiting the ability of international law to part ways with the VP paradigm. But a lot of water has flown since then. The discipline has become a lot more embedded within the formal machineries of global governance. The pressures that come from having to keep its "side of the deal" are a lot greater, and the room it has left for any intellectual-identity-changing maneuvers is a lot smaller today. If the international law profession were to admit today that, for the last 120 years, the entire foundation of its purported claim to scientificity (international law as knowledge of positive social facts) and worldly expertise (international law as a technology of power) was, in fact, to a very large extent grounded in the assumption that (a) God or some undisclosed God-like entity remains an active player in international affairs and (b) if things go wrong, this God-like entity will always step in to clean up the mess, the damage it would suffer in the world outside its own social and theoretical planes would be lethal and irreversible. There would be no forgiveness, no coming back, no second chances. The fate that befell phrenology and other debunked pseudosciences would pale in comparison.

Has the discipline become too big to fail? It is hard to say for sure, but it certainly seems so. The absent structural center that is missing in VP's officially declared theoretical account is absent from it for a reason that definitely goes beyond what can be fixed by simple "theoretical honesty."

19.4 CONCLUSION

Scotus's posing of the problem of free will, I argue in this chapter, resembles in terms of its basic structure the same theoretical paradox which confronts the VP tradition. VP's question "How can a decentralized international legal process be expected to give rise to a regulatory dynamic that is both sufficient and suitable for the promotion of international peace, security, sustainable development, and other universal values?" is essentially homologous to Scotus's "Why cannot the 'blessed in heaven' commit sin?" The theoretical solution that Scotus proposes to this problem – God gave the "blessed in heaven" an additional measure of steadfastness (*firmitas*) – historically laid the blueprint for a narrative strategy that in various forms would be replayed over the next few centuries in many different contexts ranging from the Protestant debates about predestination to Kant's theory of morality to Classical Liberal arguments in favor of laissez-faire economics. Notably, however, the context that matters most for our purposes – the VP tradition – is the one in which it was not directly replicated, and it is precisely by reconstructing the logic of this failure that we can start to map out and decipher the basic extent and configuration of that regime of Sartrean bad faith that I alluded to at the beginning of this chapter.

The refusal to replicate within the international law context the model offered by Scotus, Kant, and Smith, it has to be admitted, was not without good reasons, if within the category of good reasons one is prepared to include reasons of ideological self-aggrandizement and disciplinary rent-seeking. One way or another, however, this refusal or failure has not passed without consequences.

In describing the general meaning of bad faith, Sartre notes at some point that the practice of bad faith generally entails "a certain art of forming contradictory concepts which unite in themselves both an idea and the negation of that idea."[125] The twist here, he immediately adds, is that the same theoretical practice also tends to be characteristic of the act of critical self-reflection, or what Sartre calls the culture of sincerity and candor with oneself. The only thing that appears to be different is the surface motivation. The underlying mindset is exactly the same. The quest for sincerity presupposes, ultimately, the same form of self-transcendence or self-alienation as bad faith: "Total, constant sincerity as a constant effort to adhere to oneself is by nature a constant effort to dissociate oneself from oneself."[126] To be able to acknowledge and evaluate "what one is," one must distance oneself from oneself: to separate the judging and critiquing part of one's self from that which is being judged and critiqued. But "[w]hat then is sincerity except precisely a phenomenon of bad faith?"[127] The punchline does not come immediately – the argument drags on for another page or so – but when it does, it is as ruthless as it can be: "Bad faith is possible only because sincerity is

[125] Sartre, *Being and Nothingness*, 79.
[126] Sartre, *Being and Nothingness*, 88–9.
[127] Sartre, *Being and Nothingness*, 86.

conscious of missing its goal inevitably, due to its very nature."[128] The project of self-critique – the quest for sincerity, including sincerity in the sense of (finding) the courage to know oneself – sooner or later always fails, whether because of its hubris or because of its sheer metaphysic unsustainability, and when that happens, inevitably, a culture of bad faith gradually arises.

The discipline's failure to debunk the theoretical unsustainability of the VP tradition was not, ultimately, a function of any inherent intellectual limitation or its lack of ability for critical introspection. Quite on the contrary: to a large extent it was precisely its uncompromising commitment to the latter that eventually drove it to develop that falsely naive culture of theoretical cover-up that we see with the likes of Lowe, Corbett, and Brownlie.

Looking back at the last 120 or so years, every generation of international lawyers since Triepel and Anzilotti has sought to launch a project of "candor and sincerity," debunking the discipline's unholy union with the VP paradigm. Alejandro Alvarez, Eugene Korovin, Alf Ross, Myres McDougal, Charles Chaumont, Mohammed Bedajoui, David Kennedy, Karen Knop, Anne Orford, B. S. Chimni – the list runs on and on. For a brief fleeting moment, each of these critical interventions seemed to succeed: the project of critique broke the surface – the "truth" momentarily came into view, the incoherence of the positivist dogma became undeniable – but sooner or later the wave inevitably crested, dissipated, and ran into the sand.

It is a moot point to ask what could have been done differently. Paradigm displacement is neither a science one can codify nor an art one can learn through practice. It is a function, rather, of fundamental politico-economic reforms that take place within the respective social planes. Inasmuch as no such reforms have (yet) taken place within international law's social base, it would be pointless to expect VP's reign to end.

In the meantime, the continuing stability of this reign seems to have induced within the broader theoretical landscape of international law a situation not dissimilar to that described by Friedrich Nietzsche in his commentary on Victorian-era liberal humanism:

> They have got rid of the Christian God [but they] feel obliged to cling all the more firmly to Christian morality. . . . When one gives up Christian belief one thereby deprives oneself of the right to Christian morality. For the latter is absolutely not self-evident: one must make this point clear again and again . . . Christianity is a system . . . If one breaks out of it a fundamental idea, the belief in God, one thereby breaks the whole thing to pieces: one has nothing

[128] Sartre, *Being and Nothingness*, 89.

> of any consequence left in one's hands. ... Christian morality ... stands or falls with the belief in God.[129]

Like Victorian liberalism, the VP paradigm endures as an artifact of a revolution arrested: an experiment in theoretical secularism that collapsed precisely at that point where it was meant to take the kind of leap of courage which its underlying politico-economic conditions could not allow.

The essential contours of the deal which the VP tradition offered the discipline of international law have not really changed since the days of Triepel and Anzilotti. What lies at the root of its sales-pitch – embrace the proposed method so as to be able to acquire a more reliable grasp of *international law as a real-world process* and to develop a more effective understanding of its potential *as a political mechanism* – is the same classical bargain that Nietzsche detected with Victorian humanists: to master the world, turn to science and equip yourself with its tools and you will never need to worry about where you will then find your source of direction or guidance. But the particular version of science it brought with it, in the end, turned out to be nothing more than a crudely repackaged mixture of Kantian moral theory and Smithian economics, and the secularist bargain it advertised came out to be nothing more than a fraud.

RECOMMENDED READING

Fassbender, Bardo, and Anne Peters, eds. *The Oxford Handbook of the History of International Law*. Oxford: Oxford University Press, 2012.

Kammerhofer, Jörg, and Jean d'Aspremont, eds. *International Legal Positivism in a Post-Modern World*. Cambridge: Cambridge University Press, 2014.

Kennedy, David. "A New World Order: Yesterday, Today, and Tomorrow." *Transnational Law Contemporary Problems* 4, no. 2 (1994): 329–76.

Kennedy, Duncan. *A Critique of Adjudication: (fin de siècle)*. Cambridge, MA: Harvard University Press, 1997.

Marks, Susan. *The Riddle of All Constitutions: International Law, Democracy, and the Critique of Ideology*. Oxford: Oxford University Press, 2000.

Olsen, Frances E. "The Family and the Market: A Study of Ideology and Legal Reform." *Harvard Law Review* 96, no. 7 (1983): 1497–578.

[129] Friedrich Nietzsche, *Twilight of the Idols and the Anti-Christ* (New York: Penguin Books, 2003), 80–1.

Select Bibliography

Abbattista, Guido. "Chinese Law and Justice: George Thomas Staunton and the European Discourses on China in the Eighteenth and Nineteenth Centuries." In *Law, Justice and Codification in Qing China*, edited by Guido Abbattista, 1–138. Trieste: Edizioni Università di Trieste, 2017.

Abu-Odeh, Adnan. "Two Capitals in an Undivided Jerusalem." *Foreign Affairs* 71, no. 2 (1992): 183–8.

Adler, Hans, and Wulf Köpke, eds. *A Companion to the Works of Johann Gottfried Herder*. Rochester, NY: Camden House, 2009.

Ago, Roberto. "Positive Law and International Law." *The American Journal of International Law* 51, no. 4 (1957): 691–733.

Ahdar, Rex, ed. *Research Handbook on Law and Religion*. Cheltenham: Edward Elgar, 2018.

AHR Forum, "Historiographic 'Turns' in Critical Perspective." *American Historical Review* 117, no. 3 (2012): 698–813.

Alban, Donald Jr., Robert H. Woods Jr., and Marsha Daigle-Williamson. "The Writings of William Carey: Journalism as Mission in a Modern Age." *Mission Studies* 22, no. 1 (2005): 85–113.

Aleinikoff, T. Alexander. *International Legal Norms and Migration: An Analysis*. Geneva: International Organization for Migration, 2002.

"International Legal Norms and Migration: A Report." In *Migration and International Legal Norms*, edited by T. Alexander Aleinikoff and Vincent Chetail, 1–27. The Hague: T.M.C. Asser Press, 2003.

Alexander, Lawrence, and Frederick Schauer. "Rules of Recognition, Constitutional Controversies, and the Dizzying Dependence of Law on Acceptance." In *The Rule of Recognition and the U.S. Constitution*, edited by Matthew Adler and Kenneth Einar Himma, 175–92. New York: Oxford University Press, 2009.

Allain, Jean. "The Jus Cogens Nature of Non-refoulement." *International Journal of Refugee Law* 13, no. 4 (2001): 533–58.

Allard, Silas W. "Reimagining Asylum: Religious Narratives and the Moral Obligation to the Asylum Seeker." *Refuge: Canada's Journal on Refugees* 29, no. 1 (2013): 121–9.

"Global and Local Challenges to Refugee Protection." *International Journal of Legal Information* 46, no. 1 (2018): 45–52.
"Christianity and a Global Law for Migration." In *Christianity and Global Law*, edited by Rafael Domingo and John Witte, Jr., 351–64. London: Routledge, 2020.
Allott, Philip. *The Health of Nations*. Cambridge: Cambridge University Press, 2002.
Althusser, Louis. "From *Capital* to Marx's Philosophy." In *Reading Capital*, edited by Louis Althusser and Etienne Balibar, 11–70. London: New Left Books, 1970.
Althusser, Louis, Étienne Balibar, Roger Establet, Pierre Macherey, and Jacques Rancière. *Lire e Capital*, Tome 1 & 2. Paris: Maspero, 1965.
Alvarez, Jose. *International Organizations as Law-Makers*. Oxford: Oxford University Press, 2005.
American Bar Association. *Model Rules of Professional Conduct*. Chicago: ABA Book Publishing, 2019.
Amirav, Hagit, and Evangelos Chrysos, "The Christian Commonwealth in Anti-Heretical Texts: The Case of The Emperor Justinian's Writings." In *New Themes, New Styles in the Eastern Mediterranean: Christian, Jewish, and Islamic Encounters, 5th–8th Centuries*, edited by Hagit Amirav and Francesco Celia, 19–38. Leuven: Peeters, 2017.
Amorosa, Paolo. *Rewriting the History of the Law of Nations: How James Brown Scott Made Francisco de Vitoria the Founder of International Law*. Oxford: Oxford University Press, 2019.
Anderson, Glaire. "Islamic Spaces and Diplomacy in Constantinople (Tenth to Thirteenth Centuries C.E.)." *Medieval Encounters* 15, no. 1 (2009): 86–113.
Anderson, Judith Icke. *William Howard Taft: An Intimate History*. New York: Norton, 1981.
Andreae, Johannes. *In quintum Decretalium librum Novella Commentaria*. Turin, 1963.
Andrén, Carl-Gustaf. "De mänskliga rättigheternas religiösa och rättsliga bakgrund: Debatten inom Förenta nationerna och Europarådet i slutet på 1940-talet." *Svensk teologisk kvartalskrift* 51, no. 4 (1975): 158–66.
Angelou, Athanasios D. "'Who Am I?' Scholarios' Answers and the Hellenic Identity." In *Philhellen: Studies in Honour of Robert Browning*, edited by Costas N. Constantinides, Nikolaos M. Panagiotakes, Elizabeth Jeffreys, and Athanasios D. Angelou, 1–19. Venice: Istituto Ellenico di Studi Bizantini e Postbizantini di Venezia, 1996.
Angelov, Dimiter. *Imperial Ideology and Political Thought in Byzantium (1204–1330)*. Cambridge: Cambridge University Press, 2007.
Anghie, Antony. "Francisco De Vitoria and the Colonial Origins of International Law." *Social & Legal Studies* 5, no. 3 (1996): 321–36.
"Europe and International Law's Colonial Present." *Baltic Yearbook of International Law Online* 6, no. 1 (2006): 79–84.
Imperialism, Sovereignty, and the Making of International Law. Cambridge: Cambridge University Press, 2007.
"International Law in a Time of Change: Should International Law Lead or Follow?" *American University International Law Review* 26, no. 5 (2011): 1315–76.
Annicchino, Pasquale. *Law and Religious Freedom: The Rise and Decline of the American Model*. London: Routledge, 2018.

Antoninus of Florence. *Summa Theologica*. Vol. 3. Graz: Akademische Druck & Verlagsanstalt, 1959.

Aquinas, Thomas. *The Summa Theologiæ of St. Thomas Aquinas*. 2nd rev. ed., translated by Fathers of the English Dominican Province. London: Burns, Oates & Washbourne, 1920.

Summa Theologiae. Translated by Fathers of the English Dominican Province. New York: Benzinger Bros, 1947.

Arana, Marie. *Silver, Sword, and Stone: Three Crucibles in the Latin American Story*. New York: Simon and Schuster, 2019.

Arendt, Hannah. *The Origins of Totalitarianism*. New York: Harcourt, 1976.

The Origins of Totalitarianism. Orlando: Houghton Mifflin Harcourt, 1994.

"We Refugees." In *Altogether Elsewhere: Writers on Exile*, edited by Marc Robinson, 110–19. Boston: Faber and Faber, 1994.

Arminius, Jacobus. *The Complete Works of James Arminius*. Grand Rapids, MI: Baker Book House, 1956 [1853].

Arnim, Ludwig Achim von. *Werke und Briefwechsel: Historisch-kritische Ausgabe*. Vol. 11, *Texte der deutschen Tischgesellschaft*, edited by Stefan Nienhaus. Tübingen: Niemeyer, 2008.

Arrignon, Jean-Pierre, and Jean-François Duneau. "La frontière chez deux auteurs byzantins: Procope de Césarée et Constantine VII Porphyrogénète." In *Géographica Byzantina*, edited by Hélène Ahrweiler, 17–30. Paris: Sorbonne, 1981.

Årsheim, Helge. *Making Religion and Human Rights at the United Nations*. Boston: Walter de Gruyter, 2018.

Asad, Talal. *Formations of the Secular: Christianity, Islam, Modernity*. Stanford: Stanford University Press, 2003.

d'Aspremont, Jean, and Jörg Kammerhofer. "Introduction: The Future of International Legal Positivism." In *International Legal Positivism in a Post-Modern World*, edited by Jörg Kammerhofer and Jean d'Aspremont, 1–20. Cambridge: Cambridge University Press, 2014.

Aubert, Didier. "Surveys and Romance: Methodist Missionaries' Photographs of the South American 'Field' in the Early 20th Century." *IdeAs* 6 (2015), http://journals.openedition.org/ideas/1066.

Auslin, Michael R. *Negotiating with Imperialism: The Unequal Treaties and the Culture of Japanese Diplomacy*. Cambridge, MA: Harvard University Press, 2004.

Azpilcueta, Martin de [Doctor Navarrus]. *Relectio in cap. Ita Quorumdam*. Rome: 1580; Coimbra: 1550.

Backhouse, Roger. *The Ordinary Business of Life*. Princeton: Princeton University Press, 2002.

Badiou, Alain. *St. Paul: The Foundation of Universalism*. Stanford: Stanford University Press, 2003.

Baldwin, David A. *Economic Statecraft*. Princeton: Princeton University Press, 1985.

Ball, Philip. *Critical Mass*. New York: Farrar, Straus and Giroux, 2006.

Banda, Fareda, and Lisa Fishbayn Joffe, eds. *Women's Rights and Religious Law: Domestic and International Perspectives*. Abingdon: Routledge, 2016.

Banu, Roxana. *Nineteenth-Century Perspectives on Private International Law*. Oxford: Oxford University Press, 2018.

Barker, Ernest. *Social and Political Thought in Byzantium, from Justinian I to the Last Palaeologus: Passages from Byzantine Writers and Documents*. Oxford: Clarendon Press, 1957.

Barkun, Michael. *Crucible of the Millennium: The Burned-Over District of New York in the 1840s*. Syracuse, NY: Syracuse University Press, 1986.

Bartolo da Sassoferrato. [*Collected Works*]. Venice: Apud Iuntas, 1570; Robbins Collection, University of California-Berkeley.

Barber, Malcolm. *The Crusader States*. New Haven: Yale University Press, 2012.

Barber Crosby, Margaret. *The Making of a German Constitution: A Slow Revolution*. Oxford: Berg Publishers, 2008.

Barducci, Marco. *Hugo Grotius and the Century of Revolution, 1613–1718: Transnational Reception in English Political Thought*. Cambridge: Cambridge University Press, 2017.

Bary, Wm. Theodore de. "Introduction." In *Confucianism and Human Rights*, edited by Wm. Theodore de Bary and Tu Weiming, 1–26. New York: Columbia University Press, 1998.

Bash, Anthony. *Ambassadors for Christ: An Exploration of Ambassadorial Language in the New Testament*. Tübingen: J. C. B. Mohr, 1997.

Baszkiewicz, Jan. "Quelques remarques sur la conception de dominum mundi dans l'oeuvre de Bartolus." In *Bartolo da Sassoferrato: Studi e documenti per il VI centenario*. Vol. 2, edited by Università degli studi di Perugia, 7–25. Milan: Giuffrè, 1962.

Bates, M. Searle. *Religious Liberty: An Inquiry*. New York: International Missionary Council, 1945.

Baumgartner, Konrad. "Die Familie Friedrich Carl von Savigny und Sailer." *Zeitschrift der Savigny-Stiftung für Rechtsgeschichte: Germanistische Abteilung* 135, no. 1 (2018): 359–80.

Beard, Jennifer. *The Political Economy of Desire: International Law, Development and the Nation State*. Abingdon: Routledge-Cavendish, 2007.

"The International Law in Force: Anachronistic Ethics and Divine Violence." In *Events: The Force of International Law*, edited by Fleur Johns, Richard Joyce, and Sundhya Pahuja, 18–28. New York: Routledge, 2011.

"Charities, Election Campaigning and the *Australian Constitution*." *Melbourne University Law Review* 43, no. 2 (2019): 462–514.

Beard, Jennifer, and Gregor Noll, "Parrhēsia and Credibility: The Sovereign of Refugee Status Determinations." *Social & Legal Studies* 18, no. 4 (2009): 455–77.

Beck, H.-G. *Nomos, Kanon und Staatsraison in Byzanz*. Vienna: Osterreichische Akademie der Wissenschaften, 1981.

Beetham, David. *The Legitimation of Power*, 2nd ed. New York: Palgrave Macmillan, 2013.

Beier, A. L. *The Problem of the Poor in Tudor and Early Stuart England*. London: Methuen, 1983.

Bell, G. K. A., ed. *The Stockholm Conference 1925: The Official Report of the Universal Christian Conference on Life and Work Held in Stockholm, 19–30 August, 1925*. London: Oxford University Press, 1926.

Bellah, Robert N. "The Final Word: Can Christianity Contribute to a Global Civil Religion?" In *Christianity and Human Rights: An Introduction*, edited by John Witte, Jr. and Frank S. Alexander, 351–66. Cambridge: Cambridge University Press, 2010.

Bellomo, Manlio. *The Common Legal Past of Europe, 1000–1800*. Translated by Lydia G. Cochrane. Washington, DC: Catholic University of America Press, 1995.

Belloni, Annalisa. *Professori giuristi a Padova nel secolo XV: profili bio-bibliografici e cattedre*. Frankfurt: Klostermann, 1986.

Benhabib, Seyla. *The Rights of Others: Aliens, Residents and Citizens*. New York: Cambridge University Press, 2004.

Benton, Lauren. *Law and Colonial Cultures: Legal Regimes in World History, 1400–1900*. New York: Cambridge University Press, 2002.

Benton, Lauren, and Lisa Ford. *Rage for Order: The British Empire and the Origins of International Law, 1800–1850*. Cambridge, MA: Harvard University Press, 2016.

Benton, Lauren, and Richard J. Ross, eds. *Legal Pluralism and Empires, 1500–1850*. New York: New York University Press, 2013.

Bentwich, Norman. "The Wilderness of Legal Charity." *Law Quarterly Review* 49 (1933): 520–7.

Berger, Peter, and Thomas Luckmann. *The Social Construction of Reality: A Treatise in the Sociology of Knowledge*. New York: Anchor Books, 1967.

Berkowitz, Roger. *The Gift of Science Leibniz and the Modern Legal Tradition*. Cambridge, MA: Harvard University Press, 2009.

"From Justice to Justification: An Alternative Genealogy of Positive Law." *UC Irvine Law Review* 1, no. 3 (2011): 611–30.

Berman, Harold J. "The Influence of Christianity upon the Development of Law." *Oklahoma Law Review* 12, no. 1 (1959): 86–101.

Law and Revolution. Vol. 1: *The Formation of the Western Legal Tradition*. Cambridge, MA: Harvard University Press, 1983.

Law and Revolution. Vol. 2: *The Impact of the Protestant Reformation in the Western Legal Tradition*. Cambridge, MA: Harvard University Press, 1983.

Berman, Nathaniel. "But the Alternative Is Despair: European Nationalism and the Modernist Renewal of International Law." *Harvard Law Review* 106, no. 8 (1993): 1792–903.

"Legalizing Jerusalem or, of Law, Fantasy, and Faith." *Catholic University Law Review* 45, no. 3 (1996): 823–35.

"In the Wake of Empire." *American University International Law Review* 14, no. 6 (1999): 1521–54.

"The Nationality Decrees Case, or, of Intimacy and Consent." *Leiden Journal of International Law* 13, no. 2 (2000): 265–95.

"'The Sacred Conspiracy': Religion, Nationalism, and the Crisis of Internationalism." *Leiden Journal of International Law* 25, no. 1 (2012): 9–54.

"'In a Place Parallel to God': The Draft, the Demonic, and the Conscientious Cubist." *Journal of Law and Religion* 32, no. 2 (2017): 311–39.

Berman, Paul. *Global Legal Pluralism: A Jurisprudence of Law Beyond Borders*. Cambridge: Cambridge University Press, 2012.

Besson, Samatha. "The Legitimate Authority of International Human Rights: On the Reciprocal Legitimation of Domestic and International Human Rights." In *The Legitimacy of International Human Rights Regimes: Legal, Political and Philosophical Perspectives*, edited by Andreas Follesdal, Johan Karlssson Schaffer, and Geir Ulfstein, 32–83. Cambridge: Cambridge University Press, 2014.

Betts, Alexander. *Survival Migration: Failed Governance and the Crisis of Displacement*. Ithaca: Cornell University Press, 2013.
Bhuta, Nehal. "What Should Freedom of Religion Become?" In *Freedom of Religion, Secularism and Human Rights*, edited by Nehal Bhuta, 1–20. Oxford: Oxford University Press, 2019.
Bickers, Robert. *The Scramble for China: Foreign Devils in the Qing Empire, 1832–1914*. London: Allen Lane, 2011.
Black, Ann, Hossein Esmaeili, and Nadirsyah Hosen. *Modern Perspectives on Islamic Law*. Cheltenham: Edward Elgar, 2013.
Blakeney, Michael. "Sequestered Piety and Charity: A Comparative Analysis." *The Journal of Legal History* 2, no. 3 (1981): 207–26.
Bloch, Ernst. *The Spirit of Utopia*. Translated by Anthony A. Nassar. Stanford: Stanford University Press, 2000.
Blockley, Roger C. *East Roman Foreign Policy: Formation and Conduct from Diocletian to Anastasius*. Leeds: Francis Cairns, 1992.
Blois, Matthijs de. "Blessed [Are] the Peacemakers … Grotius on the Just War and Christian Pacifism." *Grotiana* 32, no. 1 (2011): 20–39.
Blower, Brooke L. "From Isolationism to Neutrality: A New Framework for Understanding American Political Culture, 1919–1941." *Diplomatic History* 38, no. 2 (April 2014): 345–76.
Blumenberg, Hans. *The Legitimacy of the Modern Age*. Translated by Robert M. Wallace. Cambridge, MA: MIT Press, 1983.
Bluntschli, Johann Caspar. *Gesammelte kleine Schriften*. Vol. 1, *Geschichte des Rechtes der religiösen Bekenntnisfreiheit*. Nördlingen: C. H. Beck, 1879.
Gesammelte kleine Schriften. Vol. 2, *Das römische Papstthum und das Völkerrecht*, Nördlingen: C. H. Beck, 1881.
Boer, Roland, and Christina Petterson. *Idols of Nations: Biblical Myth at the Origins of Capitalism*. Philadelphia: Augsburg Fortress Publishers, 2014.
Boggs, Mary. "William Alexander Parsons Martin, Missionary to China, 1850–1916." MA thesis, McCormick Theological Seminary, 1949.
Bohmer, Carol, and Amy Shuman. *Rejecting Refugees: Political Asylum in the 21st Century*. London: Routledge, 2008.
Bonansea, Bernardine. "Duns Scotus' Voluntarism." In *John Duns Scotus, 1265–1965*, edited by John Ryan and Bernardine Bonansea, 83–121. Washington, DC: Catholic University of America Press, 1965.
Borgwardt, Elizabeth. *A New Deal for the World: America's Vision for Human Rights*. Cambridge, MA: Harvard University Press, 2005.
Borutta, Manuel. *Antikatholizismus: Deutschland und Italien in Zeitalter der europäischen Kulturkämpfen*. Göttingen: Vandenhoeck & Ruprecht, 2011.
Bossy, John. *Peace in the Post-Reformation*. Cambridge: Cambridge University Press, 1998.
Bouwman, Bastiaan. "From Religious Freedom to Social Justice: The Human Rights Engagement of the Ecumenical Movement from the 1940s to the 1970s." *Journal of Global History* 13, no. 2 (2018): 252–73.
Bowers, Amy, and Kristin Carpenter. "Challenging the Narrative of Conquest: The Story of Lyng v. Northwest Indian Cemetery Protective Association." In *Indian Law Stories*, edited by Carole E. Goldberg, Kevin K. Washburn, and Philip P. Frickey, 497–504. New York: Foundation Press, 2010.

Boyle, Alan, and Christine Chinkin. *The Making of International Law*. Oxford: Oxford University Press, 2007.

Braun, Johann. "Eduard Gans (1797–1839): Ein homo Politicus zwischen Hegel und Savigny." In *Deutsche Juristen Jüdischer Herkunft*, edited by Helmut Heinrichs, Harald Franzki, Klaus Schmalz, and Michael Stolleis, 45–57. Munich: Beck Verlag, 1993.

Breton, Stanislas. *A Radical Philosophy of St. Paul*. Translated by Joseph N. Ballan. New York: Columbia University Press, 2011.

Brett, Annabel S. *Changes of State: Nature and the Limits of the City in Early Modern Natural Law*. Princeton: Princeton University Press, 2011.

Brinkley, Alan. *The Publisher*. Toronto: Penguin Random House, 2010.

Brockey, Liam. *Journey to the East*. London: Harvard University Press, 2007.

Brownlie, Ian. *International Law at the Fiftieth Anniversary of the United Nations*. The Hague: The Hague Academy of International Law, 1995.

Brueggemann, Walter. *Theology of the Old Testament: Testimony, Dispute, Advocacy* Minneapolis: Fortress Press, 1997.

The Land: Place as Gift, Promise and Challenge in Biblical Faith. Minneapolis: Fortress Press, 2002.

Brundage, James A. *The Medieval Origins of the Legal Profession: Canonists, Civilians, and Courts*. Chicago: University of Chicago Press, 2008.

Brunus, Conradus. *De legationibus libri quinquei*. In Conradus Brunus, *Opera tria [. . .]. De legationibus libri quinque [. . .] De caeremoniis libri sex [. . .] De imaginibus liber unus [. . .]*. Moguntiae apud S. Victorem: Ex officina Francisci Behem, 1548.

Brunyate, John. "The Legal Definition of Charity." *Law Quarterly Review* 61 (1945): 268–85.

Bryan, Robert. "The Legal Profession." In *American University Men in China*. Shanghai: Comacrib Press, 1936.

Buckle, Stephen. *Natural Law and the Theory of Property: Grotius to Hume*. Oxford: Clarendon Press, 1991.

Burchfield, Robert William. "The Ormulum." In *Dictionary of the Middle Ages*. Vol. 9, edited by Joseph R. Strayer. New York: Charles Scribner's Sons, 1987.

Burnidge, Cara Lea. *A Peaceful Conquest: Woodrow Wilson, Religion, and the New World Order*. Chicago: University of Chicago Press, 2016.

Büttner, Urs. *Poiesis des 'Sozialen': Achim von Arnims frühe Poetik bis zur Heidelberger Romantik (1800–1808)*. Berlin: De Gruyter, 2015.

Buxton, William, and Lawrence Nichols. "Talcott Parsons and the 'Far East' at Harvard." *American Sociologist* 31, no. 2 (2000): 5–17.

Caciola, Nancy. *Discerning Spirits: Divine and Demonic Possession in the Middle Ages*. Ithaca: Cornell University Press, 2003.

Callewaert, Teresa. *Theologies Speak of Justice: A Study of Islamic and Christian Social Ethics*. Uppsala: Acta Universitatis Upsaliensis, 2017.

Callinicos, Alex. *Social Theory*. Cambridge: Polity, 2007.

Cameron, Alan, Jacqueline Long, and Sherry Lee. *Barbarians and Politics at the Court of Arcadius*. Oakland: University of California Press, 1993.

Cameron, Averil. "Mount Athos and the Byzantine World." In *Mount Athos: Microcosm of the Christian East*, edited by Graham Speake and Metropolitan Kallistos Ware, 11–28. Oxford: Peter Lang Verlag, 2012.

Campbell, Chloe. *Race and Empire*. New York: Manchester University Press, 2007.

Camus, Albert. *The Rebel*. Translated by Anthony Bower. New York: Alfred A. Knopf, 1954.

Cantwell Smith, Wilfred. *The Meaning and End of Religion: A New Approach to the Religious Traditions of Mankind*. New York: Macmillan, 1962.

Capps, Patrick. "Natural Law and the Law of Nations." In *Research Handbooks in International Law*, edited by Alexander Orakhelashvili, 61–92. Cheltenham: Edward Elgar, 2011.

Carrillo de Albornoz, Angel Francisco. *Roman Catholicism and Religious Liberty*. Geneva: World Council of Churches, 1959.

Carty, Anthony. *The Decay of International Law? A Reappraisal of the Limits of Legal Imagination in International Affairs*. Manchester: Manchester University Press, 1986.

Cassese, Antonio. *International Law*. 2nd ed. Oxford: Oxford University Press, 2005.

Cavallar, Georg. *Imperfect Cosmopolis: Studies in the History of International Legal Theory and Cosmopolitan Ideas*. Cardiff: University of Wales Press, 2011.

Certain Sermons or Homilies Appointed to be Read in Churches. London: Church of England, 1563.

Chakrabarty, Dipesh. *Provincializing Europe: Postcolonial Thought and Historical Difference*. Reissued with preface by author. Princeton: Princeton University Press, 2008.

Chamedes, Giuliana. *A Twentieth Century Crusade: The Vatican's Battle to Remake Christian Europe*. Cambridge, MA: Harvard University Press, 2019.

Chanock, Martin. *Law, Custom, and Social Order*. London: Cambridge University Press, 1985.

Chenu, Marie-Dominique. "*Officium*: Théologiens et canonistes." In *Études d'histoire du droit canonique dédiées à Gabriel Le Bras*. 2 vols, vol. 2, 835–39. Paris: Sirey, 1965.

Chibi, Andrew A. *Henry VIII's Bishops: Diplomats, Administrators, Scholars and Shepherds*. Cambridge: James Clarke & Co, 2003.

Chidester, David. *Empire of Religion*. Chicago: University of Chicago Press, 2014.

Ching, Julia. "Human Rights: A Valid Chinese Concept?" In *Confucianism and Human Rights*, edited by Wm. Theodore de Bary and Tu Weiming, 67–82. New York: Columbia University Press, 1998.

Chiniquy, Charles. *The Priest, the Woman, and the Confessional*. London: Gibson, 1874.

Chochran, Robert F., Jr., and Zachary R. Calo, eds. *Agape, Justice, and Law: How Mighty Christian Love Shape Law?* Cambridge: Cambridge University Press, 2017.

Chroust, Anton-Hermann. "The Corporate Idea and the Body Politic in the Middle Ages." *The Review of Politics* 9, no. 4 (1947): 423–52.

Chrysos, Evangelos. "Some Aspects of Roman-Persian Legal Relations." *Kleronomia* 8, Issue A (1976): 1–56.

"The Title Βασιλευς in in Early Byzantine International Relations." *Dumbarton Oaks Papers* 32 (1978): 29–75.

"Die Nordgrenze des Byzantinischen Reiches im 6. bis 8. Jahrhundert." In *Die Völker Südosteuropas im 6. bis 8. Jahrhundert*, edited by Bernhard Hänsel, 27–40. Munich: Südosteuropa Gesellschaft, 1987.

"Legal Concepts and Patterns for the Barbarians' Settlement on Roman Soil." In *Das Reich und die Barbaren*, edited by Evangelos Chrysos and Andreas Schwarcz, 13–24. Vienna: Böhlau, 1989.

"Perceptions of the International Community of States during the Middle Ages." In *Ethnogenese und Überlieferung*, edited by Karl Brunner, 293–307. Vienna: Oldenbourg, 1994.

"The Roman Political Identity in Late Antiquity and Early Byzantium." In *Byzantium – Identity, Image, Influence: Major Papers: XIX International Congress of Byzantine Studies, Copenhagen 18–24 August 1996*, edited by Karsten Fledelius and Peter Schreiner, 7–16. Copenhagen: Danish National Committee for Byzantine Studies, 1996.

"Conclusion: De foederatis iterum." In *Kingdoms of the Empire: The Integration of Barbarians in Late Antiquity*, edited by Walter Pohl, 185–206. Leiden: Brill, 1997.

"Byzantines and Foreigners." In *Fifty Years of Prosopography: The Later Roman Empire, Byzantium and Beyond*, edited by Averil Cameron, 119–36. Oxford: Oxford University Press, 2003.

"The Empire, the gentes and the regna." In *Regna and Gentes: The Relationship between Late Antique and Early Medieval Peoples and Kingdoms in the Transformation of the Roman World*, edited by Hans-Werner Goetz, Jörg Jarnut, and Walter Pohl, 13–19. Leiden: Brill, 2003.

Churchill, Winston. "Foreword." In *Europe Unites*. London: United Europe Movement, 1948.

Cicero, *De officiis*. Translated by Walter Miller. Cambridge, MA: Harvard University Press, 1913.

De inventione. Translated by C. D. Yonge. Whitefish, MT: Kessinger Publishing, 2004.

Clapham, Andrew. *Brierly's Law of Nations*. 7th ed. Oxford: Oxford University Press, 2012.

Clark, Christopher, and Wolfram Kaiser, eds. *Culture Wars*. Cambridge: Cambridge University Press, 2003.

Clarke, Peter D. *The Interdict in the Thirteenth Century: A Question of Collective Guilt*. Oxford: Oxford University Press, 2007.

Clayton, Lawrence, and David Lantigua, eds. *Bartolomé de las Casas and the Defense of Amerindian Rights: A Brief History with Documents*. Tuscaloosa: University of Alabama Press, 2020.

Coates, Benjamin Allen. *Legalist Empire: International Law and American Foreign Relations in the Early Twentieth Century*. New York: Oxford University Press, 2016.

Coates, P. D. *The China Consuls*. Hong Kong: Cambridge University Press, 1988.

Cobb, John B., Jr. "Alfred North Whitehead." In *Founders of Constructive Postmodern Philosophy: Peirce, James, Bergson, Whitehead, and Hartshorne*, edited by David Ray Griffin, John B. Cobb, Jr., Marcus P. Ford, Pete A. Y. Gunter, and Peter Ochs, 165–95. Albany: State University of New York Press, 1993.

Cobb, John B. *Transforming Christianity and the World: A Way beyond Absolutism and Relativism*. Maryknoll: Orbis Books, 1999.

Cohen, Felix S. "Transcendental Nonsense and the Functional Approach." *Columbia Law Review* 35 (1935): 809–49.

Cohen, Morris. "Property and Sovereignty." *Cornell Law Review* 13, no. 1 (1927): 8–30.

Collins, Richard. "Classical Legal Positivism in International Law Revisited." In *International Legal Positivism in a Post-Modern World*, edited by Jörg Kammerhofer and Jean d'Aspremont, 23–49. Cambridge: Cambridge University Press, 2014.

Condorelli, Orazio, ed. *Niccolò Tedeschi (Abbas Panormitanus) e i suoi Commentaria in Decretales*. Rome: Il Cigno Galileo Galilei, 2000.

Condorelli, Orazio. *"Unum corpus, diversa capita": Modelli di organizzazione e cura pastorale per una varietas ecclesiarum (secoli XI-XIV)*. Rome: Il Cigno Galileo Galilei, 2002.

Conner, Alison. "Anglo-American Law at Soochow." In *China's Christian Colleges*, edited by Daniel Bays and Ellen Widmer, 147–72. Stanford: Stanford University Press, 2009.

Cooper, Melinda. *Family Values: Between Neoliberalism and the New Social Conservatism*. New York: Zone Books, 2017.

Corbett, Percy Ellwood. "The Consent of States and the Sources of the Law of Nations." *British Yearbook of International Law* 6 (1925): 20–30.

The Study of International Law. New York: Doubleday, 1955.

Cornet, Enrico. *Le guerre dei Veneti nell' Asia 1470–1474: Documenti cavati dall' archivio ai Frari in Venezia*. Vienna: Tendler, 1856.

Cortés, Hernán. *Letters from Mexico*. Edited and translated by Anthony Pagden. New Haven: Yale University Press, 1986.

Cortright, David, and George A. Lopez. *The Sanctions Decade: Assessing UN Strategies in the 1990s*. Boulder: Lynne Rienner, 2000.

Cortright, David, and George A. Lopez, eds. *Smart Sanctions: Targeting Economic Statecraft*. Lanham: Rowman & Littlefield, 2002.

Costello, Cathryn, and Michelle Foster. "Non-refoulement as Custom and Jus Cogens? Putting the Prohibition to the Test." *Netherlands Yearbook of International Law* 46 (2015): 273–327. The Hague: T.M.C. Asser Press, 2016.

Crawford, James. *Chance, Order, Change: The Course of International Law*. Leiden: Brill, 2014.

Crawford, James, and Susan Marks. "The Global Democracy Deficit: An Essay in International Law and Its Limits." In *Re-imagining Political Community: Studies in Cosmopolitan Democracy*, edited by Daniele Archibugi, David Held, and Martin Köhler, 72–90. Stanford: Stanford University Press, 1998.

Creel, George. *How We Advertised America*. New York: Arno Press, 1972.

D'Amato, Anthony. "The Theory of Customary International Law." *Proceedings of the Annual Meeting (American Society of International Law)* 82 (1988): 242–60.

Danchin, Peter G. "Islam in the Secular *Nomos* of the European Court of Human Rights." *Michigan Journal of International Law* 32, no. 4 (2011): 663–747.

Daniell, David, ed. *Tyndale's New Testament*. New Haven: Yale University Press, 1989.

Davis, Adam. "The Social and Religious Meanings of Charity in Medieval Europe." *History Compass* 12, no. 12 (2014): 935–50.

Davis, Kathleen. *Periodization and Sovereignty: How Ideas of Feudalism and Secularization Govern the Politics of Time*. Philadelphia: University of Pennsylvania Press, 2017.

Deane, Hugh. *Good Deeds and Gunboats*. San Francisco: China Books & Periodicals, 1990.

Decock, Wim. *Theologians and Contract Law: The Moral Transformation of the Ius Commune (ca. 1500–1650)*. Leiden: Martinus Nijhoff Publishers, 2013.

DeCoursey, Matthew, ed. *The Thomas More/William Tyndale Polemic: A Selection*. Sheffield, UK: Early Modern Literary Studies, 2010.

de las Casas, Bartolomé. *Historia de las Indias*. Vol. 3. Mexico: Fondo de Cultura Económica, 1986.

In Defense of the Indians. Translated by Stafford Poole. Dekalb: Northern Illinois University Press, 1992.

De La Torre, Miguel A. *Embracing Hopelessness*. Minneapolis: Fortress Press, 2017.

deLisle, Jacques, and Avery Goldstein, eds. *China's Global Engagement: Cooperation, Competition, and Influence in the Twenty-First Century*. Washington, DC: The Brookings Institution, 2017.

Dell'Oro, Aldo. *I* libri de officio *nella giurisprudenza romana*. Milano: Giuffrè, 1960.

Denning, Margaret. "The American Missionary and U.S. China Policy during World War II." In *United States Attitudes and Policies toward China*, edited by Patricia Neils, 211–18. Armonk, NY: M. E. Sharpe, 1990.

Derrida, Jacques. *Writing and Difference*. Chicago: University of Chicago Press, 1978.

Derrida, Jacques, and Gianni Vattimo. *Religion*. Stanford: Stanford University Press, 1998.

Desautels-Stein, Justin. "The Rule of Law." In *Tipping Points in International Law: Commitment and Critique*, edited by John D. Haskell and Jean d'Aspremont. *Forthcoming*, Cambridge: Cambridge University Press, 2021.

Dingjan, François O. S. B. *Discretio: Les origines patristiques et monastiques de la doctrine sur la prudence chez Thomas d'Aquin*. Assen: Van Gorcum & Comp. N. V. – Dr. H. J. Prakke & H. M. G. Prakke, 1967.

Dirsch, Felix. *Authentischer Konservatismus*. Berlin: LIT, 2012.

Divine, Robert A. *Second Chance: The Triumph of Internationalism in America during World War II*. New York: Atheneum, 1967.

Doe, Norman, ed. *Christianity and Natural Law: An Introduction*. New York: Cambridge University Press, 2017.

Dölger, Franz. *Byzanz und die europäische Staatenwelt: Ausgewählte Vorträge und Aufsätze*. Darmstadt: Wissenschaftliche Buchgesellschaft, 1964.

Donahue, Charles. "Medieval and Early Modern Lex Mercatoria: An Attempt at the Probatio Diabolica." *Chicago Journal of International Law* 5, no. 1 (2004): 21–37.

"Benvenuto Stracca's De Mercatura: Was There a Lex Mercatoria in Sixteenth-Century Italy?" In *From Lex Mercatoria to Commercial Law*, edited by Vito Piergiovanni, 69–120. Berlin: Duncker & Humblot, 2005.

Dorais, Geneviève. "Missionary Critiques of Empire, 1920–1932: Between Interventionism and Anti-Imperialism." *The International History Review* 39, no. 3 (2017): 377–403.

Dorsett, Shaunnagh, and Shaun McVeigh. "An Essay on Jurisdiction, Jurisprudence, and Authority: The High Court of Australia in Yorta Yorta (2001)." *Northern Ireland Legal Quarterly* 56, no. 1 (2005): 1–20.

"Jurisprudences of Jurisdiction: Matters of Public Authority." *Griffith Law Review* 23, no. 4 (2014): 569–88.

Dostoyevsky, Fyodor. *The Brothers Karamazov*. Translated by Richard Pevear and Larissa Volokhonsky. New York: Vintage, 1990.

Dowling, Maria. *Humanism in the Age of Henry VIII*. London: Croom Helm, 1986.

Drew, Phillip. *The Law of Maritime Blockade*. Oxford: Oxford University Press, 2017.

Duffy, Eamon. "The Godly and the Multitude in Stuart England." *The Seventeenth Century* 1, no. 1 (1986): 31–55.

Dungan, David. *Constantine's Bible: Politics and the Making of the New Testament*. Minneapolis: Fortress Press, 2007.

Duranti, Marco. *The Conservative Human Rights Revolution: European Identity, Transnational Politics, and the Origins of the European Convention*. New York: Oxford University Press, 2017.

Durantus, Guillelmus. *Rationale divinorum officiorum*. 3 vols., vol. 2, edited by Anselme Davril and Timothy M. Thibodeau. Turnhout: Brepols, 1995–2000.

Durham, W. Cole, Jr., and Brett Scharffs. *Law and Religion: National, International and Comparative Perspectives*. 2nd ed. New York: Wolters Kluwer, 2019.

Dussel, Enrique. "Las Casas, Vitoria, and Suárez, 1514–1617." In *Human Rights from a Third World Perspective: Critique, History, and International Law*, edited by José-Manuel Barreto, 172–207. Newcastle upon Tyne: Cambridge Scholars Publishing, 2013.

Dvornik, Francis. *Early Christian and Byzantine Political Philosophy: Origins and Background*. 2 vols. Washington, DC: Dumbarton Oaks Center for Byzantine Studies, Trustees for Harvard University, 1966.

Dyson, R. W., ed. *Aquinas Political Writings*. Cambridge: Cambridge University Press, 2002.

Eagly, Ingrid V., and Steven Shafer. "A National Study of Access to Counsel in Immigration Court." *University of Pennsylvania Law Review* 164, no. 1 (2015): 1–91.

Echo-Hawk, Walter R. *In the Courts of the Conqueror: The 10 Worst Indian Law Cases Ever Decided*. Golden, CO: Fulcrum Publishing, 2010.

Eckel, Jan. *The Ambivalence of Good: Human Rights in International Politics Since the 1940s*. New York: Oxford University Press, 2019.

Eco, Umberto. *Faith in Fakes: Travels in Hyperreality*. London: Vintage, 1998 [1973].

Edwards, James R., Jr. "A Biblical Perspective on Immigration Policy." In *Debating Immigration*, edited by Carol Swain, 46–62. New York: Cambridge University Press, 2007.

Einarsen, Terje. "Drafting History of the 1951 Convention and the 1967 Protocol." In *The 1951 Convention Relating to the Status of Refugees and Its 1967 Protocol: A Commentary*, edited by Andreas Zimmermann, Felix Machts, and Jonas Dörschner, 37–73. Oxford: Oxford University Press, 2011.

Elias, Norbert. *The Civilizing Process*. Oxford: Blackwell, 1969.

Eliot, T. S. "The Waste Land." In *The Waste Land: Authoritative Text, Contexts, Criticism*, edited by Michael North, 5. New York: W.W. Norton & Company, 2001.

Eliyahu, Ashtor. *Levant Trade in the Later Middle Ages*. Princeton: Princeton University Press, 1983.
Emon, Anver M. *Islamic Natural Law Theories*. New York: Oxford University Press, 2010.
Emon, Anver, Mark Ellis, and Benjamin Glahn. *Islamic Law and International Human Rights Law*. Oxford: Oxford University Press, 2012.
Englander, David. *Poverty and Poor Law Reform in Nineteenth-Century Britain, 1834–1914: From Chadwick to Booth*. London: Routledge, 1998.
Erasmus, *The Education of a Christian Prince*. Edited by Lisa Jardine. Cambridge: Cambridge University Press, 1997.
Esmaeilli, Hossein, Marboe Irmgard, and Javaid Rehman. *The Rule of Law, Freedom of Expression and Islamic Law*. Oxford: Hart, 2017.
Eusebius. "Oration of Eusebius in Praise of Constantine." In *Church History, Life of Constantine the Great, and Oration in Praise of Constantine*. Translated by Ernest Cushing Richardson et al., 646–720. New York: Christian Literature Co., 1890.
Evans, Carolyn. *Freedom of Religion under the European Convention of Human Rights*. Oxford: Oxford University Press, 2001.
Evans, Malcolm D. *Religious Liberty and International Law in Europe*. New York: Cambridge University Press, 1997.
Executive Office of Immigration Review. *FY 2016 Statistics Yearbook*. Falls Church, VA: U.S. Department of Justice, 2017.
FY 2018 Statistics Yearbook. Falls Church, VA: U.S. Department of Justice, 2019.
Faitini, Tiziana. "Shaping the Profession: Some Thoughts on Office, Duty, and the Moral Problematisation of Professional Activities in the Counter-Reformation." *Journal of Early Modern Christianity* 7, no. 1 (2020): 177–200.
Fallon, R. H. "Legitimacy and the Constitution." *Harvard Law Review* 118, no. 6 (2005): 1787–835.
Fassbender, Bardo, and Anne Peters, eds. *The Oxford Handbook of the History of International Law*. Oxford: Oxford University Press, 2012. See especially Bardo Fassbender and Anne Peters, "Introduction: Towards a Global History of International Law," 1–24.
Fedele, Dante. "'Templorum praerogativae cum Legatorum domibus communicabantur:' Il tempio nel dibattito sull'inviolabilità della sede diplomatica nella prima età moderna." In *La territorializzazione del sacro: Valenza teologico-politica del tempio*, edited by Tiziana Faitini, 195–222. Brescia: Morcelliana, 2016.
"The Status of Ambassadors in Lucas de Penna's Commentary on the *Tres Libri*." *Tijdschrift voor Rechtsgeschiedenis* 84, no. 1–2 (2016): 165–92.
Naissance de la diplomatie moderne (XIIIe-XVIIe siècles): L'ambassadeur au croisement du droit, de l'éthique et de la politique. Baden-Baden: Nomos Verlag; Zürich: Dike Verlag, 2017.
"Religious Freedom and Diplomacy." In *The Wiley-Blackwell Encyclopedia of Diplomacy*. 4 vols., vol. 4, edited by Gordon Martel, 1597–1610. Hoboken, NJ: Wiley-Blackwell, 2018.
"Rosier, Bernard de (1400–1475)." In *The Wiley-Blackwell Encyclopedia of Diplomacy*. 4 vols., vol. 4, edited by Gordon Martel, 1654–58. Hoboken, NJ: Wiley-Blackwell, 2018.

Fedotov, Georgy Petrovich. "Eskhatologiya i kul'tura" [Eschatology and Culture]. *Novy Grad* [New City] 13 (1938): 45–56.

Fisch, Jörg. *The Right of Self-Determination of Peoples: The Domestication of an Illusion*. New York: Cambridge University Press, 2015.

Fitzgerald, David Scott. *Refuge beyond Reach: How Rich Democracies Repel Asylum Seekers*. New York: Oxford University Press, 2019.

Fitzmaurice, Andrew. *Sovereignty, Property and Empire, 1500–2000*. Cambridge: Cambridge University Press, 2014.

Fitzmaurice, G. G. *The General Principles of International Law Considered from the Standpoint of the Rule of Law*. The Hague: The Hague Academy of International Law, 1957.

Fitzpatrick, Matthew P. *Purging the Empire: Mass Expulsions in Germany, 1871–1914*. New York: Oxford University Press, 2015.

Flynn, Maureen. *Sacred Charity: Confraternities and Social Welfare in Spain, 1400–1700*. London: Palgrave Macmillan, 1989.

Foreign Relations of the United States, 1880–1881. Vol. 1. Washington, DC: Government Printing Office, 1880.

Foreign Relations of the United States, 1881–1882. Washington, DC: Government Printing Office, 1882.

Forrester, Katrina. *In the Shadow of Justice: Postwar Liberalism and the Remaking of Political Philosophy*. Princeton: Princeton University Press, 2019.

Forst, Rainer. *The Right to Justification: Elements of a Constructivist Theory of Justice*. New Directions in Critical Theory. Translated by Jeffrey Flynn. New York: Columbia University Press, 2012.

Foucault, Michel. *The History of Sexuality: An Introduction*. New York: Pantheon, 1978.

"Technologies of the Self." In *Technologies of the Self: A Seminar with Michel Foucault*, edited by Luther H. Martin, Huck Gutman, and Patrick H. Hutton, 16–49. London: Tavistock, 1988.

The Hermeneutics of the Subject: Lectures at the College de France, 1981–82. Edited by Frédéric Gros, translated by Graham Burchell. New York: Picador, 2001.

"19 February 1975." In *Abnormal: Lectures at the Collège de France, 1974–1975*. Edited by Valerio Marchetti and Antonella Salomoni, translated by Graham Burchell, 167–99. London: Verso, 2003.

"Society Must Be Defended": Lectures at the Collège de France, 1975–76. Edited by Mauro Bertani and Alessandro Fontana, translated by David Macey. New York: Picador, 2003.

Security, Territory, Population: Lectures at the Collège de France, 1977–1978. Edited by Michel Senellart, François Ewald, and Alessandro Fontana, translated by Graham Burchell. Basingstoke: Palgrave Macmillan, 2009.

The Government of Self and Others: Lectures at the Collège de France, 1982–1983. Edited by Frédéric Gros, François Ewald and Alessandro Fontana. New York: Picador/Palgrave Macmillan, 2011.

Abnormal: Lectures at the Collège de France 1974–1975. Edited by Graham Burchell. London: Verso, 2016.

Fraenkel, Ernst. *The Dual State: A Contribution to the Theory of Dictatorship*. New York: Octagon Books, 1969.

Franck, Thomas. *The Power of Legitimacy Among Nations*. Oxford: Oxford University Press, 1990.

Frank, William, ed. *Duns Scotus on the Will and Morality*. Washington, DC: Catholic University of America Press, 1997.

Freeman, Michael D. A., ed. *Lloyd's Introduction to Jurisprudence*. 6th ed. London: Sweet & Maxwell, 1994.

Frere, Walter, and William Kennedy. *Visitation Articles and Injunctions of the Period of the Reformation*. Vol. 3. London: Longmans, Green & Co, 1910.

Frick, Marie-Luisa, and Andreas Th. Muller, eds. *Islam and International Law: Engaging Self-Centrism from a Plurality of Perspectives*. Leiden: Brill, 2013.

Friedman, Jerome. "Jewish Conversion, the Spanish Pure Blood Laws and Reformation: A Revisionist View of Racial and Religious Antisemitism." *Sixteenth Century Journal* 18, no. 1 (1987): 3–30.

Friedmann Marquardt, Marie, Timothy J. Steigenga, Philip J. Williams, and Manuel A. Vásquez. *Living "Illegal": The Human Face of Unauthorized Immigration*. New York: New Press, 2011.

Friesel, Ofra. "Race versus Religion in the Making of the International Convention Against Racial Discrimination, 1965." *Law and History Review* 32, no. 2 (2014): 351–83.

Fromm, Erich. *The Fear of Freedom*. London: Routledge, 2001 [1942].

Fromont, Cecile. "Collecting and Translating Knowledge across Cultures: Capuchin Missionary Images of Early Modern Central Africa." In *Collecting Across Cultures: Material Exchanges in the Early Modern Atlantic World*, edited by Daniela Bleichmar and Peter Mancall, 134–54. Philadelphia: University of Pennsylvania Press, 2011.

Frost, Amanda. "Alienating Citizens." *Northwestern University Law Review Online* 114, no. 1 (2019): 241–67.

Fubini, Riccardo. "L'ambasciatore nel XV secolo: due trattati e una biografia (Bernard de Rosier, Ermolao Barbaro, Vespasiano da Bisticci)." *Mélanges de l'École française de Rome: Moyen-Âge* 108, no. 2 (1996): 649–51.

Fullerton, Maryellen. "Borders, Bans, and Courts in the European Union." *Roger Williams University Law Review* 23, no. 2 (2018): 393–418.

Gallagher, Clarence. *Church Law and Church Order in Rome and Byzantium: A Comparative Study*. Aldershot: Ashgate Variorum, 2002.

Gamwell, Franklin I. *The Meaning of Religious Freedom: Modern Politics and Democratic Resolution*. Albany: State University of New York Press, 1995.

Garloff, Katja. "Figures of Love in Romantic Antisemitism: Achim von Arnim." *German Quarterly* 80, no. 4 (2007): 427–48.

Gatrell, Peter. *The Making of the Modern Refugee*. Oxford: Oxford University Press, 2013.

Gauchet, Marcel. *The Disenchantment of the World: A Political History of Religion*. Translated by Oscar Burge. Princeton: Princeton University Press, 1997.

Gedicks, Frederick Mark. "True Lies: Canossa as Myth." *Journal of Contemporary Legal Issues* 21 (2013): 133–44.

Geest, Sjaak van der, and Jon Kirby. "The Absence of the Missionary in African Ethnography, 1930–65." *African Studies Review* 35, no. 3 (1992): 59–103.

Gennadius II, Patriarch of Constantinople. *Oeuvres complètes de Georges Scholarios*. Edited by Louis Petit, Xénophon A. Siderides, and Martın Jugie. Paris: Maison de la Bonne Presse, 1936.

Gentili, Alberico. *De iure belli libri tres*. Vol. 2. Translated by John C. Rolfe. Oxford: Clarendon Press, 1933.

Gerhard, Gesine. "Change in European Countryside: Peasants and Democracy in Germany 1935–1955." In *War, Agriculture, and Food: Rural Europe from the 1930s to the 1950s*, edited by Paul Brassley, Yves Segers, and Leen Van Molle, 195–209. New York: Routledge, 2012.

Ghanea, Nazila. "The 1981 UN Declaration on the Elimination of All Forms of Intolerance and of Discrimination Based on Religion or Belief: Some Observations." In *The Challenge of Religious Discrimination at the Dawn of the New Millennium*, edited by Nazila Ghanea, 9–31. Dordrecht: Springer, 2004.

Godefroy, Lucien. "Mensonge." In *Dictionnaire de théologie catholique: contenant l'exposé des doctrines de la théologie catholique, leurs preuves et leur histoire*, edited by Alfred Vacant et al., t. X, col. 555–69. Paris: Letouzey et Ané, 1903–72.

Goldmann, Lucien. *Immanuel Kant*. New York: Verso, 2011.

Gong, Gerrit. *The Standard of "Civilization" in International Society*. Oxford: Clarendon Press, 1984.

Goodman, Sarah. "Asking for Too Much: The Role of Corroborating Evidence in Asylum Proceedings in the United States and United Kingdom." *Fordham International Law Journal* 36, no. 6 (2013): 1733–66.

Goodwin-Gill, Guy S., and Jane McAdam. *The Refugee in International Law*. Oxford: Oxford University Press, 2007.

Gordon, Robert. "J. Willard Hurst and the Common Law Tradition in American Legal Historiography." *Law and Society Review* 10, no. 1 (1975): 9–55.

Goria, Fausto. "'Romani', cittadinanza ed estensione della legislazione imperiale nelle costituzioni di Giustiniano." In *La nozione di 'Romano' fra cittadinanza ed universalità: Atti del II seminario di studi storici da Roma alla terza Roma*, 277–342. Naples: E.S.I., 1984.

Gottofredo da Trani. *Summa Super Titulis Decretalium*. Aalen: Scientia Verlag, 1968 [1519].

Grabill, Joseph. *Protestant Diplomacy and the Near East*. Minneapolis: University of Minnesota Press, 1971.

Grafton, Anthony, and Lisa Jardine. *From Humanism to the Humanities: Education and the Liberal Arts in Fifteenth- and Sixteenth-Century Europe*. London: Duckworth, 1986.

Gratian, *The Treatise on Laws*. Translated by Augustine Thompson. Washington, DC: Catholic University of America Press, 1993.

Grayson, Cary T. *Woodrow Wilson: An Intimate Memoir*. New York: Holt, Rinehart, and Winston, 1960.

Greenberg, Udi. "Protestants, Decolonization, and European Integration, 1885–1961." *Journal of Modern History* 89, no. 2 (2017): 314–54.

"Catholics, Protestants, and the Tortured Path to Religious Liberty." *Journal of the History of Ideas* 79, no. 3 (2018): 461–79.

"Catholics, Protestants, and the Violent Birth of European Religious Pluralism." *American Historical Review* 124, no. 2 (2019): 511–38.

"Is Secularism Protestant? A Genealogy of a Critical Idea." *Journal of the American Academy of Religion* 88, no. 1 (2020): 74–91.

Greenblatt, Stephen. *Renaissance Self-Fashioning: From More to Shakespeare*. Chicago: University of Chicago Press, 1980.

Grelle, Francesco. "Le categorie dell'amministrazione tardoantica: *officia, munera, honores.*" In *Società romana e impero tardoantico*. Vol. 1, *Istituzioni ceti economie*, edited by Andrea Giardina, 37–56. Roma: Laterza, 1986.

Griffin, David Ray. "Introduction to SUNY Series in Constructive Postmodern Thought." In *Founders of Constructive Postmodern Philosophy: Peirce, James, Bergson, Whitehead, and Hartshorne*, edited by David Ray Griffin, John B. Cobb, Jr., Marcus P. Ford, Pete A. Y. Gunter, and Peter Ochs. Albany: State University of New York Press, 1993.

Process Theology: On Postmodernism, Morality, Pluralism, Eschatology, and Demonic Evil. Anoka, MN: Process Century Press, 2017.

Griffin, David Ray, ed. *Deep Religious Pluralism*. Louisville, KY: Westminster John Knox Press, 2005. See especially David Ray Griffin, "John Cobb's Whiteheadian Complementary Pluralism," 39–66.

Griffiths, Paul J. *Problems of Religious Diversity*. Oxford: Blackwell Publishing, 2001.

de Groot, Hugo. *De iure belli ac pacis*. Edited by B. J. A. de Kanter-van Hettinga Tromp. Leiden: Brill, 1939.

Grotius, Hugo. *De Jure Belli Ac Pacis Libri Tres*. Lausanne, 1625.

De Jure Belli ac Pacis Libri Tres (1646 edition), *The Classics of International Law*. Edited by James Brown Scott, translated by Francis Kelsey. Oxford: Clarendon Press, 1925.

"Adamus Exul." In *The Celestial Cycle*, edited by Watson Kirkconnell. Toronto: University of Toronto Press, 1952.

Prolegomena to the Law of War and Peace. Translated by Francis Kelsey. New York: Liberal Arts Press, 1957.

Meletius, Sive De Iis quae inter Christianos Conveniunt Epistola. Edited and translated by G. H. M. Posthumus Meyjes. Leiden: Brill, 1988.

The Freedom of the Seas. Kitchener: Batoche Books, 2000 [1609].

"Defense of Chapter V of the *Mare Liberum*." In *The Free Sea*, edited by David Armitage, 75–130. Indianapolis: Liberty Fund, 2004.

The Rights of War and Peace. Edited by Richard Tuck, translated by John Clarke. Indianapolis: Liberty Fund, 2005 [1625].

Commentary on the Law of Prize and Booty. Edited by Martine Julia van Ittersum, translated by John Clarke. Indianapolis: Liberty Fund, 2006 [1868].

Mare Liberum 1609–2009. Edited by Robert Feenstra. Leiden: Brill, 2009.

The Truth of the Christian Religion. Translated by John Clarke. Indianapolis: Liberty Fund, 2012 [1627].

Gruber, Mayer I. "André LaCocque, *Jesus the Central Jew*." *Review of Rabbinic Judaism* 22, no. 2 (2019): 277–307.

Grütters, Carolus. "The Return of the Children." In *Law and Judicial Dialogue on the Return of Irregular Migrants from the European Union*, edited by Madalina Moraru, Galina Cornelisse, and Philippe De Bruycker. Oxford: Hart, 2020.

Gu, Ming Dong. "Sinologism, the Western World View, and the Chinese Perspective." *Comparative Literature and Culture* 15, no. 2 (2013), https://doi.org/10.7771/1481-4374.2213.

Gullino, Giuseppe. "Vitale Lando." *Dizionario Biografico Degli Italiani* 63 (2004).

Gurney, Evan. "Thomas More and the Problem of Charity." *Renaissance Studies* 26, no. 2 (2012): 197–217.

Gurvitch, Georges. *Sociology of Law*. New York: Philosophical Library and Alliance Book Corporation, 1942.
Habermas, Jürgen. "Constitutional Democracy: A Paradoxical Union of Contradictory Principles?" *Political Theory* 29, no. 6 (2001): 766–81.
"The Concept of Human Dignity and the Realistic Utopia of Human Rights." *Metaphilosophy* 41, no. 4 (2010): 464–80.
Haentjes, A. H. *Hugo de Groot als godsdienstig Denker*. Amsterdam: Ploegsma, 1946.
Häring, Theodor. *The Ethics of the Christian Life*. Translated by James S. Hill. New York: G.P. Putnam's Sons, 1909.
Hale, Robert. "Coercion and Distribution in a Supposedly Non-Coercive State." *Political Science Quarterly* 38, no. 3 (1923): 470–94.
Hall, David L., and Roger T. Ames, *Thinking Through Confucius*. Albany: State University of New York Press, 1987.
Hamilton, Mark. *Jesus, King of Strangers: What the Bible Really Says About Immigration*. Grand Rapids, MI: William B. Eerdmans, 2019.
Hamlin, Hannibal. "The Bible." In *The Oxford Handbook of Early Modern English Literature and Religion*, edited by Andrew Hiscock and Helen Wilcox, 545–61. Oxford: Oxford University Press, 2017.
Hampton, Timothy. "What Is a Colony before Colonialism? Humanist and Antihumanist Concepts of Governmentality from Foucault to Montaigne." In *Early Modern Humanism and Postmodern Antihumanism in Dialogue*, edited by Jan Miernowski, 93–115. Switzerland: Palgrave Macmillan, 2016.
Harris, Jonathan. "Being a Byzantine after Byzantium: Hellenic Identity in Renaissance Italy." *Kambos: Cambridge Papers in Modern Greek* 8 (2000): 25–44.
Hartmann, Wilfried, and Kenneth Pennington, eds. *The History of Medieval Canon Law in the Classical Period, 1140–1234: From Gratian to the Decretals of Pope Gregory IX*. Washington, DC: Catholic University of America Press, 2008.
Hartwick, Wolf-Daniel. *Romantischer Antisemitismus: Von Klopstock bis Richard Wagner*. Göttingen: Vandenhoeck & Ruprecht, 2005.
Harvey, Barbara. *Living and Dying in England, 1100–1540*. Oxford: Clarendon Press, 1993.
Harvey, David. *The Limits to Capital*. London: Verso, 2006.
Haskell, John D. "Divine Immanence: The Evangelical Foundations of Modern Anglo-American Approaches to International Law." *Chinese Journal of International Law* 11, no. 3 (2012): 429–67.
"A Case in the Politics of Form: Yearbooks of International Law." *Netherlands Yearbook of International Law* 50 (2019): 21–35.
Haskell, John D., and Jessica Fish. "Law as Eschatology." *Journal of Catholic Legal Studies* 53, no. 2 (2014): 185–210.
Hathaway, James C. "The Global Cop-Out on Refugees." *International Journal of Refugee Law* 30, no. 4 (2018): 591–604.
Hayek, Friedrich A. *The Road to Serfdom*. London: Routledge, 1944.
"The Use of Knowledge in Society." *American Economic Review* 35 (1945): 519–30.
Heal, Felicity. "Reciprocity and Exchange in the Late Medieval Household." In *Bodies and Disciplines*. Vol. 9, edited by Barbara Hanawalt and David Wallace, new edition, 179–98. Minneapolis: University of Minnesota Press, 1996.
Held, David, and Anthony McGrew, eds. *The Global Transformations Reader: An Introduction to the Globalization Debate*. Cambridge: Polity Press, 2000. See

especially David Held and Anthony McGrew, "The Great Globalization Debate: An Introduction," 1–45; David Held, "International Law," 167–71; and David Held, "Regulating Globalization?," 420–30.

Hegel, G. W. F. *Hegel's Philosophy of Right*. Translated by T. M. Knox. Oxford: Clarendon Press, 1942 [1820].

The Philosophy of History Translated by J. Sibree. Kitchener, ON: Batoche Books, 2001 [1824].

Heilbroner, Robert. *The Worldly Philosophers: The Lives, Times and Ideas of the Great Economic Thinkers*. New York: Simon & Schuster, 2000.

Heimburger, Robert W. *God and the Illegal Alien*. New York: Cambridge University Press, 2018.

Helmholz, Richard H. *The Canon Law and Ecclesiastical Jurisdiction from 597 to the 1640s*. Oxford: Oxford University Press, 2004.

"The Law of Charity and the English Ecclesiastical Courts." In *The Foundations of Medieval English Ecclesiastical History*, edited by Philippa Hoskin, Christopher Brooke, and Barrie Dobson, 111–23. Woodbridge: Boydell Press, 2005.

The Spirit of Classical Canon Law. 3rd ed. Athens, GA: University of Georgia Press, 2010.

"University Education and English Ecclesiastical Lawyers 1400–1650." *Ecclesiastical Law Journal* 13, no. 2 (2011): 132–45.

Henkin, Louis. *International Law: Politics, Values and Functions*. The Hague: The Hague Academy of International Law, 1989.

Henne, Thomas, and Carsten Kretschmann, "Der Christlich Fundierte Antijudaismus Savignys und Seine Umsetzung in Der Rechtspraxis." *Zeitschrift der Savigny-Stiftung für Rechtsgeschichte: Germanistische Abteilung* 119, no. 1 (2002): 250–315.

Henry of Susa [Hostiensis]. *Summa*. Aalen: Scientia Verlag, 1962 [1537].

Herdt, Jennifer A. "Calvin's Legacy for Contemporary Reformed Natural Law." *Scottish Journal of Theology* 67, no. 4 (2014): 414–35.

Hergenröther, Joseph Adam Gustav. *Catholic Church and Christian State*. London: Burns and Oates, 1873.

Hertz, Deborah. "Dueling for Emancipation: Jewish Masculinity in the Era of Napoleon." In *Jüdische Welten: Juden in Deutschland vom 18. Jahrhundert bis in die Gegenwart*, edited by Marion A. Kaplan and Beate Meyer, 69–85. Göttingen: Wallstein Verlag, 2005.

Hertzke, Allan D., and Timothy Samuel Shah, eds. *Christianity and Freedom*. Vol. 2, *Contemporary Perspectives*. New York: Cambridge University Press, 2016.

Herzberg, Arno A. "The Situation of the Lawyer in Germany." *American Bar Association Journal* 27, no. 5 (1941): 294–5.

Hick, John. *Philosophy of Religion*. 2nd ed. Englewood Cliffs, NJ: Prentice-Hall, 1973.

Hilarion (Alfeyev), Metropolitan. *Tainstvo very: vvedeniye v pravoslavnoye dogmaticheskoye bogosloviye* [Sacrament of Faith: Introduction to Orthodox Dogmatic Theology]. Moscow: Izdatel'stvo bratstva svyatitelya Tikhona, 1996.

Hill, Thomas E. "The Kantian Conception of Autonomy." In *The Inner Citadel: Essays on Individual Autonomy*, edited by John Christman, 91–151. New York: Oxford University Press, 1989.

Hindle, Steve. *On the Parish? The Micro-politics of Poor Relief in Rural England c.1550–1750*. Oxford: Clarendon Press, 2004.

Hirschfeld Davis, Julie, and Michael D. Shear. *Border Wars: Inside Trump's Assault on Immigration*. New York: Simon & Shuster, 2019.
Hispalensis, Isidorus. *De officiis ecclesiasticis*. Edited by Christopher M. Lawson. Turnhout: Brepols, 1989.
Hobbes, Thomas. *Leviathan*. Edited by Richard Tuck. Cambridge: Cambridge University Press, 1991 [1651].
Hodgson, Godfrey. *The Colonel: The Life and Wars of Henry Stimson, 1867–1950*. New York: Knopf, 1990.
Hoffmann, Tobias. "Conscience and Synderesis." In *The Oxford Handbook of Aquinas*, edited by Brian Davies and Eleonore Stump, 255–64. Oxford: Oxford University Press, 2012.
Hoffmeier, James K. *The Immigration Crisis*. Wheaton, IL: Crossway, 2009.
Hogan, Linda. *Keeping Faith with Human Rights*. Washington, DC: Georgetown University Press, 2015.
Hollinger, David A. *After Cloven Tongues of Fire: Protestant Liberalism in Modern American History*. Princeton: Princeton University Press, 2013.
Protestants Abroad: How Missionaries Tried to Change the World but Changed America. Princeton: Princeton University Press, 2017.
Holthausen, Ferdinand, ed. *Vices and Virtues: Being a Soul's Confession of Its Sins with Reason's Description of the Virtues: A Middle-English Dialogue of about 1200 A.D.*, repr. London: Oxford University Press, 1967 [1888].
Hooker, Richard. *The Works of That Learned and Judicious Divine, Mr. Richard Hooker, in Eight Books of the Laws of Ecclesiastical Polity*. London: R. White, 1723.
Horkheimer, Max. "The Jews and Europe." *Zeitschrift für Sozialforschung* 7, no. 1–2 (1939): 115–37.
Horodowich, Elizabeth. *The Venetian Discovery of America*. Melbourne: Cambridge University Press, 2018.
Horwitz, Morton. *The Transformation of American Law, 1780–1860*. Cambridge, MA: Harvard University Press, 1979.
Houston, R. A. "What Did the Royal Almoner Do in Britain and Ireland, c.1450–1700?" *English Historical Review* 125, no. 513 (2010): 279–313.
Howland, Donald. *International Law and Japanese Sovereignty*. London: Palgrave Macmillan, 2016.
Howse, Robert. "The World Trade Organization 20 Years On: Global Governance by Judiciary." *European Journal of International Law* 27, no. 1 (2016): 9–77.
Huc, Evariste. *A Journey Through the Chinese Empire*. New York: Harper, 1856.
Hudson, Manley. "The Prospect for International Law in the 20th Century." *Cornell Law Quarterly* 10, no. 4 (1925): 419–59.
Hugh of Saint Victor. "De institutione novitiorum." In *L'œuvre de Hugues de Saint-Victor*, edited by Hugh B. Feiss and Patrice Sicard. Turnhout: Brepols, 1997.
Humphrey, John. *Human Rights and the United Nations: A Great Adventure*. New York: Transnational Publishers, 1984.
Human Rights Watch. *"At Least Let Them Work": The Denial of Work Authorization and Assistance for Asylum Seekers in the United States*. New York: Human Rights Watch, 2013.
Hunt, Michael H. *The Making of a Special Relationship: The United States and China to 1914*. New York: Columbia University Press, 1983.

Hurd, Elizabeth Shakman. *Beyond Religious Freedom: The New Global Politics of Religion*. Princeton: Princeton University Press, 2015.

Hussey, J. M. *The Orthodox Church in the Byzantine Empire*. Oxford: Clarendon Press, 1990.

Hutchison, William R. *Errand to the World: American Protestant Thought and Foreign Missions*. Chicago: University of Chicago Press, 1987.

Hyppolite, Jean. *Genesis and Structure of Hegel's Phenomenology of Spirit*. Evanston: Northwestern University Press, 1974.

Ignatieff, Michael. *Human Rights as Politics and Idolatry*. Edited by Amy Gutmann. Princeton: Princeton University Press, 2001.

Inboden, William. *Religion and American Foreign Policy, 1945–1960: The Soul of Containment*. New York: Cambridge University Press, 2008.

Innovation Law Lab. *Building the Resistance: Innovation Law Lab Impact Report*, 2018. https://innovationlawlab.org/reports/Impact-2018.pdf.

Invernizzi-Accetti, Carlo. "Catholic Social Doctrine and Human Rights: From Rejection to Endorsement?" *Humanity: An International Journal of Human Rights, Humanitarianism, and Development* 9, no. 2 (2018): 271–95.

Israel, Jonathan I. *Enlightenment Contested: Philosophy, Modernity, and the Emancipation of Man 1670–1752*. Oxford: Oxford University Press, 2008.

Ittersum, Martine Julia van. *Profit and Principle: Hugo Grotius, Natural Rights Theories and the Rise of Dutch Power in the East Indies 1595–1615*. Leiden: Brill, 2006.

Iustiniani Novellae, recognovit Rudolfus Schoell. Opus Schoellii morte interceptum absolvit Guilelmus Kroll (Corpus Iuris Civilis, vol. III). https://droitromain.univ-grenoble-alpes.fr/Corpus/Novellae.htm.

Jackson, Robert H. "The Challenge of International Lawlessness." *American Bar Association Journal* 27, no. 11 (1941): 690–3.

Jang, Wang Shik. "A Philosophical Evaluation of Western and Eastern Civilization from a Whiteheadian Perspective." *Process Studies* 33, no. 1 (2004): 135–48.

Janis, Mark W. "Sovereignty and International Law: Hobbes and Grotius." In *Essays in Honour of Wang Tieya*, edited by Ronald St. John Macdonald, 391–400. Dordrecht: Martinus Nijhoff, 1994.

Janis, Mark W., and Carolyn Evans, eds. *Religion and International Law*. The Hague: Martinus Nijhoff, 1999.

Jenkins, Allan K., and Patrick Preston. *Biblical Scholarship and the Church: A Sixteenth-Century Crisis of Authority*. Burlington, VT: Ashgate, 2007.

Jenkins, Philip. *Jesus Wars: How Four Patriarchs, Three Queens, and Two Emperors Decided What Christians Would Believe for the Next 1,500 Years*. New York: HarperOne, 2011.

Jennings, Willie James. *The Christian Imagination: Theology and the Origins of Race*. New Haven: Yale University Press, 2011.

Jensen, Steven L. B. *The Making of International Human Rights: The 1960s, Decolonization, and the Reconstruction of Global Values*. New York: Cambridge University Press, 2016.

Jessup, Philip C. *Elihu Root*. Vol. 1. New York: Dodd, Mead, 1938.

Jia, Bing Bing. *International Case Law in the Development of International Law*. The Hague: The Hague Academy of International Law, 2015.

Johns, Fleur, Richard Joyce, and Sundhya Pahuja. *Events*. Oxford: Routledge, 2011.

Johnson, Luke Timothy. "Religious Rights and Christian Texts." In *Religious Human Rights in Global Perspective*. Vol. 1, *Religious Perspectives*, edited by John Witte, Jr., and Johan D. van der Vyver, 65–95. The Hague: Martinus Nijhoff, 1996.

Johnson, William Alexander. *On Religion: A Study of the Theological Method in Schleiermacher and Nygren*. Leiden: Brill, 1963.

Johnston, Anna. *Missionary Writing and Empire, 1800–1860*. New York: Cambridge University Press, 2003.

Johnstone, Andrew. "Isolationism and Internationalism in American Foreign Relations." *Journal of Transatlantic Studies* 9, no. 1 (March 2011): 7–20.

Against Immediate Evil: American Internationalists and the Four Freedoms on the Eve of World War II. Ithaca: Cornell University Press, 2014.

Jolly, Roslyn. "Robert Louis Stevenson, Henry Maine and the Anthropology of Comparative Law." *Journal of British Studies* 45, no. 3 (2006): 556–80.

Jones, Gareth H. *History of the Law of Charity, 1532–1827*. Cambridge: Cambridge University Press, 1969.

Jouannet, Emmanuelle. *Vattel and the Emergence of Classical International Law*. Oxford: Hart, 2017.

Joyce, Richard. *Competing Sovereignties*. New York: Routledge, 2012.

Kalaitzidis, Pantelis. *Orthodoxy and Political Theology*. Geneva: World Council of Churches, 2012.

"Towards an Orthodox Political Theology: The Churches' Theological Foundations and Public Role in the Context of the Greek Economic Crisis." In *Political Theologies in Orthodox Christianity: Common Challenges, Divergent Positions*, edited by Kristina Stoeckl, Gabriel Ingeborg, and Aristotle Papanikolaou, 151–78. London: Bloomsbury T&T Clark, 2017.

Kammerhofer, Jörg, and Jean d'Aspremont, eds. *International Legal Positivism in a Post-Modern World*. Cambridge: Cambridge University Press, 2014.

Kanstroom, Daniel. *Deportation Nation: Outsiders in American History*. Cambridge, MA: Harvard University Press, 2010.

Kant, Immanuel. *Groundwork of the Metaphysics of Morals*. Translated by H. J. Paton. New York: Harper & Row, 1964 [1785].

Lectures on Philosophical Theology. Translated by Allen W. Wood and Gertrude M. Clark. Ithaca: Cornell University Press, 1978.

Kantorowicz, Ernst H. *The King's Two Bodies: A Study in Medieval Political Theology*. Princeton: Princeton University Press, 2016 [1957].

Kaplan, Benjamin J. "Diplomacy and Domestic Devotion: Embassy Chapels and the Toleration of Religious Dissent in Early Modern Europe." *Journal of Early Modern History* 6, no. 4 (2002): 341–61.

Kapur, Ratna. "The 'Ayodhya' Case: Hindu Majoritarianism and the Right to Religious Liberty." *Maryland Journal of International Law* 29, no. 1 (2014): 305–65.

Kaser, Max. *Ius gentium*. Cologne: Böhlau, 1993.

Kazin, Michael. *A Godly Hero: The Life of William Jennings Bryan*. New York: Knopf, 2007.

Keal, Paul. *European Conquest and the Rights of Indigenous Peoples: The Moral Backwardness of International Society*. Cambridge: Cambridge University Press, 2003.

Kearns, David, and Ryan Walter. "Office, Political Theory, and the Political Theorist." *Historical Journal* (2019): 1–21.

Keith, Arthur Berriedale, ed. *The Belgian Congo and the Berlin Act*. Oxford: Clarendon Press, 1919.

Keller, Adolf. *Christian Europe Today*. New York: Harper, 1942.

Kelley, Patrick William. "Human Rights and Christian Responsibility: Transnational Christian Activism, Human Rights, and State Violence in Brazil and Chile in the 1970s." In *Religious Responses to Violence: Human Rights in Latin America Past and Present*, edited by Alexander Wilde, 95–122. Notre Dame: University of Notre Dame Press, 2015.

Kelly, J. M. *A Short History of Western Legal Theory*. Oxford: Clarendon Press, 1992.

Kennedy, David. "Images of Religion in International Legal Theory." In *The Influence of Religion on the Development of International Law*, edited by Mark W. Janis, 137–45. Dordrecht: Martinus Nijhoff, 1991.

"A New World Order: Yesterday, Today, and Tomorrow." *Transnational Law Contemporary Problems* 4, no. 2 (1994): 329–76.

"When Renewal Repeats: Thinking against the Box." *NYU Journal of International Law & Politics* 32, no. 2 (2000): 335–500.

Kennedy, Duncan. "Form and Substance in Private Law Adjudication." *Harvard Law Review* 89, no. 8 (1976): 1685–1778.

A Critique of Adjudication (fin de siècle). Cambridge, MA: Harvard University Press, 1997.

"Savigny's Family/Patrimony Distinction and Its Place in the Global Genealogy of Classical Legal Thought." *American Journal of Comparative Law* 58, no. 4 (2010): 811–42.

"Three Globalizations of Law and Legal Thought: 1850–2000." In *The New Law and Economic Development: A Critical Appraisal*, edited by David Trubek and Alvaro Santos, 19–73. Cambridge: Cambridge University Press, 2006.

Kenny, Anthony. *Medieval Philosophy*. Oxford: Oxford University Press, 2005.

The Rise of Modern Philosophy. Oxford: Oxford University Press, 2006.

Kessler, Lawrence. "Foreign Missions and Home Support." In *United States Attitudes and Policies toward China*, edited by Patricia Neils, 78–96. Armonk, NY: M. E. Sharpe, 1990.

Kidd, Thomas. *Who Is an Evangelical? The History of a Movement in Crisis*. New Haven: Yale University Press, 2019.

Kimball, Warren F. *The Juggler: Franklin Roosevelt as Wartime Statesman*. Princeton: Princeton University Press, 1991.

Kingsbury, Benedict, and Benjamin Straumann. "The State of Nature and Commercial Sociability in Early Modern International Legal Thought." *Grotiana* 31, no. 1 (2010): 22–43.

Klare, Karl. "Contracts Jurisprudence and the First-Year Casebook." *New York University Law Review* 54 (1979): 876–99.

van Kleffens, E. N. *Sovereignty in International Law: Five Lectures*. The Hague: The Hague Academy of International Law, 1953.

Klenner, Hermann. "Savigny's Research Program of the Historical School of Law and Its Intellectual Impact in 19th Century Berlin." *American Journal of Comparative Law* 37, no. 1 (1989): 67–80.

Knox, Dilwyn. "Disciplina: The Monastic and Clerical Origins of European Civility." In *Renaissance Society and Culture*, edited by Ronald G. Musto and John Monfasani, 107–36. New York: Italica, 1991.

Knuuttila, Simo. "Duns Scotus and the Foundations of Logical Modalities." In *John Duns Scotus: Metaphysics and Ethics*, edited by Ludger Honnefelder, Rega Wood, and Mechthild Dreyer, 127–43. New York: Oxford University Press, 1996.

Koder, Johannes, and Ioannis Stouraitis. *Byzantine War Ideology between Roman Imperial Concept and Christian Religion: Akten Des Internationalen Symposiums (Vienna, 19–21 May 2011)*. Vienna: Verlag der Österreichischen Akademie der Wissenschaften, 2012.

Koeck, Heribert Franz. "Holy Places." In *Max Planck Encyclopedia of Public International Law*, edited by Rüdiger Wolfrum. Oxford: Oxford University Press, 2008.

Koenigsberger, Helmut. "The Unity of the Church and the Reformation." *Journal of Interdisciplinary History* 1, no. 3 (1971): 407–17.

Konstantin, Antonov. "Politicheskoe izmerenie russkoy religioznoy filosofii" [The Political Dimension of Russian Religious Philosophy]. *Gosudarstvo, Religiia, Tserkov' v Rossii i za Rubezhom* [State, Religion and Church in Russia and Worldwide] 32, no. 3 (2014): 265–94.

Koskenniemi, Martti. *The Gentle Civilizer of Nations: The Rise and Fall of International Law, 1870–1960*. New York: Cambridge University Press, 2001.

From Apology to Utopia: The Structure of International Legal Argument. Cambridge: Cambridge University Press, 2006.

"Empire and International Law: The Real Spanish Contribution." *University of Toronto Law Journal* 61, no. 1 (2011): 1–36.

"Histories of International Law: Dealing with Eurocentrism." *Rechtsgeschichte* 19 (2011): 152–77.

"Introduction" to *The Function of Law in the International Community*, by Hersch Lauterpacht, xxix–xlvii. Oxford: Oxford University Press, 2011.

"Vitoria and Us: Thoughts on Critical Histories of International Law." *Rechtsgeschichte: Zeitschrift des Max-Planck-Instituts für europäische Rechtsgeschichte* 22 (2014): 119–38.

"Sovereignty, Property and Empire: Early Modern English Contexts." *Theoretical Inquiries in Law* 18, no. 2 (2017): 355–89.

"Imagining the Rule of Law: Rereading the Grotian 'Tradition'." *European Journal of International Law* 30, no. 1 (2019): 17–52.

"Enchanted by the Tools? An Enlightenment Perspective." *American University International Law Review* 35, no. 3 (2020): 397–426.

Koskenniemi, Martti, Mónica García-Salmones Rovira, and Paolo Amorosa, eds. *International Law and Religion: Historical and Contemporary Perspectives*. Oxford: Oxford University Press, 2017. See especially Martti Koskenniemi, "International Law and Religion: No Stable Ground," 3–21.

Koskenniemi, Martti, Walter Rech, and Manuel Jimenez Fonseca, eds. *International Law and Empire: Historical Explorations*. Oxford: Oxford University Press, 2017.

Kossman, E. H., and A. F. Mellink, eds. *Texts Concerning the Revolt of the Netherlands*. Cambridge: Cambridge University Press, 1974.

Krisch, Nico. "The Decay of Consent: International Law in the Age of Global Public Goods." *American Journal of International Law* 108, no. 1 (2014): 1–40.

Krishnaswami, Arcot. *Study of Discrimination in the Matter of Religious Rights and Practices*. New York: United Nations, 1960.

Kroncke, Jedidiah J. "The Flexible Orientalism of Islamic Law." *UCLA Journal of Islamic and Near Eastern Law* 4, no. 1 (2005): 41–73.

"Law and Development as Anti-Comparative Law." *Vanderbilt Journal of Transnational Law* 40, no. 2 (2012): 477–555.

The Futility of Law and Development: China and the Dangers of Exporting American Law. New York: Oxford University Press, 2016.

Kulka, Otto D. "The Critique of Judaism in Modern European Thought: Genuine Factors and Demonic Perceptions." In *Demonizing the Other: Antisemitism, Racism and Xenophobia*, edited by Robert S. Wistrich, 197–209. London: Routledge, 1999.

Kurz, Nathan. "'A Sphere above the Nations?' The Rise and Fall of International Jewish Human Rights Politics, 1945–1975." PhD dissertation, Yale University, 2015.

Kuttner, Stephan. "Joannes Andreae and His Novella on the Decretals of Gregory IX." *The Jurist* 24 (1964): 393–408.

Kyrlezhev, Alexander, Andrey Shishkov, and Vladimir Shmaliy. "Dialog religii i nauki: novye podhody (itogi diskussii)" [The Dialogue of Religion and Science: New Approaches (An Overview)]. *Gosudarstvo, Religiia, Tserkov' v Rossii i za Rubezhom* [State, Religion and Church in Russia and Worldwide] 33, no. 1 (2015): 164–83.

Lachaud, Frédérique. *L'éthique du pouvoir au Moyen-Âge: L'office dans la culture politique (Angleterre, vers 1150-vers 1330)*. Paris: Garnier, 2010.

LaCocque, André. "Jesus's Hermeneutics of the Law, Reading the Parable of the Good Samaritan." In *Creation, Life and Hope: Essays in Honor of Jacques Doukhan*, edited by Jiri Moskala. Berrien Springs, MI: Seventh Day Adventist Theological Seminary, 2000.

Jesus, the Central Jew: His Times and His People. Atlanta: SBL Press, 2015.

Lacroix, Justine, and Jean-Yves Pranchère. *Human Rights on Trial: A Genealogy of the Critique of Human Rights*. New York: Cambridge University Press, 2018.

Laderman, Charlie. *Sharing the Burden: The Armenian Question, Humanitarian Intervention, and Anglo-American Visions of Global Order*. New York: Oxford University Press, 2019.

LaFeber, Walter. *The New Cambridge History of American Foreign Relations*. Vol. 2, *The American Search for Opportunity, 1865–1913*. Cambridge: Cambridge University Press, 2013.

Lahusen, Benjamin. *Alles Recht geht vom Volksgeist aus: Friedrich Carl v. Savigny und die moderne Rechtswissenschaft*. Berlin: Nicolaische Verlagsbuchhandlung, 2013.

Lai, Junnan. "Sovereignty and 'Civilization': International Law and East Asia in the Nineteenth Century." *Modern China* 40, no. 3 (2014): 282–314.

Lambert, Gregg. *Return Statements: The Return of Religion in Contemporary Philosophy*. Edinburgh: Edinburgh University Press, 2016.

Langland, William. *The Vision of William Concerning Piers the Plowman* [1377]. Edited by Walter W. Skeat. Oxford: Clarendon Press, 1874.

Piers the Ploughman. London: Penguin Books, 1959.

Lantigua, David. *Infidels and Empires in a New World Order: Early Modern Spanish Contributions to International Legal Thought*. Cambridge: Cambridge University Press, 2020.

Lapradelle, Albert-Geouffre de. *Les Principes Généraux du Droit International*. Paris: Centre Européen de la Dotation Carnegie, 1932.

Lauterpacht, Elihu, and Daniel Bethlehem. "The Scope and Content of the Principle of Non-refoulement: Opinion." In *Refugee Protection in International Law: UNHCR's Global Consultations on International Protection*, edited by Erika Feller, Volker Türk, and Frances Nicholson, 87–177. Cambridge: Cambridge University Press, 2003.

Laveley, Emile de. "The Clerical Party in Belgium." *Fortnightly Review* 18 (1872): 503–18.

Lavenia, Vincenzo. "Martín De Azpilcueta (1492–1586): Un Profilo." *Archivio Italiano Per La Storia Della Pietà* 16 (2003): 15–148.

Lazikani, Ayoush S. *Cultivating the Heart: Feeling and Emotion in Twelfth- and Thirteenth-Century Religious Texts*. Cardiff: University of Wales Press, 2015.

Lefebvre, Alexandre. *Human Rights and the Care of the Self*. Durham, NC: Duke University Press, 2018.

Leff, Arthur. "Unspeakable Ethics, Unnatural Law." *Duke Law Journal* 28, no. 6 (1979): 1229–49.

Leibniz, Gottfried Wilhelm. "Codex Iuris Gentium." In *Leibniz: Political Writings*, 2nd ed., edited by Patrick Riley, 65–176. Cambridge: Cambridge University Press, 1988.

Leopold, Richard William. *Elihu Root and the Conservative Tradition*. Boston: Little, Brown, 1954.

Lepine, David. "Cathedrals and Charity: Almsgiving at English Secular Cathedrals in the Later Middle Ages." *English Historical Review* 126, no. 522 (2011): 1066–96.

Lerner, Natan. "Proselytism, Change of Religion, and International Human Rights." *Emory International Law Review* 12, no. 1 (1998): 477–561.

Lesaffer, Randall. "Roman Law and the Intellectual History of International Law." In *The Oxford Handbook of the Theory of International Law*, edited by Anne Orford and Florian Hoffmann. Oxford: Oxford University Press, 2016.

"Letter of King Duarte to Eugenius IV." In *The Expansion of Europe: The First Phase*, edited by James Muldoon. Philadelphia: University of Pennsylvania Press, 1977.

Lewis, Thomas A. "Cultivating Our Intuitions: Hegel on Religion, Politics, and Public Discourse." *Journal of the Society of Christian Ethics* 27, no. 1 (2007): 205–24.

Lindkvist, Linde. *Religious Freedom and the Universal Declaration of Human Rights*. New York: Cambridge University Press, 2017.

Lipsius, Justus. *Politica: Six Books of Politics Or Political Instruction*. Edited and translated by Jan Waszink. Assen: Van Gorcum, 2004.

Liu, Lydia H. "Shadows of Universalism: The Untold Story of Human Rights around 1948." *Critical Inquiry* 40, no. 4 (2014): 385–417.

Lloyd, Howell A. "Constitutional Thought in Sixteenth-Century France: The Case of Pierre Rebuffi." *French History* 8, no. 3 (1994): 259–75.

Locke, John. *A Letter Concerning Toleration*. Edited by Mario Montuori. The Hague: Martinus Nijhoff, 1963 [1689].

Lockhart, Laurence, Raimondo Morozzo Della Rocca, and Maria Francesca Tiepolo, eds. *I Viaggi in Persia Degli Ambasciatori Veneti Barbaro E Contarini*. Rome: Istituto Poligrafico dello Stato, Libreria dello Stato, 1973.

Loeffler, James. *Rooted Cosmopolitans: Jews and Human Rights in the Twentieth Century*. New Haven: Yale University Press, 2018.

Lopez, Robert S. *The Commercial Revolution of the Middle Ages, 950–1350*. Englewood Cliffs, NJ: Prentice Hall, 1971.

Lorca, Arnulf Becker. "Universal International Law: Nineteenth-Century, Histories of Imposition and Appropriation." *Harvard Journal of International Law* 51, no. 2 (2010): 475–552.

"Eurocentrism in the History of International Law." In *Oxford Handbook History of International Law*, edited by Bardo Fassbender and Anne Peters, 1034–57. Oxford: Oxford University Press, 2012.

Lorimer, James. *The Institutes of the Laws of Nations*. Edinburgh: T. & T. Clark, 1872.

Lovegrove, Deryck W. *Established Church, Sectarian People: Itinerancy and the Transformation of English Dissent, 1780–1830*. Cambridge: Cambridge University Press, 1988.

Lovin, Robin. "Authority, Legitimacy and Sovereignty: Religion and Politics in the Roman Empire before Constantine." *Studies in Christian Ethics* 29, no. 2 (2016): 177–89.

Lowe, Vaughan. "The Iraq Crisis: What Now?" *International and Comparative Law Quarterly* 52 (2003): 859–71.

International Law. Oxford: Oxford University Press, 2007.

Lubac, Henri de. *Corpus Mysticum: The Eucharist and the Church in the Middle Ages*. Translated by Gemma Simmonds, Richard Price, and Christopher Stephens. London: SCM-Notre Dame University Press, 2006.

Luther, Martin. "Bondage of the Free Will." In *Discourse on the Will*. Translated and edited by Ernst Winter. London: Continuum, 2002.

Luther, Martin, and Desiderius Erasmus. *Luther and Erasmus: On the Bondage of the Will and on the Freedom of the Will*. Edited by E. G. Rupp and P. S. Watson. London, 1969.

Lyndwood, William. *Lyndwood's Provincial*. Edited by John Bullard and Bell Chalmer. London: Faith Press Ltd, 1929.

MacCulloch, Diarmaid. *Christianity, the First Three Thousand Years*. New York: Viking, 2009.

Macherey, Pierre. *A Theory of Literary Production*. London: Routledge, 1978.

Mahmood, Saba. *Religious Freedom in a Secular Age: A Minority Report*. Princeton: Princeton University Press, 2015.

Malalas, John. *The Chronicle of John Malalas: A Translation*. Translated by Elizabeth Jeffreys, Michael Jeffreys, Roger Scott, and Brian Croke. Melbourne: Australian Association for Byzantine Studies, 1986.

Malanczuk, Peter, ed. *Akehurst's Modern Introduction to International Law*. 7th rev. ed. London: Routledge, 1997.

Malik, Charles H. "Human Rights and Religious Liberty." *Ecumenical Review* 1, no. 4 (1949): 404–9.

"Asia and Africa Ask Searching Questions." *Presbyterian Life* 5, no. 24 (1954): 7–9, 36.

Malipiero, Domenico. "Annali veneti dall'anno 1457 al 1500." In *Archivio Storico Italiano* 7. Firenze: Gio. Pietro Viesseux, 1843.

Manela, Erez. *The Wilsonian Moment: Self-Determination and the International Origins of Anticolonial Nationalism*. New York: Oxford University Press, 2007.

Mann, Michael. *The Sources of Social Power*. Vol. 3, *Global Empires and Revolution, 1890–1945*. Cambridge: Cambridge University Press, 2012.

Manning, Stephen, and Juliet Stumpf. "Big Immigration Law." *UC Davis Law Review* 52, no. 1 (2018): 407–34.

Marcocci, Giuseppe. "Trading with the Muslim World: Religious Limits and Proscriptions in the Portuguese Empire (c.1480–1570)." In *Religion and Trade: Cross-Cultural Exchanges in World History, 1000–1900*, edited by Cátia Antunes, Leor Halevi, and Francesca Trivellato, 91–107. New York: Oxford University Press, 2014.

Maritain, Jacques. *Man and the State*. Chicago: University of Chicago Press 1951, repr. 1998.

Marks, Susan. *The Riddle of All Constitutions: International Law, Democracy, and the Critique of Ideology*. Oxford: Oxford University Press, 2000.

Marquardus de Susannis. *Tractatus de Judaeis et aliis infidelibus*. Venice, 1558.

Marrone, Stephen. "Revisiting Duns Scotus and Henry of Ghent on Modality." In *John Duns Scotus: Metaphysics and Ethics*, edited by Ludger Honnefelder, Rega Wood, and Mechthild Dreyer, 175–89. New York: Oxford University Press, 1996.

Marsden, R. G. "Naval or Victualling Stores: The Right of Pre-Emption." *Journal of the Society of Comparative Legislation* 4, no. 1 (1902): 45–50.

Marsh, Robert. "Weber's Misunderstanding of Traditional Chinese Law." *American Journal of Sociology* 106, no. 2 (2000): 281–302.

Martz, Linda. *Poverty and Welfare in Habsburg Spain*. Cambridge: Cambridge University Press, 1983.

Marx, Karl. "The Philosophical Manifesto of the Historical School of Law." First published in the Supplement to the *Rheiniche Zeitung* No. 221, August 9 (1842). https://marxists.catbull.com/archive/marx/works/1842/08/09.htm.

Mattingly, Garrett. *Renaissance Diplomacy*. Boston: Houghton Mifflin, 1955.

Maurer, Noel. *The Empire Trap: The Rise and Fall of U.S. Intervention to Protect American Property Overseas, 1893–2013*. Princeton: Princeton University Press, 2013.

Mawani, Renisa. "Law, Settler Colonialism, and 'the Forgotten Space' of Maritime Worlds." *Annual Review of Law and Social Science* 12 (2016): 107–31.

Максимов, Юрий Валерьевич. [Maximov, Yuri Valerievich] *Византийские Сочинения Об Исламе: Антимусульманская Апологетическая Литература Vii–Xv Вв*. [Byzantine Writings On Islam: Anti-Muslim Apologetic Literature Vii–Xv Centuries] Vol. 1. Изд-во СПбГУ [St. Petersburg: SPbSU Publishing House], 2006.

Maxwell, David. "The Missionary Movement in African and World History." *Historical Journal* 58, no. 4 (2015): 901–30.

Mazower, Mark. *No Enchanted Palace: The End of Empire and the Ideological Origins of the United Nations*. Princeton: Princeton University Press, 2009.

McClure, Julia. "The Charitable Bonds of the Spanish Empire: The Casa De Contratación as an Institution of Charity." *New Global Studies* 12, no. 2 (2018): 157–74.

McConnell, Michael, Robert Cochran Jr., and Angela Carmella, eds. *Christian Perspectives on Legal Thought*. New Haven: Yale University Press, 2001.

McDougall, Walter A. *Promised Land, Crusader State: The American Encounter with the World since 1776*. Boston: Houghton Mifflin, 1997.

McEachern, Claire. *The Poetics of English Nationhood, 1590–1612*. Cambridge: Cambridge University Press, 1996.

McIntosh, Marjorie. *Controlling Misbehavior in England, 1370–1600*. Cambridge: Cambridge University Press, 1998.
McLoughlin, William. *Revivals, Awakenings and Reform*. Chicago: University of Chicago Press, 1978.
McNair, Arnold. "So-Called State Servitudes." *British Yearbook of International Law* 6 (1925): 111–27.
McVeigh, Shaun. "Office and the Conduct of the Minor Jurisprudent." *UC Irvine Law Review* 5, no. 1 (2015): 499–511.
Mead, Walter. *Special Providence*. New York: Routledge, 2002.
Meade, Walter Russell. *God and Gold: Britain, America and the Making of the Modern World*. New York: Alfred A. Knopf, 2008.
Mediolanensis, Ambrosius. *De officiis*. Translated by Ivor J. Davidson. Oxford: Oxford University Press, 2002.
Melloni, Alberto. *Innocenzo IV: La Concezione E L'esperienza Della Cristianità Come Regimen Unius Personae*. Vol. 4. Genova: Marietti, 1990.
Ménager, Daniel. *L'ange et l'ambassadeur. Diplomatie et théologie à la Renaissance*. Paris: Garnier, 2013.
Mertens, Bernd. *Gönner, Feuerbach, Savigny: Über Deutungshoheit und Legendenbildung in der Rechtsgeschichte*. Tübingen: Mohr Siebeck, 2018.
Metropolitan Museum of Art, New York. *Byzantium and Islam: Age of Transition, 7th–9th Century*. Edited by Brandie Ratliff and Helen C. Evans. New York: Metropolitan Museum of Art, 2012.
Meyendorff, John. *The Primacy of Peter*. London: Faith Press, 1963.
"Pentarchy." In *Dictionary of the Middle Ages*, edited by Joseph R. Strayer. New York: Charles Scribner's Sons, 1982.
Michaels, Ralf. "Globalizing Savigny? The State in Savigny's Private International Law and the Challenge from Europeanization and Globalization." In *Aktuelle Fragen zu politischer und rechtlicher Steuerung im Kontext der Globalisierung*, edited by Michael Stolleis and Wolfgang Streeck, 119–144. Baden-Baden: Nomos, 2007.
Michaud, Maud. "The Missionary and the Anthropologist." *Studies in World Christianity* 22, no. 1 (2016): 57–74.
Miegge, Giovanni. *Religious Liberty*. New York: Associated Press, 1957.
Miller, Jon, and Gregory Stanczak. "Redeeming, Ruling, and Reaping: British Missionary Societies, the East India Company, and the India-to-China Opium Trade." *Journal for the Scientific Study of Religion* 48, no. 2 (2009): 332–52.
Mills, Matthew. "The Development of the Public Benefit Requirement for Charitable Trusts in the Nineteenth Century." *Journal of Legal History* 37, no. 3 (2016): 269–302.
Mitchell, Maria. *The Origins of Christian Democracy*. Ann Arbor: University of Michigan Press, 2012.
Mitoma, Glenn. "Charles H. Malik and Human Rights: Notes on a Biography." *Biography* 33, no. 1 (2010): 222–41.
Modak-Truran, Mark C. "Reenchanting International Law." *Mississippi College Law Review* 22, no. 2 (2003): 263–301.
"A Process Theory of Natural Law and the Rule of Law in China." *Penn State International Law Review* 26, no. 3 (2008): 607–52.

Moeller, Bernd. *Imperial Cities and the Reformation: Three Essays*. Edited by H. C. Erik Midelfort and Mark U. Edwards, Jr. Philadelphia: Fortress Press, 1972.
Moltmann, Jürgen. *Ethics of Hope*. Minneapolis: Fortress Press, 2012.
More, St. Thomas. *The Yale Edition to the Complete Works of St Thomas More*. Vol. 6, *Parts I & II, A Dialogue Concerning Heresies*, edited by Thomas M. C. Lawler, Germain Marc'hadour, and Richard C. Marius. New Haven: Yale University Press, 1981.
More, Thomas. *A Dyaloge Wherin be Treated Dyuers Maters*. London: John Rastell, 1529.
Morgan, Lewis Henry. *Ancient Society*. Chicago: Charles H. Kerr, 1910.
Morison, Elting Elmore. *Turmoil and Tradition: A Study of the Life and Times of Henry L. Stimson*. Boston: Houghton Mifflin, 1960.
Morris, Colin. *The Papal Monarchy: The Western Church from 1050 to 1250*. Oxford: Clarendon Press, 1989.
Morsink, Johannes. *Inherent Human Rights*. Philadelphia: University of Pennsylvania Press, 2015.
Mortimer, Sarah. "Law, Justice, and Charity in a Divided Christendom: 1500–1625." In *International Law and Religion*, edited by Martti Koskenniemi, Mónica García-Salmones Rovira, and Paolo Amorosa, 25–42. Oxford: Oxford University Press, 2017.
Motomura, Hiroshi. *Immigration Outside the Law*. New York: Oxford University Press, 2014.
Mousin, Craig B. "You Were Told to Love the Immigrant, But What If the Story Never Happened? Hospitality and United States Immigration Law." *Vincentian Heritage* 33, no. 1 (2016). https://via.library.depaul.edu/vhj/vol33/iss1/8.
"Can One Still Call It Ignorance or Improper Bias?" In *Migration and Religious Freedom: Essays on the Interaction between Religious Duty and Migration Law*, edited by Carolus Grütters and Dario Dzananovic, 71–100. Nijmegen: Wolf Legal Publishers, 2018.
"Rights Disappear When US Policy Engages Children as Weapons of Deterrence." *AMA Journal of Ethics* 21, no. 1 (2019): E58–66.
Moyn, Samuel. *Christian Human Rights*. Philadelphia: University of Pennsylvania Press, 2015.
Not Enough: Human Rights in an Unequal World. Cambridge: Harvard University Press, 2018.
Mulder, John M. *Woodrow Wilson: The Years of Preparation*. Princeton: Princeton University Press, 1978.
Muldoon, James. "A Canonistic Contribution to the Formation of International Law." *Jurist* 28, no. 3 (1968): 265–79.
"The Contribution of the Medieval Canon Lawyers to the Formation of International Law." *Traditio* 28 (1972): 483–97.
Popes, Lawyers, and Infidels: The Church and the Non-Christian World, 1250–1550. Philadelphia: University of Pennsylvania Press, 1979.
"Medieval Canon Law and the Formation of International Law." *Zeitschrift der Savigny-Stiftung für Rechtsgeschichte: Kanonistische Abteilung* 81, no. 1 (1995): 64–82.
Empire and Order: The Concept of Empire, 800–1800. New York: Palgrave Macmillan, 1999.

"From Frontiers to Borders: The Medieval Papacy and the Conversion of Those Along the Frontiers of Christendom." *Quaestiones Medii Aevi Novae* 16 (2011): 101–21.
"Colonial Charters: Possessory or Regulatory?" *Law and History Review* 36, no. 2 (2018): 355–81.
Murano, Giovanna. "Una raccolta di minute autografe di consilia di Alessandro Tartagni (1423/24–1477)." *Bulletin of Medieval Canon Law* 31, no. 1 (2014): 237–48.
Mystikos, Nicholas. *Letters*. Edited and translated by Romilly James Heald Jenkins and Leendert Gerrit Westerink. Washington, DC: Dumbarton Oaks Center for Byzantine Studies, 1973.
Nader, Laura. "Promise or Plunder?" *Global Jurist* 7, no. 2 (2007): 1–21.
Namli, Elena. *Human Rights as Ethics, Politics, and Law*. Uppsala: Acta Universitatis Upsaliensis, 2014.
"Orthodox Theology, Politics, and Power." In *Political Theologies in Orthodox Christianity: Common Challenges, Divergent Positions*, edited by Kristina Stoeckl, Gabriel Ingeborg, and Aristotle Papanikolaou, 265–82. London: Bloomsbury T&T Clark, 2017.
Nandy, Ashis, Shikha Trivedy, Shail Mayaram, and Achyut Yagnik. *Creating a Nationality: Ramjanmabhumi Movement and the Fear of the Self*. Oxford: Oxford University Press, 1998.
Nardin, Terry. "Legal Positivism as a Theory of International Society." In *International Society: Diverse Ethical Perspectives*, edited by David R. Mapel and Terry Nardin, 17–35. Princeton: Princeton University Press, 1998.
"The Moral Basis of Humanitarian Intervention." *Ethics and International Affairs* 16, no. 2 (2002): 57–70.
Nash, Margaret. *The Ecumenical Movement in the 1960s*. Johannesburg: Ravan, 1975.
Neff, Stephen C. *Justice Among Nations: A History of International Law*. Cambridge, MA: Harvard University Press, 2014.
Nellen, Henk. *Hugo de Groot: Een Leven in Strijd om de Vrede 1583–1645*. Amsterdam: Balans, 2007.
Hugo Grotius: A Lifelong Struggle for Peace in Church and State, 1583–1645. Translated by J. C. Grayson. Leiden: Brill, 2014.
Nellen, Henk, and Edwin Rabbie, eds. *Hugo Grotius, Theologian: Essays in Honour of G.H.M. Posthumus Meyjes*. Leiden: Brill, 1994.
Nelson, Eric. *The Hebrew Republic: Jewish Sources and the Transformation of European Political Thought*. Cambridge, MA: Harvard University Press, 2010.
Nelson, Norman E. "Cicero's De Officiis in Christian Thought 300–1300." In *Essays and Studies in English and Comparative Literature*, 59–160. Ann Arbor: University of Michigan Press, 1933.
Nevius, John. *China and the Chinese*. New York: Harper, 1869.
Nichols, Christopher McKnight. *Promise and Peril: America at the Dawn of a Global Age*. Cambridge, MA: Harvard University Press, 2011.
Nicol, Donald M. "Byzantine Political Thought." In *The Cambridge History of Medieval Political Thought c.350–c.1450*, edited by J. H. Burns, 51–79. Cambridge: Cambridge University Press, 1988.
Nicoletti, Michele, and Luigi Sartori. *Teologia politica*. Bologna: EDB, 1991.
Niebuhr, Reinhold. *An Interpretation of Christian Ethics*. San Francisco: Harper & Row, 1935.

Nienhaus, Stefan. *Geschichte der deutschen Tischgesellschaft*. Tübingen: Niemeyer, 2003.

Nietzsche, Friedrich. *Twilight of the Idols and the Anti-Christ*. New York: Penguin Books, 2003.

Nigg, Walter. *Great Saints*. London: Siders, 1948.

Warriors of God: The Great Religious Orders and Their Founders. New York: Knopf, 1959.

Nijman, Janne E. "Grotius' *Imago Dei* Anthropology: Grounding *Ius Naturae et Gentium*." In *International Law and Religion*, edited by Martti Koskenniemi, Mónica García-Salmones Rovira, and Paolo Amorosa, 87–110. Oxford: Oxford University Press, 2017.

Nijman, Janne E., and Wouter Werner. "Populism and International Law: What Backlash and Which Rubicon?" *Netherlands Yearbook of International Law* 49 (2018): 3–17.

Ninkovich, Frank. "Theodore Roosevelt: Civilization as Ideology." *Diplomatic History* 10, no. 3 (July 1986): 221–45.

Global Dawn: The Cultural Foundation of American Internationalism, 1865–1890. Cambridge, MA: Harvard University Press, 2009.

Noble, David F. *Beyond the Promised Land: The Movement and the Myth*. Toronto: Between the Lines, 2005.

Nolde, O. Frederick. *Power for Peace: The Way of the United Nations and the Will of Christian People*. Philadelphia: Muhlenberg Press, 1946.

Free and Equal: Human Rights in Ecumenical Perspective. Geneva: World Council of Churches, 1968.

Noll, Mark. *Turning Points: Decisive Moments in the History of Christianity*. 3rd ed. Grand Rapids, MI: Baker Academic, 2012.

Normore, Calvin G. "Duns Scotus's Modal Theory." In *The Cambridge Companion to Duns Scotus*, edited by Thomas Williams, 129–60. Cambridge: Cambridge University Press, 2003.

Nurser, John S. *For All Peoples and All Nations: The Ecumenical Church and Human Rights*. Washington, DC: Georgetown University Press, 2005.

Nye, Joseph S. *Soft Power: The Means to Success in World Politics*. New York: Public Affairs, 2004.

Nygren, Anders. *Agape and Eros*. Philadelphia: Westminster Press, 1953.

Obolensky, Dimitri. *The Byzantine Commonwealth: Eastern Europe, 500–1453*. London: Phoenix Press, 2000.

Oddie, Geoffrey. *Imagined Hinduism: British Protestant Missionary Constructions of Hinduism, 1793–1900*. London: Sage, 2006.

Ogata, Sadako. "Foreword." In *Refugee Convention 1951: The Travaux Preparatoires Analysed with a Commentary*, edited by Paul Weis, 4–5. Geneva: UNHCR, 1990.

Ogden, Shubert M. *On Theology*. New York: Harper & Row, 1986.

Is There Only One True Religion or Are There Many? Dallas: SMU Press, 1992.

Olcott, Charles S. *The Life of William McKinley*. Vol. 2. Boston: Houghton Mifflin, 1916.

Olsen, Frances. "The Family and the Market: A Study of Ideology and Legal Reform." *Harvard Law Review* 96, no. 7 (1983): 1497–1578.

Ong, S. P. "Jurisdictional Politics in Canton and the First English Translation of the Qing Penal Code." *Journal of the Royal Asiatic Society* 20, no. 2 (2010): 141–65.

Oppenheim, Lassa. *International Law: A Treatise*. Vol. 1, *Peace*. London: Longmans, Green, and Co., 1905.

"The Science of International Law: Its Task and Method." *American Journal of International Law* 2, no. 2 (1908): 313–56.

Orakhelashvili, Alexander. "The Idea of European, International Law." *European Journal of International Law* 17, no. 2 (2006): 315–47.

Orentlicher, Diane F. "Relativism and Religion." In *Human Rights as Politics and Idolatry*, edited by Amy Gutmann, 141–58. Princeton: Princeton University Press, 2001.

Orford, Anne. *Reading Humanitarian Intervention: Human Rights and the Use of Force in International Law*. Cambridge: Cambridge University Press, 2003.

Osborne, Catherine. *Eros Unveiled: Plato and the God of Love*. Oxford: Clarendon Press, 1994.

Ostrogorsky, Georg. "The Byzantine Empire in the World of the Seventh Century." *Dumbarton Oaks Papers* 13 (1959): 1–21.

History of the Byzantine State. rev. ed. New Brunswick, NJ: Rutgers University Press, 1969.

O'Sullivan, Mortimer, and Robert James M'Ghee. *Romanism As It Rules in Ireland*. London: Seeley and Burnside, 1840.

Ottmann, Henning. "Politische Theologie als Begriffsgeschichte: Oder: Wie man die politischen Begriffe der Neuzeit politisch-theologisch erklären kann." In *Der Begriff der Politik: Bedingungen und Gründe politischen Handelns*, edited by Volker Gerhardt, 169–88. Stuttgart: Metzler, 1990.

Oxford English Dictionary. Oxford: Oxford University Press, 1989. www.oed.com/.

Ozment, Steven. *The Reformation in the Cities: The Appeal of Protestantism to Sixteenth-Century Germany and Switzerland*. New Haven: Yale University Press, 1975.

Özsu, Umut. "The Ottoman Empire, the Origins of Extraterritoriality, and International Legal Theory." In *The Oxford Handbook of the Theory of International Law*, edited by Anne Orford and Florian Hoffman, 123–37. Oxford: Oxford University Press, 2016.

Pagden, Anthony. *The Burdens of Empire: 1539 to the Present*. New York: Cambridge University Press, 2015.

Pagden, Anthony, and Jeremy Lawrance, eds. *Vitoria: Political Writings*. Cambridge: Cambridge University Press, 1991.

Pahuja, Sundhya. "Laws of Encounter: A Jurisdictional Account of International Law." *London Review of International Law* 1, no. 1 (2013): 63–98.

Patterson, David. *Anti-Semitism and Its Metaphysical Origins*. New York: Cambridge University Press, 2015.

Paulin, Roger. "Review of Stefan Nienhaus, *Geschichte der deutschen Tischgesellschaft*." *Modern Language Review* 100, no. 1 (2005): 251–3.

Paz, Reut Yael. *A Gateway between a Distant God and a Cruel World: The Contribution of Jewish German-Speaking Scholars to International Law*. Leiden: Martinus Nijhoff, 2012.

"Religion, Secularism and International Law." In *The Oxford Handbook of International Legal Theory*, edited by Anne Orford and Florian Hoffmann, 923–38. Oxford: Oxford University Press, 2016.

Pedersen, Susan. *The Guardians: The League of Nations and the Crisis of Empire*. New York: Oxford University Press, 2015.

Peiponen, Matti. "Ecumenical Action in World Politics: The Creation of the Commission of the Churches on International Affairs (CCIA), 1945–1949." PhD dissertation, University of Helsinki, 2014.

Pelagius. *Pelagius' Commentary on St Paul's Epistle to the Romans*. Translated by Theodore de Bruyn. Oxford: Clarendon Press, 1993.

Pelikan, Jaroslav. *The Excellent Empire: The Fall of Rome and the Triumph of the Church*. San Francisco: Harper & Row, 1987.

Pellet, Alain. "The Normative Dilemma: Will and Consent in International Law-Making." *Australian Yearbook of International Law* 12 (1989): 22–53.

Penna, Lucas de. *Commentaria in tres posteriores libros Codicis Iustiniani*. Lugduni: Apud Ioannam Iacobi Iuntae F., 1582.

Pennington, Kenneth. *Pope and Bishops: The Papal Monarchy in the Twelfth and Thirteenth Centuries*. Philadelphia: University of Pennsylvania Press, 1984.

Popes, Canonists, and Texts (1150–1550). Vol. 412. Aldershot: Variorum, 1993a.

The Prince and the Law, 1200–1600: Sovereignty and Rights in the Western Legal Tradition. Berkeley: University of California Press, 1993b.

"Sovereignty and Rights in Medieval and Early Modern Jurisprudence: Law and Norms without a State." In *Roman Law as Formative of Modern Legal Systems*, edited by Jaroslaw Reszczyńsk, Piotr Ścislicki, and Janusz Sondel. Krakow: Jagiellonian University Press, 2003.

Pennycook, Alastair. "The Modern Mission: The Language Effects of Christianity." *Journal of Language Identity and Education* 4, no. 2 (2005): 137–55.

Perry, Michael J. *Toward a Theory of Human Rights: Religion, Law, Courts*. Cambridge: Cambridge University Press, 2007.

Peters, Edward. *Inquisition*. Berkeley: University of California Press, 1989.

Peterson, Derek. "Colonizing Language? Missionaries and Gikuyu Dictionaries, 1904 to 1914." *History in Africa* 24 (1997): 257–72.

Peterson, Nicolas, and Anna Kenny, eds. *German Ethnography in Australia*. Acton: Australian National University Press, 2017.

Petkoff, Peter. "New Worlds and New Churches: The Orthodox Church(es) and the European Union." In *God and the EU: Faith in the European Project*, edited by Jonathan Chaplin and Gary Wilton, 70–88. Abingdon: Routledge, 2016.

Pfister, Lauren. "Rethinking Mission in China: James Hudson Taylor and Timothy Richard." In *The Imperial Horizons of British Protestant Missions, 1880–1914*, edited by Andrew Porter, 183–212. Grand Rapids, MI: William B. Eerdmans, 2003.

Philpott, Daniel. *Revolutions in Sovereignty: How Modern Ideas Shaped Modern International Relations*. Princeton: Princeton University Press, 2001.

Pierce, Sarah. *Immigration-Related Policy Changes in the First Two Years of the Trump Administration*. Washington, DC: Migration Policy Institute, 2019.

Pinkard, Terry. *Hegel: A Biography*. Cambridge: Cambridge University Press, 2000.

Pitsakis, C. G. "A propos de la citoyenneté romaine dans l' Empire d' Orient: Un survol à travers les textes grecs." *Méditerranées* 12 (1997): 73–100.

Pitts, Jennifer. *A Turn to Empire: The Rise of Imperial Liberalism in Britain and France*. Princeton: Princeton University Press, 2005.

Boundaries of the International: Law and Empire. Cambridge, MA: Harvard University Press, 2018.

Placher, William C. *A History of Christian Theology: An Introduction*. Louisville, KY: Westminster John Knox Press, 1983.

Platon (Igumnov), Archimandrite. *Pravoslavnoye nravstvennoye bogosloviye* [Orthodox Moral Theology]. Sergiyev Posad: Izdaniye Svyato-Troitse-Sergiyevoy Lavry, 1994.

Politis, Nicolas. "The Status of the Individual in International Law." In *The New Aspects of International Law*, 18–31. Washington, DC: Carnegie Endowment for International Peace, 1928.

Pollard, Alfred. *Records of the English Bible: The Documents Relating to the Translation and Publication of the Bible in English, 1525–1611*. London: Henry Frowde, 1911.

Porphyrogenitus, Constantine VII. *De ceremoniis aulae Byzantinae libri duo*. Vol. 2. 1830.

Porsdam, Helle. *Civil Religion, Human Rights and International Relations: Connecting People Across Cultures and Traditions*. Cheltenham: Edward Elgar, 2012.

Porter, Jean. *Ministers of the Law: A Natural-Law Theory of Legal Authority*. Grand Rapids, MI: William B. Eerdmans, 2010.

Porterfield, Allen W. "Some Popular Misconceptions Concerning German Romanticism." *Journal of English and Germanic Philology* 15, no. 4 (1916): 479–511.

Potts, Timothy C. *Conscience in Medieval Philosophy*. Cambridge: Cambridge University Press, 1980.

Predelli, Riccardo, ed. *I Libri Commemoriali Della Republica Di Venezia: Regesti*. Vol. 2. Venice, 1878.

Preston, Andrew. *Sword of the Spirit, Shield of Faith: Religion in American War and Diplomacy*. New York: Alfred A. Knopf, 2012.

Prior, Michael. "The Right to Expel: The Bible and Ethnic Cleansing." In *Palestinian Refugees: The Right to Return*, edited by Nasser Aruri, 9–35. London: Pluto, 2001.

Purcell, Edward, Jr. *The Crisis of Democratic Theory: Scientific Naturalism and the Problem of Value*. Lexington: University Press of Kentucky, 1973.

Quaglioni, Diego. "Inter Iudeos et Christianos commertia sunt permissa: 'Questione ebraica' e usura in Baldo degli Ubaldi (c. 1327–1400)." In *Aspetti e problemi della presenza ebraica nell'Italia centro-settentrionale (secoli XIV e XV)*, edited by Sofia Boesch Gajano, 275–305. Rome: Ripoli, 1983.

Queller, Donald E. *The Office of Ambassador in the Middle Ages*. Princeton: Princeton University Press, 1967.

Quigley, William. "Five Hundred Years of English Poor Laws, 1349–1834: Regulating the Working and Nonworking Poor." *Akron Law Review* 30, no. 1 (1996): 73–129.

Quinet, Edgar. *Ultramontanism, or, the Roman Church and Modern Society*. New York: Gates & Stedman, 1845.

Peñafort, Raymond of [Raimundus de Pennaforte]. *Summa de iure canonico*. Edited by Xaverio Ochoa and Aloisio Diez. Rome: Commentarium pro religiosis, 1975.

Reath, Andrews. "Autonomy, Ethical." In *Routledge Encyclopedia of Philosophy*. Vol. 1, edited by Edward Craig, 586. London: Routledge, 1998.

Rebuffi, Pierre. *Bulla Coenae Domini Pape Pauli III*. Paris: 1537.
Reed, James. *The Missionary Mind and American East Asia Policy, 1911–1915*. Cambridge, MA: Council on East Asian Studies, Harvard University, 1983.
Rees, Brinley Roderick. *Pelagius: Life and Letters*. Martlesham: Boydell Press, 1998.
Rehman, Javaid, and Susan Breau, eds., *Religion, Human Rights and International Law: A Critical Examination of Islamic State Practices*. Leiden: Brill, 2007.
Reichberg, Gregory, Henrik Syse, and Endre Begby, eds. *The Ethics of War: Classic and Contemporary Readings*. Malden, MA: Blackwell, 2006.
Reichwein, Adolf. *China and Europe*. New York: Barnes & Noble, 1925.
Reinbold, Jenna. *Seeing the Myth in Human Rights*. Philadelphia: University of Pennsylvania Press, 2017.
Reinhardt, Nicole. "How Individual Was Conscience in the Early-Modern Period? Observations on the Development of Catholic Moral Theology." *Religion* 45, no. 3 (2015): 409–28.
Reinsch, Diether Roderich. "Ausländer und Byzantiner im Werk der Anna Komnene." *Rechtshistorisches Journal* 8 (1989): 257–74.
Renaud, Terence. "Human Rights as Radical Anthropology: Protestant Theology and Ecumenism in the Transwar Era." *Historical Journal* 60, no. 2 (2016): 493–518.
Reséndez, Andrés. *The Other Slavery: The Uncovered Story of Indian Enslavement in America*. New York: Houghton Mifflin Harcourt, 2016.
Riley-Smith, Jonathan. *The Crusades: A History*. 2nd ed. New Haven: Yale University Press, 2005.
Röben, Betsy Baker. *Johann Caspar Bluntschli, Francis Lieber und das moderne Völkerrecht 1861–1881*. Baden-Baden: Nomos, 2003.
Rolin-Jaequemyns, Gustave. *Retablissement des relations diplomatiques entre la Belgique & le Vatican*. Brussels: Weissenbruch, 1884.
Roncaglia, Alessandro. *A Brief History of Economic Thought*. Cambridge: Cambridge University Press, 2017.
Rosenberg, Emily S. *Financial Missionaries to the World: The Politics and Culture of Dollar Diplomacy*. Cambridge, MA: Harvard University Press, 1999.
Rosenblatt, Helena. *Liberal Values: Benjamin Constant and the Politics of Religion*. New York: Cambridge University Press, 2008.
Rosergio, Bernardus de. "Ambaxiatorum Brevilogus." In *De legatis et legationibus tractatus varii*, edited by Vladimir E. Hrabar, 3–28. Dorpat: C. Mattiesen, 1906.
Roumy, Frank. "L'origine et la diffusion de l'adage canonique Necessitas non habet legem (VIIIe-XIIIe s.)." In *Medieval Church Law and the Origins of the Western Legal Tradition: A Tribute to Kenneth Pennington*, edited by Wolfgang P. Müller and Mary E. Sommar, 301–19. Washington, DC: Catholic University of America Press, 2006.
Roussel, Napoleon. *Catholic and Protestant Nations Compared in Their Threefold Relations to Wealth, Knowledge, and Morality*. London: Ward, 1855.
Rubin, Miri. *Charity and Community in Medieval Cambridge*. Cambridge: Cambridge University Press, 1987.
Rubinstein, Murray. "American Board Missionaries and the Formation of American Opinion towards China." In *America Views China: American Images of China Now and Then*, edited by Jonathan Goldstein, Jerry Israel, and Hilary Conroy, 67–79. Bethlehem, PA: Lehigh University Press; London: Associated University Press, 1991.

Rückert, Joachim. *Unrecht durch Recht: Zur Rechtsgeschichte der NS-Zeit*. Tübingen: Mohr Siebeck, 2018.
Ruff, Mark Edward. *The Battle for the Catholic Past in Germany, 1945–1980*. New York: Cambridge University Press, 2017.
Runciman, Steven. *The Byzantine Theocracy*. Cambridge: Cambridge University Press, 1977.
The Great Church in Captivity: A Study of the Patriarchate of Constantinople from the Eve of the Turkish Conquest to the Greek War of Independence. New York: Cambridge University Press, 1968.
Rürup, Reinhard. "Emancipation and Crisis: The 'Jewish Question' in Germany 1850–1890." *The Leo Baeck Institute Yearbook* 20, no. 1 (1975): 13–25.
Russell, Frederick H. *The Just War in the Middle Ages*. Cambridge: Cambridge University Press, 1975.
Russell, Peter. *Prince Henry "the Navigator": A Life*. New Haven: Yale University Press, 2000.
Sabattani, Aurelius. *De vita et operibus Alexandri Tartagni de Imola*. Milan: Giuffrè, 1972.
Sahin, Emrah. *Faithful Encounters: Authorities and American Missionaries in the Ottoman Empire*. Montreal: McGill-Queen's University Press, 2018.
Said, Edward, *Orientalism*. New York: Vintage Books, 1979.
Samuelson, Paul. *Economics*. New York: McGraw-Hill, 1976.
Sandars, Thomas Collett. *The Institutes of Justinian with English Introduction, Translation, and Notes*. 15th imp. London: Longmans, Green, and Co., 1922.
Sands, Philippe. *East West Street: On the Origins of "Genocide" and "Crimes Against Humanity."* New York: Alfred A. Knopf, 2016.
Sartre, Jean-Paul. *Search for a Method*. Translated by Hazel E. Barnes. New York: Alfred A. Knopf, 1963.
Being and Nothingness. Translated by Hazel E. Barnes. London: Routledge, 2006.
von Savigny, Friedrich Carl. *System of the Modern Roman Law*. Translated by William Holloway. Westport, CT: Hyperion Press, 1979 [1867].
Vom Beruf unsrer Zeit für Gesetzgebung und Rechtswissenschaft. Heidelberg: Mohr und Zimmer, 1814.
"Stimmen für und wider neue Gesetzbücher." *Zeitschrift für geschichtliche Rechtswissenschaft* 3, no. 1 (1816): 1–52. Reprinted by Jacques Stern, ed., *A.F.J. Thibaut und F.C. von Savigny: zum hundertjährigen Gedächtnis des Kampfes um ein einheitliches bürgerliches Recht für Deutschland* (Berlin 1914; 2nd ed. Darmstadt 1959).
Schermaier, Martin. "Res Communes Omnium: The History of an Idea from Greek Philosophy to Grotian Jurisprudence." *Grotiana* 30, no. 1 (2009): 20–48.
Schlag, Pierre. "The Brilliant, the Curious, and the Wrong." *Stanford Law Review* 39, no. 4 (1987): 917–27.
"Normativity and the Politics of Form." *University of Pennsylvania Law Review* 139, no. 4 (1991): 801–932.
"Law as the Continuation of God by Other Means." *California Law Review* 85, no. 2 (1997): 427–40.
"The De-differentiation Problem." *Continental Philosophy Review* 42, no. 1 (2009): 35–62.

Schmitt, Carl. *The* Nomos *of the Earth in the International Law of the* Jus Publicum Europaeum. Candor, NY: Telos Publishing, 2003.

Political Theology: Four Chapters on the Concept of Sovereignty, 2nd ed., translated by Georg Schwab. Chicago: University of Chicago Press, 2005.

Schmitt, Jean-Claude. *La raison des gestes dans l'Occident médiéval*. Paris: Gallimard, 1990.

Schoenholtz, Andrew I. "The New Refugees and the Old Treaty: Persecutors and Persecuted in the Twenty-First Century." *Chicago Journal of International Law* 16, no. 1 (2015): 81–126.

Schrijver, Nico. "A Missionary Burden or Enlightened Self-Interest? International Law in Dutch Foreign Policy." *Netherlands International Law Review* 57, no. 2 (2010): 209–44.

Schröder, Jan. "Savignys Spezialistendogma und die 'soziologische' Jurisprudenz." *Rechtstheorie* 7 (1976): 23–52.

Schulz, Raimund. *Die Entwicklung des römischen Völkerrechts im vierten und fünften Jahrhundert n. Chr.* Stuttgart: Franz Steiner Verlag, 1993.

Schwartz, Eduard. "Die Kanonessammlungen der alten Reichskirche." *Zeitschrift der Savigny-Stiftung für Rechtsgeschichte, Kanonistische Abteilung* 25, no. 1 (1936): 1–114.

Schwöbel, Christine E. J. "Organic Global Constitutionalism." *Leiden Journal of International Law* 23, no. 3 (2010): 529–53.

Scott, James Brown. *The Spanish Origin of International Law*. Oxford: Clarendon Press, 1934.

Scotus, John Duns. *God and Creatures: The Quodlibetal Questions*. Princeton: Princeton University Press, 1975.

Scully, Eileen. *Bargaining from Afar*. New York: Columbia University Press, 2001.

Seeley, Robert Benton. *Essays on Romanism*. London: Seeley and Ditton, 1839.

Selbin, Eric. *Revolution, Rebellion, Resistance: The Power of Story*. London: Zed Books, 2010.

Sepúlveda. Juan Ginés de. "Aquí se contiene una disputa." In *Tratados de Fray Bartolomé de las Casas*. Vol 1. Mexico: Fondo de Cultura Económica, 1965.

"Del reino y los deberes del rey." In *Tratados políticos de Juan Ginés de Sepúlveda*. Madrid: Instituto de Estudios Políticos, 1963.

Serkin, Cristopher, and Nelson Tebbe. "Condemning Religion: RLUIPA and the Politics of Eminent Domain." *Notre Dame Law Review* 85, no. 1 (2009): 1–54.

Shah, Diaz, ed. *Islam and the Law of Armed Conflict*. Cheltenham: Edward Elgar, 2015.

Shah, Timothy Samuel, Alfred Stepan, and Monica Duffy Toft, eds. *Rethinking Religion and World Affairs*. Oxford: Oxford University Press, 2012.

Shah, Timothy Samuel, and Allan D. Hertzke, eds., *Christianity and Freedom*. Vol. 1, *Historical Perspectives*. New York: Cambridge University Press, 2016.

Shahîd, Irfan. *Byzantium and the Arabs in the Fifth Century*. Washington, DC: Dumbarton Oaks Research Library and Collection, 1989.

Byzantium and the Arabs in the Sixth Century. Washington, DC: Dumbarton Oaks Research Library and Collection, 1995.

Shaw, Malcolm. *International Law*. 8th ed. Cambridge: Cambridge University Press, 2017.

Shepard, Jonathan. "The Byzantine Commonwealth 1000–1550." In *The Cambridge History of Christianity*. Vol. 5, *Eastern Christianity*, edited by Michael Angold, 1–52. Cambridge: Cambridge University Press, 2006.

Shishkov, A. V. "Dva ponimaniya traditsii v russkom pravoslavnom bogoslovii" [Two Understandings of Tradition in Russian Orthodox Theology]. *Vestnik Russkoy khristianskoy gumanitarnoy akademii* [Review of the Russian Christian Academy for the Humanities] 18, no. 3 (2017): 22–9.

Shmeman, Alexander. *Sobraniye statey 1947–1983* [Collection of Articles 1947–1983]. Moscow: Russkiy put', 2009.

Shortall, Sarah. "Theology and Politics of Christian Human Rights." *Journal of the History of Ideas* 79, no. 3 (2018): 445–60.

Sieghart, Paul. *The International Law of Human Rights*. Oxford: Oxford University Press, 1983.

Silantyev, Roman. "Rossiya ni v chem ne obyazana oriyentirovat'sya na Yevropeyskiy sud po pravam cheloveka" [Russia should not be guided by the European Court of Human Rights]. *Gosudarstvo, Religiia, Tserkov' v Rossii i za Rubezhom* [State, Religion and Church in Russia and Worldwide] 31, no. 2 (2013): 286–90.

Simeonova, Liliana. "Constantinopolitan Attitudes toward Aliens and Minorities, 860s–1020s." *Études balkaniques* 11, no. 3 (2001): 91–112.

Simma, Bruno, and Andreas Paulus. "The Responsibility of Individuals for Human Rights Abuses in Internal Conflicts: A Positivist View." *American Journal of International Law* 93, no. 2 (1999): 302–16.

Singer, Joseph. "Sovereignty and Property." *Northwestern University Law Review* 86, no. 1 (1991): 1–56.

Sitzia, Francesco. "Romanità dell'impero: ius civile e ius gentium." In *La nozione di romano tra cittadinanza e universalità*, 263–75. Naples: E.S.I., 1984.

Skinner, Quentin. *The Foundations of Modern Political Thought*. Vol. 1, *The Renaissance*. Cambridge: Cambridge University Press, 1978.

Skouteris, Thomas. *The Notion of Progress in International Law Discourse*. The Hague: T.M.C. Asser Press, 2010.

Slack, Paul. *The English Poor Law, 1531–1782*. London: Palgrave Macmillan, 1990.

Slade, Ruth. "English Missionaries and the Beginning of the Anti-Congolese Campaign in England." *Revue belge de Philologie et d'Histoire* 33, no. 1 (1955): 37–73.

Sloterdijk, Peter. *Critique of Cynical Reason*. Minneapolis: University of Minnesota Press, 1987.

Slotte, Pamela. "Whose Justice? What Political Theology? On Christian and Theological Approaches to Human Rights in the Twentieth and Twenty-First Centuries." In *International Law and Religion: Historical and Contemporary Perspectives*, edited by Martti Koskenniemi, Mónica García-Salmones Rovira, and Paolo Amorosa, 196–216. New York: Oxford University Press, 2017.

Slotte, Pamela, and Miia Halme-Tuomisaari, eds. *Revisiting the Origins of Human Rights*. Cambridge: Cambridge University Press, 2015.

Smith, Alan. *The Emergence of a Nation State: The Commonwealth of England, 1529–1660*. London: Longman, 1984.

Smith, Ben. *Traditional Imagery of Charity in Piers Plowman*. The Hague: Mouton & Co., 1966.
Smith-Christopher, Daniel L. *A Biblical Theology of Exile*. Minneapolis: Augsburg Fortress, 2002.
Snyder, Jack, ed. *Religion and International Relations Theory*. New York: Columbia University Press, 2011.
Soelle, Dorothee. *The Window of Vulnerability: A Political Spirituality*, translated by Linda M. Maloney. Minneapolis: Fortress Press, 1990.
Soltes, Ori Z. "Cultural Plunder and Restitution and Human Identity." *John Marshall Law School Review of Intellectual Property Law* 15, no. 3 (2016): 460–71.
Sorensen, Roy. *A Brief History of the Paradox: Philosophy and the Labyrinths of the Mind*. Oxford: Oxford University Press, 2003.
Sowell, Thomas. *On Classical Economics*: New Haven: Yale University Press, 2006.
Spalding, Elizabeth Edwards. *The First Cold Warrior: Harry Truman, Containment, and the Remaking of Liberal Internationalism*. Lexington: University Press of Kentucky, 2006.
Spinoza, Baruch. *Ethics: Treatise on the Emendation of the Intellect and Selected Letters*. Edited by Seymour Feldman, translated by Samuel Shirley. Indianapolis: Hackett, 1992.
Stantchev, Stefan. "Devedo: The Venetian Response to Sultan Mehmed II in the Venetian-Ottoman Conflict of 1462–79." *Mediterranean Studies* 19, no. 1 (2010): 43–66.
"Inevitable Conflict or Opportunity to Explore? The Mechanics of Venice's Embargo against Mehmed II and the Problem of Western-Ottoman Trade after 1453." *Mediaevalia* 32, no. 1 (2011): 155–96.
"The Medieval Origins of Embargo as a Policy Tool." *History of Political Thought* 33, no. 3 (2012): 373–99.
Spiritual Rationality: Papal Embargo as Cultural Practice. Oxford: Oxford University Press, 2014.
Starke, J. G. *Introduction to International Law*. 8th ed. London: Butterworths, 1977.
von Stauffenberg, Alexander Schenk. "Die Germanen im Römischen Reich." *Die Welt als Geschichte: Zeitschrift für universalgeschichtliche Forschung* 1 (1935): 72–100.
Stein, Peter. *Legal Evolution*. New York: Cambridge University Press, 1980.
Stensvold, Anne, ed. *Religion, State and the United Nations: Value Politics*. London: Routledge, 2017.
Stephanson, Anders. *Manifest Destiny: American Expansionism and the Empire of Right*. New York: Hill & Wang, 1995.
Stevens, Robert. "J. B. Powell and the Missouri-China Connection." *Missouri Historical Review* 82, no. 3 (1988): 267–79.
Stoeckl, Kristina. *The Russian Orthodox Church and Human Rights*. London: Routledge, 2014.
Stoeckl, Kristina, and Ksenyia Medvedeva. "Double Bind at the UN: Western Actors, Russia and Traditionalist Agenda." *Global Constitutionalism* 7, no. 3 (2018): 383–421.
Stolleis, Michael. *Staat und Staatsräson in der frühen Neuzeit: Studien zur Geschichte des öffentlichen Rechts*. Frankfurt am Main: Suhrkamp, 1990. See especially "Löwe und Fuchs: Eine politische Maxime im Frühabsolutismus," 21–36; "Grundzüge der Beamtenethik (1550–1650)," 197–231.

Stolzenberg, Nomi. "The Profanity of Law." In *Law and the Sacred*, edited by Austin Sarat, Lawrence Douglas, and Martha Merrill Umphrey, 29–90. Stanford: Stanford University Press, 2007.

Stout, Jeffrey. *Democracy and Tradition*. Princeton: Princeton University Press, 2004.

Stow, Kenneth R. *Catholic Thought and Papal Jewry Policy, 1555–1593*. New York: Jewish Theological Seminary of America, 1977.

Stracca, Benvenuto. *De Mercatura seu Mercatore Tractatus*. Venice: 1553.

Straub, Johannes. "*Germania provincia:* Reichsidee und Vertragspolitik im Urteil des Symmachus und der Historia Augusta." In *Colloque Genevois sur Symmaque à l'occasion du mille six cinquième anniversaire du conflit de l'autel de la Victoire*, edited by François Paschoud, 209–30. Paris: Belles lettres, 1986.

Stumpf, Christoph A. *The Grotian Theology of International Law: Hugo Grotius and the Moral Foundations of International Relations*. Berlin: Walter de Gruyter, 2006.

Sturm, Douglas. "Property: A Relational Perspective." In *Economic Life: Process Interpretations and Critical Responses*, edited by W. Widick Schroeder and Franklin I. Gamwell, 29–77. Chicago: Center for the Scientific Study of Religion, 1988.

Solidarity and Suffering: Toward a Politics of Relationality. Albany: State University of New York Press, 1998.

"Taking Human Rights Seriously: Relationality and Subjectivity." *Process Studies* 33, no. 2 (2004): 237-57.

Su, Anna. *Exporting Freedom: Religious Liberty and American Power*. Cambridge, MA: Harvard University Press, 2016.

Suarez, Francisco. *Selections from Three Works of Francisco Suarez*. Oxford: Clarendon Press; London: Humphrey Milford, 1944.

Sullivan, Winnifred Fallers. *The Impossibility of Religious Freedom: New Edition*. Princeton: Princeton University Press, 2018.

Sullivan, Winnifred Fallers, and Robert Yelle, "Law and Religion: An Overview." In *Encyclopedia of Religion*. 2nd ed., 5325–32. New York: Macmillan Reference USA, 2005.

Sumner Maine, Henry. *Ancient Law: Its Connection with the Early History of Society and Its Relation to Modern Ideas*. London: Oxford University Press, 1861.

Sun, Pinghua. *Human Rights Protection System in China*. Heidelberg: Springer, 2014.

Sunstein, Cass. *Legal Reasoning and Political Conflict*. Oxford: Oxford University Press, 1996.

Sylvest, Casper. "'Our Passion for Legality': International Law and Imperialism in Late 19th Century Britain." *Review of International Studies* 34, no. 3 (2008): 403–23.

Tartagnus, Alexander. *Consilia seu responsa*. Vol. 7. Venice: 1590.

Tautu, Aloysius, ed. *Acta Honorii III (1216–1227) et Gregorii IX (1227–1241)*. Vatican City, 1950.

Taylor, Paul M. *Freedom of Religion: UN and European Human Rights Law and Practice*. Cambridge: Cambridge University Press, 2005.

Thirlway, Hugh. *Concepts, Principles, Rules and Analogies: International and Municipal Legal Reasoning*. The Hague: The Hague Academy of International Law, 2002.

Thomas, Keith. "Cases of Conscience in Seventeenth-Century England." In *Public Duty and Private Conscience in Seventeenth-Century England: Essays Presented to*

G.E. Aylmer, edited by John Morrill, Paul Slack, and Daniel Woolf, 29–56. Oxford: Clarendon Press, 1993.
Thompson, John A. "Woodrow Wilson and a World Governed by Evolving Law." *Journal of Policy History* 20 (January 2008): 113–25.
A Sense of Power: The Roots of America's Global Role. Ithaca: Cornell University Press, 2015.
Thompson, Roger. "Reporting the Taiyuan Massacre: Culture and Politics in the China War of 1900." In *The Boxers, China, and the World*, edited by Robert Bickers and R. G. Tiedemann, 65–92. Lantham: Rowman & Littlefield, 2007.
Tibble, Steve. *The Crusader Armies*. New Haven: Yale University Press, 2018.
Tibebu, Teshale. *Hegel and the Third World: The Making of Eurocentrism in World History*. Syracuse: Syracuse University Press, 2011.
Tierney, Brian. *The Idea of Natural Rights: Studies on Natural Rights, Natural Law and Church Law*. Grand Rapids, MI: William B. Eerdmans, 1997.
Tillich, Paul. *The Interpretation of History*, translated by Elsa L. Tamley. New York: C. Scribner's Sons, 1936 [1926].
Systematic Theology. Vol. 1. Chicago: University of Chicago Press, 1951.
Todd, Margo. *Christian Humanism and the Puritan Social Order*. Cambridge: Cambridge University Press, 2002.
Toews, John Edward. *Becoming Historical: Cultural Reformation and Public Memory in Early Nineteenth-Century Berlin*. Cambridge: Cambridge University Press, 2004.
"The Immanent Genesis and Transcendent Goal of Law: Savigny, Stahl, and the Ideology of the Christian German State." *American Journal of Comparative Law* 37, no. 1 (1989): 139–69.
Tolan, John Victor. *Saracens: Islam in the Medieval European Imagination*. New York: Columbia University Press, 2002.
Tolley, Howard. *The U.N. Commission on Human Rights*. Boulder: Westview Press, 1987.
Topidi, Kyriaki, and Lauren Fielder, eds. *Religion as Empowerment: Global Legal Perspectives*. Abingdon: Routledge, 2016.
Tourme-Jouannet, Emmanuelle. *Le Droit International*. 2nd ed. Paris: Presses Universitaires de France, 2016.
Toynbee, Arnold. *Christianity and Civilization*. London: CMS, 1940.
"The Idea of Europe and the Unity of Europe – Europeans' Common Destiny." In *The European Round Table Discussion in Rome, October* 1953. Strasbourg: Council of Europe, 1953.
Tracy, David. *Blessed Rage for Order: The New Pluralism in Theology*. New York: Seabury Press, 1975.
Trapman, Johannes. "Grotius and Erasmus." In *Hugo Grotius, Theologian: Essays in Honour of G.H.M. Posthumus Meyjes*, edited by Henk J. M. Nellen and Edwin Rabbie, 77–98. Leiden: Brill, 1994.
Treitinger, Otto. *Die oströmische Kaiser-und Reichsidee: nach ihrer Gestaltung im höfischen Zeremoniell*. Darmstadt: H. Gentner, 1956.
Trexler, Richard C. *The Spiritual Power: Republican Florence under Interdict*. Leiden: Brill, 1974.
Triepel, Heinrich. *Völkerrecht und Landesrecht*. Leipzig: C. L. Hirschfeld, 1899.

Trivellato, Francesca, Leor Halevi, and Catia Antunes, eds. *Religion and Trade: Cross-Cultural Exchanges in World History, 1000–1900*. Oxford: Oxford University Press, 2014.

Tuck, Richard. *The Rights of War and Peace: Political Thought and the International Order from Grotius to Kant*. New York: Oxford University Press, 1999.

Tudesch, Niccoló dei [Panormitanus]. *Lectura super Tertio Quarto Et Quinto Decretalium*. Lyon: 1521–2.

Tully, James. *An Approach to Political Philosophy: Locke in Contexts*. Cambridge: Cambridge University Press, 1993.

Turner, Bryan. "Revisiting Weber and Islam." *British Journal of Sociology* 61, no. 1 (2010): 161–6.

Tyrrell, Ian. *Reforming the World: The Creation of America's Moral Empire*. Princeton: Princeton University Press, 2010.

Ullmann, Walter. "This Realm of England Is an Empire." *Journal of Ecclesiastical History* 30, no. 2 (1979): 175–203.

Unger, Roberto Mangabeira. *Knowledge and Politics*. New York: Free Press, 1975.

United Nations High Commissioner for Refugees. *Global Trends: Forced Displacement in 2017*. Geneva: UNHCR, 2018.

Global Trends: Forced Displacement in 2018. Geneva: UNHCR, 2019.

Uzlaner, Dmitry. "Delo 'Pussi raiot' i osobennosti rossiiskogo postsekuliarizma" [The Pussy Riot Case and the Peculiarities of Russian Post-Secularism]. *Gosudarstvo, Religiia, Tserkov' v Rossii i za Rubezhom* [State, Religion and Church in Russia and Worldwide] 31, no. 2 (2013): 93–133.

Valenzuela, Pia. "Between Scylla and Charybdis." In *International Law and Religion*, edited by Martti Koskenniemi, Mónica García-Salmones Rovira, and Paolo Amorosa, 43–63. Oxford: Oxford University Press, 2017.

Vattel, Emer de. *Le droit des gens ou Principes de loi naturelle* [Law of Nations or the Principles of Natural Law]. Washington, DC: Carnegie Institution of Washington, 1916.

The Law of Nations, Or, Principles of the Law of Nature, Applied to the Conduct and Affairs of Nations and Sovereigns. Edited by Béla Kapossy and Richard Whatmore. Indianapolis: Liberty Fund, 2008.

Veeser, Cyrus. *A World Safe for Capitalism: Dollar Diplomacy and America's Rise to Global Power*. New York: Columbia University Press, 2002.

Veit, Walter. "Missionaries and Their Ethnographic Instructions." *Royal Society of Victoria* 127, no. 1 (2015): 73–82.

Vitoria, Francisco de. *De Indis et De jure belli relectiones*. Edited by Ernest Nys, translated by John Pawley Bate. Washington, DC: Carnegie Institution of Washington, 1917.

Political Writings. Edited by Anthony Pagden and Jeremy Lawrance. Cambridge: Cambridge University Press, 1991.

Vodola, Elisabeth. *Excommunication in the Middle Ages*. Berkeley: University of California Press, 1986.

Vogel, Cyrille. *Medieval Liturgy: An Introduction to the Sources*. Washington, DC: Pastoral Press, 1986.

Vryonis, Speros. *Byzantium: Its Internal History and Relations with the Muslim World: Collected Studies*. London: Variorum Reprints, 1971.

Vysheslavtsev, Boris. *Etika preobrazhennogo Erosa*. Moscow: Biblioteka eticheskoy mysli, 1994.
Waldron, Jeremy. "The Image of God: Rights, Reasons, and Order." In *Religion and Human Rights: An Introduction*, edited by John Witte, Jr. and M. Christian Green, 216–35. Oxford: Oxford University Press, 2012.
Wallerstein, Immanuel. *The Modern World-System I: Capitalist Agriculture and the Origins of the European World-Economy in the Sixteenth Century*. Berkeley: University of California Press, 2011 [1974].
Walsh, Rachael, and Lorna Fox O'Mahony. "Land Law, Property Ideologies and the British-Irish Relationship." *Common Law World Review* 47, no. 1 (2018): 7–34.
Walsham, Alexandra. *Charitable Hatred: Tolerance and Intolerance in England, 1500–1700*. Manchester: Manchester University Press, 2006.
Walzer, Michael. *The Paradox of Liberation: Secular Revolutions and Religious Counterrevolutions*. New Haven: Yale University Press, 2015.
Warren, Heather A. *Theologians of a New World Order: Reinhold Niebuhr and the Christian Realists, 1920–1948*. New York: Oxford University Press, 1997.
Warren, James A. *God, War, and Providence: The Epic Struggle of Roger Williams and the Narragansett Indians against the Puritans of New England*. New York: Simon & Schuster, 2018.
Watts, Edward J. *The Final Pagan Generation*. Oakland: University of California Press, 2015.
Webb, Sidney, and Beatrice Potter Webb. *English Local Government: English Poor Law History: Part I, The Old Poor Law*. New York: Longmans, Green, and Co., 1927.
Weingast, Barry. "Adam Smith's Industrial Organization of Religion: Explaining the Medieval Church's Monopoly and Its Breakdown in the Reformation." October 17, 2015, https://papers.ssrn.com/sol3/papers.cfm?abstract_id=2675590.
Weiss, Thomas G. "Sanctions as a Foreign Policy Tool: Weighing Humanitarian Impulses." *Journal of Peace Research* 36, no. 5 (1999): 499–509.
Welch, Sharon. *A Feminist Ethic of Risk*. Minneapolis: Fortress Press, 2000.
Wellman, David Joseph. "'Trump, the Cross and the Lynching Tree: White Christian Nationalists and the Future of American Political Identity." In *Gender-Nation-Religion: Ein internationaler Vergleich von Akteursstrategien und Diskursverflechtungen*, edited by Maren Behrensen et al., 81–100. Frankfurt: Campus Verlag, 2018.
Wellman, James, Jr., and Clark B. Lombardi, eds. *Religion and Human Security: A Global Perspective*. Oxford: Oxford University Press, 2012.
Werner, Yvonne Maria. "The Catholic Danger: The Changing Patterns of Swedish Anti-Catholicism 1850–1965." In *European Anti-Catholicism in a Comparative and Transnational Perspective*, edited by Yvonne Maria Werner and Jonas Harvard, 135–48. Amsterdam: Rodpi, 2013.
Wertheim, Stephen. "The League That Wasn't: American Designs for a Legalist-Sanctionist League of Nations and the Intellectual Origins of International Organization, 1914–1920." *Diplomatic History* 35, no. 5 (2011): 797–836.
"The League of Nations: A Retreat from International Law?" *Journal of Global History* 7, no. 2 (2012): 210–32.
Tomorrow, the World: The Birth of U.S. Global Supremacy. Cambridge, MA: Harvard University Press, 2020.

Westlake, John. *Chapters on the Principles of International Law*. Cambridge: Cambridge University Press, 1894.
Wheeler, Nicholas. *Saving Strangers: Humanitarian Intervention in International Society*. Oxford: Oxford University Press, 2000.
White, Ronald, and Charles Hopkins. *The Social Gospel*. Philadelphia: Temple University Press, 1976.
White, Stephen. "The Book of Common Prayer and the Standardization of the English Language." *The Anglican* 32, no. 20 (2003): 4–11.
Whitehead, Alfred North. *Science and the Modern World*. New York: Free Press, 1967 [1925].
Process and Reality. Corrected ed., edited by David Ray Griffin and Donald W. Sherburn. New York: Free Press 1978 [1929].
Adventures of Ideas. New York: Free Press, 1933.
Whyte, Jessica. *The Morals of the Market: Human Rights and the Rise of Neoliberalism*. London: Verso, 2019.
Wieacker, Franz. *Privatrechtsgeschichte der Neuzeit unter besonderer Berücksichtigung der deutschen Entwicklung*. Göttingen: Vandenhoeck & Ruprecht Verlag, 1967.
Wiebe, Robert H. *The Search for Order, 1877–1920*. New York: Hill and Wang, 1967.
Wiffels, Alain. "Early-Modern Scholarship on International Law." In *Research Handbook on the Theory and History of International Law*, edited by Alexander Orakhelashvili, 23–60. Cheltenham: Edward Elgar, 2011.
Wilcox, Helen. "Sacred and Secular Love: 'I Will Lament, and Love'." In *The Oxford Handbook of Early Modern English Literature and Religion*, edited by Andrew Hiscock and Helen Wilcox, 613–33. Oxford: Oxford University Press, 2017.
Wilde, Marc de. "Offering Hospitality to Strangers: Hugo Grotius's Draft Regulations for the Jews." *Tijdschrift voor Rechtsgeschiedenis* 85, no. 3–4 (2017): 391–433.
Willard, John. "Illustrations of Cy Pres." *Harvard Law Review* 8, no. 2 (1894): 69–92.
Williams, Robert A. *The American Indian in Western Legal Thought*. Oxford: Oxford University Press, 1990.
Williams, Samuel. *The Middle Kingdom*. New York: Wiley & Putnam, 1848.
Winkelmann, Friedhelm. "Die Bewertung der Barbaren in den Werken der oströmischen Kirchenhistoriker." In *Das Reich und die Barbaren*, edited by Evangelos K. Chrysos and Andreas Schwarcz, 221–35. Vienna: Böhlau, 1989.
Winter, Jay, and Antoine Prost. *René Cassin and Human Rights: From the Great War to the Universal Declaration*. New York: Cambridge University Press, 2013.
Witte, John, Jr. *Law and Protestantism: The Legal Teachings of the Lutheran Reformation*. New York: Cambridge University Press, 2002.
Witte, John, Jr., and Frank S. Alexander, eds. *The Teachings of Modern Christianity on Law, Politics, and Human Nature*. New York: Columbia University Press, 2005.
Witte, John, Jr. *God's Joust, God's Justice: Law and Religion in the Western Tradition*. Grand Rapids, MI: William B. Eerdmans, 2006.
The Reformation of Rights: Law, Religion, and Human Rights in Early Modern Calvinism. Cambridge: Cambridge University Press, 2007.
Witte, John, Jr., and Frank S. Alexander, eds. *The Teaching of Modern Roman Catholicism on Law, Politics, & Human Nature*. New York: Columbia University Press, 2007.

Christianity and Law: An Introduction. Cambridge: Cambridge University Press, 2008.

Christianity and Human Rights: An Introduction. Cambridge: Cambridge University Press, 2010. See especially John Witte, Jr. "Introduction," 8–44.

Witte, John, Jr., and M. Christian Green, eds. *Religion and Human Rights: An Introduction*. Oxford: Oxford University Press, 2012. See especially John Witte, Jr., and M. Christian Green, "Introduction," 3–24.

Wogan-Browne, Jocelyn, Nicholas Watson, Andrew Taylor, and Ruth Evans. *The Idea of the Vernacular: An Anthology of Middle English Literary Theory, 1280–1520*. Pennsylvania: Pennsylvania State University Press, 1999.

Wolff, Christian. *The Law of Nations Treated According to the Scientific Method*, ed. Thomas Ahnert. Indianapolis: Liberty Fund, 2017 [1749].

Wolff, Robert Paul. *In Defense of Anarchism*. New York: Harper, 1970.

The Autonomy of Reason: A Commentary on Kant's Groundwork of the Metaphysics of Morals. New York: Harper & Row, 1986.

Wolter, Udo. "The *Officium* in Medieval Ecclesiastical Law as a Prototype of Modern Administration." In *Legislation and Justice*, edited by Antonio Padoa-Schioppa, 17–36. Oxford: Oxford University Press, 1997.

Wong, Ching Him Felix. "The Images of the Taiping Heavenly Kingdom as Shown in the Publications in France, Germany, and Italy during the Second Half of the Nineteenth Century." *Journal of Chinese Studies* 55 (2012): 139–74.

Woods, John E. *The Aqquyunlu: Clan, Confederation, Empire*. Rev. and expanded edition. Salt Lake City: University of Utah Press, 1976.

Woolf, Cecil N. Sidney. *Bartolus of Sassoferrato: His Position in the History of Medieval Political Thought*. Cambridge: Cambridge University Press, 2012.

Wong, Timothy Man-kong. "Printing, Evangelism, and Sinology: A Historical Appraisal of the Sinological Publications by Protestant Missionaries in South China." *Journal of the History of Christianity in Modern China* 8 (2009): 47–64.

Wu, Albert Monshan. *From Christ to Confucius: German Missionaries, Chinese Christians, and the Globalization of Christianity, 1860–1950*. New Haven: Yale University Press, 2016.

Yin, Zhiguang. "Heavenly Principles? The Translation of International Law in 19th-Century China and the Constitution of Universality." *European Journal of International Law* 27, no. 4 (2016): 1005–23.

Youens, Susan. *Schubert, Müller, and Die schöne Müllerin*. Cambridge: Cambridge University Press, 1997.

Zacour, Norman P. *Jews and Saracens in the Consilia of Oldradus De Ponte*. Vol. 100. Toronto: Pontifical Institution of Medieval Studies, 1990.

Zelinsky, Vladimir. "Predaniye, pamyat' i sokrytoye 'Ya'" [Tradition, Memory and the Hidden "I"]. In *Materialy mezhdunarodnoi bogoslovskoi konferentsii "Zhivoye Predaniye"* [Materials of the International Theological Conference "Living Tradition"], edited by Yevgeni Krest'yaninov and Sergei Minov, 12–23. Moscow: Svyato-Filaretovskaya moskovskaya vysshaya pravoslavno-khristianskaya shkola, 1999.

Zemanek, Karl. *The Legal Foundations of the International System*. The Hague: The Hague Academy of International Law, 1997.

Zhaojie, Li. "The Impact of International Law on the Transformation of China's Perception of the World: A Lesson from History." *Maryland Journal of International Law* 27, no. 1 (2012): 128–53.

Zolberg, Aristide R. "Why Not the Whole World? Ethical Dilemmas of Immigration Policy." *American Behavioral Scientist* 56, no. 9 (2012): 1204–22.

Zubovich, Gene. "American Protestants and the Era of Anti-racist Human Rights." *Journal of the History of Ideas* 79, no. 3 (2018): 427–43.

"For Human Rights Abroad, against Jim Crow at Home: The Political Mobilization of American Ecumenical Protestants in the World War II Era." *Journal of American History* 105, no. 2 (2018): 267–90.

Index